COMMERCIAL REAL EST...
PREPARATION AND...
SECOND EDI...
By Mark A. Se...

As a subscriber to our book, **Commercial Real Estate Leases, Preparation and Negotiation,** by Mark A. Senn (0-471-81675-2), we are sending you this new two-volume edition with two accompanying microcomputer diskettes, on approval.

The completely updated Second Edition of Volume 1, *Preparation and Negotiation,* provides comprehensive, detailed guidance that will enable the real estate professional to prepare, renew, and negotiate commercial real estate leases. The legal origins and practical consequences of each lease provision are discussed along with explanations of the intricate legal rules, with regard to landlords' and tenants' goals. Also included are chapters on relevant insurance principles and comparison of evolving economic terms.

The brand new Volume 2, *Forms,* is comprised entirely of time-tested, proven forms used in commercial real estate transactions. Complete forms are provided with innumerable form provisions and clauses that are keyed to the corresponding discussions in the companion volume. With these forms, you can propose new or substitute provisions and promptly prepare complete leases or complete ancillary documents. The forms are duplicated on the two accompanying microcomputer diskettes.

As a subscriber to our book, we are sending you this new two volume edition with two **free** microcomputer diskettes at a special price of $160.00, a $20.00 savings over our regular price of $180.00.

If you are not thoroughly satisfied with this new two-volume edition, just return the books and diskettes to us within 30 days along with the enclosed invoice, and we will cancel the billing.

Sincerely,

WILEY LAW PUBLICATIONS
A Division of John Wiley & Sons, Inc.
One Wiley Drive
Somerset, NJ 08875

1-800-225-5945

THE REAL ESTATE LAW LIBRARY FROM WILEY LAW PUBLICATIONS

COMMERCIAL REAL ESTATE LEASES: PREPARATION AND NEGOTIATION
SECOND EDITION

COMMERCIAL REAL ESTATE LEASES
PREPARATION AND NEGOTIATION
Second Edition

MARK A. SENN
**Member of the Bars
of the States of
California and Colorado**

Wiley Law Publications
JOHN WILEY & SONS
New York · Chichester · Brisbane · Toronto · Singapore

Copyright © 1990 by John Wiley & Sons, Inc.

Library of Congress Cataloging-in-Publication Data

Senn, Mark A.
   Commercial real estate leases : preparation and negotiation/ Mark A. Senn.—2nd
ed.
      p.   cm.— (Real estate practice library)
   Includes bibliographical references.
   ISBN 0-471-51501-9
   1. Commercial leases—United States.   I. Title.   II. Series.
   KF593.C6S4   1990
   346.7304'3462—dc20
[347.30643462]   90-12391
                                                                           CIP

Printed in the United States of America

10   9   8   7   6   5   4   3   2   1

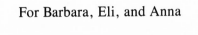
For Barbara, Eli, and Anna

For Barbara, Eli, and Anna

PREFACE TO SECOND EDITION

The second edition of this book is a substantial expansion and virtually complete revision of the first edition. For all practical purposes, it is a new book. In the six years since the publication of the first edition, commercial real estate lease law and practice have changed considerably. The law and practice of assignments and subleases have grown dramatically, as have the rules regarding mitigation of damages following a tenant's breach. The forms of public liability insurance have been so substantially changed as to necessitate the inclusion of a new detailed discussion. The environmental issues in commercial leasing have much greater importance than they had when the first edition was published. The law has even been active in such obscure areas as provisions for notices and nonwaiver. As a consequence of these changes, this second edition became necessary.

This book enables the real estate professional to prepare, review, and negotiate commercial real estate leases. The legal principles and practical consequences of each lease provision are discussed with regard to the landlord's and tenant's goals. Furthermore, the book explains the effects of lease provisions on the landlord's lenders. Chapters on relevant insurance principles and comparison of evolving economic terms are included. Also covered are calculations for office space. I have tried to explain the legal rules and practical consequences of real estate leases in enough detail to enable the user to draft effective lease documents. A main feature of the book is the inclusion of specific examples of lease clauses that address precise needs while taking into account the legal precedents affecting them.

A significant change is the publication of *Commercial Real Estate Leases: Forms*. This new volume contains forms for office building, shopping center, and single-tenant leases as well as many new and unique form provisions and clauses. Thus, the user will have in one place not only complete forms and recapitulations of forms discussed in this book, but also many additional forms for the real estate practitioner's consideration. The *Forms* volume also contains a computer disk for the user's convenience.

Aldous Huxley said that as the area of light increases, the perimeter of darkness increases. This has certainly been my experience with commercial real estate leases. As I consider my involvement with them, I find that issues I had thought were resolved must be reopened, and that issues I had never considered must be discussed. I am constantly humbled and benefited by the work of others and by the ideas of my colleagues — both the experts and novices. I have tried to convey some of my excitement about these new ideas and the gaining of a better understanding of old ideas. Some ideas, such as commercial rent regulation,[1] are germinating and will fill the pages of future supplements and editions.

I have again endeavored to mention every published article about commercial real estate leases that I could find. Of course, I am indebted to a great many people for their assistance in the completion of this work. Jim Kreger of Leprino Foods Company graciously assisted with the chapter on insurance. Vicki M. Young of the American Arbitration Association gave me her collection of cases on arbitration issues. Dennis Moyer of Hogan & Hartson in Washington, D.C., and Gary York of Dewey, Ballantine, Bushby, Palmer & Wood in Los Angeles were kind enough to send copies of helpful articles that appeared in their local legal publications. Robert S. Stein of Stein, Lubin & Lerner in San Francisco assisted with some questions of California law. BetaWest Properties, Ltd., allowed the use of several forms developed for it. Kathleen M. Wannamaker checked all of the cites and "greased" the proofreading process, while Maureen Greenberg, Lue Ann Lokken, and Donna Steir assembled the typescript. My publishers, Tom Conter and Ken Gesser, developed a tactful offhand way of asking how the manuscript was progressing while appearing to ask about my health. I deeply appreciate all the assistance.

Denver, Colorado   Mark A. Senn
June 1990

---

[1] Rosenberg, *Commercial Rent Regulation: Preserving the Diversity of the Neighborhood Commercial District,* 15 Ecology L.Q. 281 (1988).

ABOUT THE AUTHOR

Mark A. Senn was graduated with honors from Stanford University in 1969, and received his J.D. from the University of California at Berkeley (Boalt Hall) in 1972. He is the founding partner of Senn Lewis Hoth & Strahle, P.C., Denver, Colorado. After practicing in a major San Francisco law firm, Mr. Senn moved to Denver, where his practice emphasizes real estate, particularly commercial real estate leases. In addition to acting as a receiver of many properties and lecturing on receivership, he has also participated in Colorado's committee on opinion letters in real estate loan transactions. He has spoken throughout the country for such groups as the Northwest Center for Professional Education, the International Council of Shopping Centers, the National Mall Monitor, and many continuing legal education programs. Mr. Senn is editor of *Negotiating Real Estate Transactions* (John Wiley & Sons 1988) and has published articles on topics such as escrows, self-help for commercial landlords, and drafting expansion options and "free-rent" provisions.

SUMMARY CONTENTS

DETAILED CONTENTS

SHORT REFERENCE LIST

Short Reference	Full Reference
BOMA	Building Owners and Managers Association
Friedman	M.R. Friedman, Friedman on Leases (Practicing Law Institute 1983)
2 Powell	R. Powell, 2 The Law of Real Property (P.J. Rohan ed., rev. 1977)
Restatement	Restatement of the Law of Property (Second) (Landlord and Tenant) (1977)
Schoshinski	R. Schoshinski, American Law of Landlord and Tenant (Lawyers Co-operative Publishing Co. 1980)
3 Thompson	G.W. Thompson, 3 Commentaries on the Modern Law of Real Property (1980 repl. vol. by J.S. Grimes)

PART I

INTRODUCTION

CHAPTER 1

DEFINING THE COMMERCIAL LEASE

§ 1.1   Old Law and New Business

For more than seven centuries real estate leases have led the evolution of law and commerce. From the pastures of feudal England to the skyscrapers of modern America, real estate leases have affected—and been affected by—every aspect of legal theory and commercial practice. Sometimes legal theory predominates at the expense of commercial practice; at other times commercial practice holds sway, and legal theory is given short shrift. At all times one can see the law wend its way along an uncharted path.

Here and there, it bobs and weaves as, for example, it encounters the dense thicket of a landowner's duty to strangers. A sensible rule from feudal England seems out of place in modern American commerce. The rule persists, but so many exceptions are allowed that there is almost no rule at all. Finally, an impatient court cuts through the thicket and refuses to follow the rule. Legal theory has given way to commerce, and each may continue on its way.

Wherever the law goes, its first steps exert their influence. The law has been unable to rid itself of a decision made in the sixteenth century that the landlord's giving of one required consent excuses the requirement of any further consent. Although the decision has been mercilessly criticized for centuries, a New York court followed the rule in 1971. Law again prevailed over commerce.

The law has been compelled to address unforeseen commercial realities. Environmental laws that no one imagined ten years ago affect leases that never considered them. Caught off guard, the law uses its old precepts for the new problems of commerce.

Commercial real estate leases compel landlords and tenants to resolve the many legal and commercial differences between their interests in the leased

3

property. Formidable dilemmas complicate their resolution of these differences. As a result of their common heritage, legal and commercial matters are inextricably bound together; any agreement must be considered in light of both its legal consequences and its commercial consequences. Many centuries of nearly immutable legal precedents must be brought to bear on commercial differences that arise from rapidly changing conditions. As a result, landlords, tenants, and real estate professionals must understand not only old and new legal principles but also emerging commercial practices.

§ 1.2   Ownership and Possession

Leases temporarily separate the ownership of property from the possession of property. At the end of the term of the lease, possession of the property reverts to the landlord; during the lease, that reversion is the landlord's only interest in the property. On the other hand, although the tenant does not own the property, its interest in the property—a leasehold—gives it the most important incident of ownership: possession. To all appearances, the tenant owns the property during the term of its lease. This separation of ownership from possession gives rise to the tensions discussed in § **2.1**.

In the agrarian economy that created and nurtured leases, the exchange of possession for rent was fair and simple. The landlord used property that it could not occupy and the tenant used property that it could not own.[1] The feudal landlord's obligations to its tenant were almost fully discharged when the landlord delivered possession of the property. The landlord's only other obligation was to protect its tenant's peaceable possession of the property. Although that obligation survives to this day as the covenant of quiet enjoyment, the nature of the lease as a legal instrument is now evolving dramatically from its feudal ancestors.

§ 1.3   Is the Lease a Conveyance or a Contract?

The feudal belief that a landlord's only obligation to its tenant was the delivery and preservation of possession grew out of the medieval legal belief that the lease was a conveyance of property and not a contract with regard to property. Courts viewed the lease as the landlord's conveyance of the property to the tenant for a term of years. Once the landlord put the tenant in possession, and so long as the landlord preserved the tenant's possession, there was nothing left for the landlord to do; it only waited for rent. Because the tenant's performance of its covenant to

---

[1] *See generally* 2 R. Powell, The Law of Real Property § 230(1)(P.J. Rohan ed. rev. 1977) [hereinafter Powell] (expansion of this theme).

pay rent was not dependent upon any further performance from the landlord, the landlord's and tenant's covenants were said to be independent.

This rule was sensible when leases concerned agricultural lands. A prospective tenant could inspect the lands and assure itself of their productivity. If there were any improvements on the lands, they were insubstantial and not germane to the lease. After the tenant took possession, it cultivated the lands without the landlord's further involvement.

With the passing of agrarian society, the lease continued to be used as a means of separating ownership from possession. Beginning with the Industrial Revolution, leases were used with regard to property used for modern commercial purposes. In contrast to agricultural lands, commercial property consisted primarily of improvements located in urban areas. As part of the bargain in commercial leases, landlords frequently promised to repair the premises or to provide light and heat. When landlords made those promises, they did away with the reasoning behind independent covenants because their duties did not end when they put their tenants in possession. Still, the rule of independent covenants persisted: the landlord's failure to repair the premises, or to provide light and heat, did not excuse the tenant's independent covenant to pay rent.[2] Not even destruction of the premises excused the payment of rent.[3]

In recent years, this rule of independent covenants has begun to disappear,[4] and the lease has been considered at least a hybrid conveyance and contract, or simply a contract.[5] In addition to statutes that afford relief from the rule of independent covenants,[6] the erosion of the rule has been evident from the doctrines of constructive eviction,[7] implied warranty of habitability,[8] and

---

[2] Yuan Kane Inc. v. Levy, 26 Ill. App. 3d 889, 326 N.E.2d 51 (1975) (tenant's promise to pay is independent of landlord's promise to repair leased premises).

[3] Chase & Taylor, *Landlord and Tenant: A Study in Property and Contract*, 30 Vill. L. Rev. 571 (1985).

[4] Blackstone called the lease a contract more than 200 years ago, although he did not suggest the dependency of the covenants. 2 W. Blackstone, Commentaries on the Laws of England ch. 9 (1766).

[5] *See* A. Casner, American Law of Property § 3.11 (1952); Note, *The California Lease— Contract or Conveyance?*, 4 Stan. L. Rev. 244 (1952); McGovern, *The Historical Conception of a Lease for Years*, 23 UCLA L. Rev. 501 (1976); Chase & Taylor, *Landlord and Tenant: A Study in Property and Contract*, 30 Vill. L. Rev. 571 (1985) (discussing doctrine of independent covenants, law governing destruction of premises, warranty of habitability, and covenant of good faith and fair dealing, in the context of this continuing debate). *See also* R. Schoshinski, American Law of Landlord and Tenant § 1.1 (1980) [hereinafter Schoshinski]; 3 G.W. Thompson, Commentaries on the Modern Law of Real Property §§ 1110-1116 (repl. vol. 1980) [hereinafter Thompson]. *See generally* Restatement (Second) Property (Landlord and Tenant) §§ 1-6 (1977) [hereinafter Restatement]; M.R. Friedman, Friedman on Leases § 1.1 (2d ed. 1983) [hereinafter Friedman]. Zaldin, *The Double Nature of a Lease—A Hybrid Document*, in Shopping Centre Leases (H.M. Haber ed. 1976), discusses the Canadian precedents.

[6] *See, e.g.*, Cal. Civ. Code § 1932(2) (West 1976) (eliminating rule that destruction of premises did not terminate lease).

[7] See § 28.2.

[8] See § 5.11.

commercial frustration,[9] all of which have been employed to avoid the rule's harsh effects upon tenants. On the other hand, landlords have benefited from the application of contract principles such as anticipatory breach, which allows a landlord to recover the rent reserved at the time of breach without waiting until the end of the term.[10]

As another consequence of the lease being considered a contract, a valuable contract defense—the landlord's failure to mitigate its damages after the tenant's breach—is now often available to the tenant. A landlord cannot collect damages on account of its tenant's breach if the landlord could have avoided or reduced its damages.[11] A different rule prevailed when the lease was viewed as a conveyance: after its tenant's breach, the landlord could allow its damages to accumulate without trying to reduce or avoid them. Also, a contract, as opposed to a conveyance, requires the landlord to act reasonably in its performance; this means, for instance, that the landlord's consent to assignment of the lease may not be unreasonably withheld.[12] The view that a lease is a contract (or hybrid conveyance and contract) and not a conveyance is, by and large, a great benefit to the tenant.[13]

This application of contract law to real property has involved more than established contract principles such as mitigation of damages. It also involves the modern contract principles of the Uniform Commercial Code, which was promulgated in 1952 by the National Conference of Commissioners on Uniform State Laws, and was first enacted by Pennsylvania in 1954. For example, New York has a statute[14] regarding unconscionable lease provisions and several cases involving alleged unconscionability in commercial leases;[15] unconscionable contracts are a prominent part of the Uniform Commercial Code.[16] The Bankruptcy Code provisions regarding leases[17] rely on the Uniform Commercial Code's discussion of "adequate assurances of future performance" by one who defaults,[18] as does a Connecticut court[19] that has infused real property law with

---

[9] See § 10.1.

[10] 52 C.J.S. *Landlord and Tenant* § 512 (1968).

[11] See § 30.15.

[12] See § 12.7.

[13] 2 Powell § 221(1).

[14] N.Y. Real Prop. Law § 235-C (McKinney Supp. 1981), *discussed in* Catalina, *The Unconscionability Doctrine in Leaseholds*, 6 Real Est. L.J. 59 (1977).

[15] See cases in Goldstein, *Disputes in Business Leases: An Overview*, 18 Real Prop., Prob. & Tr. J. 709 (1983).

[16] U.C.C. § 2-302 (1957).

[17] 11 U.S.C. § 365, as amended by Leasehold Management Bankruptcy Amendments Act of 1983, Pub. L. No. 98-353 (1984).

[18] U.C.C. § 2-609 (1952).

[19] Conference Center Ltd. v. TRC-The Research Corp. of New England, 189 Conn. 212, 455 A.2d 857 (1983).

the Uniform Commercial Code's concept of commercial insecurity. Lastly, viewing a lease as a contract imparts the contract doctrine of an implied covenant of good faith and fair dealing, which might be applicable to such matters as operating expense escalations.[20] The lease that slowly shed the trappings of ancient conveyances has promptly donned the latest fashion in contracts.

Beyond doubt, the modern lease is a contract by which rent is exchanged for possession and services. In commercial leases, these services include the landlord's payment of real estate taxes and assessments, public liability and property damage insurance, public utilities such as gas and electricity, and maintenance ranging from janitorial service to complete renovation.

The landlord's cost of fulfilling its share of the lease bargain has risen rapidly and uncontrollably. As a result of the law's inference of the landlord's covenants in leases and the increasing cost of the landlord's performance of those covenants, one of the dilemmas of the landlord-tenant relationship has been underscored: the fusion of legal principles and practical consequences.

The legal principles are that leases are contracts and that landlords must provide services as part of the bargain. Today, however, landlords cannot control the costs of those services. The practical consequence is that landlords have created new forms of leases in which those costs, and often all the responsibilities of ownership, are passed through to their tenants. In doing so, modern landlords have looked backward several centuries and found that their earliest ancestors were lenders. This discovery invites a comparison of leases and loans, and it leads to some important conclusions about leases.

§ 1.4   Comparison of Leasing and Secured Lending

Suppose that a careless real estate professional chose a mortgage form instead of a lease form in order to reflect the agreement of a landlord and tenant. If the landlord's name were used instead of the mortgagee's or lender's name and if the tenant's name were used instead of the mortgagor's or borrower's name, an embarrassment, but not a catastrophe, follows. On examination, the following analogies — among others — would appear: landlord and mortgagee; tenant and mortgagor; leased property and mortgaged property; rent and installment payments; term and maturity. In fact, these are the essential terms of a lease, just as they are the essential terms of a mortgage. One may say that the tenant is buying a leasehold on an installment plan financed by its landlord.

The responsibility for certain additional expenses (taxes, insurance, and maintenance, for example) typically falls on the borrower just as it falls on the tenant to one degree or another. The borrower's conduct is controlled in much the

---

[20] Barak, *Protecting Tenants With an Implied Covenant of Good Faith*, 3 Prac. Real Est. Law. 27 (1987) (leaning heavily on Kendall v. Ernest Pestana, Inc., 40 Cal. 3d 488, 709 P.2d 837, 220 Cal. Rptr. 818 (1985)).

same ways as the tenant's; for example, a prohibition of assignment is expressed as a due on sale clause. The borrower is required to preserve the mortgaged property, just as the tenant is obligated to preserve the leased property. Upon casualty damage or taking by eminent domain, the lender and the landlord alike share the insurance proceeds or condemnation award. On default by the borrower, the lender's rights and remedies are remarkably similar to the landlord's rights and remedies. In fact, the essential difference between the landlord and the lender is that the landlord has ownership but not possession, while the lender has neither ownership nor possession. When the tenant defaults or the term ends, the landlord will regain possession. When the borrower defaults, the lender will gain both possession and ownership.

These similarities are far from coincidences. The lease and mortgage have common ancestors.[21] The common origin of the lease and mortgage has more than historical interest; it helps the real estate professional to understand several modern relationships. The similarity of leases and loans also helps to explain why a California court found that a mortgage loan broker had breached its fiduciary duty to its principal (the borrowers) by arranging a sale-leaseback transaction instead of a loan transaction. The sale-leaseback required the borrowers to sell their property and then to lease it as tenants from the investor to whom they had sold it. Although the economic consequences of the sale-leaseback were similar to the economic consequences of the loan that the borrowers wanted, the broker erred by failing to explain to the borrowers that their rights and liabilities after default were considerably different in the two transactions.[22]

§ 1.5   Role of the Lender

Most landlords use borrowed money to buy and develop their property; as John Stuart Mill observed more than a century ago, "The English landlords, as they themselves are constantly telling us, are a bankrupt body, and the real owners of the bulk of their estates are the mortgagees."[23] The real estate professional cannot understand the lease without understanding the goals of real estate lenders and the lease provisions that affect these goals.

Real estate lenders have three related goals:

---

[21] *See generally* II F. Pollock & F. Maitland, The History of English Law ch. IV, at 5 (1895); 2 W. Blackstone, Commentary on the Laws of England ch. 10, at III (1766); T. Plucknett, A Concise History of the Common Law ch. 9, at 609 (5th ed. 1956); S. Baker, An Introduction to English Legal History 252 (2d ed. 1979).

[22] UMET Trust v. Santa Monica Medical Inv. Co., 140 Cal. App. 3d 864, 189 Cal. Rptr. 922 (1983).

[23] Mill, *Civilization: Signs of the Times*, XXV Westminster Rev. 1-28 (Apr. 1836), *reprinted in* The Emergence of Victorian Consciousness 93 (G. Levine ed. 1967).

1.   The availability of uninterrupted cash flow from which their loans may be repaid

2.   The certainty that they will have no substantial obligations or impediments if they must foreclose their loans and succeed to the landlord's title

3.   The existence of their security, that is, the improvements on the property, and any money that becomes available if those improvements are destroyed by casualty or taken by the exercise of eminent domain.[24]

The existence of a first lender, as well as the likelihood that there will be replacement lenders or other lenders, compels the landlord to consider the lender's requirements in preparing its lease documents. The lender's requirements are natural boundaries for certain provisions of the lease. The relevant lender's concerns are added to each chapter of this book. They help the landlord to prepare a lease that its present and future lenders will accept, and also guide the tenant who has been told by its landlord that the landlord's lenders will not allow a request made by the tenant.

The role of the lender and the affinity of leases to secured loans come together in two further observations. First, the mortgage that the landlord signs in connection with its loan is comparable to the lease that a tenant signs with the landlord. In other words, the lender is the landlord in the mortgage and the landlord is the lender in the lease. As a result, one may say that the landlord is its lender's tenant and that the tenant is its landlord's borrower. These notions will be helpful when the relationship of the tenant and its landlord's lender is discussed. Second, as the first observation shows, the landlord and the lender have more than their histories in common; their positions are analogous. Thus, the tenant has no better alliance with its landlord's lender than it does with its landlord.

There is one important exception to these observations: ground leases. Some of these unique leases (which are not discussed in this book) turn these observations

---

[24] *See generally* Smith & Lubell, *Real Estate Financing: What Lenders Want in Leases*, 6 Real Est. Rev. 11 (1977); Nugent, *Long Term Ground Leases and Leasehold Financing*, in Practicing Law Institute, 10 Commercial Real Estate Leases 65 (1984); Strum, *The Mortgagee Looks at the Lease as a Basis for Mortgage Financing*, in Practicing Law Institute, 10 Commercial Real Estate Leases 17 (1984); Grillo, *Review and Consideration of Leases in Connection with Mortgage Loans*, in Practicing Law Institute, 10 Commercial Real Estate Leases 121 (1984); Hyde, *The Real Estate Lease as a Credit Instrument from the Lender's Viewpoint*, reprinted with permission in Practicing Law Institute, 10 Commercial Real Estate Leases 161 (1984); Krasnove, *Lender Considerations Relative to Commercial Leases*, in ALI-ABA Course of Study, Advanced Issues in Commercial Real Estate Leasing 103 (1983); Nellis, *Checklist of Lender's Requirements for Reviewing Commercial Leases*, in ALI-ABA Course of Study, Advanced Issues in Commercial Real Estate Leasing 109 (1983); Lawson & McNally, *A Lender's View of Shopping Centre Leases*, in Shopping Centre Leases 81 (H.M. Haber ed. 1976); Nellis, *What Lenders Look for in Reviewing Commercial Leases*, Leasing Prof., July 1985 at 1; Wilborn, *An Analysis of Commercial Space Leases from the Perspective of a Secured Lender*, in Practicing Law Institute, Commercial Real Est. Leases 1989, 23 (1989).

upside down. In them, tenants have almost all the incidents of ownership including (in some instances) the right to encumber the reversion, which, of course, they do not own. As a result, the tenant becomes the borrower, and the lender and tenant are more closely allied. Put differently, the commercial lease is a credit instrument for the benefit of landlords and their lenders, but the ground lease is a credit instrument for the benefit of tenants and their lenders. Real estate professionals must remember these important differences between these kinds of leases; each is appropriate in its place and entirely inappropriate in any other place.

CHAPTER 2

ORGANIZATION AND SCOPE

§ 2.1   Landlord's Control versus Tenant's Rights

This book defines, assesses, and resolves the legal and practical conflicts between landlords and tenants. Toward these ends, it is divided into nine parts:

Part I   Introduction (**Chapters 1** and **2**)

Part II   The Essential Lease Provisions (**Chapters 3** through **6**)

Part III   Additional Expenses for the Tenant (**Chapters 7** through **9**)

Part IV   Controlling the Tenant's Conduct (**Chapters 10** through **15**)

Part V   Giving the Tenant Rights (**Chapters 16** and **17**)

Part VI   Preserving the Premises (**Chapters 18** through **23**)

Part VII   Protecting the Landlord (**Chapters 24** through **29**)

Part VIII   Default and Arbitration (**Chapters 30** and **31**)

Part IX   Miscellaneous Provisions (**Chapter 32**)

Beginning with **Chapter 3** each chapter encompasses one or more lease provisions. These provisions are examined from the perspectives of both the landlord, the tenant, and, in appropriate circumstances, the lender. What emerges is a discussion of lease provisions in the order that they are commonly presented in a lease.

Although the organization of this book and the organization of a typical lease are similar, leases may be arranged in any order. The inclusion of a chapter in one part does not mean that it could not have been included in another part; for example, mechanics' liens could be included as sensibly in **Part VI** as it is in **Part VII**, and purchase options could be part of the chapter about the term instead of the chapter about the premises. Completion of the premises is considered in the chapter about the term rather than in the chapter about the premises. This apparent anomaly results from the dependence of the term on the completion of the premises and illustrates the relationship of one provision to another. As these examples illustrate, the book's organization has been selected with the hope that it provides a convenient overview of the lease and not with the intention of sacrificing the substance to the form.[1]

Part II contains essential lease provisions: the landlord and tenant, the term, the premises,[2] and the rent. A lease must have these provisions.[3] A document that is missing any of these provisions is not a lease.[4] For example, a tenant cannot renew a lease in which the renewal rental rates are set forth in an exhibit if the exhibit is lost, because an essential lease term is missing.[5] A lease with no more than these provisions will be governed by the many judge-made rules that Anglo-Saxon and American jurisprudence has accumulated for many centuries: the common law.[6] Because many common law rules are inappropriate for modern commercial leases, landlords and tenants take pains to supplant the common law with the private law of their leases.

Part III describes several costs associated with owning real property: taxes, insurance, and utilities. Tenants are the "owners" of the premises for the terms of their leases; therefore, in one way or another, these costs are usually passed on to them.

As **Part IV** shows, the landlord imposes control over the tenant's rights in the premises by prescribing their use, requiring compliance with laws affecting the

---

[1] The "one provision—one chapter" approach was used successfully in Commercial Real Property Lease Practice (Cal. CEB 1976, Supp. 1984), which recommended that lease provisions be organized in three groups: provisions concerning commencement of the term; provisions that govern the relationship of landlord and tenant during the term; and provisions concerning expiration or termination of the lease. Even with the different structure, the order of provisions in this book and that book are still similar.

[2] The term "premises" is a curious word derived from a time when conveyances began with introductory material that included a description of the property. When later parts of the conveyance mentioned the property, they used the term "premises" in much the same way as a syllogism would refer to its earlier premises. The word is plural.

[3] See **§ 32.1** for leases that unintentionally arise when the landlord and tenant agree on the essential lease terms.

[4] *See* 2 R. Powell, The Law of Real Property § 222(1) (P.J. Rohan ed. revis. 1971) [hereinafter Powell] § 222(1) (expansion of this theme); Restatement Second Property (Landlord and Tenant) § 2.2 (1977) [hereinafter Restatement]; Annot., 85 A.L.R.3d 414, *Requirements as to certainty and completeness of terms of lease in agreement to lease* (1978).

[5] Bartsch v. Gordon N. Plumb, Inc., 138 Ill. App. 3d 188, 485 N.E.2d 1105 (1985), *appeal denied*, Apr. 2, 1986 (some question whether the exhibit ever existed).

[6] Smoken, *Filling the Gap in a Real Property Lease*, 35 DePaul L. Rev. 437 (1985) (explains many of these rules and suggests they are what landlord and tenant would have agreed upon if they had thought about it; emphasis is Illinois law).

premises, limiting the tenant's ability to transfer its rights in the lease and the premises, and regulating signs. In addition, the landlord may go so far as to impose detailed rules and regulations about the most mundane matters. Finally, in shopping center leases only, the landlord may require the tenant to join an association of fellow tenants or to contribute to the promotion of the shopping center in other ways.

So far, this book and the hypothetical lease it follows show the tenant's assumption of the burdens—but not the benefits—of ownership. In **Part V**, the tenant is given rights in property it has not leased, and is assured of some services from the landlord.

However, the tenant is reminded in **Part VI** that it must preserve the premises for their eventual return to the landlord. The tenant must repair and maintain the premises and must refrain from making alterations to them. Furthermore, the tenant must not let the premises become the subject of a mechanics' lien in favor of anyone who furnishes materials or services for the improvement of the premises. **Part VI** also considers two extraordinary circumstances: casualty damage and condemnation. All in all, the tenant learns it must give the premises back to the landlord just as they were given to the tenant.

Although the premises may be adequately protected and the landlord's rights in the premises assured, the landlord itself needs further comfort in the form of indemnification and security for payment of the rent. Also, the landlord excuses itself from any liability to the tenant that is implied by the lease, as well as any liability that is expressed in the lease but arises after the landlord disposes of the premises. **Part VII** explains these provisions. Incidentally, although the landlord gives over temporary possession, it preserves two incidents of ownership: the right to enter the premises and the right to encumber the premises without regard to the tenant's possession.

The landlord continues this hypothetical lease by stating the events that constitute defaults by the tenant and by prescribing its remedies. The tenant responds in kind with regard to its landlord's defaults. The landlord and tenant may agree upon arbitration as a means of resolving their differences. **Part VIII** discusses such defaults, remedies, and arbitration.

Part IX includes housekeeping matters, some of which are as important as any other part of the lease.

§ 2.2   Using and Abusing Forms

Real estate professionals that regularly represent landlords usually have form leases at hand.[7] They may also have form provisions that landlords will add or substitute if requested. Tenants' professionals are rarely in a position to prescribe an entire lease, but, they commonly propose additional or substitute provisions.

---

[7] *See* Dodds, *A Leasing Primer: From the Ground Up*, 1 J. Real Est. Dev. 11 (1986) (practical discussion of preparing lease forms with an emphasis on office building leases).

Having those proposals readily available enables the tenants' professionals to propose a provision acceptable to it and not just an "idea" that is then written by the landlords' professionals and subject to further negotiation and refinement. Although undue reliance on forms inhibits the professionals' ability to accept new ideas or to meet new challenges, forms are such an important part of the leasing business that one can only hope for their sensible use, not for their elimination. Properly used, they can avoid repetition of a great deal of work.

Some suggestions for the use of form agreements or provisions must be made:

1. Find the source and age of the form, if possible, and find out whether it has been used successfully or dismissed as a poor effort, whether it has been revised, whether it has been the source of litigation, whether it was used in a landlord's market or tenant's market, and where it was used. An old form must be carefully reviewed to be certain it complies with subsequent statutory or case law developments. A form used in a sophisticated real estate market is probably inappropriate in a small town.

2. Find out whether the form or provision was written as a strong landlord's lease or as a strong tenant's lease. Obviously, the sole proprietor will have signed a lease that is less favorable for a tenant than the lease that the national retail chain will have signed; if the real estate professional relies upon the sole proprietor's form for a national client, a disservice is done to the national chain. On the other hand, if a real estate professional suggests that the user of 2 percent of a building should have the same rights as the user of 30 percent of the building, the landlord typically will dismiss the proposal out of hand and possibly conclude that the matter should be dropped to avoid the expense necessary to come to an agreement.[8]

3. Read the form in its entirety. This enables the real estate professional to understand the transaction in which the form arose. Be sure a form provision's style is compatible with the document in which it will be used. Conform defined terms such as "lessee" or "demised premises" to the corresponding terms in the proposed document.

4. In order to facilitate the next user's task, put each form in a collection. With regard to each form in the collection, add a statement of the circumstances in which the form was created and the goal that it was meant to achieve. Form leases can be kept in their entirety. In addition, however, real estate professionals organize their forms on a provision-by-provision basis. This is particularly helpful for provisions that will invariably be used in one form or another (such as use provisions in shopping center leases) but may not be identical to the last form used.

---

[8] For a helpful discussion of the differences between negotiations with small tenants and large tenants, see Alexander & Muhlebach, *Negotiating the Shopping Center Lease with a National Tenant*, 2 J. Real Est. Dev. 79 (1986).

Unfortunately, form books are not necessarily safe. Several forms that are recommended in prominent form books have not only given rise to litigation but have been criticized and found ineffective for the very purposes the form books say they will achieve.[9]

Stationers' forms are no safer. One Illinois restaurant owner probably has some well-earned thoughts about such forms. When his printed form "Store Lease" expired, he and his landlord entered into a new printed form, designated an "Office Lease." Unlike the old store lease, the new office lease had a printed provision allowing the landlord to terminate the lease. When the landlord took steps to do so, the tenant claimed that the office lease should be reformed by the deletion of the termination provision. The tenant claimed that he and the landlord were mutually mistaken. In the alternative, the tenant claimed that only he was mistaken and that the landlord had deceived him. The tenant lost because he could not prove a mutual mistake, nor could he prove fraud when the provision was apparent from reading the lease.[10]

Real estate professionals should review their forms periodically. Brokers and developers should assure themselves that their forms are still lawful. Lawyers should change their forms in order to clarify confusing provisions and to conform to changing practices. When a new real estate development is contemplated, the landlord should try to have its prospective lenders approve the lease form that will be used.

Most real estate professionals develop their own checklists to assist them in thorough reviews of leases. A checklist is an easy way for real estate professionals not to lose sight of provisions favorable to them when wading through a form that is new to them.[11]

The forms in this book have been prepared only to illustrate the legal and practical matters discussed in the text. They do not necessarily conform to the law of any state, nor do they represent solutions for all problems. All of the forms are meant to be considered along with the text that accompanies them. Some of the forms have been selected as examples of how not to solve a leasing problem.[12]

§ 2.3   Need for Clarity of Expression

When asked why he clarified an ambiguous provision in a litigated lease, counsel to one landlord said: "I am living today; I might not be living next week or years

---

[9] For several examples, see D. Mellinkoff, The Language of the Law 279-82 (1963).

[10] Greatamerican Fed. Sav. & Loan Ass'n v. Grivas, 137 Ill. App. 3d 267, 484 N.E.2d 429 (1985).

[11] For good examples, see Goldman, *Checklist for Leases in a Commercial Lease*, 2 Prac. Real Est. Law. 83 (1986), and Lewis, *Checklist for Lease Negotiation*, 2 J. Real Est. Dev. 32 (1986).

[12] For helpful suggestions on draftsmanship, see *Report of the Committee on Leases, Section of Real Property, Probate and Trust Law, American Bar Association, Drafting Shopping Center Leases*, 2 Real Prop., Prob. & Tr. J. (1967), and Friedman, *Store Leases*, 37 N.Y. St. B.J. 126 (1965), both of which are reprinted in Practicing Law Institute, 10 Commercial Real Estate Leases (1984). For Canadian examples, see Dick, *Drafting a Shopping Centre Lease*, in Shopping Center Leases (H.M. Haber ed. 1976).

to come, and I would rather have my job finished now than later."[13] This is the task of the real estate professional — to state clearly the agreement of landlord and tenant.[14]

Real estate professionals often leave ambiguous provisions as they find them.[15] They seem to do this because they believe that any clarification will result in a provision that is clearly "bad" for their clients. Rather than take that perceived risk, they are willing to risk arguing the question of ambiguity later, if enforcement of the provision is sought. This view has drawbacks. The first is that the real estate professional may be the only person who believes that the provision is ambiguous; therefore, the argument loses. If the matter results in litigation in which the parol evidence rule is invoked to prevent extrinsic testimony, there is no argument at all. Furthermore, if the real estate professional has led a client to act in reliance on a faulty interpretation of the ambiguity, the client will have been served poorly. Finally, ambiguity can lead to litigation in which courts are driven to conclusions that neither the landlord nor the tenant expected.[16] The proper course of conduct, of course, is to raise the question of a possible ambiguity and to have it made clear.

If anything is clear about legal writing, it is that legal writing is ambiguous. Although confused ideas give rise to some ambiguity, the words themselves are the real culprits. And/or is among the many words and phrases for which real estate professionals have provided ready refuge.[17] The phrase has no clear meaning; this alone is sufficient cause to abandon it. If a landlord signs a lease with "ABC Corporation and/or assigns," and ABC Corporation assigns its interest in the lease, the landlord cannot be certain whether it has an agreement with ABC Corporation and the assignee, or ABC Corporation or the assignee, or the assignee alone, or no one. If two entities are intended, use "and"; if either of two entities is intended, use "or"; if either one or both of two entities are intended, use "A or B, or both of them" or "A and B, or either of them."

---

[13] S.P. Dunham & Co. v. 26 East State St. Realty Co., 134 N.J. Eq. 237, 35 A.2d 40, 47 (Ch. Div. 1943). Fisher Properties, Inc. v. Arden-Mayfair, Inc., 106 Wash. 2d 826, 726 P.2d 8 (1988), involves the construction of a lease at the end of its term of more than 50 years. Although it is sui generis, the case shows the ways in which provisions that were well understood at the inception of the lease become touchstones of dispute with the passage of time.

[14] For legal draftsmanship generally, see R. Dickerson, The Fundamentals of Legal Drafting (1965); D. Mellinkoff, Legal Writing — Sense and NonSense (1982). For a discussion of the approach taken by the District of Columbia Court of Appeals to ambiguities in leases, see Hill, *Ambiguity in Leases*, 29 Harv.L.J. 63 (1986).

[15] "It is submitted that the utility of vague standards in drafting is limited to situations where the parties' intentions are not definite regarding topics that are not vital to their interests; but the cases show that there are topics in which the pressure for sharp disagreement and litigation is constant and upon which there should be clear agreement in advance." Landis, *Problems in Drafting Percentage Leases*, 36 B.U.L. Rev. 190, 222 (1956).

[16] *See* Falcon Research & Dev. Co. v. Craddock, 101 N.M. 122, 679 P.2d 264 (1984) (both landlord and tenant appealed trial court's decision about the amount of escalation).

[17] The discussion in D. Mellinkoff, The Language of the Law 279-82 (1963), cannot be too highly recommended. See § **3.17**.

Ambiguity is compounded by the omnipresent legalese that survives despite its heritage of meaninglessness. Consider "herein." Does it refer to the sentence, the paragraph, or the agreement in which it appears? Ambiguity can be easily be avoided by saying "in this sentence," "in this paragraph," or "in this agreement."

The following words and phrases do not appear in the forms in this book: herein, hereinafter, hereinbefore, hereinbelow, hereinabove, heretofore, therein, thereafter, said, and/or, lessor, lessee, whereas, wherein, shall, provided however, or notwithstanding anything herein to the contrary. The forms do not appear to suffer from their loss.

Examples of faulty draftsmanship can be, and are, multiplied endlessly. Consider a simple provision that goes astray: the tenant may renew the lease if it gives notice "within thirty days from expiration." This statement has been held to allow notice within 30 days after expiration.[18] A purchase option that could be exercised "at the end of the term" meant a reasonable time after the end of the lease.[19] Does a purchase price "based on" an appraisal mean the appraised value or a higher amount purportedly "based on" the appraisal? Reversing the trial court, a Texas appellate court ruled that the purchase price was only the appraised value.[20] In a case of needless litigation involving poor drafting,[21] the lease said that the tenant could exercise its renewal on the expiration date of the lease. The tenant gave notice before that date, the landlord refused to recognize this renewal, and the court upheld the validity of the renewal over the landlord's specious objections. In a Minnesota case, a landlord unsuccessfully maintained that a purchase option that could be exercised at the end of the 10th year could not be exercised 90 days before the end of the 10th year.[22] Each word must be chosen with care.

Despite Bertrand Russell's belief that it is impossible to combine intelligibility and precision, clarity of expression can be enhanced by the use of short defined terms instead of repeating lengthy names or descriptions. Commonly *landlord* (*or lessor*) and *tenant* (*or lessee*) replace full names and descriptions. The choice is a personal one; however, since the age-old terms *landlord* and *tenant* are more difficult to confuse than *lessor* and *lessee*, costly errors may be avoided by use of the otherwise undesirable archaism. This book chooses *landlord* and *tenant* as the lesser of two evils.

The property that is leased is commonly referred to as the *premises*. This term is preferable to *leased premises* which is redundant, and also to *demised premises* which occasionally prompts an inquiry about who died. Some leases use *leased*

---

[18] McQuinn v. City of Guntersville, 277 Ala. 328, 169 So. 2d 771 (1964).

[19] Getty Ref. & Mktg. Co. v. Zweibel, 604 F. Supp. 774 (D. Conn. 1985).

[20] Corriveau v. 3005 Inv. Corp., 697 S.W.2d 766 (Tex. Ct. App. 1985).

[21] *See* Willard E. Robertson Corp. v. Benson Continental Motors, Inc., 476 So.2d 7 (La. Ct. App. 1985).

[22] Crosstown Bell, Inc. v. Northwestern Bell Tel. Co., 381 N.W.2d 911 (Minn. Ct. App.), *review denied*, May 16, 1986.

premises or *demised premises* to refer to the tenant's space and *use premises* to refer to the building of which the tenant's space is a part. In those leases, confusion is almost unavoidable.

Thoughtless use of a defined term can lead to unwanted results. For example, leases often use the term *base monthly rent* to define a fixed obligation and the term *rent* to mean the tenant's other monetary obligations under the lease. If the landlord has agreed to abate base monthly rent as an inducement to the tenant's entry into the lease, but the lease simply says that rent will be abated, the landlord will have to pay the tenant's other monetary obligations. Thus, whenever a defined term is used (especially an inclusive one), the real estate professional must consider its meaning in each context in which it is used.

The need for precision is clearest in two particular instances: the escalation of rent pursuant to an index, and the calculation of percentage rent. Errors in these provisions have readily ascertainable monetary consequences. Extreme caution is therefore required; it is often helpful to translate the verbal expression to a mathematical one and to work through examples outside of the lease itself.

§ 2.4   Poor Use of a General Provision: The Most Favored Tenant Provision

The inadvertent misuse of defined terms is akin to the reckless use of general provisions. *Most favored tenant* provisions are prime examples of this mistake. The first tenants in a new development often demand that the landlord assure them that no later tenants will get more favorable lease terms than they did. Their concern is understandable: if subsequent leasing falters, the landlord may make concessions in order to attract tenants and the first tenants should also have those concessions. Problems arise, however, when a lease states that the landlord will give the first tenant the same favorable agreements that the landlord gives subsequent tenants. Presumably, this provision would be effected by an amendment to the first tenant's lease.

Such a general provision is completely unworkable because of the many possible variations of rights and obligations between the landlord and the subsequent tenant. Although it may seem like a great benefit to the tenant, and may even be intended to be so, the tenant will find itself unable to determine what the "most" favorable terms are. For example, does a tenant of 1,000 square feet derive any benefit from an option to expand to 30,000 feet over a two-year period, just because a later larger tenant gets that option? Does a subsequent tenant to whom the landlord lends money (with interest) for leasehold improvements have an advantage over a tenant whose premises are constructed according to building standard specifications? If it does, what can the landlord do about it after the first tenant has taken occupancy?

If the first tenant wants to assure itself of the more favorable rental rates that may be given to subsequent tenants, most favored tenant provisions become impossible. For example, if one lease has cost of living adjustments and the other one has fixed increases, the economic effect on the first tenant cannot be correctly understood until the end of its term. However, its term may end before the end of the subsequent tenant's term. If that occurs, increases in the subsequent tenant's rent after the end of the first tenant's term may make the net economic cost to the subsequent tenant greater than the net economic cost to the first tenant. For another example, how can the first tenant, which operates a jewelry store, say that its percentage rental rate is less favorable than the subsequent tenant, which operates a sporting goods store. Real estate professionals would agree that they should not be given the same percentage rental rate, but they would probably disagree as to what each rate should be. If a landlord were to take a more scientific approach and promise a tenant the same sort of economic deal, when compared in a way such as § **6.13** describes, a landlord and tenant would still argue about assumptions and the sorts of problems described in this paragraph would nevertheless be irresoluble.

If a landlord must give most favored tenant protection, the provision should be carefully limited in duration and in scope. For example, use:

FORM 2-1
MOST FAVORED TENANT—LONG FORM

Beginning on the date of this lease and ending on the second anniversary of that date, landlord will offer to amend this lease if landlord enters into a lease of any part of the building that gives any other tenant of the building at no cost more than three (3) directory strips for each 1,000 square feet of its premises. The amendment will provide Tenant at no cost such greater number of directory strips for each 1,000 square feet of its premises as was given to the other tenant.

Such a provision is preferable to:

FORM 2-2
MOST FAVORED TENANT—SHORT FORM

Landlord will not give any other tenant more directory strips than it gave Tenant.

Most favored tenant provisions are given only to the most desirable tenants in the biggest possible markets. If they must be given, landlord should consider some further limitations:

1. A tenant's sole remedy on account of landlord's breach should be for specific performance of landlord's promise. In no event should the tenant have a right to terminate the lease or seek damages.

2. The protection should not extend to leases that are not comparable to the size of the first tenant's premises, for example, within 15 percent of their size. A less desirable way for the landlord to express that notion is that leases below a specified size and leases above a specified size will not enable the first tenant to compel modification of its lease.

3. The provision should limit the total monetary rent reduction and the total
    monetary cost to landlord to stated sums, for example, no more than
    $10,000 annual reduction in rent or no more than $10,000 in actual out-
    of-pocket costs to landlord to comply with the provision. The landlord
    should be certain that the limitation on rent reduction or cost effect is
    aggregated for all the subsequent leases.
4. The provision should not be binding upon landlord's lender that succeeds
    to landlord's title.

Administration of these provisions are fraught with problems. Is the landlord
supposed to disclose to the first tenant every subsequent tenant's lease (which is
the tenant's preference, but the landlord's burden), or is landlord merely to certify
periodically that it has not entered into a more favorable lease, or is the tenant
relegated to catching the landlord if it happens to learn of a breach? If the landlord
must disclose subsequent leases, the most favored tenant provisions raise a
significant tenant-relation issue for landlord. Most subsequent tenants will not
consent to this in advance and will be angered by it if it occurs without their
consent. If their prior consent is asked because of a most favored tenant provision
under an earlier lease, they will ask for similar most favored tenant protection and
for information about the first tenant's lease.

Finally, a landlord who proposes to give such a provision must be certain that
its lender's underwriting assumptions are not belied by the action of the
provision; its lender's consent to such a provision is imperative for a landlord.

§ 2.5 Good Use of a General Provision: Assuring Uniform Treatment of Tenants

For all its faults, the most favored tenant provision has a worthwhile relative.
Assuming that the tenant has not been able to negotiate an all-inclusive most
favored tenant provision (and perhaps even if it has), the tenant will still want
certain provisions of its lease carried into other leases without modification. In a
sense, the tenant wants a "least" favored tenant provision by which it seeks to
assure itself that it will not be treated more poorly than other tenants.

A clear example is the provision for measurement of the premises. If the
landlord's operating expenses are allocated in the proportion that a tenant's area
bears to the entire area of all tenants, all premises must be measured in the same
way. If one tenant's premises are measured with regard to mezzanines and
identical premises of another tenant are not, the first tenant will pay a greater
share of operating expenses than the second tenant. That is just one way in which
uniformity is necessary. Uniformity is also appropriate with regard to store
hours, sharing of expenses, prohibitions of overloading utility services, and
obligations to merchants associations. In all of those provisions, the tenant should
be assured that all tenants will be treated in the same way.

At least two cases of disparate treatment of tenants have reached the courts. In
one case, the lease provided that all tenants would share the cost of real estate

taxes but that the landlord could exclude certain tenants from those who shared that cost. As a result, the other tenants bore a disproportionate share of the real estate taxes. A Wisconsin court agreed with the tenant that the provision was unconscionable.[23] Other courts would have enforced the provision as written.

In another case, typewritten additions to a printed shopping center lease provided that the tenant would not be obligated to pay its share of common area maintenance or real estate taxes unless "at least ninety-five percent (95%) of the other tenants of the Shopping Center are also required to comply with the terms and conditions as herein provided." The owner unsuccessfully maintained that this meant other tenants were paying their shares of those amounts pursuant to provisions of their leases, even though the provisions were not the same as in the complaining tenant's lease. The provision was enforced as written.[24] As a matter of drafting, the tenant would probably have been even better off with a provision that tied its payment obligation to "tenants occupying at least 95% of the leasable area of the shopping center."

Both the most favored tenant provision and its worthwhile relative require attention to one further detail: the distinction between sellers of goods and sellers of services. The fast-food franchisee and the optometrist are in entirely different businesses. They should not be treated equally. Consequently, any provision for uniformity among tenants must be limited to uniformity among comparable tenants.

§ 2.6 Scope

This book is confined to written[25] office building leases,[26] shopping center leases, and single tenant building leases. Single tenant buildings are often called *free standing buildings*; because buildings are generally free standing, this term is not very helpful. The lease of the single tenant building is what some real estate professionals call a *net lease*; for these purposes, one may envision an industrial

---

[23] Foursquare Properties Joint Venture I v. Johnny's Loaf & Stein, Ltd., 116 Wis. 2d 679, 343 N.W. 2d 126 (Ct. App. 1983).

[24] Great Falls Hardware Co. of Reston v. South Lakes Village Center Assoc., Ltd., _____ Va. _____ , 380 S.E.2d 642 (1989).

[25] This assumption of a written — and signed — lease obviates any discussion of those parts of the statute of frauds which deal with the need for a "writing." *See* 2 Powell § 222(1). *See generally* 3 G.W. Thompson, Commentaries on the Modern Law of Real Property §§ 1097-1101 (1980 repl. vol.) (statute of frauds and leases). *But see* Trinity Carton Co. v. Falstaff Brewing Corp., 767 F.2d 184 (5th Cir.), *reh'g denied,* 775 F.2d 301 (5th Cir. 1985), *cert. denied,* 106 S. Ct. 1202 (1986) (applying Louisiana law and holding that an oral lease is valid if landlord and tenant did not condition their agreement on written agreement).

[26] *See* R. Simpson, Leasing Concepts: a Guide to Leasing Office Space ch. 2 (1983) (one of the rare general discussions of office leases); Hershman, *Practical Aspects of Commercial Leasing,* Prac. Real Est. Law, Jan. 1985, at 12; Di Sciullo, *Negotiating a Commercial Lease From the Tenant's Perspective,* Real Est. L.J., Summer 1989, at 27.

building[27] or single tenant retail store standing alone on a parcel of land that surrounds it.[28] An understanding of these three types of leases will encompass the vast majority of commercial real estate leases.[29]

The term *net lease* is awful. It has no single meaning. It refers to leases in which tenants pay only insurance costs, it refers to leases in which tenants pay all expenses of operation and maintenance, and it refers to leases in shopping centers and office buildings and industrial parks. Occasionally, this book uses the term (with doubt and regret) as a name for leases in which the tenant is intended to assume all the burdens of ownership: taxes, insurance, operation and maintenance, liability to third persons, and compliance with laws.[30] The net lease is contrasted with the *gross lease*, under which the tenant usually pays only rent and the landlord retains all other burdens of ownership;[31] The term gross lease, however, is likewise not uniformly defined.

Several types of real estate leases have been deliberately omitted: ground leases;[32] residential and apartment leases; leases to or from governmental agencies; proprietary and cooperative leases; sale-leaseback transactions;[33] and leases of air rights. The federal income tax consequences of real estate leases are also outside the scope of this book.

Although numerous statutes and court decisions are mentioned, no part of this book should be relied upon without research of the laws and decisions that govern a proposed transaction. For example, in order to avoid the effect of a particular state statute,[34] a California real estate lease is likely to include a provision such as "the destruction of the premises will not terminate this lease"; however, the

---

[27] *See Pro-Tenant Industrial Lease—A Landlord Analysis*, Leasing Prof., June 1987, at 1 (discussion of landlord's response to industrial tenant's form lease); Gerro, *The Nuts and Bolts of Negotiating Industrial Leases*, L.A. Law., Jan. 1986, at 22.

[28] *See* Friedman, *Lease Provisions for Developing a Single-Tenant Retail Store*, J. Real Est. Devel., Spring 1989, at 51; Halper, *The Self-Occupancy Ground Lease* (pts. I & III), 18 Real Est. Rev. 32 (1988), 19 Real Est. Rev. 39 (1989) (complete discussions).

[29] *Report of the Real Estate Financing Committee, Subcommittee on Commercial Lease Checklist, A Practical Guide to Reviewing a Commercial Lease*, 19 Real Prop. Prob. & Tr. J. 891 (1984). *See also* Kuklin, *What to Look for in Space Leases*, 4 Prac. Real Est. Law. 69 (1988).

[30] *See* Howard & Howard, *Suggestions for Negotiating a Net Lease*, 28 Prac. Law. 39 (1982); *see generally* Kemph, *Drafting Commercial Leases*, 10 Real Est. L.J. 99 (1981); Smith & Lubell, *Real Estate Financing: Leases: Net and Not So Net*, 8 Real Est. Rev. 14 (1979). Cohen, *What To Look For When You Negotiate Net Leases*, Prac. Real Est. Law., Sept. 1988, at 23.

[31] 2 Powell § 242(1)(b)(i) n.19.

[32] *See* Nelson & Schnall, *An Introduction to Ground Leases (with Form)*, 4 Prac. Real Est. Law. 21 (1988) (discussion of the salient issues in ground leases); Whalen, Commercial Ground Leases (1988).

[33] For illuminating discussions of sale-leaseback transactions, see Segal, *Structuring a Sale-Leaseback of Commercial Property*, 2 Prac. Real Est. Law. 21 (1986); Black, *Sale Leaseback Transactions: Advantages and Disadvantages*, Prob. & Prop., May/June 1989, at 23. For special emphasis on the income tax aspects of sale-leaseback transactions, see Maller, *Structuring a Sale-Leaseback Transaction*, 15 Real Est. L.J. 291 (1987);

[34] Cal. Civ. Code § 1932(2) (West 1976). *See also* P. Rohan, Real Estate Transactions § 2.01(1) (Supp. 1984) (collection of relevant statutes).

relevant forms in this book make no mention of such a provision. Similarly, since Texas law prohibits certain assignments and subleases,[35] a Texas lease may not make any provision for these matters. At common law, and in most other states, assignments and subleases are allowed unless expressly prohibited. As a result, using a Texas lease outside of Texas could have the unintended result of allowing assignments and subleases.

This book may refer to a case in one state that is not the rule in a real estate professional's own state. In fact, trial courts and intermediate appellate courts within a state may disagree with one another. As important as knowing the law in one's own state is knowing the direction of the law in that state and others. For example, a real estate professional who advises a landlord that it can arbitrarily and capriciously decline a tenant's requested consent to an assignment or sublease may be making a mistake; although judicial decisions may support the advice, a court is likely to reconsider older precedents in view of emerging rules in that area of the law. See § **12.6**.

§ 2.7   A Balanced Lease

"You can't always get what you want," it has been said, "but if you try sometimes you can get what you need."[36] Although lease negotiations were probably not in the speaker's mind, the observation holds true in that context. Neither the landlord nor the tenant gets what it wants, but with reasonable negotiations they should get what they need. The lease has a midpoint at which the legitimate interests of the landlord and tenant are perfectly balanced. This midpoint exists whether the lease is for premises built to suit a Fortune 500 company or for a "mom-and-pop" store. The midpoint changes; the principle does not.[37]

Real estate professionals should prepare leases with this midpoint in mind and should work toward the midpoint in the negotiations. This is true whether they are preparing slight modifications to form leases in multi-tenant projects or drafting unique leases. By seeking the midpoint and no more for their respective clients, real estate professionals can save time and money and avoid the acrimonious feelings that develop when negotiations become pitched battles.[38]

---

[35] Tex. Rev. Civ. Stat. Ann. art. 5237 (Vernon 1962); Lehrer v. Wegenhoft, 203 S.W.2d 245 (Tex. Civ. App. 1947), *writ ref'd n.r.e.*

[36] Rolling Stones, "Let It Bleed," London Records, Inc. NPS-4.

[37] Halper, Emanuel B., *Can You Find a Fair Lease?*, 14 Real Est. L.J. 99 (1985) is, like everything else he writes, required reading. *See* Kuklin, *On the Knowing Inclusion of Unenforceable Contract and Lease Terms,* 56 Cincinnati L. Rev. 845 (1988) (cerebral discussion of moral, economic, and sociological consequences).

[38] I am indebted to the late Bill Christie of Pillsbury, Madison & Sutro, San Francisco, for teaching me this important lesson. He prepared a lease on behalf of a landlord and submitted it to me. As a young lawyer, I had only perfunctory comments about it and mentioned its apparent fairness to him. He explained what I call the principle of the midpoint—that he prepared a first draft of lease in the form that he anticipated a reasonably negotiated lease would ultimately take.

PART II

THE ESSENTIAL LEASE PROVISIONS

CHAPTER 3

INTRODUCTORY PROVISIONS

§ 3.1   Presenting Basic Lease Information

A concise presentation of basic lease information in a cover sheet to the lease assists the landlord's administration of several similar leases in a single development, enables the real estate professional to review quickly the important terms of any lease, and appropriately closes out a lease transaction. A lease often has a table of contents and rarely an index, which is far less useful than a table of contents.

Forms are set forth in *Commercial Real Estate Leases: Forms* for presenting basic lease information in office building leases, shopping center leases, and single tenant building leases. Provisions for renewals, options, and other tenant benefits are not set forth in these forms because landlords generally do not want to bring these opportunities to a tenant's attention. However, the landlord's internal lease abstracts must describe those sorts of negotiated matters, and the basic lease information should be amended to reflect them. A form of office building lease summary is also set forth in *Commercial Real Estate Leases: Forms*.

§ 3.2   Identifying the Lease

The modern lease customarily begins by identifying itself and the landlord and tenant:

FORM 3-1
INTRODUCTION

THIS LEASE is made on _____, 19____ , by _____ ("landlord"), and _____ ("tenant").

When basic lease information is set forth in a form like those in *Commercial Real Estate Leases: Forms*, the introduction may be:

FORM 3-2
INTRODUCTION—AN ALTERNATIVE

THIS LEASE is entered into by landlord and tenant described in the basic lease information on the date set forth for reference only in the basic lease information.

Although the real estate professional can complete Form 3-1 without much thought, some considerations should come to mind.

§ 3.3   Date of the Lease

The first date stated in the lease may do much more than help to identify the lease. It may be the commencement date of the term. If it is not, it may still be the date that some of the tenant's obligations begin; for example, although the term may begin when the premises are available for occupancy, the lease may subsequently provide the tenant's obligations to pay real estate taxes starts "on the date first written above."

The date of the lease may be an important point of reference. Perhaps the tenant is obligated to pay any increase in real estate taxes over a base year, and the base year is the one in which the lease is signed. If the tenant occupies the premises in a later year and, if real estate taxes increase, it will automatically be obligated to pay an increase. The date of the lease may also affect:

1. **The term of the lease**. "This lease will expire five years after the date of this lease."
2. **A renewal right**. "Tenant must give notice of its election to renew this lease on or before the fourth anniversary of the date of this lease."
3. **An increase in rent**. "On the first day of the sixtieth full month after the date of this lease, the monthly rent will be increased to $5,000."

In each of these examples, unless the tenant occupies the premises on the date of the lease, the tenant may have less than it believed—a shorter term, a shorter period to decide whether to renew its lease, or a faster escalation of its rent. Note the importance of the date of the lease in **Form 2-1**.

The same care must be exercised when the term is mentioned. A lease may give a tenant "free rent" during the term, but require that all other expenses (such as operating expenses) be paid during the term. In that case, the free rent period is not entirely free. Furthermore, the tenant may have obligations during the term that do not coincide with its occupancy. A lease may require the tenant to indemnify the landlord against liabilities. If the tenant is given a period at the beginning of the term to improve its premises and prepare them for its occupancy, the tenant will have an insurance obligation during that period. The tenant without adequate insurance will have an uncovered risk.

Throughout the lease, the real estate professional must watch for references to the date of the lease and the term of the lease.

§ 3.4 Tradenames and Service Marks

First of all, the landlord may wish to protect the name of its development as a service mark or tradename according to federal or local law. By way of examples, there are federal service mark registrations for the names of Crestwood Plaza in Kansas City, Missouri, and K Mart Plaza, and for the logos of Northwest Plaza in St. Ann, Missouri, and Horton Plaza in San Diego, California.[1] The tenant's tradename is considered in § **10.12**.

§ 3.5 Individuals

A lease to a married person should be signed by that person's spouse. Cosignature deters fraudulent spousal transfers if the business fails, and also assures the landlord that the proprietor's likely heir will be liable if the proprietor dies. Since

---

[1] *See* Schiff & Haddad, *What's in A Name?*, 2 J. Real Est. Dev. 75 (1986) (valuable discussion of this important matter).

death does not terminate a tenant's obligations under a lease,[2] the proprietor's estate will be burdened by the lease. To avoid a crushing liability, a sole proprietor tenant ought to insist upon inclusion of a provision such as:

FORM 3-3
TENANT—DEATH OF A SOLE PROPRIETOR

If tenant dies or becomes disabled (as defined in this paragraph), tenant or tenant's personal representative may cancel this lease by notice given to landlord within _____ days after the date on which tenant dies or becomes disabled. The lease will terminate without further liability to tenant on the _____ day after landlord's receipt of the notice. The term "disabled" means that tenant is unable to conduct its business at the Premises because of tenant's physical or mental illness, or injury.

If the tenant cannot get that provision, term life and disability insurance may be desirable. Sole proprietorships usually prompt a landlord to ask for credit enhancement: a guaranty or a large deposit.

When there is more than one tenant, all tenants are jointly and severally obligated. Many leases state this rule in the manner shown in § **32.17**. Co-owners are considered in § **3.6**.

Finally, when dealing with individuals, the tenant should assure itself that the individual is the fee simple owner of the premises. A life tenant, for example, is usually unable to grant a lease that extends beyond his or her death.[3]

§ 3.6   Co-Owners and Co-Tenants

All co-owners—joint tenants and tenants in common—should sign a lease as landlord.[4] When a lease is signed by less than all joint tenants, and the nonsigning joint tenant is the last to survive, the lease will end at the time of the death of the penultimate joint tenant, and the nonsigning joint tenant will be free of the lease.[5] When a defaulting tenant claimed that its lease was invalid because only one of three co-owners had signed it as landlord, the District of Columbia Court of Appeals first observed that the tenant had occupied the premises for more than three years before raising its claim. The court then distinguished the nonsigning co-owners' claims against the signing co-owners for their fair shares

---

[2] *See* 2 R. Powell, The Law of Real Property § 1 (P.J. Rohan ed. 1971 revis.)[hereinafter Powell] (expansion of this theme). Annot., 42 A.L.R. 4th 963, *Death of lessee as terminating lease* (1985), in accord with the text and discussing special exceptions to the general rule.

[3] Annot., 14 A.L.R.4th 1054, *Life tenant's death as affecting rights under lease given by him* (1982).

[4] 3 G.W. Thompson, Commentaries on The Modern Law of Real Property §§ 1071-1972 (1980 repl. vol.) [hereinafter Thompson].

[5] Tenhet v. Boswell, 18 Cal. 3d 150, 133 Cal. Rptr. 10, 554 P.2d 330 (1976).

of rental income (which the court acknowledged) from any infirmity of the lease on account of the number of signers (which the court denied).[6]

Co-tenants have fiduciary duties to one another that preclude one from acting in its own interest to the detriment of the other.[7]

A lease from a married person should be signed by the landlord's spouse. This is imperative in leases made in states that recognize community property and in leases that grant a right to purchase the premises.

§ 3.7   Corporations

If the tenant is a corporation, its certificate of incorporation or charter should be reviewed in order to be certain that it has the power and authority to make a lease; under modern corporation laws, such matters are usually found in omnibus articles. An incumbency certificate and a specific resolution of the tenant's board of directors ought to be examined. The resolution may say:

FORM 3-4
TENANT—CORPORATE RESOLUTION

RESOLVED, that the lease dated _____, _____, between _____, as landlord, and the Company, as tenant, in the form attached to these minutes, with respect to certain real property, known as _____ Street, City of _____, County of _____, State of _____ is approved and that _____, as president of the Company, and _____, as secretary of the Company, on behalf of the Company are authorized and directed to execute and deliver the lease to the landlord.

Nevertheless, later in the lease, the tenant's signatories will represent that the tenant has the requisite power and authority to enter into the lease and that they are authorized to sign on its behalf (see § **32.18**). When the signatory on behalf of the corporate landlord is not authorized to sign the lease, but the tenant does not claim lack of authority for two years after the lease is signed, tenant cannot escape its liability under the lease.[8] Leases that are adopted by corporate resolution should be amended by corporate resolution. Local law governs the necessity or desirability of affixing the corporate seal.

If the tenant is incorporated in a state other than the one in which the premises are located, both the landlord and tenant should consider tenant's need for qualification to do business as a foreign corporation[9] and the appointment of a

---

[6] Washington Ins. Agency, Inc. v. Friedlander, 487 A.2d 599 (D.C. 1985).

[7] Rosenthal v. Mahler, 141 A.D.2d 625, 529 N.Y.S.2d 365 (1988).

[8] Dobbs v. Titan Properties, Inc., 178 Ga. App. 389, 343 S.E.2d 419 (1986).

[9] A lease incidental to the business in which the corporation is engaged does not require qualification as a foreign corporation, 36 Am. Jur. 2d *Foreign Corporations* § 343 (1968).

local agent for service of process.[10] Finally, if the landlord is leasing all or substantially all its assets in a transaction that is not in the ordinary course of its business, approval by its board of directors or shareholders may be necessary.[11]

If a principal shareholder of a corporate tenant is essential to the tenant's success, the landlord may want to assure that shareholder's active involvement in its business; this is accomplished simply by requiring the principal shareholder to guarantee the lease (thus insuring his or her interest in the business) and providing that it is a default under the lease for the principal shareholder to devote less than all of his or her energy to the operation of the tenant's business. Since control of a corporation passes with the transfer of its stock, the landlord will want to restrict stock transfers in the manner described in § **12.9**.

A cautious practice in drafting a lease is to go directly from the introductory description of a corporate tenant to the signature blocks at the end of the lease. This will assure that they are identical. In one case, the introduction described the tenant as "Grebe and Simon, d/b/a The Burnt Wood, Inc." This would usually result in personal liability for Grebe and Simon. However, the signature block was prepared and signed in the form for a corporate tenant and the lease was held to be a corporate, not a personal, obligation.[12]

Corporate officers are always well advised to show that they are signing as officers, for example, by signing "Jones Corporation, a _____ corporation, by John J. Jones, as its president."[13] Corporate officers who each sign a corporate lease twice (once described as officers and once without description) have been held jointly and severally personally liable, the second signature suggesting a cosignature.[14]

On the other hand, a corporation whose name appeared as tenant, in a lease that was signed by its sole shareholder personally, had a corporate obligation since the corporation paid the rent, the corporation's name was on the door of the premises, the corporation's property was in the premises, and the corporation did not make any suggestion that it was not bound by the lease for more than a year after the lease commenced.[15]

---

[10] See Annot., 59 A.L.R.2d 1131, *Leasing of real estate by foreign corporation, as lessor or lessee, as doing business within state statutes prescribing conditions of right to do business* (1958).

[11] Model Bus. Corp. Act Ann. § 79 (2d 1971).

[12] L.R. Property Management, Inc. v. Grebe, 96 N.M. 22, 627 P.2d 864 (1981). In the face of compelling evidence, what appears to be a personal obligation may be held to be a corporate obligation. Savois v. Taylor, 447 So.2d 1219 (La. Ct. App. 1984).

[13] In Diversified Realty, Inc. v. McElroy, 41 Wash. App. 171, 703 P.2d 323 (1985), the landlord's assertion that the tenant (a corporation) and its principal officer were jointly liable on a lease was contradicted by the principal officer's execution of the lease in his representative capacity only. The principal officer was the president (and vice president, in this case).

[14] Spicer v. James, 21 Ohio App. 3d 222, 487 N.E.2d 353 (1985).

[15] Holloway v. Acadian News Agency, Inc., 488 So.2d 328 (La. Ct. App. 1986). *See also* Booker v. Trizec Properties, Inc., 184 Ga. App. 782, 363 S.E.2d 13 (1987), *cert. denied*, 184 Ga. App. 909 (1988) (involving professional law corporation and unsuccessful alter-ego theory by landlord).

§ 3.8 Partnerships

A lease with a partnership raises questions about the purposes for which the partnership was formed. In addition, in contrast to corporations (whose existence is generally perpetual), a partnership should have a specific term that exceeds the term of the lease and any available extensions or renewal terms. The authority and required number of signatory partners should be determined from the partnership agreement. Often, a resolution of the partnership is adopted in much the same form as a corporate resolution. Limited partnerships may be required to qualify as foreign limited partnerships if they are organized outside of the state in which the premises are located. The observations in this paragraph pertain to partnerships both as landlords and as tenants.

Just as certain transfers of corporate stock are prohibited, so also are transfers of partnership interests by those whose involvement is necessary for the tenant-partnership's success. Transfers of partnership interests effectively result in an assignment of the lease and are usually prohibited by broad anti-assignment provisions such as those set forth in § **12.9**; a prohibition of assignments by a tenant is not necessarily breached by assignments of partnership interests.[16]

Because all the partners of a general partnership are liable for the acts and debts of the partnership, partnership tenants should ask for the landlord's agreement that retiring or withdrawing partners will be relieved from liability under the lease so long as new partners assume the obligations under the lease.

FORM 3-5
TENANT—LIABILITY OF CERTAIN PARTNERS

So long as tenant's new partners assume tenant's obligations under this lease accruing after the date of their assumption and agree to be bound by this lease after that date, any partner in tenant who retires or dies will be released from any liability under this lease that accrues after the date of retirement or death. This paragraph applies to present and future partners in tenant and to any successor partnership that becomes tenant under this lease.

Landlords should resist this general provision if the lease is based on the creditworthiness of particular partners. Those partners should not be able to escape from their liabilities.

§ 3.9 Agents, Representatives, and Guardians

The authority of persons acting in representative capacities must be verified by reference to the instruments that empower them and the statutes that govern

---

[16] Madison 52nd Corp. v. Luxemburg, 204 N.Y.S.2d 185, 8 N.Y.2d 955, 168 N.E.2d 851 (1960); Wester & Co. v. Nestle, 669 P.2d 1046 (Colo. Ct. App. 1983); Barnett v. Buchan Baking Co., 45

them.[17] A trust, for example, often does not allow its trustee to enter into leases of more than a certain term. A guardian may have no power to bind its ward after the ward's minority; a 20-year lease with a guardian may be cut short when the ward reaches lawful age.[18] In some cases, court approval may be necessary in order to have an effective lease. An agent's authority must be written.[19] Usually, the written authorization is a power of attorney. If a tenant's lawyer renews his client's lease without written authorization, the landlord may be able to avoid the renewal.[20] By the same token, a notice of termination given by a landlord's lawyer is invalid if the lease requires such notices from the landlord.[21]

A prudent representative will want to be sure its liability is appropriately limited by including the following provision:

FORM 3-6
LANDLORD — REPRESENTATIVE'S EXCULPATION

Landlord is acting solely in its representative capacity as [trustee under the John Jones Irrevocable Trust dated _____ , (the "trust")], in entering into this lease. Landlord has no personal liability under this lease. Landlord's liability under this lease will be limited to the trust's assets as they may exist from time to time.

§ 3.10   Charitable Associations, Campaign Committees, and Government Entities

Charitable associations, political campaign committees, and government entities present problems for landlords because their unique budgetary structures leave some question as to their continuing ability to pay. For charitable associations and campaign committees, landlords may demand substantial prepayments or a responsible person's guarantee of payment and performance.

Governmental entities are also troublesome landlords. The statutes, charters, and administrative codes that constitute them often limit their power to lease. As one might expect, a fundamental question is whether the lease is in furtherance of public benefit or private gain. Even a lease for private gain may have direct public benefit, such as increased employment. If the municipality can be convinced that

---

Wash. App. 152, 724 P.2d 1077 (1986); *aff'd*, 108 Wash. 2d 405, 738 P.2d 1056 (1987); Hoops v. Tate, 104 Cal. App. 2d 486, 231 P.2d 560 (1951).

[17] Annot., 95 A.L.R.2d 258, *Power and authority in the absence of determining clause in will, of executor or administrator to lease out, or to rent, decedent's real estate* (1964).

[18] 3 Thompson § 1074.

[19] *See* Winters, *Detrimental Reliance in an Agency Setting: The Demise of Apparent Authority*, 33 Loy. L. Rev. 1162 (1988) (discussing Breaux v. Schlumberger Offshore Servs., 817 F.2d 1226 (5th Cir. 1987), and the relevant Louisiana law).

[20] III Lounge, Inc. v. Gaines, 217 Neb. 466, 348 N.W.2d 903 (1984), *appeal after remand*, 227 Neb. 585, 419 N.W.2d 143 (1988).

[21] See § **30.6**.

the premises are not useful to the public—as is often the case with land near railroad tracks or land that is virtually surrounded by private enterprise—the obstacles to a lease are diminished. Still, the real estate professional must be aware of limitations on the duration of such leases, because they are often limited to the term of the public officials who approved them.[22]

Municipalities may impose affirmative action hiring programs in their leases.[23] Finally, there are often requirements for notice and hearing on proposed leases, thus making a proposed lease contingent on proper approval.[24]

§ 3.11   Tax-Exempt Organizations

Leases involving tax-exempt organizations mandate consideration of an exemption from real property taxation. These considerations are as important to the tenant of a tax-exempt landlord[25] as they are to a tax-exempt tenant and its landlord.[26] The inquiry is governed by various state laws; generalizations are necessarily vague. As a general rule, when a governmental unit leases its land, the tenant's leasehold is taxable; of course, the government's reversion is not taxable. When a taxable landlord leases to a governmental unit, the premises remain fully taxable.[27] When both the landlord and tenant are tax-exempt, the landlord's real property tax exemption is not lost;[28] again, this example occurs under one state's laws.

There may also be adverse federal income tax consequences in leasing to tax-exempt entities, because the time period over which depreciation deductions must be taken may be affected.[29]

---

[22] *See* Mardikes, Cone, & Van Horn, *Governmental Leasing: A Fifty State Survey of Legislation and Case Law*, 18 Urban Law. 1 (1986).

[23] Alioto's Fish Co. v. Human Rights Comm'n, 120 Cal. App. 3d 594, 174 Cal. Rptr. 763 (1981), *cert. denied*, 455 U.S. 944, 102 S. Ct. 1441 (1982).

[24] Annot., 47 A.L.R.3d 19, *Power of municipal corporation to lease or sublet property owned or leased by it* (1973).

[25] Annot., 54 A.L.R.3d 402, *Comment note: Availability of tax exemption to property held on lease from tax exempt owner* (1973).

[26] Annot., 55 A.L.R.3d 430, *Property tax: exemption of property leased by and used for purposes of otherwise tax exempt body* (1974); 2 Powell § 241 n.21.

[27] City of Desert Hot Springs v. Riverside County, 91 Cal. App. 3d 441, 154 Cal. Rptr. 297 (1979).

[28] Christ the Good Shepherd Lutheran Church v. Mathieson, 81 Cal. App. 3d 355, 146 Cal. Rptr. 321 (1978). In one case, the City and County of San Francisco leased property for use as parking garages in urban renewal projects. The city agreed to pay real property taxes and did so, paying the taxes to itself. A taxpayers' suit which called the arrangement an illegal tax exemption was rebuffed because the city was considered to be paying for services. Cane v. City & County of San Francisco, 78 Cal. App. 3d 654, 144 Cal. Rptr. 316 (1978). However, a landlord who leased its property for school use was allowed a property tax exemption as a matter of state constitutional law (because of the nature of the use for school purposes). Oates v. County of Sacramento, 78 Cal. App. 3d 745, 143 Cal. Rptr. 337 (1978).

[29] I.R.C. § 168 (1986, as amended).

§ 3.12   Tenants with Sovereign Immunity

A lease to a tenant with sovereign immunity, such as a foreign consulate, is particularly troublesome. Under the Foreign Missions Act,[30] all foreign government offices are required to notify the State Department before they acquire, sell, or otherwise dispose of real estate in the United States; leasing is included in those terms by definition. The State Department has 60 days to review the notification and it can require divestiture of any premises leased without compliance. As a result, a lease to a foreign government office must be conditioned on no objection from the State Department.[31]

If the landlord is able to avoid the pitfalls of the Foreign Sovereign Immunities Act of 1976 (FSIA),[32] it may still falter before the Vienna Convention on Diplomatic Relations,[33] which deals with privileges of individuals in foreign missions, and the Vienna Convention on Consular Relations,[34] which covers consulates. These conventions effectively preclude dispossession of the sovereign. As one commentator has said, the landlord may "have a right without a remedy."[35]

The FSIA and these conventions allow the foreign sovereigns to waive their immunities. Waivers sufficient to assure a landlord of a right to prosecute a possessory action successfully are extremely rare, and disputes seem to be resolved through negotiation rather than litigation.[36]

§ 3.13   Franchisors and Franchisees

Often, franchised operations, including many fast-food restaurants, offer financial strength, efficiency, national advertising, and substantial drawing power. On the other hand, the successful operations of one franchisee are vulnerable to adverse publicity about other franchises. On balance, though, franchised operations are usually attractive shopping center tenants.[37]

---

[30] Public Law 97-241, 96 Stat., 273 (1982).

[31] A great deal of the discussion in this section is derived from Odell, *Foreign Governments as Tenants*, N.Y.S. B.J., Jan. 1984, at 28, which clearly and comprehensively explains the issues.

[32] 28 U.S.C. §§ 1330, 1332(a)(2)-(4), 1391(f), 1441(d), 1602-1611(1976). The landlord's remedies are greater if the premises are used for nondiplomatic purposes (such as a commercial enterprise) than if they are used for diplomatic purposes.

[33] 23 U.S.T. 3227, T.I.A.S. 7502.

[34] 21 U.S.T. 77, T.I.A.S. 6820.

[35] Richards, *The Tenant With Sovereign Immunity*, 11 Real Est. L.J. 232 (1983).

[36] Odell, *Foreign Governments as Tenants*, N.Y.S. B.J., Jan. 1984, at 28. The extremely knowledgeable author has never seen such a waiver, but he also says he has never seen a dispute that could not be resolved through negotiation.

[37] Welsh, *Franchises in Shopping Centres*, in Shopping Centre Leases (H.M. Haber ed. 1976).

Typically, a franchisor approaches a shopping center with the intention of entering the market or assuring itself of a desirable new location. For the most part, these franchisors anticipate that they will find a franchisee to operate at the premises, but they do not yet know who that franchisee will be. Franchisors tend to be coy about their intentions to find a franchisee for the premises. This is unfortunate, because many problems can be avoided with proper planning. Therefore, the landlord must press the franchisor about its intentions.

When the franchisor lets the landlord know that it intends for a franchisee to operate at the premises (which may be when negotiations begin or when a franchisee is presented), the landlord will also learn that the franchisor wishes to sublease the premises to the franchisee. For the reasons explained in § **12.2**, a sublease, as opposed to an assignment, enables the franchisor to maintain control of the premises if the franchisee fails. The problem that this creates is that only the landlord and franchisor are bound to each other by the lease, while only the franchisor and franchisee are bound to each other by the franchise agreement and the sublease. However, the lease, the franchise agreement, and the sublease all affect the tenant's use of the premises. The landlord must harmonize these three documents.

Checklist

To do so, whether it agrees in advance to allow a franchisee to operate in the premises, or whether it is presented with a prospective franchisee after the lease is signed, the landlord should insist that:

_____ 1.   The landlord has the right to review the franchise agreement. This enables the landlord to determine whether the franchise agreement contradicts the lease, for example, by allowing the franchisee to operate in the premises in a way that is forbidden by the lease.

_____ 2.   The landlord has the right to review the prospective franchisee's financial strength and experience in operations. This enables the landlord to judge how successful the proposed franchisee is likely to be.

_____ 3.   The landlord's form of lease will be used as the form of the sublease. This requirement assures the landlord that the sublease is substantially identical to the lease and avoids any possible inconsistencies between them. Even though the sublease is subject to the lease by law, the landlord does not want to find itself in the position of demanding the franchisee's performance under a lease that the franchisee may never have seen.

_____ 4.   The franchisor will not be released by the sublease. This assures the landlord that it has the financial strength that it anticipated when it entered into the lease with the franchisor.

_____ 5.   The franchisee will make the same use of the premises as the lease requires and will use the franchisor's name in doing so.

_____ 6.   Neither the sublease nor the franchise agreement will be amended without the landlord's consent.

_____ 7.   The premises will not be further subleased, nor will the sublease be assigned. This gives the landlord some control over the occupant of the premises.

_____ 8.   A default under the sublease is a default under the franchise agreement, and a default under the franchise agreement is a default under the sublease, and the franchisor's failure to terminate the sublease and franchise agreement on account of such a breach is a breach of the lease. This puts the franchisor in the position of a virtual guarantor of franchisee's performance of the franchise agreement. Stated another way, it assures the landlord that the premises will be operated in a manner consistent with franchisor's standards. In that light, the provision is not so objectionable.

The landlord's ability to win many of these agreements is dependent upon the desirability of the franchisor. A strong franchisor may resist any restrictions on its dealings with the premises. As the landlord retreats from its requirements, it can take comfort in the fact that many strong franchisors became strong franchisors because of their ability to select successful franchisees.[38]

§ 3.14   Guarantors

Although guarantors are not parties to the lease, their presence is so important that they must be considered from the outset of negotiations. Guarantors enter the lease negotiation when the landlord becomes concerned that the tenant may not be able to perform its obligations under the lease. The landlord thinks first to ask for a large security deposit (cash, marketable securities, or a letter of credit). However, most experienced landlords do not bother to ask for a large security deposit, because a tenant that can post a large security deposit is not a tenant from whom it will be needed, and a tenant from whom it should be asked is usually unable to post it.

As a result, landlords ask for the assurance of a guaranty from a creditworthy guarantor. Although many guaranties are furnished by friends and relatives, the landlord should look for a responsible guarantor among all those who will benefit from the tenant's operation: principal shareholders, parent or subsidiary corporations, major suppliers or customers, and franchisors.

---

[38] *See* Sagehorn, *Resolving Conflicting Provisions in Retail Leases and Franchise Agreements*, 2 Prac. Real Est. Law. 7 (1986) (excellent provision-by-provision analysis of the issue). *See also Leasing Retail Space to the Franchise Tenant*, Leas. Prof., Dec. 1989, at 1.

Since the guaranty is an important economic justification of the lease, the landlord should be sure that it has the right to terminate the lease if the guarantor dies or becomes insolvent, or if the guarantor tries to rescind or terminate the guaranty. The landlord will use its right to terminate the lease on those occasions as an opportunity to reevaluate the tenant's creditworthiness. If the landlord has the right to terminate the lease, the tenant should demand a right to provide a comparable substitute guarantor within a reasonable period of time. Furthermore, the landlord's right to terminate the lease should not entitle it to sue for damages as it could if there were a breach of the lease.

Very often, guarantors are principal stockholders or key employees. The efforts of these people may be essential for the tenant's prosperity. This is particularly true in retail leases. As a result, some landlords require the continued involvement of these people as a condition to the continuation of the lease. Moreover, some landlords provide that they may terminate the lease if these people open competing businesses within a specified distance from the retail premises.[39]

To a landlord, a lease guaranty must, at the very minimum, continue even though the lease is modified or assigned, even though the tenant becomes bankrupt, and even though the tenant or its assignees or other guarantors are released. To a guarantor, these provisions mean unlimited liability. In addition to disputing these provisions of the guaranty, a guarantor should try to limit its guaranty in duration and amount and ought to insist that the lease not be modified to its prejudice, for example, by increasing the rent or the size of the premises or the term of the lease.

§ 3.15 Guaranty of Lease

A form guaranty of lease in common use is:

FORM 3-7
GUARANTY OF LEASE

LANDLORD: _____
TENANT: _____
LEASE: Lease dated _____
GUARANTOR: _____
DATE: _____

Tenant wishes to enter into the lease with landlord. Landlord is unwilling to enter into the lease unless guarantor assures landlord of the full performance of tenant's obligations under the lease. Guarantor is willing to do so.

Accordingly, in order to induce landlord to enter into the lease with tenant, and for good and valuable consideration, receipt and adequacy of which are acknowledged by guarantor:

---

[39] See § 10.13.

1. Guarantor unconditionally guarantees to landlord, and the successors and assigns of landlord, tenant's full and punctual performance of its obligations under the lease, including without limitation the payment of rent and other charges due under the lease. Guarantor waives notice of any breach or default by tenant under the lease. If tenant defaults in the performance of any of its obligations under the lease, upon landlord's demand, guarantor will perform tenant's obligations under the lease.

2. Any act of landlord, or the successors or assigns of landlord, consisting of a waiver of any of the terms or conditions of the lease, or the giving of any consent to any matter related to or thing relating to the lease, or the granting of any indulgences or extensions of time to tenant, may be done without notice to guarantor and without affecting the obligations of guarantor under this guaranty.

3. The obligations of guarantor under this guaranty will not be affected by landlord's receipt, application, or release of security given for the performance of tenant's obligations under the lease, nor by any modification of the lease, including without limitation the alteration, enlargement, or change of the premises described in the lease, except that in case of any such modification, the liability of the guarantor will be deemed modified in accordance with the terms of any such modification.

4. The liability of guarantor under this guaranty will not be affected by (a) the release or discharge of tenant from its obligations under the lease in any creditors', receivership, bankruptcy, or other proceedings, or the commencement or pendency of any such proceedings; (b) the impairment, limitation, or modification of the liability of tenant or the estate of tenant in bankruptcy, or of any remedy for the enforcement of tenant's liability under the lease, resulting from the operation of any present or future bankruptcy code or other statute, or from the decision in any court; (c) the rejection or disaffirmance of the lease in any such proceedings; (d) the assignment or transfer of the lease or sublease of all or part of the premises described in the lease by tenant; (e) any disability or other defense of tenant; or (f) the cessation from any cause whatsoever of the liability of tenant under the lease.

5. Until all of tenant's obligations under the lease are fully performed, guarantor: (a) waives any right of subrogation against tenant by reason of any payments or acts of performance by guarantor, in compliance with the obligations of guarantor under this guaranty; (b) waives any other right that guarantor may have against tenant by reason of any one or more payments or acts in compliance with the obligations of guarantor under this guaranty; and (c) subordinates any liability or indebtedness of tenant held by guarantor to the obligations of tenant to landlord under the lease.

6. This guaranty will apply to the lease, any extension or renewal of the lease, and any holdover term following the term of the lease, or any such extension or renewal.

7. This guaranty may not be changed, modified, discharged, or terminated orally or in any manner other than by an agreement in writing signed by guarantor and landlord.

8. Guarantor is primarily obligated under the lease. Landlord may, at its option, proceed against guarantor without proceeding against tenant or anyone else obligated under the lease or against any security for any of tenant's or guarantor's obligations.

9. Guarantor will pay on demand the reasonable attorneys' fees and costs incurred by landlord, or its successors and assigns, in connection with the enforcement of this guaranty.

10. Guarantor irrevocably appoints tenant as its agent for service of process related to this guaranty.

Guarantor has executed this guaranty as of the date.

[Signature block for guarantor]
[Acknowledgment]

Paragraph 3 is important to avoid any termination of the guaranty as a result of lease amendments. In a Colorado case,[40] the landlord and assignee of the lease entered into an "amendment" of the lease by which the premises were changed and enlarged and the rent was increased. One of the original co-tenants was not a party to the "amendment." Despite a provision of the guaranty similar to that in paragraph 3 of **Form 3-7**, the Colorado Supreme Court found that the landlord had not only increased the guarantor's risk by entering into the "amendment," but also that the originally guarantied obligation had been extinguished and a new one created for which the guarantor was not liable. The court said, "It is clear that where no part of the original premises is covered by the new agreement, that new agreement goes beyond a mere modification of the original, and therefore falls outside of even a consent for modifications clause as broad as that contained in the . . . guarantee."[41]

Paragraph 4 avoids the rule that a landlord's consent to an assignment of a lease that prohibits assignment exonerates the guarantor unless the guarantor consents.[42] An assignee for collateral purposes that cures a tenant's default may have a subrogated claim against the guarantor.[43]

Paragraph 6 of this guaranty is a trap for the landlord who renews or extends a lease without knowing whether the guarantor still exists. For this reason, many landlords refuse to give extensions or renewals unless the guarantor confirms its guaranty. Some landlords will not amend a lease without the guarantor's consent because, as a general rule, the guarantor will be excused if its risk is increased without its consent.[44] Judicial decisions are divided on the question of whether the guarantor's liability continues beyond the original term in the absence of any express provision.[45]

---

[40] Green Shoe Mfg. Co. v. Farber, 712 P.2d 1014 (Colo. 1986).

[41] *Id.* at 1017. *See also* York Manor Corp. v. Astorino, 212 N.Y.S.2d 613 (Sup. Ct. 1961). Florentine Corp., Inc. v. Peda I, Inc., 287 S.C. 382, 339 S.E.2d 112 (1985) (guarantor found liable because the guarantor agreed to remain liable after future lease amendments). For a Georgia decision upholding the guarantor's ability to consent to future modifications (here, a 600 square foot enlargement of the premises and rent increase from $1,153 to $1,435 per month), see Dyna- Comp Corp. v. Selig Enters., Inc., 143 Ga. App. 462, 238 S.E.2d 571 (1977).

[42] Grammes v. St. Paul Trust Co., 147 Ill. 634, 35 N.E. 820 (1893).

[43] Bachmann v. Glazer & Glazer, Inc., 316 Md. 405, 559 A.2d 365 (1989).

[44] Fassett v. Deschutes Enters, Inc., 69 Or. App. 426, 686 P.2d 1034, (*review denied*, 298 Or. 150, 690 P.2d 506 (1984); 3 Thompson § 1226.

[45] Annot., 10 A.L.R. 3d 582, *Liability of lessee's guarantor or surety beyond the original period fixed by lease* (1966).

When reviewing guaranties, the real estate professional must distinguish between a guaranty of payment and a guaranty of performance. As their names imply, one goes no further than to assure the tenant's monetary obligations, and one goes on to assure the tenant's performance of all of its obligations, including the non-monetary obligations. These other obligations, for example, may include continuous operation in a shopping center. With the exception of individual controlling shareholders, most guarantors believe that their guaranties create only a monetary obligation and no more.

The real estate professional should be certain that the guarantor's obligations are not limited strictly to the tenant's obligations. The tenant's obligations may be curtailed by bankruptcy, but the guarantor's obligations should not be so limited. Consider paragraph 4 of **Form 3-7**. A guarantor may raise the landlord's failure to mitigate its damages in response to the landlord's claim against it.[46]

Some real estate professionals repose little faith in guaranties given by sole stockholders or a small group of stockholders for the obligations of a closely held corporation. Their doubt arises from a belief that the stockholder or stockholders will put all they have into the company and thus be unable to make good on their guaranties. In fact, some proposed guarantors use that argument to persuade a landlord that their guaranties are not meaningful. To the contrary, respond the landlords, a guaranty will assure that the guarantor makes every possible sacrifice one way or another in its commitment to the tenant's success.

§ 3.16   Contesting Guaranties

As a result of the relative simplicity of preparing a comprehensive form of guaranty, guaranties are not commonly contested with regard to whether a particular obligation is included in the scope of the guaranty. Rather, guaranties are commonly contested on the basis that something happened after the guaranty was signed that excused the guarantor's performance. The magical incantation that guarantors invoke is that the landlord's conduct has materially increased the guarantor's risk under the guaranty. To increase the guarantor's risk, however, is not the same as to increase the guarantor's liability under the guaranty.

This distinction is very important and well-illustrated in an Oregon court's decision.[47] In that case, the guaranty included rent during the renewal term, which was calculated by reference to a cost of living index. When the tenant exercised its renewal option, the landlord and tenant agreed to increase the monthly rent by $550 per month, even though the cost of living index adjustment was only $380 per month. In a suit on the guaranty, the guarantor asserted that the agreement between the landlord and tenant had materially increased his risk under the guaranty. The landlord offered to accept from the guarantor only what

---

[46] Vespoli v. Pagliarulo, 212 Conn. 1, 560 A.2d 980 (1989).

[47] Fassett v. Deschutes Enters, Inc., 69 Or. App. 426, 686 P.2d 1034, *review denied*, 298 Or. 150, 690 P.2d 506 (1984).

would have been guarantied pursuant to the cost of living index adjustment and thus to forego the increased liability. The court rejected this approach and said:

> We have concluded that [the guarantor's] risk was materially increased when the parties negotiated the monthly rental to $1,600 instead of $1,430 without notifying [the guarantor] or obtaining a subsequent modification of the new amount. Consequently, [the guarantor] was discharged. He therefore cannot be held liable for the lower figure earned by [the landlord] or for any other sum.

Not all cases. however, shelter the guarantor. In a South Carolina case,[48] the guarantor defended on the basis that the guaranty had been discharged by a lease modification pursuant to which the tenant moved to larger space for the same amount of rent. The court held the guarantor to the guaranty for several reasons. The guaranty contained a provision similar to that in paragraph 3 of **Form 3-7**, and two of the individual guarantors had signed the modification in their corporate capacities, while the third individual guarantor was aware of the modification. The landlord was saved by the rule that lease modifications contemplated or permitted by the guaranty do not destroy it.

The liability of a guarantor presupposes the proper execution of the guaranty. There are a surprising number of cases in which a guarantor's, co-tenant's, or co-signatory's liability is confused by the documents. For example, in a Washington case,[49] the Court of Appeals was confronted with a nearly illiterate provision:

> 26.   Binding effect: This agreement shall be binding upon the parties personally in addition to their corporations, hereto their heirs [*sic*], successors and assigns. IN WITNESS WHEREOF, the parties hereto set their hands the day and year first above written.
> LESSOR: Diversified Realty, Inc.
>   By: /s/ Jack C. Foster
>   President
> LESSEE: McElroy Trucking, Inc.
>   By: /s/ Johnny McElroy
>   President
>   /s/ Donna McElroy
>   Donna McElroy,
>   Sec.-Treasurer

The question was whether the McElroys were personally obligated. Needless to say, the McElroys said they were not because of their apparent execution in corporate capacities, while the landlord relied upon the phrase, "This Agreement shall be binding upon the parties personally. . . ." The case is as instructive as it is amusing. One judge had found the lease "clear and unambiguous" in denying

---

[48] Florentine Corp., Inc. v. Peda I, Inc., 287 S.C. 382, 339 S.E.2d 112 (1985).

[49] Diversified Realty, Inc. v. McElroy, 41 Wash. App. 171, 703 P.2d 323, 324 (1985). Similarly, in Sebastian Intern., Inc. v. Peck, 195 Cal. App. 3d 803, 240 Cal. Rptr. 911 (1987), the guarantor signed "Kenneth Peck, Vice President" and later claimed he was acting in a representative and not an individual capacity; he lost.

the McElroys' motion for summary judgment on the ground that it was a corporate obligation. The arbitrator to which the first judge referred the matter also believed the lease was unambiguous, but found that it bound only the corporation. On appeal, two judges found that the lease was ambiguous and that parol evidence was necessary, while a third dissenting judge found that the provision unambiguously bound the individuals.

Some practitioners wonder why guarantors do not simply cosign leases. The answer is that often the liabilities are different. For instance, the guarantor may be obligated only to pay amounts due under the lease, while the tenant might be obligated to maintain a full stock of goods in the premises. The liability of the guarantor may be limited to a fixed dollar amount, although the tenant's is not. Finally, the guarantor usually likes to keep a direct lease obligation off its financial statements and account for the obligation (if at all) as a contingent obligation. However, in the case of a corporate tenant whose obligations are to be guarantied by an active stockholder or officer, the landlord may be more successful against the guarantor by requiring the guarantor to cosign the lease.

Checklist

In conclusion, prudent real estate practitioners require that guarantors join in, endorse, or ratify all lease modifications that may affect the guarantor's risk. These include:

_____ 1. Changes in the rent (except those prescribed by the lease, such as the consumer price index adjustments)

_____ 2. Changes in the premises

_____ 3. Assignments

_____ 4. Subleases

_____ 5. Releases of co-tenants or other guarantors

_____ 6. Alterations made by the landlord for reimbursement by the tenant over the term of the lease

_____ 7. Extensions or renewals of the term.

§ 3.17 "and/or Assigns"

This expression is often added after the tenant's name with the intention that the tenant be allowed to assign the lease. The expression is dangerous.[50] To the landlord, it means that the landlord may have a new tenant of whom it knows nothing and that the original tenant may not be liable on the lease. The original tenant should not get any comfort from this phrase, because it may be as liable as

---

[50] See § 2.3.

its assignee. Rights of assignment and limitations on those rights should be stated in their proper places.[51]

§ 3.18   Grant or Agreement of Lease

After the lease is identified, and the landlord and tenant are introduced, the agreement is stated. When a lease more closely resembles a conveyance, there is a grant instead of an agreement. The archaic grant and the associated habendum clause may say: "Landlord hereby grants and demises the premises to tenant to have and to hold for a term of five years commencing January 1, 1850, upon the terms and conditions hereof."

Although there is some legal authority for the proposition that the technical terms grant and demise are necessary in order to create the landlord's implied covenant of quiet enjoyment,[52] and to imply the landlord's authority to make the grant or demise,[53] the great weight of authority does not support these intricacies. Furthermore, since a well-drafted lease includes not only an express covenant of quiet enjoyment (as explained in **Chapter 28**) but also an express representation of authority (as discussed in **§ 32.18**), the implication of these covenants from technical terms of conveyance is unnecessary.

In fact, in deference to the trend toward treating leases as contracts and not as conveyances, a simple agreement of lease is sufficient:

FORM 3-8
AGREEMENT OF LEASE

Landlord leases the premises to tenant, and tenant leases the premises from landlord, according to this lease.

This simple provision has one dangerous pitfall. The lease must be made in the present, that is, "landlord leases . . . ," and not in the future, that is, "landlord will agree to . . . ." The difference is that the former creates an executed lease and the latter creates an executory agreement to lease. Traditionally, the consequences of a tenant's failure to take possession of its premises according to an executory agreement to lease have been less serious than the consequences of its failure to take possession pursuant to an executed lease.

When the lease is executed, the landlord has been held to be entitled to recover rent due under the lease. When the lease is executory, the landlord is often unable

---

[51] See **Chapter 12**.

[52] I American Law of Property § 3.46 (A. Casner ed. 1952); 3 Thompson § 1129.

[53] I American Law of Property § 3.46 (A. Casner ed. 1952).

to recover rent; however, the landlord can recover damages for the breach of the executory contract and, in some cases, these damages have been held to be the difference between the rent that the tenant agreed to pay and the rental value of the premises.[54] If a landlord defaults under a contract to lease, the tenant must first sue to get possession, then the lease begins.[55] Of course, the tenant can also sue for damages.

---

[54] Annot., 85 A.L.R. 3d 514, *Liability of lessee who refuses to take possession under executed lease or executory agreement to lease* (1978).

[55] See M. R. Friedman, III Friedman on Leases ch. 34 (1983); R. Schoshinski American Law of Landlord and Tenant § 1:8 (1980); 3 Thompson §§ 1062-66.

CHAPTER 4

THE PREMISES

§ 4.1   An Approach to Description of Premises

The description of the single tenant building is simpler than the description of premises in an office building or shopping center. In the former, the tenant has the entire premises to itself and (with the exception of means of access in some instances) the premises are self-contained. To approach the issue differently, the tenant of a single tenant building is virtually the owner of the premises, because it takes everything the landlord has and assumes the landlord's responsibilities. The description of the single tenant building is discussed in § **4.2**.

In contrast, as one of many tenants in a multitenant development, the tenant in an office building or shopping center occupies less than all of what the landlord owns.[1] Furthermore, an office building or shopping center tenant is dependent upon other parts of the development that it shares with other tenants. Naturally, the development, the place of the tenant within it, and the shared parts of the development must be expressed in these leases.[2]

In shopping centers, the shared parts of the development are usually called *common areas*. All shopping center tenants, their customers and suppliers, and the general shopping public, may use the common areas. The idea behind common areas in a shopping center is that they are all equally available for use even though they are not all equally likely to be used. Common areas enable customers to go from one store to the next, even if the customers do not choose to do so. As a result, the walkway in front of a remotely situated tenant is as much a common area as is the walkway in front of the most prominent major tenant.

The office building is an entirely different matter. Unlike the shopping center, it is not an integrated development. The only true common area seems to be the lobby that all tenants and their visitors must use to reach the offices. In fact, as § **4.10** illustrates, there are other areas of an office building that serve all the tenants: boiler rooms, elevator shaft, and janitors' closets, for example. The common areas that serve all the tenants of a building may be called *building common areas*.

The corridors on the 17th floor of an office building must be used by the tenants on that floor and their visitors. Common areas on the 17th floor are available to be used by a tenant of the 10th floor, but that use is not intended or likely. This is particularly true if the 17th floor tenant occupies the entire floor; then, only that tenant and its visitors will use the floor's common areas. The common areas that serve the tenants of a single floor may be called *floor common areas*.

A final, and obvious, observation must be made about these building common areas. They are expensive. They are more expensive than the common areas in a shopping center, even one with an enclosed mall. Like interior common areas in

---

[1] Annot., 24 A.L.R.2d 123, *Easements or privileges of tenant of part of building as to other parts not included in the lease* (1952).

[2] For the unique needs of one kind of tenant, see *Leasing Office Space to the Telecommunications Company,* Leasing Prof., Apr. 1988, at 1.

an enclosed mall, interior common areas in an office building are heated, lit, and cooled. Shopping center common areas are built horizontally and require less structure, while the common areas of a typical office building require much more structure; they are built up. As a result, allocating common areas in an office building is a complicated and costly task.

With these thoughts in mind, the real estate professional can appreciate more fully the description and measurement of the premises.

§ 4.2   Description of Single Tenant Building

The single tenant building is described in the lease by street address. If it is not unwieldy, the legal description is also set forth in the body of the lease, but long legal descriptions, such as metes and bounds descriptions, are usually attached as exhibits. This description assumes that the lease covers all of the landlord's property at a particular location:

FORM 4-1
PREMISES—SINGLE TENANT LEASE

The premises are the land and building commonly known as _____ Street, City of _____, County of _____, State of _____, and more partic- ularly described as:
Lot 1,
Block 1,
LANDLORD'S SUBDIVISION,
according to the plat recorded _____,
19_____, in book _____, page _____ of maps,
City of _____
County of _____
State of _____.
The land consists of approximately _____ square feet. The building consists of approximately _____ square feet on the ground floor, a basement, and a mezzanine and includes without limitation all heating, ventilating, air conditioning, mechani- cal, electrical, elevator and plumbing systems, roof, walls and foundations, and fixtures within it. The premises include all appurtenances, easements, and rights of way related to it.

The description should say clearly whether basement space is included.[3] A site plan or survey of the premises is helpful as an exhibit to the lease. The failure to

---

[3] Ambiguous drafting will generally favor the tenant; the tenant's need for the basement space will lend credence to its position. Ben-David v. Mateo, 512 N.Y.S.2d 684, 128 A.D.2d 398 (1987).

attach a site plan to which the lease refers is not fatal so long as the premises are adequately described.[4]

The landlord should take the legal description directly from its deed or owner's policy of title insurance. A tenant should ask for a current title report and its landlord's representation of the condition of title, because tenants accept the premises subject to matters of record.[5] If there are any limitations on its title—for example, if a neighboring owner is entitled to pass over part of the premises in order to get to its property—the description of the premises should go on to say:

subject to the rights of ingress and egress set forth in the agreement dated _____, 19____, between _____ and _____, recorded _____, 19 _____, in book _____, page _____, _____ County Recorder's office, State of _____.

§ 4.3   Description of Shopping Center Premises

Shopping center premises are described in the body of the lease and depicted in a site plan of the shopping center that is an exhibit to the lease.[6] A typical description is the street address, if there is one for the premises, or something to the effect of:

FORM 4-2
PREMISES—SHOPPING CENTER LEASE

The Premises are:
Store 1,
Hillcrest Shopping Center,
City of _____,
County of _____,
State of _____.
The premises are depicted on Exhibit A to this lease. The premises do not include, and landlord reserves the exterior walls and roof of the premises, the land beneath the premises, and the pipes, ducts, conduits, wires, fixtures, and equipment above the suspended ceiling, and structural elements that serve the premises or the shopping center. Landlord's reservation includes the rights to install, inspect, maintain, use, repair, and replace those areas and items and to enter the premises in order to do so.

---

[4] Crown CoCo, Inc. v. Red Fox Restaurant of Royalton, Inc., 409 N.W.2d 919, 73 A.L.R. 4th 225 (Minn. Ct. App.), *review denied*, Oct. 21, 1987.

[5] See § **32.4**.

[6] *See generally* 2 R. Powell, The Law of Real Property § 242(2)(a) (P.J. Rohan ed., rev. 1977) [hereinafter Powell].

The legal description of the shopping center is almost invariably attached to the lease as an exhibit. Landlords often omit it in order to make recording more difficult. The legal description is important to the tenant because:

1. it determines the area in which the tenant's exclusive use (if any) is .effective;
2. it specifies the extent of the common areas, as set forth in § **17.4**;
3. it tells the tenant whether adjacent land is affected by the parking ratios, exclusive use, and other rights given to the tenant by the lease.

The description of the premises should clearly exclude the walls and roof; otherwise, unless prohibited by other provisions of the lease, the tenant will have the right to attach signs to the walls on the perimeter of its premises and to the roof above its premises.[7] Prudent tenants do not rely solely on their common law rights, but rather negotiate their rights and a specification of their signs before they sign a lease. The tenant should insist upon a drawing that shows the location of pipes, ducts, electrical conduits, and columns in its premises, and it should be certain that they do not interfere with the ceiling height or the selling area. Too many columns may make it impossible to show Oriental carpets, for example, and a picture framing shop puts its work areas away from overhead water pipes that may burst. When a shopping center is not yet built, tenants usually ask that structural elements occupy no more than 1 or 2 percent of their premises.

The description of the premises is the basis for the allocation of maintenance and repair obligations between landlord and tenant. If the premises include all areas beneath the roof (thus including ductwork, conduit, and heating, ventilating and air conditioning equipment), the tenant may be obligated to maintain and repair something that it has never seen. Although such an obligation appears to save costs for the landlord, it is not desirable because the landlord does not want all of its tenants working on the air conditioning system. Consequently, landlords and tenants are both interested in an accurate description of the premises.

§ 4.4   Measurement of Shopping Center Premises

This provision expresses the usual method of measuring the area of shopping center mall premises:

FORM 4-3
PREMISES—DEFINITION OF "FLOOR AREA"
IN A SHOPPING CENTER LEASE

The term "floor area" means, with respect to each store area separately leased, the number of square feet of floor space on all floor levels in the premises, including any mezzanine area, measured from the exterior faces of exterior walls, store fronts,

---

[7] Page v. Martini, 293 S.W. 253 (Tex. Civ. App. 1927).

walls fronting on the enclosed malls or interior common areas, corridors and service areas, and the center lines of party walls or common partitions. No deduction or exclusion from floor area will be made by reason of columns, stairs, elevators, escalators, shafts, or other interior construction.

With slight modifications, this form would be appropriate for a shopping center without a mall.

Mezzanines, second floors, and basements are often measured at 50 percent of ground floor area. The tenant should measure existing premises; if the premises are being constructed, the tenant should demand that the premises be measured "as-built" and that rent and cost sharing ratios be appropriately adjusted. Since common area maintenance charges are shared in proportion to floor area, tenants should insist that all floor areas be measured in the same way; otherwise, the tenant may pay more than its fair share. For example, if a tenant's mezzanine is included in its floor area and a neighboring department store's mezzanine is not, the tenant's proportionate share will be relatively greater than the department store's. Of course, as § 17.7 discusses, a disproportionate sharing can result if the department store is not required to contribute to common area maintenance charges in the same way as other tenants.

Although the measurement of shopping center premises is not as susceptible to abuse as the measurement of office building premises, the real estate professional must still be careful. For example, some landlords measure their premises to the outside of building walls. Unless the tenant knows that its prospective landlord uses that method, the tenant cannot compare the effective cost of those premises to the effective cost of premises that are measured to the inside of building walls. The rent per square foot may be the same for both premises, or the total rent may be the same for both premises, but the rent per square foot inside the walls will be different.

§ 4.5   Appurtenances in a Shopping Center

Appurtenances are rights and benefits that a lease impliedly vests in a tenant even though the lease makes no express reference to them.[8] Some jurisdictions imply only those appurtenances that are essential to the tenant's use and enjoyment of its premises,[9] while others imply appurtenances that are reasonably necessary for the tenant's use and enjoyment of its premises.[10] If there are four doorways serving the premises, but the premises are adequately served by three, one of the doors is not necessary for the premises and therefore is not an appurtenance.

---

[8] *See generally* Friedman, *Appurtenances: What a Lease Does Not State,* 72 A.B.A. J. 151 (1966).

[9] Page v. Martini, 293 S.W. 253 (Tex. Civ. App. 1927).

[10] Hemmingway, *Selected Problems in Leases of Community and Shopping Centers,* 16 Baylor L. Rev. 1 (1964); Friedman, *Store Leases,* 37 N.Y. St. B.J. 126 (1965); III M.R. Friedman, Friedman on Leases § 3.2 (1983) [hereinafter Friedman]. Morris, *Shopping Centers—The Role of the Lawyers,* 1955 U. Ill. L.F. 681.

Appurtenances must be in existence at the time the lease is made. If an addition is made to the building of which the premises are a part, unless the landlord promised to make the addition as an appurtenance, the addition cannot be an appurtenance because it did not exist at the time the lease was made. Since an appurtenance is considered to be a part of the premises, or at least a right that is implied by the lease, the loss of an appurtenance may be the basis for a claim of eviction or a claim for damages. Therefore, determining the appurtenances is an important task.

The trouble with appurtenances is that they arise by implication; in other words, if a court concludes their use was contemplated by the landlord and tenant as well as essential or reasonably necessary (depending upon the local law) for the enjoyment of the premises, there is an appurtenance. A judge, however, is not the proper arbiter of the tenant's needs; the tenant is. The landlord is no less concerned than the tenant because, if the landlord contemplates demolition of something that is found to be an appurtenance to a tenant's premises, the tenant may try to terminate the lease or to sue the landlord for damages.

The desirable appurtenances in a shopping center include not only the matters discussed with regard to office building premises in § **4.15**, but also parking, access through another tenant's space (in a mall for example), and display windows. A tenant that proposes to move into an existing shopping center should walk through the shopping center and its premises to determine what other factors make the space valuable to it: for example, particular entrances may be important because they assure a traffic pattern. The tenant should get the landlord's assurance in the lease that these unique qualities will not be eliminated or impaired. If they are, the tenant should have the option to reduce its minimum rent, to pay only a percentage rent, or to cancel the lease, depending upon the severity of the loss.

§ 4.6 Designating Certain Areas

The tenant will want certain matters designated on the site plan: the common areas, the angle of the striping, the location of planters and other barriers, the parking areas reserved for the tenant or other tenants,[11] the location of handicapped or loading- zone spaces, the size of the spaces, entrances and exits, curb cuts, loading areas, means of access to the premises, and the size and location of buildings.

Tenants often forget the importance of the visibility of their premises. Without a contrary agreement, the landlord may install a kiosk or automated teller

---

[11] A tenant that believes the landlord has not delivered the promised parking cannot pay partial rent for 18 months and then vacate, claiming constructive eviction; constructive eviction requires the tenant to vacate the premises promptly. RNR Realty, Inc. v. Burlington Coat Factory Warehouse of Cicero, Inc., 168 Ill. App. 3d 210, 522 N.E.2d 679, *appeal denied,* 121 Ill. 2d 586, 122 Ill. Dec. 446, 526 N.E.2d 839 (1988).

machine in the common area directly in front of the premises. This can be avoided by designating on the site plan an unobstructed vista (or sight line easement) that the landlord must preserve for the tenant. A Florida tenant successfully protected its visibility with a prohibition of "any other buildings or improvements in the Shopping Center which would in any way affect the access or visibility of the demised premises."[12]

The site plan is also the best place to show where other tenants will be located. If the tenant's business benefits from proximity to another tenant, the location of the other tenant should be located in the site plan. Other tenants prefer that their competitors be located as far away as possible; within the bounds of permissible trade practices discussed in § **10.8**, the site plan should show the competitors' locations. The landlord should limit its representations in this regard to the initial or existing occupancy of the shopping center and should disclaim any promise that the site plan will not change during the term of the lease.

The site plan should show the places at which signs will be located and refer to the sign criteria set forth as an exhibit to the lease for a further description of the appearance of signs. An inauspiciously placed sign may impair visibility of the tenant's premises.

The site plan should also show the so-called *outparcels,* that is, all those parts of the shopping center that the landlord intends to lease or sell profitably after the shopping center is prospering. The development of the outparcels can greatly effect the tenant. A building on an outparcel may impair visibility of the tenant's premises. The parking demands of an outparcel may far exceed the outparcel's capacity, despite the apparent strictures imposed by building and zoning codes, if the buyer of the outparcel negotiates the typical cross-parking arrangements with the shopping center owner. The overflow parking may impair the parking reserved or intended for the tenant.

§ 4.7 Preserving Flexibility in Shopping Center Development

When the landlord and tenant discuss the site plan of a proposed development, they are most likely to disagree completely. The tenant wants the landlord's assurance that the final development will be the same as the proposed development that first caught the tenant's attention. The tenant wants to know that the site plan is a complete and accurate depiction of the matters described in § **4.6**.

The tenant may propose that the landlord promise to develop the shopping center strictly according to the site plan. The landlord will be aghast at such a suggestion. It believes that it should have flexibility to develop the shopping center as it pleases, and it will remind the tenant that they both want a successful development.

---

[12] L. Luria & Son, Inc. v. Fingerman, 497 So. 2d 682 (Fla. Dist. Ct. App. 1986).

The landlord and tenant may come to an agreement that assures the tenant that landlord's changes to the site plan will not:

1. Be substantial
2. Reduce parking below a specified ratio
3. Affect the visibility of the premises or access to them
4. Put any other tenant's storeline in front of the premises
5. Remove the tenant from a specified proximity to proposed anchor tenants or shopping center entrances or parking areas.[13]

A site plan should not depict any more than the landlord's present (or presently proposed) development. If it must show areas that the landlord intends to develop in the future, those areas should be marked as "excluded" or "possible future development"; any implication that they are part of the development should be studiously avoided.[14] The landlord and tenant resume this discussion when they encounter the common areas and parking areas discussed in **Chapter 17**.

§ 4.8 Description of Office Building Premises

Office building premises are identified in the lease itself in several ways:

1. Existing premises may be identified by suite number, for example, Suite 2720.
2. Premises that are to be built may be assigned a suite number but are also described by an approximate number of square feet on a particular floor (for example, "approximately 5,280 square feet on the sixth floor"), or simply by the approximate dimensions and floor.
3. Full floor premises (whether or not already built) are identified by floor number, although elevators, shafts, stairwells, and other common areas of the building are usually expressly excluded from the premises.[15]

The identification continues with the name and street address of the building in which the premises are located and the legal description of the land on which the building is located. The legal description is often set forth in an exhibit to the lease.

In addition to the identification in the lease, the premises are shown in an exhibit to the lease. This exhibit is the typical floorplate of the building in which

---

[13] Pollock, *Clauses in a Shopping Center Lease,* 20 Prac. Law. 63 (1974).

[14] *See* La Pointe's, Inc. v. Beri, Inc., 73 Or. App. 773, 699 P.2d 1173 (1985) (form lease prevailed over contradictory site plan). See also § **17.4**.

[15] A full-floor tenant has no rights to the stairwells serving its premises. Wilfred Laboratories, Inc. v. Fifty-Second St. Hotel Ass'n, Inc., 519 N.Y.S.2d 220, 133 A.D.2d 320 (1987), *appeal dismissed*, 71 N.Y.2d 994, 529, 524 N.E.2d 878, N.Y.S.2d 277 (1988).

the premises are located; commercial space on the first floor is shown on a unique floorplate.

This, however, is merely identification. It will enable the tenant to find its premises. It will not tell the tenant what it really needs to know about its premises: their usefulness and their cost. In order to determine their cost, the landlord will consult architects, space planners, and similar professionals. In order to determine its cost, the tenant must first understand the area of its premises, because rental rates are given on a square foot basis. To understand the area, the tenant must understand the unique method of measuring office building premises.

§ 4.9   An Approach to Measurement of Office Building Premises

Consider the office building occupant. She leaves her car in the parking lot on the third floor of the building, enters the building lobby, awaits the elevator at the elevator lobby, takes the elevator to her floor, visits the women's room, and walks down the corridor (past the janitorial supply room) to the door to her office. This tenant may feel that she is paying only for the area inside her office. She is wrong. Office building tenants pay for almost every part of the building. In some cases, they pay for more than every part of the building.

The process by which tenants pay for virtually the rest of the building is sometimes called grossing up, but is not to be confused with grossing up operating expenses discussed in **§ 6.12**. Each office is allocated a proportionate share of almost all of those parts of the building that are not included in offices; a 5,000 square foot office may be grossed up to a 5,500 square foot office. In this way, tenants pay "rent" for the entire building.

This grossing up process is carried out with reference to several important terms of art. For these purposes, this book has employed the standards known as *BOMA,* an acronym for Building Owners and Managers Association. BOMA is an increasingly common but not universal standard. Since the BOMA terms are used differently by different landlords, the measurement of office building space is an expensive Tower of Babel.[16] The task of the real estate professional is to translate all the different measurements into the same units and to assign a cost to each unit. Only in this way can any progress be made toward advising a tenant of the comparative costs of its prospective premises.

§ 4.10   Introduction to BOMA Measurement

BOMA* uses these defined terms in its measurement standards:

---

[16] *Incredible Shrinking Square Foot,* N.Y. Times, Aug. 5, 1984, § 8 at 1.

* Permission to reprint granted by BOMA International. Copies are available from: BOMA International, 1250 Eye Street, N.W., Suite 200, Washington, D.C. 20005.

(a) "Finished Surface" shall mean a wall, ceiling or floor surface, including glass, as prepared for tenant use, excluding the thickness of any special surfacing materials such as paneling, furring strips, and carpet.

(b) "Dominant Portion" shall mean that portion of the inside finished surface of the permanent outer building wall which is 50% or more of the vertical floor-to-ceiling dimension measured at the dominant portion. If there is no dominant portion, or if the dominant portion is not vertical, the measurement for area shall be to the inside finished surface of the permanent outer building wall where it intersects the finished floor.

(c) "Major Vertical Penetrations" shall mean stairs, elevator shafts, flues, pipe shafts, vertical ducts, and the like, and their enclosing walls, which serve more than one floor of the building, but shall not include stairs, dumb-waiters, lifts, and the like, exclusively serving a tenant occupying offices on more than one floor.

(d) "Office" shall mean the premises leased to a tenant for which a measurement is to be computed. Furthermore, the Construction Area of a floor shall be computed by measuring to the outside finished surface of permanent outer building walls. The Construction Area of a building shall be the sum of the Construction Area of all enclosed floors of the building, including basements, mechanical equipment floors, penthouses, and the like.

§ 4.11 Usable Area

Illustration 4-1 reproduces the BOMA definition of *usable area*. BOMA goes on to say:

> This method measures the actual occupiable area of a floor or an office suite and is of prime interest to a tenant in evaluating the space offered by a landlord and in allocating the space required to house personnel and furniture. The amount of Usable Area on a multitenant floor can vary over the life of a building as corridors expand and contract and as floors are remodeled. Usable Area on a floor can be converted to Rentable Area by the use of a conversion factor.

Usable Area is not the same as useful area. The useful area of office premises is determined by the layout of those premises. In turn, the layout depends upon such things as the placement of windows and mullions (because they dictate the size of the exterior offices) and the depth of the premises (because it governs how much space is lost to circulation). Thus, the usefulness of the premises is decided by the architects and space planners who are familiar with the tenant's requirements. A simple way to remember usable area is that it is the area for which the tenant buys carpet.

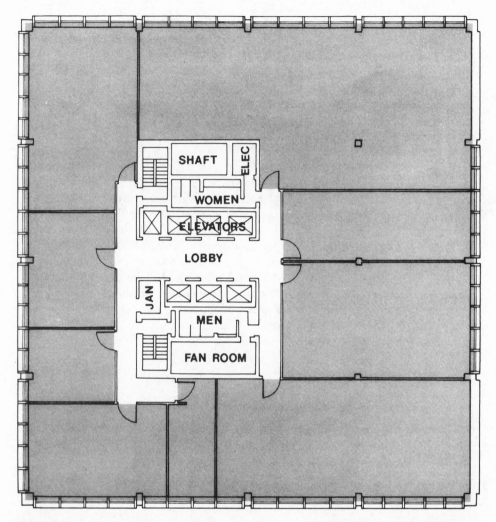

Illustration 4-1.   Usable area (shown in gray). The Usable Area of an office shall be computed by measuring to the finished surface of the office side of corridor and other permanent walls, to the center of partitions that separate the office from adjoining Usable Areas, and to the inside finished surface of the dominant portion of the permanent outer building walls. No deductions shall be made for columns and projections necessary to the building. The Usable Area of a floor shall be equal to the sum of all Usable Areas on that floor. Reprinted by permission.

§ 4.12   Rentable Area

Illustration 4-2 reproduces the BOMA definition of rentable area. BOMA goes on to say:

> This method measures the tenant's pro rata portion of the entire office floor, excluding elements of the building that penetrate through the floor to areas below. The Rentable Area of a floor is fixed for the life of a building and is not affected by changes in corridor sizes or configuration. This method is therefore recommended for measuring the total income producing area of a building and for use in

computing the tenant's pro rata share of a building for purposes of rent escalation. Lenders, architects, and appraisers will use Rentable Area in analyzing the economic potential of a building.

It is recommended that on multitenant floors the landlord compute both the Rentable and Usable Area for any specific office suite.

In contrast to usable area, for which the tenant buys carpet, architects and space planners say that rentable area is what gathers dust. The distinction between usable area and rentable area leads to the apocryphal story of the merchant who specialized in carpet remnants bought from office building tenants that had ordered carpet on the basis of their rentable areas and not their usable areas.

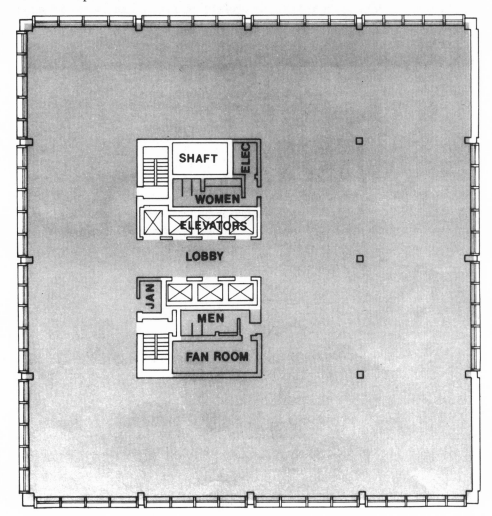

Illustration 4-2. Rentable area (shown in gray). The Rentable Area of a floor shall be computed by measuring to the inside finished surface of the dominant portion of the permanent outer building walls, excluding any major vertical penetrations of the floor.

No deductions shall be made for columns and projections necessary to the building.

The Rentable Area of an office on the floor shall be computed by multiplying the Usable Area of that office by the quotient of the division of the Rentable Area of the floor by the Usable Area of the floor resulting in the "R/U Ratio" described herein. Reprinted by permission.

§ 4.13 Importance of Measurement

Before drawing any conclusions from the BOMA terminology, the real estate professional should note that neither rentable area nor usable area is what it seems. Although rentable area includes the fan room, and the tenant pays for the space, it will not be allowed to enter or use the fan room. Of even greater importance is the fact that usable area does not mean *useful* area. When the premises are prepared for the tenant's occupancy, walls will separate the interior offices and the usable area will diminish. If the premises are designed poorly, more of the usable area will vanish into inaccessible parts of the premises.

The rentable area includes virtually everything on the floor except the major vertical penetrations described in § **4.10**. It will not change during the lease. Accordingly, for some purposes, it is a better standard. Rental rates are given in terms of rentable area.

The *conversion factor* relates rentable area to usable area:

$$\text{conversion factor} = \frac{\text{rentable area}}{\text{usable area}}$$

This conversion factor is a critical factor in computing rents.

If a tenant is looking for 5,000 square feet of usable area, it must convert the cost per square foot of rentable space to the cost per square foot of usable space. If one building has a 1.10 conversion factor and another building has a 1.15 conversion factor, the tenant must rent either 5,500 or 5,750 square feet of rentable area in order to have 5,000 square feet of usable area. To solve one of the examples:

$$\text{if conversion factor} = \frac{\text{rentable area}}{\text{usable area}} = 1.10, \text{ then}$$

$$\text{rentable area} = 1.10 \times \text{usable area} = 1.10 \times 5,000 = 5,500$$

Thus, in one building the tenant must pay for 250 more square feet of rentable area in order to have its desired usable area.

To approach the problem from a different direction, if the cost per square foot of rentable area is $25 and the conversion factor is 1.08, the rent per square foot of usable area is $27.[17]. This amount—$27—is often referred to as the *effective rent per square foot*; it is

$$\frac{\text{actual rent}}{\text{actual Usable Area in square feet}}$$

---

[17] *See generally* Ahner, *Ten Questions to Ask when Leasing Office Space (And the Answers You Should Get!)*, 23 Law Off. Econ. & Mgmt. 494 (1983); Hershman, *Practical Aspects of Commercial Leasing,* 1 Prac. Real Est. Law. 12 (1985).

Real estate professionals sometimes mention *loss factors* (instead of conversion factors) when discussing rentable and usable areas. In the example in which the 1.15 conversion factor arose out of the 5,750 rentable square foot area and the 5,000 usable square foot area, the loss factor may be expressed as a percentage of which the numerator is 750 (the amount by which the rentable area exceeds the usable area) and the denominator is 5,750 (the rentable area); that percentage is 13 percent. Although the areas are the same, a 13 percent loss factor looks better than a 15 percent conversion factor. The confusion arises, of course, from comparing the lost area (750) to the rentable area in the loss factor analysis as opposed to the usable area in the conversion factor analysis.

Since the total rentable area of a building will usually not fluctuate, the total rentable area is used as the denominator and each tenant's rentable area is used as the numerator in computing the proportions in which tenants share operating expenses as discussed in § **6.10**. In a building of 100,000 square feet of rentable area, a tenant with 8,500 square feet of rentable area pays 8.5 percent of operating expenses. A tenant should ask for an explanation of the calculation of the total rentable area of the building and should ask that its maximum share be stated. Since the total rentable area may be increased by the conversion of common areas to rentable area, the tenant should also insist that its share should be reduced if the total rentable area is increased.

In an office building lease,[18] the tenant must be certain that its share of operating expenses is based upon the total area regardless of whether it is leased or occupied. If the tenant's share is based upon leased or occupied space, it will pay more than its share; it will share the cost of operating unleased or vacant space in the building. For example, if the tenant leases and occupies 5,000 square feet of a 100,000 square foot building, its share is 5 percent. If only half the building is leased and occupied, then that tenant's share is 5,000/50,000 or 10 percent. If the tenant is the only tenant and occupant of the building, it pays all the expense of operating the building.

Once again, the BOMA terms have been used as an illustration only. The real estate professional must begin with definitions in the lease—or demand them if they are not defined—in order to compare rental rates. For example, if the BOMA terms are used in a lease, but the exclusion of major vertical penetrations is not made, no valid comparisons can be made to a lease that uses the defined terms properly.

Unfortunately, the tenant's work is not finished when it finally determines its actual rent cost and its proper share of operating expenses. The tenant's rent cost cannot be ascertained until the tenant learns which (if any) costs of operating the building are included in its rent and which costs are passed on to it as its share of operating expenses. These issues are discussed in § **6.10**.

Even then, the tenant cannot fully understand its costs until it understands the economic consequences of the construction of its premises. This is discussed in § **6.13**.

---

[18] See § **17.6** regarding sharing common area expenses in shopping centers.

§ 4.14   An Illustration of Office Building Measurement

An analysis of a three-story building may look like the illustration in **Table 4-1**.

In this example, the landlord may believe that it should average the three R/U conversion factors in order to be able to offer space without resort to a floor-by-floor calculation. The average is 1.051 ([1.0861 + 1.0353 + 1.0318] divided by 3). Tenants on the second and third floors are hurt because their actual R/U conversion factors are more favorable, but tenants on the first floor are benefited because their R/U conversion factor is less favorable.

Changing the R/U conversion factor for the floors means changing the rentable areas of the floors, because the rentable area is derived from the usable area by the definition of rentable area in § **4.12**. As a result of the change, and with the loss of some accuracy in rounding fractions, the last two columns of the earlier example look like:

Rentable area	Multitenant R/U Conversion factor
14,022	1.05
14,864	1.05
14,864	1.05
43,750	1.05 (average)

The building rentable area and usable areas do not change. The only change is in the floors.

Before leaving this thought, one opportunity for abuse should be observed. Using these examples, consider the possibility of leasing the building with the rentable area of the second and third floors given on the average basis, as shown in the last example, and the rentable area of the first floor given on the actual basis first discussed. The rentable area of the building would be:

First Floor	14,500
Second Floor	14,864
Third Floor	14,864
	44,228

or 478 square feet of rentable area larger. Certainly, this is phantom space — and tenants everywhere are paying for it.

§ 4.15   Appurtenances in an Office Building

When dealing with existing office building premises, a visit to the building can be very informative. In the order in which they appear to a visitor going through the

Table 4-1

ANALYSIS OF THREE-STORY BUILDING

Floor	Construction Area[a]	Non-Rentable[b]	Common Areas Building[c]	Common Areas Floor[d]	Single tenant usable[e]	Multi-tenant corridor[f]	Multi-tenant usable[g]	Rentable area[h]	Multi-tenant R/U Conversion factor[i]
1	15,000	250	750	150	13,850	500	13,350	14,500	1.08
2	15,000	100	50	200	14,650	500	14,150	14,650	1.0453
3	15,000	150	-0-	200	14,650	500	14,150	14,600	1.03
	45,000	500	800	550	43,150	1,500	41,6 50	43,750	1.05*

* (average)

[a] Construction area of a floor is computed by measuring to the outside finished surface of permanent outer building walls.

[b] This non-rentable area arises from major vertical penetrations as defined in § **4.10.**

[c] Building common areas are areas which serve all tenants of the building. For example, a mail room or public lobby on the first floor serves tenants on all three floors.

[d] Floor common areas are areas which are most likely to serve only tenants on the floor. Examples are bathrooms and janitorial and telephone closets.

[e] Single tenant usable is what remains of the construction area after the non-rentable, building common, and floor common areas are deducted. A full-floor tenant could make use of the single tenant usable area.

[f] In order to have several unrelated tenants on the same floor, a multitenant corridor is needed. It reduces the single tenant usable area.

[g] Multitenant usable is what remains after multitenant corridors are deducted from single tenant usable area. See the definition of usable area in § **4.11.**

[h] Rentable area is calculated according to the BOMA definition set forth in § **4.12.** Note that construction area is measured to the *outside* finished surfaces while rentable area is measured to the inside finished surfaces; this example sets the difference at 250 square feet for each floor.

[i] Multitenant R/U conversion factor is, of course, rentable area divided by multitenant usable area on each floor.

premises, the tenant should evaluate its need for the following improvements, some or all of which may be appurtenances: parking;[19] means of access to the building (for example, bridges, footpaths); building doors and entries to the building; the lobby; the directory;[20] the corridors; elevators; signs (common in Manhattan) in the elevators that announce the tenants' floors; directories on each of the floors; bathrooms; stairways; telephone, telecommunication, and utility connections (not visible); and the basement. Improvements that the tenant believes it will want or need should be discussed and any agreement about them should be expressed in the lease.

The existence of appurtenances underscores the importance to a landlord of its reserved right to change the common areas of its development. **Section 17.2** expands this idea.

§ 4.16   Personal Property

If tangible personal property is included in the premises, the lease should have a separate schedule that describes it. A real estate professional reading a lease must be certain that the general term *premises* is properly used with reference to the personal property; otherwise, real property concepts and personal property concepts may be confused. For example, in a lease that requires that the premises be returned to the landlord subject to wear and tear, will the personal property also be returned subject to wear and tear, even though it is more than likely that the personal property has been completely worn out? If it is worn out, should the landlord or tenant replace it? When substantial personal property is involved, a separate personal property lease is an easy solution.

§ 4.17   Storage Space

Tenants ought to inquire whether there is storage space available for their use. When considering a storage space agreement, tenants should ask:

---

[19] See *The Tenant's Office Building Parking Checklist,* Leasing Prof., May 1989, at 1, for a long list of the questions that a tenant can ask. Absent an agreement in the lease, a landlord is not required to assure its tenants of parking. In Hoyt v. Brokaw, 359 N.W.2d 310 (Minn. Ct. App. 1984), discussions preceding execution of the lease were deemed merged into the lease.

[20] Some courts have held that a listing on the building directory is an appurtenance. 92 Liberty St. Corp. v. Dooney, 116 N.Y.S.2d 44 (App. Term 1952) (involving rights of subtenants); Surrey v. H.&F. Sellmann, Inc., 6 Misc. 2d 614, 164 N.Y.S.2d 87 (Sup. Ct. 1957) (involving indispensable signs for third floor barber shop). But at least one court has held that such a listing is not an appurtenance in a case involving unusual circumstances growing out of a holdover tenancy of rent-controlled premises. Leventhal v. 128 West 30th St. Corp., 158 N.Y.S.2d 398 (Sup. Ct. 1956).

1. Where is it in relation to the premises?

2. Is it subject to the terms of the lease (for example, its destruction allows termination in certain circumstances), or is it subject to a separate license?

3. Is the rent paid for the storage space part of the minimum rent for purposes of calculating percentage rent in a retail lease?

4. When does tenant have access to it?

5. How is the storage space secured?

A landlord's form of storage space agreement in an office building may be found in *Commercial Real Estate Leases: Preparation and Negotiation.*

§ 4.18   Lenders' Concerns about Premises

The lenders' principal concerns about the premises are (1) that its mortgage encumber the entire premises and (2) that the premises not be dependent on other property that is not encumbered by its mortgage. The first instance gives rise to the possibility that, in order to preserve the lease income, the lender may have to cure defaults on property in which it has no interest and that it may be unable to do so. The second instance gives rise to the possibility that the tenant may not be able to use its premises for reasons beyond the landlord's or lender's control if the right to use the other property is terminated. Both of these instances may result in a cessation of the income stream on which the lender depends.

§ 4.19   Options

Some leases include one or more of these rights: options, or rights of first refusal, to expand the premises (as discussed in §§ **4.20** through **4.22**), and options, or rights of first refusal, to purchase the premises (as discussed in §§ **4.23** and **4.25**). Options to extend or to renew the term of a lease are discussed in §§ **5.13** through **5.15**. All of these options impose obligations on the landlord and restrict the landlord's use of its property. A landlord may lose a large tenant because another tenant's expansion options involve part of the prospective tenant's premises. Purchase options may set the upper bound of the value of the landlord's property; even a purchase option without a fixed price (such as a right of first refusal) affects the marketability of the landlord's property.

For these reasons, landlords avoid granting options. Only rarely does a landlord's form lease make reference to any options; the landlord will not want to suggest that any options are available. As a result, tenants must bear the burden of raising the subject of options and negotiating them successfully.

§ 4.20   Options to Expand Premises

Tenants in multitenant developments—office buildings and shopping centers—may want the right to expand their premises if they prosper. Law firms add more lawyers and, less frequently, retailers add more floor space. Tenants must consider suggesting several sorts of expansion options. The tenant's best case is that it may expand as much as it pleases at any time at its option at a favorable rate. The landlord's best case is that the tenant will be compelled to take specified additional space at a fixed date on then-prevailing terms and conditions. An expansion option will reduce the value of the option premises if the option may be exercised in so short a period (usually less than 5 years) that other prospective tenants for the space are reluctant to risk the need to move.[21]

In order to see how the expansion option works, consider this tenant-oriented expansion option:[22]

FORM 4-4
PREMISES—EXPANSION OPTION

(a)   Tenant has the right, but not the obligation, to add to the premises any or all of the spaces shown on Exhibit _____ (each an "expansion space") on the respective anniversaries of the commencement date of this lease according to the further provisions of this paragraph. Tenant must exercise its right to add any expansion space (if at all) by written notice to landlord given at least _____ (____) days before to the anniversary on which the relevant expansion space may be added to the premises. If tenant does not exercise its right in a timely manner, tenant will have irretrievably lost its right to the relevant expansion space.

(b)   Any expansion space with respect to which tenant exercises its rights will be delivered by landlord to tenant either (1) in its condition on the date on which the expansion premises are added to the premises if the expansion space has been previously occupied or (2) with the building standard tenant finish allowance available on the date on which the expansion premises are added to the premises if the expansion space has not been previously occupied; however, if the relevant expansion space has been occupied, landlord will use so much of the occupant's security deposit as it lawfully can use to repair and restore the expansion space. Any expansion space will become part of the premises on the relevant anniversary of the commencement date, and the premises will then be deemed to include any such expansion space. All of the provisions of this lease will apply to any expansion space. Landlord will not be obligated to grant any concessions or allowances with respect to any expansion space except as set forth in this paragraph.

(c)   The base monthly rent for any expansion space will be the base monthly rent per rentable square foot of the premises in effect on the date on which the expansion space becomes part of the premises. The base monthly rent will be increased as of the day on which the expansion space becomes part of the premises by an amount

---

[21] See Gilson, *Opting for Expansion Rights*, Wash. Law, Sept./Oct 1988, at 14 (valuable discussion).

[22] For further discussion and two more forms, see *Tying Up the Office Landlord With Pro-Tenant Expansion Rights*, Leasing Prof., Sept. 1989, at 1.

equal to the product of (1) the number of rentable square feet of the expansion space multiplied by (2) the base monthly rent per rentable square foot of the premises in effect on the day on which the expansion space becomes part of the premises. Tenant's share [of operating expenses] will be increased as of the day on which any expansion space becomes part of the premises by a fraction whose numerator is the sum of the rentable square feet of the premises and the new expansion space, and whose denominator is the rentable square feet of the premises. The base monthly rent and tenant's share [of operating expenses] will be increased in a similar manner whenever expansion space is added to the premises. The landlord's share [of operating expenses] with respect to the expansion space will be the landlord's share then prevailing for new leases in the building.

(d) Tenant will not have any rights according to this paragraph if, at the time tenant is obligated to give any notice, or at the time landlord delivers possession of the expansion premises, either (1) an event of default then exists, or (2) tenant has assigned the lease with respect to, or sublet, more than _____ rentable square feet of the premises.

In this form an exhibit shows the expansion areas and the anniversaries on which they may be added.

§ 4.21 "Build-Out" Expansion Option

The "build-out" expansion option is one lease concession that aggressive landlords use to lure tenants in soft commercial real estate markets. This option gives the tenant the right to lease more space in the same building at a particular point in the lease term, and it requires the landlord to improve the space if the tenant decides to take it.

Any expansion option is a tenant concession. When a landlord gives a tenant an expansion option, it provides in the lease that, on a particular date, the tenant has the right to rent additional space in the same building or shopping center. It is a concession because, until the tenant exercises the option, the additional space usually stays vacant, depriving the landlord of income. Also, the option often lets the tenant rent the additional space on favorable terms, for example, the same base rent per square foot as its current space.

The concession is even greater, and even costlier to the landlord, if it promises to renovate the tenant's additional space. Usually the tenant agrees to accept the expansion space "as is." This means, of course, that the tenant normally makes any improvements at its own cost. Some landlords, however, promise to do the work at their own expense for desirable tenants. The concession can be worth the price if the tenant stays solvent. If not, the landlord invests in improving the space only to find that the tenant cannot pay the increased rent.

Although the build-out expansion option can be an effective tenant lure, it can hurt a landlord. Many landlords have found that their decision to let the tenant lease more space through a build- out expansion option was unwise, because the tenant became insolvent after signing the lease—or, if not insolvent, at least unable to pay rent for the enlarged space.

One solution to this problem may be a lease provision that lets the landlord verify the tenant's financial condition when it seeks to exercise the expansion option. This provision allows the landlord to cancel the option if it decides the tenant is not creditworthy.

Expansion options that involve renovating the additional space have a number of other vices that the landlord should recognize:

1. If the tenant cannot use the expansion space itself, it may be able to profit by assigning the advantageous lease or subleasing the space.
2. The tenant knows that, even if it is insolvent, the landlord must get the additional space ready for the tenant on demand. The tenant may use this leverage to renegotiate the lease or escape from it entirely.
3. Lenders are concerned whenever a landlord makes a financial commitment to a tenant. There is always the danger that the landlord may default, in which event the lender will have to spend money to renovate the tenant's expansion space or risk losing the tenant. The risk for the lender is multiplied if it cannot tell whether the tenant is creditworthy.

The provision in **Form 4-5** reduces the risks associated with most build-out options. It lets the landlord check whether the tenant's credit is good before it is obligated to build out the additional space.

When the tenant seeks to exercise its option, which it must do by a specific date, it has to requalify its credit if it wants to expand. It must send the landlord its most recent quarterly and annual financial statements, consisting of income statements, balance sheets, and statements of cash flow.

If the tenant has a guarantor that has promised to pay the rent if the tenant does not, the guarantor must supply the same information. The tenant and guarantor must also authorize credit-rating agencies to give the landlord credit reports on them.

The landlord should have the information reviewed by an accountant or someone with similar financial expertise. The landlord should also give the information to any lender that is financing the project.

Three signals may indicate that the tenant might have trouble paying its rent:

1. The tenant's net worth is less, or no higher, than it was when it moved in
2. Its cash flow is low
3. It has previously undisclosed liabilities.

Form 4-6 permits the tenant to lease additional space only if it first gives the landlord its most recent financial statements, and only if the landlord decides that the tenant is creditworthy. Another section of the form says that, if the landlord approves the tenant's credit and lets it lease the extra space, the landlord agrees to renovate the extra space.

Paragraph (a) explains when and how the tenant can exercise the option. Paragraph (b) lists some of the reasons the landlord can use to deny giving the tenant the extra space, for example, its lack of creditworthiness. Paragraph (d) gives the landlord the right to ask the tenant for an additional security deposit.

FORM 4-5
PREMISES—CREDIT VERIFICATION AS A CONDITION TO EXPANSION

(a)   *Tenant's Rights.* Subject to paragraph (c), tenant has the right, but not the obligation, to add to the premises the space shown on Exhibit _____ (the "expansion space") on the _____ anniversary of the commencement date of this lease according to the further provisions of this paragraph. Tenant must exercise its right to add the expansion space by written notice to landlord given at least _____ (____) days prior to the anniversary on which the expansion space may be added to the premises. If tenant does not exercise its right in a timely manner, tenant will have irretrievably lost its right to the expansion space.

(b)   *Documents Tenant Must Submit.* The notice given by tenant to landlord pursuant to paragraph (a) will be accompanied by:

(i)   The current quarterly financial statement (which may be unaudited but must be certified by the president or chief financial officer) and last annual financial statement (which must be audited) of tenant and any guarantor ("guarantor") that has furnished a guaranty ("guaranty") of this lease. The financial statements (the "financial statements") required by this paragraph include income statements, balance sheets, statements of cash flow, and footnotes; and

(ii)   Tenant's and guarantor's written authorization to all credit-rating agencies of the release of their credit reports.

(c)   *When Option May Be Invalid.* Tenant will not have any rights under paragraph (a) if tenant does not give landlord notice strictly according to this paragraph, or if at the time either that tenant gives landlord notice under paragraph (a) or that the expansion space is delivered to tenant:

(i)   An event of default exists;

(ii)   The original occupant of the premises occupies less than _____% of the rentable square feet of the premises;

(iii)   Any lender whose deed of trust, mortgage, or other security interest affects either the premises or the landlord does not approve tenant's creditworthiness;

(iv)   Landlord does not approve tenant's or guarantor's creditworthiness. In determining tenant's creditworthiness, landlord may consider the financial statements of tenant and guarantor and may compare them to financial statements submitted by tenant and guarantor in connection with the entry into this lease;

(v)   Guarantor has endeavored to rescind or terminate the guaranty.

(d)   *Security Deposit.* At landlord's request, tenant will deliver an amount sufficient to make the security deposit equal to one month's rent for the premises and the expansion space, and tenant will deliver guarantor's ratification of its guaranty of the lease as amended by the addition of the expansion space.

Some tenants use "build-out" expansion options as a way to line their own pockets. Once the landlord had signed a lease containing a commitment to renovate expansion space, the tenant may decide not to take the additional space itself. Instead, before the option is exercised, it assigns or sublets its original space at a profit.

Before the tenant exercises the expansion option, its lease is a valuable commodity. It contains a commitment by the landlord to invest money into expansion space. A prospective assignee or subtenant may pay the tenant a bonus to occupy the original space, knowing the lease also entitles it to occupy the additional, renovated space after the option ripens.

When it is time for the option to be exercised, the tenant exercises it for the subtenant (in the case of a sublease) or the assignee exercises it itself (in the case of an assignment). Then the landlord is forced to make costly renovations for an assignee or subtenant it never met, while the tenant keeps the assignee's or subtenant's rent.

Form 4-5 is designed to prevent the tenant from realizing a profit on the expansion option because the tenant can lease the additional space only if it is currently occupying a certain percentage of the original space. If the tenant has assigned or sublet more than the designated portion of its original space, the expansion option is void.

A tenant could bargain for a set standard that the landlord would have to use to evaluate its credit; **Form 4-5** does not tie the landlord to any criteria of creditworthiness. If the tenant meets the standard, then the landlord would have to let it lease the additional space.

Two possible standards that a tenant might want and a provision clause incorporating such standards are:

(1)   The landlord can deny the tenant the additional space only if the tenant's assets and net worth are less than they were when the lease was signed:

In determining tenant's creditworthiness, landlord may require only that the then-current financial statements of tenant and guarantor reflect total assets and net worth at least equal to those reflected in the financial statements submitted by tenant and guarantor in connection with the entry into this lease.

(2)   The landlord can deny the tenant the expansion space only if the tenant's financial condition do not meet reasonable standards of creditworthiness:

If tenant exercises its right to add the expansion space and submits the required financial statements, landlord will withhold consent only in accordance with landlord's reasonable and prevailing credit standards.

§ 4.22   Right of First Refusal to Lease Additional Space

When a landlord will not give a tenant an option to expand the premises, the tenant can fall back to a demand for a right of first refusal to lease additional space. This means that the landlord must offer space to the tenant before it leases that space to anyone else. The terms on which the tenant has the right to take additional space are those of the lease that the landlord intends to make. Those terms, unfortunately, are not always easy to identify. In a California case,[23] the

---

[23] Mitchell v. Exhibition Foods, Inc., 184 Cal. App. 3d 1033, 229 Cal. Rptr. 535 (1986).

right of first refusal was expressly intended to enable the tenant to extend the term of the lease for five years "on terms and conditions identical" to those negotiated with a third party. The landlord reached agreement with a third party for a lease containing three five-year options and several covenants with which the existing tenant could not comply because of the nature of its business. Acknowledging the inconsistency, but realizing that the right was for the tenant's benefit, the court gave the tenant the three renewal periods and did not require it to perform the impracticable covenants. The court was acutely aware of possible abuses of this right by landlord.

Just as an option to purchase should be exercised unequivocally (see § **4.23**), so also should a right of first refusal to lease additional space. When space is offered to a tenant according to its right of first refusal to lease it, and the tenant accepts the offer conditioned upon its inspection, its exercise is conditional, equivocal and ineffective.[24]

To a tenant, the virtue of a right of first refusal is that it gives the tenant an opportunity to evaluate the space before it loses it. To a landlord, the drawback is that a prospective tenant may lose interest in the space while the first tenant evaluates the opportunity. For this reason, negotiation of the right of first refusal dwells most extensively on the period during which the first tenant has the right to evaluate the opportunity.

Rights of first refusal can be used in tandem with options for the same space. For example, if a tenant has the option to take adjacent space in the tenth year of its lease, the landlord can lease the adjacent space up to the date on which the first tenant has the right to take it. However, if the first tenant expands more quickly than it anticipated, it may want the adjacent space before the tenth year of its lease. The right of first refusal, combined with the option, will give it the right to take the adjacent space if it comes up for lease. When rights of first refusal are used in tandem with options, the tenant must be certain that its exercise of a right of first refusal does not leave a gap before its rights ripen under its option. In this example, if the adjacent premises became available in the fifth year of the first tenant's lease, and the landlord's offer was for a three-year lease, the first tenant would have space for the sixth, seventh and eighth years, but not for the ninth and tenth years of its lease. The right of first refusal—or right of first offer as it is sometimes called—may look like:

FORM 4-6
PREMISES—RIGHT OF FIRST OFFER TO LEASE

(a) *Notice.* Before entering into a lease for all or any portion of the space adjacent to the premises consisting of approximately _____ (_____) square feet, as more particularly shown on Exhibit _____ (the "additional space"), during the first forty-eight (48) months of the term, and so long as tenant is not then in default under this lease, landlord will notify tenant of the monthly rent and rental

---

[24] Central Nat. Bank v. Fleetwood Realty Corp., 110 Ill. App. 3d 169, 441 N.E.2d 1244 (1982).

increases ("rental terms") on which it would be willing to lease the additional space to tenant.

If within five (5) days after receipt of landlord's notice, tenant agrees in writing to lease the additional space for a term not to exceed the remaining initial term of this lease at the rental terms, landlord and tenant will execute a lease for the additional space within ten (10) days after landlord's receipt of tenant's notice of intent to lease on all the same terms as this lease except for the rental terms, and other matters dependent upon the size of the premises such as tenant's share of the common area expenses, insurance premium payments, and security deposit. If tenant does not deliver its notice of intent to lease the additional space or portion of the additional space offered in landlord's notice within such five (5) day period, or if landlord and tenant do not enter into a fully executed lease for the additional space or such portion within such ten (10) day period, then this right of first offer to lease the additional space or portion of the additional space will lapse and be of no further effect and landlord will have the right to lease the additional space or such portion of the additional space to a third party on the same or any other terms and conditions, whether or not such terms and conditions are more or less favorable than those offered to tenant. This right of first offer to lease the additional space is personal to [name of tenant] and is not transferable.

(b)   *Time of Essence.* Time is of the essence of the provisions of this paragraph.

This right of first offer to lease is not as beneficial as some tenants may deserve. For one thing, it does not limit the landlord to making a lease on the same terms offered to the tenant if the tenant does not accept the offer. That sort of provision prevents the landlord from making a disingenuous offer to the tenant. Further refinements to **Form 4-6** are suggested by the form and discussion in § **4.25**.

Some landlords offer a first right to negotiate instead of a right of first refusal. This is meant to be a lesser right than the right of first refusal. It gives the tenant only the right to sit down with the landlord and to try to come to an agreement before the landlord offers the space to the public. The tenant has no assurance that the terms that are offered to the general public are the same as those that were offered to it. These sorts of provisions seem ripe for a first tenant's assertion that the landlord did not deal in good faith when its opportunity to negotiate arose. Thus, the first right to negotiate should be avoided.

§ 4.23   Options to Purchase

Wall Street wisdom holds that either the buyer or the seller has made a mistake in any sale transaction. The abundant litigation spawned by options to purchase supports this wisdom.[25] Commonly, landlords (optionors) realize that the sale they have agreed to make is not advantageous to them when the tenant exercises its purchase option—understandably so, because it is obvious that tenants

---

[25] *See, e.g.,* Texaco, Inc. v. Golart, 206 Conn. 454, 538 A.2d 1017 (1988) (landlord unsuccessfully opposed fixed price purchase option as unconscionable). See also cases in § **2.3**.

exercise their options to purchase only when the option price turns out to be a bargain. Thus litigation often ensues when the landlord resists the tenant's option.

Options to purchase raise the same questions that other options raise: the effect of a breach,[26] assignment,[27] termination,[28] and the means of giving notice. Options to purchase also raise questions about the rule against perpetuities; however, these options do not violate the rule against perpetuities if they are part of the lease and must be exercised during the term of the lease. A California case[29] held that an option to purchase did not violate the rule as restraint on alienation even though it could be exercised in any of four five-year option terms after the initial five-year term; the option was executed simultaneously with the lease in a document separate from the lease but integrated into it.

A Texas appellate court, however, found that an option to purchase at any time 30 years after the making of the lease violated the rule against perpetuities. The ruling was based on the binding-effect provision — for heirs and assigns — and the possibility that an heir might be born who would exercise the option more than 21 years after a grantee had died; thus, the possibility existed that the interest might not vest for 21 years after a life in being as required by the rule against perpetuities.[30]

A tenant's option to purchase premises "at any time during the term of the lease" includes any renewal of the term.[31]

Although an option to purchase at an appraised value is lawful (and may be written with reference to the method in paragraph (b) of **Form 5-11**), an option price "based on" an appraisal was litigated when the landlord unsuccessfully demanded a price higher than the appraised price and purportedly "based on" the

---

[26] Some courts have held that the option is independent of tenant's performance under the lease. Tracy v. Albany Exch. Co., 7 N.Y. 472 (1852). Other courts have declined to allow a tenant to exercise its purchase option if it is in default under the lease. A trial is needed to determine whether late payments of rent, taxes, and insurance, as well as failure to maintain the premises properly, are trivial or technical breaches which will not nullify tenant's purchase option. 1014 Fifth Ave. Realty Corp. v. Manhattan Realty Co., 111 A.D.2d 78, 489 N.Y.S.2d 204 (1985), *rev'd*, 67 N.Y.2d 718, 490 N.E.2d 855, 499 N.Y.S.2d 936 (1986). *But see* Eskridge v. Macklevy, Inc., 468 So. 2d 337 (Fla. Dist. Ct. App.), *review denied*, 478 So. 2d 54 (Fla. 1985), in which tenant's 10-year-old defaults (subleasing and improving the premises without landlord's consent) enabled landlord to avoid tenant's purchase option.

[27] 3 G.W. Thompson, Commentaries on The Modern Law of Real Property § 1156 (1980 repl. vol. by J.S. Grimes) [hereinafter Thompson].

[28] A tenant who pledges its lease as its security for a loan and thereafter loses its lease in foreclosure also loses the purchase option in the lease. Moore & McCaleb, Inc. v. Gaines, 489 So.2d 491 (Miss. 1986).

[29] Housing Authority of Monterey County v. Monterey Senior Citizen Park, 164 Cal. App. 3d 348, 210 Cal. Rptr. 497 (1985).

[30] Garza v. Sun Oil Co, 727 S.W.2d 115 (Tex. Ct. App. 1986).

[31] Exxon Corp. v. Pollman, 712 S.W.2d 230 (Tex. Ct. App. 1986), *opinion superseded*, 729 S.W.2d 302 (Tex. Ct. App. 1986).

appraisal.[32] An option to purchase at "fair market value" is sufficiently clear to be enforced.[33] The purchase price can also be set by appraisal.[34]

An option to purchase is, of course, an offer that the tenant may accept. As such, it can be evidenced by a purchase contract that only the landlord has signed. Although attaching a purchase contract to a lease seems inappropriate, the real estate professional should not dismiss the notion out of hand; using a real estate purchase contract assures that there are no missing provisions that will enable a landlord to avoid the purchase option.[35]

A form of purchase option is:

FORM 4-7
PREMISES—OPTION TO PURCHASE

(a) *Grant.* Landlord grants tenant the option to purchase the premises at any time during the term of this lease. Tenant must exercise this option, if at all, by written notice. The notice must state a closing date no more than one hundred twenty (120) days after the date of tenant's notice.

(b) *Assignment.* This option may be assigned apart from this lease.

(c) *Conditions.* This option is conditioned upon tenant not being in default at either the time of its exercise of this option or the time of closing of this option.

(d) *Purchase Price.* The purchase price will be payable in cash or certified funds, as directed by landlord, and is: $_____.

(e) *Closing.* At closing landlord will convey the premises to tenant by general warranty deed, subject only to those exceptions or matters of record stated on the form of deed attached as Exhibit _____. At closing landlord will also supply tenant with a pinned survey of the premises. The surveyor will certify the survey to tenant and tenant's title insurance company. Landlord and tenant will each pay fifty percent (50%) of the cost of the survey, title insurance policy, and any documentary, transfer, and recording fees and charges. At closing, landlord will deliver the general warranty deed, tenant will pay the purchase price to landlord, and tenant will assume all obligations for real estate taxes and assessments applicable to the premises without adjustment or proration.

(f) *Insurance.* Landlord will provide a title insurance policy on an ALTA Form B with standard printed exceptions 1 through 4 deleted and with Form _____ (mineral protection) if minerals are severed. As soon as practicable after tenant's election to purchase the premises, landlord will cause the title insurance company to issue a commitment for title insurance and will deliver a copy of it to tenant for tenant's review. Tenant will notify landlord of its objections to exceptions to title, except that tenant may not object to any exceptions to title described in Exhibit

---

[32] Corriveau v. 3005 Investment Corp., 697 S.W.2d 766 (Tex. Ct. App. 1985), *error refused n.r.e.,* Jan. 15, 1986.

[33] Goodwest Rubber Corp. v. Munoz, 170 Cal. App. 3d 919, 216 Ca. Rptr. 604 (1985). See Leasing Prof., Jan. 1989, regarding options at fair market value option.

[34] Beclar Corp. v. Young, 750 P.2d 934 (Haw. Ct. App. 1988) (residential lease with purchase option).

[35] When the payment provisions are unenforceably vague, the tenant has no right to pay the purchase price in a lump sum if it loses its option. Christmas v. Turkin, 148 Ariz. 603, 716 P.2d 59 (Ct. App. 1986).

_____, and landlord will exercise reasonable efforts to cause such objections to be deleted within thirty (30) days after the date on which landlord receives notification from tenant. If landlord is unable to secure deletion of those exceptions, or secure, at its expense, title insurance against them, then tenant will have the option to rescind its agreement to purchase or to proceed with the purchase and waive any such exception.

Landlords should demand that purchase options end automatically on the day before any proceedings in condemnation of the premises. The tenant with a purchase option can get a windfall in condemnation because it is entitled to the amount by which the award exceeds the option price; in effect, the tenant is considered the owner of the premises.[36]

A tenant with an option to purchase should also consider the consequences of casualty damage that allows the landlord to cancel the lease. The tenant should insist upon the right (but not the obligation) to pay the landlord the difference between the option price and the insurance limits, and to get a deed to the premises. Often landlords agree to give the tenant an assignment of the insurance proceeds upon the tenant's payment of the full purchase price. This puts the tenant at risk for the insurer's defenses to the landlord's insurance policy, for example, fraud. Even if the tenant gets the insurance proceeds, it will be missing the deductible. Consequently, the purchase price must be reduced by the deductible (in other words, the landlord's self-insured risk) and the tenant must get an assignment of the insurance proceeds.

§ 4.24   Lenders' Concerns about Options to Purchase

In the usual case in which the purchase option is subordinate to the mortgage, purchase options raise the same questions as those raised by rights of first refusal and discussed in § 4.26; this follows from the fact that the mortgage will not be disturbed by the exercise of a tenant's rights. The difficult problems arise when the purchase option is superior to the mortgage or when the lender is asked to agree to be bound by a subordinate purchase option. The lender's concerns originate from the doctrine of merger, discussed in § 32.12, which has the effect of extinguishing the lease when the reversion and the leasehold are vested in the tenant. If the reversion is purchased pursuant to a right prior to the mortgage, then the mortgage may be extinguished by merger. This result also follows from the doctrine of relation back, in which it is said that the rights of the tenant relate back to the unencumbered reversion.

The lender also has concerns about the option price, which obviously fixes the upper bound of a prudent loan. Any mortgage debt in excess of the purchase price will be extinguished by the exercise of a prior option. Although many lenders seem to feel that the upper bound of a mortgage loan is the same as the option price, a lender should consider all amounts which its mortgage may secure (costs

---

[36] San Diego County v. Miller, 13 Cal. 3d 684, 532 P.2d 139, 119 Cal. Rptr. 491 (1975).

of foreclosure, accrued and unpaid interest, and incidental expenses) when determining the face amount of its mortgage loan. Lenders will reject leases that are superior to their mortgages and that give a tenant the unequivocal right to purchase at an appraised value because there is no assurance that the appraised value will be sufficient to pay off the mortgage debt. Lenders also have several other concerns with regard to purchase options that are prior to their mortgages:

1. Lenders will insist upon the payment of the purchase price — or at least the mortgage balance — to the lender at the time of the transfer of title. The purchase price should be increased to assure the lender that prepayment charges are paid.

2. Lenders will not want the tenant to have the right to prepay the mortgage during a period when the mortgage provides that it cannot be prepaid.

3. Lenders will insist that the exercise of the purchase option does not extinguish the debt by virtue of merger or relation back.

4. Lenders will not want the tenant to have a right to cancel its lease if the landlord fails to convey title or is unable to do so.

5. If the purchase option survives the lender's foreclosure or its acceptance of a deed in lieu of foreclosure, the lender will not want the tenant to have any rights of offset against the purchase price on account of landlord's default. This is in keeping with the general requirements of nondisturbance agreements. Lenders will not want to be bound to deliver general warranty deeds, but only to deliver special warranty deeds or deeds that covenant only against the lender's own acts. Lenders will not want to make any warranties about the premises.

§ 4.25   Right of First Refusal to Purchase Premises

As an alternative to an option to purchase, a right of first refusal to purchase may be a palatable suggestion for the same reasons that a right of first refusal to lease is often an attractive alternative to an option to expand.[37] The attraction of landlords to a right of first refusal may vanish quickly if courts follow the unusual ruling of a South Dakota court that such a right continues into a holdover period.[38] The court distinguished purchase options, which would not continue into a holdover term in the absence of an expansion of contrary intent,[39] from rights of first refusal.

---

[37] *See generally* Note, *The Right of First Refusal Appendant to a Lease,* 53 Iowa L. Rev. 1305 (1968).

[38] Williams v. Williams, 347 N.W.2d 893 (S.D. 1984).

[39] Blaschke v. Wiede, 649 S.W.2d 749 (Tex. Civ. App.), *error refused n.r.e.,* Oct. 5, 1983.

FORM 4-8
PREMISES—RIGHT OF FIRST REFUSAL

(a) *Grant.* Landlord grants tenant a right of first refusal to purchase the premises pursuant to this section.

(b) *Applicable Transactions.* If landlord receives an offer to sell the premises and it intends to accept the offer, or if landlord decides to make an offer to sell the premises, landlord will give a written copy of the offer to tenant. Tenant will have the right to accept the offer by written notice to landlord given within fifteen (15) days after tenant's receipt of the offer. If tenant accepts the offer, tenant will be bound to purchase the premises strictly in accordance with the terms of the offer. So long as landlord's rights are not affected, tenant has the right to bid at any foreclosure sale of the premises.

(c) *Excluded Transactions.* Tenant does not have any right of first refusal to purchase the premises in any of the following transactions: (i) sales of the premises to a related entity (as that term is defined in this paragraph); (ii) encumbrances of the premises; and (iii) any offer after the first one that landlord gives to tenant. The term "related entity" means any corporation (A) that owns 80% or more of the voting stock of landlord; (B) 80% or more of whose voting stock is owned by landlord; or (C) 80% or more of whose voting stock is owned by a corporation that also owns 50% or more of the voting stock of landlord.

(d) *Conditions.* Tenant does not have any right of first refusal to purchase the premises if, at the time landlord receives the offer or decides to make the offer, (i) tenant is in default under this lease, or (ii) an event has occurred that would be a default under this lease after either notice or the passage of time, or (iii) tenant has assigned all or part of this lease or has sublet all or part of the premises.

(e) *No Assignment.* The rights granted to tenant in this section are personal and may not be assigned by tenant in connection with an assignment of this lease or otherwise, and tenant's rights in this paragraph may not be exercised by anyone other than tenant. Any attempted assignment of tenant's rights in this paragraph will be of no effect, and will terminate these rights as of the date of the purported assignment.

(f) *Apportionment of Rent.* If tenant purchases the premises, prepaid rent will be credited against the purchase price.

(g) *No Recording.* Tenant must not allow its rights in this section to be placed of record. If it does, its rights under this section will terminate as of the time of recording. No recording of tenant's rights in this paragraph will be of any effect.

(h) *Time of the Essence.* Time is of the essence of each and every agreement and condition in this paragraph.

This provision assumes that:

1. The landlord and tenant are not individuals, so that trusts, descendants, and charitable organizations need not be included as excluded transferees. An individual would also exclude transfers made to a partnership or corporation in exchange for an interest or stock.

2. The premises are coextensive with the entire property.

3. There is only one owner, so that partition sales may be ignored.

Landlords and tenants disagree on these questions:

1. Should the tenant be entitled to a credit for any brokerage commissions that the landlord saves? The landlord may list the property for sale with an exclusion of the tenant, or it may accept an offer involving a broker with an exclusion of the tenant. The tenant feels it should have the benefit of the savings; after all, the tenant reasons, the landlord is no worse off.

2. Does the right apply to subsequent offers or does it expire if the tenant passes up the first offer?

3. Does the right survive sales and continue during the term of the lease?[40]

4. If the premises are one of several parcels involved in a single transaction, should the purchase price be allocated among the properties?

5. Does the right apply to exchanges of the premises? The Supreme Court of Kansas ruled that it did.[41] A Colorado court ruled similarly: although the tenant obviously could not match the exchange arrangement, it could have matched the cash equivalent which the landlord offered.[42] The Colorado case suggests a simple solution to a difficult problem.

6. Does the right apply to distributions in connection with corporation dissolutions? A New York court said no.[43]

7. Does the right apply to "net" leases with purchase options? A New York court held that neither the lease nor the option gave the first tenant an opportunity to exercise its right of first refusal.[44] When a court finds that the lease with purchase option is made in order to avoid the right of first refusal, the first tenant will be able to exercise its purchase option.[45] In that case, the court considered the term (which was long enough to survive the first tenant's lease), the rent (which was well below market rates), related payments (which looked like a down payment), and a previous agreement to sell (which the "lease" replaced).

8. Does the right apply to an offer to buy the premises subject to improvement if the holder of the right declines the proposed improvements? In a Georgia case,[46] a landlord agreed to sell the tenant its premises for an amount that included the landlord's repair of the roof. The agreement

---

[40] See Annot., 15 A.L.R.2d 1040, *What constitutes a "sale" of real property within purview of clause in lease making renewal clause imperative in event of such contingency* (1951) (analogous situations).

[41] Anderson v. Armour & Co., 205 Kan. 801, 473 P.2d 84 (1970).

[42] Eliminator, Inc. v. 4700 Holly Corp., 681 P.2d 536 (Colo. Ct. App. 1984).

[43] Kings Antiques Corp. v. Varsity Properties, Inc., 121 A.D.2d 885, 503 N.Y.S.2d 575 (1986), *appeal granted,* 69 N.Y.2d 603, 504 N.E.2d 396, 512 N.Y.S.2d 1026, *appeal dismissed,* 70 N.Y.2d 641, 512 N.E.2d 557, 518 N.Y.S.2d 1031 (1987).

[44] *Id.*

[45] Quigley v. Capolongo, 53 A.D.2d 714, 383 N.Y.S.2d 935 (1976), *aff'd without opinion,* 43 N.Y.2d 748, 372 N.E.2d 797, 401 N.Y.S.2d 1009 (1977).

[46] Systems Eng'g Assoc. v. Peachtree Corners, Inc., 179 Ga. App. 48, 345 S.E.2d 136 (1986).

was subject to a right of first refusal. The holder of the right agreed to buy the building without the roof repairs at a lesser price that eliminated the roof repair. The tenant said that the holder of the right of first refusal had not bought the premises on the same terms as it had agreed. A Georgia court did not agree, since the tenant could have had the same price as the holder of the right if it had not insisted upon the roof repairs.

A single lease often employs both a purchase option and a right of first refusal.[47] This allows the tenant to buy at the option price or to buy at any other price (presumably lower than the option price) that a third person offers. Such a provision is the best of all possible worlds for the tenant and the worst of all possible worlds for the landlord. The tenant is not only assured of a fixed price that may turn out to be a bargain, but it also is assured the opportunity to buy at any sales price better than the fixed price. Consequently these provisions often spawn litigation. For example, in a Pennsylvania case, Amoco had a fixed price option at $45,000 and a right of first refusal. When the landlord received an acceptable offer at $75,000, it offered the property to Amoco at that price. Instead, Amoco exercised its fixed price option at $30,000 less than the landlord's proposed contract. The Pennsylvania Supreme Court sustained a ruling that the landlord was compelled to sell to Amoco at $45,000.[48] In a very similar case, the offer was $121,000 and the fixed option price was $40,000; the landlord was compelled to sell at $40,000, thus losing $81,000.[49] However, at least one New York appellate court has held that the tenant's failure to exercise its right of first refusal extinguished its fixed price purchase option; the court's decision—to which there was a dissent—was based on its belief that the refusal to exercise the right of first refusal vitiated it and fixed the value of the property at the fixed option price.[50]

Like any option, the right of first refusal is an offer that must be accepted unequivocally by the offeree. If it is not, the offer may be lost. In a Connecticut case,[51] a landlord gave its tenant a copy of an offer that it had received with an opportunity to accept the offer pursuant to tenant's right of first refusal. The tenant indicated interest in accepting the proposed agreement but demanded its own contract. Moreover, the tenant did not send the landlord the same deposit as had been made under the proposed contract. The court held that a deposit was required from the tenant at the time it exercised its right of first refusal. The tenant found itself in a difficult position: it had been asked to make a deposit on account of a contract that was not drawn in its name. The lesson of this case is that a tenant must send back an acceptance of the contract together with any required

---

[47] Annot., 22 A.L.R.4th 1293, *Construction and effect of options to purchase at specified price and at price offered by third person, included in same instrument* (1983).

[48] Amoco Oil Co. v. Snyder, 302 Pa. Super. 472, 448 A.2d 1139, *order aff'd*, 478 A.2d 795, 505 Pa. 214 (1984).

[49] Gulf Oil Corp v. Chiodo, 804 F.2d 284 (4th Cir. 1986).

[50] Moon v. Haussler, 153 A.D.2d 1002, 545 N.Y.S.2d 623 (1989).

[51] Smith v. Hevro Realty Corp., 199 Conn. 330, 507 A.2d 980 (1986).

deposit and show by underlineation or its response that the only change to the contract is the substitution of its name for that of a prospective purchaser.

A more difficult question is presented when the contract that is offered to the tenant is legally insufficient or artlessly drafted. In these cases, the tenant must make a judgment as to whether the artlessness or legal insufficiency is so great that it is willing to sacrifice its rights. Unless it is, the tenant should accept the contract as presented.

Although real estate professionals believe that rights of first refusal are easy and advisable alternatives to purchase options, they probably are looking at only one facet of those agreements: rights of first refusal, unlike purchase options, do not allow tenants to get windfall purchase prices (which, after all, usually means only that the landlord made a poor prognostication of the future value of its property). There are, however, many other ways in which rights of first refusal are less desirable than purchase options.

One difficulty may be posed in this way: what offer must the landlord first make to its tenant?[52] If it is the first offer that the landlord proposes to make, it is probably set high in order to enable the landlord to negotiate. If it is the first offer the landlord receives, it is probably set low in order to allow the offeror to negotiate. If the offer is the last offer made by or to the landlord, it will probably be made in the heat of negotiations and will not—as a practical matter—allow much time for the tenant's consideration without the prospective purchaser asserting bad faith. For this reason, many purchasers refuse to make offers on properties that have outstanding rights of first refusal.

Another difficulty arises when the landlord is willing to accept an offer from a creditworthy buyer requiring non-recourse purchase money financing but is unwilling to offer those same terms to its less creditworthy tenant.[53] Yet another difficulty arises if the landlord is willing to accept an offer from which it reaps post-sale benefits that the tenant cannot offer. If an owner is in the food service business and receives an offer from a buyer that proposes to build a restaurant and use the owner's food service, how can a tenant that is not in the food business match the offer?

Needless to say, a tenant's right of first refusal can frustrate a third-party sale.[54] Two Georgia decisions suggest that landlords who grant rights of first refusal should act circumspectly in their draftsmanship and their conduct with other potential buyers. In one case,[55] the tenant had a right of first refusal to purchase its premises on the terms that the landlord would sell the property "whether resulting from an offer to purchase . . . received by lessor or otherwise." The

---

[52] *See* Roy v. George W. Greene, Inc., 404 Mass. 67, 533 N.E.2d 1323 (1989) (landlord required to get acceptable written offer and give tenant opportunity to make same offer).

[53] *See* Cohen, *When the Lease Is Only the Beginning: Negotiating Ancillary Documents,* Prac. Real Est. Law., Mar. 1989, at 75.

[54] Hein Enterprises, Ltd. v. San Francisco Real Estate Investors, 720 P.2d 975 (Colo. Ct. App. 1986).

[55] Hasty v. Health Serv. Centers, Inc., 258 Ga. 625, 373 S.E.2d 356 (1988).

landlord granted an option to an unrelated entity. The tenant asserted that the grant of the option enabled it to exercise its right of first refusal to purchase on the terms of the option, even though the option was subject to the tenant's right of first refusal. The Supreme Court of Georgia ruled in its favor. The effect of the case is to give the tenant a right to match an option instead of an offer and thus to give it the right to buy its premises even though they might not otherwise have been sold.

In another Georgia case,[56] a landlord offered its tenant the premises on the terms at which it proposed to sell them. After the tenant declined, the landlord granted an option to an unrelated entity, relying upon the recent Georgia case law.[57] The tenant asserted its right to buy the property. The Supreme Court of Georgia distinguished the earlier case, because the right in that case had the broader scope created by the phrase "or otherwise." The court went on, however, to rescue the tenant by holding that the grant of the option at the price the landlord was willing to accept would end the landlord's motivation to find another offer that might be the basis for the tenant's exercise of its right of first refusal. Thus the court determined that the value of the tenant's option had been reduced and that it was entitled to compensation for the lost value. The court did not tackle the measure of the tenant's loss.

§ 4.26 Lenders' Concerns about Right of First Refusal to Purchase Premises

As a general rule, lenders do not object to a tenant's right of first refusal to purchase the premises. Still, several limitations should be observed:

1. The right of first refusal should be subordinate to the mortgage and not prior to it. A prior right of first refusal may extinguish the mortgage.

2. A lender may object to a right of first refusal given to a tenant whose creditworthiness supports the mortgage loan. The lender may believe that the lease will be extinguished by merger when the tenant buys the premises. This concern may be assuaged by requiring the tenant to assume the mortgage or pay off the mortgage if it buys the premises pursuant to its right of first refusal. This will give the lender at least the credit that it had when the buyer/tenant was only a tenant.

3. If the lender has the right to call its mortgage loan upon the sale of the property, or if there are restrictions based on the purchaser's creditworthiness, these should be disclosed in any right of first refusal, and the right should be given subject to them.

---

[56] Hewatt v. Lepperd, 259 Ga. 112, 376 S.E.2d 883 (1989).

[57] Hasty v. Health Serv. Centers, Inc., 258 Ga. 625, 373 S.E.2d 356 (1988).

4. The right of first refusal should include all of the property covered by the mortgage.

5. The right of first refusal should not apply to foreclosures or deeds given in lieu of foreclosure and should be extinguished by those transactions.

§ 4.27   Landlord's Right to Relocate Premises

If a landlord leases part of a floor of an office building to a small tenant, and is then approached by a full-floor tenant, the landlord may be unable to satisfy the full-floor tenant's requirements. By the same token, the shopping center landlord may lose a substantial tenant if the landlord cannot promise that tenant the space it desires. As a result, many multitenant development leases permit the landlord to relocate the tenant.

A relocation provision in an office building lease may look like:

FORM 4-9
PREMISES—RELOCATION

Landlord reserves the right to relocate the premises to substantially comparable space within the building. Landlord will give tenant written notice of its intention to relocate the premises, and tenant will complete its relocation within thirty (30) days after landlord's notice. The base monthly rent of the new space will not exceed the base monthly rent for the former premises. If tenant does not want to relocate its premises, tenant may terminate this lease effective as of thirty (30) days after landlord's initial notice. Upon tenant's vacation and abandonment of the premises, landlord will pay to tenant a sum equal to one monthly installment of the base monthly rent payable under this lease, and will return the unused portion of the security deposit, and landlord's and tenant's obligations to each other will then end. If tenant does relocate within the building, then effective on the date of such relocation this lease will be amended by deleting the description of the former premises and substituting for it a description of the new space. Landlord agrees to pay the reasonable costs of moving tenant to the new space.

The real estate professional who writes or reviews a relocation provision should answer these questions:

1. Does the landlord have the right to relocate the tenant before the lease commences, or during the term of the lease, or both?

2. If the landlord has a right to relocate the tenant during the term of the lease, how often may it do so?

3. How much notice must the landlord give that it intends to relocate the tenant?

4. How does the new space compare to the old space? The new premises should be comparable in size, layout, and tenant finish. The rental rate for the new premises may be different from that for the old premises,

because one is less desirable than the other or because the landlord has promulgated new rent schedules. A tenant should insist that it cannot be obligated to pay more rent than it did for its other premises. In an office building, the tenant will not want to lose its view, and may insist that the landlord's right to relocate the premises be limited to a stated number of floors below the existing premises. If tenant's premises are uniquely located — for example, on a corner, or between two other tenants from whom the tenant draws customers — it may resist this provision entirely. Finally, if the tenant has made costly improvements, it must be assured that its new premises will be comparably finished at the landlord's cost.

5.   How are moving expenses allocated? The tenant should insist that reprinting its business cards and stationery and printing and mailing announcements of the new address be done at the landlord's expense. The cost of moving the tenant's inventory should also be paid by the landlord. Other costs are not so obvious — for example, specialized wiring of word-processing equipment and extraordinary moving costs of very delicate or very heavy equipment.

6.   What happens if the tenant's operations are interrupted? Although most tenants will insist that their premises be moved over a weekend or during off hours, the tenant's business may still be interrupted. As a result, the tenant should insist that its rent be abated for any period of interruption and that the landlord pay any other costs of that interruption. If the landlord agrees to pay the cost of any interruption, the landlord should clearly specify whether those are direct out-of-pocket costs or lost profits. Finally, tenants may not want to be relocated at extremely inconvenient times, such as tax season for accountants or Christmas season for retail tenants.

7.   Are the permissible locations of the new premises adequately described? In one case, the landlord was entitled to relocate the tenant within "Phase I," but the term was undefined. On the basis of extrinsic evidence, a North Carolina court concluded that the landlord had no right to relocate the tenant to the proposed new space.[58]

---

[58] Moseley & Moseley Builders, Inc. v. Landin, Inc., 87 N.C. App. 438, 361 S.E.2d 608 (1987), *cert. dismissed,* 322 N.C. 607, 370 S.E.2d 416 (1988).

CHAPTER 5

THE TERM

§ 5.1   Defining the Term

The term is an essential lease provision of immense legal and practical importance.[1] To choose one of many practical examples, typical retail tenants should not have a term that expires just before or during the Christmas season. From a legal standpoint, as the length of the term increases, the responsibilities of the tenant increase. Thus (in the absence of a contrary lease provision), a tenant under a three-year lease may not be obligated to repair an air conditioning unit, although a tenant under a 50-year lease may be required to replace a roof.

---

[1] See § **3.3** regarding the importance of the date of a lease.

The term of a lease must be certain: commencement, continuation, and end.[2] Put differently, the lease must endure for a fixed or computable period of time.[3] This rule is easy to state, but its application can be difficult. The term may begin either on an exact date or on the occurrence of an event.[4] An exact date is usually used when the premises already exist in the condition, or nearly the condition, in which the landlord is obligated to deliver them. When the premises must be built for the tenant, the commencement date is usually tied to the completion of construction. The rule against perpetuities presents a problem when commencement of a lease is based upon an event that is not certain to occur, for example, completion of construction. However, most modern thought uses what is called the *wait-and-see* approach[5] with regard to the rule against perpetuities. Assuming that the landlord and tenant intend for the event to occur within a reasonable period of time, the court will not void the lease from the outset but rather will wait and see whether their intentions were realized. The proposed Uniform Statutory Rule Against Perpetuities recommended by the National Conference of Commissioners on Uniform State Laws adopts the wait-and-see approach, but does not specifically address the commencement of leases.[6] In jurisdictions that do not recognize the wait-and-see rule, the owners of new developments should set an outside fixed date for commencement of the lease. Usually that date is three to five years after the execution of the lease, so far away that neither the landlord nor the tenant can imagine that the premises will not be ready before it.

Although scholars differ on the necessity of a certain expiration date, as opposed to one that is tied to a certain event that will occur on an uncertain date,[7] with two exceptions modern real estate practice invariably states a precise expiration date. One exception is that the term may be subject to earlier termination because of default or catastrophe (as examples), and the other is that the term is often extended by the period of any unforeseen delay in the delivery of possession. A lease that has a certain commencement date and term that

---

[2] Restatement § 1.4.

[3] *Id.*

[4] *Id.* § 1.8; 3 G.W. Thompson, Commentaries on the Modern Law of Real Property § 1088 (1980 repl. vol. by J.S. Grimes) [hereinafter Thompson].

[5] Wong v. DiGrazia, 60 Cal. 2d 525, 386 P.2d 817, 35 Cal. Rptr. 241 (1963); Restatement of the Law of Property (Second) (Landlord and Tenant) § 1.8 (1977) [hereinafter Restatement] takes this position.

[6] *See* Pedowitz, *Modernizing the Rule Against Perpetuities,* Prob. & Prop., July/Aug. 1987, at 47 (discussing the Uniform Statutory Rule Against Perpetuities Act promulgated by the National Conference of Commissioners on Uniform State Laws). Alaska has adopted the "wait-and-see" approach with regard to purchase options. Hansen v. Stroecker, 699 P.2d 871 (Alaska 1985). Connecticut has legislated a "second look." Conn. Gen. Stat. § 45-95 (1955). Omath Holding Co. v. City of New York, 149 A.D.2d 179, 545 N.Y.S.2d 557 (1989).

[7] *See* I M.R. Friedman, Friedman on Leases § 4.1 (1983) [hereinafter Friedman], and 3 Thompson § 1089; Restatement § 1.7 says that a lease may be terminable on an event.

"continues thereafter" is a month-to-month tenancy even though a monthly rent schedule for 20 years is included.[8]

The term of the lease calls into play the applicable recording statutes; in many states, leases exceeding a prescribed term must be recorded.

If the lease is to be extended by the period of any delay in delivery of possession, the landlord and tenant must be certain to agree upon the expiration date while the delay is fresh in their minds. Otherwise the landlord will not be sure when the premises are available for occupancy, and the tenant will not be certain when to leave. The first one to ask will do so because of a need to know; in that situation, the other may exact a price for certainty.

Landlords often confirm rent commencement dates by a lease addendum such as:

FORM 5-1
COMMENCEMENT DATE CERTIFICATE

This commencement date certificate is entered into by landlord and tenant pursuant to section _____ of the lease.

1. *Definitions.* In this certificate the following terms have the meanings given to them:

    (a)   Landlord: _____

    (b)   Tenant: _____

    (c)   Lease: Office lease dated _____, 19____, between landlord and tenant

    (d)   Premises: Suite _____

    (e)   Building Address: _____
    _____
    _____

2. *Confirmation of Term:* Landlord and tenant confirm that the commencement date of the lease is _____, 19____, and the expiration date is _____, 19____, and that sections _____ and _____ are accordingly amended.

3. *Acceptance of the Premises.* Tenant accepted the premises on _____, 19____, and first occupied the premises on _____, 19____.

Landlord and tenant have executed this commencement date certificate as of the dates set forth below.

TENANT: LANDLORD:

_____   _____

By: _____   By: _____

Title: _____   Title: _____

Date: _____   Date: _____

---

[8] Union Bldg. Materials Corp. v. Kakaako Corp., 5 Haw. App. 146, 682 P.2d 82, *reconsideration granted,* 5 Haw. App. 683, 753 P.2d 253 (1984).

Although often used interchangeably, the words *expiration* and *termination* have distinct legal meanings. The expiration of a lease occurs on the last day of its term.[9] The termination of a lease cuts off the term,[10] for example, by a landlord's election after a tenant's default, by condemnation, or by destruction of the premises. If it occurs at all, a termination always precedes an expiration.[11]

§ 5.2   Landlord's Failure to Deliver Possession

Usually the landlord will not have any difficulty in delivering possession of the premises at the commencement date of the term. However, the landlord may be unable to do so if the past tenant holds over after the end of its term, or if the landlord has not completed its construction of the premises.

The consequences of the landlord's failure to deliver possession because the old tenant holds over depend upon which of the two prevailing rules is applied, the English rule (which some states have adopted) or the American rule.[12] The English rule requires the landlord to deliver actual possession of the premises to its tenant[13] and to oust anyone else who may be in possession. The American rule requires the landlord to deliver only the lawful right to possession; in other words, the American rule gives the new tenant the right to oust the old tenant.[14] The American rule also requires the new tenant to pay rent even though the landlord is unable to deliver possession because another occupant wrongfully holds over. The English rule seems to comport better with the tenant's expectations, and has been adopted by the *Restatement* § 6.2.

Depending upon the jurisdiction, under the English rule, the tenant may rescind the lease or pursue a claim for damages if its landlord fails to deliver the premises at the commencement of the term. The theories of the tenant's recovery against its landlord (in the proper jurisdiction) are variously stated as the landlord's breach of its implied covenant (1) of quiet enjoyment, (2) of its right to lease the premises, (3) of delivery of possession to the tenant, or (4) of the availability of the premises to the tenant.[15] The measure of general damages will be the difference, if any, between the rental value of the premises and the rent

---

[9] Duke's Restaurant Corp. v. Day, 90 N.Y.S.2d 16 (Mun. Ct. 1949).

[10] Piedmont Interstate Fair Ass'n v. City of Spartanburg, 274 S.C. 462, 264 S.E.2d 926 (1980).

[11] 2 R. Powell, The Law of Real Property § 222(3) (P.J. Rohan ed., rev. 1977) [hereinafter Powell]; R. Schoshinski, American Law of Landlord and Tenant § 2.7 (1980) [hereinafter Schoshinski].

[12] *See generally* Annot., 96 A.L.R.3d 1155, *Implied covenant or obligation to provide lessee with actual possession* (1979).

[13] Langham's Estate v. Levy, 198 S.W.2d 747 (Tex. Civ. App. 1946), *writ ref'd n.r.e.*

[14] Teitelbaum v. Direct Realty Co., 172 Misc. 48, 13 N.Y.S.2d 886 (N.Y. Sup. 1939) (epitomizing American rule), *overruled by statute,* N.Y. Real Prop. Law § 223-a (McKinney 1962).

[15] Schoshinski § 3:2.

stipulated in the lease.[16] Special damages, for example, lost profits, may be recovered according to their proof.[17]

To protect themselves against these sorts of claims, landlords usually add a provision such as:

FORM 5-2
TERM—FAILURE TO DELIVER PREMISES

If for any reason landlord cannot deliver possession of the premises to tenant on the commencement date, (a) this lease will not be void or voidable, (b) landlord will not be liable to tenant for any resultant loss or damage, and (c) unless landlord is unable to deliver possession of the premises to tenant on the commencement date because of tenant's delays, rent will be waived for the period between the commencement date and the date on which landlord delivers possession of the premises to tenant. No delay in delivery of possession of the premises will extend the term.

Form 5-2 excuses the landlord if it cannot deliver possession "for any reason." This is considerably broader than a provision that excuses the landlord solely because of a holdover. Of course, a landlord will be hard pressed to justify a late delivery for which it is responsible.[18] In any event, the tenant should insist upon an outside date for delivery of possession.

§ 5.3 Existing Premises

A lease of existing premises allows a precise statement of the term. The provision may say:

FORM 5-3
TERM—EXISTING PREMISES

The term of this lease will begin on January 1, 19_____, and expire on December 31, 19_____.

---

[16] Foreman & Clark Corp. v. Fallon, 3 Cal. 3d 875, 479 P.2d 362, 92 Cal. Rptr. 162 (1971).

[17] 2 Powell § 225(1); Annot., 88 A.L.R.2d 1024 at 1043, *Measure of damages for lessor's breach of contract to lease or to put lessee into possession* (1963). *See* Young v. Scott, 108 Idaho 506, 700 P.2d 128 (1985) (tenant awarded damages, including lost profits and punitive damages, when landlord failed to make promised improvements). Of course, if a landlord wrongfully refuses to allow its tenant to occupy the premises, the tenant has a claim for damages. Vault, Inc. v. Michael-Northwestern Partnership, 372 N.W.2d 7 (Minn. Ct. App.), *review denied,* Sept. 13, 1985 (awarding damages and lost profits, including a projection of Consumer Price Index increases which the tenant was required to pay under the lease it obtained to replace one which its landlord breached).

[18] *See* 2401 Pennsylvania Ave. Corp. v. Federation of Jewish Agencies of Greater Philadelphia, 319 Pa. Super. 228, 466 A.2d 132 (1983), *aff'd,* 507 Pa. 166, 489 A.2d 733 (1985) (landlord could not deliver possession to new tenant because it had granted extensions to old tenant).

Often such a provision ends with a phrase such as "unless sooner terminated in accordance with the terms of this lease." The limitation of the term in the event of termination is superfluous; it goes without saying that the term will not have an opportunity to expire if it is terminated. Certain agreements collateral to the lease, such as assignments and brokerage for agreements, are affected by a termination.[19] Those agreements should be prepared with an understanding of what happens in the event of termination.

The commencement date of a term "from March 5, 19____" is ambiguous, because courts differ on the question of whether March 5 is included or excluded.[20] The determinative factor is the intent of the landlord and tenant. However, if a difference arises, intent can only be determined from litigation. The *Restatement*[21] suggests that March 5 is included in the absence of evidence of a contrary intention. Furthermore, after acknowledging that the matter has been litigated, the *Restatement* recommends that the time of commencement be immediately after midnight on the commencement date, and that the time of expiration be immediately before midnight on the date of expiration.

A landlord may wish to exonerate itself for failure to deliver possession of the premises by use of the provision similar to the one set forth in § **5.2**. Landlord and tenant may agree to early occupancy according to the provisions in § **5.10**.

When leasing existing premises, the landlord should protect itself against the possibility of the tenant's claim that the premises were delivered in an unacceptable condition. The lease should state that:

1. The premises will be delivered by the landlord—and accepted by the tenant—in their "as-is" condition;

2. The landlord is not obligated to make any improvements or repairs to the premises;

3. The tenant has had an opportunity to inspect the premises and to have its architects, engineers, or other consultants inspect the premises;

4. The tenant has found the premises fit for the tenant's use;

5. The tenant accepts the premises with all systems (roof, walls, foundation, heating, ventilating, air conditioning, telephone, sewer, electrical, mechanical, elevator, utility, and plumbing) in good working order and repair.

In a single tenant building, the tenant should demand an assignment of any warranties of workmanship, materials, or fixtures that it is obligated to repair, replace, or maintain.

---

[19] I Friedman § 4:1 n.2.

[20] *E.g.*, Marys v. Anderson, 24 Pa. 272 (1855) (holding for inclusion).

[21] Restatement § 1.4, comment (d).

§ 5.4   Completion of New Office Premises

Most office building leases require the landlord to improve the premises before the term begins. As a result, completion of the premises and the term are closely related. In fact, a typical provision may say:

FORM 5-4
TERM—OFFICE BUILDING

The term of this lease will commence on _____, 19____, and will expire on _____, 19____. Prior to the commencement date landlord will improve the premises according to its obligations in the workletter. Landlord will be deemed to have delivered possession of the premises to tenant when landlord has given tenant ten (10) days' notice that landlord has substantially completed (or will complete within ten (10) days) these improvements, subject only to the completion of landlord's architect's "punch list" items that do not materially interfere with tenant's use and enjoyment of the premises. Neither landlord nor its agents or employees have made any representations or warranties as to the suitability or fitness of the premises for the conduct of tenant's business or for any other purpose, nor has landlord or its agents or employees agreed to undertake any alterations or construct any tenant improvements to the premises except as expressly provided in this lease and the workletter. If landlord cannot deliver possession of the premises to tenant on the commencement date, (a) this lease will not be void or voidable, (b) landlord will not be liable to tenant for any resultant loss or damage, and (c) unless landlord is unable to deliver possession of the premises to tenant on the commencement date because of tenant's delays, rent will be waived for the period between the commencement date and the date on which landlord delivers possession of the premises to tenant. No delay in delivery of possession of the premises will extend the term. Tenant will execute the commencement date certificate attached to this lease as Exhibit _____ within 15 days after landlord's request.

The workletter mentioned in this form is discussed in § **5.5**. In contrast to **Form 5-4**, many tenants ask for more than 10 days' prior notice of the delivery of possession. Some tenants ask for an estimated date of delivery, with revisions as the date of delivery approaches. This helps the tenant to coordinate with its storage and transfer company. Monday is a favorite day for delivery of possession because, with the landlord's consent, the tenant can use the preceding weekend to prepare its premises. Tenants who contemplate doing work in their premises often ask for the right to enter the premises before delivery of possession. See § **5.10**.
Although **Form 5-4** does not provide for it, the tenant should not accept possession of its premises unless:

1. An appropriate certificate of occupancy has been issued
2. The building lobby is completed and safe for tenant's invitees
3. The elevators are in operation

4. The systems and related fixtures serving the premises (heating, ventilating, air conditioning, electricity, plumbing and water) are in working order

5. The important common areas (hallways and bathrooms on multitenant floors, law libraries in the case of attorney tenants, and parking lots) are ready for use.

Provisions such as the one in **Form 5-4** trouble many tenants because the landlord does not appear to be under any compulsion to deliver possession. The only consequence of a delay of completion is the extension of the commencement date. Although it appears that the fixed commencement date is not meaningful, landlords are eager to deliver possession because their rent begins only after the tenant takes possession. If a landlord is willing to commit itself to deliver possession before a fixed date, it will do so only if it is excused from delays that are beyond its control.[22] The landlord will insist upon a force majeure provision such as:

FORM 5-5
TERM—FORCE MAJEURE

If landlord is delayed or prevented from completing its work according to the workletter by reason of acts of God, strikes, lockouts, labor troubles, inability to procure labor or materials, fire, accident, riot, civil commotion, laws or regulations of general applicability, acts of tenant, or other cause without its fault and beyond its control (financial inability excepted), completion will be excused for the period of the delay and the period for completion will be extended for a period equal to the period of such delay.

Because timely completion of improvements is not "of the essence" of the lease,[23] a tenant will often ask for an outside date for delivery of possession. This outside date contemplates delays caused by the force majeure provision and goes further by requiring an absolute and fixed date. Landlords resist such provisions because they fear that a unique tenant build-out that would have to be entirely redone for any other tenant could be lost by one day's delay; such landlords often give an unthinkably remote outside date that is not comforting to the tenant. Tenants, on the other hand, take unrealistic assurance from an outside date. Unless a landlord has failed to exonerate itself from liability for late delivery, which would be unusual, the tenant's sole remedy is to terminate the lease and face the same problems again with a new landlord.

---

[22] *See* Gardener Properties v. S. Leider & Son, 199 Misc. 824, 105 N.Y.S.2d 261 (Sup. Ct. 1951), *rev'd*, 279 A.D. 470, 111 N.Y.S.2d 88, *reargument & appeal denied*, 279 A.D. 1046, 113 N.Y.S.2d 254 (1952) (lengthy and fruitless litigation by tenant whose premises could not be completed in a timely manner because of shortages of materials).

[23] McCready v. Lindenborn, 165 N.Y. 630, 59 N.E. 1125 (1899).

§ 5.5 Workletters

A landlord's workletter describes the work that the landlord must do to the premises before possession is delivered to the tenant; this work is often called tenant finish. The landlord's workletter is often complemented by a tenant's workletter that states the work that the tenant will do after landlord finishes its work.[24] In practice one contractor often does all of the work. One workletter is then used instead of two, and the significance of the workletter is solely economic, because it states how the costs of the work will be borne between the landlord and tenant.

Workletters are construction contracts. They are the proper province of experts in the construction process. Landlords prepare workletters and construction bids in concert with their construction management experts. So should tenants. Real estate professionals must read the workletters because they govern matters other than the construction process, such as the consequences of late delivery of the premises. At least one workletter in common use requires the tenant to take additional space if the landlord believes either that the premises lay out better with the additional space or that the remaining adjacent space will be more readily rentable.

Commercial Real Estate Leases: Forms contains a workletter used in an office building.

§ 5.6 —Checklist for Reviewing Workletters

An excellent checklist for reviewing workletters* is:

TERM—WORKLETTER CHECKLIST

ARCHITECT AND CONTRACTOR

_____ Who selects the architect, contractor, and subcontractors? If the tenant chooses the contractor/subcontractor:

_____ Must the choice be approved by owner and lender (e.g., in writing and not unreasonably withheld)?

_____ What insurance must the tenant get at its own expense (e.g., "all risk")?

_____ Which contractors/subcontractors can the tenant hire (e.g., union or nonunion)?

_____ Must the contractor/subcontractor be licensed by the proper authorities?

---

* "Checklist for Negotiating Work Letters" by Alan S. Parker, Esq. Reprinted by permission from the *Commercial Lease Law Insider*, Dec. 1984, P.O. Box 4167, Grand Central Station, New York, NY 10163. Copyright ©1984 by Brownstone Publishers, Inc., New York City.

[24] For a landlord's form of workletter that allows a tenant to bid the work, see *The Pro-Landlord Office Workletter Meets the Tenant's Right to Obtain Other Bids*, Leasing Prof., May 1988, at 4. See *The Office Workletter—The Tenant's Final Battleground*, Leasing Prof., Mar. 1986, at 1, for a discussion of the provision and a landlord's form of workletter.

_____ What insurance must contractors/subcontractors carry and with what policy limits (e.g., worker's compensation; employer's liability insurance; contractor's public liability insurance; personal injury insurance; explosion, collapse, or underground damage insurance; automobile liability insurance; contractor's protective contingent liability insurance; owner's protective contingent liability insurance)?

_____ Must the owner be named as an additional insured on tenant's, contractor's, and subcontractor's insurance policies?

_____ Who pays architect's and contractor's fees?

PRELIMINARY PLANS

_____ Who is responsible for providing, and paying for, preliminary plans?

_____ What should be included in preliminary plans (e.g., enough detail to estimate construction costs and to schedule future construction)?

_____ Are preliminary plans ready for the owner's review before the workletter is signed? (If so, the workletter can focus on drafting and approving final working plans.)

If preliminary plans are not ready before the workletter is signed:

_____ When are the preliminary plans due?

_____ If the owner's contractor does the work, how much input must the tenant provide to the architect to speed up preliminary plans?

FINAL WORKING PLANS

_____ When must final working plans be delivered to the owner?

_____ If the owner's contractor does the work, how much tenant input and cooperation with the architect are needed to speed up completion of final working plans?

_____ If the tenant's contractor does the work, must the tenant consult with the owner and the owner's architect to make sure the final working plans fit the overall design of the building?

_____ What should be included in final working plans (e.g., materials and finishes other than building standard; special load requirements of equipment; openings in floors and walls; utility plans; location of telephone equipment, lighting fixtures, electrical wiring and outlets; partitions; wall finishes; variations in ceiling height; floor coverings; cabinet work)?

_____ Are final working plans subject to the owner's approval?

_____ By what date must the owner approve or reject final working plans?

_____ Can the owner approve and modify final working plans?

_____ Must the tenant accept the owner's modifications?

_____ If the tenant's contractor does the work, must the tenant pay what it cost the owner to modify the final working plans?

MATERIALS AND FINISHES

_____ What will the owner build and install at its own expense (e.g., walls, floors, exterior windows, partitions, ceilings, doors)?

_____ What materials and finishes will the owner use in construction?

_____ If the owner does the work, are building standard materials and finishes specified?

_____ Can the tenant choose other than building standard?

_____ Is there any quality requirement for building nonstandard materials chosen by the tenant (e.g., equal to or better than building standard)?

_____ Are there any building standard items that the tenant must accept (e.g., light fixtures)?

_____ Must any special material or equipment be ordered; will it delay construction?

_____ If the tenant's contractor does the work, are the materials and finishes to be used acceptable to the owner?

CONSTRUCTION COSTS

_____ Who pays for the work done to the leased space?

_____ Is the owner contributing to the tenant's costs; if so, how much?

If the owner's contractor does the work:

_____ Must the owner give the tenant an estimate of construction costs by a certain date?

_____ Is the cost estimate binding on the owner? Must the tenant approve the cost estimate by a certain date (e.g., within seven business days)?

_____ What is the owner's remedy if the tenant does not approve (e.g., termination of the lease)?

_____ Must the tenant pay part of the construction costs before construction begins?

_____ Must the tenant place the total estimated construction costs in escrow (or a percentage more than the estimate—e.g., 150 percent)?

_____ Who gets the interest on the escrow money?

_____ Who can direct payment of money from escrow?

_____ What are the procedures and timetable for paying contractors, subcontractors, suppliers, etc.?

If the tenant's contractor does the work:

_____ Must the tenant give the owner a construction cost estimate?

_____ Can the owner change the construction cost estimate?

_____ When will the owner's contribution to construction costs, if any, be paid or deposited in escrow (e.g., can it be delayed until after construction begins or ends)?

_____ Will construction funding be run through an escrow account?

_____ When can the owner's contribution to construction costs be paid out (e.g., upon substantial completion of work)?

_____ Who authorizes the payout of actual construction costs and under what schedule?

CHANGES TO APPROVED PLANS

_____ Can the tenant change the approved final working plans (e.g., add an interior wall)?

_____ Are changes subject to the owner's approval? Will the owner's approval not be unreasonably withheld?

_____ Who builds the changes and who pays for them?

_____ Must the tenant increase the construction escrow, if any, by the cost of the change (or by a greater amount)?

_____ Is the owner entitled to overhead (e.g., 10 percent of cost) plus profit (e.g., 10 percent of cost) on the tenant's change requests?

_____ What happens to rental payment obligations and the timing of option periods if the changes delay the completion of construction?

CONSTRUCTION DELAYS

_____ If the owner's contractor does the work, is the owner liable for any delays in completing the construction?

_____ What remedies can the owner use if the tenant causes the delay (e.g., acceleration of rental payments; termination of lease upon notice; completion of tenant's unfinished obligations upon notice; charge tenant for additional expenses caused by the delay; retain escrow money)?

_____ For what kind of delay may the owner resort to a remedy (e.g., changes to approved plans; late delivery of preliminary plans; late delivery of final working plans; late tenant approval of owner's approved plans or construction costs; difficulty in obtaining specially ordered material; failure to perform any obligation under workletter)?

ACCESS AND COMPLETION OF CONSTRUCTION

If the tenant's contractor does the work:

_____ Is there any quality standard for completion of the work (e.g., first class and workmanlike)?

_____ Must the contractor/subcontractor warrant or guarantee its work (e.g., free from defects for one year)?

_____ Are there clean-up procedures that must be followed (e.g., storage of materials, disposal of waste)? If the owner's contractor does the work:

_____ Does the tenant have any right to enter before the completion of construction and/or the commencement date in the lease?

_____ What kind of work can the tenant do upon entry (e.g., install computer equipment or special machinery; install book cases, shades, curtains; hang pictures)?

_____ Who is liable for accidents to the tenant's employees and workers during this prelease period; who is liable for theft of materials?

_____ When will construction be completed?

_____ When must the tenant move in?

_____ When will the tenant be obligated to pay rent (e.g., upon substantial completion; a set date)?

_____ Can construction delays caused by the tenant postpone the commencement of rental obligations?

_____ Can the tenant postpone rent payments if the completion of construction was caused by the owner or events outside either party's control (e.g., labor strikes, fire)?

UTILITY SERVICE

_____ Who will provide electric service to the leased space?

_____ Where will the electricity connection be for the leased space?

_____ What will be the power and lighting capacity per square foot?

_____ Can the tenant increase the load; if so, who pays for it?

_____ Can utility lines of other tenants be run through the leased space; if so, where can they be placed?

_____ Do the owner and utility company have the right to enter to repair, alter, or replace utility lines running through the leased space?

_____ Is there a nearby connection for sprinkler service?

_____ Who provides the air supply mains, heating mains, and the various other components of the tenant's heating, ventilation, and air conditioning system?

_____ Does the tenant have special heating and air conditioning loads (e.g., heavy equipment or computers that give off heat)?

MISCELLANEOUS

_____ Is the location of the leased space adequately described in the workletter?

_____ Do the provisions (and additional remedies) of the lease also apply to the workletter?

_____ If any municipal approvals or permits are needed to start construction, who should get and pay for them?

_____ Are the tenant's payments under the workletter considered additional rent under the lease? (If so, the owner may have the same remedies prescribed by the lease for nonpayment of rent, e.g., termination, summary process.)

§ 5.7   Building Standard Specifications

Building standard specifications are an integral part of the workletter.[25] Part of the workletter set forth in _Commercial Real Estate Leases: Forms_ is devoted to building standard specifications. Building standard refers to the types of items and the quantities of those items that will be installed from the landlord as part of the landlord's initial improvement of the tenant's premises. Usually, building standard items are directly related to the number of square feet that a tenant occupies; for example, the landlord may agree to deliver one interior door for every 350 square feet of tenant area. Carpeting is usually expressed as an allowance in dollars per square foot.

Building standard specifications are often supplemented (especially in a tenant's market) by an additional allowance from the landlord for the cost of the tenant's improvements in excess of building standard. A landlord may offer a tenant improvement— or tenant finish—allowance of $15 per square foot. In that case, the tenant will not incur any cost for the initial improvement of its premises if the cost of its improvement is equal to, or less than, building standard plus $15 per square foot.

The landlord will prepare its building standard in collaboration with its architect and contractor. To a landlord, building standard is nothing more than a cost of attracting tenants. Consequently, some landlords cut corners on building

---

[25] _See also What is Building Standard Work?_, Leasing Prof., Jan. 1987, at 1.

standard specifications. To a tenant, the meaning of building standard is simple: the tenant must pay for what the landlord does not.

One specification of building standard items (without reference to quantities) is:

FORM 5-6
BUILDING STANDARD ITEMS

Tenant Interior Partitions: 3-3/4" partition consisting of 2-1/2" 25-gauge metal studs at 24" on center and 5/8" gypsum board on each side to underside of the acoustical ceiling. The partitions are painted with two coats of flat wall paint and have 4" resilient base on each side.

Tenant Interior Doors: 1-3/4" by 3' x 8' red oak hardwood veneer, solid core door, stained building standard color set in painted hollow metal frame with 6" metal head. Hardware consists of two pairs of heavy duty metal hinges, latch set with metal knob as manufactured by _____ and wall-mounted door stops.

Duplex Wall Outlets: wall-mounted 120 volt duplex receptacle with cover plate mounted at floorline in the resilient base.

Telephone Wall Outlets: wall-mounted telephone outlet with cover plate, 3/4" conduit to telephone closet, mounted at floorline in the resilient base.

Wall Switches: wall-mounted single pole toggle switch with cover plate connected to lighting branch wiring "J" boxes.

Painted Surfaces: surfaces for interior drywall partitions will be two-coat work consisting of one sealing coat and one coat of flat wall paint selected from building standard choices. Building allowance includes one color paint per room.

Wall Base: 4" high resilient base in color selected by building at base of all interior walls.

Carpeting: building standard carpeting installed in tenant areas over carpet pad. Tenant may choose from a variety of standard colors.

Acoustical Ceiling: 2' x 5' module lay-in acoustical ceiling tile as manufactured by _____ installed in an exposed tee suspension system in pattern indicated on the base building shell and core contract drawings. Ceiling height is 8'6" above concrete floor slab.

Vertical Blinds: vertical blinds at all exterior windows equal to _____ with 3-1/2" blades in off-white.

Fire Sprinklers: ceiling-mounted concealed sprinkler heads in pattern indicated on the base shell and core contract drawings.

Air Conditioning Zones: 8 interior and 4 exterior air conditioning zones per full floor in pattern indicated on the base shell and core contract drawings.

Supply Air Diffusers: 24" x 6" supply air grills as manufactured by _____ with 8" diameter, 8' long insulated flexible duct and 8" diameter spin in fitting with damper for connection to distribution ductwork in the quantity indicated on the base shell and core contract drawings.

Light Fixtures: 2' x 4', 277 volt, 3-tube fixture with parabolic lens as manufactured by _____ wired for l/3-2/3 operation with 6' wiring pigtail in the quantity indicated on the base shell and core contract drawings.

Lighting Branch Wiring "J" Box: junction box with electrical connectors wired to fixture wiring pigtails and wall switches in the quantity indicated on the base shell and core contract drawings.

Tenant Entry Door: 1-3/4" thick by 3' x 8' hardwood veneer, solid core door, stained building standard color set in painted hollow metal frame with 6" metal head and obscure glass sidelight. Hardware consists of two pair of heavy duty metal hinges, lever lockset as manufactured by _____, door closure as manufactured by _____, and wall-mounted doorstop.

Tenant Exit Door: same as tenant interior doors except hardware is the same as tenant entry door hardware.

The first obstacle that the tenant encounters is that many building standard specifications are given in terms of usable feet and not rentable feet. Thus, even though its rent obligation is calculated on the basis of its rentable area, tenant must adjust its building standard and tenant finish allowance by reference to its usable feet and the efficiency of the building.

When considering building standard in one office building as opposed to building standard in other office buildings, the tenant's first task is to reduce these building standard items to a value per rentable square foot. The landlord may say, for example, that the building standard is worth $15 per rentable square foot. The next question is to determine the unit prices for each of the items of building standard. This will enable the tenant to compare the building standard in several leases on a "unit-cost" basis. The tenant may then have the right to substitute. For example, in the building standard set forth in **Form 5-6**, the tenant may not need the number of interior doors that building standard would give it, but it may need more telephone wall outlets. Can the tenant eliminate one door at a unit cost of $350 and substitute seven telephone wall outlets at a cost of $50 each?

A related question concerns the substitution of a non-building standard item for a building standard item. With regard to **Form 5-6**, may the tenant install linoleum in the luncheon room instead of carpeting? The substitution of non-building standard items for building standard items leads directly to the question of credits. If the linoleum costs less than the carpet, is the tenant entitled to any credit? If so, how may it use its credit? Must it take another door (which it may not need) or may it elect to take a cash payment or a credit against its rent?

These kinds of questions are necessary, but they are not sufficient. In order to know the cost of its premises, the tenant must determine what expenses it will incur before it begins to install its improvements. These expenses will either reduce the tenant's allowance or, if there is no allowance, be borne solely by the tenant. By far the most important question is whether the allowance relates to the premises on a *slab to slab* basis or whether it relates to the premises on a *below finished ceiling to floor* basis. Slab to slab responsibility may require the tenant to use its allowance for everything required between the floor of the premises and the concrete deck above the dropped ceiling. Floor to ceiling responsibility does not include the area above the dropped ceiling. The area above the dropped ceiling contains air conditioning ducts and sometimes the air handling units themselves, sprinkler systems, and electrical wiring. The expense of moving a sprinkler head, heating and air conditioning units, or duct work is substantial. Very often landlords state that there will be a stated number of evenly spaced light fixtures on each floor. With the exception of the highly improbable situation in which the lighting arrangement of the tenant's premises fits perfectly with the existing light fixtures, the tenant will incur the cost of moving those fixtures. **Form 5-6**, for example, states that fire sprinklers will be indicated on the base shell and core contract drawings. If these must be moved, the tenant will bear the cost of doing so.

Real estate professionals can give little credence to the expression building standard. The term has no generally accepted meaning in the real estate industry. If it means anything, it means what the landlord wants it to mean. For example, if **Form 5-6** stated that lighting fixtures would be "building standard" and eliminated any further description, the tenant would have no idea of the fixture that it might expect. The specification given in **Form 5-6** is better than no standard, but it is still not adequate for most tenants. For example, it does not state the degree of illumination (measured in foot-candles) at desk height and thus does not enable the tenant to determine whether a desk top will be sufficiently illuminated for sorting small electronic components (which requires high illumination) or only for coffee-making (which requires less illumination). Very few lighting specifications ever state whether the landlord will furnish the light bulbs or, in fluorescent fixtures, the ballasts. Finally, **Form 5-6** does not state how many light switches there will be in the office. Does one switch control the entire office suite or does each room in the office suite control its own lights? If one switch controls the entire premises, the tenant will suffer some inconvenience but all tenants will suffer the inefficiency when they pay a share of the building's electrical bill.

The term building standard is often used with regard to colors. In **Form 5-6** carpeting and painted surfaces refer to building standard colors. A tenant should be certain that the colors that it wants for its premises are acceptable. Most landlords will allow a tenant to choose almost any color from among those offered by the manufacturer for the specified item, but will charge the tenant extra for deep hues that require additional coats of paint.

In addition to the ill-defined building standard, many leases promise "adequate" items. Adequate is not a meaningful term. For example, adequate heating, ventilating, and air conditioning is different for a reception area than it is for a computer room, a cooking area, or a conference room. Heating and air conditioning are usually measured in terms of the ability of the system to maintain specified interior temperatures when specified exterior temperatures exist. Ventilation is measured by the percentage of fresh air in recirculating air or the number of air changes a space receives per hour. The term "adequate" with regard to heating, ventilating, and air conditioning is inadequate.

Although landlords are willing to promise adequate building standard, they are usually reluctant to promise that the building standard items are sufficient to meet the requirements of applicable building codes. These codes, for example, may require fire alarms and "exit" signs at the doors. **Form 5-6** above does not promise these items if required by building codes. Furthermore, even though **Form 5-6** requires a tenant exit door, it does not obligate the landlord to install the number of exit doors that the size of the premises may require by law. A tenant should never assume that premises built according to building standard will allow lawful occupancy. In order to assure lawful occupancy, additional work may be necessary and the tenant will pay for it.

The analysis of building standard and allowances is within the province of contractors and architects.[26] Real estate professionals must have the support of these experts before they can serve the interests of landlords and tenants. There is less embarrassment in referring to an expert than in explaining a costly mistake.

§ 5.8   Completion and Acceptance of New Shopping Center Premises

A typical provision for the term of a shopping center lease is:

FORM 5-7
TERM—SHOPPING CENTER

The term will commence on the earlier of:
(a)   the date on which tenant opens the premises for business to the public, or
(b)   _____ (_____) days after the delivery of the premises to tenant by landlord.
Delivery will be established by a written notice by landlord to tenant specifying the date upon which the premises will be delivered to tenant.

This provision is comparable to the same provision in an office building lease insofar as each of them is tied to the completion of the premises. Shopping center leases, however, usually give the tenant a *fixturing period* during which the tenant completes its premises and stocks its shelves. Since a tenant may complete

---

[26] *See* II Friedman ch. 23; Goldstein, *When a Landlord Constructs or Alters Business Premises,* 23 Prac. Law. 59 (1977).

its fixturing in a shorter period, shopping center leases provide that the term begins when the tenant opens for business to the public.

The commencement date of the shopping center lease is very important to the landlord and the tenant. In a new development, the landlord may be unable to get permanent financing until a specified leasable area has been occupied and accepted by rent- paying tenants. Furthermore, leases for anchor tenants may excuse the anchor tenant from occupying or paying rent until other tenants have occupied their premises and begun to pay rent. For the tenant, the commencement date determines when it can order its goods, how long it must carry those goods without sales revenue, and whether it will be open for its best season.[27]

Landlords often insist that their tenants participate in a grand opening of a new shopping center. In fact, they sometimes insist that tenants defer their openings until the grand opening, although most landlords will allow tenants to do business earlier so long as they participate in the grand opening when it occurs. If a tenant does not open when it should, the landlord may be able to get a court order compelling the tenant to do so. In order to avoid the delay, uncertainty, and cost of such an order, landlords usually demand an amount of liquidated damages for each day after the tenant's opening date. Most leases provide that rent accrues from the date on which the tenant is supposed to take possession. Although the landlord should reserve the right to terminate the lease if the tenant does not occupy the premises when possession is available, termination is not likely to be a useful remedy. By the time the case reaches the courts the tenant will have moved in and no one, including the judge, will want to terminate the lease. If the landlord's financing has an occupancy requirement, termination is a wholly unrealistic right.

Tenants are reluctant to open in their off-seasons. Occasionally, they will agree to open and to pay only percentage rent until their seasons begin; this relates their costs to their revenues by requiring rent only as sales justify it, but it does not necessarily justify opening in the off-season. Many tenants ask for more than a mere deferral of their commencement date or an adjustment of their rent.

Shopping center landlords and tenants discuss *force majeure* in the same way as do office building landlords and tenants.

Many tenants in new shopping centers impose degrees of completion that (if not met) enable the tenant to cancel the lease. Typical milestones are:

1. completion of the foundations
2. completion of the premises
3. completion of the development
4. opening of the development.[28]

[27] Wilson, *Opening Clauses and Carrying on Business Clauses,* in Shopping Centre Leases 329 (H.M. Haber ed. 1976).

[28] Pollock, *Clauses in a Shopping Center Lease,* 20 Prac. Law. 63, 68 (1974).

Shopping center premises are delivered to the tenant in a variety of degrees of completion.[29] Some premises are delivered to the tenant "as-is." This is often true of space that has been already built-out and used by a previous occupant. The premises delivered "as-is" are renovated by the tenant to fit its particular needs. The landlord may contribute to this renovation.

Shopping center premises are also delivered on what is known as a "shell and allowance" basis. This means that the tenant is given a shell and a sum of money with which to build-out the premises to its liking. This is customary in first generation developments. The shell may vary from one in which the floor, ceiling, walls, and the utilities (including those in the space above the ceiling) are completed to one in which only the roof and demising walls are completed. Needless to say the tenant must understand the degree of improvement that it will have to make to the shell in order to fix its costs of the lease.

Finally, some premises are delivered on a "turn-key" basis in which the landlord builds the tenant's premises. The tenant opens the front door, stocks the shelves and opens for business. In order to avoid the uncertainties of construction costs, landlords prefer shell and allowance arrangements, unless of course, the tenant will accept the premises as is.

Just as the office building tenant insisted upon completion of other parts of the office building, the shopping center tenant insists on completion of other parts of the shopping center. In fact, as § 5.7 shows, the shopping center tenant is typically more demanding.

§ 5.9   Requiring Completion of Other Parts of the Shopping Center and Occupancy by Other Tenants

In shopping centers, tenants may insist that other tenants (usually anchors and a fair share of satellites) open for business before their own rent obligations begin; a variation allows a tenant to pay only percentage rent and common area costs until the "fill-up" occurs or until the tenant reaches a specified sales volume. There is a big difference between a provision that defers minimum rent until fill-up and a provision—often called a *go dark* provision—that gives a tenant the right to terminate its lease if specified tenants are lost or a certain level of occupancy in the shopping center is not maintained.

In one case,[30] a Texas court held that a landlord's covenant that certain major tenants would open for business within 120 days after the tenant opened and would "remain as tenants" located as shown in an exhibit "at all times during the

---

[29] *See* Fisher, *Emerging Trends in the Financing of Shopping Center Tenant Improvements*, Prac. Real Est. Law., May 1985, at 33.

[30] Lilac Variety, Inc. v. Dallas Texas Co., 383 S.W.2d 193 (Tex. Civ. App. 1964); *see also* Miles Shoes, Inc. v. Brainerd Village, Inc., (Tenn. Ct. App., E.D., Dec. 11, 1967) (unreported), cited by Pollack, *Clauses in a Shopping Center Lease*, 20 Prac. Law. 63 (1974).

term of this lease" was breached when one of the major tenants closed its doors and discontinued the conduct of business, although it did not remove its fixtures and it continued to pay rent.

In a California case, a restaurant tenant entered into a lease in which the landlord agreed that it would enter into long-term leases with three anchor tenants. Two of the anchors moved out within three years after they took occupancy. The restaurant tenant asserted a claim against the landlord for a breach of the landlord's agreement; the tenant's theory was that there was an implied covenant to maintain the leases with the anchors even though the agreement was only to enter into leases with the anchors. The appellate court agreed.[31] Consequently, landlords must distinguish between initial occupancy and continuous occupancy when promising anchor tenants.

A strong tenant completion provision, including co-tenancy, will require that the following be true:

1. A substantial portion of the shopping center (including the landscaping) has been substantially completed in accordance with the site plan except for minor details that, if not completed, will not prevent the use of the common areas or the functioning of the shopping center.

2. The building in which the premises are to be located has been substantially completed except for minor details.

3. Sufficient parking areas have been completed, striped, and illuminated to meet the minimum parking requirements of the lease.

4. The premises have been substantially completed except for minor details, that, if not completed, will not prevent their full use and enjoyment.

5. The landlord has entered into leases for space to be occupied by specified tenants, and those leases (a) set forth the approximate square foot area to be occupied by each of the specified tenants and their location on the site plan, (b) by their terms run for at least ten (10) years, and (c) are not cancellable by the tenants except in case of a taking by eminent domain or a destruction by casualty.

6. A permanent or temporary certificate of occupancy has been issued by the appropriate authority in localities where official certificates of occupancy are issued, otherwise, by landlord's architect certifying that the shopping center, the building in which the premises are located, and the store premises may be lawfully occupied.

7. All utilities have been connected and are in adequate supply.

8. The storm and sewer drainage are adequate.

9. Stores occupying at least _____ square feet of the leasable area shown on the site plan, including certain specified key tenants, have opened before

---

[31] Cordonier v. Central Shopping Plaza Assocs., 82 Cal. App. 3d 991, 147 Cal. Rptr. 558 (1978).

the tenant or simultaneously with it or within a given period after the tenant opens.

10.   Tenant has received at least 30 days' notice from landlord authorizing it to enter the premises, to fixture them, and otherwise make them ready for business.[32]

§ 5.10   Allowing Early Occupancy

Even with the most extensive build-out, a tenant will need some time for such matters as installing its furniture (in the case of office tenants) or installing trade fixtures and stocking its shelves (in the case of shopping center and single tenant building tenants). Of course, the tenant does not want to pay rent for this unproductive time. So it will ask that the term (and the rent) not begin until the 30th (or 60th) day after the landlord tells the tenant that the premises are ready for its occupancy. This is more than free rent. It is exoneration from the terms of the lease that obligate the tenant to pay taxes and utilities, to comply with laws, and to indemnify the landlord against third-party claims. Although the landlord may concede a free rent period, it may provide:

FORM 5-8
TERM—EARLY OCCUPANCY

At tenant's request made at any time after a temporary certificate of occupancy has been issued for the premises, landlord may permit tenant to occupy so much of the premises as tenant wishes to occupy prior to the commencement date. Landlord will cooperate with tenant in order to facilitate tenant's moving into the premises. If tenant occupies the premises prior to the commencement date with landlord's permission, all of the provisions of this lease will be in effect from the beginning of the occupancy; however, rent otherwise due under this lease will be abated up to the commencement date, and tenant will pay as rent landlord's actual costs (but in no event more than the base monthly rent that would have been due in the absence of any applicable abatements) incurred by reason of tenant's early occupany.

§ 5.11   Implied Warranty of Fitness

Perhaps the greatest modern innovation in traditional landlord-tenant law is the implied warranty of fitness in residential leases. This rule holds that a lease of a dwelling carries with it a warranty by the landlord that the premises are in a condition suitable for residential use, that is, habitable or tenantable. Until this implied warranty was fashioned by the courts, the accepted wisdom had been that

---

[32] Report of the Committee on Leases, 2 Real Prop., Prob. & Tr. J. 222 (1967). *Drafting Shopping Center Leases.*

a lease was a conveyance in which there were no implied warranties. This rule was sensible when leases were of agrarian land on which there were little or no improvements.

Although there were judicial exceptions to this rule against implied warranties—the short-term lease of furnished rooms,[33] and the existence of latent defects known to the landlord[34]—caveat emptor prevailed. Of course, this rule was inapplicable if the landlord deceived the tenant or concealed a known defect.[35] Occasionally, courts relied upon the implied covenant of quiet enjoyment to find that the tenant was excused from its lease obligations because the landlord's conduct interfered with the tenant's possession of the premises; this remedy was of limited usefulness to a tenant because it required interference with possession and did not pertain to the landlord's failure to maintain the premises.

In the early 1800s, courts went beyond the boundaries of the quiet enjoyment theory and created constructive eviction as a claim for a tenant who had not actually been evicted from the premises but whose use and enjoyment of the premises had been diminished by the landlord's conduct. On this theory, the tenant was entitled to abandon the premises and to stop paying the rent. Although this approach was much more helpful to tenants than the quiet enjoyment approach, constructive eviction compelled the tenant to vacate the premises and face the possibility that the landlord might prevail in the ensuing litigation.

In the 1960s, courts went beyond the quiet enjoyment and constructive eviction theories when they ruled that leases of residential premises contained an implied warranty of habitability.[36] One of the earliest cases that followed this theory of the implied warranty of habitability was, in fact, a case involving a commercial lease.[37]

This implied warranty has been almost universally endorsed with regard to residential tenancies.[38] The plight of tenement dwellers whose negligible negotiating strength was no match for urban housing shortages led courts to add this warranty as a new element of leases or to find it within the penumbra of the well-accepted implied covenant of quiet enjoyment. When it was adopted as a new element, courts found that the tenant's obligation to pay rent was dependent upon the landlord's delivery of habitable housing; this is another modern departure from the traditional independence of lease covenants.

When courts regarded the delivery of substandard housing as a breach of the covenant of quiet enjoyment, they did so by saying that the tenant was constructively evicted and that the covenant was breached. The practical difference between a breach of the implied warranty of habitability and a breach of the

---

[33] Schoshinski § 3:11.

[34] *Id.* § 3:12.

[35] Looney v. Smith, 198 Misc. 99, 96 N.Y.S.2d 607 (Sup. Ct. 1950).

[36] *See generally* 3 Thompson § 1230 (discussing this implied warranty and the obligations for repairs).

[37] Reste Realty Corp. v. Cooper, 53 N.J. 444, 251 A.2d 268 (1969).

[38] 2 Powell § 225(2); *see* Schoshinski §§ 3:16-3:28 (development of the implied warranty of habitability in residential tenancies). N.Y. Real Prop. Law § 235-b (McKinney 1975) is a typical statute.

covenant of quiet enjoyment, or constructive eviction, is that under the former theory, residential tenants can litigate the implied warranty while remaining in the premises; under the latter, generally, the tenant must give up possession in order to claim constructive eviction.

Residential housing is, of course, in a completely different class than commercial tenancies. There is a national housing policy and legislation intended to effect the policy, but there is no similar national policy for commercial tenants. An abandoning commercial tenant must show that its premises are untenantable, not simply uncomfortable, in order to prevail in a claim of constructive eviction.[39] Dwellings provide what some people view as a fundamental right to housing, while commercial premises enable business to be conducted.[40] Residential housing codes spawned the covenant of habitability; they are inapplicable to commercial premises (which do, however, have relevant building codes). One commentator has said: "The principal difference distinguishing residential from commercial leases is that the latter are instruments of credit."[41] A California court was less abstract in denying a commercial tenant's defense that it was not obligated to pay rent because the landlord did not fulfill its obligation to repair the premises:

A lessor's breach of a covenant contained in a commercial lease is a substantially different matter [from the dependent covenants in a residential lease]. The parties are more likely to have equal bargaining power, and, more importantly, a commercial tenant will presumably have sufficient interest in the demised premises to make needed repairs and the means to make the needed repairs himself or herself, if necessary, and then sue the landlord for damages.[42]

In that case the commercial tenant could not remain in possession and litigate. It had to vacate and sue for damages, or stay in possession and sue for damages. In either event, it had to pay rent.

There is a small body of law that considers the similarities of the residential and commercial tenant.[43] Neither the residential tenant nor the commercial

---

[39] Thirsk v. Coldwell Banker/Barton & Ludwig Realtors, 172 Ga. App. 236, 322 S.E.2d 544 (1984).

[40] A Minnesota case—apparently standing alone—held a landlord liable for its failure to tell its jewelry store tenant that a burglar could enter (as one did) through a thin ceiling. Vermes v. American Dist. Tel. Co., 312 Minn. 33, 251 N.W.2d 101 (1977).

[41] Murphy, *It's a Good Form, But Who'll Sign It—The Confessions of a Draftsman of Leases for Commercial Office Space,* 2 Real Est. L.J. 211 (1973).

[42] Schulman v. Vera, 108 Cal. App. 3d 552, 561, 166 Cal. Rptr. 620, 625 (1980). *See also* Petroleum Collections, Inc. v. Swords, 48 Cal. App. 3d 841, 122 Cal. Rptr. 114 (1975).

[43] *See generally* Note, *Landlord-Tenant—Should a Warranty of Fitness Be Implied in Commercial Leases?,* 13 Rutgers L.J. 91 (1981); Greenfield & Margolies, *An Implied Warranty of Fitness in Nonresidential Leases,* 45 Alb. L. Rev. 855 (1981); Levinson & Silver, *Do Commercial Property Tenants Possess Warranties of Habitability?,* 14 Real Est. L.J. 59 (1985) (recommending such warranties for small commercial tenants under California law); Bopp, *The*

tenant is realistically in a position to inspect the premises and the systems that support the premises. Both the commercial landlord and the residential landlord are in a position to spread the risk of defects among their several units.

Although there is some superficial attraction to the notion that the residential lease ought to be distinguished from the commercial lease, because the latter is profit-motivated, this distinction leads to absurd results. Should a wealthy tenant of a luxurious apartment be entitled to more benefit from the implied warranty than a poor commercial tenant who sets up shop in dilapidated commercial premises? How should the courts treat a person who lives in her place of business or who rents a room above his store?

All tenants, commercial and residential, have rights under the Uniform Commercial Code to claim that goods have implied warranties of merchantability and fitness for a particular use. Many people view the implication of these sale warranties as expressions of social policy. On close examination, many of the underpinnings of the implied warranty of fitness are as applicable to commercial tenancies as they are to residential tenancies.

The Texas Supreme Court found no reason to distinguish residential leases from commercial leases, and found that there is an implied warranty of suitability of commercial premises for their intended use.[44]

When her landlord failed to provide the heat that her commercial lease required, a New Jersey commercial tenant used heaters to raise the temperature in her premises and deducted the cost of additional electricity from her rent.[45] The court rejected the landlord's contention that the tenant could not offset against the rent but could only terminate the lease. Declining to distinguish residential from commercial tenancies, the court's remedy is the "repair-and-deduct" method traditionally used in residential tenancies. This decision may herald a new approach for commercial tenants.

The real estate professional should be aware of the possibility that this warranty of fitness will be implied in commercial leases. Courts which have recognized this new rule have relied upon the constructive eviction theory or have said that the implied covenant to put the tenant in possession carries with it a covenant that the premises will be usable for the purpose for which they were leased.[46] Other courts have refused to recognize the implied covenant in commercial leases.[47] Although the *Restatement* § 5.1 emphasizes that it takes no

---

Unwarranted Implication of a Warranty of Fitness in Commercial Leases—An Alternative Approach, 41 Vand. L. Rev. 1057 (1988); Pinto, *Modernizing Commercial Lease Law: The Case for an Implied Warranty of Fitness*, 19 Suffolk U.L. Rev. 929 (1985).

[44] Davidow v. Inwood Professional Group-Phase I, 747 S.W.2d 373 (Tex. 1988) (cases and other discussions cited).

[45] Westrich v. McBride, 204 N.J. Super. 550, 499 A.2d 546 (1984).

[46] Hodgson v. Chin, 168 N.J. Super. 549, 403 A.2d 942 (App. Div. 1979).

[47] Yuan Kane Inc. v. Levy, 26 Ill. App. 3d 889, 326 N.E.2d 51 (1975); Service Oil Co. v. White, 218 Kan. 87, 542 P.2d 652 (1976); Van Ness Indus., Inc. v. Claremont Paint & Decorating Co., 129 N.J. Super. 507, 324 A.2d 102 (1974); Buker v. National Management Corp., 16 Mass. App. 36, 448 N.E.2d 1299, *review denied*, 389 Mass. 1104, 451 N.E.2d 1167 (1983).

position on the question, commentators have supported adoption of the theory in commercial leases.

One author suggested that the doctrine of dependent covenants should be applied in commercial leases when rent is sought for uninhabitable premises.[48] Significantly, another commentator stressed the desirability of this new rule because it would enable insurers to recover by subrogation against landlords whose breach of the covenant had led those insurers to make payments to tenant-insureds.[49] If insurance company counsel are roused by this call to action, one may expect to see this new rule raised frequently. Ironically, a remedy which was first developed to aid the disenfranchised may be most vigorously promoted by one of the wealthiest sectors of the economy.

Strict liability in tort is one theory that has made no progress in the commercial lease arena, although the California Supreme Court extended the concept of strict liability in tort to residential housing and held an apartment owner liable for injuries sustained by a tenant as a result of a hidden construction defect.[50] In this case, the hidden defect existed when the owner purchased the property, and, of course, the owner was unaware of it.

Strict liability was first embraced by California courts in the 1960s as a basis for recovery from manufacturers and distributors for injuries sustained by the buyer of a defective product. Many other courts followed California's lead. The rationale for strict liability has been the ability of a manufacturer or distributor both to spread the risk of loss among its many sales of the product and to avoid the risk of loss through insurance or reserves. In contrast, consumers have been considered unable to inspect products for hidden defects or otherwise to protect themselves from harm. Until this case, real estate had not been considered a "product" that fell within the purview of strict liability. Those who believe that the implied warranty of fitness is as appropriate for commercial tenancies as it is for residential tenancies will certainly endeavor to apply strict liability standards to commercial premises. However, one California Court of Appeal declined to apply this doctrine to commercial tenancies.[51]

Fireman's Fund Ins. Co. v. BPS Co., 23 Ohio App. 3d 56, 491 N.E.2d 365 (1985). A study published in 1986 concluded that the following jurisdictions have ruled against the implied warranty for fitness in a commercial lease: Alabama, Arkansas, California, Colorado, Connecticut, D.C., Delaware, Florida, Idaho, Illinois, Indiana, Kansas, Maine, Massachusetts, Missouri, New Hampshire, New Jersey, New York, North Carolina, Ohio, Oregon, Pennsylvnia, Tennessee, Texas, Utah, Vermont, Washington, and West Virginia. *Tenant Loses Complaint About Fitness of Space,* Com. Lease L. Insider, Nov. 1986, at 1. Texas has since changed its position. Davidow v. Inwood Professional Group–Phase I, 747 S.W.2d 373 (Tex. 1988).

[48] Schoshinski § 3:29.

[49] Brennan, *The Implied Warranty of Fitness in Commercial Leases and the Subrogating Insurance Company,* 18 Forum 683, 684 (1983).

[50] Becker v. IRM Corp., 38 Cal. 3d 454, 698 P.2d 116, 213 Cal. Rptr. 213 (1985).

[51] Mora v. Baker Commodities, Inc., 210 Cal. App. 3d 771, 258 Cal. Rptr. 669 (1989).

§ 5.12   Lenders' Concerns about Term

Traditionally, lenders have carefully scrutinized the terms of the leases of major tenants in order to be certain that they continued for the life of the loan. As loan terms have become shorter, lenders' concerns in this regard have diminished. Of course, the lease terms are very important for landlords who propose to use those leases to replace short term loans from time to time. Lenders, like landlords, do not like to see all of the leases expire at about the same time. Rather, they prefer staggered expiration dates that facilitate releasing.

As a general rule, lenders reject a tenant's right to terminate its lease on account of the landlord's default. Lenders require that a tenant's remedies be limited to a suit for damages or a suit for specific performance. Some go so far as to reject leases in which the tenant has the right to offset its judgment against its rent if it is successful in a suit for damages. In some limited cases discussed in § **30.1**, a lender may allow a tenant the right to cure certain of the landlord's defaults and to offset that amount against rent.

§ 5.13   Option to Extend or Renew a Lease

Consider the retail tenant who develops a faithful clientele. Its customers associate its business with its location. When the end of the tenant's term comes, moving its premises will unavoidably affect its business. Just as certainly, the landlord will offer the premises to one of the tenant's competitors, who will benefit from the association of the premises and the earlier tenant's business. Office building tenants may be less tied to their locations, but they too will suffer the same disruption of moving offices. To protect themselves, retail tenants, and to a lesser degree all tenants, should insist upon renewal or extension rights. Landlords benefit from renewals or extensions. Usually, they avoid the payment of a commission that would be due if a new tenant were found. They also avoid the cost of renovating the premises for a new tenant, the risk of vacancy until a new tenant is found, and the uncertainty of a new tenant's performance.[52]

Renewals and extensions both prolong the term of the lease, but they are technically different.[53] A renewal is a new lease that requires a new agreement. It is often said that renewals must be in writing. Extensions continue the same lease and are often implied from the continuation of the tenancy.[54] Put differently, a lease that is renewed ends for an instant between the original term and the renewal term, and a lease that is extended continues without interruption. Most real estate professionals use these terms without regard to their technical difference. In fact, at least one state court has endorsed the idea that they are the same.[55] Another

---

[52] For an overview of the topic and variety of form provisions, see *Options to Extend—Review the Basics*, Leasing Prof., Aug. 1986, at 1.

[53] 3 Thompson § 1120.

[54] 2 Powell § 245(1).

[55] Smith v. Arthur D. Little, Inc., 276 Cal. App. 2d 391, 81 Cal. Rptr. 140 (1969).

state court virtually eliminated any distinction between renewals and extensions by ruling that an option to renew "upon the same terms and conditions" means an option to extend, thus obviating a new written agreement.[56] Some states hold to the common law distinction, with the result that the improper exercise of a renewal right has led to a forfeiture of the renewal term. The real estate professional should be familiar with the law that governs the lease and, as a precaution, may wish to state that the terms are used synonymously.

Well-written provisions do not leave the tenant's rights at the mercy of obscure distinctions:

FORM 5-9
TERM—OPTION TO EXTEND AT NEW BASE MONTHLY RENT

Tenant may extend the term until the fifth anniversary of the expiration date by written notice of its election to do so given to landlord at least one year prior to the expiration date. The extended term will be on all of the terms and conditions of the lease applicable at the expiration date; however, tenant will have no further right to extend the term and the base monthly rent will be $_____. Tenant will not have any rights under this paragraph if (a) an event of default exists on the expiration date or on the date on which tenant gives its notice, or (b) tenant occupies less than _____ rentable square feet of the premises on the expiration date, or (c) tenant exercises its rights less than one year before the expiration date.

The first question that comes to mind with regard to the renewal provision is whether the tenant can exercise its option if it is in default of the lease.[57] In the absence of a dispositive provision in the lease, some courts have ruled that the tenant must have performed its lease covenants as a condition to renewal. Unless they find a landlord's waiver of performance, courts enforce an express condition of tenant's performance.[58] For example, the Supreme Judicial Court of Maine barred a renewal when the tenant was in default at the time it notified the landlord of its intention to extend the term.[59] However, courts have also recognized the contract doctrine of substantial performance in order to avoid the tenant's loss of valuable rights.[60] Some landlords prefer to state that the tenant's renewal right is conditioned upon it having performed all of its obligations under the lease. A tenant may object to this because it gives the landlord an opportunity to avoid a renewal on account of a past (and cured) default. The tenant will insist upon having a renewal right if no event of default (as described in § **30.4**) has occurred

---

[56] Anderson v. Lissandri, 19 Mass. App. 191, 472 N.E.2d 1365 (1985).

[57] 3 Thompson § 1123.

[58] 51C C.J.S. Landlord & Tenant 62(1)(b) (1968).

[59] Homstead Enters. v. Johnson Prods., Inc., 540 A.2d 471 (Me. 1988). The lease said, "Provided that Lessee is not in default hereunder, Lessee shall have the option . . . ." The court used extension and renewal interchangeably. *Accord* TSS-Seedman's, Inc. v. Nicolas, 143 A.D.2d 223, 531 N.Y.S.2d 827 (1988).

[60] Annot., 23 A.L.R.4th 908, *Right to exercise option to renew or extend lease as affected by tenant's breach of other covenants or conditions* (1983).

and is continuing. Some tenants go further. They reason that the loss of a renewal right is equivalent of a termination of the lease and that the landlord should not be able to terminate the lease without an impartial judicial determination; thus, they object to a loss of renewal rights unless the lease has been terminated by a court order. Landlords who insist on a renewal right conditioned upon no default having occurred do so because they are concerned that the tenant will cure the existing default and immediately default again.[61] Of course, if other conditions must be met (such as no assignment or sublease having been made, or a specified level of sales having been reached), the lease should specify them.

Renewal and extension options are often concessions by the landlord. As such, the landlord may give them only to desirable tenants. The same landlord may not think of giving these options to every tenant. However, the options may usually be assigned with the lease.[62] Consequently, many landlords provide that these options terminate on an assignment or sublease; put differently, these options may be exercised only if no assignment or sublease has been made.

§ 5.14   — Notice

The method by which the option must be exercised should also be set forth.[63] Generally, leases provide for exercise of options by written notice, because a document provides tangible evidence. In states that adhere to a distinction between renewals and extensions, a writing may be necessary. Courts generally require notice that complies with the requirements of the lease, but they often allow any notice if no method is prescribed.[64] Still, courts are hesitant to invalidate a tenant's exercise of its option merely because the tenant failed to give the written notice that the lease required; for example, an Illinois landlord improperly refused a timely extension notice that arrived with 20 cents postage due even though the lease required postage prepaid.[65] Many cases have allowed options to be exercised orally.[66]

If notice must be given by a specific date, the landlord is well advised to emphasize that the tenant will have no rights under the option unless it has

---

[61] Posen, *Options to Renew or Extensions of Term,* in Shopping Centre Leases 441 (H.M. Haber ed. 1976).

[62] Annot., 29 A.L.R.2d 834, *Assignee's right to enforce lessor's covenant to renew or extend lease* (1984).

[63] *See* Willard E. Robertson Corp. v. Benson Continental Motors, Inc., 476 So. 2d 7 (La. Ct. App. 1985).

[64] Annot., 29 A.L.R.4th 903, *Sufficiency as to method of giving oral or written notice exercising option to renew or extend lease* (1984); Annot., 32 A.L.R.4th 452, *Waiver or estoppel as to notice requirement for exercising option to renew or extend lease* (1984).

[65] Gold Standard Enters., Inc. v. United Inv. Management Co., 182 Ill. App. 3d 840, 131 Ill. Dec. 261, 538 N.E.2d 636 (1989).

[66] Leonhardi-Smith, Inc. v. Cameron, 108 Cal. App. 3d 42, 166 Cal. Rptr. 135 (1980).

exercised option in a timely manner. Nevertheless, courts have been reluctant to deprive tenants of valuable rights merely because they exercise their rights tardily without any prejudice to the landlord. This is particularly true when the tenant has previously exercised other options tardily without objection by the landlord. The judicial decisions vary with the facts of each case; for example, in California, some appellate decisions are indulgent,[67] while some are strict.[68] Some courts analyze the question of late notice in this way: if the notice is sent before the deadline but is not received until after the deadline, the tenant is more likely to be excused than if the notice is both sent and received after the deadline.[69] Generally, courts will not grant relief to a tenant unless its delay was slight, without harm to the landlord, and unless a great hardship (such as the loss of improvements made at the tenant's expense) would result from the denial of relief.[70] A 1987 study suggested that 11 states strictly enforce deadlines, 10 states excuse late renewals when special circumstances exist, and 29 states have not ruled on forgetful tenants, although some of them have excused tenants that were not so forgetful as to be considered negligent.[71]

An Illinois court excused a tenant's late exercise in part because the exercise date fell on a weekend and in part because the landlord was not adversely affected. That decision went on to say that "strict performance of conditions . . . may be excused under proper circumstances even where the failure to provide the stipulated notice is due solely to the negligence of the lessee."[72] Some strong tenants are able to demand that their option rights continue after the stated exercise date until the 30th day after the landlord gives them notice of the passage of the date.

A New York court[73] forgave a tenant whose written exercise for renewal was given on April 4 instead of February 1. In doing so, the court observed that the tenant had spent $25,000 for improvements in converting the premises from a beauty store to a gift boutique; the tenant had ordered its spring line; the tenant had established good will at the premises; the monthly rent would increase from $475 to $625; and the landlord was not harmed by the late notice.

A Connecticut court has also held that the degree of the tenant's neglect may be determinative; the more negligent the tenant is, the less likely a court is to enforce its renewal option.[74] The court appeared to be influenced by the fact that

---

[67] 108 Cal. App. 3d at 42.

[68] Simons v. Young, 93 Cal. App. 3d 170, 155 Cal. Rptr. 460 (1979).

[69] Annot., 29 A.L.R.4th 956, *What constitutes timely notice of exercise of option to renew or extend lease* (1984).

[70] Annot., 27 A.L.R.4th 266, *Circumstances excusing lessee's failure to give timely notice of exercise of option to renew or extend lease* (1984); Norwesco, Inc. v. Community Petroleum Prods., Inc., 38 Conn. Supp. 585, 456 A.2d 340 (1982).

[71] *See* Com. Lease L. Insider, July 1987, at 1 (discussion and collection of cases).

[72] Providence Ins. Co. v. LaSalle Nat'l Bank, 118 Ill. App. 3d 720, 455 N.E.2d 238 (1983).

[73] Grunberg v. George Assocs., 104 A.D.2d 745, 480 N.Y.S.2d 217 (1984).

[74] R&R of Conn., Inc. v. Steigler, 4 Conn. App. 240, 493 A.2d 293 (1985).

the tenant had given two earlier notices (by first class mail and not certified mail) that the landlord denied receiving. Another Connecticut case refused to enforce a renewal term for which the tenant did not give notice by registered mail as the lease required; there was some question as to whether any notice had been given.[75] In Connecticut, relief seems to be available only if (1) the tenant's failure was mere neglect, not gross and willful neglect, (2) the potential harm to the landlord is small, and (3) the delay is slight.[76]

A tenant who can show that its tardy exercise of a renewal option was caused by an ambiguous provision may get equitable relief.[77] In a New York case there was some justifiable confusion about the date by which notice was to be given. When notice is required to be given "only at the end of the tenth year of the lease," notice may properly be given within the last quarter of the tenth year.[78]

An intermediate appellate court of Colorado refused to enforce a tenant's tardy exercise of its option to extend its term when the only excuse was the tenant's negligence and inadvertence.[79] The court noted that the tenant would not lose its investment in its improvements and fixtures because the lease authorized the tenant to remove them and because the landlord had offered to buy them for their fair market value. A California appellate court was also unforgiving when the tenant refused to give timely notice.[80] Finding the tenant's negligence to be the cause of its own problems, the court disregarded not only the tenant's improvements but also the tenant's conduct in making improvements as evidence of its exercise of its renewal option.

An option to renew is the landlord's offer to prolong the term of the lease. As such, the offer must be accepted in precisely the terms in which it was given: "By this letter, we extend the term of the lease dated May 1, 1982 between you, as landlord, and us, as tenant, pursuant to paragraph ____ of that lease." A conditional acceptance may be construed as a counteroffer that terminates the option; for example, the tenant should not say: "So long as you repair the leak in the roof, we will extend the term. . . ."

Nevertheless, judicial prestidigitation can save an errant tenant. When a tenant exercised an option by saying, "We now wish to exercise this option with a further provision allowing us to cancel the lease on 90 days' written notice," the

---

[75] Seven Fifty Main St. Assocs. Ltd. v. Spector, 5 Conn. App. 170, 497 A.2d 96 (1985), *cert. denied,* 197 Conn. 815, 499 A.2d 804 (1985).

[76] Tartaglia v. R.A.C. Corp., 15 Conn. App. 492, 545 A.2d 573, *cert. denied,* 209 Conn. 810, 548 A.2d 443 (1988).

[77] Bank of New York v. Ulster Heights Properties, Inc., 114 A.D. 431, 494 N.Y.S.2d 345 (1985).

[78] Crosstown Bell, Inc. v. Northwestern Bell Tel. Co., 381 N.W.2d 911 (Minn. Ct. App. 1986), *review denied,* May 16, 1986; *see* Tritt v. Huffman & Boyle Co., 121 A.D.2d 531, 503 N.Y.S.2d 842, *appeal denied,* 68 N.Y.2d 611, 502 N.E.2d 1007, 510 N.Y.S.2d 1025 (1986).

[79] Trueman-Aspen Co. v. North Mill Inv. Corp., 728 P.2d 343 (Colo. Ct. App.) (not selected for official publication), *cert. denied,* No. 86SC271, Oct. 20, 1986.

[80] Bekins Moving & Storage Co. v. Prudential Ins. Co., 176 Cal. App. 3d 245, 221 Cal. Rptr. 738 (1985), *review denied,* Apr. 16, 1986.

Utah Supreme Court decided that the notice was not conditional but was unconditional with a subsequent request for a modification.[81] Although the landlord appeared to accept the renewal, a contrary decision could easily have been reached. An evasive notice—that the tenant was "in a position to renew the lease"—and payment of rent in the renewal term were sufficient to bind a tenant who later denied that it had renewed its lease.[82] Equivocal renewals may be ineffective.[83]

Of course, notices should be given by the proper entity to the proper entity strictly according to the lease.[84]

The real estate professional should note that the amount of advance notice will vary from lease to lease. A landlord may need more notice that 10 percent of its premises will be vacated than it will if only 2 percent will be.

§ 5.15   —Terms of Renewal

The renewal terms are often said to be "on the same terms and conditions as the initial term of the lease." The first question that arises is whether those terms and conditions include the right to renew, thus creating a perpetual lease. Some courts have held that they do,[85] even though a majority seems to conclude they do

---

[81] Upland Indus. Corp. v. Pacific Gamble Robinson Co., 684 P.2d 638 (Utah 1984).

[82] Zuckerman Group v. Raveis, 4 Conn. App. 568, 495 A.2d 300, *cert. dismissed,* 197 Conn. 811, 499 A.2d 62 (1985). *See* Central Nat. Bank v. Fleetwood Realty Corp., 110 Ill. App. 3d 169, 441 N.E.2d 1244 (1982) (tenant lost its option because of conditional, equivocal exercise). *See also* Joyous Holdings, Inc. v. Volkswagen of Oneonta, Inc., 128 A.D.2d 1002, 513 N.Y.S.2d 841 (1987) (tenant exercised its renewal contingent upon the landlord making certain repairs; when landlord challenged exercise, court sided with it).

[83] Jay Gee Commerce, Inc. v. Havas, 89 Nev. 157, 508 P.2d 1015 (1973) (tenant left message "Call me about the lease" and later claimed it was renewal); Exchange Oil & Gas Corp. v. Giullot, 251 So. 2d 479 (La. Ct. App.), *writ denied,* 259 La. 899, 253 So. 2d 222 (1971) (tenant with one-year lease and ten-year renewal option unsuccessfully claimed that leaving check for rent for first year of renewal term was renewal); 120 Bay Street Realty Corp. v. City of New York, 44 N.Y.2d 907, 379 N.E.2d 167, 407 N.Y.S.2d 639 (1978) (tenant's expression of intention to renew was insufficient to act as renewal).

[84] Annot., 34 A.L.R.4th 857, *Sufficiency as to parties giving or receiving notice of exercise of option to renew or extend lease* (1984). When a landlord uses ordinary mail to inquire about a tenant's intentions to renew, the tenant's response by overnight mail cannot be challenged as ineffective by the landlord. Tehrani v. Century Medical Center, P.C., 7 Conn. App. 301, 508 A.2d 814 (1986).

[85] Becker v. Submarine Oil Co., 55 Cal. App. 698, 204 P.245 (1921). In Camerlo v. Howard Johnson Co., 710 F.2d 987 (3d Cir. 1983), the court held that a perpetual renewal right did not violate the rule against perpetuities or create a restraint on alienation unless a contrary statute obtained. *See also* McLane & McLane v. Prudential Ins. Co., 735 F.2d 1194 (9th Cir. 1984) (inadvertent second renewal right created by stating that terms of first lease term would remain "in full force and effect" for renewal term).

not, in the absence of proof of contrary intent.[86] An option to extend "this lease" entitled a tenant to an extension on the same terms as the original term.[87] A right to lease for "successive terms" has been held to confer perpetual rights in at least one case.[88]

Options to purchase that were available in the initial term will survive into the renewal term if the renewal term is "on the same terms and conditions." A Nebraska court said: "When a lease confers on the [tenant] an option to purchase the property at any time during the term of the lease, and the lease is thereafter extended on the same terms and conditions, the option to purchase is also extended for the period of the extended term."[89]

Another question is whether the rent concessions and other allowances that were given under the initial term of the lease will be due again for the renewal term. On the one hand, it seems impossible to improve the premises again, but on reflection, it is possible to give a tenant a second allowance for improvement of the premises. The allowance could be used for renovation even if it is not necessary for initial construction. Rent abatements are as sensible during a renewal term as they are under the initial term. The real estate professional can readily see that it is important for the landlord and tenant to specify which terms will be the same as those of the first term of the lease.

Rent, of course, is the most important of the essential lease provisions during a renewal or extension. The premises are obvious and the term is usually stated with ease. If the lease does not prescribe a rent (or a method for determining rent) during an extension or renewal term, the previously prevailing rent under the lease will be presumed. Only rarely do real estate professionals forget to state a rent for renewal or extension terms. Landlords, who are reluctant to give other options from the outset, want to do nothing more than agree to market rental during a renewal term. Tenants, on the other hand, want not only a specified rental, but also a bargain rental. The negotiation of these provisions usually ends between the two positions. However, the tenant who is unable to win a bargain renewal rate should nevertheless accept an option to renew at a market rent. For a retail tenant, the premises themselves may have become an asset by virtue of the public's association of the tenant's business and the tenant's location. For any tenant, the cost of moving is considerable and can be avoided by exercising a market-rent renewal option.

A provision for renewal at market rental[90] may be:

---

[86] 3 Thompson § 1125. Lattimore v. Fisher's Food Shoppe, Inc., 313 N.C. 467, 329 S.E.2d 346 (1985).

[87] McCutchin v. SCA Servs. of Ariz. Inc., 147 Ariz. 234, 709 P.2d 591 (Ct. App. 1985).

[88] Pechenik v. Baltimore & Ohio R.R., 157 W. Va. 895, 205 S.E.2d 813 (1974). *Contra* Pults v. City of Springdale, 23 Ark. App. 182, 745 S.W.2d 144 (1988).

[89] III Lounge, Inc. v. Gaines, 217 Neb. 466, 348 N.W.2d 903 (1984), *appeal after remand*, 227 Neb. 585, 419 N.W.2d 143 (1988).

[90] See *Fair Market Renewal Option—The Second Generation*, Leasing Prof., June 1988, at 1.

FORM 5-10
TERM—OPTION TO EXTEND AT MARKET RENT

(a) *Option Period.* So long as tenant is not in default under this lease, either at the time of exercise or at the time the extended term commences, tenant will have the option to extend the initial five (5) year term of this lease for an additional period of five (5) years (the "option period") on the same terms, covenants, and conditions of this lease, except that the monthly rent during the option period will be determined pursuant to paragraph (b). Tenant will exercise its option by giving landlord written notice ("option notice") at least one hundred eighty (180) days but not more than two hundred seventy (270) days prior to the expiration of the initial term of this lease.

(b) *Option Period Monthly Rent.* The initial monthly rent for the option period will be determined as follows:

(1) Landlord and tenant will have fifteen (15) days after landlord receives the option notice within which to agree on the then-fair market rental value of the premises, as defined in paragraph (b)(3), and rental increases to the monthly rent for the option period. If they agree on the initial monthly rent and rental increases for the option period within fifteen (15) days, they will amend this lease by stating the initial monthly rent and rental increases for the option period.

(2) If they are unable to agree on the initial monthly rent and rental increases for the option period within fifteen (15) days, then, the initial monthly rent for the option period will be the then-fair market rental value of the premises as determined in accordance with paragraph (b)(4) and the periodic rental increases will be consistent with current market standards for rent increases at that time, in amounts and at frequencies determined by the appraisers pursuant to paragraph (b)(4).

(3) The "then-fair market rental value of the premises" means what a landlord under no compulsion to lease the premises and a tenant under no compulsion to lease the premises would determine as rents (including initial monthly rent and rental increases) for the option period, as of the commencement of the option period, taking into consideration the uses permitted under this lease, the quality, size, design and location of the premises, and the rent for comparable buildings located in the vicinity of _____. The then-fair market rental value of the premises and the rental increases in the monthly rent for the option period will not be less than that provided during the initial term.

(4) Within seven (7) days after the expiration of the fifteen (15) day period set forth in paragraph (b)(2), landlord and tenant will each appoint a real estate appraiser with at least five (5) years' full-time commercial appraisal experience in the area in which the premises are located to appraise the then-fair market rental value of the premises. If either landlord or tenant does not appoint an appraiser within ten (10) days after the other has given notice of the name of its appraiser, the single appraiser appointed will be the sole appraiser and will set the then-fair market rental value of the premises. If two (2) appraisers are appointed pursuant to this paragraph, they will meet promptly and attempt to set the then-fair market rental value of the premises. If they are unable to agree within thirty (30) days after the second appraiser has been appointed, they will attempt to elect a third appraiser meeting the qualifications stated in this paragraph within ten (10) days after the last day the two (2) appraisers are given to set the then-fair market rental value of the premises. If they are unable to agree on the third appraiser, either landlord or tenant, by giving ten (10) days' prior notice to the other, can apply to the then-presiding

judge of the _____ County Court for the selection of a third appraiser who meets the qualifications stated in this paragraph. Landlord and tenant will bear one-half (1/2) of the cost of appointing the third appraiser and of paying the third appraiser's fee. The third appraiser, however selected, must be a person who has not previously acted in any capacity for either landlord or tenant.

Within thirty (30) days after the selection of the third appraiser, a majority of the appraisers will set the then-fair market rental value of the premises. If a majority of the appraisers are unable to set the then-fair market rental value of the premises within thirty (30) days after selection of the third appraiser, the three (3) appraisals will be averaged and the average will be the then-fair market rental value of the premises.

In order to assure itself of a bargain renewal rental rate, a tenant may suggest a fixed dollar amount. Landlords will usually reject such a proposal. Some landlords will accept the renewal rate based on some cost of living adjustment, for example, the change in a consumer price index.

In order to know the renewal rent before it exercises its option, the tenant should insist that the comparison index be set before the date on which the renewal must be exercised. In turn, the landlord will want to move the first index back to a date before the term. For example, consider a 10-year lease that begins June 1, 1991, and contains a renewal option that must be exercised by March 1, 2001. The beginning index may be January 1, 1991, and the comparison index may be January 1, 2001, thus enabling the tenant to know its renewal rate before it exercises its option. Provisions that are tied to a consumer price index allow a floor (a minimum increase) and a ceiling (a maximum increase). The tenant will insist on a ceiling and the landlord will insist on a floor. If the tenant wins a renewal rate adjusted for the cost of living, and then wins a ceiling on the increase, the tenant has, in effect, successfully set the upper bound on its renewal rental rate.

Renewal rental rates can also be set by arbitration[91] or appraisal; **Form 5-12** uses appraisal if the landlord and tenant cannot agree. In either case, the landlord and tenant must be careful to specify the parameters for appraisal or arbitration. For example, is the lease itself—and perhaps the existence of other renewal options—to be considered in evaluating the premises? How are the tenant's improvements to be considered? As in any arbitration, the question for resolution by the arbitrators should be precisely stated. Tenants often insist on arbitration or appraisal provisions without realizing that they may be no better off than with a fair market rental renewal rate provision. Although arbitration and appraisal provide some comfort insofar as they are impartial, their goal is usually to set a fair market rental rate within the bounds prescribed by the landlord and tenant. The same effect can be reached by prescribing a fair market rental rate for renewal terms.

There is one possible virtue to arbitration or appraisal. As the end of the term approaches, the landlord will advise the tenant of the renewal rental rate. If the tenant does not agree with the landlord, they will pursue arbitration or appraisal.

---

[91] Pearce & Tomkin, *Agreement to Agree a Revised Rent,* 131 New L.J. 859 (1981).

What happens when the appraisal or arbitration concludes that the rental rate is higher than that which the landlord set, or lower than that which the tenant offered? Or, as is more likely to be the case, when the arbitrated rate falls between the landlord's and tenant's offers?

If the tenant believes the rent should be $20, and the landlord believes it should be $25, the tenant may not want to be bound by arbitration just in case arbitration concludes that the landlord is right. Similarly, the landlord will not want to be bound to an arbitrated amount that the landlord believes to be less than the fair market rent. On the other hand, if the tenant is correct and the rent is $20 per square foot, it should have no right to decline the renewal option. It should be bound to the renewal term if the arbitrators or appraisers agree. By the same token, if the landlord is correct in its estimate of the fair market rental, the landlord should be bound to the renewal term. However, the tenant will want an opportunity to reconsider its renewal option if the appraisers conclude that the fair market rent is $24.50 per square foot, just as the landlord will want to reconsider if the appraisers set fair market rent at $20.50 per square foot. Accordingly, each should be bound to a renewal term within some range above (in the case of the tenant) or below (in the case of the landlord) its initial estimate.

A tenant whose landlord offers a renewal rent equal to a market rate has a good argument that its rent should be somewhat less than the market rate because the landlord saves a commission on a lease to a new tenant and initial construction cost for a new tenant. In order to avoid the risk of vacancy during releasing, a landlord may try to lure a tenant with a better than market renewal rate. On the other hand, since the renewal option does not bind the tenant, the landlord may not wish to agree to any bargain rate but rather to await the time of renewal and then negotiate the renewal rate.

A landlord claimed that a renewal option at a rent equal to a third party's offer was unenforceable because it failed to state a rent; noting that the landlord had never entertained a third party's offer, a Florida court disagreed, feeling it had a sufficient standard by which to set a renewal rent.[92]

A renewal right at a "reasonable market value price" is sufficiently clear to be enforced.[93]

When a lease gives a renewal option at a rate to be negotiated within a range of rates, the landlord and tenant have a "reasonable" period in which to agree before the option expires; a disgruntled tenant can sue for a judicial determination of the rent in that period but cannot sue for damages after that period ends.[94] Presumably, a refusal to negotiate in good faith would give rise to a suit for damages.

Many landlords and tenants throw up their hands when considering the renewal rental rate and agree that the rent will be "mutually agreed upon." This solution is no more than an agreement to agree on an essential lease provision. Traditionally, it has been no agreement at all. Courts usually refuse to set the rent

---

[92] Ludal Development Co. v. Farm Stores, Inc., 458 So. 2d 781 (Fla. Dist. Ct. App. 1984), *review denied*, 467 So. 2d 1000 (Fla. 1985).

[93] Northrup v. Hushard, 514 N.Y.S.2d 304, 129 A.D.2d 1005 (1987).

[94] Charter Medical Corp. v. Bealick, 103 Nev. 368, 741 P.2d 1359 (1987).

when the landlord and tenant have not. One California court considered an extension option "under the same terms and conditions except for the rent which will be determined by mutual agreement at that time" and concluded that it was unenforceable.[95] Similarly, a Texas court that considered a provision that "the monthly lease payments [during the renewal term] will be increased to an amount mutually acceptable to the parties hereto," held that the provision was "unenforceable and void for uncertainty and indefiniteness."[96] A Georgia court refused to enforce a renewal right at "the same rental as may have been offered lessor by any other reputable person," holding that "reputable person" was insufficient guidance for a determination.[97] A renewal option "on reasonable terms" is too vague to allow enforcement, according to the Utah Supreme Court.[98]

However, some recent judicial decisions have indulged this malfeasance.[99] These courts apparently believe that the landlord and tenant would have acted reasonably and in good faith and have concluded that a fair market rental was meant to be their agreement. Some courts rule that a fair market rent was intended, while others rule that the rent is what is "reasonable as between the parties." If the real estate professional is compelled to use a "to be determined" provision, the "reasonable as between the parties" is a helpful addition. It may take the tenant's own improvements into consideration. A 1985 study of jurisdictions (including the District of Columbia and Virgin Islands) concluded that 19 states will enforce a renewal option when no rent is set, 19 states will not, and 14 states are undecided.[100]

A Colorado appellate court construed a "mutually agreed to" option provision to mean that the option was

> contingent upon the Tenants and Landlord each acting in their complete discretion, reaching complete agreement prior to the end of the original Lease term, as to the monthly rental rate, any escalation factor to be applied to the monthly rental, other financial obligations of the Tenants and all other terms and conditions of the Lease.[101]

---

[95] ETCO Corp. v. Hauer, 161 Cal. App. 3d 1154, 208 Cal. Rptr. 118 (1984).

[96] Kaplan v. Floeter, 657 S.W.2d 1 (Tex. Ct. App. 1983). Presumably the court's redundancy was for emphasis.

[97] McCormick v. Brockette, 167 Ga. App. 325, 306 S.E.2d 344, 345 (1983).

[98] Cottonwood Mall Co. v. Sine, 767 P.2d 499 (Utah 1988).

[99] P.J.'s Pantry v. Puschak, 188 N.J. Super 580, 458 A.2d 123 (App. Div. 1983) (trial court should establish renewal fair market rent if the landlord and tenant do not.)

[100] *Which Courts Enforce Renewal When No Rent Set?*, Com. Lease L. Insider, Apr. 1985, at 7-8. The decision of the California court in ETCO Corp. v. Hauer, 161 Cal. App. 3d 1154, 208 Cal. Rptr. 118 (1984), has probably changed one state which formerly would enforce the agreement to a state which will not enforce the agreement. However, 7 Rohan, Current Leasing Law & Techniques § 4.02 (1982), says, "[T]he current trend upholds such a renewal provision and many courts will establish a reasonable rental consideration if the parties fail to agree [citing cases]."

[101] Scrima v. Goodley, 731 P.2d 766 (Colo. Ct. App. 1986).

One can hardly distinguish such a construction from an unenforceable agreement-to-agree. The dissent would have imported an obligation to negotiate in good faith in order to avoid the illusion caused by the majority.

Finally, regardless of the method the landlord and tenant select to determine renewal rent, their choice must be clear. In one case,[102] the lease said:

> The base rental [during the renewal term] shall be computed upon the existing base rental for the base term together with an increase that may be computed based solely upon increases in real estate taxes, insurance, utilities and building management expenses.

These expenses had increased 59 percent. The tenant asserted that these increased expenses should be "passed through," so that its base rental would increase from $5.04 to $5.69 per square foot. The court held that the base rental was to be multiplied according to this provision in order to reach the base rental in the renewal term; this meant a rent of $8.01 (159% × $5.04).

Ironically, the landlord was not entirely pleased with this outcome. The lease provided a free rent period that, the landlord argued, would not be provided in the renewal period. Thus, the landlord contended, the base rental for the initial term was really $5.60 per square foot (when the free rent was not considered) and the renewal rental should be $8.90 per square foot (159% × $5.60). The court rejected this approach and based the renewal rent on the effective base rent.

This case illustrates not only the importance of clear writing but also the importance of specifying whether renewal rent is based on the effective rent or stated rent rate.[103]

§ 5.16   Tenant's Option to Terminate Lease

Often tenants ask for the right to cancel their leases.[104] They do this for many reasons: they may be uncertain whether the premises will be sufficient for a business that they expect to flourish, they may be uncertain whether the premises will be too much for a business that is just starting up, or they may want to know the extent of their costs if they decide not to continue in business.[105]

A landlord has no reason to allow its tenant to cancel its lease. After all, the landlord went to the trouble of entering into the lease in anticipation of the tenant's performance. Still, if landlords are offered enough money to pay for their

---

[102] Falcon Research & Dev. Co. v. Craddock, 101 N.M. 122, 679 P.2d 264 (1984).

[103] For another example of abysmal draftsmanship, this one confounding a CPI adjustment and stepped up rent, see Bakas Restaurant, Inc. v. Charos, 111 A.D.2d 360, 490 N.Y.S.2d 17 (1985).

[104] *Tying Retail Option And Termination Rights to Performance,* Leas. Prof., April 1989, at 1.

[105] See *How to Negotiate and Structure Lease Buy-Outs,* Com. Lease L. Insider, Aug. 1986, at 1, for an informative discussion and form. For a form of retail lease termination agreement and a discussion of it, see *Negotiating the Retail Lease Termination Agreement,* Leasing Prof., July, 1987, at 1.

sunk costs—usually commissions and tenant improvements—and the rent accruing until their (estimated) releasing of the premises, landlords may grant these options.

Landlords should never grant an option to cancel without first considering and consulting their lenders. Termination of lease by a landlord that has assigned its lease to its lender is invalid.[106] Most mortgages prohibit the landlord's acceptance of surrender. Lenders will certainly want the cancellation premium, and some lenders will simply refuse a lease that gives the tenant a cancellation right.

With these sobering thoughts in mind, a real estate professional may suggest a provision such as:

FORM 5-11
TERM—TENANT'S OPTION TO CANCEL THE LEASE

Tenant may cancel this lease according to this paragraph.

(a)   Tenant will give landlord at least thirty (30) days' prior written notice of tenant's election to cancel this lease.

(b)   Tenant may cancel this lease only as of the last day of a month (the "cancellation date"). The cancellation date will be stated in tenant's notice and will be no less than _____ (_____) days after the date of tenant's notice. At least ten (10) days before the cancellation date, as a condition of tenant's election, tenant will pay landlord in bank funds (1) the unamortized portion of the commission paid by landlord to _____ in connection with this lease, and (2) the unamortized cost of the improvements (without consideration of any salvage value) made by landlord pursuant to _____, both as of the cancellation date, and (3) $_____. The amortizations will be on a straight-line basis over the initial term of the lease.

(c)   Landlord may reject tenant's election to cancel this lease if an event of default has occurred at the time of its election.

(d)   If landlord does not reject tenant's election to cancel this lease, tenant will cure any event of default under this lease that exists on the cancellation date, and tenant's obligation to cure any such default within the period of time specified in this lease will survive the cancellation date.

(e)   On or prior to the cancellation date, tenant will surrender possession of the premises to landlord in accordance with the provisions of this lease, as if the cancellation date were the expiration date of this lease.

(f)   Upon cancellation, landlord and tenant will be relieved of their obligations under this lease, except for those accruing prior to the cancellation date.

---

[106] F.W. Woolworth Co. v. Buford-Clairmont Co., 769 F.2d 1548 (11th Cir., 1985).

CHAPTER 6

RENT

§ 6.1 Fixed Rent

The basic rent provision states:

FORM 6-1
RENT—BASIC PROVISION

Tenant will pay landlord the monthly rent in equal consecutive monthly installments on or before the first day of each month during the term of this lease. The
monthly rent will be paid in advance at the address specified for landlord in the
basic lease information, or such other place as landlord designates, without prior
demand and without any abatement, deduction or setoff. If the commencement date
occurs on a day other than the first day of a calendar month, or if the expiration date
occurs on a day other than the last day of a calendar month, then the monthly rent for
the fractional month will be prorated on a daily basis.

Because the common law rule does not apportion rent, this provision prorates the
first and last months' rent. Rent is payable at the premises unless the lease
requires otherwise.

The importance of requiring that rent be paid without deduction or setoff
cannot be overemphasized.[1]

The term *fixed rent,* when used in a lease that requires the tenant to pay its share
of other costs, creates an ambiguity. An Arizona court resolved the ambiguity in
the tenant's favor by holding that the tenant was required to pay only the fixed
rent.[2] The basic lease information had said "fixed minimum rent" from which
"minimum" had been deleted. When a lease involves rent escalations, a term
such as "base rent" should be used; see *Commercial Real Estate Leases: Forms*.

Some leases require the tenant to pay the first month's rent at the time of
execution of the lease. Usually the security deposit is also payable on execution.
In fairness, prorations should be made on the basis of actual days elapsed, not 30
days as some leases provide.

In the rare instance in which the payment of fixed rent is the tenant's only
monetary obligation, the lease may be called a *gross lease*: the landlord receives
a gross amount from which it must pay real estate taxes, insurance, maintenance,
and all other incidents of ownership before it realizes a net return on its
investment. In most situations, the term is misleading and uninformative. Some
landlords use the term to denote a lease in which the tenant pays for insurance,
and other landlords use the same term to refer to an office lease in which the
tenant pays its share of operating expenses in excess of a base year's operating
expenses. Commercial leases in which the tenant's sole obligation is to pay a fixed
rent—what some would call a *true gross lease*—are very rare. Aside from
residential rental agreements, they are found in short-term commercial arrangements in which the landlord is confident of its associated costs. Furthermore,

---

[1] *See* S.L. Motel Enters. v. East Ocean, Inc., 751 S.W.2d 114 (Mo. Ct. App. 1988) (tenant
mistakenly overpaid rent and then failed to pay rent due later on basis of alleged offset right;
landlord successfully terminated lease for nonpayment of rent); GTM Invs. v. Depot, Inc., 694
P.2d 379 (Colo. Ct. App. 1984) (another case enforcing a phrase such as "without any
deductions or set-off whatsoever").

[2] Cecil Lawter Real Estate School v. Town & Country Shopping Center Co., 143, Ariz. 527, 694
P.2d 815 (Ct. App. 1984).

almost any gross lease will impose some maintenance obligations. In other words, knowing the name of a lease is not a substitute for reading it.

In most leases, the fixed rent provision in **Form 6-1** works in tandem with several other provisions that either impose costs in addition to the fixed rent (called *pass-throughs*), or adjust fixed rent (called *escalations*). Pass-throughs include operating expenses, real estate taxes, and utilities. Escalations include cost of living adjustments, and percentage rent in the shopping center lease. Still other lease provisions require the tenant to reimburse costs incurred by the landlord; provisions for attorneys' fees and repairs are typical examples of this kind of provision. When a lease requires the tenant to pay amounts in addition to rent, the landlord is well advised to denominate those amounts as *additional rent*. This assures the landlord of the expedited remedies available for nonpayment of rent; otherwise, it has only a contract claim and is subject to judicial delays attendant upon most other litigation.

FORM 6-2
RENT—ADDITIONAL RENT

Tenant will pay landlord as additional rent without deduction or offset all amounts that this lease requires tenant to pay (the "additional rent"), including without limitation any increase in the monthly rent resulting from the provisions of [cost of living adjustment paragraph], at the place where the monthly rent is payable. Landlord will have the same remedies for a default in the payment of additional rent as it has for a default in the payment of monthly rent.

This provision assumes that there is a cost of living adjustment, and that each provision imposing an additional charge states when it is due.

Although the provision for a late payment charge is often among the default provisions, or among the miscellaneous provisions, it can also accompany the rent provision. In drafting these provisions, the real estate professional must be careful to prepare a provision for liquidated damages, as opposed to a penalty (which courts will not enforce) or interest (which may violate usury restrictions). This one-time charge, as opposed to a continuous 2 percent per month charge, does not look like interest and is clearly designated as liquidated damages.

FORM 6-3
RENT—LATE PAYMENT CHARGE

If tenant fails to pay any monthly rent or additional rent on the date they are due and payable, the unpaid amounts will be subject to a late payment charge equal to 2% of the unpaid amounts. This late payment charge is intended to compensate landlord for its additional administrative costs resulting from tenant's failure, and has been agreed upon by landlord and tenant, after negotiation, as a reasonable estimate of the additional administrative costs that will be incurred by landlord as a result of tenant's failure. The actual cost in each instance is extremely difficult, if not impossible, to determine. This late payment charge will constitute liquidated damages and will be paid to landlord together with such unpaid amounts. The payment of this late payment charge will not constitute a waiver by landlord of any default by tenant under this lease.

This provision expresses the factors that lead to judicial approval of late charge provisions.[3]

The late charge provision is usually coupled with a provision that the tenant will pay interest on past due amounts from the date on which they are due until the date on which they are paid in full with interest. Standing alone, a late charge provision does not give the tenant any less reason to pay four weeks late than one day late. Interest charges provide that reason.

§ 6.2   "Free Rent" Arrangements

In some soft real estate markets, landlords try to attract tenants with offers of rent abatements or "free rent."[4] Instead of a five-year lease at $15 per foot, they offer a five-year lease with two years "rent free" and three years at $25 per foot. The total rent—$75—is the same; the tenant, however, enjoys a period of lower occupancy cost when it is starting up its business, and the landlord looks forward to the $25 rate that attracts buyers and facilitates refinancing. The $15 rate is often called the *effective rate,* while the $25 rate is called the *face rate.*

Often, at the end of the free rent period, tenants approach their landlords to renegotiate their leases. They may wish to extend the terms of their leases at the effective rate, thus precluding the landlord from the benefit of increased rates at the end of the initial term. If the market has not improved since the lease was made, the landlord may find it very difficult to avoid a tenant default. In any event, the landlord may lose the benefit that it had perceived when it made the lease.

In order to avoid these calamities and to give the landlord some assurance of the tenant's ability to pay the face rate, free rent provisions are often written to require rent on alternating months. Thus, instead of one year without rent, there might be two years with rent payable in every other month. The landlord has some of its face rate rent, and its risks are reduced; the tenant has some benefit of the effective rate and gets in the habit of making rent payments.

Whenever a free rent provision is used, the real estate professional must be certain to specify what is free. Landlords will rarely abate operating expenses. Most lenders will insist upon the tenant's payment of those costs.

If there are escalations in a renewal term that are tied to the rental rate, the real estate professional must be certain to define whether the face rate or effective rate is the basis. If there is a renewal term with rent at the same rate as the initial term,

---

[3] Krupp Realty Co. v. Joel, 168 Ga. App. 480, 309 S.E.2d 641 (1983).

[4] *See A Thoughtful Landlord Approach to Free Rent Deals,* Leas. Prof., July 1989, at 1.

does this mean the same effective rate or the same face rate? When escalations are based on cost of living adjustment or a fixed percentage step up, does the increase pertain to the face rate or the effective rate? No free rent provision can be written without consideration of the federal income tax consequences that may spread the rent across the entire term and give the landlord a tax liability when it has no revenue.[5]

§ 6.3 Stepped Up Rent

Fixed rent lost its appeal when the landlord's revenue was eroded by unexpected costs and inflation. In an effort to protect themselves against unexpected costs and inflation, landlords used provisions by which the fixed rent is escalated by fixed amounts at fixed intervals. Originally, this increasing rent was given the euphonious name of "crescendo rental,"[6] but it is now called stepped up rent.

FORM 6-4
RENT—STEPPED UP RENT

Tenant will pay landlord as rent ("the rent"):

$_____ per month commencing on _____ 1, 19_____, and continuing up to and including _____ 1, 19_____;

$_____ per month commencing on _____ 1, 19_____, and continuing up to and including _____ 1, 19_____;

$_____ per month commencing on _____ 1, 19_____, and continuing up to and including _____ 1, 19_____;

$_____ per month commencing on _____ 1, 19_____, and continuing up to and including _____ 1, 19_____.

The rent will be paid on or before the first day of each month during the term of this lease. The rent will be paid in advance at the address specified for landlord in the basic lease information, or at such other place as landlord designates, without prior demand and without any abatement, deduction, or setoff. If the commencement date occurs on a day other than the first day of a calendar month, or if the expiration date occurs on a day other than the last day of a calendar month, then the rent for such fractional month will be prorated on a daily basis.

Instead of stating the stepped up rent in dollars, these provisions often use percentages, such as "rent will increase 6% on each anniversary of the

---

[5] I.R.C. § 467 (1986).

[6] Sohmer Co. v. C.H. Welling Inv. Co., 63 Misc. 439, 118 N.Y.S. 450 (Sup. Ct. 1909).

commencement date." In order to avoid confusion about compounding (as discussed in § **6.6**), stating a dollar rent is preferable.

Stepped up rent provisions are useful in short-term leases when the landlord and tenant are willing to trade precision for simplicity. The landlord knows its income, and the tenant knows its expense. Each believes that it is better off with this certainty than with an unpredictable rent adjustment based on a cost of living index or actual expenses.

Two precautions are necessary for proper use of a stepped up rent provision. First, if the tenant has the right to renew or extend the lease "on the same terms and conditions," there is a patent (and easily avoidable) ambiguity about the rent in the renewal or extension term:[7] is the renewal rent the rent fixed for the first step of the initial term, or the last step of the initial term, or some step in between? Second, the use of stepped up rent may have unexpected federal income tax consequences.[8]

§ 6.4   An Approach to Cost of Living Adjustments

When landlords realized that increased costs and inflation reduced the returns on their investments and that stepped up rent provisions were imprecise, they began to provide that the fixed rent would be periodically escalated by *cost of living adjustments* (COLAs).[9] COLAs appear to be a more precise approach than stepped up rent provisions; however, even COLAs have a degree of imprecision that the real estate professional can minimize.[10]

COLAs have been enthusiastically embraced by landlords as a solution to their problems with increasing costs and inflation.[11] Curiously, there appears to be no empirical support for the proposition that the cost of operating a real estate development fluctuates with the cost of living. Little thought has been given to the plight of tenants whose costs of doing business are also increasing. Still less thought has been devoted to decide whether COLAs themselves compel inflation and are self-fulfilling prophecies.[12]

The first obstacle to proper cost of living adjustments (which were once called "a challenge to an imaginative legal mind")[13] is the choice of the index by which

---

[7] *Id., discussed in* N. Hecht, Long Term Lease Planning and Drafting ch. 4 (1974).

[8] *See* I.R.C. § 467 (1986), as amended.

[9] Annot., 87 A.L.R.3d 986, *Lease provisions providing for rent adjustment based on event or formula outside control of parties* (1978).

[10] Note, *Lease Escalation Clauses Using the Consumer Price Index—How Well Do They Work?*, 7 Okla. City U.L. Rev. 489 (1982).

[11] A thorough discussion of this kind of provision, including a form and examples, is set forth in *How to Get More Rent in Times of Low Inflation,* Com. Lease L. Insider, Nov. 1985, at 1.

[12] "COLA is the engine that fuels runaway inflation . . . COLA feeds on itself: the more you try to keep up with rising prices, the more inflation you create." L. Iacocca, Iacocca: An Autobiography 304-05 (1984).

[13] Morris, *Shopping Centers—The Role of the Lawyer,* U. Ill. L.F. 681 (1955).

the cost of living is measured. There is an abundance of indexes.[14] By far the most common index is the consumer price index (CPI), whose popularity is attributable to the impartiality of its preparer (the federal government) and its ready availability (as noted in § **6.7**).[15]

Actually, two primary CPIs are published by the Bureau of Labor Statistics (BLS) of the United States Department of Labor. One index (CPI-U), which is technically titled "All Items and Major Group Figures for All Urban Consumers but usually called the "all urban index," pertains to all urban consumers. The other index (the CPI-W), which is technically titled "All Items and Major Group Figures for Urban Wage Earners and Clerical Workers" but usually called the "wage earner index," pertains to urban wage earners and clerical workers only. The CPI-U is intended to include 80 percent of the total noninstitutional civilian population, while the CPI-W includes approximately half the population included in the all urban index. There are subindexes on the CPI-U and CPI-W bases for many geographic areas. There are also special indexes and experimental indexes that are not used in commercial leases.

The CPIs measure the cost of a hypothetical market basket of consumer goods, such as medical care, entertainment, clothing, food and beverages, and housing. Ironically, the foremost determinant of commercial lease escalations does not consider any commercial real estate costs. The propriety of the consumer price indexes is a fascinating topic that is well beyond the scope of this book; however, excellent discussions of these indexes and other indexes are available.[16]

Until recently, the CPIs were calculated from a base year of 1967, in which the cost of the items included in the indexes was presumed to be 100. Therefore, those indexes were followed by the indication of (1967 = 100). Beginning with the release of data for January 1988, the standard reference base period for the CPIs was changed to 1982-84 = 100.

The rebasing by the BLS, after review by the Office of Federal Statistical Policy and Standards, Office of Management and Budget, is in keeping with the government's long-standing policy that index bases should be updated periodically. The BLS chose the 1982-84 period to coincide with the time period of the updated CPIs expenditure weights, which are based upon the Consumer Expenditure Surveys for 1982, 1983, and 1984.

As a convenience to users, the BLS will continue to compile and publish the all items indexes for U.S. City Average and for the individual local areas for which CPIs are published on their former official reference base (1967 = 100 in most cases). However, with release of the January 1988 CPI, the BLS discontinued calculation and publication of the all items index (1957-59 = 100).

Adoption of the new base period does not affect the measurement of percent changes in an index series from one time period to another, except for rounding

---

[14] *See generally* Sherman, *Hedges Against Inflation in Leases of Real Property,* in Real Prop., Prob. & Tr. J., *reprinted in* Real Estate in Midcentury 296 (F.S. Lane ed. 1974).

[15] *See generally* Note, *Lease Escalation Clauses Using the Consumer Price Index—How Well Do They Work?,* 7 Okla. City U.L. Rev. 489 (1982).

[16] *See generally* The Consumer Price Index, ch. 19, *reprinted from* BLS Handbook of Methods, Bulletin 2285.

differences. Index point changes are, however, usually affected. The example below illustrates the different effects of rebasing on index points and percent changes:

Base	Dec. 1985 Index	Dec. 1986 Index	Index Point Change	Percent Change
1967 = 100	327.5	331.1	3.6	1.1
1982-84 = 100	109.3	110.5	1.2	1.1

In addition, factors to convert an index from a 1982-84 base to a previous base index for other series are available. These provisions will enable most users to continue to utilize the former official reference base through the entire period of their leases. The BLS does, however, urge users to incorporate the change in reference base in new leases or at the time of renegotiations.

The following tables provide conversion factors that can be used to convert data from their former (1967 = 100) base to the current base (1982-84 = 100):

All items	Conversion Factors CPI-U	CPI-W
United States	0.3338279	0.3357175
Denver	0.2998875	0.3004331
Kansas City	0.3367728	0.3412969
St. Louis	0.3366814	0.3398984

These conversion factors were derived by taking the reciprocal of the 1982-84 Average Index on the former base and multiplying that reciprocal by 100. Multiplication by these factors converts indexes on the 1967 = 100 reference base to the 1982-84 = 100 reference base. Division by these factors converts an index on the 1982-84 base to the former base. Whenever possible, actual historical tables should be used. Because of rounding differences, the use of the conversion factors may not duplicate the official series.

Monthly indexes are published for the four largest metropolitan areas.

Northeast.   New York-Northern New Jersey-Long Island, NY-NJ-CT. Philadelphia-Wilmington-Trenton, PA-DE-NJ-MD

North Central.   Chicago-Gary-Lake County, IL-IN-WI

West.   Los Angeles-Anaheim-Riverside, CA

Bimonthly indexes are published for the next 11 largest areas, including Detroit, for which an index has historically been published monthly. Those indexes and their names are:

Boston-Lawrence-Salem, MA-NH

Pittsburgh-Beaver Valley, PA

Cleveland-Akron-Lorain, OH

Detroit-Ann Arbor, MI

St. Louis-East St. Louis, MO-IL

Baltimore, MD

Dallas-Fort Worth, TX

Houston-Galveston-Brazoria, TX

Miami-Fort Lauderdale, FL

Washington, DC-MD-VA

San Francisco-Oakland-San Jose, CA

The index for Cleveland-Akron-Lorain, OH is published in odd-numbered months rather than in even-numbered months as the Cleveland, Ohio index was historically. The Detroit, MI index is published only in even numbered months, rather than monthly, as the Detroit, Mich. index was historically.

A semiannual average index is published for 12 areas that previously had monthly publications. These indexes and their names are:

Buffalo-Niagara Falls, NY

Cincinnati-Hamilton, OH-KY-IN

Kansas City, MO-KS

Milwaukee, WI

Minneapolis-St. Paul, MN-WI

Atlanta, GA

Anchorage, AK

Denver-Boulder, CO

Honolulu, HI

Portland-Vancouver, OR-WA

San Diego, CA

Seattle-Tacoma, WA

The index is based on an average of six months' data.

As one may expect, landlords want rapidly rising indexes and tenants do not. Since the primary indexes are national, they are not directly affected by local fluctuations and so move more slowly. Landlords and tenants often assume that the CPIs for the city or vicinity of the premises are appropriate; however, local CPIs may be unfair to a tenant whose sales are national and thus escalating at a slower rate. The wholesale price index, which is also published by the BLS, seems to be the most sluggish index and thus is a favorite of tenants.[17]

§ 6.5   Preparing the Cost of Living Adjustment Provision

The cost of living adjustment provision is not nearly as complicated as the efforts to write it suggest. The provision, simply put, endeavors to (1) measure the change, (2) in an index, (3) over time. To prepare the provision, one must identify the starting point against which change will be measured, identify the index, and state the intervals over which change will be measured. A typical provision for these purposes is:

FORM 6-5
RENT—CPI RENT ADJUSTMENT

The rent in paragraph _____ will be adjusted according to this paragraph on each January 1 and July 1 during the term of this lease.

(a)   In this paragraph,

(1)   "base year" means the full calendar year during which the term of this lease commences.

(2)   "price index" means the Consumer Price Index published by the Bureau of Labor Statistics of the United States Department of Labor, U.S. City Average, All Items and Major Group Figures for Urban Wage Earners and Clerical Workers (1982-84 = 100).

(3)   "price index for the base year" means the average of the monthly price indexes for each of the twelve (12) months of the Base Year.

(b)   The January 1 adjustment will be based on the percentage difference between the price index for the preceding month of December and the price index for the base year. The July 1 adjustment will be based on the percentage difference between the price index for the preceding month of June and the price index for the base year.

(1)   If the price index for June in any calendar year during the term of this lease is greater than the price index for the base year, then the rent in paragraph _____ payable on the next July 1 (without regard to any adjustments under this paragraph) will be multiplied by the percentage difference between the price index for June and the price index for the base year, and the product will be added to the rent in paragraph _____ effective as of July 1. The adjusted annual rent will be payable until it is readjusted pursuant to the terms of this lease.

(2)   If the price index for December in any calendar year during the term of this lease is greater than the price index for the base year, then the rent in paragraph _____ payable on the next January 1 (without regard to any adjustments under this paragraph) will be multiplied by the percentage difference between the price index for December and the price index for the base year, and the product will be added to

---

[17] *See CPI-U vs. CPI-W: Which Yields More Rent*, Com. Lease L. Insider, Apr. 1986, at 1 (thorough analysis of this index in the period from 1983 to 1985).

the rent in paragraph _____ effective as of January 1. The adjusted annual rent will be payable until it is readjusted pursuant to the terms of this lease.

If a substantial change is made in the price index, then the price index will be adjusted to the figure that would have been used had the manner of computing the price index in effect at the date of this lease not been altered. If the price index (or a successor or substitute index) is not available, a reliable governmental or other nonpartisan publication evaluating the information used in determining the price index will be used.

No adjustments will be made due to any revision that may be made in the price index for any month.

(c)   The statements of the adjustment to be furnished by landlord as provided in subparagraph (b) will consist of data prepared for the landlord by a firm of certified public accountants (which may be the firm now or then currently employed by landlord for the audit of its accounts). The statements thus furnished to tenant will constitute a final determination as between landlord and tenant of the relevant adjustment.

(d)   The rent in paragraph _____ (exclusive of the adjustments under this paragraph) will not be reduced.

(e)   The landlord's delay or failure, beyond July 1 or January 1 of any year, in computing or billing for these adjustments will not impair the continuing obligation of tenant to pay rent adjustments.

(f)   Tenant's obligation to pay rent as adjusted by this paragraph will continue up to the expiration of this lease and will survive any earlier termination of this lease.

This provision contemplates that two adjustments will be made each year, that the changes in the index may not be available on the date on which adjustments must be made, that the index may no longer be published, that the landlord forgets to make the adjustment to the base rent, and that the change in the index is downward. Unlike some provisions, this one does not require arbitration if the landlord and tenant are unable to agree upon a substitute index if the CPI is no longer published; see **Form 31-1**.

Tenants should be aware of escalations that start from the date of signing the lease. If there is a delay in occupancy, rent will be escalating before the tenant takes possession. Since it uses the average index for the first calendar year as the base, this provision gives the tenant the balance of the first calendar year of its occupancy without escalation. Many landlords calculate escalation with reference to a stated month, usually the month before the term begins. The astute real estate professional will want to negotiate this provision for the tenant's benefit.

Escalations such as the cost of living adjustment are intended to keep rent abreast of inflation and operating costs. When landlords pass through operating expenses and escalate rent, they say that the escalation is designed only to protect the rent from erosion by inflation. Since market rents may not keep up with inflation (depending upon the chosen index), landlords may get rent in excess of market rents. Needless to say, tenants do not warm up to this prospect. Some landlords simply adjust the minimum rent to market rent during the term; although this may prevent a lease from developing bonus value, the determination of market rent may be very difficult to make.

§ 6.6   Refining the Cost of Living Adjustment

In a net lease, of course, the tenant pays all real estate taxes, insurance, maintenance, and other operating costs. The landlord receives an amount from which it must pay only its mortgage debt. Assume that the debt service is a fixed amount, which is 80 percent of the original rent payment. As a result, the landlord realizes only 20 percent of the rent payment as spendable income. If a cost of living adjustment (COLA) is applied to the entire rent payment, the landlord is getting a substantial windfall. This is illustrated:

Net rent payment	$7,500
(less) debt service (80% × $7500)	−6,000
Landlord's base spendable income	$1,500
COLA of 5% applied to net rent payment	
105% × $7,500)	$7,875
(less) debt service	−6,000
Landlord's adjusted spendable income	$1,875
COLA of 5% applied landlord's base spendable	
income (105% × $1,500)	$1,575
Landlord's windfall	$ 300

This distortion can occur in other leases as well. Assume that the rent per square foot is $25.00. The landlord has agreed to pay $4.00 of the rent for operation expenses and the tenant has agreed to pay any amount in excess of $4.00. If a COLA is applied to $25.00, the landlord has another windfall: an escalation over $4.00 which it was never allowed to keep in the first place.

COLA of 5% applied to rent per square foot	
(105% × $25)	$26.25
(less) landlord's share of operating expenses	−4.00
Landlord's adjusted base rent	$22.25
Rent per square foot	$25.00
(less) landlord's share of operating expenses	−4.00
Landlord's base rent	$21.00

The tenant's defense is to demand that the COLA be applied to landlord's base rent only. In this example, the adjusted rent would be (($21.00 × 105%) + $4.00), or $26.05, instead of $26.25.

The landlord may be prompted to ask for a floor on the CPI increase, demanding that the rent be adjusted upward by some stated percentage at each annual adjustment period, for example, "the rent will be increased by the greater of (a) 3%, or (b) the cost of living adjustment pursuant to paragraph ____." This is simply a stepped up rent without any of the risk that led to indexing in the first place; the landlord wants more money and there is no justification for it (other than market conditions), because the landlord is insulated from risk by other provisions of the lease. The tenant should note that this increase occurs without regard to the actual behavior of the CPI. It is an increase in rent. If the tenant is compelled to accede to such a provision, it should be assured that the next increase that is based on the CPI should be only as great as the amount by which the CPI increase exceeds the increases that have been made without regard to it. This allows the tenant to avoid escalations that are based on "fictitious" increases, and it allows for actual CPI experience to be accommodated before stepped up rent is paid. For example, assume that the CPI was unchanged in one year. The landlord would get an automatic rent increase of 3 percent, according to the lease. If, the next year, the CPI increases by 5 percent, the landlord should get a 3 percent increase (a total increase of 6 percent, not 8 percent) so that the tenant recovers the previous fictitious increase.

Just as the landlord may demand a floor on the COLA, the tenant may demand a ceiling on the COLA. These provisions are written in two ways. One says that the tenant will pay only a fixed share of the actual increase, for example, 80 percent;[18] this limitation is appropriate when the landlord is insulated from certain costs by virtue of pass-through provisions such as those discussed in § 6.11. The other way says that the increase in any period shall not exceed a fixed percentage, for example, 5 percent. The purpose is to avoid any distortions arising from extraordinary CPI experience; however, landlords object to this rationale because they are at risk if extraordinary increases become the norm.

While the tenant is arguing about the ceiling on its exposure to CPI increases, another opportunity arises for the tenant to ingratiate itself with its landlord. As soon as the tenant concedes the merit of the landlord's argument that it needs inflation protection because "the dollar isn't what it used to be," the tenant should ask that the landlord's contribution to operating expenses (for example, the $4.00 in the preceding example) be escalated by the same CPI factor. The reason behind this is that the landlord is getting inflation-proof rent, and thus the tenant should get inflation-proof operating expense contributions from the landlord. Put differently, landlord's income increases with inflation but its costs (to the extent it has agreed to pay any) do not. Landlords are very rarely persuaded by this argument, but as a compromise, they usually agree to escalate only that part of the base rent that exceeds the landlord's contribution to operating expenses.

---

[18] See Gilson, *The CPI Clause—Read It Carefully,* Wash. Law., May/June 1987 at 24, for a revealing discussion about varieties of escalations based on a fraction of the CPI.

§ 6.7 Common Mistakes in Cost of Living Adjustments

The most catastrophic mistake that can be made in the cost of living provision is the failure to identify the index or the way in which it works. The leading case in this ignominious area arose in Missouri with a lease that provided in part:

> The Fixed Minimum Rent herein provided for shall be adjusted by any percentage increase from the base period of the United States Department of Labor Statistics Consumer Price Index (U.S. City average). The term "base period" shall refer to the period for which said index is published which includes the commencement date of the Lease. "Sufficient Percentage Rent" as used herein is defined as such Percentage Rent which, when added to the then Fixed Minimum Rent, equals or exceeds such Fixed Minimum Rent when adjusted to the aforesaid Index.[19]

The court observed that the lease did not identify which of the two consumer price indexes was meant, that it did not indicate the rent period to which the calculation was to apply, and that it did not indicate the point to which the increase was to be measured. In conclusion, the court followed the common judicial preference in such matters. It declined to make an agreement for people who could not make their own, and it dismissed the landlord's claim for escalated rent.

A later Missouri case was more indulgent.[20] There, the court was called upon to construe a rent escalation equal to "the increase of cost of living index over base period of April 1, 1977, to April 1, 1982."[21] The court concluded that the contract was "clearly not ambiguous," even though the previous Missouri case balked at a provision that did not distinguish between two consumer price indexes.[22] The real estate professional may find these cases hard to reconcile.

In yet another mistake that need never have happened, a landlord and tenant agreed on escalations based upon the "cost of living figures for the City of Spokane, issued by the United States Bureau of Labor Statistics." Unfortunately for the landlord, there were no such figures, and the court refused to compel payment of escalations until there was such an index.[23]

Those cases are unavoidable miscarriages of justice. They are miscarriages of justice because, even though the landlord and tenant agreed on some CPI adjustment, the courts did not enforce their agreement. They are unavoidable because the only judicial alternative to leaving the landlord and tenant with their unenforceably unclear agreement is to make an agreement for them. Unfortunately, these decisions give tenants no reason to insist upon clarity, because tenants are rewarded for ambiguity by avoiding a CPI adjustment.

---

[19] Johnston v. First Nat'l Bank & Trust Co. of Joplin, 624 S.W.2d 500, 502 (Mo. Ct. App. 1981).

[20] Satterfield v. Layton, 669 S.W.2d 287 (Mo. Ct. App. 1984).

[21] *Id. at* 288.

[22] Johnston v. First Nat'l Bank & Trust Co. of Joplin, 624 S.W.2d 500, 502 (Mo. Ct. App. 1981).

[23] Seattle First Nat'l Bank v. Earl, 17 Wash. App. 830, 565 P.2d 1215 (1977), *review denied* (1978).

Sadly, judicial efforts to interpret poor provisions may offend both the landlord and the tenant. In one case, the provision at issue stated:

> The annual minimum lease fee payable to Lessors shall be adjusted at one year intervals . . . . The Consumer Price Index as prepared by the United States Department of Labor shall be used as the basis of comparison . . . . [S]aid index obtained shall be compared with the prior index figure for May 1, 1972 and the $78,000 annual rent figure shall be varied (either increased or decreased) in the same ratio that the price index for the period bears to the price index figure of May 1, 1972. The formula for the rent is as follows: New rent for the next succeeding year is to $78,000 as the average price index for the past year is to price index of May 1, 1972.[24]

This provision could have met the same judicial aversion as the previous provisions. Although the issue does not seem to have been raised, this provision did not identify the consumer price index. The question actually presented was whether the increase was to be measured against the difference of the (1) average of the 12 months consumer price indexes for the comparison year, or (2) consumer price indexes that were 12 months apart. The court noted the "ineptness of expression," but ruled in favor of the latter approach.[25] In doing so, it said that the familiar rule that ambiguity is construed most strongly against the drafter should not apply since both landlord and tenant contributed to the vagueness.

At the risk of belaboring the point, one further case must be reported. In this instance, the poorly drafted provision was enforced to the chagrin of the tenant. That provision was:

> That upon the expiration of the primary term of this Lease and Agreement, that is to say from January 11, 1976, through and including January 10, 1981, Tenant is granted the option to lease these premises for two (2) additional five (5) year consecutive terms with the same terms and conditions as hereinabove set forth for each of the five (5) year consecutive periods, with the exception that the amount of minimum base rental in the sum of Four Hundred Dollars ($400.00) as set forth hereinabove shall at the expiration of the first five (5) year lease period be changed as follows:
>
> (a)   The sum of the base rental shall be changed to reflect the increase or decrease in the cost of living index occurring during the first five (5) years for the term of this Lease and Agreement shall either increase or decrease the amount of base rental to be paid (in the sum of $400.00 per month) by the same percentage which the consumer price index has risen or fallen during the first five (5) years of this lease.
>
> The percentage of increase or decrease, if any, at the end of said five (5) year period shall be multiplied by the monthly rental of $400.00 and the product of such multiplication shall be the amount of the Tenant's minimum rental for each month during the second five (5) year period of this lease, subject to paragraph (b) below. The consumer price index is and shall be the price index computed by the United

---

[24] Centennial Enters. Inc. v. Mansfield Dev. Co., 193 Colo. 463, 568 P.2d 50 (1977); *see also* Rubright, *Rent Escalation and the Consumer Price Index,* 10 Colo. Law. 769 (1981).

[25] Centennial Enters. Inc. v. Mansfield Dev. Co., 193 Colo. 463, 465, 568 P.2d 50, 52 (1977).

States Bureau of Labor Statistics, being the national consumer price index for the urban wages and clerical workers, generally referred to as the "Cost of Living Index."

(b)   The sum of the base rental shall also be changed to reflect the yearly increase or decrease in the cost to Landlord of property taxes and utilities. The percentage of any increase or decrease of these items from date hereof until the termination of the first five (5) year period shall be multiplied by monthly rental derived under paragraph (a) above, and such multiplication shall be the amount of the Tenant's monthly rental for each month during the second five (5) year period commencing with the first month to the second five (5) year period.[26]

The landlord followed the provision literally to calculate the rent during the renewal period. The calculation—with which the tenant did not disagree—was:

(1)   Amount of base   ×   percentage of increase or
      rent   decrease in cost of living
                                    index

                              plus

(2)   Amount of   ×   percentage of increase or
      monthly rental   decrease cost of property
      derived from (1)   taxes and utilities

The tenant relied upon what it felt was an inconsistency within the lease. The court was not persuaded and held for the landlord. The result was a threefold increase in minimum rent during the renewal term.[27]

These sorts of mistakes arise from the preparer's failure to grasp the simplicity of the cost of living provision. They are compounded by the failure of the other real estate professionals to read the provisions carefully. All of these cases would have been avoided by reference to the consumer price index that is readily available from the United States Department of Labor, or by joint review of the operation of the provision in a hypothetical situation.

The final observation about cost of living adjustments is the most important for a tenant: beware of compounding. Suppose a five-year lease has base annual rent of $20,000 and annual CPI adjustments.

Year	CPI Change	Rent
First	N/A	$20,000.00
Second	5%	21,000.00
Third	3%	21,630.00
Fourth	4%	22,495.20
Fifth	2%	22,945.10

---

[26] Lemley v. Bozeman Community Hotel Co., 200 Mont. 470, 651 P.2d 979, 980 (1982).
[27] 651 P.2d at 981.

Note that the actual CPI increase has been 14 percent and that the overall rent as increased should be $22,800 (114% × $20,000). However, the actual rent increase is 14.72 percent ($22,945.10/$20,000). The difference is the effect of compounding. The real estate professional should insist on behalf of a tenant that all adjustments relate back to the first index. In this example, the adjustments would be:

105% of the base annual rent, or $21,000.00 for the second year;
108% of the base annual rent, or $21,600.00 for the third year;
112% of the base annual rent, or $22,400.00 for the fourth year;
114% of the base annual rent, or $22,800.00 for the fifth year.

This effect is considerably more dramatic if the adjustments are quarterly or even semiannual.

§ 6.8 Porters' Wage Escalations

As the preceding sections in this chapter have shown, escalation provisions have moved from the crude stepped up rent provisions to the apparently more precise cost of living adjustments (COLAs). The ostensible goal has been to insulate the landlord against increased operating expenses and inflation. On the way to even more precise operating expense provisions, landlords came across porters' wage escalations.[28] These mechanisms are the missing link in the evolution of escalations from COLAs to actual operating expense pass-throughs.

Calling porters' wage escalations the missing link is to emphasizes that these escalations are neither COLAs nor operating expense pass-throughs. Porters' wage escalations are somewhere between them. Although (like COLAs) they escalate the base rent as a response to increased costs, they are not COLAs because they are not tied to a broadbased cost of living index; in fact, they are a narrow category of commercial expense. Although (like operating expense pass throughs) they are related to the landlord's cost of furnishing services, they are not operating expense escalations because they raise the base rent without regard to the landlord's actual costs for its services.

This nice distinction is underscored by a New York court decision.[29] The tenant had won the landlord's agreement that operating expenses would not include costs for which the landlord was reimbursed by others; this exclusion

---

[28] *See* Treanor, *Pitfalls of Escalation Clauses,* 2 Prob. & Prop. 4 (1988) (extended discussion of porter's wage clauses with examples). *See also* Goldstein, *Disputes in Business Leases: An Overview,* 18 Real Prop., Prob. & Tr. J. 709 (1983).

[29] J. Henry Schroder Bank & Trust Co. v. South Ferry Bldg. Co., 99 A.D.2d 736, 472 N.Y.S.2d 382 (1984); *see also* City of Hope v. Fisk Bldg. Assocs., 63 A.D.2d 946, 406 N.Y.S.2d 472 (1978) (somewhat similar question involving CPI and utility pass-throughs).

(which is included in **Form 6-8**) is meant to assure the tenant that the landlord is not reimbursed twice for the same cost—once from a third person, and again from the tenant through the operating expense provision. The tenant argued that the porters' wage escalation paid by other tenants was a reimbursement for labor costs and that the operating expense provision should exclude labor costs. Concluding that the porters' wage escalation was only a device to avoid inflation, and not an actual operating expense, an appellate court held for the owner.

Porters' wage escalations adjust rent by reference to the increase in a class of building workers' wages. The first step in using the porters' wage escalation is the definition of the porters' wage. Does it include fringe benefits, sick leave, and vacations, for example, all of which increase the porters' wage itself? Once the porters' wage is defined, the escalation is easy to determine, is beyond the influence of the landlord and tenant, and is fixed for the duration of the union contracts. The precision of these escalations is, however, dubious. Their conceptual underpinning—that the landlord's operating expenses increase in direct relation to labor costs—is infirm.

At its origins, the porters' wage escalation was a one-percent increase in rent for each one-cent increase in the porters' wage. In fact, this escalation has been called the penny wage escalation, even though, as it developed, it took on several forms. One form escalated rent by the same percentage as the porters' wage increased. Another escalated the rent on a penny-for-penny basis: a one-cent per hour increase in the porters' wage meant a one-cent per foot increase in rent. Clearly, these have significantly different economic consequences. Today, the usual porters' wage escalation provides that the rent per square foot will increase at one cent (or one and one-half cents) for each one-cent increase in the porters' wage.

So long as wages increase more quickly than other operating expenses, landlords stand to profit from the porters' wage escalation. Because this escalation is not related to a landlord's actual cost, landlords are not compelled to reveal their actual operating expenses. Some tenants have said that porters' wage escalations give landlords no reason to oppose porters' union demands; this contention fails to consider that leases with porters' wage escalations must still compete with leases without these escalations, and that landlords without competitive lease costs will have empty buildings. Porters' wage escalations can be staggering and completely unrelated to any imaginable operating expense experience. However, tenants have no claim against their landlords if the actual operating expenses are less than the porters' wage escalation. Some landlords use porters' wage escalations together with one or more other operating expense escalations. The real estate professional must be very careful to analyze the porters' wage escalation with hypothetical examples in order to be certain that its apparent simplicity does not disguise a substantial liability.[30]

---

[30] I Friedman 5.402; *see* Rahm, *Escalation Clauses in Urban Office Leases,* 12 Real Est. Rev. 27 (1982) (a frightening example of how this escalation can work).

§ 6.9 Operating Expense Escalations

Fixed rent became unfashionable when increased costs and inflation made it unpalatable for a landlord. Stepped up rent was employed as a simple method to assure the landlord that some part of its increased costs would be paid by the tenant and that its spendable income would be safe from inflation. Cost of living adjustments (COLAs) replaced stepped up rent because COLAs approximated actual expenses and inflation experience more closely than did stepped up rent.

In another step toward precision, landlords created operating expense escalations.[31] These provisions pass the landlord's operating expenses through to its tenants. Some leases pass through all operating expenses and other leases pass through real estate taxes, utilities, or insurance, or a combination of these. When variable-rate mortgages have been used, landlords have also tied escalations to a portion of the landlord's interest cost.

The tenant wants to fix its occupancy costs. To the extent that operating expenses are passed through without limitation, the tenant's occupancy cost remains uncertain. A tenant cannot arrive at any approximation of its occupancy costs without a thorough understanding of its obligation for operating expenses. To do so, a tenant must ignore labels and concentrate on costs. One office building lease may have all its operating expense provisions in a single paragraph entitled "Operating Expenses," while another office building lease may cover operating expenses in three different paragraphs entitled "Operating Expenses," "Taxes," and "Energy Costs." (By the same token, one shopping center lease may discuss common area maintenance charges in a single paragraph, while another may discuss common area maintenance, taxes, and insurance in three separate paragraphs. Of course, in a shopping center lease, the costs of merchants' associations or promotional funds must be considered as well.) When a lease provides for COLAs, those adjustments must also be considered.

When comparing leases, the real estate professional must identify the total cost of the lease. This includes the base rent, any escalations to the rent, and all operating expenses. These in turn require assumptions about the rate at which price indexes, operating expenses, and other costs of the lease will increase. Clearly, the reliability of these assumptions is as important as identifying the ways in which the occupancy cost is determined.

§ 6.10 Operating Costs in Office Building Leases

If operating costs are passed through in full, the lease is sometimes called a *net lease.* (The single tenant lease is also sometimes called a net lease.) If part of

---

[31] *See generally* Strum & Kuklin, *Commercial Leases and the Inflationary Economy,* in ABA Section of Real Prop., Prob. & Tr. Law, Financing Real Estate During the Inflationary 80's at 411 (B.J. Strum ed. 1981). See Gerbie, *Fighting Hidden Costs in Commercial Leases,* 4 Prac. Real Est. Law. 87 (1988), for ways in which tenants can protect themselves.

these expenses is passed through and part is paid by the landlord, the lease is said to have a *stop,* that is, a maximum amount at which the landlord's contribution to these expenses stops and the tenant's contribution begins. Leases with a stop are also known as *full service leases* or *modified net leases,* which means that the per square foot cost in the lease rate includes the base rent and some operating expenses. For example, a full service lease rate may be $22.50, of which $19.00 is the base rent and $3.50 is the landlord's contribution to its operating expenses, that is, the stop. In operation, the tenant will pay at least $22.50 per square foot. If the operating expenses are $4.00, the tenant's rent will be adjusted to $23.00. However, if the actual operating expenses are $2.00, the tenant will still pay $22.50.

If all office building leases were written on this basis, they could be compared by making an assumption about the likely pass through of operating expenses in the different buildings. Unfortunately, office building leases are written in many different ways.[32] For example, the lease in the preceding paragraph may have been written as a lease of $18.00 for base rent and $4.50 for operating expense. If the actual operating expenses were $4.00, the tenant with an $18.00/$4.50 rate would be better off than a tenant with a $19.00/$3.50 rate; the latter must pay $23.00. Of course, if operating expenses already exceed $4.50, both tenants will pay pass throughs. A landlord may give a tenant the comfort of a $4.50 operating expense, but at the same time state that base rent will escalate at 5 percent annually. In this lease, the tenant is spared an operating expense increase for some longer period of time than a tenant with a $3.50 operating expense. However, the occupancy cost will still be increased by 5 percent of the base rent in each year. In order to compare these two leases, the real estate professional must make assumptions about the rate at which operating expenses will increase.

The problems associated with full service leases may be avoided by going to an office building that employs a net lease. In a net lease, the tenant pays its pro rata share of all actual operating expenses. In comparison to a full service lease with a $19.00 base rent and a $3.50 expense stop, a net lease may state that the base rate is $19.00 and that the tenant pays its pro rata share of all actual operating expenses of the building. If the actual operating expenses are $3.25, the net lease tenant pays $3.25, but the full service lease tenant pays $3.50. So long as the tenant's pro rata share is less than $3.50, the tenant is better off with the net lease. But, when actual expenses exceed $3.50, both the tenant with a full service lease and the tenant with a net lease will have the same lease cost.

Both of these methods of computing the landlord's contribution to operating expenses may be expressed with regard either to the aggregate operating expenses or to each component of the operating expenses. For example, the landlord may say that it will contribute $7.00 toward all operating expenses, or it may say that it will contribute up to $3.50 toward real estate taxes, up to $1.25 toward insurance, up to $.75 toward janitorial, and so on for each operating

---

[32] For a discussion of operating expenses in mixed use developments, see *Operational Concerns and Cost Pass Throughs for the Urban High Rise Landlord,* Leas. Prof. (Mar. 1989), at 1.

expense. In practice, expense-by-expense escalations are not used because of the time that would be involved to express, negotiate, and report each one. However, separate bases are often set forth for real estate taxes, insurance, and utilities. When separate bases are used, tenants are better able to compare their costs of several prospective leases if, and only if, the other leases use the same format for their escalation of operating expenses. Landlords have an opportunity to manipulate separate escalations.

In the following chart, the landlord has agreed to separate contributions for several classes of operating expenses: up to $2.50 for taxes; up to $.75 for insurance; up to $.50 for janitorial; up to $1.75 for utilities; up to $2.25 for all other. The landlord has agreed to make separate contributions that add up to $7.75, but it has not agreed to contribute $7.75 in all events. The distinction is illustrated by two hypothetical years:

	Actual Expenses First Year	Contributions Landlord	Contributions Tenant	Actual Expenses Second Year	Contributions Landlord	Contributions Tenant
Taxes	$3.00	$2.50	$ .50	$3.50	$2.50	$1.00
Insurance	1.00	.75	.25	1.50	.75	.75
Janitorial	.50	.50		.75	.50	.25
Utilities	1.75	1.75		1.50	1.50	
All Others	2.50	2.25	.25	2.00	2.00	
	$8.75	$7.75	$1.00	$9.25	$7.25	$2.00

In the first year, the landlord contributes $7.75, its maximum contribution, because each of the items of expense to which it has agreed to contribute is equal to or greater than its agreed contribution. The tenant's contribution is a relatively modest $1.00, or about 12 percent of the total expenses. However, in the second year, the total operating expenses have increased, but there are savings in some expense categories. As a result, the landlord's contribution is $7.25 and the tenant's contribution is $2.00. The landlord's contribution has decreased $0.50, from $7.75 to $7.25, and the tenant's contribution has increased $1.00, from $1.00 to $2.00. The tenant's contribution (as a percentage of expenses) has increased from about 12 percent to more than 20 percent.

If the landlord had promised to contribute an aggregate amount of $7.75, the tenant would have been considerably better off, because it would have contributed only $1.50 ($9.25 less $7.75). The trick is that the landlord has benefited from the "netting" of savings against increases.

Although this manipulation of the bases is important, the tenant's most important questions remain. What significance is the base amount? How does the cost of this lease compare to the cost of other leases? A landlord who agrees to contribute a base amount or a base year amount has agreed to do no more than apply some part of the rent to operating expenses. If the rent is $25.00 and the landlord's contribution is $6.00, the landlord will keep $19.00 (from which it may pay its debt service), and the tenant will pay any amount by which the operating expenses exceeds $6.00. If the landlord had offered a $22.00 rent, including a $3.00 landlord's contribution, the economic effect to the landlord would have been the same. However, if two landlords offered rent of $22.00, but one had a $3.00 contribution and the other had a $4.00 contribution, a tenant would choose the landlord with the $4.00 contribution, because the tenant would begin to contribute to the payment of operating expenses as soon as they exceeded $3.00 in the first lease. Consequently, tenants must remember that the landlord's contribution to operating expenses is merely a matter of adjusting the landlord's revenue and that the tenant is best off with the greatest contribution from its landlord.

After a tenant learns whether it has a full service lease or a net lease, the tenant should satisfy itself that the total rentable area of the building has been properly, or at least consistently, calculated. The tenant should require the landlord to state the maximum percentage of operating expenses that the tenant must bear. The tenant should know that its share will not increase as a result of a reduction in the rentable area of the building; if a lease's definition of "rentable area" allowed it, such a reduction could occur if a portion of the rentable area were converted to utility and maintenance areas. The tenant should also ask for assurance that its share will decrease if the rentable area of the building is increased, for example, by the conversion of common areas to rentable areas. Finally, the tenant will want its lease to provide that the landlord will not recover more than 100 percent of its operating costs. This can happen if the rentable area of the building is computed in such a way as to exceed the gross area of the building; an example of that computation is set forth in § **4.14**.

Although the case appeared in the appellate courts on a procedural question regarding class actions, one California decision suggests the importance of defining not only the rentable area but also the operating costs.[33] In that case, a tenant suggested that its landlord had breached the lease by (1) failing to include garage space in determining the total rentable area of the building when computing amounts to be added to rent for increase in taxes and building services and (2) computing an increase in rent with reference to taxes on the entire property and not just the building. The trial court and the appellate court both found the relevant lease provisions ambiguous, although the substantive issues were not considered in the appellate decision.[34]

When a landlord recovers on overpayment of management fees, a tenant that was overcharged may be able to recover its share of the overpayment from its landlord.[35] One commentator has suggested the applicability of the implied covenants of good faith and fair dealing in operating expense escalations.[36]

---

[33] Hamwi v. Citinational-Buckeye Inv. Co., 72 Cal. App. 3d 462, 140 Cal. Rptr. 215 (1977).

[34] Id.

[35] Haines, Lundberg & Waehler v. Breitbart, 141 A.D.2d 346, 529 N.Y.S.2d 92 (1988).

[36] See Barak, *Protecting Tenants With an Implied Covenant of Good Faith,* 3 Prac. Real Est. Law. 27 (1987); Barak, *Building Operations Audits: What to Give Tenants Who Think They Have Everything,* L.A. Law., Oct. 1987, at 19 (both emphasizing California case law regarding "implied covenant of good faith and fair dealing," "fiduciary duty," and "punitive damages recoverable for tortious breach of the implied covenant of good faith and fair dealing").

§ 6.11   Preparing an Office Building
Operating Expenses Provision

An office building lease may employ this provision to describe operating expenses for which the tenant is responsible:

FORM 6-6
OPERATING EXPENSES (SHORT FORM)

In addition to the monthly rent payable during the term, tenant will pay tenant's share of the amount by which operating expenses paid or incurred by landlord in each calendar year or partial calendar year during the term exceed landlord's share for such period. If operating expenses are calculated for a partial calendar year, landlord's share will be appropriately prorated. If landlord's share exceeds operating expenses for any full year or partial year, then tenant will have no obligation to pay any part of the operating expenses for such period, and tenant will not be entitled to any adjustment of monthly rent. As used in this lease, the term "operating expenses" means (a) all reasonable costs of management, operation, and maintenance of the project, including without limitation, real property taxes (and any tax levied in whole or in part in lieu of real property taxes), wages, salaries and compensation of employees, janitorial, maintenance, guard and other services, reasonable reserves for operating expenses, that part of office rent or rental value of space in the project used by landlord to operate the project, power, water, waste disposal and other utilities, materials and supplies, maintenance and repairs, insurance, and depreciation on personal property, and (b) the cost (amortized over such reasonable period as landlord determines together with interest on the unamortized balance at the prime rate from time to time prevailing) of any capital improvements (i) that are made to the project by landlord during the term and that reduce other operating expenses, or (ii) that are made to the project by landlord after the date of this lease and that are required under any governmental law or regulation that was not applicable to the project at the time it was constructed. Operating expenses will not include depreciation on the project (other than depreciation on exterior window coverings provided by landlord and carpeting in public corridors and common areas), costs of improvements made for other tenants of the project, real estate brokers' commissions, mortgage interest and capital items other than those referred to in clause (b) above.

This form refers to a *landlord's share*, and is appropriate for a full service lease. Some landlords prefer an exhaustive list of operating expenses, such as:

FORM 6-7
OPERATING EXPENSES (LONG FORM)

The term "operating expenses" means all operating expenses of any kind or nature with respect to the building complex and includes without limitation:
   (a)   the cost of building supplies;
   (b)   costs incurred in connection with all energy sources for the building, such as propane, butane, natural gas, steam, electricity, solar energy, and fuel oil;

(c)   the costs of water and sewer service, janitorial services, general maintenance and repair of the building complex, including the heating and air conditioning systems and structural components of the building;

(d)   landscaping, maintenance, repair, and striping of all parking areas used by tenants of the building;

(e)   insurance, including fire and extended coverage and public liability insurance and any rental insurance and all risk insurance (if landlord decides to carry any of them) but tenant will have no interest in such insurance or the proceeds of such insurance, and any deductible paid by landlord.

(f)   labor costs incurred in the operation and maintenance of the building complex (including any health club, cafeteria or other special facilities available to tenants of the building complex), including wages and other payments;

(g)   costs to landlord for workmen's compensation and disability insurance;

(h)   payroll taxes and welfare fringe benefits, including professional building management fees, architectural, engineering, and space planning costs, legal, accounting, inspection, and consultation fees incurred in connection with the building complex;

(i)   a general overhead and administrative charge equal to two percent (2%) of all other operating expenses incurred by landlord;

(j)   any expense attributable to costs incurred by landlord for any capital improvements or structural repairs to the building complex required by any change in the laws, ordinances, rules, regulations or otherwise that were not in effect on the date landlord obtained its building permit to construct the building complex required by any governmental or quasi-governmental authority having jurisdiction over the building complex, which costs will be amortized over the useful life of the capital improvement or structural repair; and

(k)   any costs incurred by landlord in making capital improvements or other modifications to the building complex or any part of the building complex that reduce the operating expenses. These costs will be amortized over the useful life of such improvement or modification; however, the annual amortization amount will not exceed the reduction in operating expenses as projected by landlord's accountant for the relevant year, and the amortization schedule will be extended accordingly, if necessary.

Like the previous form, this form includes certain capital costs within the ambit of operating expenses: costs of compliance with new laws and costs that reduce other operating expenses (usually energy costs, but also replacement of manually operated elevators with automatic elevators). The tenant should insist that these costs be amortized over the useful life of the assets to which they relate. The tenant should only allow the amortized cost of cost-saving devices to the extent of the cost saving. Some landlords include capital expenditures (such as carpeting) made with respect to the common areas. Other landlords include the cost of replacing capital assets (such as window shades or curtains) that are included in the premises as part of building standard construction. At least one court has enforced a "pass through" provision that required tenants to share in the landlord's mortgage payment even when the landlord prepaid its mortgage in full.[37]

---

[37] Black v. Of Kitchen Things II, Inc., 121 Misc. 2d 64, 467 N.Y.S.2d 167 (Civ. Ct. 1983).

Leases should make it clear that the obligation to pay a share of operating expenses as finally adjusted survives the end of the lease.[38]

In order to eliminate any incentive that a landlord may have to overestimate its operating expenses, some tenants ask for interest on their overpayments.

Landlords and tenants always argue about the landlord's management fees. Landlords say that those fees cover actual costs and are no different from other costs that are passed through to tenants. Tenants consider those fees to be improper profit centers for landlords. Generally, landlords and tenants agree that the management fees should not exceed similar fees for comparable services available in the vicinity of the building. Tenants usually resist management fees that are based on amounts for which the landlord merely writes a check, such as utility charges and real estate taxes. Tenants also resist costs from which they get no benefit or less benefit than their landlords, such as management fees based on brokerage costs or an on-site office.[39]

As a result of litigation in which disgruntled tenants complained that they were deceived by a representation that the expense stop was at least equal to the first year's operating expenses, prudent landlords provide:

Tenant acknowledges that landlord has not made any representation or given tenant any assurances that the operating expenses base will equal or approximate the actual operating expenses per square foot of rentable area of the premises, for any calendar year during the term.

In any event, a tenant should demand that many costs be excluded from the definition of operating expenses because they are not truly operating expenses.[40] These possible exclusions are:

FORM 6-8
OPERATING EXPENSES—EXCLUSIONS

(a)   Costs of decorating, redecorating, or special cleaning or other services not provided on a regular basis to tenants of the building;

(b)   Wages, salaries, fees, and fringe benefits paid to administrative or executive personnel or officers or partners of landlord unless employed at competitive rates as independent contractors;

(c)   Any charge for depreciation of the building or equipment and any interest or other financing charge;

---

[38] *See* Columbia Assocs. v. Propper Oil Co., 402 N.W.2d 223 (Minn. Ct. App. 1987) (case in which lease was silent but landlord prevailed against tenant's claim that end of lease was end of tenant's obligation for certain operating expense adjustments).

[39] Nadel, *Determining a Tenant's Actual Rental Obligations Under Its Lease,* Real Est. L.J., Winter 1990, at 296.

[40] *See What Operating Expenses Should Tenant Pay For?,* Com. Lease L. Insider, Feb. 1986, at 1 (extensive lists and form). See *Tenant Checklist for Office Lease Operating Expenses,* Leasing Prof., Dec. 1987, at 1.

(d)   Any charge for landlord's income taxes, excess profit taxes, franchise taxes, or similar taxes on landlord's business;

(e)   All costs relating to activities for the solicitation and execution of leases of space in the building;

(f)   All costs and expenses of operating the garage space and commercial space in the building;

(g)   All costs for which tenant or any other tenant in the building is being charged other than pursuant to [the operating expense] clause;

(h)   The cost of any electric current furnished to the premises or any rentable area of the building for purposes other than the operation of building equipment and machinery and the lighting of public toilets, stairways, shaftways, and building machinery or fan rooms;

(i)   The cost of correcting defects in the construction of the building or in the building equipment, except that conditions (not occasioned by construction defects) resulting from ordinary wear and tear will not be deemed defects for the purpose of this category;

(j)   The cost of any repair made by landlord because of the total or partial destruction of the building or the condemnation of a portion of the building;

(k)   Any insurance premium to the extent that landlord is entitled to be reimbursed for it by tenant pursuant to this lease or by any tenant of the building pursuant to a similar lease other than pursuant to clauses comparable to this [paragraph];

(l)   The cost of any items for which landlord is reimbursed by insurance or otherwise compensated by parties other than tenants of the building pursuant to clauses similar to this [paragraph];

(m)   The cost of any additions or capital improvements to the building subsequent to the date of original construction;

(n)   The cost of any repairs, alterations, additions, changes, replacements, and other items that under generally accepted accounting principles are properly classified as capital expenditures to the extent they upgrade or improve the building;

(o)   Any operating expense representing an amount paid to a related corporation, entity, or person that is in excess of the amount that would be paid in the absence of such relationship;

(p)   The cost of tools and equipment used initially in the construction, operation, repair, and maintenance of the building;

(q)   The cost of any work or service performed for or facilities furnished to any tenant of the building to a greater extent or in a manner more favorable to such tenant than that performed for or furnished to tenant;

(r)   The cost of alterations of space in the building leased to other tenants;

(s)   The cost of overtime or other expense to landlord during its defaults or performing work expressly provided in this lease to be borne at landlord's expense;[41] and

(t)   Amounts paid (including interest and penalties) in order to comply with or cure violations of statutes, laws, notes, or ordinances by landlord or any part of the building.

---

[41] Strum & Kuklin, *Commercial Leases and the Inflationary Economy,* in ABA Section of Real Prop., Prob. & Tr. Law, Financing Real Estate During the Inflationary 80's, 411 (B.J. Strum ed. 1981).

Some tenants—particularly in California—ask that an increase in real estate taxes arising out of a sale of the building be excluded from operating expenses; these increases may arise from reassessments prompted by the recording of a deed indicating a sales price in excess of the prevailing assessment. If the landlord accedes to the tenant's request, the landlord will absorb the increase—or at least that tenant's share of it. This presents a risk to the landlord and to any prospective buyer of the building; of course, their lenders are also at risk. Since property is sold from time to time and assessments often increase, landlords know they have a real risk with this concession. As a result, if they must give it, they agree to exclude either any increase arising out of a sale consummated within, for example, three years after execution of the lease or only the first increase during the term (leaving open the possibility of subsequent sales that would not involve a limitation on tenant's obligation to pay its share of real estate taxes).

§ 6.12 "Grossing Up" Operating Expenses

A gross up provision is used in order to avoid an inadvertent distortion of the responsibility for operating expenses: if a building is less than substantially occupied by tenants, but operating expenses are allocated among tenants on the basis of their rentable areas as a percentage of the total rentable area in the building, then the bulk of the expenses will fall upon the landlord despite the intention of both landlord and tenants that all costs be borne by the tenants. An example illustrates the problem.

If a building is fully occupied and it is the intention of a landlord and its tenants that the tenants pay all of the operating expenses, then a tenant that occupies 10 percent of the building will pay 10 percent of the operating expenses. If only half of the building is occupied, but the tenants in occupancy pay their shares in a similar fashion, then 50 percent of the operating expenses will be paid by the tenants in occupancy and 50 percent of the operating expenses will be paid by the landlord. This is contrary to the intention of the landlord and tenant. In order to avoid this unintentional misallocation, one of two tacks can be taken. Each tenant could pay on the basis of its rentable share as a percentage of the occupied space; in that event, the hypothetical tenant would pay 20 percent of the operating expenses (10 percent divided by 50 percent = 20 percent). The other tack would be to double the expenses to assume full occupancy and then give the tenant its 10 percent share on the basis of full occupancy. The economic consequence to the landlord and its tenants is identical in either approach.

In practice, a variation of this second approach is used. Because pro forma building operations are usually predicated on the basis of 90 percent to 95 percent occupancy, and because there are economies of scale that reduce the unit cost of operating expenses as the number of units increases, operating expenses are commonly "grossed up" to an assumed occupancy of 90 percent to 95 percent of the building and allocated on the basis of the proportion that each tenant's space bears to the entire rentable space on the building.

Another illustration may be helpful. Consider a tenant that occupies one floor of a 10-floor building pursuant to a lease that requires the tenant to pay its share of operating expenses based upon the proportion of the tenant's space to the total space of the building. If the tenant is the sole occupant of the building and a landlord provides janitorial service at a cost of $100 (which the landlord is entitled to recover in operating costs), tenant will get $100 worth of janitorial services and will pay $10 for them. In order to avoid this result, a gross up provision is used. The janitorial service's operating expense is increased to $1,000; the tenant's cost is $100 instead of $10. That $100 cost is fair, because the tenant is the only user of the janitorial service. Of course, if the per floor cost of the janitorial service were to decline as the number of floors served increased, then the tenant would have a slight advantage from the gross up provision.

A gross up provision provides:

FORM 6-9
OPERATING EXPENSES—"GROSSING UP"

The operating expenses that vary with occupancy and that are attributable to any part of the term in which less than 95% of the rentable area of the building is occupied by tenants will be adjusted by landlord to the amount that landlord reasonably believes they would have been if 95% of the rentable area of the building had been occupied.

Needless to say, grossing up is applicable only to variable expenses, that is, those that vary with occupancy; it is entirely inappropriate to gross up the cost of the first-floor security guard, since it is unaffected by occupancy.

As the examples in this section illustrate, the gross up provision does not allow the landlord to recover imaginary costs and thus enjoy a windfall; it recovers the same costs it paid but the tenants pay for what they received. Some real estate professionals insist that costs will not be grossed up so as to allow the landlord to recover any amounts in excess of its costs.

The gross up provision is particularly important to the tenant that is paying operating expenses on the basis of a base year. If the base year is artificially low because the building is not fully occupied, then the tenant will bear the brunt of increased occupancy because it will pay the cost in excess of the artificially low base year.

Finally, the gross up provision is helpful not only at the outset of a lease but also during a lease. If a large tenant leaves the building, for example, the same distortions can occur.[42]

---

[42] Gilson, *'Grossing Up' Operating Costs—It's Only Fair,* Wash. Law., Sept./Oct. 1987, at 16.

§ 6.13 Comparing Several Office Leases

The many ways in which office leases may be written complicate any comparison of different leases.[43] As § **4.13** has shown, the distinction between rentable area and usable area (not to mention useful area) underlies any comparison based strictly on rentable area or usable area. As § **5.7** illustrates, the cost of initial improvements to the premises is not based merely on dollars and areas. In addition, operating costs can be passed on to a tenant in many different ways.

This section presents a three-part analysis of three different lease proposals in **Table 6-1**.[44] In order to arrive at a meaningful comparison of the different economic consequences of these leases, Part I sets forth the economic terms of the lease. Part II extends these economic terms into cash flows at the inception of the leases, at the end of each of five years of the leases, and in total at the end of the leases. Part III summarizes the economic terms and arrives at a basis for comparison. A painstaking study of this analysis is a worthwhile conclusion to the real estate professional's consideration of office building rent. The analysis in **Table 6-1** shows the real cost of a lease. It also has some surprises.

Table 6-1

Part 1

		NEW LEASE "A"	NEW LEASE "B"	NEW LEASE "C"
1.	RENT RATES & AREA			
2.	Usable area (USF[a] required)	5,100	4,850	5,000
3.	Rentable/Usable ratio	1.07	1.14	1.11
4.	Gross rent rate ($/RSF[b]/Yr)	25.00	22.75	17.00
5.	Net rent escalation (annual rate)	0	0	15%
6.	Deposit required ($)	0	0	7,100
7.	TENANT FINISH COSTS			
8.	Standard allowance ($/USF)	8.00	10.00	0.00
9.	Upgrade allowance ($/USF)	0.00	0.00	0.00
10.	Estimated actual finish costs ($/USF)	18.00	18.00	18.00

---

[43] *See* Bellows, *A Real Estate Leasing Analysis,* Legal Econ., Sept./Oct. 1985, at 57 (shorter form of analysis in this section).

[44] For a similar analysis, see Powell, *Give Tenants the Lease Analysis They Need,* Com. Real Est. Inv. J., Winter 1986, at 32.

RENT

Table 6-1 *(continued)*

	NEW LEASE "A"	NEW LEASE "B"	NEW LEASE "C"
11. OPERATING COSTS			
12. Expense stop ($/RSF/Yr)	4.75	5.80	5.75
13a. Estimated actual expenses: Year 1 ($/RSF)	4.00	4.00	4.00
13b. Estimated actual expenses: Year 2 ($/RSF)	4.25	4.25	4.25
13c. Estimated actual expenses: Year 3 ($/RSF)	5.00	5.00	5.00
13d. Estimated actual expenses: Year 4 ($/RSF)	5.25	5.25	5.25
13e. Estimated actual expenses: Year 5 ($/RSF)	6.00	6.00	6.00
14. CASH INCENTIVES			
15a. No. months free rent: Gross	12	0	0
15b. No. months free rent: Net	0	24	0
16. No. months buyout of existing lease	3	0	0
17. Moving allowance ($)	10,000	0	0
18. Cash incentive to lease ($)	120,000	0	250,000
19. MISCELLANEOUS			
20. Moving expense ($)	10,000	10,000	10,000
21. Storage area:			
21a. area required (RSF)	100	120	120
21b. rent rate ($/SF/Yr)	7.00	5.00	5.00
22. Parking places:			
22a. number required	4	4	4
22b. monthly rate ($/Mo)	60.00	100.00	0.00
23. Other annual cost ($/Yr)	0.00	0.00	0.00

[a] Usable square feet

[b] Rentable square foot

Lines 2-3 relate to the discussions in §§ **4.11** and **4.12**. Throughout this analysis, the real estate professional must be careful to distinguish USF from RSF.

Line 4 is the full service (sometimes known as gross) cost of the lease.

Lines 5-6 show that the new lease "C" is the only one of the leases that has an escalation of the net rent (the gross rent rate minus the expense stop in line 12) and it is the only lease that requires a deposit.

Table 6-1 (*continued*)

Part 2

NEW LEASE "A" ANALYSIS	INCEPTION	YEAR 1	YEAR 2	YEAR 3	YEAR 4	YEAR 5	TOTAL
24. Months gross free rent		12	0	0	0	0	12
25. Months net free rent		0	0	0	0	0	0
26. Months existing lease less buyout		3	0	0	0	0	3
27. Net lease rate ($/RSF)		20.25	20.25	20.25	20.25	20.25	
28. Gross lease rate ($/RSF)		25.00	25.00	25.25	25.50	26.25	
29. *Cash flows*							
30a. Gross rent - New lease (less free rent)($)		0	136,425	137,789	139,154	143,246	556,614
30b. Gross rent - Old lease (less buyout)($)		43,313	29,250	0	0	0	72,563
31. Storage, parking & other annual costs ($)		3,580	3,580	3,580	3,580	3,580	17,900
32. Tenant finish costs ($)	51,000[c]						
33. Moving cost less reimbursement ($)		0					0
34. Deposit ($)		0					0
35. Cash incentive to lease ($)	−120,000[d]						0
36. Total cash flows ($)	−69,000	46,893	169,255	141,369	142,734	146,826	647,077

[c] This is USF (5,100) multiplied by $10, which is the difference between estimated actual finish cost in line 10 ($18) and the landlord's standard allowance in line 8 ($8).

[d] See line 18.

Table 6-1 *(continued)*

NEW LEASE "B" ANALYSIS	INCEPTION	YEAR 1	YEAR 2	YEAR 3	YEAR 4	YEAR 5	TOTAL
37. Months gross free rent		0	0	0	0	0	0
38. Months net free rent		12	12	0	0	0	24
39. Months existing lease less buyout							0
40. Net lease rate ($/RSF)		16.95	16.95	16.95	16.95	16.95	0
41. Gross lease rate ($/RSF)		22.75	22.75	22.75	22.75	22.95	
42. *Cash flows*							
43a. Gross rent - New lease (less free rent) ($)		32,068	32,068	125,785	125,785	126,891	442,596
43b. Gross rent - Old lease (less buyout) ($)		57,750	29,250	0	0	0	87,000
44. Storage, parking & other annual costs ($)		1,000	1,000	1,000	1,000	1,000	5,000
45. Tenant finish costs ($)	38,800						38,800
46. Moving costs less reimbursement ($)	10,000						10,000
47. Deposit ($)	0						
48. Cash incentive to lease ($)	0						
49. Total cash flows ($)	48,800	90,818	62,318	126,785	126,785	127,891	583,396

	Item	Yr 0	Yr 1	Yr 2	Yr 3	Yr 4	Yr 5	Total
50.	Months gross free rent	0	0	0	0	0	0	
51.	Months net free rent	0	0	0	0	0	0	
52.	Months existing lease less buyout	0	0	0	0	0	0	
53.	Net lease rate ($/RSF)	0	11.25	12.95	14.88	17.11	19.68	
54.	Gross Lease Rate ($/RSF)	0	17.00	18.69	20.63	22.86	25.68	
55.	*Cash flows*							
56a.	Gross rent - New lease (less free rent) ($)		94,350	103,716	114,486	126,872	142,504	581,928
56b.	Gross rent - old lease (less buyout) ($)		57,750	29,250	0	0	0	87,000
57.	Storage, parking & other annual costs ($)		600	600	600	600	600	3,000
58.	Tenant finish costs ($)	90,000						90,000
59.	Moving costs less reimbursement ($)	10,000						10,000
60.	Deposit ($)	7,100						7,100
61.	Cash incentive to lease ($)	−250,000						−250,000
62.	Total cash flows ($)	−142,900	152,700	133,566	115,086	127,472	143,104	529,028

Table 6-1 *(continued)*

Part 3

CASH FLOWS (in dollars)	NEW LEASE "A"	NEW LEASE "B"	NEW LEASE "C"
63. Inception	−69,000	48,800	−142,900
64. Year 1	46,893	90,818	152,700
65. Year 2	169,255	62,318	133,566
66. Year 3	141,369	126,785	115,086
67. Year 4	142,734	126,785	127,472
68. Year 5	146,826	127,891	143,104
69. Total cash flows	647,077	583,397	529,028
70. Arithmetic rate per usable square foot	25.38	24.06	21.16
Discounted cash flow			
71. 10%	371,254	403,751	335,173
72. 12%	341,468	377,636	307,183
73. 14%	314,524	353,932	281,841
Present value rate per usable square foot			
74. 10%	14.56	16.65	13.41
75. 12%	13.39	15.57	12.29
76. 14%	12.33	14.60	11.27

Lines 8-10 show the tenant's cost ($18/USF) and the tenant allowances for tenant finish costs. These costs will be incurred in the amount by which the tenant's estimated actual finish costs exceed the standard allowance that will have been paid by the tenant at the inception of the lease as shown on lines 32, 45, and 58.

Line 12 is the expense stop, or landlord's contribution to operating costs.

Lines 13(a)-13(e) are the tenant's estimate of actual operating expenses. In this analysis, all of the buildings will have the same estimated actual expenses.

Lines 15(a)-15(b) show that new lease "A" completely abates rent for the first year while new lease "B" abates the net rent but not the expense stop. As a result, line 43(a) shows charges of $32,068 for each of the first two years (5529 RSF x $5.80/RSF).

Line 16 shows that new lease "A" will pay three months of the rent required under the tenant's existing lease. This incentive is reflected on line 30(b) in which the tenant's cost under its old lease is one-quarter (3 months) of the year less than its costs in lines 43(b) and 56(b).

Line 18 shows cash payments paid to the tenant in connection with new lease "A" and new lease "B."

Lines 20-23 show several lesser costs that would be incurred by the tenant in connection with moving and maintaining the lease. The moving cost is $10,000 in every case and will be paid at the inception of the lease. The other incidental costs are shown on lines 31, 44, and 57.

Part 2 is an extension of the amounts shown in Part 1 and a spreading of those amounts over the terms of the respective years.

Lines 32-35, 45-48, and 58-61 all show costs that will have been paid by the tenant before the lease begins. Note that new lease "A" and new lease "C" are both negative numbers, indicating that the tenant will put money in its pocket before the lease begins. The fact that it does so leads to the conclusion that new lease "B" is more expensive than the other leases, even though new lease "B" is less expensive than the other leases during the term of the lease. As shown by comparing the totals in lines 36, 49, and 62, without discounting, new lease "A" is most expensive despite the tenant's initial cash in hand at the inception of the lease. However, when the cash flows are discounted in Part 3, new lease "B" emerges as most expensive.

Lines 27, 40, and 53 are the gross rent rates from line 4 minus the expense stops from line 12. Note in line 41 that a new lease "B" has an unchanging rent rate until the fifth year, when estimated actual expenses exceed the expense ($5.80). Note that line 53 is escalated at the rate of 15 percent per year as shown in line 5.

Lines 30(b), 43(b), and 56(b) all show a $29,250 charge to the tenant in the second year. This results from one-half of the year's rent ($18/RSF/year $\times$ 3,000 RSF $\div$ 2 = $27,000) plus one-half of the amount by which estimated annual expenses ($4.25 RSF) exceed the expense stops ($2.75/RSF) for 3,000 feet (($4.25 − $2.75) $\times$ 3,000 $\div$ 2 = $2,250).

Part 3 summarizes the totals from lines 36, 49, and 62, and then derives the rental rate per usable square foot by dividing the total cash flows by 5 (the term) and then the number of usable feet in the new leases.

Lines 71-73 reduce the total cash flows to their present value by three different assumptions about the return on invested capital; for example, if the tenant assumes that its invested capital grows at 12 percent annually, then new lease "B" would cost it $377,636, because the tenant would have to invest that amount of money at 12 percent per annum in order to yield its total obligation of $583,397 in five years. Lines 74-76 express arithmetic rate per usable square foot at present value by dividing the corresponding values in lines 71-73 by the respective areas of the premises. The surprising conclusion is that new lease "A," which has the highest gross rent rate and the highest USF, is not the most expensive lease. To the contrary, the lease with the lowest USF and an average gross rent rate turns out to be the most expensive lease.

§ 6.14   Operating Expenses in Shopping Centers

Shopping center tenants pay for the operating expenses of their centers according to several separate provisions of the lease. These include the common area maintenance provision (§ **17.6**), the utilities provision (§ **8.2**), and the real estate tax provision (§ **7.4**). The common area maintenance provision may, like the office building operating expense provision, be divided into several component provisions. In computing its occupancy costs, the shopping center tenant must also consider the cost of the merchants association, described in **Chapter 15**.

§ 6.15   Operating Expenses in Single Tenant Leases

Leases of single tenant premises—net or long-term leases—do not have provisions entitled "Operating Expenses," but rather pass on operating expenses to the tenant by virtue of several distinct paragraphs: real estate taxes, repairs and maintenance, insurance, and utilities. These leases often make a general statement that the landlord's rent is supposed to be paid "net" of any operating expenses. Such a provision may be:

FORM 6-10
OPERATING EXPENSES—"NET" RENT PAYMENTS

The rent will be a net rental payment. All costs of maintenance, repairs, utilities, taxes, insurance, and any and all other expenses necessary in connection with the operation or maintenance of the premises will be paid solely by tenant during this lease.

As a general statement of the intentions of the landlord and tenant, this provision is unobjectionable. However, it is not an adequate substitute for a thorough explanation of the tenant's obligations for each of these costs.

§ 6.16   An Approach to Percentage Rent

The practice of requiring the payment of percentage rent in addition to, or in lieu of, a minimum rent came into currency after the Depression, some say, because tenants sought to avoid the crushing effects of fixed rent in slow periods.[45] Landlords obliged by setting the fixed rent at 70 to 80 percent of fair market rentals and hoping that the balance (and more) would be realized through the percentage rent. Percentage rent is sometimes characterized (and perhaps justified) as a bonus paid in recognition of the valuable location of the shopping center.[46]

A percentage rent provision is usually buttressed by related provisions in a retail lease. Those provisions are an express covenant of continuous operation (§ **10.10**), a prescribed manner of doing business (§ **10.12**), restrictions on assignments or subleases (§ **12.7**), and a radius provision (§ **10.13**). Together these provisions are intended to assure the landlord of percentage rent.[47]

Percentage rent may be calculated in any one of several ways.[48] The most common are:

1. A specific percentage of gross sales as rental, with a guaranteed minimum rent

2. A specific percentage of gross sales as rental, with no guaranteed minimum

---

[45] *See* Halper, *Can You Find a Fair Lease?*, 14 Real Est. L.J. 99 (1985) (a flavor of the era).

[46] Various theories about the origins of percentage rent abound. *See* Note, *The Percentage Lease- Its Function and Drafting Problems*, 61 Harv. L. Rev. 317 (1948); Van Doren, *Some Suggestions for the Drafting of Long Term Net and Percentage Leases*, 51 Colum. L. Rev. 186 (1951). *See generally* N. Hecht, Long Term Lease Planning and Drafting 77-98 (1974); Schloss, *Inflation-Proofing Retail Investments*, 7 Real Est. Rev. 36 (1978); Schloss, *How Inflation-Proof Are Those Percentage Leases?*, 11 Real Est. Rev. 99 (Fall 1981); Blair, *Are Percentage Rents Unfair to Tenants?*, 7 Real Est. Rev. 42 (1978) (economics of percentage rent from landlords' and tenants' perspectives).

[47] Cohen, *Advice for Landlords and Tenants on Percentage Rent,* Prac. Real Est. Law., Nov. 1989, at 13, has a very helpful discussion of percentage rent. *See* Thigpen, *Good Faith Performance Under Percentage Leases,* 51 Miss. L.J. 315 (1980-81) (concluding than an implied covenant of good faith performance is not always employed in resolving disputes under percentage rent leases).

[48] *See generally* Annot., 58 A.L.R.3d 384, *Calculation of rental under commercial percentage lease* (1974).

3. As set forth in item 2, but with a minimum established after a fixed period of time and based upon a percentage of the average rental developed during the "no minimum period"

4. A specific fixed rent that provides for additional rental based upon a percentage of gross sales over a given amount of sales

5. A percentage of profits.[49]

Considering the ways in which sales can be manipulated, as discussed in § **6.23**, some landlords have thought about requiring a percentage of their tenants' cost of goods; these landlords feel that a tenant has no reason to understate its cost of goods, although it does have reasons (income taxes and percentage rent) to understate sales. Net profits are an extremely poor basis for percentage rent.[50]

Among these, by far, the most common method is the third. For example, a lease may provide that the tenant will pay "an amount by which 6% of gross sales exceeds minimum rent." Disregard for the moment any ineptitude in the expression, and assume that the minimum rent is $50,000. The tenant knows that it will have no obligation for percentage rent unless its sales exceed $833,333, because it is only at that level of sales that 6 percent exceeds the minimum rent. The sales volume required to trigger percentage rent obligation is often called the *breakpoint*. In formulaic terms,

percentage rate × breakpoint = annual rent.

Although a tenant's breakpoint is usually equal to its annual minimum rent divided by its percentage, there is no immutable rule that it must be. In fact, the percentage rent provision may be written without regard to the minimum rent, as, for example, "tenant will pay (a) minimum rent of $10,000, and (b) percentage rent in an amount by which 3% of gross sales exceeds $75,000." In that case, the breakpoint is $2,500,000, the minimum rent is $10,000, and the two are unrelated. Some landlords try to reduce the breakpoint by the proportion of the premises devoted to office, storage, and other uses that do not produce revenue. If ten percent of the premises in this example were "nonproductive," the breakpoint would be $2,250,000. This approach is based on the unfounded assumption that those uses are not productive.

Reference to a fixed amount can lead to an error. If the landlord proposes minimum annual rent of $50,000 and a percentage of 6 percent, the tenant may say "Let's make it simple. Since my breakpoint is $833,333, let's just say 6 percent of gross sales in excess of $833,333 in any year." By eliminating the reference to minimum rent, the tenant may have succeeded in avoiding percentage rent in partial years in which it sells at the rate of more than $833,333 but less than a full year elapses. The same distortion will occur if the tenant operates for less than a full year as a result of interruptions by casualty damage or condemnation.

---

49 McMichael, Leases—Percentage, Short and Long Term 21 (5th ed. 1959).

50 Caeli Assoc. v. Firestone Tire & Rubber Co., 226 Neb. 752, 415 N.W.2d 116 (1987), illustrates the hapless plight of the disappointed landlord.

In any event, the breakpoint is a deceptive notion, because, as § **6.20** illustrates, percentage rent may be due on a considerably lower volume of sales.

When (as is usually the case) a tenant pays a percentage of gross sales to the extent that the percentage exceeds "minimum rent," the landlord must be careful that the "minimum rent" is only the base rent and that it does not include additional amounts payable as rent (such as the tenant's share of common area maintenance, real estate taxes, and insurance). This error is made when the defined term rent is used to mean all amounts payable under the lease (except percentage rent) and percentage rent is defined, for example, as "the amount by which 6% of gross sales exceeds rent payable." Of course, tenants will not correct this error in their favor. In fact, when the provision is correctly stated, tenant may ask that percentage rent be payable against all amounts payable under the lease. In this way, tenants' lease costs are credited against their percentage rent obligation.

A tenant who renews a lease that has stepped up rent in the renewal term must pay on the basis of the breakpoint in the original term, unless the lease makes other provisions for the renewal term.[51] Tenant's real estate professional must be sure that the breakpoint is adjusted for increased minimum rent in renewal terms. In periods of rent abatement, landlords may insist on a zero base for gross sales so that some percentage rent might be generated despite the abated minimum rent. Tenants respond that minimum rent and percentage rent should be stated.

The percentage rent provision is composed of six essential components:

1. A definition of gross sales, in which the landlord will endeavor to state as broad a definition as possible and the tenant will try to set forth a restrictive scope

2. A statement of exclusions from gross sales, in which the landlord will be stingy and the tenant will be generous

3. A percentage

4. A computation and payment period

5. A method of recordkeeping by the tenant

6. A method of verification by the landlord.

§ 6.17   Definition of Gross Sales

In its effort to define gross sales as broadly as possible, the landlord should be certain to include (without limitation) revenues from services, sales, or rentals made:

---

[51] Kay-Bee Toy & Hobby Shops, Inc. v. Pyramid Co. of Plattsburgh, 126 A.D.2d 703, 511 N.Y.S.2d 308 (1987).

1. By the tenant, or
2. by any licensee, subtenant, assignee, concessionaire, vending machine or other occupant of the premises or part of the premises,
3. for cash, credit, exchange, or other value,
4. whether or not collected or collectible,
5. in,
6. from,
7. on, or
8. through
9. the premises,
10. including orders made by telephone or mail order,
11. whether or not filled or delivered at the premises, and
12. sales made off the premises but delivered or filled at the premises,
13. at retail or wholesale.

FORM 6-11
PERCENTAGE RENT—DEFINITION OF GROSS SALES

"Gross sales" means the actual sales or rental price of all goods, wares, and merchandise sold, leased, licensed, or delivered, and the actual charges for all services performed by the tenant or by any subtenant, licensee, or concessionaire in, at, from, or arising out of the use of the premises, wholesale and retail, whether for cash, credit, exchange, or otherwise, without reserve or deduction for inability or failure to collect. Gross sales will include without limitation, sales, rentals, and services (a) when the orders for them originate in, at, from, or arising out of the use of the premises, whether delivery or performance is made from the premises or from some other place, (b) made or performed by mail, telephone, or telegraph orders, (c) made or performed by means of mechanical or other vending devices in the premises, (d) that tenant or any subtenant, licensee, concessionaire, or other person in the normal and customary course of its business would credit or attribute to its operations in any part of the premises. Any deposit that is not refunded will be included in gross sales. Each installment sale or credit sale will be treated as a sale for the full price in the month during which the sale is made, regardless of whether or when tenant receives payment for it. Gross sales will not be reduced by any franchise, occupancy, capital stock, income, or similar tax based on income or profits.

This broad definition of gross sales is the battleground on which the landlord and tenant will meet in § **6.18** when exclusions and deductions from percentage rent are discussed. Before leaving the definition, some famous areas of its inequity should be observed.

If a tenant is forced to divide the proceeds of its sales with someone—as is the case in consignment sales or telegraphic sales of flowers—the tenant bears an unfair burden of the percentage rent attributable to the sales. For example, if the tenant sells consigned goods for $100, and is obligated to pay 5 percent of gross sales in percentage rent, and is also obligated to pay the consignor 50 percent of the sales price of those goods, the tenant will pay $5 percentage rent on what is actually a $50 sale, not a $100 sale. The effective percentage is 10 percent.

The solution appears to be the exclusion of consignment sales from gross sales, but this answer is more apparent than real. If all consignment sales were excluded, the tenant might set up a related corporation that consigned all the goods the tenant sold, thus entirely avoiding percentage rent. A better conclusion allows consignment sales to be accounted for on the basis of the tenant's net sales (gross sale price less the amount paid to the consignor), but sets a maximum percentage of gross sales that may be made as consigned sales.

A similar problem arises with respect to sales of lottery tickets. Usually, the tenant-seller keeps a commission on lottery ticket sales and remits the balance to the state. If the entire sale is included, the tenant pays percentage rent on phantom revenue. An Illinois court ruled that the tenant was obligated to include only its commission in gross sales because the tenant was not entitled to the entire sales price.[52] However, a Michigan court held that the entire amount of a tenant's sales of traveler's checks is included in gross sales even though the tenant keeps only a commission, as in the sale of lottery tickets.[53]

Another problem with some definitions of gross sales is the treatment of trade-ins. If a portion of the sales price is paid in trade—such as a $1,000 mink coat against which $200 is allowed on the trade-in of an old one—the $1,000 purchase price is presumably included in gross sales. When the $200 trade-in is sold, should its sales price be included in the gross sales? If so, the tenant has paid on $200 twice. The solution seems to be to allow the subsequent sale of the trade-in to be excluded from gross sales.[54] Forfeited installment sales and repossessions present analytically similar problems: is the entire second sale to be included in gross sales, or is only the excess over the first sale to be included?

Tenants who factor their receivables or chattel paper should ask two questions:

1. Is the amount of the sale the face amount of the invoice or is it the amount received on sale?

2. If the discount transaction is made with recourse, what happens if the buyer demands repurchase?

A less well-known (but possibly more expensive) problem arises from the inclusion of a licensee's or subtenant's *sales* (which landlords prefer) as opposed to subtenant's *subrents* (which tenants prefer). Assume that a tenant who pays 6 percent of gross sales as percentage rent subleases a department for a monthly rent of $1,000 and no percentage rent. If the subtenant's sales are included in the

---

[52] Anest v. Bellino, 151 Ill. App. 3d 818, 503 N.E.2d 576, *appeal denied*, 114 Ill. 2d 543, 508 N.E.2d 725 (1987).

[53] McComb v. McComb, 9 Mich. App. 70, 155 N.W.2d 860 (1967).

[54] Comment: *Percentage Lease Agreement*, J. Washburn U. Topeka 121, 128 (1957).

tenant's sales, the tenant will pay percentage rent on its subtenant's sales.[55] In this example, if the subtenant's sales were $17,000 each month, the tenant could lose $20 per month in its subleases: $(\$17,000 \times 6\%) - \$1000 = -\$20$.[56] Obviously, if the subtenant's sales are included in the tenant's sales, a subtenant should be obligated to pay percentage rent comparable to the tenant's percentage rent. If the subtenant's sales are not included in the tenant's gross sales, its rent should still be included. A landlord may insist that it be paid percentage rent on the subleased part of the premises at least equal to the rate of percentage rent paid by tenant on the rest of the premises; in other words, the landlord should not lose percentage rent it would have had if the tenant had used the subleased part of the premises.

When a tenant uses discount coupons an analogous question arises: Do gross sales include the price of goods sold before or after reduction for the face value of the coupon? If the full price is included, the tenant pays percentage rent on revenue it never receives, and the landlord presumably also benefits from the increased sales that discount promotions are intended to assure. A Connecticut court ruled that only the net amount should be included in gross sales.[57] The landlord's failure to include wholesale sales has hurt a Florida landlord whose tenant operated a wholesale sales operation from part of its retail premises,[58] as well as a Kansas landlord whose tenant sold goods to affiliates at a 25% discount, relying on "inter-store transfers" exclusion, although the court held the discounted sales were not retail sales for purposes of computing percentage rent.[59]

The professional tenant (doctor, lawyer, accountant, or dentist, for example) must satisfy itself that the payment of a percentage of its fees is not a prohibited "fee splitting" arrangement. For example, a New York dentist's payment of 20 percent of his gross revenues for his use and occupancy of a fully equipped dental facility did violate several canons of professional conduct.[60] Informal inquiries put to the American Medical Association and American Dental Association lead to the conclusion that a shopping center lease with percentage rent but no appearance of payment for referrals would be acceptable. The American Bar Association[61] believes that percentage lease agreements are proscribed sharings

---

[55] *See* Flowers v. Wrights, Inc., 199 Utah 378, 227 P.2d 768 (1951) (subtenant's rent, not sales, are included in tenant's gross sales, unless lease provides otherwise).

[56] *See* G.R. Kinney v. White, 48 So. 2d 733 (Fla. 1950).

[57] Papa Gino's of Am., Inc. v. Brodmanor Assocs., 5 Conn. App. 532, 500 A.2d 1341 (1985).

[58] Spiegel v. Stanley Nelson, Inc., 458 So. 2d 1175 (Fla. App. 1984), *review denied,* 471 So. 2d 44 (Fla. 1985).

[59] Fairlawn Plaza Dev., Inc. v. Fleming Co., 210 Kan. 459, 502 P.2d 663 (1972). *But see* Michigan Ave. Nat. Bank of Chicago v. Evans, Inc., 176 Ill. App. 3d 1047, 531 N.E.2d 872 (1988), *appeal denied,* 125 Ill. 2d 567, 537 N.E.2d 811 (1989) (use provision "primarily retail" left open possibility of wholesale sales that were thus included in gross sales).

[60] Sachs v. Saloshin, 138 A.D.2d 586, 526 N.Y.S.2d 168 (1988). For a case involving a physician, see People v. Angelakos, 70 N.Y.2d 670, 512 N.E.2d 305, 518 N.Y.S.2d 784 (1987). *See also* Baliotti v. Walkes, 115 A.D.2d 581, 496 N.Y.S.2d 242 (1985), *appeal dismissed,* 68 N.Y.2d 664, 496 N.E.2d 241, 505 N.Y.S.2d 1028 (1986). New York seems to have the bulk of the reported cases.

[61] ABA/BNA Lawyers Manual on Professional Conduct.

of legal fees with a nonlawyer. Local rules must be researched by a real estate professional representing a professional in a percentage rent arrangement.

Finally, landlords must examine the definition of gross sales in the light of each tenant's prospective use in order to be certain that all possibly significant sources of revenue are expressly included. Theater leases are famous examples because landlords (who never fail to include ticket sales in gross sales) routinely omit the far more substantial revenue from candy, popcorn, and other concessions.[62]

§ 6.18   Deductions and Exclusions from Gross Sales

In order to avoid a very common confusion in percentage rent provisions, the real estate professional must distinguish between deductions and exclusions. A deduction is an amount by which gross sales are reduced; the most frequent example of a deduction is sales tax. Sales tax is received by the tenant but paid out to the taxing authority. It is deducted from gross sales so that the tenant does not pay percentage rent on amounts that it does not keep. Exclusions are amounts that should never be, or never have been, included in gross sales: returns to shippers are exclusions because they have not been part of gross sales in the first place.[63] Amounts paid by Medi-Cal to a convalescent hospital and restricted to particular purposes are not gross sales, the court concluding that neither the landlord nor the tenant intended those revenues to be part of gross sales.[64]

The reason for the distinction is important. If a tenant is allowed to deduct from gross sales an amount that was not initially included in gross sales, the tenant will be able to reduce gross sales artificially. In the previous example, the tenant could have $1 million in gross sales (after deducting sales tax) and it could have a $100,000 return to shipper. If the return is deducted from gross sales, gross sales will be only $900,000. Put somewhat differently, nothing should be deducted from gross sales unless it has previously been included in gross sales.

Most percentage rent leases provide that some revenue will be deducted or excluded from gross sales. Common deductions and exclusions are:

1.   Exchanges of merchandise between tenant's stores when the exchange is made solely for the convenience of the tenant's operations and not for the purpose of consummating a sale made in, at, or from the premises, or for the purpose of depriving the landlord of the benefit of a sale that would otherwise have been made at the premises. This common exclusion is meant as an accommodation to the tenant that has more than one retail outlet, because interstore transfers are sometimes accounted as sales by

---

[62] Taft Realty Corp. v. Yorkhaven Enter., Inc., 146 Conn. 338, 150 A.2d 597 (1959); Gould v. Paramount Theatre Corp., 507 P.2d 1115 (Colo. Ct. App. 1973).

[63] *See generally* Landis, *Problems in Drafting Percentage Leases,* 36 B.U.L. Rev. 190, 200 (1956).

[64] Western Medical Enter., Inc. v. Albers, 166 Cal.3d 383, 212 Cal. Rptr. 434 (1985).

the transferor-store. If a tenant has more than one retail outlet, interstore transfers are likely.[65]

(When one outlet has no percentage rent or a more favorable percentage rent arrangement, interstore transfers are inevitable; the tenant will avoid percentage rent by delivering its goods at the store that has less or no percentage rent. At least one case has held that a percentage lease implies the tenant's obligation not to divert sales in order to avoid percentage rent;[66] when the tenant's motive is not simply to deprive the landlord of percentage rent, however, the courts are more lenient toward the tenant. This is particularly true when the tenant has a sound business reason to move a particular line of its goods to another location and the lease does not require sales of that product at the premises.[67] One court has ruled that the tenant was not required to include sales at another store (to which the tenant had moved its fur business), so long as it did not refer customers to the other store.[68] When a tenant takes readily accessible adjacent premises that are not subject to percentage rent, and manages both businesses from one location, the tenant is considered to be operating only one business and is liable for percentage rent on sales occurring in both locations.[69])

2. Returns to suppliers or manufacturers.

3. Cash or credit refunds to customers on transactions (such as trade-ins, exchanges, cancellations, allowances, deposit returns, discounts, and credits) previously included in gross sales, and only to the extent that they were included. Tenants should note that returns of Christmas sales will probably occur in the first part of the new year, but that percentage rent will have been paid on those sales when the previous year is closed out. To be sure, the tenant's gross sales in the next year will be reduced by those returns, but there will be a distortion of each year's percentage rent unless the tenant is allowed to reduce the prior year's gross sales by returns written the first 60 or 90 days of the new year.

4. Sales of trade fixtures, machinery, and equipment after their use in the tenant's business. These deductions are indirectly limited by the provision in § 10.12 that prohibits "going out of business sales" and are intended to assure that the tenant does not make a business of selling its

---

[65] *But see* Fairlawn Plaza Dev., Inc. v. Fleming Co., 210 Kan. 459, 502 P.2d 663 (1972) (sales excluded because they were not retail sales).

[66] Goldberg, 168-05 Corp. v. Levy, 256 A.D. 1086, 11 N.Y.S.2d 315 (1939).

[67] Wahlder v. Osborne, 410 So. 2d 808 (La. App. 1982), *writ denied,* 414 So. 2d 378 (La. 1982), (tenant moved its tire sales in order to protect them from theft); Stern v. Dunlap Co., 228 F.2d 939 (10th Cir. 1955) (tenant's better goods were moved to a new location; lease did not require those goods to be sold at premises).

[68] Mutual Life Ins. Co. of N.Y. v. Tailored Woman, Inc., 309 N.Y. 248, 128 N.E.2d 401 (1955).

[69] Cissna Loan Co. v. Baron, 149 Wash. 386, 270 P. 1022 (1928).

trade fixtures. Some leases exclude these sales only if the tenant promptly replaces the items that it has sold.

5. Amounts collected and paid by the tenant to any governmental agency for any sales or excise tax. Another way to state this is to allow deduction of taxes that are added to the selling price, separately stated, collected by the tenant from its customers, and delivered by the tenant to the taxing authority. This deduction should be carefully expressed so that no inference is made that the tenant may deduct income taxes, franchise taxes, or other taxes not levied on sales. Some landlords argue that excise taxes should not be excluded from gross sales, because excise taxes are often imposed on manufacturers and included in the purchase price; in contrast to sales taxes, excise taxes are not added to the purchase price and are not collected by landlord on behalf of a taxing authority to which they are remitted. Tenants prefer a general exclusion of "taxes on gross receipts whether or not characterized as sales taxes."

6. Sales to employees at a discount. Landlords sometimes allow deductions for "amounts of discounts on sales to employees." These penalize the landlord because a discounted sale is further reduced unless the employee paid the full price and got a separate rebate of the discount. Landlords are better off specifying a percentage of gross sales that may be so deducted.

7. Interest, financing charges, service charges, credit charges, and carrying charges received on credit sales, installment sales, and layaway sales. Interest charged by retailers is often offset by interest paid by retailers who borrow against their accounts. Along this line, some retailers are given the right to deduct the discounts that they pay to credit card companies.

8. Credits or payments in settlement of claimed losses.

9. Fire or casualty sales or (one-time) bulk sales when the tenant is going out of business.

10. Loss leader sales. The idea is that sales made at the tenant's cost or close to it should be deducted because there is little or no overhead and profit in the price. These deductions should be a limited percentage of gross sales.

11. Receipts incidental to the tenant's main business (such as receipts from vending machines, stamp machines, money orders, cigarette machines, public telephone, lottery tickets, and video games). Sometimes these are limited to sales to employees or to a percentage of gross sales. Emphasizing that these receipts are incidental to the tenant's business, courts have excluded some of them from gross sales.[70] The popularity of video games compels a landlord to be careful about general exclusions such as

---

[70] Herbert's Laurel-Ventura, Inc. v. Laurel-Ventura Holding Corp., 58 Cal. App. 2d 684, 138 P.2d 43 (1943).

"vending machine sales."[71] There is no compelling reason to allow the tenant to exclude its share of these sales even though one can support an argument that the entire sales price should not be included.

12. Amounts received for wrapping, delivery, or installation services. These minimal amounts are deducted because these services are usually provided at or below the tenant's cost.[72]

13. Service charges on items purchased from the premises.

14. The cost of trading stamps and similar promotional devices.

15. Goods given in exchange for trading stamps.

16. Revenues from subtenants or concessionaires whose purpose is to draw customers to the premises. This is directly contrary to the definition of gross sales and should be a limited exclusion if it is granted.

17. Punitive damages and trebled damages received in antitrust litigation. Most landlords would not think to include in gross sales any damages that a tenant receives in antitrust litigation; however, when the tenant is awarded damages for losses that it sustained as a result of anticompetitive practices, the landlord should be given its share of the same recovery, because it lost percentage rent. This exclusion takes for granted that the landlord can share in the basic award. The federal courts divide on the question of whether a landlord has standing to assert its own antitrust claim when anticompetitive practices have affected its percentage rent.[73]

18. Receipts of the tenant-operated cafeteria.

19. Mail order catalog sales. The theory is that the premises are irrelevant to these sales and that the landlord should not profit from them.

20. Gift certificates until redeemed at the premises. This deduction merely defers a gross sale. Gift certificates are included at their actual sales price, not their face amount. If gift certificate sales are included at the time of sale, then later redemptions are excluded up to the amount previously included in gross sales.

21. Losses or bad debts for credit sales (including tenant's credit cards), and unpaid balance of uncollectible layaway plans. These losses occur when a credit card customer claims that its purchase was defective and refuses to pay the credit card company; the credit card company then charges back the retailer whose accounts it has purchased. If the retailer offers its own credit system, the effect of nonpayment should be the same as a

---

[71] A South Carolina landlord lost percentage rents on video games because of such an exclusion. Moore v. Greenville Restaurants, 287 S.C. 295, 337 S.E.2d 892 (Ct. App. 1985).

[72] *See* Washington Nat'l Corp. v. Sears, Roebuck & Co., 474 N.E.2d 116 (Ind. Ct. App. 1985) (a lease in which these exclusions for gift wrapping, alterations, bicycle set-ups, auto labor, maintenance agreements, and appliance repair were approximately $85,000 in one year).

[73] Annot., 27 A.L.R.Fed. 866, *Standing of lessor under percentage of profits or gross receipts lease to sue for treble damages under 4 of Clayton Act (15 USCS 15) for antitrust violations decreasing profits or gross receipts* (1976).

return if the sale has been included in gross sales. If a customer defaults in payments on a layaway item and the tenant has included the full sale at the time the layaway began, the tenant must reduce its gross sales by the unpaid balance.

22. Certain deposits. Refundable deposits are usually excluded from gross sales until the sale is made. Nonrefundable deposits are part of gross sales when received.

23. Bulk sales. Sales of the tenant's entire stock in trade are usually excluded. In this context, the term bulk sales has a narrow and specific meaning; it is the kind of sale that is subject to Article 6 of the Uniform Commercial Code. It is not a wholesale sale made in bulk with the intention that the buyer will resell the goods item-by-item; if these "bulk sales" are excluded, the tenant may be able to avoid percentage rent on its wholesale business. Tenants should try for the exclusion of close-out sales at the end of a season, but landlords usually want these sales also.

A strong tenant will occasionally win the right to reduce its percentage rent obligation by the amount of any taxes, insurance, common area charges, and merchants association dues that it pays. From the tenant's standpoint, these amounts reduce percentage rent and not gross sales.

§ 6.19   How to Choose an Appropriate Percentage Rate

The shortest part of the percentage rent provision is the most important: the percentage. Traditionally, the percentage has been lowest for high volume/low profit-margin goods, such as food; conversely, the percentage has been highest for low volume/high profit-margin goods, such as jewelry. Another inverse rule-of- thumb relationship is between the tenant's floor area and its percentage rate.[74]

As tenants diversify their product lines, some real estate professionals believe that different percentages should be applied to different goods sold by the same tenant. For example, a supermarket that sells food and automobile accessories should pay at different rates for each of these product lines. Although super-markets insist that they cannot segregate their sales on a product-by-product basis, they can segregate food sales from nonfood sales.

A tenant who carries several classes of goods should insist on a percentage that recognizes the blend of its products. **Table 6-2** is a guide, not a rule.

§ 6.20   Computation and Payment Period

Another part of the percentage rent provision states the computation and payment period:

---

[74] Tucker, *Rent, Rent Records, Report and Audit,* in National Association of Realtors, Guide to Commercial Property Leasing 39 (1963).

FORM 6-12
PERCENTAGE RENT—COMPUTATION AND PAYMENT PERIOD

Tenant will pay landlord percentage rent in the amount by which 6% of tenant's gross sales during each year exceeds the minimum rent paid by tenant for such year. Beginning within ten (10) days after the month in which the term commences and continuing within ten (10) days after each month during the term, tenant will furnish landlord a statement of gross sales during the preceding month and tenant will pay landlord the amount by which 6% of gross sales during the preceding month exceeds the minimum rent paid for such month.

Table 6-2

COMPANY	Amusement Centers	Art Shops	Auto Accessories	Bakeries	Barber/Beauty Shops	Books and Stationery	Bowling Lanes	Bridal Shops	Candy
John P. Turman, Carter & Associates, ATLANTA, GA	15-20	6-8	—	8-10	6-8	6	—	6	8-10
Maryann Gilligan Rose, The Rouse Co., Inc., BOSTON, MA	—	—	—	7-8	1	2	—	—	10
Amiel J. Mokhiber, Jr., Maloney, Inc., CHICAGO, IL	10-15	6-8	3-4	6-8	6-8	5-7	—	6-8	8-10
Marvin S. Schwartz, Lewis & Fink, Inc., CLEVELAND, OH	10-15	8-10	3-5	6-10	8-10	5-8	9-10	6-8	8-10
Herbert D. Weitzman, Henry S. Miller Co., DALLAS, TX*	—	5-8	2-6	4-8	5-8	5-7	6-8	—	6-8
Thomas Young, Grubb & Ellis, DENVER, CO	—	6-8	4-6	6	6	5-6	—	6	6-8
J. McGregor Dodds, Reaume & Dodds, DETROIT, MI	—	6	3-5	4-6	6	5-6	—	—	5-6
Bruce H. Wood, Homart Development, HOUSTON, TX*	15	7-8	6	8	6	6	—	6	10
Kathy Lasco, Leo Eisenberg Co., KANSAS CITY, MO*	8-10	8	3-4	6	6-8	3-5	8	6	7-9
Brent F. Howell, Coldwell Banker, LOS ANGELES, CA	10	6-8	3-4	5-8	5-10	5-7	6-10	6-7	6-9
Lewis W. Stirling, III, Stirling Properties, NEW ORLEANS, LA	—	8-10	—	5-8	6-8	4-8	—	5-7	6-10
Charles Aug, Garrick-Aug Associates, NEW YORK, NY*	12-15	8-10	4	6-7	8-10	4-5	10	7	8-10
Michael Hirschfeld, The Hirschfeld Cos., NEW YORK, NY*	10-15	8-10	3-5	6-8	8	6	8-10	6	8
Ted deSwart, Strouse, Greenberg & Co., PHILADELPHIA, PA*	10	8-10	6	8	8	6	12-15	6-8	8-10
Albert Bullier, Jr., Bullier & Bullier, PORTLAND, OR	12-15	7-10	4-5	4-6	8-10	5-7	9-10	6	6-8
Karl D. Ehrlich, Richard Ellis Inc., SAN FRANCISCO, CA*	10-15	7-10	4-6	6-10	8	6-8	—	6-10	8-10

COMPANY	Electrical Appliances	Fabrics	Florists	Florists (Garden Supply)	Furniture	Furs	Garage (Storage)	Gas Stations cents per gallon	Gift Shops
John P. Turman — ATLANTA	—	6-10	7	6	4-8	—	—	—	—
Maryann Gilligan Rose — BOSTON	—	—	—	—	—	—	—	—	—
Amiel J. Mokhiber, Jr — CHICAGO	4-6	8-10	6-8	5-6	6-8	4-6	—	—	6-8
Marvin S. Schwartz — CLEVELAND	3-5	8-12	6-8	4-5	7-10	4-5	40-55	50-70	4-6
Herbert D. Weitzman — DALLAS	5-7	4-8	—	5-6	5-8	4-6	40-80	60-65	—
Thomas Young — DENVER	4-6	8-10	5-6	5-6	6-7	4-6	50-75	50-75	5-6
J. McGregor Dodds — DETROIT	4-6	5-8	—	5-6	6	6	50	50	—
Bruce H. Wood — HOUSTON	7	8-10	7	5-6	10	4-6	—	—	0
Kathy Lasco — KANSAS CITY	3	8-10	5-7	6	6-8	3-5	70-75	70-80	—
Brent F. Howell — LOS ANGELES	4-6	8-12	6	4-6	7-10	4-6	—	—	—
Lewis W. Stirling, III — NEW ORLEANS	5-8	8-10	6-8	4-6	8-10	—	50-75	50-75	6
Charles Aug — NEW YORK	5-6	12-15	4-5	5-6	5-6	5-6	50	50-60	7-8
Michael Hirschfeld — NEW YORK	7-8	8-10	7	6	8	5	50	60	8
Ted deSwart — PHILADELPHIA	6	10-15	6	5	8	3-5	—	—	6-8
Albert R. Bullier, Jr. — PORTLAND	6	10-12	5-7	5	7-10	4-6	40-55	60-75	—
Karl D. Ehrlich — SAN FRANCISCO	6-8	10	6-8	5-7	3-10	5	—	—	—

Leases frequently confuse *paid* and *payable*. If the tenant has not actually paid the minimum rent for the month, it should not be allowed to deduct the minimum rent payable (but unpaid) from its percentage rent obligation.

Although the provision seems harmless, it can result in the tenant paying more than the stated percentage of 6 percent of gross sales on an annual basis. **Table 6-3** illustrates the distortions from monthly, quarterly, and annual percentage rent payments.

The point is very simple: if the tenant is not allowed to make an annual recalculation of its percentage rent obligation, good months will not be averaged with poor months, and an overpayment can result.

Table 6-2 (*continued*)

Carpet Stores	Children's Clothing	Cocktail Lounge	Computer Stores	Copy Services	Deli Specialty Foods	Department Stores	Discount Stores	Drug Stores (Chain)	Drug Stores (Individual)	Drug Stores (Prescription)	Dry Cleaning & Laundry	Dry Cleaning & Laundry (Coin Operated)
—	5-6	—	2-4	6	6-8	1½-3	1-2	3½-4	5	—	—	—
—	1	—	—	—	30	—	—	—	—	—	—	—
3-4	5-6	7-10	4-5	8-10	6-8	1-3	0-2	1½-3	3-5	4-6	6-8	7-10
3-4	4-6	7-9	4-5	8-10	4-6	1-2½	½-2	1½-3	2-4	3-6	6-10	7-10
3	3-6	4-6	—	—	3-8	1-3	1-4	1-4	2-6	4-6	5-7	5-8
3-5	5-6	6-8	4-5	5-6	5-5	0	0-2	0-2	3-5	4-6	6-8	6-10
—	5-6	8-10	—	—	6-8	1-2½	1-3	2-4	2-6	4-6	4-6	—
6	6	8	3	7	6-10	2½	2	3	3	3	8	—
3-5	4-6	8-10	3	8	6-8	0	0-1	1-3	2-4	6-8	5-8	5-8
3-4	5-7	6-9	3	5	5-6	0-2	0-2	1-3	2-5	5-8	6-8	8-10
—	5-8	7-10	3-5	6-10	6-8	1-3	1-4	1-3	3-5	—	6-8	6-10
3-4	5-6	8-10	4-5	6-8	6-8	1½-3	1½-2	2-3	3-5	5	8	6
4	5-8	8-10	4-5	6-8	6-8	1½-3	1½-2	2-4	4-5	7-9	6-8	8-10
2-5	3-6	6-8	5-6	10	6	1-3	1-3	1-3	2-5	4-6	5	8-10
—	5-7	—	3-5	—	5	1-3	1½-2½	2-3	4-5	7-9	7-9	10
—	6-7	6-7	3-6	—	6-10	½-2	2-5	2-5	2-5	—	8-10	10

Photography	Pianos and Musical Instruments	Radio, Television, Hi-Fi	Record Shops	Restaurants	Restaurants (With Bar)	Shoe Repair	Sporting Goods	Tobacco/Cigars	Women's Dress Shops	Women's Furnishings	Women's Shoes	Variety Stores
4-8	4-5	2-5	6	6	5-6	10	3-5	6	5-6	6-8	6	—
4	—	—	—	10	32	2	—	1	40	6	3	18
5-7	4-7	3-6	5-7	5-8	5-8	8-10	4-6	6-10	4-6	5-7	5-7	3-5
7-10	4-6	3-5	5-7	4-6	5-7	8-10	4-6	8-10	5-6	5-7	4-6	3-4
6-8	5-7	3-6	4-7	4-6	4-6	8-10	3-6	—	2-5	4-7	5-7	3-4
5-6	4-6	3-5	5-6	5-10	5-10	6-8	3-5	—	3-5	4-7	6-7	1½-5
5-6	6	6	6	6	5-10	4-6	6	?-10	?	?	6	3-5
8-10	5	3	7-8	5-6	5-8	6-10	3-5	8	5	6-7	5-7	2-4
5-8	5	4	6	5-7	5-8	8	2-4	3	4-6	4-6	5-7	1-3
5-8	3-5	3-7	5-6	5-7	5-8	—	4-6	5	4-7	5-7	6-7	2-4
6-10	4-5	3-6	5-8	7-10	7-10	6-10	4-7	6-10	5-7	3-8	5-8	1-5
6	5	4-5	7-8	6-10	8-10	10	3-4	8-10	4-6	5-6	6-7	4-5
8	4-5	4-7	6	5-7	8-10	10	6-7	8	6	6	6	7
6	5	6	6	6	6	8	5-6	6	6	6	6	4-6
6-8	4-6	3-5	5-6	5-6	6-8	10	4-6	—	4-7	5-7	5-7	3-4
8-10	4-6	3-5	6-8	6-8	5-8	10	4-6	6-10	5-6	6-8	6-7	3-5

Table 6-2 (*continued*)

COMPANY	Men's Shoes (Volume)	Motion Picture Theaters	Nutrition Centers	Office Supply	Optical	Paint, Wallpaper Supplies	Parking Lots & Garages (Attendant)	Parking Lots & Garages (Non-Attendant)	Phone Stores
John P. Turman — ATLANTA	3-5	5	8	—	5-6	5-7	—	—	6-8
Maryann Gilligan Rost — BOSTON	—	—	4	—	8	—	—	—	40
Amiel J. Mokhiber, Jr. — CHICAGO	3-5	5-6	7-10	4-6	3-5	6-8	—	—	7-10
Marvin S. Schwartz — CLEVELAND	3-5	4-6	7-10	4-6	3-5	6-8	40-50	1-2	7-10
Herbert D. Weitzman — DALLAS	3-6	3-6	5-8	3-9	3-6	5-7	40-55	1½-2½	5-8
Thomas Young — DENVER	3-5	4-6	5-6	—	3-5	4-7	—	—	6-10
J. McGregor Dodds — DETROIT	4-6	3-5	5-6	—	3-6	6	50	1-1½	6
Bruce H. Wood — HOUSTON	5	5-6	8-10	8	6	6	—	—	8
Kathy Lasco — KANSAS CITY	2-4	4-6	6-8	2-4	2-4	6	70-75	1	6-8
Brent F. Howell — LOS ANGELES	3-6	5-6	6-10	—	3-5	4-6	—	0-1½	6-10
Lewis W. Stirling, III — NEW ORLEANS	3-5	4-6	6-10	5	3-6	6-8	—	0-2	7-10
Charles Aug — NEW YORK	4-5	5	9-10	6	4-5	7-8	45-50	1½	8-10
Michael Hirschfeld — NEW YORK	5	4-5	7-10	8	4	6	—	—	7
Ted deSwart — PHILADELPHIA	3-5	2-5	5-8	6	2-5	6-8	—	—	6-8
Albert R. Buller, Jr. — PORTLAND	3-5	5-6	7-10	5-6	3-5	6	40-55	—	7-10
Karl D. Ehrlich — SAN FRANCISCO	3-5	5-7	8-10	—	3-5	6-8	—	—	8-10

Percentage lease tables. *Current figures for these cities are unavailable, the above reflect 1989 rates. Copyright © 1990 by Buildings. Reprinted with permission from Buildings, The Facilities Construction & Management Magazine, January 1990.

The right to *recalculate* on an annual basis should not be confused with a right to *pay* on an annual basis. The landlord should not have to wait until the end of each year to receive its percentage rent; not only does the landlord lose the use of the money, but it also risks no payment if the tenant abandons the premises. On the other hand, the tenant should not be put to the trouble of calculating and paying percentage rent at the end of each month. Thus a quarterly payment period is popular. As a variation on these themes, some percentage leases provide that the averaging procedure will be done on a quarterly basis; thus, if percentage rent were paid for the first quarter and gross sales in the second quarter were so low that percentage rent was overpaid on a two-quarter basis, a credit would be due the tenant. This approach gives the landlord the benefit of interim payments while giving the tenant the benefit of interim averaging.

Another costly distortion occurs when the first computation period is less than a full year. This may occur as a result of the commencement and termination date or as the result of casualty damage that abates the rent. Consider the previous example as though the tenant's occupancy began on September 1. Then its sales and minimum rent would be:

	Sales	Minimum rent
September	10,000	400
October	10,000	400
November	10,000	400
December	15,000	400
	45,000	1,600

Table 6-2 (*continued*)

	Grocery Stores (Chain)	Grocery Stores (Conveni-ence)	Hardware	Hobby Shops, Toys	Hosiery and Knit Goods	Ice Cream Parlors	Jewelry (Costume)	Jewelry (Exclusive)	Leather Goods	Liquors and Wines	Meat Markets	Men's Clothing	Men's Stores
	1	—	—	6	8	8-10	8-10	6	6	—	—	5-6	5-6
	—	—	--	6	2	9	12	2	4	1	2	4	2
	1-1½	2-4	3-5	5-7	6-8	7-10	8-10	5-8	6-8	3-6	2-5	4-6	5-7
	½-1½	1-2½	3-5	4-6	7-10	6-8	8-10	6-8	6-8	—	2-4	4-6	5-7
	1-1½	1-3	2-5	5-6	5-8	—	6-8	4-7	6-8	4-6	2½-5	4-6	5-7
	1-1½	1-3	4-6	5-6	6-7	6-7	7-8	5-6	5 6	4-6	4-5	4-6	5-6
	1-2	—	4-6	5-6	6	—	5-6	6	6	—	3-4	4-6	5-6
	1½	2	3-5	6	6-8	8-10	10	6	6-8	5	5	6	5-6
	1	1-3	2-3	5-6	6	7	6-8	8-10	5	4-6	2-4	5	5
	1-1½	1-3	2½-6	5-10	7-10	6-10	6-10	6-10	6-8	3-6	2½-6	5-7	6-7
	1-2	1-3	2-6	6-8	8-10	10	8	8	6-8	2-5	—	4-8	6-8
	1-2½	2-4	3-4	6-7	6-8	8	8-10	6-8	6	3-6	5	5	5
	1½	2-3	3-5	6	6-8	8	8	5-6	7	4	4	6-10	6-10
	1-4	2-6	2-5	6	6	8	8-10	8	6-8	2-5	5-7	3-6	6
	1-1½	2-3	3½-5	6-8	5-7	6-8	8	5-7	6-8	—	2-4	4-6	6
	—	—	—	6-8	8-10	10	8-10	6-8	6-7	—	—	5-7	5-7

The percentage rent due for the period is $1,100: $2,700 (6% of $45,000) less $1600. This is more than the percentage rent which would have been paid for the entire year. The distortion arises because only the best months are considered (in which nearly one-half the sales occurred) and no offset is given for poorer months.

The problem can be avoided by making the computation periods run from September 1 to August 30, but this is an inconvenience for the landlord. A simple way is to agree upon the share of annual sales that will occur in the partial year, and to compute annual sales on that basis. In this example, the landlord and tenant might agree that 50 percent of the tenant's annual sales will occur in the period

Table 6-3

				Percentage Rent Due		
	Gross sales	6% of gross sales	Minimum rent paid	Monthly	Quarterly	Annually
January	5,000	300	400	0	—	—
February	5,000	300	400	0	—	—
March	7,500	450	400	50	0	—
April	7,500	450	400	50	—	—
May	7,500	450	400	50	—	—
June	5,000	300	400	0	0	—
July	5,000	300	400	0	—	—
August	5,000	300	400	0	—	—
September	10,000	600	400	200	0	—
October	10,000	600	400	200	—	—
November	10,000	600	400	200	—	—
December	15,000	900	400	500	900	—
	92,500	5,550	4,800	1,250	900	750
Effective percentage rate:				6.5%	6.1%	6%

from September 1 to December 31. On that basis, total annual sales would have been $90,000 (2 × $45,000) and the tenant's percentage rent would have been $600: ($90,000 × 6%) = $4800. This is considerably closer to the $750[75] amount that would actually have been due in the first example.

These distortions can also be avoided if the tenant is not required to pay any percentage until it reaches its breakpoint on an annual basis.

§ 6.21   Recordkeeping

An obligation to pay percentage rent necessarily implies an obligation to keep books and records that are sufficient for its computation.[76] The usual provision is:

FORM 6-13
PERCENTAGE RENT—RECORDKEEPING

(a)   Each statement of gross sales furnished by tenant will be certified as correct by tenant or an employee of tenant authorized so to certify and will show the computations of gross sales for tenant and each of its subtenants, licensees, and concessionaires separately.

(b)   For the purpose of ascertaining the amount of gross sales, tenant will record each and every sale at the time of the transaction on either a cash register having a sealed, continuous, cash register tape with cumulative totals that numbers, records, and duplicates each transaction entered into the register, or on serially prenumbered sales slips. If tenant chooses to record each sale by using a cash register, the continuous cash register tape will be sealed or locked in such a manner that it is not accessible to the person operating the cash register. If tenant chooses to record each sale on individual sales slips, the sales slips (including those canceled, voided, or not used) will be retained in numerical sequence for three (3) years.

(c)   Tenant will prepare, preserve, and maintain each lease year for a period of not less than three (3) years these books, accounts, and records:

(1)   Daily cash register summary tapes (normally referred to as "Z tapes") and sealed, continuous, cash register tapes or prenumbered sales slips;

(2)   A single, separate bank account into which all receipts of business or other revenue from operations on or from the premises are deposited;

(3)   All bank statements detailing transactions in or through any business bank account;

(4)   Daily or weekly sales recapitulations;

(5)   A sales journal;

---

[75] Lasker, *Shopping Center Leases are Not Nonnegotiable*, 6 Real Est. Rev. 116 (1976). A lengthy analysis of this problem is presented in Landis, *Problems in Drafting Shopping Center Leases*, 36 B.U.L. Rev. 190, 206 (1956). Reprinted by permission from the Real Estate Review, Fall 1981, Volume 11, No. 3, Copyright 1981, Warren, Gorham & Lamont Inc., 210 South Street, Boston, Mass. All Rights Reserved.

[76] Note, *The Percentage Lease—Its Function and Drafting Problems*, 61 Harv. L. Rev. 37 (1948); Morehead Hotel & Apartment Co. v. Lampkin, 267 Ky. 147, 101 S.W.2d 670 (1937).

(6)   A general ledger or a summary record of all cash receipts and disbursements from operations on or from the premises;

(7)   Copies of all tax returns filed with any governmental authority that reflect in any manner sales, income, or revenue generated in or from the premises, including, but not limited to, federal income tax returns and state sales or use tax returns;

(8)   Other records or accounts that landlord may reasonably require in order to ascertain, document, or substantiate gross sales.

To this, a tenant may wish to add provisions that assure the confidentiality of its reports and records. Landlords cannot reasonably resist this request, but they can reserve the right to disclose the tenant's reports and records to prospective lenders or purchasers and to a court in judicial proceedings pertaining to the records and reports.

A tenant may not want to warrant absolutely the accuracy of amounts of gross sales allocable to its licensees, subtenants, and concessionaires; the tenant may prefer to warrant only "to the best of its knowledge." Since the tenant's duty to provide reports is separate from the landlord's right to audit the tenant's books and records, a tenant may lose its lease for failure to supply required reports, even though the landlord is aware of the percentage rent owed to it because of its own audit.[77]

The tenant should avoid a requirement for audited statements because they are expensive; the tenant should suggest instead that the statement be certified by one of its officers. A landlord may be willing to accept such statements from a nationally recognized tenant, but it may be reluctant to accept them from an untried operation. To an accountant, the phrase "certified by a public accountant" with reference to financial statements means audited. To audit is to prepare a statement according to generally accepted accounting principles. Those principles pertain to accrual methods of accounting. There are no generally accepted accounting principles for cash receipts and disbursements basis accounting. When a lease asks for an audited statement of gross sales, it is asking for the impossible: an accrual treatment of a cash basis accounting. All that a public accountant can do is render its opinion that gross sales have been fairly presented on the basis specified in the lease.[78] Finally, the term certified public accountant has a specific meaning. Certification is a state examination procedure. A firm of certified public accountants means that the firm's members have passed the state examination. Public accountants are subject to little or no regulation in most states.

A tenant with several locations will reduce its bookkeeping by insisting on the same reporting period for all stores.

---

[77] Frog, Inc. v. Dutch Inns, Inc., 488 A.2d 925 (D.C. Ct. App. 1985).

[78] Codification of Accounting Standards and Procedures, Statement on Accounting Standards No. 14 (Am. Inst. of Certified Public Accountants 1972) explains generally accepted accounting standards and the sorts of reports that are issued in connection with compliance with contractual agreements.

Landlords occasionally ask for reports that are not reasonably related to the protection of their legitimate interests; these include periodic balance sheets and income tax returns. Income tax returns are not informative if they relate to more than one enterprise of the tenant or if they relate to a different accounting period than the one used in the lease. Balance sheets may reveal sensitive information that enables the landlord to negotiate renewals or extensions more successfully. Many landlords believe that the tenant's financial statements will tell them whether a bankruptcy is imminent; actually, landlords can foretell bankruptcy more quickly and reliably by visiting the premises and looking at the tenant's stock and the number of its customers.

§ 6.22 Verification

In order to avoid the results of the tenants' errors in calculating percentage rent, a verification procedure is essential. A typical verification provision states:

FORM 6-14
PERCENTAGE RENT—LANDLORD'S RIGHT
TO AUDIT TENANT'S RECORDS

All of the books, records, and other documents will be maintained at the premises and in the manner recited in this paragraph, and will be open to inspection, examination, or audit by landlord or landlord's designated representative, upon giving tenant five (5) days' prior notice of landlord's intention to exercise its rights under this paragraph. In connection with an examination or audit, landlord will have the right to inspect the records of sales from any other store operated by tenant, but only if the examination is reasonably necessary to ascertain gross sales from the premises. If upon inspection or examination of tenant's available books and records of account, landlord determines that tenant has failed to maintain, preserve, or retain the documents, books, and records that this lease requires tenant to maintain in the manner set forth in this paragraph, landlord will give the tenant sixty (60) days to cure the deficiencies. Further, if tenant is found to be deficient in maintaining any of documents, books, or records, tenant will reimburse landlord for all reasonable expenses incurred by landlord in determining the deficiencies, including without limitation, any audit or examination fees incurred by landlord.

If tenant fails to cure the deficiencies within sixty (60) days after notice, landlord may, at its option, either hold tenant in default of the lease, or, at tenant's expense and for tenant's benefit, retain an independent accounting or bookkeeping firm to prepare and maintain the documents, books, and records. If landlord elects the latter option, the representatives of the accounting or bookkeeping firm will have full right of entry and access to the premises and existing financial records, and full cooperation by tenant, for the purpose of establishing and maintaining the documents, books, and records. Any expenses incurred by landlord in furtherance of its rights under this paragraph will be additional rent payable by tenant upon receipt of an invoice.

If an audit or examination by landlord, or its representative, discloses that tenant has failed to report all gross sales accurately, and that the total amount of the underreported gross sales exceeds 2% of the gross sales previously reported by tenant for any period examined, or the total amount of the underreported gross sales results in tenant owing additional percentage rent in excess of $_____, tenant will reimburse landlord for all reasonable expenses incurred by landlord in performing the examination, in addition to all additional percentage rent found to be owed by tenant pursuant to this paragraph. Additional percentage rent will bear interest at the lesser of ____% per annum or the highest rate allowed by law from the date on which the additional percentage rent was due until it is paid in full with interest. If an examination by landlord or its representative discloses that tenant has overreported gross sales and that as a result of the overreporting the tenant has overpaid percentage rent, landlord will give tenant credit against future rent due and owing by tenant for the balance of the overpaid rentals after deducting from the overpayments all reasonable expenses incurred by landlord in conducting its examination.

If tenant subleases, licenses, or in any manner allows use of space in the premises, for the purpose of making sales of goods (the "subtenant"), tenant is responsible for ensuring that the subtenant's books and records conform to the requirements in this lease. Tenant will include in its monthly report of gross sales and revenue, but separately noted, the gross sales of the subtenant. In addition, tenant will report as additional gross sales all rentals, commissions, revenue or income received by tenant from the subtenant as payment for use of the premises, or part of the premises. The failure of any subtenant to maintain its books and records of account as required in this paragraph, or to report correctly gross sales will be deemed a failure on the part of the tenant to conform to the requirements of this lease.

The verification provision, as this example indicates, should contain the following elements: an obligation for the tenant to retain relevant books and records (unless required elsewhere in the percentage rent provision); a time within which verification must be undertaken (in order to avoid the retention of useless records); the scope of the verification (whether mere inspection is allowed or whether an audit is permitted); the person who bears the cost of verification if an error is found; the size of the errors that give rise to liability for the cost of verification; and the consequences of an underpayment or overpayment.

If the tenant's operation at the premises is one of several of its stores, the verification cannot be accurate without access to the books and records of the several stores. If the verification is confined to an audit of gross sales, the landlord may be unable to review deductions and exclusions from gross sales.

The usual provision states that the landlord will refund to the tenant any overpayment of percentage rent that its verification reveals. Why should it? If the landlord paid to show the tenant its errors, the landlord should get its costs back; perhaps it should share in the refund after its costs are paid. The preceding form allows the landlord its costs.

Tenants should think twice about being bound by the landlord's verification if it is conducted by the landlord's employees. In that case, there should be recourse to an independent verification if the landlord and tenant do not agree. A mutually acceptable independent accountant should be the only binding arbiter of the percentage rent reports.

Verification procedures differ widely in the size of the error that gives rise to the tenant's obligation to pay for it. The provision should be clear that the error must be found in the percentage rent due and not in the gross sales; the preceding form, however, refers to errors in gross sales. If the tenant has made offsetting errors in its gross sales, and in its exclusions or deductions, the percentage rent may still be correct. The landlord and tenant should consider carefully the size of the error that determines who pays the audit fees. The tenant should resist any provision that gives the landlord the right to cancel the lease if an error is found, unless the tenant does not promptly pay the balance due; of course, repeated errors may suggest some chicanery.

Finally, some tenants ask for a limit on the number of random audits the landlord can conduct, fearing that audits could be used to harass them. Because fruitless audits cost the landlord money, there is no reason it would act capriciously.

§ 6.23   Controlling Percentage Rent

Both the landlord and the tenant may wish to control percentage rent. The landlord will want to be certain that it receives percentage rent. The tenant will want to be sure that in its opinion the percentage rent is not excessive.[79]

For some time, landlords have used the simple device of reserving the right to terminate a lease if the tenant's sales do not reach and maintain a specified level after a specified period of the lease;[80] for example, "landlord may terminate this lease if tenant's gross sales in each lease year after the first lease year do not exceed $300,000." Tenants have responded to this provision by demanding that they have the right to avoid termination of their leases by paying an amount equal to what their percentage would have been if the specified level of sales had been achieved. Although many landlords have agreed with this suggestion, some have rejected it, because they have felt that insufficient sales revealed a tenant's inability to draw customers and thus to augment sales of fellow tenants. If the tenant must concede this point, it should insist that the landlord's right to terminate the lease be conditioned upon other tenants achieving appropriately similar success; put differently, the landlord should not be able to terminate the tenant's lease if the entire shopping center is languishing.

Be all that as it may, this practice has been shaken by a federal court decision in Hawaii.[81] This case held that a landlord's refusal to renew a tenant's lease because the tenant did not achieve sufficient sales was price fixing in violation of Section 1 of the Sherman Anti-Trust Act.[82] This opinion has been severely criticized for several reasons, not the least of which is that it held that a shopping center can be a

---

[79] *See Tenant Strategies for Negotiating Percentage Rent,* Leasing Prof., Sept. 1987, at 1.

[80] I Friedman § 6.8.

[81] Bartley's Town & Country Shops v. Dillingham Corp., 530 F. Supp. 499 (D. Haw. 1982).

[82] 15 U.S.C. 1 (1980).

market for purposes of monopolization. Since there are doubts about the support that this decision will find, many landlords will continue to include termination provisions. Others will go—or have already gone—to other means of controlling percentage rent; they escalate the minimum rent each year according to a cost of living adjustment (COLA).

Tenants often ask for the right to cancel their leases if sales do not meet reasonable projections. Although landlords do not want unsuccessful tenants, they do not want tenants to decide for themselves whether poor performance justifies cancellation. As a compromise, landlords often agree to a provision that the tenant may expand its use beyond the use provision if its initial use fails. Of course, the expanded use must be carefully defined so as to avoid a breach of another tenant's exclusive use. Often these expanded uses are allowed on a temporary basis in order to determine whether the initial use was really the problem.

Without control, the tenant's percentage rent can easily be greater than its minimum rent. Thus there are many ways by which successful tenants try to control their percentage rent. Some of the more common methods are:

1. Prescribing a maximum amount of total rent (the sum of percentage rent and minimum rent) per square foot of the premises.

2. Requiring a sliding scale for increasing sales, for example, 5 percent of gross sales up to $1 million, 4 percent of gross sales over $1 million and up to $1.5 million, and so on up to an amount of gross sales above which no percentage rent is due. In preparing this kind of provision, the landlord should avoid the abysmal draftsmanship that says "if gross sales exceed $2,000,000, no percentage rent will be due" or similar language that ends the tenant's entire percentage rent obligation, and not just its obligation for percentage rent on gross sales of over $2 million.

3. Providing that a lower flat percentage would be due on sales over a specified amount.

4. Offsetting against percentage rent liability the common area maintenance charges, real estate taxes, merchants association dues, and insurance which it pays. The tenant may be able to negotiate a cumulative right of offset by which any amount by which its offsets exceed its percentage rent liability in any year is carried forward into the following years.

Some tenants control percentage rent in a crude way—they cheat.

Of course the simplest method is for the tenant to put cash receipts directly into its pocket. Other tenants ring up less than the full sales price, thus creating cash register tapes with deflated gross sales. Customers who examine their receipts will catch this tenant; however, in many businesses (for example, the take-out food business) customers do not usually examine their receipts.

Another device is used when tenants have two stores leased in the same area. If one of them requires percentage rent and the other does not, or if they both require percentage rent but they do so at different rates, opportunities for the miscreant are many. The tenant may make sales from the flat rent (or lower percentage rent) store and may accept returns at the percentage rent store, thus enlarging the deductions from gross sales. Occasionally, sales slips and return receipts are printed in such a way as to leave no trace of the store in which the transactions originated.

Some retailers have been known to "slip" their cash register tapes. This cumbersome ruse involves "zeroing out" some sales. When a tenant rings up a sale, it inserts a piece of paper between the tape and the printing head before ringing up the sale. Then, with the paper still in position, an amount equal to the sale — but negative — is rung up. Finally, the tape is rolled back so that the next entry is in the right position and the unprinted spaces are not shown. The effect is that the landlord's inspection of the tape does not reveal the zeroed-out sale.

Other retailers have used unnumbered receipts between the numbered receipts. The effect is "one for the landlord — one for the tenant, one for the landlord — one for the tenant." When the landlord reviews the receipt books, the receipts appear sequentially without interruption. Close examination may reveal stubs of the unnumbered receipts. Other tenants whose leases exclude sales of tobacco from gross sales have rung up large amounts of sales on the "T" key.

Finally, some retailers charge by mail for large purchases and do not take any money at the premises.

The landlord's best defense to the cheating tenant is, of course, an audit of the tenant's books.[83] The profile of a cheating tenant is one:

1. Whose gross sales are always just below the "breakpoint"
2. Who paid percentage rent once but never again
3. Who operates several stores that are more successful at other locations
4. Who acts as the shopping center's "rabble-rouser."

§ 6.24 Lenders' Concerns about Rent

The first thing that lenders want in the rent provision is a statement that the rent will be paid without deduction, offset, prior notice, or demand. Some lenders will accept the tenant's right to offset certain overpayments against rent, for example, those arising from the landlord's overestimation of operating expenses, or those arising from recalculation of percentage rent.

Since cost of living adjustments are not an infallible substitute for escalations based on actual experience, lenders object to leases in which the tenant's only obligation to pay increased operating expenses is tied to a COLA. Rather, lenders prefer to see pass-throughs of actual costs.

---

[83] *Auditing Your Percentage-Rent Tenant: When It Pays, When It Doesn't,* Com. Lease L. Insider, Aug. 1989, at 1.

Lenders do not usually look to anticipated percentage rent as the source of repayment of their loans. Thus, landlords are often free to allow tenants to deduct from their percentage rent certain other amounts that they have paid. Typically these amounts include merchants association dues, promotional fund and advertising fund contributions, real estate taxes, common area maintenance expenses, and insurance.

Naturally, lenders prefer leases that require that the rent be paid on the first of each month, because this normally coincides with the date on which their payments are due. Although the lender's position and the landlord's position are often identical, one aspect of rent provisions pits them against each other. That provision has to do with the right of the tenant to prepay rent or to buy its way out of the lease. If the tenant pays too much rent in advance, and the landlord defaults on its mortgage, the lender may succeed to a lease in which the tenant has a right not to pay rent to the extent of its prepayment. Similarly, if the tenant buys its way out of a lease, the lender may be deprived of the cash flow on which it relied in making its mortgage loan. Prepayments of rent and buyouts of leases are commonly used by desperate landlords in order to raise money. One can readily see why their interests are then different from those of their lenders.

With regard to prepayments of rent, an important question arises. What happens if the landlord has made a collateral assignment of its leases to its lender and, in connection with that assignment, has given up to the lender the right to make modifications or amendments to its leases? With the rare exception of states that have enacted statutes putting tenants on notice of the limitations of their landlords' acceptance of prepaid rent,[84] the lender is in a difficult position. For one thing, its rights under a collateral assignment of rents are usually not available until a default in the mortgage has occurred. Even if the lease provides that the tenant may not pay rent in advance, the landlord and tenant (who is unaware of the terms of its landlord's mortgage) may amend that provision. The best opportunity that a lender has to protect itself against such prepayments is to have a separate agreement with the tenant that rent will not be prepaid. This agreement is usually found in a nondisturbance and attornment agreement such as that set forth in § **24.3**.

Often landlords give shopping center tenants the right to pay only percentage rent for a part of the term of the lease, for example, until major tenants open for business. In office buildings, landlords often give away free rent. Lenders must be very careful with these provisions in order to be certain that the minimum rent reserved under the lease is sufficient to support the loan. If there is a strong likelihood that the tenant will not be obligated to pay rent for a substantial period of time, the balance of the term for which the tenant has a rent obligation may be too short to support the loan.

Leases often give tenants the right to cancel their leases if the tenants do not achieve anticipated sales, or if major tenants do not open for business or do not continue in business after opening, or for some other reason that affects the

---

[84] *See, e.g.,* N.Y. Real Prop. Law § 291-f (McKinney 1968).

tenants' businesses. These provisions are problematic for lenders because there is no certainty of lease revenue. As a result, they may be disregarded in considering the loans that lenders would make in reliance upon lease income.

Obviously, the uninterrupted income stream from leases is the lender's most pressing concern. The revenue from those leases creates the value on which the lender will rely if it must foreclose its loan and sell its collateral.

PART III

ADDITIONAL EXPENSES FOR THE TENANT

CHAPTER 7

TAXES AND ASSESSMENTS

§ 7.1   Introduction

The simplest provisions for taxes and assessments are found in leases of single tenant buildings. There, the term "taxes and assessments" is defined and the tenant is given responsibility for their payment. A definition of taxes and assessments is set forth in § **7.2**, and a typical provision for their payment by a single tenant is set forth in § **7.3**. Although it is unusual, the landlord in a lease of a single tenant building may agree to pay taxes and assessments in a base year or base amount, with the tenant agreeing to pay any amount in excess of the base. Because that kind of provision is far more common in office building and shopping center leases,[1] it will be considered in those multitenant contexts.

In office building leases, real estate taxes may be part of operating expenses; in shopping center leases, real estate taxes attributable to the common areas may be part of the common area maintenance charges. However, in both types of leases, real estate taxes may also be considered in an entirely separate provision.

That provision may allocate all real estate taxes among all the tenants in the proportions that the areas of their respective premises bear to one another. This is a *net* provision. On the other hand, the lease may provide that tenants will share ratably all real estate taxes over a base amount or over an amount paid or assessed in a base year. This is often referred to as a *real estate tax expense stop.* It is an amount — expressed either in dollars or by reference to a base year — above which

---

[1] For a very helpful discussion of real estate taxes and assessments, see Hall, *The Retail Tenant's Obligations for Real Estate Taxes — An Insurance Policy for Landlord's Profit?*, Leasing Prof., June 1985, at 1.

the landlord has no further liability. Over that amount, the tenants will have all the liability.

Leases that charge real estate taxes separately from other operating expenses are somewhat more difficult to analyze than the leases discussed in § **6.13**,[2] all of which had one operating expense charge that presumably included real estate taxes. However, the analysis is not really different. Rather, the charges for other operating expenses and the real estate taxes must be projected and then added together to prepare the assumptions necessary in order to compare the leases.

A provision for a "net payment by all tenants" is discussed in § **7.4**. A provision for a base amount is discussed in § **7.5** and a provision for a base year is discussed in § **7.6**. Although these forms have been prepared for office building leases, they can be readily altered to fit an otherwise appropriate shopping center lease.

Because real estate taxes seem to increase without bounds or reason, landlords should allocate them to their tenants or at least limit their own responsibility for them. For a case illustrating the folly of a landlord undertaking to pay real estate taxes in a long-term lease, consider a Florida landlord's plight.[3] There, in a lease (including renewal rights) of 33 years, the taxes increased from approximately $15,000 in the first year to nearly $190,000 in the twentieth year. Since the lease did not require the tenant to pay taxes, the landlord was required to pay them. The landlord claimed commercial frustration, arguing that performance was impossible. The court refused to find that performance of the lease had been frustrated; it had simply become more expensive and less profitable.

§ 7.2 Definition of Taxes

For at least two reasons, landlords should strive for the broadest possible definitions of *taxes*.[4] One reason is that the definition will control what the tenant pays and what the landlord pays. Another is that the methods of taxation are always changing and landlords must endeavor to anticipate new taxes. Many leases use the term *impositions* in order to be certain that special assessments, sewer charges, and other costs not usually called taxes are included. In fact, a California court ruled that a tenant who is obligated to pay "taxes" is not obligated to pay assessments.[5]

A broad definition of taxes used in any kind of lease is:

[2] *See generally* Goldstein, *Drafting a Tax Escalation Clause in a Lease*, 25 Prac. Law. 53 (1979).

[3] Valencia Center Inc. v. Publix Super Markets, Inc., 464 So. 2d 1267 (Fla. Dist. Ct. App.), *cert. denied*, 475 So. 2d 696 (Fla. 1985). *Accord* Gunhus, Grinnell v. Englestad, 413 N.W.2d 148 (Minn.Ct. App.), *review denied*, Nov. 24, 1987 (lease not unconscionable merely because it cost landlord $30,000 annually as a result of increased utility costs and property taxes).

[4] See *Tenant Checklist for Real Estate Taxes*, Leasing Prof., Apr. 1987, at 3, which also sets forth a landlord's form of real estate tax provision for an office lease.

[5] Wells v. Union Oil Co. of California, 25 Cal. App. 2d 165, 76 P.2d 696 (1938); *see also* I Friedman § 5.201, and E. Halper, Shopping Center and Store Leases, § 5.02(b) (Supp. 1984).

FORM 7-1
TAXES—DEFINITION

"Taxes" means the aggregate amount of real estate taxes, water and sewer rents, and any general or special assessments (exclusive of penalties and interest) imposed upon the property, including without limitation (1) assessments made upon or with respect to any air and development rights at any time appurtenant to the property, (2) any fee, tax, or charge imposed by any governmental authority for any vaults, vault space, or other space within or outside the boundaries of the property, except that if the vault fee, tax, or charge is payable by any tenant (including tenant) directly to the governmental authority, the vault fee, tax, or charge will not be considered as part of taxes for the tax year in which the vault fee, tax, or charge is so paid, and (3) any assessments levied after the date of this lease for public benefits to the property (excluding an amount equal to the assessments payable in whole or in part during or for the first tax year, which assessments, if payable in installments, will be deemed payable in the maximum number of permissible installments) in the manner in which taxes and assessments are imposed as of the date of this lease. If, because of any change in the taxation of real estate, any other tax or assessment (including without limitation, any franchise, income, profit, sales, use, occupancy, gross receipts or rental tax) is imposed upon landlord as the owner of the property or the building, or the occupancy, rents or income from either of them, in substitution for any taxes, such other tax or assessment, computed as if the property were landlord's sole asset, will be deemed part of taxes. All expenses, including attorneys' fees and disbursements, experts' and other witnesses' fees, incurred in contesting the validity or amount of any taxes or in obtaining a refund of taxes will be considered as part of the taxes for the tax year in which the expenses are incurred.

Another definition of taxes is in Form **7-2**.

Tenants usually ask that some taxes be excluded from the definition because the taxes are unique to the landlord, controllable by the landlord, or unrelated to the lease of the premises. Those exclusions are:

1. Inheritance taxes
2. Gift taxes
3. Transfer taxes
4. Franchise taxes
5. Excise taxes
6. Net income taxes
7. Profit taxes
8. Capital levies.

Landlords usually exclude these taxes from their definition. Tenants also ask their landlords to exclude late payment charges and penalties from the definition of taxes, and landlords usually agree to do so, but only on the condition that the tenants have not defaulted in their obligations to pay taxes.

§ 7.3 Taxes and the Single Tenant Building

The single tenant building subject to a net lease may provide:

FORM 7-2
TAXES—SINGLE TENANT BUILDING

(a) *Obligation for Payment.* Tenant will pay all taxes (collectively the "tax"), including without limitation real estate and personal property taxes and assessments assessed, levied, confirmed, or imposed during the term of this lease (other than net income taxes) whether or not now customary or within the contemplation of landlord and tenant: (1) upon, measured by, or reasonably attributable to the cost or value of tenant's equipment, furniture, fixtures, and other personal property located in the premises or by the cost or value of any leasehold improvements made in or to the premises by or for tenant regardless of whether title to such improvements is in tenant or landlord; (2) upon or measured by the monthly rent, including without limitation any gross receipts tax or excise tax levied by the federal government or any other governmental body with respect to the receipt of monthly rent; (3) upon or with respect to the possession, leasing, operation, management, maintenance, alteration, repair, use, or occupancy by tenant of the premises or any portion of the premises; (4) upon this transaction or any document to which tenant is a party creating or transferring an interest or an estate in the premises; (5) upon the premises and all personal property, furniture, fixtures, and equipment, and all replacements, improvements, or additions to them, whether owned by landlord or tenant; and (6) impositions based in whole or in part on monthly rent, whether made in addition to or in substitution for any other tax.

(b) *Taxes Payable in Installments.* Unless landlord has exercised its rights under paragraph _____ (f) and if, by law, any tax may at the option of the taxpayer be paid in installments (whether or not interest accrues on the unpaid balance of such tax), tenant may exercise the option to pay the tax (and any accrued interest on the unpaid balance of such tax) in installments, and in that event tenant will pay the installments that become due during the term of this lease and before any fine, penalty, further interest or cost may be added to them.

(c) *Taxes for Period other than Term.* Any tax, including taxes that have been converted into installment payments, relating to a fiscal period of the taxing authority, a part of which is included within the term and a part of which is included in a period of time prior to the commencement or after the end of the term, will, whether or not such tax or installments are assessed, levied, confirmed, imposed upon or in respect of, or become a lien upon the premises, or become payable, during the term, be adjusted between landlord and tenant as of the commencement or end of the term, so that tenant will pay the portion of the tax or installment that the part of the fiscal period included in the term bears to the entire fiscal period, and landlord will pay the remainder.

(d) *Other Impositions.* Tenant will not be obligated to pay local, state, or federal net income taxes assessed against landlord; local, state, or federal capital levy of landlord; or sales, excise, franchise, gift, estate, succession, inheritance, or transfer taxes of landlord.

(e) *Right to Contest Taxes.* Tenant will have the right to contest the amount or validity, in whole or in part, of any tax by appropriate proceedings diligently conducted in good faith, only after paying such tax or posting security that landlord reasonably requires in order to protect the premises against loss or forfeiture. Upon the termination of any proceedings, tenant will pay the amount of the tax or part of the tax as finally determined, the payment of which may have been deferred during the prosecution of the proceedings, together with any costs, fees, interest, penalties, or other related liabilities. Landlord will not be required to join in any contest or proceedings unless the provisions of any law or regulations then in effect require that the proceedings be brought by or in the name of landlord. In that event landlord will join in the proceedings or permit them to be brought in its name; however, landlord will not be subjected to any liability for the payment of any costs or expenses in connection with any contest or proceedings, and tenant will indemnify landlord against and save landlord harmless from any costs and expenses.

(f) *Estimated Payments.* If any lender requires landlord to do so, then, in each December during the term or as soon after December as practicable, landlord will give tenant written notice of its estimate of amounts payable under paragraph ____ (a) for the ensuing calendar year. On or before the first day of each month during the ensuing calendar year, tenant will pay to landlord one-twelfth (1/12th) of the estimated amounts; however, if notice is not given in December, tenant will continue to pay on the basis of the prior year's estimate until the month after notice is given. If at any time or times it appears to landlord that the amounts payable under paragraph ____(a) for the current calendar year will vary from its estimate by more than 10%, landlord will, by written notice to tenant, revise its estimate for the year, and subsequent payments by tenant for the year will be based upon the revised estimate.

(g) *Final Settlement.* Within ninety (90) days after the close of each calendar year or as soon after such ninety-day period as practicable, landlord will deliver to tenant a statement of amounts payable under paragraph ____ (a) for the calendar year prepared by certified public accountants designated by landlord, or prepared by landlord and certified by one of its officers, and the certified statement will be final and binding upon landlord and tenant. If the statement shows an amount owing by tenant that is less than the estimated payments previously made by tenant for the calendar year, the statement will be accompanied by a refund of the excess by landlord to tenant. If the statement shows an amount owing by tenant that is more than the estimated payments previously made by tenant for the calendar year, tenant will pay the deficiency to landlord within thirty (30) days after the delivery of the statement.

Landlords should be certain that they can demand monthly deposits if their lenders require it or if the tenant defaults in any of its monetary obligations under the lease. Landlords should resist the suggestion that interest be paid on tax deposits.

Form 7-2 assumes that the "premises" are separately assessed from any development of which they may be a part. Tenants should insist on separate assessments in order to avoid allocation issues.

Tenants should be certain to win the right to contest taxes in the manner of paragraph (e) of **Form 7-2**.

Tenants should insist upon the right to pay assessments in installments if law allows it. In this way, the tenant's payment will more closely correspond to the use it gets from the subject matter of the assessment. In connection with a lease that required the tenant to pay taxes and assessments, and in which the landlord had elected to pay an assessment in installments (although the tenant reimbursed it), the tenant was held obligated to pay the balance of the assessment when the landlord decided to pay off the assessment in connection with refinancing its property.[6] If the tenant had won the landlord's agreement to pay assessments only in installments, the tenant would have saved an expense from which it had no benefit.

Occasionally, hoping to avoid additional taxes, a single tenant will ask the landlord not to include the premises in any new special improvement district. The trouble with this request is that special improvement districts are usually not consensual; they are formed according to law whether or not all landowners want them. Moreover, even if a landlord could opt out of a special improvement district, would it be well-advised to do so and thus risk putting its property at a competitive disadvantage when the time for releasing or sale comes?

There is an unusual situation in which a similar request may be justified. If part of the costs of a development (for example, streets or sewers) are paid through a special assessment district, the landlord, of course, has avoided those costs; however, the tenant pays them in the pass-through of taxes and assessments. If the rent rate for the premises is the same as the rent rate for comparable premises in which there is no special assessment, the tenants pay twice for the special improvements: once in a return on the landlord's investment via the rent, and again as a special assessment via the pass-through. Put differently, the total occupancy cost (rent and pass-throughs) should be the same for both premises.

Finally, tenants must be certain to provide that their obligation for taxes and assessments is pro rata, that is, that taxes and assessments are apportioned so that the tenant pays only that part of taxes and assessments fairly allocable to the term. In the absence of a pro rata provision, a tenant may be surprised to learn that it is obligated to pay taxes for a full tax year even though it occupied the premises for only part of the tax year.[7] In effect, the lease should prorate taxes as though the tenant were buying the premises at the beginning of the term and selling the premises at the end of the term.

§ 7.4 Net Tax Provision in a Multitenant Development

This is a *net* tax provision used in a multitenant development:

---

[6] Mott Haven Furniture Co. v. Finance Adm'r, 130 Misc. 2d 667, 497 N.Y.S.2d 213 (1985). *See also* Waldbaum, Inc. v. Finance Adm'r, 141 A.D. 2d 10, 532 N.Y.S.2d 539 (1988), *reversed*, 74 N.Y.2d 128, 542 N.E.2d 1078, 544 N.Y.S.2d 561 (1989).

[7] Folberg v. Clara G.R. Kinney Co., 104 Cal. App. 3d 136, 163 Cal. Rptr. 426 (1980).

FORM 7-3
TAXES—NET TAX PROVISION IN A
MULTITENANT DEVELOPMENT

(a)   In addition to the base monthly rental payable during the term of this lease, tenant will pay as additional rental tenant's percentage share of the amount of property taxes levied against the Building for each calendar year of the term of this lease.

(b)   On or before the first day of the term of this lease, or as soon after that day as practicable, landlord will give tenant written notice of landlord's estimate of the additional rental payable under paragraph (a) for the remainder of that calendar year. During December of each calendar year or as soon after December as practicable, landlord will give tenant notice of its estimate of the payments to be made pursuant to paragraph (a) for the ensuing calendar year. On or before the first day of each month during the ensuing calendar year, tenant will pay to landlord one-twelfth (1/12th) of the estimated amount; however, if the notice is not given in December, tenant will continue to pay on the basis of the prior year's estimate until the month after the notice is given. If at any time or times it appears to landlord that the payments to be made under paragraph (a) for the current calendar year will vary from its estimate by more than 5%, landlord will, by notice to tenant, revise its estimate for the year, and subsequent payments by tenant for the year will be based upon the revised estimate.

(c)   Within ninety (90) days after the close of each calendar year or as soon after the ninety-day period as practicable, landlord will deliver to tenant (i) a statement of property taxes for the calendar year certified by certified public accountants designated by landlord, which certified statement will be final and binding upon landlord and tenant, and (ii) a statement of the payments made or to be made under paragraph (a) for the calendar year that has been prepared on the basis of the certified statement. If on the basis of those statements tenant owes an amount that is less than the estimated payments for the calendar year previously made by tenant, landlord will credit the excess to the next succeeding monthly installment of rent. If on the basis of those statements tenant owes an amount that is more than the estimated payments for such calendar year previously made by tenant, tenant will pay the deficiency to landlord within thirty (30) days after delivery of those statements.

(d)   If this lease commences on a day other than the first day of the calendar year or ends on a day other than the last day of a calendar year, the amount of the payments pursuant to this paragraph payable by tenant with respect to the year in which such commencement or end occurs will be prorated on the basis that the number of days of the term included in the year bears to 365. The end of this lease will not affect the obligations of landlord and tenant pursuant to paragraph (c) to be performed after that end.

(e)   The term "property taxes" means any form of real or personal property taxes, assessments, special assessments, fees, charges, levies, penalties, service payments in lieu of taxes, excises, assessments and charges for transit, housing or any other purposes, impositions or taxes of every kind and nature whatsoever, assessed or levied or imposed by any authority having the direct or indirect power to tax, including, without limitation, any city, county, state, or federal government, or any improvement or assessment district of any kind, whether or not consented to or joined in by tenant, against the building or any legal or equitable interest of landlord in the building or any personal property of landlord used in the operation of the building, whether now imposed or imposed in the future, whether or not now customary or in the contemplation of landlord and tenant on the date of this lease, excepting only taxes measured by the net income of landlord from all sources.

This provision raises many of the questions that operating expense provisions raise. Can the landlord collect more than 100 percent of its real estate tax expenses? Can the tenant audit the landlord's records? Can the tenant contest the real estate taxes? A small tenant's right to contest taxes is not likely to be used; no cost-benefit analysis could support it. However, a group of small tenants or a single large tenant may find this right important.

When tenants ask for the right to contest real estate taxes, many landlords respond that they are as interested as their tenants in low assessments. Even though they can pass on all the costs of real estate taxes, these landlords argue, they want to have competitively priced properties. So, they conclude, they will contest high assessments. Some tenants believe that they should have the right to decide what is "high." They also contend that no harm can come from both the landlord and the tenant having a right to contest assessments.

The right of the tenant of a multitenant property to protest taxes may not be allowed by statute. For example, New York's highest court has ruled that a "fractional lessee who is obligated to pay rent which includes a variable pro rata share of the landlord's real property taxes" does not have standing to contest those taxes.[8] The court distinguished decisions in which a tenant was contractually obligated to pay taxes directly on an undivided tax liability; in those cases, a New York tenant seems to have the right to contest taxes. The case was confused by a lease provision that enabled the tenant to reduce its percentage rent by the real estate taxes it had paid; consequently, the tenant's liability was considered "remote." Contest rights must be drafted with reference to the relevant state tax law. If a tenant cannot contest taxes under any circumstances, then it must win the landlord's agreement to do it at tenant's expense (to the extent the cost of the contest exceeds the savings).

Tenants should insist that they recover their costs of any contest. Although fair, this is troublesome. If the tenant succeeds in winning a refund, there will be money with which to reimburse its costs. If the tenant prevents a high assessment before it is made, there is no money with which to pay the tenant. The landlord must either pay the tenant with the landlord's money — surely not its preference — or it must assess the other tenants for the cost of the contest. Most leases do not give the landlord that right. Of course, the tenants should not be entitled to recover more than the cost saving they effect.

---

[8] Atlantic Leasing Co. v. Castro Convertible Corp., N.Y.L.F., Jan. 12, 1984, at 12, col. 5B (Civ. N.Y.1983); *see* First Nat'l Bank of Highland Park v. Mid-Central Food Sales, Inc., 129 Ill. App. 3d 1002, 473 N.E.2d 372, *appeal denied*, May 1985 (court applied real estate tax provision literally and charged tenant for taxes billed after its term).

§ 7.5   Base Amount Tax Provision in a Multitenant Development

A provision for a *real estate tax stop* (expressed in dollars) is:

FORM 7-4
TAXES—BASE AMOUNT TAX PROVISION

(a)   Tenant will pay all real estate taxes assessed against the building, building complex, or premises during the term of this lease; however, landlord agrees to expend as its share of real estate taxes during any calendar year $_____ (the "base real estate taxes").

"Real estate taxes" will include: (1) any form of tax or assessment (including any so-called "special" assessment), license fee, license tax, business license fee, business license tax, commercial rental tax, levy, charge, penalty, or tax, imposed by any authority having the direct power to tax, including any city, county, state, or federal government, or any school, agricultural, lighting, water, drainage, or other improvement or special district, against the premises, the building, or building complex, or any legal or equitable interest of landlord in any of them; (2) any tax on landlord's right to rent the premises or against landlord's business of leasing the premises; and (3) any assessment, tax, fee, levy, or charge in substitution, partially or totally, of or in addition to any assessment, tax, fee, levy, or charge previously included within the definition of real estate taxes that may be imposed by governmental agencies for services such as fire protection, street, sidewalk and road maintenance, refuse removal, and for other governmental services formerly provided without charge to property owners or occupants. All new and increased assessments, taxes, fees, levies, and charges will be included within the definition of real estate taxes for purposes of this lease. Tenant will pay landlord the entire amount of (i) any tax allocable to or measured by the area of the premises or the rental payable under this lease, including without limitation, any gross income, privilege, sales or excise tax levied by the state, any political subdivision of the premises, city, municipal, or federal government, with respect to the receipt of such rental, or upon or with respect to the possession, leasing, operating, management, maintenance, alteration, repair, use, or occupancy by tenant of the premises or any portion of the premises; and (ii) any tax upon this transaction or any document to which tenant is a party, creating or transferring an interest or an estate in the premises. "Real estate taxes" will not include landlord's federal or state income, franchise, inheritance, or estate taxes.

(b)   Within ninety (90) days after the end of each calendar year, landlord will furnish tenant a written comparative statement showing the calculations described in this paragraph and state the increases, if any, for the then-current year. Commencing with the next month following such statement, tenant will pay landlord a lump sum equal to one-twelfth (1/12th) of the annual increase for each month of the immediate preceding calendar year and for each month of the current calendar year that has passed since the commencement date of this lease. With the same payment, tenant will commence payment to the landlord of one-twelfth (1/12th) of the annual increase by adding that amount to the regular monthly rent installments. The increased monthly rent installments will continue until landlord gives tenant the next written notice calculating any additional rent increases for future calendar years, to which the same procedures for payment will apply. If the total additional rent payments by tenant to landlord for any future calendar years are found at year end to vary from the actual additional rents due for that year, tenant will pay landlord any deficiency as additional rent upon notice of the actual amount, and landlord will credit any excess to the next succeeding additional rent installments becoming due. Any such excess in the last year of this lease will be refunded by landlord to tenant within sixty (60) days after the expiration of the lease, but only if tenant is not in default and has vacated the premises.

Even though the term of this lease has ended and tenant has vacated the premises, when the final determination is made of tenant's share of real estate taxes for the year in which this lease ends, tenant will pay any increase due over the estimated real estate taxes within sixty (60) days after delivery of a statement for them, and, conversely, within sixty (60) days after the end of the term, landlord will rebate any overpayment due of estimated real estate taxes. Tenant will not be relieved of its obligation to pay to landlord any amount due pursuant to this paragraph if landlord fails, for any reason, to provide its comparative statement within the time provided.

A landlord may say that it will pay $3.00 per leasable square foot toward taxes assessed against, for example, a 200,000 square foot shopping center. Another way of saying the same thing is that the landlord will pay $600,000 toward those taxes: $3.00 per square foot multiplied by 200,000 square feet. In either case, the tenants will be obligated to pay any amount over $3.00, or their shares of amounts over $600,000, as the case may be. When the landlord's contribution is expressed as a total amount (in this example $600,000), both landlord and tenant must consider expansion of the shopping center (when the landlord's share will be unfairly low) or contraction of the shopping center by casualty or condemnation (when the landlord's share will be too high).

The landlord is saying to itself that it has reduced its revenue from the lease by $3.00, or from the leases by $600,000, and that its leases are net as to the balance (assuming all other costs are passed through to tenants). To tenants, this contribution seems to be a magnanimous gesture. Its real significance, however, must be determined by the tenant's further inquiry. Is the $3.00 contribution equal to the actual amount of the taxes? There is no requirement that it be so; a tax bill will tell more of the story. As shown, the contribution may simply be the result of the landlord's analysis of its revenue (with due regard to competing landlords).

Even if the contribution is based upon the landlord's intention to pay fully the taxes assessed in the year of the lease, there is still little comfort for the tenant. In the first place, that year's assessments may not be available; as a result, the landlord is actually paying an amount equal to the prior year's taxes. Furthermore, a lease signed in one year may not begin until the next year (because of construction, for example); in this situation, the tenant will again be one year behind in the landlord's contribution. The outcome of both these scenarios is that the lease has a built-in tax escalation on the day the tenant moves in, not in the next year as the tenant may have believed.

Are any tax contests pending? If the base year's taxes are contested and reduced, the landlord and tenant will be in unexpected positions. If the landlord has agreed to pay $3.00 (because that amount was supposed to pay taxes for the first year of the lease), and if the first year's taxes are only $2.50 as the result of a contest, then the landlord may be contributing to taxes for several years of the lease (until taxes reach $3.00 and the tenant takes over). If the base year's taxes are reduced, the landlord will be saving a part of its planned contribution to taxes (the difference between the original taxes and the adjusted taxes). A tenant may ask that any such savings be passed on to it in the form of either the landlord's contribution of its savings to other operating expenses that would be borne by the tenant, or reduced rent. The basis for this request is that the landlord has calculated the tenant's rent on the assumption that the landlord will be paying a portion of that rent for taxes ($3.00 in this example). If, in fact, the landlord saves part of that tax expense (by paying only $2.50), the rent is 50 cents too high and the tenant should have the benefit of the savings.

In any provision for the escalation of taxes, such as those in this section and § 7.6, the landlord must avoid any confusion between an increase in taxes and an increase in the assessed valuation or tax rate. All things being equal, taxes will increase if either the assessed valuation or the tax rate is increased. The landlord wants to recover any increase in taxes, regardless of whether increase is attributable to a change in the assessed valuation or the tax rate.

§ 7.6   Base Year Tax Provision in a Multitenant Development

This is a base year tax provision in a multitenant development:

FORM 7-5
TAXES—BASE YEAR TAX PROVISION

The rental payable during each calendar year in the term of this lease subsequent to the tax year ending ⸻, 19⸻ (the "base tax year") will be increased by tenant's percentage share of the total dollar increase, if any, in real property taxes (and any tax levied wholly or partly in lieu of real property taxes) levied against the building for the tax year, over the taxes for the base tax year. Taxes for the base tax year will be determined by multiplying the assessed valuation of the building for the base tax year by the tax rate actually in effect for the tax year ending ⸻, 19⸻.

During December of each calendar year, or as soon after each December as practicable, landlord will give tenant written notice of its estimate of amounts payable under the preceding paragraph ⸻ for the ensuing calendar year. On or before the first day of each month during the ensuing calendar year, tenant will pay to landlord one-twelfth (1/12th) of the estimated amounts; however, if notice is not given in December, tenant will continue to pay on the basis of the prior year's estimate until the month after notice is given. If at any time the amounts payable under the preceding paragraph _____ for the current calendar year will vary from the estimate by more than 5%, landlord will, by written notice to tenant, revise its estimate for the year, and subsequent payments by tenant for the year will be based upon such revised estimate.

Within ninety (90) days after the end of each calendar year or as soon after the ninety-day period as practicable, landlord will deliver to tenant a statement of amounts payable under this section for the calendar year. The statement will be certified by certified public accountants designated by landlord, and the certified statement will be final and binding upon landlord and tenant. If the statement shows an amount owing by tenant that is less than the estimated payments for the calendar year previously made by tenant, the statement will be accompanied by a refund of the excess by landlord to tenant. If the statement shows an amount owing by tenant that is more than the estimated payments for the calendar year previously made by tenant, tenant will pay the deficiency to landlord within thirty (30) days after delivery of the statement.

If, for any reason other than the default of tenant, this lease ends on a day other than the last day of a calendar year, the amount of increase (if any) in rental payable by tenant applicable to the calendar year in which the end occurs will be prorated on the basis that the number of days from the commencement of such calendar year to and including the end date bears to 365.

What is the base year? Because the landlord must pay the base year's taxes and the tenant must pay amounts in excess of the base year's taxes, the landlord would prefer a pre-Columbian base year. The tenant would prefer a base year that is far in the future.

Sometimes the base year is the year in which the lease begins. This is akin to a base year in which the building is completed and has its drawbacks. Completion varies. A simple way to measure completion is by the issuance of a certificate of occupancy, but this, too, is misleading. Some taxing authorities abate taxes in part or in full during construction and perhaps for some time after completion. When a lease provided that the tenant would pay all real estate taxes in excess of a base year's taxes, but (unknown to landlord and tenant) the real estate taxes were abated for the base year, a Louisiana court would not enforce the mutual mistake. As a result, the base year may be unduly low, only to be followed by a substantial increase.[9]

Some leases have tried to avoid this problem by averaging the taxes imposed during the first few years of the term; if the "term" is the measuring device, then a year during the term in which no assessment is made may be part of the average and the average itself will be low.[10] An averaging provision can be useful if it is tied to assessments of land and building, after substantial completion of the

---

[9] Falstaff Brewing Corp. v. Consolidated Fibres, Inc., 487 So. 2d 138 (La. Ct. App.), *writ denied*, 493 So. 2d 638 (La. 1986).

[10] *See* Rodolitz v. Neptune Paper Prods., Inc., 22 N.Y.2d 383, 239 N.E.2d 628, 292 N.Y.S.2d 878 (1968); (taxes assessed only against land in first year and against land and buildings in next two years of three-year average). *See generally* I Friedman § 5.401 (1983).

building and issuance of a certificate of occupancy. Another possible base year is the year in which the building is first assessed as fully operational.

Second, are there substantial additional improvements to be made after the base year? Office buildings often have substantial tenant finish work to do after the certificate of occupancy is issued for the building.[11] Phased developments present the same possibility. These improvements can result in higher assessments and increased taxes. Additional improvements or phased developments can also be pitfalls for the landlord. If the lease defines the base year as the one in which substantial completion occurs, what is the base year if the project is fully developed over several years?

This problem arises more often in shopping centers that are completed according to the site plan and then enlarged. If the base year is the year in which the initial improvements are completed, the tenant has been held responsible for a large increase over the base year that occurred when the additional improvements were made.[12] If one were to generalize, one might say that a small tenant is likely to prevail in its claim that it should not be liable for real estate taxes arising from the landlord's improvements subsequent to the lease. A tenant of a substantial portion of the building, which could have foreseen a tax increase arising from improvements which it knew would be made after its lease, will be liable for its share of them.[13]

Finally, are any tax contests pending? In contrast to the previous provision, in which the landlord had a fixed dollar obligation, here the landlord's obligation is only whatever the taxes may be in a specified year. The real estate professional must first determine the actual amount (if known) and will insist that the dollar amount be specified as the landlord's contribution. In this situation, a successful contest decreases the landlord's contribution and decreases the base amount over which the tenant shares. Thus, when taxes are tied to a base year as opposed to a base amount, the tenant suffers from a successful contest. Consequently, when considering these provisions, the real estate professional must ask whether a contest is in progress or contemplated and should provide that, in any event, the landlord's share will always be the original tax bill for purposes of the lease.

---

[11] Faberge Inc. v. Fisher Sixth Ave. Co., 40 A.D.2d 788, 338 N.Y.S.2d 383 (Sup. Ct. 1972).

[12] National Commercial Bank & Trust Co. v. Richard I. Rubin & Co., 51 A.D. 2d 818, 379 N.Y.S.2d 527 (1976), aff'd, 41 N.Y.2d 937, 363 N.E.2d 362, 394 N.Y.S.2d 638 (1977).

[13] See Credit Exchange, Inc. v. 461 Eighth Ave. Assocs., 69 N.Y.2d 994, 511 N.E.2d 47, 517 N.Y.S.2d 903, reargument denied, 70 N.Y.2d 748, 514 N.E.2d 392, 519 N.Y.S.2d 1034 (tenant exonerated from increased real estate taxes attributable to expansion of building).

CHAPTER 8

UTILITIES

§ 8.1   Utilities in Single Tenant Building Lease

In keeping with the guiding principles of these leases, the tenant of a single tenant building is solely responsible for every aspect of its utilities. A typical provision may say:

FORM 8-1
UTILITIES—SINGLE TENANT BUILDING

Tenant will pay the appropriate suppliers for all water, gas, electricity, light, heat, telephone, power, and other utilities and communications services used by tenant on the premises during the term, whether or not such services are billed directly to tenant. Tenant will also procure, or cause to be procured, without cost to landlord, any and all necessary permits, licenses, or other authorizations required for the lawful and proper installation and maintenance upon the premises of wires, pipes, conduits, tubes, and other equipment and appliances for use in supplying any such service to and upon the premises. Landlord, upon request of tenant, and at the sole expense and liability of tenant, will join with tenant in any application required for obtaining or continuing any such services.

Tenants should insist upon assurance that their desired utilities are available at the premises:

FORM 8-2
UTILITIES—TENANT'S ASSURANCE OF UTILITIES

Landlord warrants to tenant that electricity, water, sanitary and drainage sewers, telephone, and natural gas will be available at the outside wall of the building

199

throughout the term of this lease. If any such utility service becomes unavailable or is interrupted for more than _____ (_____) consecutive days (without default by tenant), tenant may terminate this lease by notice to landlord given within _____ (_____) days after such services become unavailable, or within _____ (_____) days after the ninetieth (90th) day of interruption, as the case may be. The notice will specify a termination date no more than thirty (30) days after the date of such notice. This lease will end on the termination date, and rent and other charges will be appropriately prorated between landlord and tenant as of the termination date.

Landlords often respond to this provision by suggesting that the tenant inspect the utility systems and assure itself of their adequacy before entering into the lease.

In giving these assurances, landlords should be careful to distinguish between the *premises* (which may include land that is not served by utilities) and the *building on the premises* (served by utilities). In these leases of single tenant buildings, the *premises* should include the land between the building and the property line so that the tenant will be obligated to make repairs of utility lines and not just the utility systems in the building.[1]

§ 8.2   Utilities in Shopping Center Lease

Shopping centers are often constructed so that each tenant's premises are separately metered; still, some shopping centers apportion utilities costs on the basis of the areas of the premises that are served.[2] When utilities directly serve the premises, the general provision states:

FORM 8-3
UTILITIES—SHOPPING CENTER LEASE

Tenant will pay all initial utility deposits and fees, and all monthly service charges for water, electricity, sewage, gas, telephone, and any other utility services furnished to the premises and the improvements on the premises during the entire term of this lease. If any such services are not separately metered or billed to tenant but rather are billed to and paid by landlord, tenant will pay to landlord its pro rata share of the cost of such services, as determined by landlord, together with its pro rata share of the cost of making such determination. Landlord will not be liable for any reason for any loss or damage resulting from an interruption of any of these services.

This provision is used in tandem with the common area maintenance charge provision so that the tenant pays for all utilities to its premises and for its share of

---

[1] *See* Smith's Properties, Inc. v. Munford, Inc., 165 Ga. App. 204, 300 S.E.2d 3 (1983).

[2] A very helpful discussion of energy costs in multitenant developments is found in Cassettes 6 & 7, ALI-ABA, *Advanced Issues in Commercial Leasing* (Houston, Nov. 1983).

utilities to the common areas. When the shopping center premises are built out on a shell and allowance basis, the tenant must assure itself that the utilities are available at the boundary of the premises and not at some distance away from them. The cost of bringing utilities to the premises can be significant.

§ 8.3   Utilities in Office Building Lease

Generally, office building tenants pay their shares of utilities as part of the operating expenses that they pay; the provision in § **6.11** includes utilities as part of building operating expenses. In addition, these tenants pay for utilities when they request landlord's services in excess of normal business hours.

There is, however, no reason why the cost of utilities cannot be separately charged as an escalation in its own right. Such a provision is:

FORM 8-4
UTILITIES—OFFICE BUILDING ENERGY ESCALATION

For purposes of this paragraph "building energy costs" means the costs and expenses incurred or borne by landlord for steam, oil, electricity, or any other fuel or energy source purchased or used for the building (other than electricity that is redistributed to tenants on a rent inclusion or a submetering basis). Forty percent (40%) of the building's payment to the public utility for the purchase of electricity will be deemed to be payment for electricity purchased or used for the building. The term "proportionate share" means a fraction whose numerator is the rentable area of the premises and whose denominator is the total rentable area of the building (excluding garage space). The total rentable area of the premises is _____ square feet, and the rentable area of the building is _____ square feet. The term "base year" means the full calendar year prior to the year in which the term of this lease commences. The term "comparison year" means the calendar year in which the term of this lease commences and each subsequent calendar year.

If the building energy costs for any comparison year are greater than those for the base year, tenant will pay to landlord, as additional rent, a sum equal to tenant's proportionate share of the excess (the "energy payment") of the building energy costs and for such comparison year over those for the base year.

(a)   After the end of each comparison year, landlord will submit to tenant a statement, certified by landlord, setting forth the building energy costs for the preceding comparison year and the energy payment, if any, due to landlord from tenant for the comparison year. The rendition of the statement to tenant will constitute prima facie proof of the accuracy of the statement. If the statement shows an energy payment due from tenant to landlord with respect to the comparison year, then tenant will pay landlord (i) any unpaid portion of the energy payment within ten (10) days after receipt of such statement; (ii) within ten (10) days after receipt of such statement, an amount equal to the product obtained by multiplying the total energy payment for the preceding comparison year by a fraction whose denominator is twelve (12) and whose numerator is the number of months of the current comparison year that have elapsed prior to the first day of the month immediately following the rendition of the statement; and (iii) commencing as of the first day of the month immediately following the rendition of the statement and on the first day of each succeeding month until a new statement is rendered, one-twelfth (1/12th) of the total energy payment for the comparison year. These monthly payments based on the total energy payment for the preceding comparison year will be adjusted to reflect known increases in rates for the current comparison year applicable to the categories involved in computing building energy costs, whenever the increases become known prior to or during the current comparison year. The payments required to be made under (ii) and (iii) will be credited toward the energy payment due from tenant for the then-current comparison year, subject to adjustment as and when the statement for the current comparison year is rendered by landlord.

Tenant will make energy payments due for the first comparison year on the basis of reasonable estimates prepared by landlord. Payments will be made monthly on the first day of each month during the first comparison year. The payments based on the estimates will then be adjusted by landlord and tenant after the end of the first comparison year on the basis of landlord's actual costs for that year.

Landlord's certified public accountant may rely on landlord's allocations and estimates wherever allocations or estimates are needed for building energy costs. The statements of the building energy costs thus furnished by landlord to tenant will constitute a final determination as between landlord and tenant of the building energy costs for the periods represented by the statements unless, within sixty (60) days after they are furnished, tenant gives notice to landlord that it disputes their accuracy. The notice will specify the particular respects in which tenant believes the statements are inaccurate. Pending resolution of the dispute, tenant will pay the additional rent to landlord in accordance with the statements furnished by landlord. After payment of the additional rent, tenant will have the right, during reasonable business hours and upon not less than five (5) business days' prior written notice to landlord, to examine landlord's books and records with respect to the statements, so long as such examination is commenced within thirty (30) days and concluded within sixty (60) days after the rendition of the statement in question.

(b)   Any dispute will be resolved by arbitration in accordance with the provisions of paragraph [arbitration provision].

(c)   The base monthly rent will not be reduced by virtue of this paragraph.

(d)   If the commencement date of the term of this lease is not the first day of the first comparison year, then the additional rent due under this paragraph for the first comparison year will be a proportionate share of the additional rent for the entire comparison year. At the end of this lease, the unpaid proportionate share of the additional rent for the comparison year during which the end occurs will immediately become due and payable by tenant to landlord. Landlord will as soon as practicable cause statements of the building energy costs for that comparison year to be prepared and furnished to tenant. Landlord and tenant will make appropriate adjustments of amounts then owing.

(e)   Landlord's and tenant's obligation to make the adjustments referred to in subparagraph (3) will survive this lease.

(f)   Any delay or failure of landlord in billing any energy payment will not impair the continuing obligation of tenant to make the energy payment.

The tenant must be certain that the utility expenses are not duplicated in the operating expenses. Furthermore, the tenant should have some assurance about the average utility use of the other tenants. A tenant whose utility use per square foot is low is foolish to share utility costs on a per square foot basis with other tenants whose per square foot use is higher; when the costs are allocated, the low-use tenant will share the higher overall cost created by the other tenants.

§ 8.4   Direct Metering, Submetering, and Electric Rent Inclusion

A significant exception to the practice of including utilities in office building operating expenses occurs commonly in New York City. There, certain utilities may be provided on a direct metering, submetering, or electric rent inclusion basis.

Direct metering (which is also known as individual metering) involves a direct contract between the tenant and the public utility. As a general rule, this method is most attractive to tenants because they pay only for what they use. This is particularly true of significant tenants whose bulk usage may entitle them to lower utility prices. Landlords can administer a direct metering system so that they profit from it. They may, for example, insist that their tenants buy meters and light bulbs from them at prices that include a profit for the landlord. In addition, landlords can charge for utilities used in the common areas and mark up the costs of those utilities. Of course, the tenant must be certain that its utility bill relates only to its own usage and not to common area usage.

Submetering is used when the landlord buys utilities in bulk and resells them to the tenant, perhaps at higher rates.[3] In addition to reselling the utilities at higher rates, landlords often add an administrative charge that bears no relationship to any cost it incurs, because its cost is built into the resale and overhead should be paid from its resale. Submetering commonly causes injustice because tenants pay first-user or low-volume rates and the landlord profits by its volume purchases. One large shopping center owner annually charged its tenants about $100,000 more for its electricity than the utility company's direct costs for the same electricity.[4] One approach that tenants can take is to insist that their cost be the average cost per unit charged to the landlord and not the first-user or low-volume charge.

Electric rent inclusion is a device by which the cost of the tenant's utilities is included in the rent.[5] Thus, a rent of $25 per square foot may include $1.25 for utilities on a rent inclusion basis. The amount of the utility charge included in the rent is based upon an estimate of the tenant's requirements — or connected load — and is subject to adjustment by the landlord's survey of the tenant's actual use.

---

[3] Annot., 75 A.L.R.3d 1204, *Landlord supplying electricity, gas, water, or similar facility to tenant as subject to utility regulation* (1977).

[4] Public Serv. Comm'n v. Howard Research & Dev. Corp., 271 Md. 141, 314 A.2d 682, 75 A.L.R.3rd 1193 (1974).

[5] Collins, *Electric Rent Inclusion Fosters Energy Gluttony,* 12 Real Est. Rev. 93 (1982); I Friedman 5.205 (1983).

The cost is not based on a meter reading of the tenant's actual use. As a result, the right to contest the landlord's survey and the right to insist upon its own survey must be demanded by the tenant.

Electric rent inclusion raises some of the same questions that are raised by submetering. Is the tenant's utility cost based on the higher first-user cost or on the landlord's actual average cost? Is the electricity cost that is included in the rent duplicated in the operating expenses, thus allowing the landlord double recovery?

Tenants who face direct metering, submetering, or electric inclusion leases often retain separate experts in utility usage in order to assure themselves of the greatest possible understanding of these provisions.

INSURANCE

§ 9.1   A Method of Management

The real estate professional can safely ignore the insurance provisions of a lease. This seemingly indefensible statement is unquestionably correct if one assumption is made: that during the term of the lease no one will be hurt on or about the premises, and nothing will happen to the premises or the project of which they are a part. Unless real estate professionals are willing to guarantee that improbable state of affairs, they must address the insurance provisions of the lease.

Many real estate professionals are unnecessarily intimidated by insurance provisions.[1] Although insurance provisions can be complicated, the real estate

---

[1] The only available and current book about insurance and leases is H. Brooks & D. Malecki, Insuring the Lease Exposure (2nd ed. 1989), half of which is devoted to personal property leases

professional can readily grasp the fundamental concepts and recognize the issues that demand greater expertise. Some insurance terminology, such as *all-risk* insurance, is misleading. Some insurance terms, such as *co-insured,* are easily confused with other terms, such as *additional insured.* To epitomize the confusion, when the old standard liability policy (the *comprehensive general liability policy*) was changed, it was renamed the *commercial general liability policy* and its abbreviation, CGL, was unchanged; as a result, CGL stands for two different policies. This chapter explains the insurance matters that are most commonly found in leases and then offers forms that may be used in office building, shopping center, and single tenant building leases.

A landowner generally bears the risk of liability to people who sustain bodily injury or property damage on the landowner's property, and is also at risk for damage to the improvements on its property. When the landowner becomes a landlord and separates its ownership of the property from possession of the property, it tries to avoid or minimize these risks. Consequently, the lease is a method of risk management for the landlord.

§ 9.2   Finding Risk Management Provisions

A lease may have one or more risk management strategies.[2] For example, there is *risk retention*; the landlord retains the risk of property damage arising from uninsurable risks such as nuclear war. There is *risk avoidance,* such as a prohibition against storage of explosives on the premises. There is *express risk allocation,* such as the tenant's obligation to indemnify the landlord against losses arising out of the tenant's use of the premises and the exculpation of the landlord from liability to its tenant for certain (perhaps all) losses that the tenant suffers.

The lease also implicitly allocates risks from the landlord to the tenant. For example, if the tenant must continue to pay rent during any period of restoration following damage to the premises, some of the risk of damage—the loss of income—is effectively transferred to the tenant. If the tenant must surrender the premises in the condition in which they were delivered, or if the tenant has an unqualified obligation to maintain or repair the premises, the tenant bears the risk of damage to the premises.

Furthermore, the lease allocates risks in almost imperceptible ways. For example, if the landlord's insurer does not waive its rights of subrogation against

---

and half of which is devoted to real estate leases. *See generally* G. Castle, R. Cushman & P. Kensicki, The Business Insurance Handbook (1981); Ellis & Goodrich, *Everything You Need to Know About Insurance in Commercial Leases (with Forms),* Prac. Real Est. Law., July 1989, at 23; Fischer, *Insurance and Restoration Provisions in Commercial Leases,* 3 Prac. Real Est. Law. 73 (1987); Dauer & Pierce, *Who is Obligated Under a Lease?,* 2 J. Real Est. Dev. 87 (1987); Dauer & Pierce, *The Liability Considerations of the Lease,* 3 J. Real Est. Dev. 71 (1987).

[2] Properly speaking, insurance is not a risk management strategy but only a method of assuring payment by the one who bears the risk.

the tenant, the insurer may sue the tenant if it must pay a loss that the tenant caused. Many leases do not make provision for termination after certain risks for which insurance is usually not available, such as earthquake or flood. In these cases, the risk of loss is shifted to a tenant if it has no legal right to terminate its lease after its premises are destroyed.

The real estate professional who reads only the insurance provisions of the lease will not be aware of many risks for which insurance is required or appropriate.[3] By way of illustration, most leases provide that the tenant will indemnify the landlord against certain losses. Although this indemnification is not found among the insurance provisions, the tenant can obtain appropriate insurance in order to be protected against this risk. The office building use provision discussed in **§ 10.2** often allocates to the tenant any increase in the landlord's insurance rates that is caused by the tenant's use.[4] This is another example of an agreement regarding insurance that is not part of the insurance provision.

The insurance provisions of most leases give almost no guidance regarding insurance that the tenant should obtain for its own benefit. If any provision is made, it is typically that the tenant must insure its inventory, fixtures, and improvements; in fact, this provision is largely for the landlord's benefit, because it insures tenant's capability to rebuild, restock, and resume its business. Tenants have insurable interests in their leasehold improvements (even if they become the landlord's property when installed), because they have the use and enjoyment of them during the term; the appropriate coverage is called an improvements and betterments policy. Every tenant is concerned about the continuation of its income after damage to its premises; because this is of no concern to landlords, their leases do not mention the need for insurance and tenants are left to deduce it for themselves. Finally, an individual tenant must consider life insurance if his or her estate will continue to be obligated under the lease.

In conclusion, the landlord and tenant must identify the risks they bear under the lease, and must insure themselves against losses from those risks.

§ 9.3   The Law and Basic Terms

There are very few (if any) legal principles of real estate law that directly govern insurance in leases; of course, contract law and insurance law exert paramount control.[5] In the absence of any requirement, neither the landlord nor the tenant

---

[3] A helpful checklist is set forth in Even, *A Critique of Lease Terms and Their Effect on Insurance Administration,* 7 Forum 130 (1972).

[4] Lindblad, *Risk Implications in Lease Agreements,* Ins. L.J., June 1979, at 307-12.

[5] For the insurance principles, see J. Appleman, 4 Insurance Law and Practice §§ 2191-94 (1969, Supp. 1982), and H. Brooks & D. Malecki, Insuring the Lease Exposure (2nd ed. 1989).

needs to insure the premises.[6] This is true even though both the landlord and the tenant have an insurable interest in the premises for purposes of property insurance; that is, they have profit, advantage, or benefit by the continued existence of the premises and will sustain loss from damage to the premises.[7]

The insurance contract is a contract of indemnity; its purpose is to place the insured in the same position as the insured would have been if the insured's loss had not occurred. This idea is a fundamental principle of insurance law. It follows from this tenet that an insured cannot improve its position as a result of an insured loss, but can only be returned to its position before the loss.

In keeping with the principle that the insurance contract is a contract of indemnity, the real estate professional can see the differences and similarities of the two broad categories of risk: the insured's liability to third parties for bodily injury or property damage, and the insured's risk of loss of its own property. The proceeds of liability insurance are payable to a third party and the insured receives nothing from them; the insured's liability is paid by its insurer to the extent of the policy limits and the insured remains where it was before the loss. The proceeds of property insurance are payable to the insured and not to any third party (except, perhaps, the insured's lender to the extent of its loan against the property); the insured (or lender) gets the insured value of its property and remains where it was before the casualty. Thus, even though the claims are paid differently, liability insurance and property damage insurance return the insured to its position before the loss.

Before turning to specific insurance coverages, the real estate professional should bear in mind that individuals (or entities) and not properties or risks are insured; thus, one correctly says that "Jones is insured against certain fire risks" and not "Jones's property is insured against certain fire risks."

§ 9.4 Liability Insurance

For many years, comprehensive general liability insurance was written as a basic policy with many possible endorsements or a single broad form endorsement. In

---

[6] A New York tenant who was unable to obtain the required insurance limits because of a crisis in the liability insurance markets was not excused by the force majeure provision and lost its lease. Kel Kim Corp. v. Central Mkts., 133 Misc. 2d 529, 507 N.Y.S.2d 359 (Sup. Ct. 1986), *aff'd*, 131 A.D.2d 947, 516 N.Y.S.2d 806, *aff'd*, 70 N.Y.2d 900, 519 N.E.2d 295, 524 N.Y.S.2d 384 (1987).

[7] A tenant with an option to purchase, however, does not have an insurable interest to the extent of the value of the property in the absence of a binding obligation to purchase it; the tenant's insurable interest may include the value of the use of the building during the unexpired term of the lease, the value of the leasehold improvements, and the value of the contents and the tenant's personal property. Travelers Indem. Co. v. Duffy's Little Tavern, 478 So. 2d 1095 (Fla. Dist. Ct. App. 1985), *review denied*, 488 So. 2d 68 (Fla. 1986), *appeal after remand*, 541 So. 2d 689 (Fla. Dist. Ct. App. 1989). This discussion is based on the ISO form. There may be important differences, however, between these forms and those offered by other insurers. The real estate professional should read the ISO liability forms for a full appreciation of all their terms, which seem to be an attempt at "plain English."

1986 the Insurance Services Offices, Inc. (ISO) promulgated the *commercial general liability policy,* which, like its predecessor, is known as the CGL policy.[8] The new policy simplifies former practice by subsuming the old basic policy and many of the common endorsements in one policy. The coverages are explained further in this § **9.4**.

Before the real estate professional considers the coverages, two extremely important changes in the policies must be observed. The ISO forms now offer both claims-made and occurrence coverages. A *claims-made policy* insures against claims that are made during the term of the policy. An *occurrence policy* covers events that occurred during the term of the policy, even if the claims are made after the term of the policy. An insured has greater protection with traditional occurrence coverage than with the newer claims-made coverage. Conversely, insurance companies have greater liability exposure with occurrence policies than with claims-made policies; the asbestos litigation, for example, has led to questions about the respective responsibilities of many insurers over several decades. Although the intricacies of these two types of coverages are beyond the scope of this work, the real estate professional should be generally aware of these two types of policies and the trend toward claims-made policies.

The second important change introduced in the new ISO forms has to do with the limits of insurance. Under the old CGL policy, an insured with a $1 million limit of insurance was protected for all claims up to $1 million each [9] during the term of the policy; for example, an insured was protected against five $1 million claims during the policy but not protected against the entirety of a $1.5 million claim. Under the new forms, the limits of insurance are aggregated for all claims during the term of the policy; as a result, an insured is protected against a single $1 million claim or five $200,000 claims, but no more than $1 million for all claims.[10] Some policy forms include the costs of defense in the limits of insurance, thus reducing the insured's protection. There are also separate sublimits for medical payments, personal injury, advertising injury, and fire damage legal liability coverages, as explained in this § **9.4**.

---

[8] ISO published several pamphlets explaining the CGL entitled "Introduction and Overview," "Workshop Student's Guide," "Workshop Exercises," and "Reference Materials." (They are available from ISO, 160 Water St., New York, NY 10038.) They provide detailed explanations of the changes in coverages and the newly available coverages. The discussion in the text concerns the ISO policy forms; however, not all insurance companies are members or affiliates of ISO and many file and sell different liability policies. As always, the real estate professional must read the policy.

[9] Occurrence and claims are separate concepts although they are frequently confused. An occurrence gives rise to a claim or more than one; for example, a single auto accident may injure three people. The distinction is important for several reasons, not the least of which is that deductibles pertain to occurrences and not claims; in the auto accident example, there would be one deductible even though there were three claims.

[10] This example presumes that the occurrence limits are at least $200,000. An occurrence limit is the most that will be paid on all claims in one occurrence and an aggregate limit is the most that will be paid for all occurrences.

Commercial general liability insurance is a "line" of insurance in which there are two sublines: *products/completed operations* and *premises/operations*. For commercial leases, the premises/operations subline is most relevant. That subline includes the older sublines called manufacturers and contractors (M&C); owners, landlord and tenants (OLT); personal injury and advertising injury; medical payments; and fire damage legal liability.

The CGL policy has three basic insurance coverages: bodily injury and property damage; personal injury and advertising injury; and medical payments. Bodily injury and property damage coverage provides broad indemnification against loss from liability for those occurrences. However, it is subject to several exclusions, including the expected consequences of the insured's conduct (in other words, the insured's intentional acts); liquor-related accidents if the insured is in the liquor business; injuries to employees, who are presumably covered by worker's compensation insurance; and pollution incidents. The CGL policy provides what used to be called contractual liability coverage, that is, insurance for bodily injury or property damage that an insured assumes by contract such as a lease; this is the method by which a tenant insures its indemnification of its landlord against loss on account of bodily injury or property damage. The CGL policy also provides fire damage legal liability insurance for fire damage to premises rented to the insured, but only if the insured has liability for the fire; this coverage is subject to a separate limit and is inapplicable to personal property in the insured's care, custody, or control, as to which the tenants must usually get a separate policy.

The second basic coverage in the CGL policy is personal injury and advertising injury. As distinguished from bodily injury which involves physical harm, personal injury generally means false arrest, malicious prosecution, wrongful eviction, and defamation. Advertising injury includes violation of a person's right of privacy, misappropriation of advertising ideas, and copyright infringement. This coverage is also subject to a sublimit.

The final basic coverage in the CGL policy is medical payments coverage. It pays medical expenses for bodily injury occurring on or on ways to premises owned or rented by the insured. Unlike other liability insurance policies, medical payments coverage obtains regardless of the insured's negligence.

The last basic question about the CGL policy is who is covered by it. An individual and spouse are insured. A partnership and all its partners and their spouses are insured, but only with respect to conduct of the business. For other organizations, executive officers and directors are insured, as are shareholders, but in all cases only in those capacities.

The landlord has the benefit of the tenant's liability policy if it is named as an additional insured; it has a defense and primary coverage to the limits of the policy. Nevertheless, the landlord may have liability exposure for which it buys insurance separately. Such an exposure may occur if the liability arises from a part of the property owned by the landlord but not leased to the tenant. Another exposure may arise from personal injury or property damage caused by additions or improvements to the premises made by the landlord and by other independent action of the landlord. Of course, the tenant may fail to add the landlord as an additional insured; the resultant loss to the landlord is not covered by the tenant's liability policy.

§ 9.5 Property Insurance

Insurance is at the root of the relationship between the repairs and maintenance, casualty, and surrender provisions of most leases. All these provisions may prescribe the condition of the premises at the end of the term. If the surrender provision requires the tenant to return the premises in their condition at the time they were delivered, "ordinary wear and tear and casualty damage excepted," while the casualty provision requires the landlord to repair the premises after casualty damage, and the maintenance provision requires the tenant to maintain and repair the premises, then the lease, taken as a whole, does not tell landlord and tenant who should repair the premises after an accidental fire caused by the tenant. When confronted with inconsistent provisions such as these, the real estate professional's first task is to organize them and then to determine the risks that the landlord and tenant must insure.

Landlords will be compelled by their lenders to maintain property insurance on the premises. Tenants will want to maintain property insurance for their contents and their improvements to the premises. The real estate professional can make an important contribution to any lease by assuring that the landlord's and tenant's coverages are consistent and not overlapping.

The *standard fire policy* protects the insured against direct loss by fire and lightning and the cost of removal from premises that are endangered by fire and lightning. In addition, the standard policy covers the cost of water and smoke damage incidental to an insured occurrence. Fire insurance with extended coverage covers not only the occurrences included within the standard fire policy, but also includes loss from windstorm, hail, explosion, lightning, riot and civil commotion, damage by aircraft, and damage by a vehicle. The fire policy may be endorsed to include risks of vandalism and malicious mischief, and has optional coverages for falling objects, weight of snow, sleet, or ice, collapse, water damage, glass breakage (not the same as plate glass coverage described in § 9.14), and accidental sprinkler damage.

The standard fire policy and the extended fire coverage policy are called *named perils coverages* because they name the perils that they cover. In order for the insured to recover on a standard fire policy or extended coverage fire policy, the insured must prove that there was a loss and that the loss occurred as a result of one of the named perils. The named perils policies (that is, the standard fire coverage and the extended fire coverage policies) exclude losses from water, flood, operation of building codes, nuclear reaction, power failure, and damage to electrical apparatus from artificially generated currents.

Some of these risks may be covered by an *all-risk policy,* which is written differently from both fire policies. In order to recover on an all-risk policy, the insured must only prove that a loss occurred; it need not show which peril caused the loss, but only that the loss is not specifically excluded. If the insurer denies coverage, it has the burden of showing that the peril was excluded. Since the all-risk policy usually excludes flood, earthquake, and losses from nuclear reaction, the term *all-risk* is a misnomer.

A *difference in condition policy* (DIC) usually covers earthquakes, floods, and many other losses, but it is subject to high deductibles, and can be very expensive if the property is in a flood or earthquake zone.

Since the tenant as occupant and user of the landlord's property is the most likely cause of damage to that property, tenants must protect themselves from claims arising from that damage. One method is to insist upon being named on the landlord's policy; since the insurer cannot assert a claim against its own insured, the tenant is protected—but only to the limits of the policy and the extent of the covered perils. Another approach is to insist upon a waiver of subrogation as discussed in § **9.11**; again, the tenant is protected to the policy limits but exposed for greater losses. Finally, the tenant can buy its own fire legal liability policy, as discussed in § **9.4**.

§ 9.6   Actual Cash Value and Replacement Cost

Because the property insurance policy (like any other insurance policy) is a contract of indemnity, and is not meant to be used to improve the insured's position as a result of a loss, fire policies may be obtained only for the insured's loss. Property damage policies are usually written in one of two ways: *actual cash value* (ACV) and *replacement cost*. Although its definition is subject to dispute, ACV usually means replacement cost less physical depreciation. ACV must never be confused with depreciated book value or other accounting valuation; depreciated book value considers tax-related depreciation and is almost invariably less than the ACV. When an insured insures for the property's actual cash value, or when an insured insures a property for its replacement cost but does not rebuild after damage, it receives the actual cash value of the premises.

The ACV may be inadequate to pay for the repairs. Under ACV coverage, the insured that loses a five-year-old awning gets a five-year-old awning or its cash equivalent. To avoid paying the shortfall themselves, landlords usually insure on a replacement cost basis in which depreciation is not deducted. Under replacement cost coverage, the insured gets "new for old" and the five-year-old awning would be replaced with a new awning. Once again, an insured that insures for replacement cost but does not rebuild receives no more than the ACV. Since building and zoning codes change, landlords often incur costs in excess of ACV or replacement cost in order to comply with new laws. This risk can be insured with an increased cost of construction endorsement. This endorsement, however, may not cover the cost of demolition, for which the insured should be certain to get demolition and debris removal coverage; if a building with asbestos burns, the presence of asbestos ash in the debris may require special handling. The value to which the premises must be insured is a critical factor in avoiding the painful consequences of co-insurance.

§ 9.7   Co-Insurance

Co-insurance arose when some buyers of insurance noticed that most fire damage results in less than a total loss, and that they would be covered for the vast majority of losses if they insured their properties for a fraction of their actual values. Insurance companies believed that this practice penalized the insureds who bought insurance in an amount more closely related to the true value of the premises; a less charitable view holds that insurance companies were upset at the loss of revenues for the higher coverages. Accordingly, insurers required that insureds carry some specified portion, usually 80 to 90 percent of the sound insurable value of the premises, in order to recover fully for their losses. As a penalty for failing to do so, insurers now reduce any loss payment in the proportion that the actual amount of the insurance was less than the amount of the insurance that the insured was required to carry. The owner was said to be a co-insurer because it was self-insuring a loss with the premiums it saved.

Suppose that the owner of a building worth $1 million was insured by a fire policy having a typical 80 percent co-insurance provision. The owner would be required to insure the building for $800,000. If the owner insured the building for only $600,000, and a $300,000 loss occurred, the insurer would pay only $225,000 of the loss; that is, $600,000/$800,000 \times $300,000 = $225,000.

The liability of being a co-insurer is quite substantial. In order to avoid it, the insured should consider an inflation guard endorsement, which reduces the risks of co-insurance. With this endorsement, the policy limits are increased by inflation or, in some cases, by fixed amounts or percentages. A policy with an inflation guard endorsement usually provides that the insurer may not claim that the insured has co-insured a risk. The insurance may nevertheless be inadequate (because the value of the property has outstripped inflation), but the insured will not suffer the consequences of co-insurance.

Alternatively, the insured may demand that the co-insurance provision be removed, and should seek its insurer's agreement with the sufficiency of the amount of insurance as evidenced by a stipulated or agreed amount or stated amount endorsement. To get that endorsement, the insured must usually insure 90 percent of the replacement cost.

§ 9.8   Contributing Policies

Because both the landlord and the tenant have insurable interests in the premises, some real estate professionals feel that they should both be insured for the value of the premises, and that, if a loss occurs, both the landlord and the tenant will recover on their policies. That is not, however, what happens, since the result would be to put either the landlord or the tenant in a better position than it had been before the loss, violating the principle of indemnity. The outcome will depend upon the provisions of the policies and, in their absence, the governing law. Either the policies will share the liability, in which case they are called *contributing,* or one will pay first and the other will pay any amount in excess of the limits of the first, in which case the first paying policy is called *primary* and the other policy is called *excess* or *secondary*.

If the policies are contributing, they will contribute in one of two ways: their pro rata liability, or their limit of liability. Pro rata liability apportions the loss over the total face amounts of the policies. Limit of liability apportions the loss on the basis of what each of the policies would have paid if there had been no other policy in effect.

To illustrate the differences in contribution, and disregarding any co-insured risks, suppose that a $1 million building were insured for $800,000 by the landlord and for $200,000 by the tenant, and that a $500,000 loss occurred. The total of the face amounts of the policy is $1,000,000. On a pro rata contribution, the landlord's insurer would pay 80 percent of the loss ($800,000/$1,000,000), or $400,000, and the tenant's insurer would pay 20 percent of the loss ($200,000/$1,000,000), or $100,000.

In the limit of liability approach, the maximum exposure of the insurers (that is, their respective policy limits) is compared and their sharing is based upon the respective percentages of their loss. In the preceding example, the limits of liability are $500,000 (the actual loss) for the insurer with the $800,000 policy, and $200,000 for the insurer with the $200,000 policy, and the total limit of liability is $700,000. Therefore, the loss would be apportioned in this way:

$800,000 policy issuer: ($500,000/$700,000) $\times$ $500,000 = $357,143
$200,000 policy issuer: ($200,000/$700,000) $\times$ $500,000 = $\underline{$142,857}$
$$\$500,000$$

Some policies prohibit other insurance, thus creating the possibility that their coverages might be voided by the existence of other insurance. Other policies provide that they will be in excess to any concurrent coverage. In any event, duplicate insurance complicates the adjustment process, and that complication delays rebuilding.

Leases that require property policies commonly require that the landlord be named as a "loss payee as its interest may appear" on any of the tenant's property insurance policies. Although this requirement has some virtues, it also has some faults. Its principal virtue is that the insurer will have no right of subrogation against either the landlord or the tenant if it pays any loss; this is true because of the general rule that an insurer has no rights of subrogation against its insured. On the other hand, if a lease requires the landlord to maintain property insurance for the premises, the landlord and tenant may both be considered insureds, and the insurer will have no subrogation rights against a tenant that negligently causes a fire.[11] Its principal vice is that the insurer cannot settle claims unless both insureds agree to the settlement.

The real estate professional should avoid two common errors in these provisions. One is the improper use of *additional insured*; that term is limited to

---

[11] Fashion Place Inv. v. Salt Lake County/Salt Lake County Mental Health, 776 P.2d 941 (Utah Ct. App. 1989).

liability coverages only. The other is the improper use of *named insured*; a named insured is liable for premiums and other obligations under the policy (such as reporting requirements), and thus landlords do not want to be named insureds. When the landlord and tenant are both to be insureds in the fire policy, the lease should provide which one of them is responsible for settlement of claims on the policy. The fire policy that is purchased to cover two insureds can be endorsed to provide that one insured may recover against the insurer even though the other insured has made misrepresentations in the application for insurance.

§ 9.9   Insuring the Rent Stream

By endorsement to its fire policy, an insured can buy rental value or rental income insurance that assures the payment of rent if the premises are rendered untenantable by fire. These coverages traditionally had distinct meanings (depending whether the insured was the landlord or the tenant), but are now used interchangeably. In fact, rent insurance, rental value insurance, and business interruption insurance (discussed in § 9.10) are often subsumed in the *business income coverage*. This insurance may be purchased by either the landlord or the tenant, depending upon which has an insurable interest in the rent stream. If the tenant is obligated to continue to pay rent during the period of any repair of fire damage, then the tenant has an insurable interest, and it is the only possible insured under a rent insurance policy. On the other hand, if tenant is not obligated to pay rent during any period when the premises are rendered untenantable by fire, then the landlord bears the risk of the lost rental, and the landlord is the only proper insured under a rent insurance policy. Landlords often buy excess rental value insurance that pays the difference between the fair rental value and the rent received for premises that have been damaged to such an extent as to result in cancellation.

In determining the amount of coverage that is necessary, the insured must consider the greatest period for which it will be obligated to pay rent (in the case of the tenant) or deprived of rent (in the case of the landlord). This determination can only be made by examining the rights of the landlord and tenant to terminate the lease if the building is not restored within some period after it is damaged by fire. These rights are found in the damage and destruction provisions. In addition to considering base rent, the insured should take into account the taxes and other operating expenses that accrue after the insured casualty.

§ 9.10   Tenant's Insurance

With the exception of leases that require a tenant to insure its personal property and inventory, leases do not usually give any consideration to the tenant's insurance. Coverages in which tenants are interested include:

Property Insurance.   The tenant will often carry insurance for its improvements and betterments, that is, insurance for its interest in fixtures, actuations, installations, or additions that are part of the premises, but not owned by the tenant, and that were acquired at the tenant's expense but are not removable by the tenant. The insurance is called *building and personal property coverage* on some forms. Many of the observations in § **9.5** regarding landlord's property insurance are relevant to the tenant. When appropriate, tenants consider boiler and machinery coverage, which is written as a separate policy.

If the landlord has agreed to restore the tenant's improvements and betterments, then the tenant seems to have no insurable interest in them. The landlord will insure them. However, if the landlord fails to restore the premises and the tenant cancels the lease pursuant to its right to do so, the tenant will lose the unamortized cost of its improvements and thus may have an insurable interest. The tenant may also have an insurable exposure if the landlord's restoration obligation—for example, to restore to the premises' original condition—is less than the condition as a result of subsequent improvements made by the tenant.

The other losses covered in this coverage are the cost of stock that was sold at the time of the fire but not delivered, and the cost of repurchasing, transporting, and reshelving inventory. If the tenant's inventory fluctuates, special reporting policies should be considered. These policies eliminate the cost of a fixed level of coverage and vary the coverage with reported inventory. In contrast to the landlord, whose property insurance policy limits are set by its lender, the tenant must decide for itself what limits its fire policy should have.

Tenants usually obtain property insurance against the risk of loss of their furniture, fixtures, and equipment. Again, the observations in § **9.5** are relevant here.

Insuring leasehold improvements is a very complicated matter. Landlords usually insure leasehold improvements made at their expense, and tenants usually do the same. If the lease is not terminated by the fire (but rather continues after repair), the cost of repair will be paid by the landlord's insurer or the tenant's insurer, depending upon which paid for the leasehold improvements.

If the lease is terminated by the fire damage, both landlord and tenant have compensable losses. The tenant has a claim for a prorated portion of the depreciated value of the leasehold improvements; that is, their remaining value to the tenant at the time of the fire. The landlord has a claim for the value of the improvements that (according to the usual rule) it was to get at the end of the lease. In this situation, there appears to be double recovery for the same loss; however, since there are two separate insurable interests, the principle of indemnity is not violated. The total recovery should be no greater than if the landlord owned the entire premises without a tenant.

The real estate professional may feel that overlapping coverage of leasehold improvements is wasteful. Why not require the landlord to insure the leasehold improvements (which its fire policy automatically includes) and to rebuild them after a fire? This may work, but the landlord and tenant may be unable to agree upon the division of insurance proceeds after a fire that terminates the lease.

Because of this possible conflict, landlords and tenants continue to insure the leasehold improvements separately.

Life Insurance.   This is necessary for an individual who is not able to negotiate a lease provision that terminates the lease automatically upon death or gives the tenant's personal representative or executor the right to cancel the lease within some period after the death. Individuals should consider disability insurance to cover rent during any period when a sole proprietor's health prevents him or her from operating the business. In certain circumstances, partners and key corporate employees should have similar insurance.

Business Interruption Insurance.   This insurance protects the tenant against the costs of operation when it is unable to operate as a result of a fire that destroys the tenant's own premises or adjoining premises whose vacancy affects the tenant. This coverage is usually written in one of three different ways: (1) *no co-insurance earnings form,* by which the small firm insures its profits and expenses with some limitations; (2) *gross earnings form,* which is similar to the no co-insurance earnings form but requires minimum insurance by virtue of its co-insurance feature; and (3) *profits form,* which assures the tenant's profits for a period of time after business resumes (in contrast to earnings forms, which stop paying when the premises should be ready for occupancy if repair is diligently pursued). Retailing and manufacturing tenants are particularly well-advised to carry this insurance.

Extra Expense Insurance.   This insurance covers the amount by which business expenses incurred during the period of restoration exceed what expenses would have been if damage had not occurred. This insurance is different from business interruption insurance, which continues the tenant's gross earnings, and it is generally recommended to be maintained in addition to that coverage. Extra expense insurance may be written as part of business interruption insurance. The rationale of extra expense coverage is that the insured's business interruption loss may be reduced if it has the ability to incur some extra expense; for example, a tenant whose premises are destroyed may have a smaller business interruption claim if it takes temporary space at some extra expense rather than sitting by idly during the reconstruction process.

Contingent Business Interruption Insurance.   In contrast to direct business interruption insurance, contingent business interruption insurance protects the tenant against losses that it suffers without direct physical injury to the insured, for example, property damage to the anchor tenants' premises.

Leasehold Interest Coverage.   This coverage protects a tenant who has an advantageous long-term lease in which the rent is less than prevailing market rate. If the premises are totally destroyed and the lease is terminated by the landlord, the tenant will be put to considerable additional expense in order to find replacement premises. This coverage protects the tenant against that risk. In addition, this coverage is used when the tenant has made a large cash investment in the lease itself, such as an advance rent payment, or a bonus payment to its assignor. Of course, the tenant's investment in the premises is also covered by the tenant's fire policy. Leasehold interest coverage should not be confused with leasehold title insurance discussed in § **32.7**.

§ 9.11   Waiver of Subrogation

When fire loss occurs, the insured's insurance company pays its insured for the amount of the loss. This payment is made without regard to fault. If the insured is at fault, but has not deliberately caused the loss, its insurer has no claim against it and must still pay the loss. If the insurer were to have a claim against its insured or the right not to pay the loss, a principal reason for insurance would be defeated. However, if a third person is at fault, the insured has a claim against that third person. Once the insured has been fully paid by its insurance company, any amount that the insured then recovered from the third party would be a double recovery and would put the insured in a better position than it had been before the loss occurred. That outcome, of course, is repugnant to the principle of indemnity. Consequently, the insurer is considered to be the only proper claimant against the person who caused the loss. In the parlance of insurance, the insurer is said to be *subrogated* to the rights that its insured has against that person. When the landlord's policy is found to be for the benefit of both landlord and tenant, the insurer has no subrogation rights against the tenant, because the tenant is, in effect, its insured.[12]

The insured's rights against that person are the basis for the rights that the insurer obtains by subrogation. If the insured waives its own rights against that third person, the insurer has no rights by subrogation. Insurers have traditionally allowed their insureds to waive their own rights and thus to preclude any claims that the insurer may make against a negligent third person.[13] Recently, however, insurers have changed their attitude towards these subrogated rights.

The change in attitude began in the early 1950s when a now-classic case drew insurers' attention to the importance of their subrogated rights.[14] The landlord leased a small piece of industrial property to a very substantial tenant. One of the

---

[12] Safeco Ins. Co. v. Capri, 101 Nev. 429, 705 P.2d 59 (1985).

[13] Strictly speaking, the landlord and tenant do not waive their rights of subrogation. The rights of subrogation belong to their insurers; however, since the insurers' rights are dependent upon the existence of their insureds' rights, a mutual release extinguishes the insurers' subrogated rights. In order to preserve their subrogated rights, insurers sometimes prohibit any release by their insureds or provide that a release will invalidate the insurance policy. If the insureds' policy allows the release, however, then the effect of the release is to waive subrogation. In a more succinct way, the waiver of subrogation is a brief but inexact way to describe what happens.

[14] Goldman v. General Mills, Inc., 184 F.2d 359 (8th Cir. 1950), *cert. denied*, 340 U.S. 947 (1951).

tenant's employees accidentally caused a fire that completely destroyed the building. The landlord's insurance company paid it approximately $110,000, which covered the landlord's acquisition cost of the property and some rental loss. The landlord, however, went on to sue the tenant for damages of approximately $342,000, on account of the loss of the building, the lost rent, and clean-up costs. The landlord's insurer intervened in order to protect its subrogated rights. The insurer's concern was that its insured might recover twice against the tenant or might reduce the insurer's claim against the tenant by the amount that the insurance company had paid, and thus prevent the insurer from recovering against the negligent tenant. The trial court ruled against the tenant for less than all of the amounts claimed, and ruled that the insurer was entitled to approximately $110,000, according to its subrogated rights. The trial court's determination turned on the fact that, although the lease required the tenant to surrender the premises in the same condition in which they were delivered to the tenant "loss by fire . . . excepted,"[15] the exception did not go so far as to exculpate the tenant from its negligence.

On appeal, the Eighth Circuit Court of Appeals construed the entire lease and concluded that the lease was drawn with the intention that the landlord acquire property insurance and that the risk of fire damage was meant to fall on the insurer and not the tenant.[16] Although the tenant won, insurers gave renewed consideration to their rights of subrogation.

As a result, the automatic waiver of subrogation that had been found in property insurance policies was replaced by more restrictive provisions. Some of those provisions allow rights of subrogation to be waived by the insured so long as it is done in writing and the insurance company is notified in writing before a loss occurs. Some insurance policies require the insured to obtain a written waiver of subrogation from the insurer before the loss occurs. In any case, many insurers have begun to impose a charge for the waiver of their rights of subrogation.

The waiver of subrogation is very important to tenants, because they are more likely to cause considerable damage to their landlords' property than are landlords likely to damage their tenants' property. Landlords usually insist on waivers of subrogation on tenants' workers compensation and automobile policies.

The preparation of a release of rights raises two important questions: (1) is the release to be of all claims or only for limits of insurance? and (2) is the release to be unilateral or bilateral? If the release is only of claims to the extent of insurance, the tenant still has exposure to the landlord for the amount of uninsured losses. If all claims are released, the releasor will pay its own deductible. This is probably not the intention of the landlord and tenant who, if they had thought about it, would not have agreed to pay their own deductible for a loss that was not their fault. With respect to the question of bilateral or unilateral waivers, tenants

---

[15] 184 F.2d at 360.

[16] *Id*. at 366.

usually have no problems waiving claims against their landlords so long as the tenants' insurers allow them to do so.

The mutual release of all claims is not fully satisfactory to a prudent tenant. A written waiver of the insurer's rights of subrogation—or evidence that the insured has the right to waive the insurer's rights of subrogation—is also desirable. Therefore, a mutual release provision is used in tandem with a waiver of subrogation:

FORM 9-1
INSURANCE—WAIVER OF SUBROGATION

Landlord and tenant waive all rights to recover against each other or against any other tenant or occupant of the building, or against the officers, directors, share-holders, partners, joint venturers, employees, agents, customers, invitees, or business visitors of each other or of any other tenant or occupant of the building, for any loss or damage arising from any cause covered by any insurance required to be carried by each of them pursuant to this paragraph or any other insurance actually carried by each of them. Landlord and tenant will cause their respective insurers to issue appropriate waiver of subrogation rights endorsements to all policies of insurance carried in connection with the building or the premises or the contents of either of them. Tenant will cause all other occupants of the premises claiming by, under, or through tenant to execute and deliver to landlord a waiver of claims similar to the waiver in this paragraph and to obtain such waiver of subrogation rights endorsements.

The tenant's interest in a waiver of subrogation by its landlord's insurer is so important that some further discussion is necessary. Once the tenant has the landlord's agreement to obtain a waiver of subrogation from its insurer, the tenant must pursue the matter to be certain that it is done. If the landlord fails to do so and if the tenant causes a loss, the landlord's insurer may still assert a very substantial claim against the tenant. In the usual lease that excuses the landlord from personal liability the tenant will have no fruitful avenue of recourse against its landlord for the landlord's breach of its promise.

In order to illustrate the steps by which this result would be reached, one must consider what happens when the landlord does not fulfill its promise to obtain its insurer's waiver of subrogation:

1. If the landlord either waives its claims against its tenant without its insurer's consent or forgets to get its insurer's waiver of subrogation, and subsequently a loss occurs, the landlord's insurer will investigate the loss, determine the cause, and pay the landlord for its loss.
2. The landlord's insurer determines that the tenant is the cause of the loss that it paid, and asserts its subrogated rights against the tenant.
3. The tenant will respond to its landlord's insurer by pointing out the waiver of subrogation contained in its lease. The landlord's insurer will respond that it never gave its waiver in the manner required in the landlord's policy.

4. The insurer will pursue its claim against the tenant and will ultimately recover the amount it paid to its insured.

5. The tenant will file suit against its landlord for breach of the landlord's agreement to obtain its insurer's waiver of subrogation.

6. The tenant will prevail in its claim against the landlord, who will be found liable to the tenant on account of its failure to obtain its insurer's waiver of subrogation.

7. The tenant, however, will be prevented from asserting any personal claim against the landlord by virtue of a limitation of the landlord's liability such as that set forth in **Chapter 29**.

8. The tenant will bear the loss.

Conclusion.   The tenant must develop a program to monitor its landlord's insurance in order to be certain that the landlord maintains insurance and that the landlord's insurers have waived and continue to waive their rights of subrogation against the tenant.

§ 9.12   Blanket Insurance, Excess Insurance, Umbrella Coverage, and Self-Insurance

Occasionally a tenant asks whether it can satisfy its insurance obligations by endorsements to its *blanket policies.* Blanket policies are policies that cover the same risks in several locations. Blanket policies are usually written for property damage risks; the corresponding breadth of coverage for liability is achieved by the "comprehensive" general liability policy. Obviously, blanket coverage is used by substantial companies having operations in several locations.

Traditionally, blanket coverage has worked this way. Suppose a company has five facilities that are each worth $5 million. Instead of five $5 million property damage policies, the insured gets one $25 million policy. If restoring one property costs $6 million, the insured is fully covered by the blanket; it would not have been if it had maintained five separate policies. The insured's only uninsured risk is if all its properties burn down at one time from a single occurrence and the aggregate loss exceeds $25 million.

However, insurers have restricted this coverage by *pro rata distribution provisions.* These provisions impose co-insurance penalties when blanket insurance is improperly used. So long as it is satisfied that there is no pro rata distribution provision in the blanket policy, the landlord should have no objection to the satisfaction of the tenant's insurance obligations by endorsements of the tenant's blanket policy.

Excess liability insurance gives layers of insurance. An insured might have $5 million in coverage of which the primary layer is $1 million issued by the primary insurer, the first excess layer is $2 million issued by the first excess insurer, and so on up to $5 million. After a loss, the insured looks to each insurer in the order of its layer of insurance up to the amount of the liability. With excess coverages, the insured must be certain that the policies cover the same risks and that there are no gaps between them, that is, they are "following form."

Occasionally, leases mistakenly refer to *umbrella coverages* as though they were the same as blanket or excess coverages. The fundamental distinction between umbrella policies and blanket policies is that umbrella policies do not cover property coverage risks; they are liability policies. Umbrella coverage, as the name implies, increases coverage afforded by multiple underlying coverages. Usually umbrella coverage is written for a very large amount if certain required underlying coverages are maintained. For example, if the umbrella policy requires that a comprehensive auto liability policy with limits of $500,000 be kept in effect, and a $2 million loss occurs, the umbrella will cover the excess loss (assuming its limits are at least $2 million).

On rare occasions, a tenant will ask for the right to *self-insure* its liability or property damage risks. The request is usually made by a substantial tenant whose sophisticated self-insurance program or financial strength underlies its insurance coverage. When a tenant asks for the right to self-insure, the landlord must evaluate the tenant's ability to respond to a liability or property damage claim in the same way as the landlord must consider the tenant's resources when setting the deductible. Some landlords will allow tenants to self-insure the public liability risk but not the property damage risk. Other landlords require that the tenant maintain a responsible self-insurance program so that the tenant can withstand uninsured risks. In the final analysis, the decision is based upon the tenant's creditworthiness. If the landlord allows the tenant to self-insure any or all of its risks, the landlord must reserve the right to rescind its consent if the tenant's creditworthiness is diminished during the term of the lease. Also, the right to self-insure cannot run to any assignee, unless the landlord is assured of the assignee's creditworthiness.

Finally, when self-insurance is allowed, the waiver, release, and mutual waiver of subrogation provisions must be carefully reconsidered. These provisions are, of course, no more than a risk-shifting device; the landlord and tenant and their insurers agree that the insurers should bear certain property damage risks. If the tenant has no insurer, and if it waives any claims against its landlord, it has self-insured a risk that its insurer would otherwise assume: the risk of the landlord's negligence. Thus, waivers may be inappropriate in this unique circumstance.

§ 9.13   Insurance Provision for Office Building Leases

Building leases commonly require insurance by a provision such as:

FORM 9-2
INSURANCE—OFFICE BUILDING

(a) *Landlord's Insurance.*   At all times during the term, landlord will carry and maintain:

(1)   Fire and extended coverage insurance covering the project, its equipment and common area furnishings, and leasehold improvements in the premises to the extent of the tenant finish allowance (as that term is defined in the work letter);

(2)   Bodily injury and property damage insurance; and

(3)   Such other insurance as landlord reasonably determines from time to time. The insurance coverages and amounts in this section (a) will be reasonably determined by landlord, based on coverages carried by prudent owners of comparable buildings in the vicinity of the project.

(b)   *Tenant's Insurance.*   At all times during the term, tenant will carry and maintain, at tenant's expense, the following insurance, in the amounts specified or such other amounts as landlord may from time to time reasonably request, with insurance companies and on forms satisfactory to landlord:

(1)   Bodily injury and property damage liability insurance, with a combined single occurrence limit of not less than $3,000,000. All such insurance will be equivalent to coverage offered by a commercial general liability form including, without limitation, personal injury and contractual liability coverage for the performance by tenant of the indemnity agreements set forth in this lease;

(2)   Insurance covering all of tenant's furniture and fixtures, machinery, equipment, stock, and any other personal property owned and used in tenant's business and found in, on, or about the project, and any leasehold improvements to the premises in excess of the allowance, if any, provided pursuant to the work letter in an amount not less than the full replacement cost. Property forms will provide coverage on a broad form basis insuring against "all risks of direct physical loss." All policy proceeds will be used for the repair or replacement of the property damaged or destroyed; however, if this lease ceases under the provisions of [casualty damage], tenant will be entitled to any proceeds resulting from damage to tenant's furniture and fixtures, machinery and equipment, stock, and any other personal property;

(3)   Worker's compensation insurance insuring against and satisfying tenant's obligations and liabilities under the worker's compensation laws of the state in which the premises are located, including employer's liability insurance in the limits required by the laws of the state in which the project is located; and

(4)   If tenant operates owned, hired, or nonowned vehicles on the project, comprehensive automobile liability will be carried at a limit of liability not less than $500,000 combined bodily injury and property damage.

(c)   *Forms of the Policies.*   Certificates of insurance, together with copies of the endorsements when applicable naming landlord and any others specified by landlord as additional insureds, will be delivered to landlord prior to tenant's occupancy of the premises and from time to time at least ten (10) days prior to the expiration of the term of each such policy. All commercial general liability or comparable policies maintained by tenant will name landlord and such other persons or firms as landlord specifies from time to time as additional insureds, entitling them to recover under such policies for any loss sustained by them, their agents, and employees as a result of the negligent acts or omissions of tenant. All such policies maintained by tenant will provide that they may not be terminated nor may coverage be reduced except after thirty (30) days' prior written notice to landlord. All commercial general liability and property policies maintained by tenant will be written as primary policies, not contributing with and not supplemental to the coverage that landlord may carry.

(d) *Waiver of Subrogation.*   Landlord and tenant each waive any and all rights to recover against the other or against any other tenant or occupant of the project, or against the officers, directors, shareholders, partners, joint venturers, employees, agents, customers, invitees, or business visitors of each other or of the other tenants or occupants of the project, for any loss or damage to the waiving party arising from any cause covered by any property insurance required to be carried by the party pursuant to this paragraph or any other property insurance actually carried by the party to the extent of the limits of the policy. Landlord and tenant, from time to time, will cause their respective insurers to issue appropriate waiver of subrogation rights endorsements to all property insurance policies carried in connection with the project or the premises or the contents of the project or the premises. Tenant agrees to cause all other occupants of the premises claiming by, under, or through tenant to execute and deliver to landlord a waiver of claims and to obtain waiver of subrogation rights endorsements.

(e) *Adequacy of Coverage.*   Landlord, its agents, and employees, make no representation that the limits of liability specified to be carried by tenant pursuant to this paragraph are adequate to protect tenant. If tenant believes that any insurance coverage is inadequate, tenant will obtain additional insurance coverage as tenant deems adequate, at tenant's sole expense.

§ 9.14   Insurance Provision for
Shopping Center Leases

Shopping center leases require liability and property damage insurance in much the same way as office building leases do:

FORM 9-3
INSURANCE—SHOPPING CENTER

(a)   Tenant will maintain in full force and effect during the entire term of this lease, at its own expense and in companies acceptable to landlord, the following policy or policies of insurance:

(1)   Commercial general liability insurance, including property damage, insuring landlord and tenant (and any mortgagee, ground landlord, or other person or persons whom landlord may designate, called "additional insured" in this lease) from and against all claims, demands, actions, or liability for injury to or death of any persons, and for damage to property arising from or related to the use or occupancy of the premises or the operation of tenant's business. No deductible will be carried under this coverage without the prior written consent of landlord. This policy must contain, but not be limited to, coverage for premises and operations, products and completed operations, blanket contractual, personal injury, operations, ownership, maintenance and use of owned, non-owned, or hired automobiles, bodily injury, and property damage. The policy must have limits in amounts not less than $＿＿ per occurrence and $＿＿ in the aggregate. This insurance will include a contractual coverage endorsement specifically insuring the performance by tenant of its indemnity agreement contained in [indemnity paragraph]. If landlord's insurance advisor reasonably concludes that these amounts of

coverage or coverages are no longer adequate, then such amount or coverage will be appropriately increased, or obtained, as the case may be.

(2)   Worker's compensation insurance with a limit of no less than that amount required by law.

(3)   "All-risk" fire insurance, including, without limitation, vandalism and malicious mischief, to the extent of 90% of the replacement value of all furnishings, trade fixtures, leasehold improvements, equipment, merchandise, and other personal property from time to time situated in, on, or upon the premises. The proceeds from any such insurance will be payable to landlord and held in trust by the landlord to be used only for the repair or replacement of the improvements, fixtures, and other property so insured.

(b)   Landlord may elect to procure and maintain insurance covering fire and such other risks of direct or indirect loss or damage as it deems appropriate, including extended and broad form coverage risks, mudslide, land subsidence, volcanic eruption, flood, and earthquake, on improvements in the shopping center. Tenant will reimburse landlord for the costs of all such insurance as part of operating expenses reimbursable pursuant to [common area paragraph]. Any such insurance coverage will be for the benefit of landlord, tenant, and any additional insured or loss payee, as their interests may appear. Tenant will not adjust losses or execute proofs of loss under such policies without landlord's prior written approval.

(c)   If this lease is canceled by reason of damage or destruction and tenant is relieved of its obligation to restore or rebuild the improvements on the premises, any insurance proceeds for damage to the premises, including all fixtures and leasehold improvements, will belong to landlord, free and clear of any claims by tenant.

(d)   All policies of insurance described in this paragraph that tenant is to procure and maintain will be issued by responsible companies, reasonably acceptable to landlord and qualified to do business in the state in which the shopping center is situated. Executed copies of such policies of insurance or, at landlord's election, certificates of such insurance, will be delivered to landlord and any additional insureds or loss payee within ten (10) days after delivery of possession of the premises to tenant and within thirty (30) days prior to the termination or expiration of the term of each existing policy. All public liability and property damage policies will contain the following provisions:

(1)   Landlord, and any additional designated insureds, although named as insured, will nevertheless be entitled to recovery under said policies for any loss occasioned to them, their servants, agents, and employees by reason of the negligence of tenant, its officers, agents, or employees.

(2)   The company writing the policy will agree to give landlord and any additional insured or loss payee not less than thirty (30) days' notice in writing prior to any cancellation, reduction, or modification of such insurance.

(3)   At the election of landlord's mortgagee, the proceeds of any insurance will be paid to a trustee or depository designated by landlord's mortgagee.

All public liability, property damage, and other casualty policies will be written as primary policies, not entitled to contribution from, nor contributing with, any coverage that landlord may carry.

(e)   Tenant's obligations to carry the insurance required by this lease may be brought within the coverage of a so-called blanket policy or policies of insurance carried and maintained by tenant, so long as (1) landlord and such other persons will be named as additional insureds under such policies as their interests may appear; (2) the coverage afforded to landlord and such other persons will not be reduced or diminished by reason of the use of such blanket policy of insurance; and (3) all other requirements set forth in this paragraph are otherwise satisfied.

(f) If tenant fails either to acquire the insurance required pursuant to this paragraph or to pay the premiums for such insurance or to deliver required certificates or policies, landlord may, in addition to any other rights and remedies available to landlord, acquire such insurance and pay the requisite premiums for them. Those premiums will be payable by tenant to landlord immediately upon demand.

(g) Landlord and tenant waive any rights each may have against the other for loss or damage to its property or property in which it may have an interest if the loss is caused by a peril of the type generally covered by property insurance with extended coverage or arising from any cause that the claiming party was obligated to insure against under this lease. Landlord and tenant on behalf of their insurers waive any right of subrogation that the insurer might otherwise have against the other. Landlord and tenant agree to cause their respective insurance companies insuring the premises or insuring their property on or in the premises to execute a waiver of any such rights of subrogation.

In contrast to office building leases, shopping center leases often require the tenant to maintain boiler coverage, unless the boiler is part of the common areas, in which event the landlord will buy the boiler coverage and include it as a common area maintenance expense. Once again, the insurance terminology is misleading, because boiler coverage actually is properly called *boiler and pressure vessel coverage* and covers not only heat-generating equipment, such as boilers, but also refrigeration and air-conditioning equipment. It covers explosions resulting from excessive pressure, not from combustion.

Boiler and pressure vessel coverage is often issued in connection with machinery coverage. *Machinery coverage* includes such things as fans and blowers, pumps or engines, and some electrical equipment. When boiler and pressure vessel coverage and machinery coverage are issued together, they are issued under the so-called boiler and machinery policy. This insurance covers the cost of the object, such as boiler or machinery, that is damaged in an accident. In addition, the boiler and machinery policy has some characteristics of the liability policy, because it provides coverage for losses for third parties' property which is in the care, custody, and control of the insured. Coverage for the insured's legal liability for bodily injury may also be included at the insured's option.

The boiler and machinery policy excludes some of the risks in the standard property insurance policy, and must be used in tandem with fire coverage. Boiler and machinery policies may be supplemented by a business interruption insurance coverage. The greatest virtue of boiler insurance is that the insurers who sell the coverage have vigorous inspection and loss prevention programs that are of great benefit to the insureds.

Plate glass insurance is another coverage that is commonly required in shopping center leases. Plate glass insurance (which is covered under the comprehensive glass policy) is different from glass breakage (which is an optional peril in the fire policy). Plate glass coverage is sometimes a separate policy with separate limits of liability; it is also included in some all-risk forms.

Plate glass insurance replaces the plate glass, while the comprehensive glass policy insures not only the glass but also all the lettering and ornamentation on it, and not only breakage, but also chemical damage and abrasion by sand.

One great virtue of the comprehensive glass policy is that it provides for immediate boarding of the windows and is likely to result in prompt replacement of the glass because of the insurer's leverage with suppliers and installers. The drawback to the separate plate glass policy is that the glass must be described in detail; there may be questions about the coverage for signs, stained glass, and other unique glass products. If the tenant is obligated to replace the plate glass, the tenant must be the insured on the comprehensive glass policy because only it has an insurable interest in the plate glass.

Wise shopping center landlords require dram shop endorsements for those tenants that serve alcoholic beverages.

§ 9.15   Insurance Provision for Single Tenant Building Leases

In keeping with the notion that the landlord of single tenant premises wants no part of the risks of ownership of the premises, the single tenant lease provisions for insurance may state:

FORM 9-4
INSURANCE-SINGLE TENANT BUILDING

All-Risk Coverage.   Tenant will, at its sole expense, obtain and keep in force from the commencement of construction of the improvements to the premises and during the term of this lease, "all-risk" coverage insurance (including earthquake and flood insurance) naming landlord and tenant as their interests may appear and such other parties as landlord or tenant may designate as additional insureds, in the customary form in the City of _____ for buildings and improvements of similar character, on all buildings and improvements now or after this date located on the premises. The amount of insurance will be designated by landlord no more frequently than once every twelve (12) months; will be set forth on an "agreed amount endorsement" to the policy of insurance; will not be less than the agreed value of the buildings and improvements; and will be subject to arbitration pursuant to [arbitration paragraph] if landlord and tenant do not agree with regard to the value. Landlord and tenant agree that the value of the existing building on the premises is $_____.

Commercial General Liability.   Tenant will, at its sole expense, obtain and keep in force during the term of this lease commercial general liability insurance with a combined single limit of not less than $_____ for injury to or death of any one person, for injury to or death of any number of persons in one occurrence, and for damage to property, insuring against any and all liability of landlord and tenant, including, without limitation, coverage for contractual liability, broad form property damage, host liquor liability, non-owned automobile liability, with respect to the premises or arising out of the maintenance, use, or occupancy of the premises. Such insurance will insure the performance by tenant of the indemnity agreement as to liability for injury to or death of persons and damage to property set forth in [indemnity paragraph]. Such insurance will be noncontributing with any insurance that may be carried by landlord and will contain a provision that landlord, although named as an insured, will nevertheless be entitled to recover under the policy for any loss, injury, or damage to landlord, its agents, and employees, or the property of such persons. The limits and coverage of all such insurance will be adjusted by agreement of landlord and tenant during every third lease year during the term of this lease in conformity with the then prevailing custom of insuring liability in the City of _____, and any disagreement regarding such adjustment will be submitted to arbitration in the manner provided in [arbitration paragraph].

Other Matters.   All insurance required in this paragraph and all renewals of it will be issued by companies authorized to transact business in the State of _____, and rated at least A Class X by Best's Insurance Reports (property liability) or approved by landlord. The "all-risk" coverage insurance will be payable to landlord, tenant, and any lender as their interests may appear. The "all-risk" coverage insurance and the general liability insurance will be carried in the joint names of tenant, landlord, and such other parties having an interest in the premises as landlord and tenant may designate. All insurance policies will be subject to approval by landlord and any lender as to form and substance; will expressly provide that such policies will not be canceled or altered without thirty (30) days' prior written notice to landlord and any lender, in the case of "all-risk" coverage insurance, and to landlord, in the case of general liability insurance; will, to the extent obtainable, provide that no act or omission of tenant that would otherwise result in forfeiture or reduction of the insurance will affect or limit the obligation of the insurance company to pay the amount of any loss sustained; and will, to the extent obtainable, contain a waiver by the insurer of its rights of subrogation against landlord. Upon issuance, each insurance policy or a duplicate or certificate of such policy will be delivered to landlord and any lender whom landlord designates. Tenant may satisfy its obligation under this paragraph by appropriate endorsements of its blanket insurance policies. Since the tenant is in complete control of the premises, and a broad indemnification of the landlord is appropriate, contractual liability coverage should be obtained by the tenant.

§ 9.16   Conclusion

For many years, the Insurance Services Office, Inc. (ISO) promulgated standard coverages throughout the country. The ISO promulgated the commercial general liability policy discussed in § 9.4. As the insurance industry became less regulated, the policies have become more varied. Consequently, coverages change constantly, and the coverages in one policy may be different from the coverages in a different policy with the same name. Provisions in ten-year-old (or even five-year-old) leases are probably out of date. The real estate professional must have these provisions reviewed by independent risk management professionals.

PART IV

CONTROLLING THE TENANT'S CONDUCT

CHAPTER 10

USE

§ 10.1 The Law

A tenant may use its premises for any purpose for which the premises are adapted and which is not either prohibited by the lease or illegal.[1] Therefore, leases usually state the use of the premises affirmatively, that is, "the premises will be used for. . . ." However, provisions that try to limit the use of the premises are strictly construed against the limitation.[2]

---

[1] R. Schoshinski, American Law of Landlord and Tenant § 5:6 (1980) (hereinafter Schoshinski); I American Law of Property § 3.39 (A. Casner ed. 1952); 3 G.W. Thompson, Commentaries on The Modern Law o Real Property § 1147 (J.S. Grimes repl. vol. 1980) (hereinafter Thompson).

[2] Schoshinski § 5:7.

Consequently, a statement that the premises "are being leased" or "may be used" for one purpose does not by itself preclude other purposes. That statement is said to be permissive.[3] For example, an Ohio supermarket lease provided:

> The leased premises may be used for the purposes of selling, distributing or otherwise handling or dealing in any and all goods, wares, merchandise, commodities or services such as are normally sold or dealt in a supermarket.

When the supermarket assigned its lease to a karate school, the landlord asserted a breach of this use provision. The landlord lost at the trial court because the court ruled that the provision was permissive. On appeal, the court granted a new trial to the landlord because it felt that the trial court should have considered other parts of the lease; however, the appellate court agreed that the provision was merely permissive.[4]

A lease of premises "to be used primarily as an automobile dealership" did not prohibit a saloon.[5] However, the provision "Lessee agrees to lease said premises for the purpose of operating a restaurant for the sale and consumption on and off the premises of food and nonalcoholic beverages," although not artful, convinced the New Hampshire Supreme Court that the tenant's sale of alcoholic beverages was forbidden.[6]

The Connecticut Supreme Court enforced a use provision that referred to the statute governing the liquor license the tenant was required to obtain. Dealing with an ambiguity, the court limited the use to that permitted by the statute in effect at the time the lease was signed, even though the scope of the statute was subsequently enlarged.[7]

To achieve a strict limitation, careful real estate professionals use words of limitation such as "only," "solely," or "and for no other purpose." So expressed, the use is said to be *restrictive,* and courts give effect to the restrictions. For example, in considering a lease that provided that the premises would be used "for the sale of tacos, enchiladas and related other Mexican foods and for no other purpose," a New York court held that the tenant defaulted when it offered video games in addition to food service.[8]

---

[3] 3 Thompson § 1147.

[4] Juhasz v. Quick Shops, Inc., 55 Ohio App. 2d 51, 9 Ohio Op. 3d 216, 379 N.E.2d 235 (1977); Forman v. United States, 767 F.2d 875 (Fed. Cir. 1985) (United States Postal Service successfully made a profit on a sublease of a post office; the state use, "for postal purposes," was not found to be a limitation).

[5] Chassereau v. Stuckey, 288 S.C. 368, 342 S.E.2d 623 (Ct. App. 1986), *discussed in* Beans, *Express Language Required to Restrict Use of Property Demised in Lease,* 39 S.C.L. Rev. 142 (1987).

[6] ELCA of New Hampshire, Inc. v. McIntyre, 129 N.H. 114, 523 A.2d 90 (1987).

[7] Hatcho Corp. v. Della Pietra, 195 Conn. 18, 485 A.2d 1285 (1985).

[8] 72nd & Broadway Gourmet Restaurant, Inc. v. Stahl Real Estate Co., 118 Misc. 2d 372, 460 N.Y.S.2d 408 (Sup. Ct. 1981). Video games have spawned many cases, perhaps not because of the games themselves or the landlord's lost percentage rent, but because of the crowds and their

Sales of lottery tickets are a modern battleground for landlords. Tenants seem to be prevailing when their landlords claim that their tenants have violated the leases by selling lottery tickets.[9] Although lottery ticket sales do draw customers, and this would appear to be beneficial to the landlord and the tenant, the argument against them is that many lottery customers do not use the balance of shopping centers and thus do not contribute to the general welfare. Landlords have no benefit from imposing unnecessary limitations on their retail tenants; if they cannot sell the goods that their customers demand, the tenants will pay less percentage rent and the landlord also suffers.

The agreement of the landlord and tenant does not conclusively determine the use of the premises. Governmental restrictions also affect uses. Consequently, the use provision and compliance with laws provision in **Chapter 11** must be considered together. Governmental restrictions arise in one of two ways: a use that is illegal at the time of the leasing, and a use that becomes illegal after the leasing.[10]

If both the landlord and tenant intend that the premises will be used for an illegal purpose, their lease cannot be valid; put differently, "contemplated legality of use is a prerequisite for an effective lease."[11] These sorts of illegal leases (in which the landlord and tenant both contemplate the illegal purpose) are further characterized as either *unenforceable* or *void;* although these terms are often used synonymously, they are distinct from one another. This characterization is important because it determines the availability of judicial redress.

Courts will not have any part of a void lease. A landlord may rescind a void lease and recover possession; a tenant under a void lease may surrender possession. A court will not enforce any of their rights under the void lease. If money has been paid or other reliance has been placed upon the lease, the courts will leave the landlord and tenant where they are.[12] In this sense, void and unenforceable are

---

members. *See* Rodking Serv. Station, Inc. v. Gribin, 109 A.D.2d 873, 486 N.Y.S.2d 786 (1985) (prohibiting video games as not incidental to the sole permitted use of the premises as a gas station); Qwakazi, Ltd. v. 107 W. 86th St. Owners Corp., 123 A.D.2d 253, 506 N.Y.S.2d 162, *appeal denied,* 68 N.Y.2d 609, 500 N.E.2d 874, 508 N.Y.S.2d 1025 (1986) (allowing video games). In Ray-Ron Corp. v. DMY Realty Co., 500 N.E.2d 1163 (Ind. 1986), a tenant who installed video games and other machines was found not to violate permitted use of "a restaurant and/or retail sale of liquor and associate commissary," because the machines generated only a small part of the tenant's profits. By the same reasoning, the tenant could begin to sell washers and dryers from a bar and justify itself by saying that the profits from appliance sales were minimal.

[9] *See* Card Appeal, Inc. v. Deli-Bake, Inc., 131 Misc. 2d 724, 501 N.Y.S.2d 560 (Sup. Ct. 1986) (stationery store); Sky Four Realty Co. v. C.F.M. Enters. Inc., 128 A.D.2d 1011, 513 N.Y.S.2d 546 (1987) (convenience store).

[10] Schoshinski § 5:12.

[11] 2 R. Powell, The Law of Real Property § 222(2) (P.J. Rohan ed. 1977) (hereinafter Powell).

[12] Dougherty v. Seymour, 16 Colo. 289, 26 P. 823 (1891); 3 Thompson at § 1092; 51C C.J.S. Landlord & Tenant 226(1) (1968).

synonymous.[13] On the other hand, courts will, for example, compel the return of a security deposit made pursuant to an unenforceable lease;[14] the *Restatement* §§ 9.1(1) and 12.4 consider these illegal leases to be unenforceable and not void.

Traditionally, illegal use cases have arisen in the context of gambling, prostitution, and liquor. Violation of zoning ordinances is a modern example of illegality of use. A lease for only one use that violates zoning ordinances is void or unenforceable, as discussed in this section. If there is a use that is legal and permitted by the lease, the lease will not be affected even if the intended use is illegal. If a use may be made legal—as, for example, a lease for a tavern may be made legal by receipt of a license—the lease will be enforceable even if the license is not obtained, unless the tenant has protected itself with a condition or right to terminate.

The landlord may enforce a lease when the tenant puts the premises to an illegal use without landlord's knowledge. The landlord may also terminate the lease (if the lease allows it to do so or if an applicable statute allows it to do so), sue to enjoin the illegal activity, or sue for damages.[15] The landlord must act promptly if the premises are used for illegal purposes. In some cases, the landlord's knowledge of the illegal purpose has not barred its recovery of rent, even though the distinction between knowledge and intention is elusive;[16] the landlord's agreement not to enforce its remedies if the tenant uses the premises for an illegal purpose suggests that the landlord intended the illegal use.[17]

A lease for a use that becomes illegal after the leasing—the usual examples are saloons after Prohibition—will terminate if the use is the principal use of the premises; however, if the use that becomes illegal is incidental or only one of several uses, the lease will not terminate.[18]

The effect of this supervening illegality is often analyzed in terms of the contract doctrine of frustration,[19] which requires proof of an agreement (1) that has not been fully performed; (2) that was made by the landlord and tenant in contemplation of a particular purpose; and (3) that cannot come about for unforeseeable reasons that the frustrated party did not cause or knowingly risk. A Washington tenant whose use required the correction of fire code violations that

---

[13] Restatement of The Law of Property (Second) (Landlord and Tenant) § 9.1, Reporter's Note 5 (1977) (hereinafter Restatement).

[14] Green v. Frahm, 176 Cal. 259, 168 P. 114 (1917).

[15] Restatement § 12.5.

[16] I American Law of Property § 3.43 (A. Casner ed. 1952); M.R. Friedman, III Friedman on Leases § 27.302 (1983) (hereinafter Friedman).

[17] 49 Am. Jur. 2d *Landlord and Tenant* § 43 (1970).

[18] *Id*. at § 269; 2 Powell § 247(4).

[19] III Friedman § 27.302; *see* Valencia Center v. Publix Super Mkts., 464 So. 2d 1267 (Fla. Dist. Ct. App.), *cert. denied*, 475 So. 2d 696 (Fla. 1985) (doctrine of impossibility in context of landlord's obligation to pay real estate taxes which increased more than tenfold).

would bankrupt the company may base a claim that the purpose of the lease has been frustrated.[20]

Before leaving the question, several aspects of illegality must be observed:

1. The illegal activity must be a continuous course of conduct, not isolated incidents.

2. The illegality must be inherent in the nature of the activity, not incidental to it. Prostitution, for example, is usually always illegal; there is no way to operate a brothel lawfully in most jurisdictions. In contrast, a tenant whose business requires a state license is operating illegally without the license, but its lease will not be subject to termination because there is a way to operate lawfully. Thus an Illinois tenant's inability to get an occupancy permit as required by the applicable building code is not a defense to the landlord's claims on the lease.[21]

3. The illegal conduct must be occurring at the premises.

Restrictive covenants affecting the premises may also have the effect of limiting their use. A landlord may sue for damages (which may be difficult to prove), or it may endeavor to terminate the lease, or it may seek a court order compelling the tenant to comply with the restrictive covenants. Of course, most landlords would prefer to compel compliance with the restrictive covenants and to keep their tenants.

The landlord does not warrant that a use is lawful merely by prescribing or permitting it.[22] A tenant may contend that the purposes of the lease have been frustrated if the use is not lawful; however, the tenant must overcome the obstacles to prove frustration.

As a warranty, a prudent tenant may ask for a statement such as:

FORM 10-1
USE—LANDLORD'S WARRANTY OF LEGALITY
OF TENANT'S USE

Landlord warrants that tenant's use of the premises according to this paragraph is lawful and that it does not breach any restriction of record, zoning ordinance, or other agreement that affects the premises.

In order to give this warranty, the landlord must carefully define the tenant's use. If the tenant has a very broad or unrestricted use provision, the landlord cannot be certain what use the tenant will make of the premises. If the tenant has a specific

---

[20] Stevedoring Serv. of Am., Inc. v. Marvin Furniture Mfg., 54 Wash. App. 424, 774 P.2d 44 (1989).

[21] Braeside Realty Trust v. Cimino, 133 Ill. App. 3d 1009, 479 N.E.2d 1031 (1985). The tenant should have insisted on a condition in the lease.

[22] Welson v. Neujan Bldg. Corp., 264 N.Y. 303, 190 N.E. 648 (1934); Dillon-Malik, Inc. v. Wactor, 151 Ariz. 452, 728 P.2d 671 (Ct. App. 1986).

use, the landlord may verify the lawfulness of the use by reference to zoning ordinances, instruments of record, and other leases (which may grant an exclusive to another tenant). After this investigation, the landlord may conclude, for example, that the premises may be used for making photocopies. However, the tenant's method of operating its store may still be unlawful; it may store paper or solvents in a way that violates fire codes. The landlord must be careful that its representation is given as of the date of the lease or as of the date of the commencement of the term; it should not warrant the continued legality of use.[23] Some landlords expressly disclaim any warranty of legality; this is particularly true in single tenant building leases.

The lease's use provisions are closely related to the provisions that require the tenant to comply with laws. Consider a license that the tenant must have in order to operate. The use provision requires the use, but the compliance with laws provision requires the license. As a general rule, the failure to obtain a license which is required as part of the government's exercise of its police power (as opposed to the government's revenue-raising power) will make the lease illegal; failure to obtain a license related to the revenue-raising power does not have the same effect.

§ 10.2   Use Provisions in Leases of Office Buildings and Single Tenant Buildings

Because leases of single tenant buildings virtually give ownership to the tenant, these leases have the broadest use provisions:

FORM 10-2
USE—LIBERAL SINGLE TENANT BUILDING

Tenant may use the premises only for lawful purposes.

Of course, this does no more than state the common law rule. Occasionally, a specific use is stated, for example, "the manufacture, storage, distribution, and sale of men's wear, and no other purpose." Tenants should insist upon the least restrictive use provision. In these leases, some landlords expressly disclaim any warranty that the premises may be lawfully used for tenant's intended purposes.

Even when the lease allows "any lawful purpose," some landlords prohibit immoral, lewd, or offensive uses. Although these words are admittedly vague, they may make it possible for a landlord to forfeit a lease when the premises are used for a massage parlor, pornographic book store, or adult movie theatre. See also **Form 10-4**.

Office building use provisions are also fairly simple:

---

[23] 49 Am. Jur. 2d *Landlord and Tenant* § 42 (1970).

FORM 10-3
USE—OFFICE BUILDING

The premises will be used for business offices and for no other purpose. The premises will be used in a careful, safe, and proper manner. The premises will not be used for any activity or in any manner that would tend to lower the first-class character of the building. Tenant will not use or occupy or permit the premises to be used or occupied for any purpose or in any manner prohibited by the laws of the United States, or the State of _____, or the ordinances of the City of _____. Tenant will not commit waste nor suffer or permit waste to be committed in, on, or about the premises. Tenant will conduct its business and control its employees, agents, invitees, and visitors in such manner as not to create any nuisance, or interfere with, annoy, or disturb any other tenant or occupant of the building or landlord in its operation of the building. Tenant will not do anything that is prohibited by the standard form of extended coverage fire policy, or that will increase the existing rate of such insurance or otherwise affect any other insurance related to the building, or cause a cancellation of landlord's insurance.

Some of these provisions go on to require the tenant to pay any increase in real estate taxes that its improvements cause, and increases in insurance cost that its use causes. Generally, even in the absence of such a provision, the tenant is responsible for increased insurance costs[24] or real estate taxes.[25]

Some cautious real estate professionals insist that incidental uses be specified—for example, lunch rooms with cooking facilities—because they feel that any other provision is merely descriptive and not limitative. If there is any possibility of doubt, the tenant should specify its incidental uses and avoid a later disagreement with the landlord.

A tenant's promise to operate "a restaurant in a hotel at a high standard" means "at a minimum, that a tenant will not allow criminal activity to take place on the premises."[26] On the other hand, a tenant's violation of United States Department of Energy regulations regarding temperature control is not an "unlawful purpose" or waste sufficient to terminate a lease.[27]

With greater frequency, office building tenants are using their premises for purposes unrelated to their main businesses. Such purposes include, for example, the sale of computer time on a time-share basis and the development and sale of software programs incidental to the business. Since these uses could certainly arouse a vexatious landlord, the lease should expressly allow the tenant's intended uses.

---

[24] Annot., 30 A.L.R.2d 489, *Relative rights and liabilities of landlord, tenant, assignee or sublessee where act is done increasing insurance rates* (1953).

[25] Annot., 68 A.L.R.2d 1289, *Clause of lease providing for payment of taxes by lessor as applicable to increase in real estate taxes occasioned by lessees improvements* (1959).

[26] Frog, Inc. v. Dutch Inns of Am., Inc., 488 A.2d 925, 929 (D.C. 1985).

[27] Rowe v. Wells Fargo Realty, Inc., 166 Cal. 3d 310, 212 Cal. Rptr. 374 (1985).

§ 10.3   Lenders' Concerns about General
Use Provisions

Landlords and their lenders usually have identical interests in the office building and single tenant lease use provisions. In an office building lease, a landlord and its lender might possibly disagree about the use provision if the landlord granted an exclusive use to retail areas of a mixed use project, or to a tenant offering a support service (such as a travel agency or cafeteria) to other office building tenants. However, such instances are rare.

§ 10.4   Use Provisions in Shopping Center Leases

Since tenants can use their premises for any lawful purpose, one can imagine a shopping center in which all the tenants sold the same products. In this imaginary marketplace, fierce competition among the tenants would drive down their prices and their sales. As a result, the landlord's percentage rent would be minimal. Many tenants would fail.

The landlord would endeavor to re-lease the premises of its failed tenants, but would be unable to attract competitors of the surviving tenants. In fact, the landlord would attract tenants wanting an opportunity to sell products that no other tenant sold. Eventually, by trial and error, the shopping center would evolve into a variety of tenants whose businesses and products were compatible and supportive of one another. At that point of equilibrium, all tenants would flourish. So would the landlord.

Unfortunately, the steady state is an unattainable ideal. Some tenants go out of business for reasons that have nothing to do with the tenant mix in the shopping center; they die or fail because of poor management or insufficient capital. When a tenant goes out of business, the landlord may not be able to find an identical replacement or may be unwilling to wait until it does. The landlord releases the premises as soon as it can to a tenant whose products are new to the shopping center, thus disturbing the equilibrium.

The tenants themselves may disturb the equilibrium. A tenant whose products become unfashionable will want to replace them with new products that have not been sold at the shopping center. Other tenants may want to supplement their successful products with related products that are new to the shopping center. In those circumstances, the tenants will have disrupted the steady state.

The imaginary shopping center sets the stage for use provisions in shopping center leases. The landlord and tenant both strive for equilibrium by means of the use restrictions. The landlord wants the range of the tenant's uses to be narrow; when it must first lease premises or re-lease a failed tenant's premises, the landlord will then be able to select a new tenant from a broad spectrum of uses without risking a use that overlaps with the narrowly specified uses of existing tenants. On the other hand, the tenant wants to express its use broadly; thus, when fashions change or new products become available, the tenant may expand its use without the fear of competition from other tenants in the shopping center.

In order to appreciate the divergent paths of landlord and tenant, the real estate professional should begin with the landlord's careful selection of tenants and meticulous preparation of the use provision. The landlord's primary concern in the use provision is how a use can be granted that anticipates (or at least does not jeopardize) the demands of future tenants. As one observer said, "Ideally, the developer should lease to tenants in the order of decreasing importance to the center."[28] Since shopping center developments do not proceed under ideal conditions, the answer, of course, is very careful draftsmanship.

The form of the use provision is generally the same as that set forth in § **10.2** in **Form 10-3**, that is, "The premises will be used for the sale of . . . and for no other purpose." Prescribing how the premises will be used, as opposed to how the tenant will use them, limits any concern about subtenants, licensees, concessionaires, and the tenant's heirs or executors.

The use should be precisely described after discussion with the landlord and tenant, inspection of the tenant's existing stores, review of the tenant's inventory, and consideration of comparable stores. The landlord's desire for specificity and the tenant's desire for generality make the use provision a subject of heated negotiation. Each use provision is the unique result of this negotiation. Consequently, there are no general form use provisions.[29] For example, some landlords require restaurant tenants to attach a sample menu to the lease as a statement of the items that will be sold. An inventory list (without prices) could be attached to a retail tenant's lease, although a tenant may rightly believe that provision to be unfairly limiting. On the other hand, the term "women's wear," for example, is too broad because it encompasses all clothing that women wear and makes it impossible to give a later exclusive for women's shoes.[30] Similarly, "and accessories" is imprecise and susceptible of application to almost any item of clothing or paraphernalia.[31]

Prices must not be mentioned; landlords should not require "medium priced children's sports shoes" or "dresses in the $40-60 price range." Quality, however, may be specified: "high-quality designer women's dresses." A New York court has enforced a requirement that a tenant's merchandise and window displays meet the standards of Bloomingdale's.[32] The standard is easier to recognize than "first class" or "sign quality." Sales may be required to be retail. As matters of definition, wholesale sales are sales made for resale and retail sales are all others. Thus, retail sales denote not so much price as the method of distribution.

---

[28] Hemingway, *Selected Problems in Leases of Community and Regional Shopping Centers,* 1 Baylor L. Rev. 20 (1964).

[29] I American Law of Property § 246 (A. Casner ed. 1952).

[30] *See* Convert-A-Bed, Inc. v. Salen, 360 So. 2d 605 (La. Ct. App. 1978) (use restriction of ladies' apparel construed to mean clothes worn by men because court held that there are clothes which are made for women and worn by women, as well as clothes made for men which are worn by women, and therefore the term "ladies' apparel" is imprecise).

[31] *See* Haber, *Use Clauses,* in Shopping Centre Leases 341 (H. Haber ed. 1976), for several specific use provisions; E. Halper, Shopping Center and Store Leases § 9.01 (Supp. 1984) has a long and very helpful discussion of specific use provisions.

[32] Mostazafan Found. v. Rodeo Plaza Assocs., 151 A.D.2d 347, 542 N.Y.S.2d 599 (1989).

When a tenant leases its premises in a shopping center, it agrees to use the premises according to the use provision. The tenant may demand that it be the only occupant of the shopping center who has the right to make that use of premises in the shopping center. In other words, the tenant asks the landlord not to allow the tenant's competitors into the shopping center; one can readily see that such an exclusive provision is nearly the mirror image of a radius provision in which the landlord asks the tenant not to compete with itself.[33]

If the landlord has not realized the importance of the use provisions in its leases, it will awaken immediately after it has been asked for an exclusive. Before it can grant the exclusive use, the landlord must carefully review the permitted uses in its existing leases in order to be certain that it has not allowed its existing tenants—or, better yet, that it has prohibited them from—the proposed exclusive use.[34] In other words, if an existing tenant is not barred from competing with the new protected tenant, the new tenant has no protection at all; the new tenant must investigate the permitted and particularly the excluded uses of existing tenants. If the landlord cannot assure its prospective tenant of an exclusive use, an advantageous lease may be lost. Thus, the landlord's inattention to its first few leases may limit the success of its shopping center.

A cautious developer may conclude that it has a solution to the problem: it will not grant any exclusives, and thus it will avoid losing any tenants because of a competing use. Unfortunately, matters are not so simple. Significant tenants are likely to demand exclusives, and without them the size of the development will be severely limited. Quite aside from this crude fact of real estate life, shopping centers flourish best with complementary tenants; so, even if tenants did not require exclusive uses, developers would eventually bring about the same result in their evolving tenant mix. Since the issue is unavoidable, landlords must learn to deal with it to their least detriment.[35]

---

[33] Colbourn, *A Guide to Problems in Shopping Center Leases,* 29 Brooklyn L. Rev. 56, 70-78 (1962).

[34] Klein v. Equitable Life Assurance Soc., 17 Ohio App. 3d 50, 477 N.E.2d 1190 (1984). The tenant cannot recover damages or obtain equitable relief based upon an exclusive use covenant for competitive activities that predate the tenant's lease. *See* Danish Maid, Inc. v. South Bay Center, Inc., 11 A.D.2d 768, 205 N.Y.S.2d 358 (1960) (damages denied where tenant had actual notice of preexisting use); Handfinger v. Stevelaw Realty Corp., 102 N.Y.S.2d 688 (Sup. Ct. 1950) (injunctive relief denied where tenant signed lease and began business though unaware of preexisting use); Salerno v. B.C. Posner Construction Co., 39 Misc. 2d 699, 241 N.Y.S.2d 598 (Sup. Ct. 1963) (damages and equitable relief denied where tenant signed lease and began business though unaware of preexisting use); Norwood Shopping Center, Inc. v. MKR Corp., 135 So. 2d 448 (Fla. Dist. Ct. App. 1961) (injunctive relief, damages, and declaratory decree denied where tenant signed lease and began business though unaware of preexisting use). If the competing use predates the tenant's lease, the landlord may, without breaching the exclusive use covenant, renew the competitor's lease after the tenant's lease begins. Furchgott's, Inc. v. Jacobs, 199 So. 2d 749 (Fla. Dist. Ct. App. 1967).

[35] *See* Silverman, *Practical Suggestions for Shopping Center Use and Exclusive Clauses,* Prac. Real Est. Law, Nov. 1989, at 65, for a helpful discussion.

§ 10.5   Drafting an Exclusive Use Provision

First of all, anchor tenants often do not have restrictive use provisions in their leases.[36] As a result, any lawful use will be allowed, and no subsequent tenant can be assured of an exclusive use. Some anchor tenants' leases have a use provision such as "any lawful use;" of course, this just states the law and is no limitation at all. If the use provision is restrictive, it may be something like "a supermarket," or "a department store." These are vague descriptions; they are not limitations. One New Jersey lease provided that the premises would be used for "a supermarket and drugstore and for any and all lawful purposes." When the tenant assigned its lease to a retail salvage center, the landlord claimed that the use provision had been breached. Finding no limitations in the lease, the court held for the tenant.[37] Many anchor tenants that will not agree to narrow use provisions will nevertheless agree not to sell certain goods; this may be a compromise that allows another tenant to get an exclusive use.

Occasionally, an anchor tenant employs a provision such as: "Tenant will have the sole right to operate a drug store in the shopping center." This appears to be a restrictive use provision, but careful examination reveals that it is nothing of the sort. It grants an exclusive use but does not limit the tenant to that use in any way; it means only that no other tenant of the shopping center may operate a drug store. Thus, even if the landlord can assure the prospective tenant that no one in the shopping center is presently in violation of the proposed use provision, and even if the landlord is willing to forego future tenants whose use would violate the prospective exclusive use provision, the landlord cannot assure the prospective tenant that an existing tenant with a broad or unrestricted use provision will not violate the proposed exclusive use. The landlord can only agree that, after execution of the new tenant's lease with its exclusive use, it "will not lease any part of the shopping center for tenant's exclusive use."

Because nothing can be done about existing tenants and their uses (except landlord's hopeless supplication for a limiting amendment), landlords must exclude them from their exclusives. However, landlords are better advised to exclude the premises of the existing tenants rather than the tenants themselves. This enables the landlord to replace the existing tenants with new tenants that have the same broad uses (including the newly protected exclusive use) as the erstwhile tenant, and there will be no breach of the new exclusive use. The real estate professional will observe that the landlord's goal in this situation is the same as it is when the landlord says "the premises will be used only for. . ." instead of "tenant will use the premises only for. . . ." In each case, the focus is the use of the premises and not the user.

In preparing the provision, the landlord may be assisted by an awareness of two broad categories of exclusive use provisions. One grants the exclusive right to

---

[36] *The Retail Exclusive Clause,* Leasing Prof., Feb. 1987, at 6, contains a form and discussion.

[37] Monmouth Real Estate Inv. Trust v. Manville Foodland, Inc., 195 N.J. Super. 262, 482 A.2d 186 (App. Div. 1984), *cert. denied,* 99 N.J. 234, 491 A.2d 722 (1985).

carry on a particular business without reference to particular products; it is often referred to as a *limited exclusive*. Another grants the exclusive right to sell specific products; it is called a *true exclusive*.

The distinction between limited and true exclusives (which is not always easy to make) may be illustrated by two provisions regarding drugs. The landlord might grant one tenant the exclusive right to operate a drug store. In the same center, the landlord might have a health food store (which sells vitamins in competition with the drug store), a beauty store (which sells cosmetics in competition with the drug store), and a newspaper stand (which sells magazines in competition with the drug store). A limited exclusive is obviously no real protection against competition in products, although it is protection against competition in store category.

A limited exclusive invites a common error in which the tenant's use concludes with a catch-all phrase such as ". . . related products and services." The goal is unimpeachable: to be certain that the use is not so narrowly expressed it prohibits activities the landlord would have allowed if they had been suggested. The result is to make unclear what the tenant cannot do. For example, a gas station was allowed to sell food products with a lease that said the premises would be used "for a gasoline service station, car wash and associated activities."[38]

Sophisticated tenants that insist upon a true exclusive are saying, in effect, "Landlord, I don't care what your other tenants call themselves, but I do care about their product lines." This initiates a very difficult process. No one who has visited a modern drug store could say that it remotely resembles an old-time apothecary shop. Many drug stores sell not only prescription drugs, but also health care and beauty aids, paper products and school supplies, nonprescription glasses, packaged ice cream, candy, nuts, and a broad variety of other consumer products. A drug store that insists upon product-line exclusives may virtually eliminate any other tenants. Moreover, clear drafting can be subjected to an inane cavil. In a Pennsylvania case the tenant unsuccessfully asserted that the landlord breached its promise not to lease space "for the sale or display of International Foods" when it allowed another tenant to sell domestic hams; the tenant argued that international meant any nation including the United States.[39]

One Vermont landlord learned the hard way how true exclusives work. He agreed with a tenant that he would not lease space to anyone offering "automotive rustproofing, insulating, waxing, painting, and the sale of automotive accessories and other products." The landlord then leased space to a tenant whose products incidentally overlapped with a few of the first tenant's products. The Vermont Supreme Court ruled in favor of the first tenant, holding that the product-exclusive provision was breached when the products were sold by another tenant.[40] The decision would have been different if the first tenant had only a business-exclusive provision in which some overlapping was inevitable.

---

[38] Snow v. Winn, 607 P.2d 678 (Okla. 1980).

[39] Gralka v. Isaacson, 388 Pa. Super. 2441, 556 A.2d 888 (1989).

[40] Addison County Automotive, Inc. v. Church, 144 Vt. 553, 481 A.2d 402 (1984).

Obviously, the preparation of exclusive use provisions requires superhuman foresight: what tenants will occupy the shopping center, and what will they sell? The negotiating and drafting opportunities are boundless; so are the pitfalls. A landlord could promise a desirable tenant that the landlord would "not allow anyone to sell" certain products. Landlords should avoid such a provision because it requires their continuous supervision.[41]

Another landlord approach is to limit the product lines. For example, it may simply refuse to give a drug store the exclusive right to sell nuts and candy; the success of the landlord's refusal is, of course, dependent upon the landlord's bargaining strength and the importance of the particular product to the drug store's overall business plan.

The landlord may propose that it will not grant an exclusive use like the tenant's to any other tenant. The tenant is not pleased with this suggestion because it is not a limitation: a subsequent tenant with no use restriction may violate the first tenant's use. Furthermore, the landlord could grant several other tenants exclusive uses that, in the aggregate, would be co-extensive with the first tenant's exclusive; one tenant could have an exclusive for shoes, another for dresses, and so on until the first tenant's exclusive for women's wear vanishes.

The landlord may suggest that it will not lease to anyone whose primary or principal products are those that the proposed tenant wishes to sell exclusively. Some tenants are pleased with this limitation. Others find this provision to be of little comfort, because it leaves open the possibility that all future tenants may compete with its products if those products are incidental to their businesses. The tenant may be more pleased by the landlord's promise that there will be no more than one future tenant with the particular incidental use.

The landlord may promise either not to lease to a competing business within a specified distance from the protected tenant, or to locate competing businesses in specified places in the shopping center.

The landlord may also agree not to lease any space to a tenant that uses more than a stated area of its premises (for example, 1000 square feet) or a stated percentage of its premises (for example, 10 percent of its premises) for the sale of the exclusive products. A landlord will prefer to use a percentage because it allows for future expansion of a successful tenant; a tenant with an exclusive will naturally want a fixed area. When using area limitations, landlords almost never consider the wall areas but rather only the floor areas; 400-square-foot premises configured as a square will have 480 square feet of wall space (if the walls are 8 feet), allowing one side for windows and an entrance. Occasionally, a limitation is expressed as an absolute dollar volume or a percentage of sales; for example, "Landlord will not lease to any tenant whose gross sales in any year include more than $50,000 of sales of electric trains." This approach presents difficulty in enforcement because tenants are usually reluctant to disclose their sales figures to competitors, even "incidental" ones. Moreover, it is impractical to limit a tenant's success by prescribing sales volumes.

---

[41] Hildebrand v. Stonecrest Corp., 174 Cal. App. 2d 158, 344 P.2d 378 (1959); Barr & Sons, Inc. v. Cherry Hill Center, Inc., 90 N.J. Super. 358, 217 A.2d 631 (1966).

When an agreeable provision has been prepared, the landlord will state that its promise—the exclusive use—is personal to the tenant, that is, that it will not run to the benefit of the tenant's assignees or subtenants. The landlord's position is that it granted the exclusive use to the tenant because of the landlord's confidence in the tenant's ability to succeed in the premises; as a result, the landlord says, it has agreed to forego other tenants whose use would violate the exclusive. To the tenant, however, this "personal" agreement means that it cannot sell a business with the same protections that have made it successful; the tenant fears that its marketability or desirability will be affected by the cessation of the exclusive on transfer. A landlord is wise to limit the tenant's exclusive use to the duration of the tenant's use of the premises for the protected use. This avoids the tenant's assignee from claiming that the landlord cannot lease to a tenant whose use infringes the past but not present use of the premises.[42]

Although tenants who have the economic power to demand broad exclusives usually have the power to avoid express covenants of continuous operation, such as those set forth in § **10.10**, landlords should try to limit the duration of exclusives to the duration of the tenants' actual occupancy of the premises. Otherwise, the landlord may find that its anchor tenant moves out during its term (while continuing to pay rent) and that the landlord is limited in leasing other parts of the shopping center because the ex-tenant's exclusive continues. The tenant may resist the landlord's proposal because it may want to move across the street (or nearby) and still have the protection of its old exclusive; put differently, the tenant may say that its rent includes the value of its exclusive and that it should have the exclusive as long as it pays rent.

The tenant must assure itself that the site plan of the shopping center and the legal description of the shopping center are identical. Often the site plan is more than all of the property whose legal description is attached to the lease; a site plan is not usually the equivalent of a survey. Frequently, shopping centers are developed by several landowners who relate their separate parcels by reciprocal easement or operating agreements. If the tenant is part of such a development, it may have the exclusive use in less than all the shopping center of which it is a part.

Another aspect of this problem arises when the landlord expands the shopping center beyond the land shown in the site plan, or builds an addition to the shopping center on adjacent property, or acquires an adjacent shopping center.[43] The tenant must plan for this possibility by defining its exclusive area as an area that extends beyond the shopping center and by defining the landlord's affiliates among those who are so restricted.[44]

---

[42] Berkeley Dev. Co. v. Great Atl. & Pac. Tea Co., 214 N.J. Super. 227, 518 A.2d 790 (1986).

[43] See cases collected in the excellent article by Haber & Messinger, *Exclusive Rights and Non-Competition Clauses,* in Shopping Centre Leases 415 (H. Haber ed. 1976); III Friedman § 28.4.

[44] *In* Edmond's of Fresno v. MacDonald Group, 171 Cal. App. 3d 598, 217 Cal. Rptr. 375 (1985), a California appellate court ruled that a tenant's exclusive included the expanded shopping center; the court was influenced by the facts that the name of the expanded center was the same

Once the tenant has ascertained the scope of the development, it must insist that the legal description of the shopping center be that of the land composing the entire development — and must record its lease for the reasons set forth in § **32.4**.

The tenant must be certain that the exclusive use provision prohibits not only other occupants of the shopping center, but also the landlord itself[45] and any purchaser of any part of the shopping center from competing with the tenant;[46] generally, courts infer that landlords have agreed not to compete with their tenants, but the express agreement is preferable. One way for a tenant to achieve this goal is to demand a provision that says, "Landlord will not use or allow any part of the shopping center to be used for . . . ." Similarly, an exclusive provision must require the landlord to enforce these exclusives at the landlord's expense. Otherwise, the tenant has only the right to sue its co-tenants that know of the tenant's exclusive.

Retail tenants are rightly concerned about the co-tenants of their shopping centers. The image, parking requirements, and shopper profile of other tenants affect their success. Consequently, some shopping center tenants demand a provision such as:

FORM 10-4
PROHIBITED USES — SHOPPING CENTER (TENANT'S FORM)

Landlord will not lease or sublease or permit the use of any portion of the shopping center, or any future expansion of it, to any tenant whose business: creates strong, unusual, or offensive odors, fumes, dust, or vapors; is a public or private nuisance; emits noise or sounds that are objectionable due to intermittence, beat, frequency, shrillness, or loudness; creates unusual fire, explosive, or other hazards; or is used, in whole or in part, as or for warehousing, the dumping or disposing of garbage or refuse, the sale of indecent or pornographic literature, catering halls, theater, movie theaters, off-track betting parlors, bars, night clubs, discotheques, bowling alleys, so-called "head shops," car washes, auto body shops, unsupervised amusement arcade or game room, amusement centers, billiard parlor, funeral parlor, automobile (used or new) dealership, skating rink, health spa, adult book store, or massage parlor.

§ 10.6   Tenant's Remedies

If a landlord violates the provisions of an exclusive use granted to a tenant, the tenant has several remedies. They are all less than perfect, and they all must be

---

as the name of the original center and that the tenant was obligated to pay its share of common area maintenance charges for the expanded center. For a somewhat similar case involving adjacent developments under separate ownership, see Kole v. Linkenhoker, 259 Ga. 82, 377 S.E.2d 671 (1989).

45 Sylvester v. Hotel Pasco, 153 Wash. 175, 279 P. 566 (1929).

46 2 Powell § 242(2)(c) (citing authorities).

promptly pursued. A tenant who does not promptly seek to enforce its exclusive rights may lose them.[47]

The tenant may sue its landlord for damages. Traditionally, the measure of damages has been the difference between the value of the premises without the competing tenant and the value of the premises with the competing tenant.[48] When this measure of damages is used, however, the award may be limited to the period from the time the breach of covenant began until commencement of the action by the lessee-covenantee.[49] In addition, the amount of damages must be established by competent expert testimony.[50]

Newer cases have used lost profits as a measure of damages.[51] Even though there may be no question about the landlord's breach, there may be difficult questions about the extent of the tenant's damages.[52] For example, a new business that has the benefit of an exclusive may not have any experience of profits by which to prove the difference between the value of the premises with and without the restriction. A North Carolina court held that a landlord's promise not to compete with its tenant implies a promise not to lease adjacent space to one of the tenant's competitors;[53] although the issue of tenant's relief was not before it, the court suggested that damages were appropriate. Finally, the tenant who prevails in litigation may be unable to collect its judgment by reason of provisions of the lease that limit the tenant's recourse, such as those set forth in **Chapter 29**.

With such limitations in mind, a tenant may take a different tack and try to terminate its lease. If the tenant's business fails, an attempt to terminate the lease on a theory of constructive eviction may be worthwhile. An Alabama court has suggested that constructive eviction may be an appropriate theory when the tenant's business is ruined by prohibited competition.[54] However, a claim of constructive eviction requires the tenant to leave the premises in which it does business, sustain concomitant losses and expenses of relocation, and obligate

---

[47] U.S. Inv. Corp. v. Village Square Shopping Center, 688 S.W.2d 44 (Mo. Ct. App. 1985).

[48] Supreme Fin. Co. v. Burnee Co., 146 Misc. 374, 262 N.Y.S. 147 (Sup. Ct. 1933). *See, e.g.,* Kennedy v. Abarno, 277 A.D. 883, 97 N.Y.S.2d 907 (1950); Carusos v. Briarcliff, Inc., 76 Ga. App. 346, 45 S.E.2d 802 (1947).

[49] Kennedy v. Abarno, supra; L&S Delicatessen, Inc. v. Carawana, 143 N.Y.S.2d 350 (Sup. Ct. 1955).

[50] Snyder v. Greenblatt, 28 Misc. 2d 403, 212 N.Y.S.2d 862 (Sup. Ct.), *aff'd,* 14 A.D.2d 888, 218 N.Y.S.2d 565 (1961).

[51] 2 Powell § 242(2)(c). *See, e.g.,* Flagg v. Andrew Williams Stores, Inc., 127 Cal. App. 2d 165, 273 P.2d 294 (1954); Hildebrand v. Stonecrest Corp., 174 Cal. App. 2d 158, 344 P.2d 378 (1959); Freedman v. Seidler, 233 Md. 39, 194 A.2d 778 (1963). However, the award should be limited to only those profits lost during the actual time the competition took place. Flagg v. Andrew Williams Stores, Inc., 127 Cal. App. 2d 165, 273 P.2d 294 (1954); Hildebrand v. Stonecrest Corp., 174 Cal. App. 2d 158, 344 P.2d 378 (1959). Moreover, the method of computing the lost profits must be reasonable. Freedman v. Seidler, 233 Md. 39, 194 A.2d 778 (1963).

[52] Parker v. Levin, 285 Mass. 125, 188 N.E. 502 (1934).

[53] Bicycle Transit Auth., Inc. v. Bell, 314 N.C. 219, 333 S.E.2d 299 (1985).

[54] Southern Sec. Servs. Inc. v. Esneault, 435 So. 2d 1309 (Ala. Civ. App. 1983).

itself to a new lease. Then, if the constructive eviction claim fails, the tenant may have two leases. If a tenant wishes to exercise its right to terminate the lease, it must do so within a reasonable time after the landlord's violation.[55] Another substantial obstacle to a termination claim is that the tenant must show it had no use of the premises as a result of the landlord's breach.[56]

For example, in a California case[57] the lease provided that the tenant could use and occupy the premises as a drug store and for no other business. The lease also provided that the landlord would not lease to any other tenant for the purpose of maintaining a drug store or selling drugs. Consequently, the landlord's breach of the exclusive use provision defeated the entire objective of the lease, rendering tenant's further occupancy of the premises a source of continuing financial loss incapable of satisfactory measurement in damages.[58] The Illinois Supreme Court upheld a restaurant tenant's repudiation of its lease when the landlord breached the exclusive use provision; the court held that the exclusive use was an essential part of the tenant's agreement to enter into the lease.[59]

The tenant may try to enjoin the landlord from breaching the exclusive use provision. Injunctive relief involves several substantial hurdles, such as the posting of a bond, but may be an adequate remedy. In a New York case[60] the competing lease was enjoined even though the first tenant's lease seemed to offer an adequate remedy at law, that is, the elimination of base rent if the landlord leased to a competitor. The court refused to allow the landlord to choose a remedy for its own breach.

The *Restatement* § 7.2 recognizes that judicial decisions hold either that the landlord's promise is valid, or that the landlord's promise and the entire lease are invalid. In order to give the tenant the benefit of its expectation, the *Restatement* says that the tenant is allowed to terminate the lease even if the landlord's promise

---

[55] *In re* Consumers World, 160 F. Supp. 238, 240 (D. Mass. 1958).

[56] Kulawitz v. Pacific Woodenware & Paper Co., 25 Cal. 2d 664, 155 P.2d 24 (1944); *In re* Consumers World, 160 F. Supp. 238 (D. Mass. 1958). In the cases that grant the remedy of termination of the lease, the tenant vacated the premises in order to assert its right to terminate. *See, e.g., In re* Consumers World, 160 F. Supp. 238 (D. Mass. 1958); Kulawitz v. Pacific Woodenware & Paper Co., 25 Cal. 2d 664, 155 P.2d 24 (1944); Medico-Dental Bldg. Co. v. Horton & Converse, 21 Cal. 2d 411, 132 P.2d 457 (1942); University Club of Chicago v. Deakin, 265 Ill. 257, 106 N.E. 790 (1914); Hiatt Inv. Co. v. Buehler, 225 Mo. App. 151, 16 S.W.2d 219 (1929).

[57] Medico-Dental Bldg. Co. v. Horton & Converse, 21 Cal. 2d 411, 132 P.2d 457 (1942).

[58] 132 P.2d at 470. *See also* Kulawitz v. Pacific Woodenware & Paper Co., 25 Cal. 2d 664, 155 P.2d 24 (1944) (lease provided premises to be used exclusively as general furniture store; landlord covenanted not to lease space in the same building for the purpose of conducting a furniture store); University Club v. Deakin, 265 Ill. 257, 106 N.E. 790 (1914) (lease provided tenant should use space for a jewelry and art shop and for no other purpose; landlord agreed not to rent any other store in the building for sale of pearls).

[59] Johnstowne Centre Partnership v. Chin, 99 Ill. 2d 284, 76 Ill. Dec. 80, 458 N.E.2d 480 (1983).

[60] *See* Papa Geno's of America, Inc. v. Plaza at Latham Assocs., 135 A.D.2d 74, 524 N.Y.S.2d 536 (1988).

is invalid. If the landlord's promise is valid, the tenant may also sue for damages or appropriate equitable relief, such as an injunction.

Finally, the tenant may ask for a provision for liquidated damages in the event of a breach by the landlord. For example, the tenant may demand that it be obligated to pay only percentage rent and that it be relieved of its minimum rent obligations. Such a provision may be an unenforceable penalty. In any event, the landlord's lender will object to any provision that interrupts cash flow.

§ 10.7 Antitrust Implications of Exclusive Uses

Exclusive uses are widely and wrongly believed to be unlawful restraints of trade. To the contrary, restrictions against competing uses have been sustained if they are incidental to an otherwise lawful agreement and are reasonable in scope (that is, as to the activities that are prohibited), time, and territory.[61] The few practically relevant limitations are found in the statutory authority—Sections 1 and 2 of the Sherman Act,[62], the Federal Trade Commission Act,[63] the several state antitrust laws (many of which are modeled on the Sherman Act)—and the common law. A landlord should never grant an exclusive use unless it has assured itself that none of these limitations is applicable.

The first question in the Sherman Act analysis is whether the exclusive use either occurs in interstate commerce or substantially affects interstate commerce.[64] If it does not, there is no federal jurisdiction.

If the nexus with interstate commerce is established, the next question is whether the restraint of trade is unreasonable. A few restraints of trade—the so-called "per se" violations—are by their very natures conclusively presumed to be unreasonable: price fixing,[65] market division by competitors, group boycotts,[66]

---

[61] 2 Powell § 242(2)(c); Annot., 1 A.L.R.4th 942, *Shopping center lease restrictions on type of business conducted by tenant* (1980). Peoples Savings Bank v. County Dollar Corp., 43 A.D.2d 327, 351 N.Y.S.2d 157 (1974), *aff'd*, 35 N.Y.2d 836, 321 N.E.2d 784, 362 N.Y.S.2d 864 (1974).

[62] 15 U.S.C.A. 1 and 2.

[63] 15 U.S.C. 45(a)(1).

[64] Harold Friedman, Inc. v. Thorofare Markets, Inc., 587 F.2d 127 (3d Cir. 1978); Savon Gas Station No. Six, Inc. v. Shell Oil Co., 309 F.2d 306 (4th Cir. 1962), *cert. denied*, 372 U.S. 911, 83 S. Ct. 725 (1963); Optivision, Inc. v. Syracuse Shopping Center Assoc., 472 F. Supp. 665 (N.D.N.Y. 1979); Payless Drug Stores N.W. v. City Prods. Corp., 1975-2 Trade Cases (CCH) ¶ 60,385 (D. Ore. 1975); Dalmo Sales Co. v. Tyson's Corner Regional Shopping Center, 308 F. Supp. 988 (D.D.C.), *aff'd*, 429 F.2d 206, 139 U.S. App. D.C. 22 (D.C. Cir. 1970).

[65] Natural Design, Inc. v. Rouse Co., 302 Md. 47, 485 A.2d 663 (1984); Mendel v. Golden-Farley of Hopkinsville, Inc., 573 S.W.2d 346 (Ky. Ct. App. 1978); *but see* Optivision, Inc. v. Syracuse Shopping Center Assocs., 472 F. Supp. 665 (N.D.N.Y. 1979).

[66] Klor's, Inc. v. Broadway Hale Stores, Inc., 359 U.S. 207, 79 S. Ct. 705 (1959); Dalmo Sales Co. v. Tyson's Corner Regional Shopping Center, 308 F. Supp. 988 (D.D.C. 1970), *aff'd*, 429 F.2d 206 (D.C. Cir. 1970).

refusals to deal,[67] and tie-in sales. In commercial real estate leases, concern about allegations of price-fixing prompts landlords to avoid mentioning prices or price ranges (for example, "high price") in their use provisions. If the restraint of trade is not a per se violation, it is analyzed under the "rule of reason" approach to determine whether it is unreasonable.

The "rule of reason" antitrust analysis requires the identification of the "market," which comprises both a geographic market and a product market. The geographic market may be the shopping center itself,[68] or it may be, for example, a three-mile radius from the shopping center,[69] the area within 30 minutes driving time from the shopping center,[70] or a part of the city.[71]

The product market requires identifying the products that are either identical or reasonably substituted for the suspect product. In an antitrust analysis of shopping center space, the product market would be the kind of space that is affected by the exclusive use.[72] To be unlawful, the exclusive use must deprive the complainant of a product (that is the space) in the geographical market.[73] The relevant geographic market is the area of commerce in which the suspect violator operates and in which a competitor can turn for product.[74]

In addition to the restraint of trade analysis under Section 1 of the Sherman Act, exclusive uses might be analyzed under the monopolization provisions of Section 2. That analysis requires proof of monopolistic power in a product and geographic market (as those terms are used in the restraint of trade cases); acquisition, maintenance and use of that power; and resultant injury. There seems to be only one commercial real estate lease case finding monopolization,[75] and it was so unusual that it seems unlikely to recur.

Real estate professionals involved with federally regulated institutions should determine whether federal law restricts exclusives given to those institutions. For example, a federal banking association may not enter into any agreement that gives it the exclusive right to operate a branch office in a regional shopping center, or in a majority of the locations of a chain store, or that excludes other

---

[67] Savon Gas Station No. Six, Inc. v. Shell Oil Co., 309 F.2d 306 (4th Cir. 1962).

[68] Payless Drug Stores N.W. v. City Prods. Corp., 1975-2 Trade Cases (CCH) ¶ 60,385, (D. Ore. 1975).

[69] Countrie Butcher Shoppe, Inc. v. Foodarama Supermarkets, Inc., 1982-1 Trade Cases (CCH) ¶ 64,580 (E.D. Pa. 1982).

[70] Deauville Corp. v. Federated Dep't Stores, Inc., 1983-2 Trade Cases (CCH) ¶ 65,559 (S.D. Tx. 1983), *aff'd in part, rev'd in part*, 756 F.2d 1183 (5th Cir. 1985).

[71] Optivision, Inc. v. Syracuse Shopping Center Assocs., 472 F. Supp. 665 (N.D.N.Y. 1979).

[72] Gamco, Inc. v. Providence Fruit & Produce Bldg., 194 F.2d 484 (1st Cir.), *cert. denied*, 344 U.S. 817, 73 S. Ct. 11 (1952).

[73] Optivision, Inc. v. Syracuse Shopping Center Assocs., 472 F. Supp. 665 (N.D.N.Y. 1979).

[74] For a step-by-step analysis, see Dunafon v. Delaware McDonald's Corp., 691 F. Supp. 1232 (W.D. Mo. 1988).

[75] Gamco, Inc. v. Providence Fruit & Produce Bldg., Inc., 194 F.2d 484 (1st Cir. 1952), *cert. denied*, 344 U.S. 817, 73 S. Ct. 11 (1952).

financial institutions "from operating in a regional shopping center or any location of a chain store where the federal association does not have an office."[76] For these purposes regional shopping center means a group of commercial establishments planned, developed, owned, or managed as a unit with off-street parking on the property, having a gross floor area of 400,000 square feet or more, and including as tenants one or more department stores.[77]

The Federal Trade Commission cases are discussed in § **10.8**. See § **10.13** regarding unlawfulness of radius restrictions.

§ 10.8   Federal Trade Commission's Response to Exclusive Uses

In the early 1970s, some exclusive use provisions were successfully challenged as anticompetitive agreements in violation of federal trade practices legislation.[78] Since then, exclusive uses and related development practices have been attacked on the federal level by the Justice Department, the Federal Trade Commission, and private litigants. State attorneys general and private litigants have attacked the practices on several state levels. The federal cases revolve around three classes of defendants: major retailers, major developers, and major retailer developers. Federal law is now sufficiently settled to allow some general observations.[79]

As a tenant, a major retailer may not:

1.   Demand a right of approval of other tenants in the shopping centers which they occupy

2.   Exact a prohibition against particular tenants or classes of tenants unless the prohibition extends no further than clearly objectionable tenants (To date, pornography shops, body and fender shops, and massage parlors

---

[76] 12 C.F.R. § 545.92(i).

[77] *Id.* at § 571.11(b).

[78] E. Halper, Shopping Center and Store Leases § 9.07 (Supp. 1984) has a very thorough discussion of the development of this area of the law.

[79] See the excellent discussion in Halper, *The Antitrust Laws Visit Shopping Center Use Restrictions,* 4 Real Est. L. Rev. 3 (1975). The relevant Federal Trade Commission orders are: Tysons Corner Regional Shopping Center, 83 F.T.C. 1598 (1974), 3 Trade Reg. Rep. (CCH) ¶ 20,532 at 20,464; Gimbels Bros. Inc., 83 F.T.C. 1320 (1973), 3 Trade Reg. Rep. (CCH) ¶ 20,478 at 20,411; Sears, Roebuck & Co., 89 F.T.C. 240 (1977), 3 Trade Reg. Rep. (CCH) ¶ 21,218 at 21,121; Federated Dep't Stores, Inc., Order, Docket C-2958, 3 Trade Reg. Rep. (CCH) ¶ 21,505 at 21,536; Food Fair Stores, Inc., Complaint, Docket 8935, 3 Trade Reg. Rep. (CCH) ¶ 20,946 at 20,798; Peoples Drug Stores, Inc., 87 F.T.C. 1 (1976), 3 Trade Reg. Rep. (CCH) ¶ 21,005 at 20,863; The Rouse Co., 85 F.T.C. 848 (1974), 3 Trade Reg. Rep. (CCH) ¶ 20,818 at 20,687; Strawbridge & Clothier, 87 F.T.C. 593 (1976), 3 Trade Reg. Rep. (CCH) ¶ 21,082 at 20,943; Rich's, Inc., 87 F.T.C. 1372 (1976), 3 Trade Reg. Rep. (CCH) ¶ 21,118 at 20,973; Tysons Corner Regional Shopping Center (City Stores), 85 F.T.C. 970 (1975), 3 Trade Reg. Rep. (CCH) ¶ 20,933 at 20,771.

have been identified as clearly objectionable. In this area, the greatest abuse has arisen in the prohibition of discounters.)[80]

3. Demand a right to approve the location of tenants in the shopping center
4. Limit the floor areas occupied by other tenants in the shopping center
5. Limit the types or brands of merchandise sold by other tenants or floor areas of other tenants used for sales of certain merchandise
6. Demand an exclusive right to sell certain merchandise or goods
7. Demand a right of first refusal on space in the shopping center
8. Restrict advertising by tenants in the shopping center
9. Prescribe minimum hours of operation by other tenants
10. Limit discounting by other tenants
11. Dictate prices or ranges of prices charged by other tenants
12. Require the landlord to impose radius restrictions on other tenants in the shopping center
13. Require that it be the only tenant of its kind (for example, drugstore) in the shopping center.

Major developers cannot:

1. Prohibit discounters or discounted prices
2. Allow any tenant to control prices, discounters or price ranges
3. Make any agreement to exclude discounters
4. Prescribe prices, or a range of prices, or price lines
5. Control price advertising.

In addition to complying with the restrictions on both major retailers and major developers, major retailer developers cannot:

1. Use the same employees in both the real estate development and retail sales division
2. Condition one lease of a tenant on that tenant making other leases
3. Condition leases on a tenant's pricing practices
4. Specify price ranges.

The real estate professional can pick a path through these forbidden practices and conclude that some restrictions are still permissible. They include agreements regarding:

---

[80] Schear & Sheehan, *Restrictive Lease Clauses and the Exclusion of Discounters from Regional Shopping Centers,* 25 Emory L.J. 609 (1976), concluded that restrictive lease provisions may have excluded discounters at one time but that it was "no longer certain" they still did at the time of the article. An earlier commentator had concluded that such lease restrictions should be considered per se violations of the antitrust laws. Note, *The Antitrust Implications of Restrictive*

1. A balanced tenant mix
2. A prohibition of odors
3. The appearance of the shopping center
4. The exclusion of clearly objectionable tenants
5. The layout of the center, including the location of nonretail tenants
6. The requirement of one or more major tenants.

Finally, these federal antitrust rules are applicable only to:

1. Shopping centers that have more than 200,000 square feet of floor area, of which at least 50,000 feet of floor area are occupied by retail tenants other than major tenants
2. Shopping centers which have at least two tenants other than the major tenant
3. Shopping centers which have at least one major tenant
4. Shopping centers providing on-site parking.

When enforcement of these antitrust laws was more active, many landlords insisted that tenants who demanded exclusives indemnify them against the consequences of litigation challenging the exclusive. Many major retailers and developers have changed their exclusionary practices. This is not to say that anticompetitive agreements are no longer made. The developer who ignores the unspoken wishes of its anchor tenants knows that those anchor tenants will not be available for the next development.

§ 10.9   Lenders' Concerns about Exclusive Uses

For at least four reasons, lenders prefer not to see leases that give exclusive uses:

1. Since exclusive uses are often vague, they increase the likelihood of a tenant asserting that its landlord has breached the lease. Many lenders feel that exclusive uses go so directly to the heart of a lease that a court may allow a tenant to terminate its lease if its exclusive use is violated.
2. Exclusive uses limit leasing activity and compel a landlord (or, worse yet, a lender after foreclosure) to turn away tenants that would be acceptable in the absence of the exclusive use.
3. Exclusive uses prompt assertion of restraint of trade claims.
4. If the lease prohibits the landlord from leasing to the tenant's competitor, or competing with the tenant within some distance from the shopping center (in what is sometimes called a *reverse radius provision*), the landlord's lender will be particularly concerned. If the lender forecloses on that shopping center and if the lender owns (or comes to own through foreclosure) another shopping center in the proscribed area in which

there is a prohibited competitor, the first tenant may assert a breach of its lease. A lender should be pleased to see that the reverse radius provision expires upon foreclosure or the giving of a deed in lieu of foreclosure.

Nevertheless, most lenders recognize that desirable tenants will often demand exclusive uses. Lenders are pleased when leases with exclusive uses are recorded; subsequent tenants are thus put on notice. Of course, no lender would accept a recorded lease that is superior to its mortgage.

§ 10.10 Express Covenant of Continuous Operation

The general rule is that the tenant is not obligated to occupy the premises unless waste results from its failure to do so.[81] A lease that provides that the tenant will use its premises for a specified purpose is merely a restriction and not a mandate; in other words, such a provision does not obligate the tenant to make continuous use of the premises for the specified use. Without breaching that provision, the tenant may close its doors and continue to pay rent.[82] A tenant's promise "to use and occupy said premises as a retail store for the sale of goods, wares and merchandise, and not use the same for any illegal purposes" does not require the tenant's continuous occupancy; it does not restrict operations (such as it would by saying "solely for" or "only") or prohibit cessation of operations.[83]

There are exceptions to the general rule.[84] One turned on the word "occupied," which was used in the use provision and construed by the court to mean

---

Covenants in Shopping Center Leases, 86 Harv. L. Rev. 1201 (1973); this view has been criticized frequently.

[81] *See generally* Kline, *Percentage Leases: May Lessee Vacate Premises?*, 19 Clev. St. L. Rev. 612 (1970); Case Note, *Implied Covenants of Continuous Operation in Commercial Leasing Settings*, 25 Ariz. L. Rev. 792 (1983); Colbourn, *A Guide to Problems in Shopping Center Leases*, 29 Brooklyn L. Rev. 56, 62-67 (1962); E. Halper, Shopping Center and Store Leases (Supp. 1984) § 9.02(c). For a discussion of recent cases and further illustration of the difficulty of enforcing these provisions, see Fishman, *What Counsel Must Know About Continuous Use Covenants*, 3 Prac. Real Est. Law. 35 (1987).

[82] McKnight-Seibert Shopping Center, Inc. v. National Tea Co., 263 Pa. Super. 292, 397 A.2d 1214 (1979); Dickey v. Philadelphia Minit-Man Corp., 377 Pa. 549, 552, 105 A.2d 580, 581 (1954); Davis v. Wickline, 205 Va. 166, 135 S.E.2d 812 (1964); Riverside Realty Co. v. National Foods Stores, Inc., 174 So. 2d 229 (La. Ct. App.), *writ refused*, 247 La. 1037, 175 So. 2d 647 (1965); McCormick v. Stephany, 57 N.J. Eq. 257, 263, 41 A. 840 (Ch. 1898), *modified*, 48 A. 25 (Ch. 1900); Hoffman v. Seidman, 101 N.J.L. 106, 127 A. 199 (N.J. Err. & App. 1925).

[83] Gerardi v. Vaal, 169 Ill. App. 3d 818, 523 N.E.2d 1327 (1988).

[84] Ayres Jewelry Co. v. O&S Bldg., 419 P.2d 628 (Wyo. 1966). *See* Lippman v. Sears, Roebuck & Co., 44 Cal. 2d 136, 280 P.2d 775 (1955); Simhawk Corp. v. Egler, 52 Ill. App. 2d 449, 202 N.E.2d 49 (1964); Tuttle v. W.T. Grant Co., 16 Misc. 2d 222, 187 N.Y.S.2d 549 (Sup. Ct. 1957), *order reversed*, 5 A.D.2d 370, 171 N.Y.S.2d 954 (1958), *judgment reversed*, 6 N.Y.2d 745, 159 N.E.2d 202, 186 N.Y.S.2d 655 (1959).

that continuous use and occupancy was required.[85] In Pennsylvania, a limitation of a tenant's use to one purpose, together with other provisions in the lease, may imply an obligation to occupy the premises.[86]

In a percentage rent lease, the landlord's profit comes from the tenant's overages; the minimum monthly rent covers only mortgage payments and sometimes all or a part of the landlord's operating costs. Also, in a shopping center, as opposed to an office building, activity is essential to success.[87] Therefore, the tenant's continuous operation of its business in the premises is vital to the landlord.

The tenant itself is not uninterested in this matter. Typically, a tenant wants to know that if it closes its business because its expectations are not realized, it will be obligated for its lease costs but not other costs such as personnel and inventory. In negotiating operating covenants, real estate professionals should consider the tenant's investment in the premises. A tenant that has built and owns its own premises, tied to the rest of the shopping center by a development agreement, is not as appropriate a candidate for an operating covenant as the tenant whose premises are delivered to it on a turn-key basis with rent concessions.

Many leases try to regulate the tenant's conduct of its business; some of these efforts are discussed in § **10.12**. This section considers the tenant's express covenants to operate continuously.[88] Implied covenants to operate continuously are considered in § **10.11**.

A common express covenant in a shopping center lease states:

FORM 10-5
USE—EXPRESS COVENANT OF CONTINUOUS OPERATION

Tenant will operate tenant's business in the premises so as to maximize the gross sales produced by such operation, and will carry in the premises at all times a stock of merchandise of such size, character, and quality as is reasonably designed to produce the greatest gross sales and the greatest possible amount of percentage rent. Tenant will carry on its business diligently and continuously at the premises through the term of this lease and will keep the premises open for business on all business days in accordance with the schedule of minimum hours specified in the basic lease information. If landlord from time to time establishes different standard retail hours for the shopping center, tenant will remain open during those hours. If tenant fails to carry on its business each business day as required pursuant to this paragraph, tenant will, at landlord's option, pay, in addition to the minimum rental due pursuant to this lease, for each day during which the premises are not open or during which

---

[85] Ingannamorte v. Kings Super Mkts., Inc., 55 N.J. 223, 260 A.2d 841 (1970).

[86] Slater v. Pearle Vision Center, Inc., 376 Pa. Super. 580, 546 A.2d 676 (1988). For a full discussion of the Pennsylvania experience with implied and express continuous operating covenants, see Segal, *Shopping for Just the Right Covenant: Part I,* Prac. Real Est. Law., Nov. 1988, at 6; *Part II,* Prac. Real Est. Law., May 1989, at 7.

[87] 2 Powell § 242(2)(c).

[88] Schoshinski § 5:3.

the required hours are not maintained, an amount equal to 25% of the per diem minimum rental then in effect. That additional rental will be deemed to be in lieu of any percentage rent that may have been earned during the period of tenant's breach.

A tenant will want to modify that provision by saying:

FORM 10-6
USE—TENANT'S LIMITATION ON THE
COVENANT OF CONTINUOUS OPERATION

Unless it wishes to do so, tenant will not operate in the premises (a) unless _____ square feet of the shopping center are open for business to the general public by tenants in their premises; (b) unless the anchor tenant(s) are open for business to the general public; (c) if it is prevented from doing so by strikes, labor disputes, the elements, fire or other casualty, unavailability of its stock in trade, or other matters beyond its control; (d) while alterations are being made to the premises; (e) for two weeks each calendar year when tenant will be on vacation, on national legal holidays, on religious holidays, and on days when inventory is taken; (f) during the last two months of the term of the lease when tenant will be moving out; and (g) in any hours or on any days when tenant demonstrates that its operations are not profitable.

The exception in (b)—the *go dark provision*—is unacceptable to the landlord and its lender; this provision is quite different from a provision (such as that in § **5.9**) for initial occupancy by an anchor tenant. If a landlord in a large shopping center is compelled to accede to this provision, it should limit the tenant's right to cease its operations to the cessation of operations by the anchor tenant nearest to the tenant. If a distant anchor tenant ceases operations, the landlord contends, the tenant's business should not be affected. In larger shopping centers, the exception in (e) will be unacceptable because the landlord will want virtually uninterrupted occupancy; if this provision is made, the national legal holidays should be specified. Since some litigation has arisen respect to the tenant's right to wind down its business before the end of the term, the right in (f) should be reserved to the tenant.[89]

The landlord's lender will be displeased by a provision as broad as (g), and the landlord's real estate professional should resist it. Its effect is to allow the tenant to close down if it is not profitable. Moreover, does it mean that the tenant may stay open only during peak business hours each day or in peak months each year? Surely no tenant expects to be profitable every hour of the day and every day of the year. The best that the landlord can do is to agree that the tenant will not be required to stay open at hours or on days when less than (for example) 75 percent of the leasable area of the shopping center is open. The landlord could allow some interruptions of business if it provided that the tenant would be presumed

---

[89] I Friedman § 6.902.

nevertheless to have gross sales (for purposes of percentage rent) during the interruption.

Landlords' attempts to terminate leases on account of a breach of an obligation to operate during certain hours have met with some successes.[90] The Ohio Supreme Court, on the strength of the default provision, the tenant's failure to take its grievance to the merchants association, and the equality of bargaining position between landlord and tenant, enforced a forfeiture when the tenant failed to operate during 11 of 71 hours weekly for 2 months.

Tenants should assure themselves that they can comply with the hours of operation in the lease as well as with applicable wage-and-hour laws. Depending upon the profile of their employees, tenants may need two shifts in order to have adequate personnel at their stores. Tenants should be certain that they can operate at other hours in addition to the prescribed hours and that security personnel and other services will be available.

§ 10.11   Implied Covenant of Continuous Operation

A far more interesting issue than the express covenant of continuous operation is presented when the lease does not expressly require the tenant's continuous operation, and a court must determine whether such a covenant is implied. This question has been litigated many times, not only in the context of occupying the premises but also in the context of changing the use of the premises (from retail to storage, for example). The result can be an unsightly vacancy in the middle of a shopping center and a reluctance on the part of prospective tenants to rent space in a shopping center that a prior tenant seems to have found undesirable.[91] The problem usually arises in the same way each time: the tenant's operations are losing money or are marginally profitable, and the tenant closes down while continuing to pay any monthly minimum rent.

When these cases first began to come before the courts, inflexible rules developed: if there was no minimum rent, an implied covenant was found; if there was insubstantial minimum rent, an implied covenant was found; and if there was substantial or not insubstantial minimum rent, no implied covenant was found. Gallonage leases, in which the rent is paid on a percentage of the sales of

---

[90] Joseph J. Freed & Assocs., Inc. v. Cassinelli Apparel Corp., 23 Ohio St. 3d 94, 491 N.E.2d 1109 (1986); Caranas v. Morgan Hosts-Harry Hines Boulevard, Inc., 460 S.W.2d 225 (Tex. Ct. App. 1970) (specified hours and tenant's refusal to install cash register according to lease helped landlord). *But, see* Bal Harbour Shops v. Greenleaf & Crosby Co., 274 So. 2d 13 (Fla. Dist. Ct. App. 1973) (vagueness hurt landlord). The practical aspects of operating covenants are discussed in Kane, *Dealing with Assignment, Use, and Operating Covenant Lease Clauses,* 2 Prac. Real Est. Law. 45 (1986).

[91] *See* Reich, *Implied Covenants of Continuous Operation,* J. Real Est. Dev. 63 (Fall 1988); Segal, *Shopping for Just the Right Covenant: Part I,* Prac. Real Est. Law., Nov. 1988, at 6; *Part II,* Prac. Real Est. Law, May 1989, at 7.

gasoline, are illustrative of the insubstantial minimum rent doctrine.[92] The so-called substantial minimum rent doctrine is no real comfort to a landlord. In the first place, a trial is usually necessary to determine whether the minimum rent is insubstantial. Second, courts generally dislike implying covenants in leases because it is tantamount to making an agreement for the landlord and tenant.[93]

However, in a case that has become the cornerstone of this area of the law, a tenant was found to have implicitly agreed to operate continuously because minimum rent was "not substantial and adequate" and the landlord had remodeled the building for the tenant and made improvements to the premises during the term, all at no cost to the tenant. The court thoughtfully set forth the requirements for an implied covenant:

1.   The implication must arise from the language used

2.   It must appear from the language used that the covenant was so clearly within the contemplation of the parties that they deemed expressing it unnecessary

3.   Implied covenants can only be justified on the grounds of legal necessity

4.   A promise can be implied only when it can be rightfully assumed that it would have been made if attention had been called to it

---

[92] Sinclair Ref. Co. v. Davis, 47 Ga. App. 601, 171 S.E. 150 (1933) (landlord's recovery was the fair rental value of the premises); Carl A. Schuberg, Inc. v. Kroger Co., 113 Mich. App. 310, 317 N.W.2d 606 (1982). The College Block v. Atlantic Richfield Co., 206 Cal. App. 3d 1376, 254 Cal. Rptr. 179 (1988), involved a percentage of a gas station operator's sales and an appellate court's remand to the trial court for determination along the lines of the substantial minimum rent doctrine.

[93] Percoff v. Solomon, 259 Ala. 482, 67 So. 2d 31 (1953); Walgreen Ariz. Drug Store Co. v. Plaza Center Corp., 132 Ariz. 512, 647 P.2d 643 (Ct. App. 1982), *discussed in* Lofy, *Implied Covenants of Continuous Operation in Commercial Lease Settings,* 25 Ariz. L. Rev. 792 (1983); Cousins Inv. Co. v. Hastings Clothing Co., 45 Cal. App. 2d 141, 113 P.2d 878 (1941); Stemmler v. Moon Jewelry Co., 139 So. 2d 150 (Fla. Dist. Ct. App.), *cert. denied,* 146 So. 2d 375 (Fla. 1962); Bastien v. Albertson's, Inc., 102 Idaho 909, 643 P.2d 1079 (1982); Chicago Title & Trust Co. v. Southland Corp., 111 Ill. App. 3d 67, 443 N.E.2d 294 (1982); Jenkins v. Rose's 5, 10 & 25 ¢ Stores, 213 N.C. 606, 197 S.E. 174 (1938); Kretch v. Stark, 26 Ohio Op. 2d 385, 193 N.E.2d 307, 92 Ohio L. Abs. 47 (1962); Monte Corp. v. Stephens, 324 P.2d 538 (Okla. 1958); Weil v. Ann Lewis Shops, Inc., 281 S.W.2d 651 (Tex. 1955); Palm v. Mortgage Inv. Co. of El Paso, 229 S.W.2d 869 (Tex. Civ. App. 1950), *writ refused n.r.e.;* Gerardi v. Vaal, 169 Ill. App. 3d 818, 523 N.E.2d 1327 (1988); Stein v. Spainhour, 167 Ill. App. 3d 555, 521 N.E.2d 641, *appeal denied,* 122 Ill. 2d 595, 125 Ill. Dec. 237, 530 N.E.2d 265 (1988) (court ordered tenant that ceased operations to pay percentage rent for last five years of term based on percentage rent paid in preceding five years); Rapids Assocs. v. Shopko Stores, Inc., 96 Wis. 2d 516, 292 N.W.2d 668 (1980) (finding that percentage rent and specified purpose did not create implied covenant of continuous operation and that right to sublease negated any such intention); Food Fair Stores, Inc. v. Blumberg, 234 Md. 521, 200 A.2d 166 (1964); KDT Indus., Inc. v. King's Mammoth, Inc., 30 Bankr. 252 (S.D.N.Y. 1983); Hicks v. Whelan Drug Co., 131 Cal. App. 2d 110, 280 P.2d 104 (1955).

5. There can be no implied covenant where the subject is completely covered by the contract.[94]

Some courts have relied upon the use provision in order to give the same result as finding an implied covenant.[95] In a lease providing the tenant would use the "premises only for the purpose of a shoe store engaged in the sale at retail of children's shoes and footwear," the court noted that the lease had required the tenant to pay percentage rent and that "to insure its continued operation the lease specified that the defendant tenant would use the premises only for such purpose."[96] The court also ruled immaterial the tenant's proffered evidence to the effect that the minimum rent was substantial. Another case came to the same conclusion, saying

> words related to the use intended are of primary importance and must be construed and interpreted to have been intended as an express covenant that the occupancy specified shall be continued during the entire lease period so as to provide a constant base upon which the agreed rent formula may be applied and the rent computed.[97]

However, in a case involving a percentage lease, a New York appellate court refused to infer a covenant to operate on the theory of good faith and fair dealing.[98]

Looking backward, the real estate professional can distinguish several judicial approaches to an implied covenant of continuous operation: refusal to imply a covenant for any reason; refusal to imply a covenant because the minimum rent is substantial, and a willingness to imply a covenant if it is not; willingness to imply a covenant if several requirements are satisfied; and a willingness to imply a covenant on the basis of the use provision. All of these approaches might be considered irrelevant to the economic realities of shopping center development. Another approach endeavors to cure that defect.

Although its courts' decisions are in a small minority, New Jersey has implied a covenant of continuous operations in several cases.[99] These cases began with one in which the court recognized that this covenant is generally implied in percentage leases and that it would be difficult to measure the harm caused by the

---

[94] Lippman v. Sears, Roebuck & Co., 44 Cal. 2d 136, 280 P.2d 775 (1955).

[95] *Id.*

[96] Simhawk Corp. v. Egler, 52 Ill. App. 2d 449, 202 N.E.2d 49, 51 (1964).

[97] Ayres Jewelry Co. v. O&S Bldg., 419 P.2d 628, 632 (Wyo. 1966).

[98] Tuttle v. W.T. Grant Co., 16 Misc. 2d 222, 187 N.Y.S.2d 549 (Sup. Ct. 1957), *order reversed,* 5 A.D.2d 370, 171 N.Y.S.2d 954 (1958), *judgment reversed,* 6 N.Y.2d 745, 159 N.E.2d 202, 186 N.Y.S.2d 655 (1959). The Court of Appeals reversed, believing there were triable issues of fact.

[99] Ingannamorte v. Kings Super Mkts., Inc., 55 N.J. 223, 260 A.2d 841 (1970); Dover Shopping Center, Inc. v. Cushman's Sons, Inc., 63 N.J. Super. 384, 164 A.2d 785 (1960).

withdrawal of one member from a "semi-cooperative enterprise" like a shopping center.[100]

In later cases, the New Jersey courts considered leases that did not have percentage rents. Thus, the implication of a covenant of continuous operation could not be so easily made. In one of those cases, the court relied upon the tenant's promise that the premises would be "used and occupied" in reaching its decision, but it was also influenced by the exclusive use given to the tenant and the landlord's obligation to maintain the common areas for the tenant and all other stores.[101] The court required the tenant to resume operations or lose its lease.

In the other case, the tenant operated a diner that was part of a truck stop. The lease gave the diner the exclusive right to sell food. Both the truck stop and the diner were operated 24 hours a day, 7 days a week. When the tenant stopped operating, the landlord sought a court order requiring it to operate. The court noted the "economic interdependence" of the diner and the truck stop, the tenant's covenant to use and occupy the premises, and the tenant's exclusive use. Here again, the court ruled that the tenant must resume operations or lose its lease.[102]

These New Jersey cases emphasized the tenant's promise to use and occupy the premises, the exclusive use given to the tenant, and the economic interdependence of the tenant and the other tenants. If the New Jersey approach is adopted by other states, landlords will have a more flexible standard for their claims. On the other hand, tenants will have no idea whether their leases will be found to be part of "an integrated shopping center" so as to lock them into the development. Does a tenant with a large draw and no exclusive become bound to the center merely because it succeeds?

A landlord is most likely to prove an implied covenant to operate continuously if:

1. The lease does not allow the tenant to assign its lease or sublet its premises. Clearly, if assignments and subleases are unrestricted, the tenant can argue that the lease did not contemplate continuous operation.[103]

2. The lease has percentage rent. The absence of percentage rent shows that continuous operations are irrelevant to the landlord's revenue from the lease. Conversely, if the minimum rent is low, a court may conclude that

[100] Dover Shopping Center, Inc. v. Cushman's Sons, Inc., 63 N.J. Super. 384, 164 A.2d 785 (1960).

[101] Ingannamorte v. Kings Super Mkts., Inc., 55 N.J. 223, 260 A.2d 841 (1970).

[102] Tooley's Truck Stop, Inc. v. Chrisanthopouls, 55 N.J. 231, 260 A.2d 845 (1970).

[103] Chicago Title & Trust Co. v. Southland Corp., 111 Ill. App. 3d 67, 443 N.E.2d 294 (1982). *But see* First American Bank & Trust Co. v. Safeway Stores, Inc., 151 Ariz. 584, 729 P.2d 938 (1986) (tenant's right to assign or sublease only extended to same business as the tenant).

the tenant was expected to operate so as to increase the minimum rent by the percentage rent.[104]

3. The tenant is substantial. A sole proprietor is less able to operate continuously than is a national chain store.

4. The tenant is an important part of the shopping center's success, for example, the first large tenant, which drew subsequent smaller tenants.[105]

5. The lease specifies the tenant's use.[106] When the use is not specified, the continuation of the use will seem less important. Even when the use is specified, a court can conclude that the tenant was merely agreeing not to use the premises for other purposes.[107]

6. The other leases in the shopping center do not have an express continuous operations covenant. If they do, the omission of the covenant in another lease seems deliberate and no covenant will be implied.[108]

Legal theories notwithstanding, landlords face substantial obstacles to enforcing implied agreements. Courts are divided on the propriety of injunctive relief to prevent breach of a continuous occupancy provision.[109]

As a result of both the judicial reluctance to order specific performance of express continuous operation covenants and the difficulty of fixing monetary damages, landlords have used novel lease provisions to counter the problems raised when a tenant goes dark but continues to pay its rent. Some landlords reserve a right to terminate the lease without the right to sue for the balance of the rent. Others prescribe an increased minimum rent as compensation for the percentage rent lost from cessation of the tenant's operations, and also for the adverse effects on the balance of the shopping center. One case suggests that a lease may require a tenant to use a stated percentage of the area of the premises.[110] Certainly, a landlord should provide that special concessions made

---

[104] Professional Bldg. of Eureka v. Anita Frocks, Inc., 178 Cal. App. 2d 276, 2 Cal. Rptr. 914 (1960).

[105] *See* Fay's Drug Co., Inc. v. Geneva Plaza Assoc., 98 App. Div. 978, 470 N.Y.S. 2d 240 (1983), *aff'd*, 62 N.Y.2d 886, 467 N.E.2d 531, 478 N.Y.S. 2d 867 (1984) (also mentioned that lease did not require percentage rent).

[106] *See* Ingannamorte v. Kings Super Mkts., Inc., 55 N.J. 223, 260 A.2d 841 (1970).

[107] Tulip Realty Co. v. City Prods. Corp., 27 Pa. D&C 62a (1961). *See* Gerardi v. Vaal, 167 Ill. App. 3d 818, 523 N.E.2d 1327 (1988) (failure to limit use proved fatal to an implied covenant sought by landlord).

[108] Tulip Realty Co. v. City Prods. Corp., 27 Pa. D&C 62a (1961).

[109] *Compare* Price v. Herman, 81 N.Y.S.2d 361 (Sup. Ct. 1948), *aff'd without opinion,* 275 A.D. 675, 87 N.Y.S.2d 221 (1949), *and* Grossman v. Wegman's Food Mkts., Inc., 43 A.D.2d 813, 350 N.Y.S.2d 484 (1973) (both denying an injunction), *with* Dover Shopping Center, Inc. v. Cushman's Sons, Inc., 63 N.J. Super. 384, 164 A.2d 785 (1960) (granting an injunction). Other cases have been gathered in Kane, *Dealing with Assignment, Use, and Operating Covenant Lease Clauses,* 2 Prac. Real Est. Law. 45, 52 (1986).

[110] *In re* Goldblatt Bros., Inc., 766 F.2d 1136 (7th Cir. 1985).

in consideration of a tenant's operation—including exclusive uses, reserved or extra parking, and rights to recapture common area expenses from percentage rent—will end if the tenant ceases operations.

In a discussion that is likely to have significant progeny, the Supreme Court of Nevada ruled that a landlord may recover damages (more than $1 million in this case) for its tenant's breach of an implied covenant of continuous operations.[111]

This discussion of the covenant of continuous operation should prompt the real estate professional to reach an appropriate express agreement or an express disclaimer. Reliance upon an implied covenant is imprudent for a landlord who might expect cash flow from overages of tenants that are free to leave. Similarly, tenants should not undertake their lease obligations without an exact understanding of their fixed costs if the leasehold is not profitable.

§ 10.12 Manner of Conducting Business

In addition to the express continuous operation provision, the shopping center lease imposes other obligations that are intended to assure the landlord of the greatest possible sales from the premises. In the absence of express covenants, some courts have declined to rule that a tenant has an implied obligation to maintain full productivity.[112]

FORM 10-7
MANNER OF CONDUCTING BUSINESS

The premises will be used solely for the purpose specified in the basic lease information. Tenant's business in the premises will be conducted under the trade name specified in the basic lease information during the business hours specified in the basic lease information. Tenant will not use or permit the premises to be used for any other purpose or under any other trade name without landlord's prior consent. Tenant will maintain an adequate number of capable employees and sufficient inventory in order to achieve the greatest possible gross sales. Tenant's advertising in the _____, _____, area will refer to the business conducted at the premises and will mention the name of the shopping center. The identity of tenant, the specific character of tenant's business, the anticipated use of the premises, and the relationship between that use and other uses within the shopping center have been material considerations to landlord's entry into this lease. Any material change in the character of tenant's business or use will constitute a default under this lease.

---

[111] Hornwood v. Smith's Food King No. 1, 722 P.2d 1284 (Nev. 1989). There, the tenant—a food store anchor—had moved into new premises near the premises it leased from the landlord, continued to pay minimum rent (percentage rent having ceased several years before the tenant moved), and subleased the former premises. The decision mentioned the importance of an anchor tenant for the financing and success of a shopping center and concluded that damages for the diminution of the shopping center's value when the tenant went dark were foreseeable and recoverable.

[112] Dickey v. Philadelphia Minit-Man Corp., 377 Pa. 549, 105 A.2d 580 (1954); Mercury Inv. Co. v. F.W. Woolworth Co., 706 P.2d 523 (Okla. 1985).

Tenant will not, without the consent of landlord, use the name of the shopping center for any purpose other than as the address of the business to be conducted by tenant in the premises, nor will tenant do or permit the doing of anything in connection with tenant's business or advertising that in the reasonable judgment of landlord may reflect unfavorably on landlord or the shopping center, or confuse or mislead the public as to any relationship between landlord and tenant.

Tenant will not (1) use or permit the use of any portion of the premises for the conduct in or on the premises of what is commonly known in the retail trade as an outlet store or second-hand store, or army, navy, or government surplus store; (2) advertise any distress, fire, bankruptcy, liquidation, relocation or closing, or going out of business sale unless such advertisements are true and landlord gives its prior written consent; (3) warehouse and stock within the premises any goods, wares, or merchandise other than that which tenant intends to offer for sale in the premises; or (4) use or permit the use on the premises of any pinball machines, video games, or other devices or equipment for amusement or recreation, or any vending machines, newspaper racks, pay telephones, or other coin-operated devices.

Generally, a tenant can change its name unless the lease prohibits it.[113] The importance of prescribing the tenant's trade name appears in two other contexts in the lease. One is the use provision. There, if the landlord believes that the use provision has been breached, it can point to the tenant's other outlets using the same name to show the change in condition. The trade name is also important when assignments or subleases are considered. There, the trade name can prevent the change of control of the premises to one who will not use the trade name; however, the trustee of a tenant in bankruptcy will not be frustrated in its assumption and assignment of a lease merely by a requirement in the lease that the business at the premises be conducted under a certain name.[114] Substantial tenants demand the right to change their trade names so long as the names of their other outlets are similarly changed and there is no conflict between the new name and that of an existing tenant in the shopping center.

Occasionally, the landlord's property has a unique name, for example, Johnson's Corner, and a tenant uses a name such as Johnson's Corner Shoe Shop. Problems arise when a tenant creates a clientele based on its name and then moves. Should it be allowed to continue to call itself Johnson's Corner Shoe Shop when it is no longer at Johnson's Corner? The landlord, of course, will want to capitalize on its old tenant's success and will look for a new shoe shop tenant to use that name. Consequently, landlords often provide that the tenant's trade name will be used only at the premises for the business conducted at the premises so long as the tenant remains in the premises.[115]

---

[113] Keystone Square Shopping Center Co. v. Marsh Supermkts., Inc., 459 N.E.2d 420 (Ind. Ct. App. 1984) (landlord who wants tenant to use its name must make appropriate lease provision).

[114] In re Vista VI, Inc., 35 Bankr. 564, 11 Bankr. Ct. Dec. (CRR) 450 (N.D. Ohio 1983) (decided before 1984 amendments to Bankruptcy Code).

[115] Norden Restaurant Corp. v. Sons of Revolution, 51 N.Y.2d 518, 415 N.E. 2d 956, 434 N.Y.S.2d 967 (1980), reargument denied, 52 N.Y.2d 1073, 420 N.E.2d 413, 438 N.Y.S. 2d 1029, cert. denied, 454 U.S. 825, 102 S. Ct. 115 (1981).

In an effort to assure the greatest possible sales (and thus percentage rent), some landlords limit the area of the premises that may be devoted to storage and office uses.[116] An Ohio court fashioned a sensible remedy for a common situation: a tenant converts part of its premises to a use that does not generate sales, as a result of which the landlord loses percentage rent. In this case, the tenant sublet a part of its premises for nonretail purposes. The landlord sued for lost percentage rent. The court awarded the landlord the historically allocable portion of percentage rent attributable to the proportion of the premises that had been sublet.[117]

Tenants insist that they should not be obligated to remain open during prescribed business hours unless a large percentage — 75 percent to 90 percent — of the leasable area of the shopping center is also open. Tenants also ask that they should not be required to do business outside of set hours, such as 8 a.m. to 10 p.m. Some tenants — banks and movie theaters, among others — must have their own hours. Tenants that furnish services (such as income tax return preparers and shoe repair stores) cannot be open for the same hours as tenants that furnish goods.

§ 10.13 Radius Restriction

The radius restriction is one of the shopping center landlord's efforts to assure itself that the tenant will generate the greatest possible sales from the premises. A radius restriction prohibits a tenant from conducting the same business within a specified distance from the shopping center.[118] In the absence of a restriction, courts usually hold that a tenant may open a competing store,[119] unless it does so in a bad-faith effort to divert sales.

A typical radius restriction states:

FORM 10-8
USE — RADIUS RESTRICTION (SHORT FORM)

During the term of this lease, tenant will not directly or indirectly operate a competing business within a radius of five (5) miles from the shopping center.

From the landlord's perspective, this commonly used provision is wholly inadequate.[120] The phrase "directly or indirectly" is vague. For example, is this provision meant to restrict the conduct of the tenant's parent, sister, or subsidiary

---

[116] Handiak, *Percentage Rent,* in Shopping Centre Leases (H. Haber ed. 1976).

[117] Joffe v. Sears, Roebuck & Co., 31 Ohio App. 3d 243, 510 N.E.2d 834 (1986).

[118] *See generally* E. Halper, Shopping Center and Store Leases § 9.06 (Supp. 1984) (radius restrictions); *Radius Clause Protects Owners,* Comm. Lease L. Insider, Feb. 1987, at 1.

[119] Kretch v. Stark, 26 Ohio Op. 2d 385, 193 N.E.2d 307 (C.P. 1961).

[120] *See* Loblaw, Inc. v. Warren Plaza, Inc., 163 Ohio St. 581, 127 N.E.2d 754 (1955) (measurement was important).

corporations? Presumably it is; however, the tenant can control neither its parent, nor its sister, and perhaps not its subsidiary.

The primary problem with the usual provision is that it does not restrict the people who are in the best position to compete with the tenant: its shareholders, directors, partners, managers, guarantors, and investors. By creating another legal entity, or a sole proprietorship, the radius provision may be avoided.

The problem with restricting these potential competitors is that they are not signatories to the lease and thus not bound by its provisions. The landlord may ask for separate agreements from them. This is cumbersome and not likely to succeed. The landlord can, however, add an additional lease default in contemplation of this possibility. A landlord may also wish to provide that such conduct amounts to the opening of a competing business, with the result that the competing sales are deemed gross sales for purposes of the lease. (This remedy, however, may be useless because the landlord may be unable to gain access to the competitor's sales reports.)

A more comprehensive radius restriction may say:

FORM 10-9
USE—RADIUS RESTRICTION (LONG FORM)

Tenant will not engage in any business that is both (a) competitive with the business or any part of it that the use provision requires tenant to operate in the premises, and (b) located within _____ ( ) miles of any point on the perimeter of the premises. For purpose of this paragraph, tenant will be deemed to be engaged in a business if it or any of its present or future employees, shareholders, or partners (while any of them is also an employee, shareholder, or partner of tenant), or any of the guarantors of tenant's obligations under this lease, is an owner, shareholder, principal, partner, employee, agent, or independent contractor of any such business, or is a lender to any such business, or is a guarantor of the debts of any such business, or is entitled to compensation, dividends, profits, or any other payments or other things of value from any such business.

This provision is a problem for the tenant. At the very least the tenant will want to exclude its existing stores that are in violation of the radius provision; if the landlord agrees to this exclusion, it will demand that the excluded stores not be enlarged or that the leases of those premises not be extended or renewed. Similarly, tenants ask that they be allowed to replace existing stores with new stores within the radius. The provision in **Form 10-9** is also impossible for a publicly held tenant; any of its shareholders may open a competing store within the radius. Furthermore, the tenant may suggest that the radius provision be eliminated if:

1. **The tenant's competitors open within the radius**. By this limitation, the tenant seeks only to protect itself against competition. The landlord may be persuaded by the fact that the landlord is losing sales in any event, whether they are lost to its tenant or its tenant's competitor. On the

other hand, the landlord may be willing to risk competitors but unwilling to give the tenant the freedom to expand within the radius.

2. **A stated part of the term has elapsed**. The tenant will argue that this period—for example, three years—gives the tenant enough time to establish itself and that it should not be further restricted.

3. **A stated aggregate rent has been paid**. For example, the tenant has paid $35 per square foot of the premises, or percentage rent is equal to the minimum rent. The tenant will argue that it has paid more than enough rent for the premises, and that it should be allowed to expand its operations as it deems best.

4. **A different trade name is used**. Tenant's rationale is that a store with a different name cannot capitalize on the existing store's reputation.

5. **The lease is assigned**. The original tenant believes it should be free of the restriction.

The landlord's problem with the tenant's suggestions in items 1 and 2 is one it will have with any occurrence test. An occurrence test, as opposed to a maintenance test, is one that, when satisfied, ends the restriction. A maintenance test ends the restriction only for so long as the test is satisfied. In these examples, if the radius provision ends when the tenant's competitor opens within the radius, the landlord is unprotected if the competitor later closes its doors. Obviously, the tenant cannot be expected to close its outlet in the radius. With regard to item 4, the landlord worries that the new store may still be an effective competitor.

If the tenant is acquired by a larger chain of similar businesses, or if the tenant itself acquires a chain of similar businesses, the acquirer or tenant may find that it is in violation of a radius provision because it has inadvertently purchased stores in the radius. A legitimate business transaction may be stalemated.

In view of the difficulty of determining the landlord's damages if a tenant breaches a radius provision, and in view of the doubt whether a court would enjoin a tenant's breach, most leases provide that all or a part of the sales in the prohibited store will be included in the sales from the premises. If this approach is taken, some real estate professionals either simply define "gross sales" at the premises to include these other sales, or allow other stores within the radius if their sales are considered part of "gross sales." One judicial decision discussed a lease that allowed the tenant to open a competing business within the radius after four years from the date of the lease, but increased the minimum rent under the lease.[121]

No discussion of radius provisions is complete without reference to the doubt that has been cast over their legality. Some commentators have suggested that radius provisions be subjected to the so-called rule of reason test under the

---

[121] Pensacola Assocs. v. Biggs Sporting Goods Co., 353 So. 2d 944 (Fla. Dist. Ct. App. 1978), *cert. denied*, 364 So. 2d 881 (Fla. 1978).

antitrust laws.[122] Still, several state courts have denied claims that radius provisions violate state antitrust laws;[123] these courts have found the radius provisions to be reasonable and ancillary to a lawful agreement. In a somewhat unrelated area, the imposition of radius provisions has been enjoined in a consent degree between the Federal Trade Commission and one large developer/tenant.[124]

The foremost antitrust analysis of radius provisions argues that:

> [R]adius clauses are anachronistic when included in modern shopping center leases since they unreasonably restrain businesses from opening competitive outlets, they do not positively affect either the landlord's rental income or other legitimate interests, and they no longer relate to any valid historical considerations. Indeed, radius clauses may run contrary to modern attitudes and policies toward anti-trust enforcement.[125]

The goal in all these provisions is to avoid the appearance of an unenforceable penalty provision or a restraint of trade. Thus, when employing a radius provision, a real estate professional should draft it with a view toward its bona fide business purpose and reasonableness in terms of scope, duration, and territory. These are the traditional standards that measure restraints of trade. A radius provision that prohibits a new business in an entire state for the term of the lease and any renewals appears less reasonable than one that prohibits a new business in the same county (or city) for the first three years of the lease. A radius provision with greater refinement is even more likely to pass muster. The goal of the radius provision should be remembered: to allow the tenant to establish itself in the shopping center and not to prohibit a successful tenant from expanding into new markets when its success justifies expansion.

---

[122] Steele, *The Shopping Center Radius Clause: Candidate for Antitrust?*, 32 S.W.L.J. 1825 (1978), Marsh, *The Federal Antitrust Laws and Radius Clauses in Shopping Center Leases*, 32 Hastings L.J. 839 (1981). *See* Plum Tree, Inc. v. N.K. Winston Corp., 351 F. Supp. 80 (S.D.N.Y. 1972) (suggestion that rule of reason applies).

[123] Pensacola Assocs. v. Biggs Sporting Goods Co., 353 So. 2d 944 (Fla. Dist. Ct. App.), *cert. denied*, 364 So. 2d 881 (Fla. 1978) (three-mile radius); Winrock Enters., Inc. v. House of Fabrics of N.M., Inc., 91 N.M. 661, 579 P.2d 787 (1978) (two-mile radius). The Georgia Supreme Court found a reasonable restriction of five years' duration in a two-mile radius. The restriction applied to a period after the end of the lease, which was effectively a franchise and bound the "franchisees" who were essential to the protected party's welfare. Watson v. Waffle House, Inc., 253 Ga. App. 671, 324 S.E.2d 175 (1984). Saginaw Joint Venture v. Elias Bros. Restaurant, Inc., 106 Mich. App. 274, 307 N.W.2d 759 (1981), invalidated a three-mile restriction because of a Michigan statute. See Charles Todd, Inc. v. Manhattan Sponging Works, Inc., 1978-1 Trade Cases (CCH) ¶ 62,024 (Tenn. Ct. App. 1978), which upheld a 25-mile restriction for three years after the lease ended.

[124] *In re* Sears, Roebuck & Co., 89 F.T.C. 240 (1977), 3 Trade Reg. Rep. (CCH) ¶ 21,218 at 21,121.

[125] Lentzner, *The Antitrust Implications of Radius Clauses in Shopping Center Leases*, 55 J. Urb. L. 1, 5 (1977).

§ 10.14   Use Provisions in a Bankruptcy Not Involving a Shopping Center Lease

When the tenant files for bankruptcy and its lease rate is less than market rental, the tenant or its trustee (which is used interchangeably with tenant in this discussion) wants to realize the difference between its rate and the market rate for its reorganization or liquidation. In that event, the landlord will try to terminate the lease in order to re-lease the premises at the greater market rental.

At this point, both landlord and trustee must consider § 365 of the Bankruptcy Code of 1978.[126] When the lease has value, the trustee will typically assume the lease according to §§ 365(a) and (b) of the Bankruptcy Code and then assign the lease according to § 365(f)(2), keeping for the tenant or its creditors the amount paid by the assignee for the lease.

In order to assign the lease, the trustee must provide adequate assurance of future performance according to § 365 (f)(2)(B), which is related to the ability of the assignee to comply with the financial obligations of the lease. Significantly, this adequate assurance is less stringent as adequate assurance in § 365(b)(3) of the Code, discussed in §§ **10.15** and **10.16**.

With regard to the term adequate assurances, one court has observed:

> The terms "adequate assurance of future performance" are not words of art; the legislative history of the [Bankrutpcy] Code shows that they were intended to be given a practical, pragmatic construction . . . . Section 2-609 of the Uniform Commercial Code, from which the bankruptcy statute borrows its critical language, provides that "when reasonable grounds for insecurity arise with respect to the performance of either party, the other may in writing demand adequate assurance of future performance . . . ." What constitutes "adequate assurance" is to be determined by factual conditions; [in the Uniform Commercial Code] the seller must exercise good faith and observe commercial standards; his satisfaction must be based upon reason and must not be arbitrary or capricious.[127]

The use provision of the lease comes into play when the trustee tries to provide "adequate assurance of future performance." The landlord claims that it has no assurance of future performance of the use provision. Unless the trustee has found a prospective assignee whose use is identical to the bankrupt tenant's use, and whose acumen might be doubted in the circumstances, the trustee must avoid strict compliance with the use provision. The trustee's success will depend in large part on the location of the premises. Adequate assurances in a shopping center lease differ dramatically from adequate assurances of other leases.

In cases not involving shopping center leases, courts have defined adequate assurances to mean that which will give the landlord the full benefit of its

---

[126] 11 U.S.C. § 365 (1988).

[127] *In re* Sapolin Paints, Inc., 5 Bankr. 412, 420-421 (Bankr. E.D.N.Y. 1980).

bargain.[128] The benefit is shown by proof of the assignee's ability to satisfy the financial conditions imposed by the lease.[129] Unless the landlord shows that it would incur an actual and substantial detriment if the deviation in use were permitted, the use provision will not be an obstacle to the trustee's assignment. Thus, courts have allowed all of the following:

1. A small bistro to use the premises when the lease said they should be used "only for television service and sale of electrical appliances."[130]

2. A discount cigar and pipe tobacco store to use the premises when the lease said that the premises should be used in a "high grade and reputable manner" as a "high class tobacco shop" and "not as a cut rate shop," the court seeming to say that a high-grade, high-class, reputable cut-rate shop was permitted.[131]

3. A store selling fine women's apparel at a discount to use "high caliber" premises in which "high standards" were observed.[132]

4. A store selling women's dresses to use premises which the lease contemplated would be used as an electronic specialty store, when the landlord's contention that the proposed assignee would be detrimental to the building or lower its dignity was supported only by the fact that, at other locations of the proposed assignee, women's dresses were sold off a pipe rack and the ceilings were painted a dark color.[133]

5. Delicatessen premises to be used as a Japanese restaurant and sushi bar.[134]

6. A high-class boutique selling clothing and accessories for both sexes to assign its lease to Diane von Furstenberg, a designer offering women's clothing and accessories.[135]

The apparent ease with which trustees have assumed and assigned these leases is disturbed by a case in which the trustee's proposed sublease would have drastically affected the landlord's rent over a long-term lease. Although it could have disposed of the matter by finding there had been no showing of adequate assurances of future performance of the financial terms of the lease, the court

---

[128] The term adequate assurances comes from U.C.C. § 2-609 (1972). The Official Comment to that section says that the term relates to the financial condition of a contracting party and its ability to meet its financial obligations.

[129] *In re* U.L. Radio Corp., 19 Bankr. 537 (Bankr. S.D.N.Y. 1982).

[130] *Id.*

[131] *In re* Peterson's Ltd., Inc., 31 Bankr. 524 (Bankr. S.D.N.Y. 1983).

[132] *In re* Evelyn Byrnes, Inc., 32 Bankr. 825 (Bankr. S.D.N.Y. 1983).

[133] *In re* Lafayette Radio Elec. Corp., 9 Bankr. 993 (Bankr. S.D.N.Y. 1981) (involving sublease according to the lease and not assignment).

[134] *In re* Grudoski, 33 Bankr. 154 (Bankr. D. Haw. 1983) (court conditioned approval on adequate assurances of proposed assignee's financial ability).

[135] *In re* Fifth Ave. Originals, 32 Bankr. 648 (Bankr. S.D.N.Y. 1983).

went on to say it could not approve the proposed sublease in violation of the terms of the lease: "If Congress intended to give this Court or the trustee the power to abrogate any contractual rights between a debtor and non-debtor contracting party other than anti-assignment and 'ipso-facto' clauses, it would have expressly done so."[136] This reasoning, which has been criticized as too narrow,[137] does not reach the question of the landlord's benefit of its bargain, and requires literal compliance by the tenant with every term of the lease.

The unavoidable conclusion is that a restrictive use provision in a valuable lease (other than a shopping center lease) is a small hurdle for most courts when they determine adequate assurance of future performance. Since courts have employed very strict constructions of use provisions, one solution might be to draft an even narrower use provision. This solution is more apparent than real, however, because courts have criticized enforcement of narrow use provisions and are aware that "lessors could employ very specific use clauses to prevent assignment and thus circumvent the [Bankruptcy] Code."[138]

§ 10.15   Use Provisions in a Shopping Center Bankruptcy

For cases filed after October 1, 1984,[139] § 365(b)(3) of the Code provides:

> For the purposes of paragraph (1) of this subsection and paragraph (2)(B) of subsection (f), adequate assurance of future performance of a lease of real property in a shopping center includes adequate assurance —
>
> (A)   of the source of rent and other consideration due under such lease, and in the case of an assignment, that the financial condition and operating performance of the proposed assignee and its guarantors, if any, shall be similar to the financial condition and operating performance of the debtor and its guarantors, if any, as of the time the debtor became the lessee under the lease;
>
> (B)   that any percentage rent due under such lease will not decline substantially;
>
> (C)   that assumption or assignment of such lease is subject to all the provisions thereof, including (but not limited to) provisions such as a radius, location, use, or exclusivity provision, and will not breach any such provision contained in any other lease, financing agreement, or master agreement relating to such shopping center; and

---

[136] *In re* Pin Oak Apartments, 7 Bankr. 364, 367 (Bankr. S.D. Tex. 1980).

[137] *In re* Evelyn Byrnes, Inc., 32 Bankr. 825 (Bankr. S.D.N.Y. 1983).

[138] *In re* U.L. Radio Corp., 19 Bankr. 537 (Bankr. S.D.N.Y. 1982).

[139] For a knowledgeable discussion of the state of the law leading up to changes in the original Code, see Rosevick & McEvily, *Use Clauses in Shopping Center Leases: The Effect of the Tenant's Bankruptcy,* 14 Real Est. L.J. 3 (1985).

(D)   that assumption or assignment of such lease will not disrupt any tenant mix or balance in such shopping center.[140]

This new section requires an assignee to be at least as experienced and creditworthy as the debtor was when the lease began, and requires absolute (as opposed to substantial) conformity to the lease and relevant shopping center agreements. Most importantly, the section protects the landlord against a substantial decline in percentage rent. Two tenants of equal creditworthiness may pay different percentage rents because of their different sales volumes. A supermarket will have considerably greater sales than a gourmet food store of the same size; the new § 365(b)(3) assures the landlord who has lost a supermarket that it will not be left with a gourmet food store.

The burdens imposed on assignments of shopping center leases in bankruptcy cases made it inevitable that landlords and their debtor-tenants would do battle over the threshold question: Are the premises part of a shopping center? A landlord who shows that they are has the benefit of the substantial adequate assurances of new § 365(b)(3), while a tenant who shows that the premises are not part of the shopping center has the lesser burden of giving adequate assurances under § 365(f)(2).

The Seventh Circuit Court of Appeals found that the debtor- tenant's premises were not part of a shopping center because there was "no evidence whatsoever that the stores were developed to be a shopping center," and "typical indicia of shopping centers, such as a master lease, fixed hours during which the stores are all open, [and] common areas or joint advertising" were all absent.[141] The premises were one of eight stores, of which seven were contiguous. The contiguous stores were under common ownership, the debtor was the "anchor" tenant, and there was joint off-street parking adjacent to all stores. This case is interesting for its discussion of the continuous operation covenant. The tenant, whose lease had a continuous operation covenant and a percentage rent provision, first used two floors for retail sales, and then used only one. Since the lease did not require that all the premises be used for sales, did not require a particular sales volume, and did not require the tenant to act so as to maximize sales, the court concluded that the failure to use both floors was not a default under the lease. This confirms the practice of requiring the premises to be used, stocked, and attended so as to maximize sales.

In another case involving the definition of a shopping center,[142] a Missouri bankruptcy court found and the district court affirmed that the premises were not part of a shopping center because the tenants of the alleged shopping center were not contractually interdependent. Although there were restrictive covenants

---

[140] 11 U.S.C. § 365(b)(3) (1988).

[141] *In re* Goldblatt Bros., Inc., 766 F.2d 1136 (7th Cir. 1985).

[142] *In re* 905 International Stores, Inc., 57 Bankr. 786 (D. Mo. 1985).

affecting the alleged shopping center (which the court treated as amounting to no more than a building code), there was separate ownership of the constituent parcels. The lease in question did not require percentage rents or any joint activities for mutual benefit of all tenants, pertained to a single tenant building with its own parking, and did not tie the debtor-tenant's lease to the continued operation of an anchor tenant.

CHAPTER 11

COMPLIANCE WITH LAWS

§ 11.1   General Compliance Provisions

Most leases have a provision entitled "compliance with laws," "requirements of law," or something to that effect. Some leases subsume this topic in the use provision.[1] Since a tenant may legally use its premises only for lawful purposes, the real estate professional may conclude that a compliance with laws provision is redundant. However, the redundancy is more apparent than real.

By leasing its premises, a landlord traditionally made no warranty that the premises complied with the legal requirements that affected them (such as zoning or building ordinances). Similarly, a tenant had no obligation to comply with those legal requirements, except that the tenant could not use the premises for illegal purposes; the landlord was required to comply with them. Of course, landlords and tenants were free to change this common law rule in their leases, and that is what the compliance with law provision was meant to do. It usually excuses the landlord from any obligations that it would otherwise have had to comply with legal requirements, and it requires the tenant to perform an obligations that it would not otherwise have had. This is a typical provision:

---

[1] *See generally* II M.R. Friedman, Friedman on Leases ch. 11 (1983) (hereinafter Friedman); Annot., 22 A.L.R.3d 521, *Who, as between landlord and tenant, must make, or bear expense of, alterations, improvements, or repairs ordered by public authorities* (1968).

FORM 11-1
COMPLIANCE WITH LAWS

Tenant will not use or occupy, or permit any portion of the premises to be used or occupied, (a) in violation of any law, ordinance, order, rule, regulation, certificate of occupancy, or other governmental requirement, or (b) for any disreputable business or purpose, or (c) in any manner or for any business or purpose that creates risks of fire or other hazards, or that would in any way violate, suspend, void, or increase the rate of fire or liability or any other insurance of any kind at any time carried by landlord upon all or any part of the building in which the premises are located or its contents. Tenant will comply with all laws, ordinances, orders, rules, regulations, and other governmental requirements relating to the use, condition, or occupancy of the premises, and all rules, orders, regulations, and requirements of the board of fire underwriters or insurance service office, or any other similar body, having jurisdiction over the building in which the premises are located. The cost of such compliance (including without limitation capital expenditures) will be borne by tenant.

If the use provision has not required compliance with insurance requirements, then this paragraph continues:

Any increase in the cost of any insurance carried by landlord attributable to tenant's activities, property, or improvements in the premises or tenant's failure to perform and observe its obligations and covenants under this lease will be payable by tenant to landlord, from time to time, on demand. A schedule or "make up" of rates for the premises or building of which the premises are a part issued by the body making its fire insurance rates will be, as between landlord and tenant, conclusive evidence of the facts stated in it and of the items and charges in the fire insurance rates then applicable. The final judgment of any court, or the admission of tenant, that tenant has violated any law or requirement of governmental or insurance authorities affecting the premises or building of which the premises are a part will be conclusive evidence of such violation as between landlord and tenant.

In the typical short-term lease, the tenant will find its exposure under this provision intolerable. By its terms, it obligates the tenant to make capital expenditures for structural alterations required by laws enacted during the term of the lease. These expenses can be substantial and of relatively little use to the tenant. Fortunately, courts are sympathetic to tenants whose landlords try to press these substantial costs on their tenants.[2]

The tenant's first approach will be to say that it should not have any exposure to the expense of making alterations to the premises so long as it uses the premises according to the lease. In other words, in a short-term lease, the tenant should not be required to incur any cost in order to comply with laws of general applicability.

---

[2] 2 R. Powell, The Law of Real Property § 241 (P.J. Rohan rev. ed. 1977) (hereinafter Powell); Finnegan v. Royal Realty Co., 35 Cal. 2d 409, 218 P.2d 17 (1950) (court went out of its way to excuse the tenant from capital expenditures).

The recurrent example is sprinkler systems.[3] However, if the landlord can prove that the tenant will benefit from the installation (for example, it has such a long lease or option to purchase that its use of the premises is likely to be lengthy), the landlord may succeed in fobbing off the expense of sprinkler installation. The tenant should be willing to agree that it will pay for any improvements that it is legally required to make if the requirement is imposed solely because of the unique nature of the tenant's use and occupancy of the premises. Of course, if the installation is necessary in order to comply with the laws covering its business, then the tenant is justly obligated to install a sprinkler system.[4]

The landlord may still insist that the cost of complying with all laws be borne by the tenant. In this case, the tenant should agree to pay ordinary costs but decline to pay extraordinary costs, costs for capital improvements, or costs of structural alterations. None of these terms has a clear definition. If the landlord still presses, the tenant should seek a maximum amount that it is obligated to pay in the aggregate over the term of the lease. As an alternative, the tenant may require the landlord to amortize the costs of the improvements over their useful lives and to charge the tenant only so much as is amortized during its lease term. Since the landlord pays for the improvements in this scenario, it may insist upon interest on the declining balance of its expenditure.

If the landlord and tenant cannot reach an agreement on those bases, the tenant may suggest that it have the right to cancel the lease if improvements are necessary and it is unwilling to pay for them. Such a provision would be particularly beneficial to the tenant toward the end of its term when it will not get much use from the improvements. If the tenant has a purchase option, it should insist that it have the option to accelerate the exercise date and buy the premises.

In arguing its case, the tenant should remember that courts have been sympathetic to the tenant who is asked to make a substantial improvement to the premises on the basis of its agreement to comply with laws.[5] In considering the analogous situation of a tenant's covenant to repair and maintain, one thoughtful

---

[3] *See* Mayfair Merchandise Co. v. Wayne, 415 F.2d 23 (2d Cir. 1969); Sadler v. Winn-Dixie Stores, 152 Ga. App. 763, 264 S.E.2d 291 (1979) (both excusing tenant from installation of sprinkler system). In *Sadler,* the landlord's theory of the tenant's liability was that installation of the sprinkler system was a repair the tenant was obligated to make.

[4] *See* 4370 Park Ave. Corp. v. Hunter Paper Co., 10 Misc. 2d 1098, 171 N.Y.S.2d 358 (Sup. Ct.), *aff'd,* 6 A.D.2d 684, 174 N.Y.S.2d 949, *appeal denied,* 6 A.D.2d 866, 175 N.Y.S.2d 1021 (1958); Baca v. Walgreen Co., 6 Kan. App. 2d 505, 630 P.2d 1185 (1981), *aff'd in part, rev'd in part,* 230 Kan. 443, 638 P.2d 898, *cert. denied,* 459 U.S. 859, 103 S. Ct. 130 (1982). In Dennison v. Marlowe, 106 N.M. 433, 744 P.2d 906 (1987), *appeal after remand,* 108 N.M. 524, 775 P.2d 7261 (1989), the New Mexico Supreme Court concluded that a tenant had been partially evicted, and was thus entitled to rent abatement, when the landlord refused to install a sprinkler system on the second floor of the premises; the tenant had no obligation to make those improvements.

[5] Fontius Shoe Co. v. Industrial Western, Inc., 42 Colo. App. 236, 596 P.2d 1209 (1979) (excuses tenant from obligation to install sprinkler system in order to comply with laws).

decision cited these factors in allocating the cost of improvements between the landlord and tenant:

1. the relationship of the cost of the curative action to the rent reserved
2. the term for which the lease was made
3. the relationship of the benefit to the tenant to that of the landlord
4. whether the curative action is structural or non-structural in nature
5. the degree to which the tenant's enjoyment of the premises will be interfered with while the curative action is being undertaken and
6. in cases involving covenants to comply with laws or orders the likelihood that the landlord and tenant contemplated the application of the particular law or orders involved.[6]

The responsibility for asbestos removal is a new issue between landlords and tenants. Many of the leases in which the question has arisen did not contemplate the issue and did not expressly provide for it. Consequently, general compliance with laws provisions such as **Form 11-1** has been the only guide for many landlords and tenants. It appears that courts are likely to impose these traditional criteria when allocating asbestos removal or abatement costs for landlords and tenants.[7]

Most provisions requiring the tenant's compliance with laws are sufficiently broad to include compliance with trade laws, the Uniform Consumer Credit Code, labor laws, and other laws that govern its operations at the premises. Tenants usually ask that their obligations under these provisions be limited to laws governing the premises, such as building and zoning codes. Most landlords agree to this limitation. However, one may wonder, for example, whether a landlord should be deprived of its percentage of a tenant's gross sales because the tenant was compelled to make refunds when its advertising was found to be deceptive.

§ 11.2   Right to Contest

Many tenants demand the right to contest laws with which they are required to comply. This is particularly true in leases of single tenant buildings. The landlord has no real basis for objection so long as it is not affected by the contest. The landlord and tenant may agree:

---

[6] Glenn R. Sewell Sheet Metal, Inc. v. Loverde, 70 Cal. 2d 266, 451 P.2d 721, 726, 75 Cal. Rptr. 889, 894 (1969).

[7] See § **11.5** for provisions regarding environmental laws.

FORM 11-2
FORM 11-2
COMPLIANCE WITH LAWS—RIGHT TO CONTEST

Tenant will have the right to contest by appropriate proceedings diligently conducted in good faith in the name of tenant or, with the prior consent of the landlord (which will not be unreasonably withheld or delayed), in the name of landlord, or both, without cost or expense to landlord, the validity or application of any law, ordinance, order, rule, regulation or legal requirement of any nature. If compliance with any law, ordinance, order, rule, regulation, or requirement may legally be delayed pending the prosecution of any proceeding without incurring any lien, charge, or liability of any kind against the premises, or tenant's interest in the premises, and without subjecting tenant or landlord to any liability, civil or criminal, for failure to comply, tenant may delay compliance until the final determination of the proceeding. Even if a lien, charge, or liability may be incurred by reason of any delay, tenant may contest and delay, so long as (a) the contest or delay does not subject landlord to criminal liability and (b) tenant furnishes to landlord security, reasonably satisfactory to landlord, against any loss or injury by reason of any contest or delay. Landlord will not be required to join any proceedings pursuant to this paragraph unless the provision of any applicable law, rule, or regulation at the time in effect requires that the proceedings be brought by or in the name of landlord, or both. In that event landlord will join the proceedings or permit them to be brought in its name if tenant pays all related expenses.

Occasionally, a tenant states its preference for a provision that is worded negatively, that is, "Tenant will not violate . . . ." After some reflection, the real estate professional can see that this apparent subtlety does import a lower level of responsibility. A leading commentator has found case-law support for a some-what similar provision.[8] One interesting theory of the origin of this nuance is a distinction made between Old Testament law, whose injunctions usually take the form of "Thou shalt not . . . ," and New Testament law, whose injunctions usually take the form of "Thou shalt. . . ." Be that as it may, a tenant is probably better off with a negatively worded provision.

§ 11.3 Landlord's Warranty of Compliance

When the tenant cannot escape a compliance with laws provision, it should demand the landlord's warranty that the premises comply with laws at the time of their delivery to the tenant. This will assure that the tenant will not be responsible for an existing default. Although the provision will vary from lease to lease in order to be congruent to the tenant's obligations, a provision related to the form in this chapter would say:

---

[8] II Friedman § 11.1 n.33.

FORM 11-3
COMPLIANCE WITH LAWS—LANDLORD'S WARRANTY

Landlord represents and warrants to tenant that on the date of delivery of possession of the premises to tenant the premises will be in compliance with all laws, ordinances, orders, rules, regulations, and other governmental requirements relating to the use, condition, and occupancy of the premises, and all rules, orders, regulations, and requirements of the board of fire underwriters or insurance service office, or any similar body having jurisdiction over the premises and the building of which the premises are a part.

A concluding caveat: Single-user tenants of older buildings with nonconforming uses should be careful of the interrelationship between the compliance with laws provision and the tenant's duty to reconstruct after substantial destruction of the premises. As a condition to the building permit for the reconstruction, the building department is likely to require that the building be rebuilt in compliance with current codes; thus, the nonconforming use must be upgraded at what may be great expense. Although insurance coverage may be available, it will be expensive. The result may be a large uninsured loss for which the tenant is responsible. Since the landlord enjoys the windfall of a better building than it leased, recovery of the extra cost of appropriate insurance or uninsured construction may properly be borne by the landlord through rent abatement.

§ 11.4 Compliance with Environmental Laws

Until the 1980s, even the most thorough lease was not likely to have specific provisions regarding environmental laws, although there may have been a general provision (such as that set forth in § 11.1) requiring the tenant's compliance with laws, and there may have been other provisions that had the same effect as a thorough provision regarding environmental laws (see § 11.5). If a violation of an environmental law did occur with premises subject to one of those older leases, landlords would rely on those general provisions and perhaps on common law theories, such as nuisance, waste, negligence per se if the violation of a statute were involved, trespass, and strict liability.

In the early 1980s, landlords began to recognize the effect that environmental laws might have upon them. The public also became more aware of the health hazards presented by asbestos (which was common in buildings built between 1870 and 1980), PCBs (which were common in hydraulic fluids), solvents, pesticides, and petroleum products. The most important aspect of many environmental laws is that they apply to persons as a result of their status, for example, owner or operator, without regard to their conduct, for example, contaminating the environment. Consequently, liability may attach to a person who is "innocent" to all appearances and certainly not at fault for omissive or commissive behavior.

Some of the relevant environmental laws are:

1.   Comprehensive Environmental Response, Compensation, and Liability Act of 1980 (CERCLA or Superfund).[9] By far the most pervasive statute, CERCLA allows the United States, a state, or an Indian tribe to recover from potentially responsible persons (PRPs), that is:

(a)   The present owner or operator of a site.[10]

(b)   A past owner or operator of a site who at the time of disposal of a hazardous substance [11] owned or operated the site at which hazardous substances were disposed of, or who transferred the site without disclosing its knowledge that the site was contaminated.

(c)   Generators of hazardous substances disposed of or placed at a site.

(d)   Transporters of hazardous substances to a site.[12]

The recovery can include all costs of removal or remedial action (in addition to costs of investigation and penalties) not inconsistent with the national contingency plan.[13] Private parties have a right of action for recovery of costs of response incurred by them consistent with the national contingency plan.[14]

Although CERCLA imposed strict liability,[15] it did allow an innocent landowner defense in which an owner had a defense to a cost recovery action if the release of the hazardous material and resultant damage were solely the result of an act or omission of a third party, and the owner exercised due care with respect to the hazardous material, and the owner took precautions against third parties' foreseeable acts.[16] However, the third-party defense was inapplicable when the third party's acts or omission occurred in connection with a contractual relationship existing directly or indirectly with the defendant owner.[17] Another defense was available if the owner took due care and precautions against foreseeable acts and the release was caused by an act of God or an act of war.[18]

---

[9] 42 U.S.C.A. § 9601 (West 1980).

[10] A tenant may be an owner, United States v. South Carolina Recycling & Disposal, Inc., 653 F. Supp. 984 (D.S.C. 1984); or an operator, United States v. Northernaire Plating Co., 670 F. Supp. 742 (W.D. Mich. 1987).

[11] Although hazardous materials or hazardous substances are defined differently in different environmental laws, they are usually toxic, ignitable, corrosive, or reactive. For lists, see 40 C.F.R. § 302 (1987) (CERCLA); 40 C.F.R. §§ 116, 117, 401.15 (1987) (CWA); 40 C.F.R. §§ 261, 261.30-.33 (1987) (RCRA); 51 Fed. Reg. 41,570 (Nov. 17, 1986) (SARA); and 49 C.F.R. pt. 172 (1987) (Dep't Transp.).

[12] 42 U.S.C.A. § 9607(a) (West 1980).

[13] *Id*. at § 9607(a)(4)(A).

[14] *Id*. at § 9607(a)(4)(B).

[15] State of N.Y. v. Shore Realty, 759 F.2d 1032 (2d Cir. 1985).

[16] 42 U.S.C.A. § 9607(b)(3) (1980).

[17] *Id*.

[18] There is also the possiblity that an "almost innocent" landowner can settle for a minimal amount. 42 U.S.C.A. § 9622(g)(1)(B).

Under CERCLA, many real estate practitioners feared that contracts such as leases ended the third party defense. The Superfund Amendment and Reauthorization Act of 1986 (SARA)[19] made it clear that contractual relationships under CERCLA included land contracts, deeds, or other instruments transferring title or possession.[20] However, SARA created the innocent buyer defense by excluding from contractual relationships transactions in which the property was acquired after the hazardous substance had been deposited on it and the buyer did not know and had no reason to know of the hazardous substance on the property.

In order for an owner to show that it had no reason to know of the hazardous substance, it must show that at the time of the acquisition it had undertaken all appropriate inquiry into the previous ownership and uses of the property consistent with commercial or customary practice. Factors to be considered in determining whether the innocent buyer defense is available include:

(a)   Whether the buyer has specialized knowledge and experience.

(b)   The relationship of the purchase price to the value of the property if not contaminated.

(c)   The reasonably ascertainable information regarding the property.

(d)   The obviousness or likely presence of contamination.

(e)   The ability to detect the contamination with appropriate inspection.

Finally, CERCLA provides that the recovery costs are a lien against the property subject to other liens. Contribution and indemnification among PRPs are possible,[21] although a PRP cannot escape its liability, and the liability of PRPs is usually joint and several.

2.   Resource Conservation and Recovery Act (RCRA)[22] imposes criminal liability on past and present storers, generators, transporters, owners (landlords and lenders), and operators (tenants or property managers) involved in improper or unpermitted treatment, storage, and disposal of hazardous wastes. The United States Environmental Protection Agency may take or impose corrective action for the release of the hazardous wastes into the environment. Property owners may have to sign applications for their tenants and may be liable for their tenants' compliance.[23]

3.   Clean Air Act[24] prohibits the release of hazardous air pollutants that may reasonably be expected to lead to an increase of mortality or to serious irreversible or incapacitating reversible illness or that are in excess of emission standards. Clean Air Act covers asbestos. Violation of Clean Air Act can lead to civil and criminal liability. Those standards are set forth in the National Emission Standards for Hazardous Air Pollutants (NESHAP).[25]

---

[19] 42 U.S.C.A. § 9601 (West 1980).

[20] *Id*. at § 9601(a)(35)(A).

[21] *Id*. at § 9613(f).

[22] 42 U.S.C. § 6901.

[23] 40 C.F.R. § 270.10(b).

[24] 42 U.S.C. § 7401-.

[25] 40 C.F.R. pt. 61 (1987).

4.   Clean Water Act[26] prohibits the discharge of pollutants into the navigable waters of the United States without a permit. Unpermitted discharge can lead to an owner's or operators strict liability for cleanup costs, joint and several liability of responsible parties, and civil and criminal liability.

5.   Toxic Substances Control Act[27] governs the testing and manufacturing of chemicals. This is the act that bans PCBs (polychlorinated biphenyls) and requires the cleanup of asbestos in schools.

6.   Regulations regarding underground storage tanks[28] that store either petroleum or hazardous substances (other than those regulated by RCRA) require testing, registration, special design and installation, reporting, and corrective action.

7.   State counterparts to CERCLA.[29]

There are also the common law theories discussed in this section.

These environmental laws prompt the protections that landlords and tenants seek in § **11.5**.

§ 11.5   Negotiating the Environmental Compliance Provision

Negotiating provisions regarding compliance with environmental laws presents not only the problems discussed in § **11.1** with regard to legal compliance generally, but also the unique problems arising out of environmental incidents: the tenant may be deprived of the use of its premises for reasons the landlord neither knew nor caused; the landlord (and its successors) may suffer from the tenant's conduct long after the tenant's lease has ended; both the landlord and the tenant may be affected by an incident that neither of them caused. The issues that landlords and tenants discuss can be temporally divided among those that govern the condition of the premises before, during, and at the end of the lease. Although landlords and tenants have many separate interests at each point, they may also have some similar interests.

When the prospective landlord and tenant meet, the condition of the premises and thus the landlord's environmental problems (if any) are fixed. Except for the rare instance in which the landlord wants the tenant to take care of the landlord's existing environmental problems, the landlord's goal is to protect itself during the lease; it wishes to enter into a lease that gives it back no less that what it gave the

---

[26] 33 U.S.C.A. §§ 1251-.

[27] 50 U.S.C.A. §§ 2601-.

[28] 40 C.F.R. pts. 280 and 281.

[29] *See, e.g.*, Cal. Health & Safety Code §§ 25800- (West 1980), the so-called Carpenter-Presley-Taylor Hazardous Substance Account Act, or California Superfund; New Jersey Spill Compensation and Control Act, N.J. Stat. Ann. § 58:10-28.11, Mass. Gen. Laws Ann. ch. 21E, § 13, Md. Env. Code Ann. §§ 7-218- (1987); Conn. Gen. Stat. § 22(a)-452.

tenant. On the other hand, the tenant wants to be sure that it is not inheriting existing environmental problems with regard to the premises. Accordingly, the burden of negotiating provisions regarding the condition of the premises at the beginning of the lease rests far more heavily on the tenant than the landlord.

The landlord will consider the tenant's proposed use and may investigate the tenant's past tenancies or property ownerships to determine whether there were environmental problems. The landlord may also investigate the tenant's financial condition in order to be certain that the tenant can respond to the environmental indemnities for which the landlord intends to ask. Obviously, when leasing premises in an office building, a landlord is not as concerned about environmental problems caused by its tenants as it is when leasing manufacturing, industrial, or warehouse premises.

As parts of the lease, the tenant will want representations and warranties from the landlord that:

1. There are no hazardous materials on the premises.
2. The landlord has no notices of any violations of environmental laws.
3. There are no asbestos-containing materials, polychlorinated biphenyls, or underground storage tanks on the premises.
4. The premises comply with all environmental laws.

The tenant will want access to the landlord's records in order to substantiate the landlord's statements, just as it will want to assure itself about prior ownerships and uses of the premises; the existence of necessary environmental permits (such as discharge permits); past, pending, or threatened private or governmental actions; and the contents of reports of environmental tests, and soils and air samples. If the landlord has any permits that are necessary for operation of the premises, tenant will insist upon their transfer to the tenant and will condition the lease upon the completion of that transfer.

These representations and investigations are particularly important if a tenant has any prospect of buying the premises pursuant to a purchase option or right of first refusal. With these efforts, the tenant is endeavoring to clothe itself in the innocent buyer defense described in § **11.4**. Although tenants can be owners[30] or operators[31] under CERCLA, no tenant seems to have been found liable under CERCLA solely as an owner or operator without more; in the cases, the tenants' liability arose out of a generation of hazardous substances.

The tenant will also insist upon indemnification for any breach of these representations by the landlord. Even though the tenant may have no liability for cleanup expenses, its use of the premises might be interrupted by cleanup operations undertaken by the landlord or a governmental entity.

Because both the landlord and the tenant are interested in determining the condition of the property at the time the lease begins, they may both insist upon

---

[30] United States v. South Carolina Recycling & Disposal, Inc., 653 F. Supp. 984 (D.S.C. 1984).

[31] United States v. Northernaire Plating Co., 670 F. Supp. 742 (W.D. Mich. 1987).

an environmental audit or site assessment that fixes the condition of the property at the beginning of the term. Although the landlord and tenant may know that any deviation from the substance of that audit at the end of the lease did not arise from the landlord's conduct, they must also realize that the deviation did not necessarily arise from the tenant's conduct. For example, a migration of underground contaminants might have occurred as a result of an adjacent landowner's conduct.

If the preleasing audit determines that an environmental problem exists, the landlord and tenant may negotiate an allocation of cleanup costs in much the same way they would negotiate the repair obligations for improvements on the premises during the tenant's occupancy.

The landlord strives for the greatest self-protection from environmental risks by the provisions it imposes on the tenant's conduct and the rights it creates or reserves for itself during the term of the lease. Some of its efforts are directed toward expanding common provisions to be sure that they address environmental issues, while other efforts are designed specially to assuage the landlord's concerns:

1. **Use**. The landlord may require the tenant to obtain all permits and attend to all regulations (such as those regarding underground storage tanks) imposed by environmental laws or necessitated by its use of the premises.

2. **Compliance with Laws**. The landlord may specifically refer to compliance with environmental laws.[32]

3. **Surrender**. The landlord may require the removal of underground storage tanks and a clean-site certification, environmental audit or site assessment at the end of the term. The landlord may also emphasize that the tenant's liability for environmental matters survives surrender of the premises.

4. **Repair and Maintenance**. The landlord may explicitly allocate to the tenant the responsibility for environmental cleanups required during the term or after the term as a result of the tenant's conduct on the premises.

5. **Insurance**. Environmental impairment insurance may be required; however, its cost and availability may make this requirement impracticable.

6. **Indemnification, Release, and Disclaimer**. Landlord may seek indemnification for the environmental risks caused by the tenant's acts. This is not, of course, a defense to a CERCLA action and its value is entirely dependent upon the tenant's ability to respond. Indemnification against the landlord's prior acts is likely to be considered against public policy. Landlord may insist upon a release of any claim by the tenant arising out of environmental incidents affecting the premises and it may disclaim

---

[32] *See* Cal. Health & Safety Code § 25359.7 (obligates tenant to give its landlord notice of hazardous material of which it knows or has reason to know; tenant's failure to do so may void lease at landlord's discretion and make tenant liable for civil penalty).

any express or implied warranty, or liability, regarding the environmental status of the premises.[33]

7. **Security Deposits and Other Financial Assurances**. In order to insure the tenant's performance of its obligations, landlord may insist upon a larger than usual security deposit, a bond, a letter of credit, or escrow.

8. **Alterations**. The landlord may condition a tenant's alteration of the premises upon the tenant's agreement not to disturb asbestos-containing materials or PCBs on the premises, or landlord may condition tenant's right to make alterations upon its lawful removal or encapsulation of those and other hazardous materials.

9. **Entry**. The landlord may reserve the right to enter the premises to inspect and conduct periodic environmental audits.

10. **Assignment**. The landlord may condition assignment on its assurance that the assignee or subtenant is environmentally responsible. In doing so, it may make it clear that it will not be unreasonable if it refuses consent to an environmentally "risky" enterprise.

11. **Default**. The landlord may emphasize that it has the right to cure any environmental defaults, such as by cleaning up the premises, and that it can terminate the lease upon the occurrence of environmental default. The landlord will wish to be solely responsible for giving notice to any governmental agencies as a result of any environmental default and negotiating the remedial action and penalty on account of it.

The tenant, having protected itself with due diligence before the lease, has a much shorter list of protective measures during the term:

1. **Right to Cure**. The tenant will want a right to cure any default by landlord under the representations and warranties about the environmental status of the property.

2. **Rent Abatement**. The tenant will want abatement of rent if a breach of landlord's representations of the environmental status of the premises results in tenant's inability to use the premises during remedial action.

3. **Limitation of Recourse**. A tenant successful in negotiating any of the preceding rights must be certain that the usual limitation of recourse against the landlord (such as that discussed in **Chapter 29**) is appropriately modified.

---

[33] A very interesting Maryland case raises the prospect that contamination may reach the level of constructive eviction or breach of the covenant of quiet enjoyment. QC Corp. v. Maryland Port Admin., 68 Md. App. 181, 510 A.2d 1101 (1986).

Both the landlord and tenant have common interest in the negotiation of responsibility for clean up during the term.[34] In that negotiation they may wish to consider:

1. Whether the mandated work is substantial or "structural."
2. Whether the work will survive the term of the lease and inure primarily to the landlord's benefit.
3. Whether the work is required by a particular use made by the tenant.
4. Whether the costs are substantial or insubstantial.
5. Whether the event necessitating the cleanup was unusual, extraordinary and unexpected and not in the contemplation of the parties.

Many of the factors to be considered with regard to the allocation of costs and accountability in order to comply with laws as discussed in § 11.1 are relevant to these negotiations.

At the end of the term, the landlord will want to be certain that all permits necessary for the continuance of the premises are transferred to landlord or to the successor occupant of the premises, and that all necessary reports are prepared and appropriately filed by the tenant.[35] Both the landlord and the tenant may wish a final environmental audit of the premises in order to know with certainty their condition at the end of the lease. This will assist the tenant if it is subsequently brought into a CERCLA claim as a result of its tenancy or use of the property. It will assist the landlord in negotiating its next lease.

FORM 11-4
COMPLIANCE WITH ENVIRONMENTAL LAWS
(LANDLORD'S FORM)

Tenant represents, warrants, and covenants to landlord that:

(a)   Tenant and the premises will remain in compliance with all applicable laws, ordinances, and regulations (including consent decrees and administrative orders) relating to public health and safety and protection of the environment, including those statutes, laws, regulations, and ordinances identified in subparagraph (g) all as amended and modified from time to time (collectively, "environmental laws"). All governmental permits relating to the use or operation of the premises required by applicable environmental laws are and will remain in effect, and tenant will comply with them.

(b)   Tenant will not permit to occur any release, generation, manufacture, storage, treatment, transportation, or disposal of "hazardous material," as that term is defined in subparagraph (g), on, in, under, or from the premises. Tenant will

---

[34] The value of Glazerman, *Asbestos in Commercial Buildings: Obligations and Responsibilities of Landlords and Tenants*, 22 Real Prop., Prob. & Tr. J. 611 (1987), cannot be overemphasized.

[35] *See, e.g.*, N.J. CCRA, N.J. Stat. Ann. §§ 13:1(K)-6 (requires filing of negative declaration or cleanup plan in connection with surrender of premises to landlord or successor).

promptly notify landlord, in writing, if tenant has or acquires notice or knowledge that any hazardous material has been or is threatened to be released, discharged, disposed of, transported, or stored on, in, under, or from the premises; and if any hazardous material is found on the premises, tenant, at its own cost and expense, will immediately take such action as is necessary to detain the spread of and remove the hazardous material to the complete satisfaction of landlord and the appropriate governmental authorities.

(c)   Tenant will immediately notify landlord and provide copies upon receipt of all written complaints, claims, citations, demands, inquiries, reports, or notices relating to the condition of the premises or compliance with environmental laws. Tenant will promptly cure and have dismissed with prejudice any such actions and proceeding to the satisfaction of landlord. Tenant will keep the premises free of any lien imposed pursuant to any environmental law.

(d)   Landlord will have the right at all reasonable times and from time to time to conduct environmental audits of the premises, and tenant will cooperate in the conduct of each audit. The audits will be conducted by a consultant of landlord's choosing. If any hazardous material is detected or if a violation of any of the warranties, representations, or covenants contained in this paragraph is discovered, the fees and expenses of such consultant will be borne by tenant and will be paid as additional rent under this lease on demand by landlord.

(e)   If tenant fails to comply with any of the foregoing warranties, representations, and covenants, landlord may cause the removal (or other cleanup acceptable to landlord) of any hazardous material from the premises. The costs of hazardous material removal and any other cleanup (including transportation and storage costs) will be additional rent under this lease, whether or not a court has ordered the cleanup, and such costs will become due and payable on demand by landlord. Tenant will give landlord, its agents, and employees access to the premises to remove or otherwise clean up any hazardous material. Landlord, however, has no affirmative obligation to remove or otherwise clean up any hazardous material, and this lease will not be construed as creating any such obligation.

(f)   Tenant agrees to indemnify, defend (with counsel reasonably acceptable to landlord and at tenant's sole cost), and hold landlord and landlord's affiliates, shareholders, directors, officers, employees, and agents free and harmless from and against all losses, liabilities, obligations, penalties, claims, litigation, demands, defenses, costs, judgments, suits, proceedings, damages (including consequential damages), disbursements or expenses of any kind (including attorneys' and experts' fees and expenses and fees and expenses incurred in investigating, defending, or prosecuting any litigation, claim, or proceeding) that may at any time be imposed upon, incurred by, or asserted or awarded against landlord or any of them in connection with or arising from or out of:

(1)   any hazardous material on, in, under, or affecting all or any portion of the premises;

(2)   any misrepresentation, inaccuracy, or breach of any warranty, covenant, or agreement contained or referred to in this paragraph;

(3)   any violation or claim of violation by tenant of any environmental law; or

(4)   the imposition of any lien for the recovery of any costs for environmental cleanup or other response costs relating to the release or threatened release of hazardous material. This indemnification is the personal obligation of tenant and will survive termination of this lease. Tenant, its successors, and assigns waive,

release, and agree not to make any claim or bring any cost recovery action against landlord under CERCLA, as that term is defined in subparagraph (g), or any state equivalent or any similar law now existing or enacted after this date. To the extent that landlord is strictly liable under any such law, regulation, ordinance, or requirement, tenant's obligation to landlord under this indemnity will likewise be without regard to fault on the part of tenant with respect to the violation or condition that results in liability to landlord.

(g)   For purposes of this lease, "hazardous material" means: (i) "hazardous substances" or "toxic substances" as those terms are defined by the Comprehensive Environmental Response, Compensation, and Liability Act (CERCLA), 42 U.S.C. § 9601, et seq., or the Hazardous Materials Transportation Act, 49 U.S.C. § 1801, all as amended and amended after this date; (ii) "hazardous wastes," as that term is defined by the Resource Conservation and Recovery Act (RCRA), 42 U.S.C. § 6901, et seq., as amended and amended after this date; (iii) any pollutant or contaminant or hazardous, dangerous, or toxic chemicals, materials, or substances within the meaning of any other applicable federal, state, or local law, regulation, ordinance, or requirement (including consent decrees and administrative orders) relating to or imposing liability or standards of conduct concerning any hazardous, toxic, or dangerous waste substance or material, all as amended or amended after this date; (iv) crude oil or any fraction thereof which is liquid at standard conditions of temperature and pressure (60 degrees Fahrenheit and 14.7 pounds per square inch absolute); (v) any radioactive material, including any source, special nuclear or by-product material as defined at 42 U.S.C. § 2011, et seq., as amended and amended after this date; (vi) asbestos in any form or condition; and (vii) polychlorinated biphenyls (PCBs) or substances or compounds containing PCBs.

FORM 11-5
COMPLIANCE WITH ENVIRONMENTAL LAWS
(TENANT'S FORM)

With respect to both the premises and the project, landlord represents and warrants to tenant:

(a)   Landlord has no knowledge and has received no notice of any pollution, health, safety, fire, environmental, sewerage or building code violation, asbestos, PCBs, PCB articles, PCB containers, PCB article containers, PCB equipment, PCB transformers or PCB-contaminated electrical equipment, as those terms are defined in any hazardous substance laws (as that term is defined in this subparagraph); neither the premises, the project nor the ground under or about the project is contaminated with or contains any hazardous or toxic substance, pollutant, con-taminants, or petroleum, including crude oil or any fraction of them, or contains any underground storage tank; the project has never been, nor is it currently used, for the generation, transportation, treatment, storage, or disposal of hazardous or toxic substances, pollutants, contaminants, or petroleum, including crude oil or any fraction thereof; the project does not contain any conditions that could result in recovery by any governmental or private party of remedial or removal costs, natural resource damages, property damages, damages for personal injuries, or other costs, expenses, or damages or could result in injunctive relief of any kind arising from any alleged injury or threat of injury; the project is not subject to investigation, nor is it currently in administrative or judicial litigation regarding any environmental condition, such as alleged noncompliance or alleged contamination.

(b)   Landlord has undertaken all appropriate inquiry into the previous ownership and uses of the project, consistent with good commercial or customary practice, in light of any specialized knowledge or experience on the part of landlord and all reasonably ascertainable information about the project.

(c)   No part of the project has been used in connection with hazardous or toxic substances, pollutants, contaminants, or petroleum, including crude oil or any fraction of them, as defined in any of the hazardous substance laws. No releases of hazardous or toxic substances, pollutants, contaminants, or petroleum, including crude oil or any fraction of them, as such terms are defined under the hazardous substance laws, has occurred from the project into the environment, and no threat of such release exists.

(d)   Landlord will indemnify and hold harmless tenant, its directors, officers, employees, and agents, and any assignees, subtenants, or successors to tenant's interest in the premises, their directors, officers, employees, and agents, from and against any and all losses, claims, damages, penalties, and liability, including all out-of-pocket litigation costs and the reasonable fees and expenses of counsel, including without limitation all consequential damages, directly or indirectly arising out of the use, generation, storage, release, or disposal of hazardous materials by landlord, its agents, or contractors prior to execution of this lease or at any time after execution, or by any prior owner or operator of the premises or the project; and from and against the cost of any required repair, cleanup, or detoxification and any closure or other required plans to the full extent that such action is attributable, directly or indirectly, to the presence or use, generation, storage, release, threatened release, or disposal of hazardous materials by any person on, under, or in the project prior to execution of this lease.

(e)   The provisions of this lease relating to hazardous substances will survive the expiration or termination of this lease.

(f)   If any cleanup, repair, detoxification, or other similar action is required by any governmental or quasi-governmental agency as a result of the storage, release, or disposal of hazardous materials by landlord, its agents, or contractors, at any time, or by any prior owner, possessor, or operator of any part of the project, and such action requires that tenant be closed for business or access be denied for greater than a 24-hour period, then the rent will be abated entirely during the period beyond 24 hours. If the closure or denial of access persists in excess of 30 days then, at tenant's election by written notice to landlord, this lease will end as of the commencement of such closure.

(g)   In this paragraph, "hazardous materials" shall include but is not limited to substances defined as "hazardous substances," "hazardous materials," or "toxic substances" in the Comprehensive Environmental Response, Compensation and Liability Act of 1980, as amended, 42 U.S.C. § 9601, et seq.; the Hazardous Materials Transportation Act, 49 U.S.C. § 1801, et seq.; the Resource Conservation and Recovery Act, 42 U.S.C. § 6901, et seq.; and those substances defined as hazardous, toxic, hazardous wastes, toxic wastes, or as hazardous or toxic substances by any law or statute now or after this date in effect in the state in which the premises are located; and in the regulations adopted and publications promulgated pursuant to those laws (all collectively "hazardous substance laws").

CHAPTER 12

ASSIGNMENTS AND SUBLEASES

§ 12.1　An Approach to Provisions for Assignments and Subleases

The assignment and sublease provisions are among the most important and heavily negotiated parts of any lease. They are a focal point of the unavoidable "zero-sum game" landlord-tenant tension: the control gained by one is the control lost by the other. Also, these provisions are very likely to have significant economic consequences; again, one gains only at the expense of the other. Without the ability to assign its lease, a tenant may be unable to sell a profitable business or reduce its losses in an unprofitable business. However, without control over assignments and subleases, the shopping center owner cannot preserve and enhance the tenant mix that contributes to the success of its development, and an office building owner cannot be certain who occupies its building. This chapter first defines the relevant terms and then approaches assignments and subleases as processes in which the legal and practical requirements of both landlord and tenant dictate the possible lease provisions.

§ 12.2   Assignment and Sublease Defined

An *assignment* of one's interest in a lease[1] is a disposition of all the assignor's rights in the lease and its interest in the premises. An assignment may be made of all the rights in all of the premises or it may be of all the rights in part of the premises; in the latter event, it is called an *assignment pro tanto* or a *partial assignment*. Assignments are usually made by tenants. Similar dispositions by landlords occur in the context of sales or encumbrances of the premises.

A *sublease* is the tenant's creation of a lease-within-a-lease. The tenant transfers less than all its rights in all of the premises or in the part of the premises that it subleases. The relationship of the tenant and its subtenant is like the relationship of the landlord and the tenant. The most important analogy between the original landlord and the tenant-sublandlord is that each has a reversion, that is, the right to repossess the leased or subleased premises when the lease or sublease ends.

The distinction[2] between an assignment and a sublease has been made for centuries:

> An assignment is properly a transfer, or making over to another, of the right one has in any estate; but it is usually applied to an estate for life or years. And it differs from a lease only in this: that by a lease one grants an interest less than his own, reserving to himself a reversion; in assignments he parts with the whole property, and the assignee stands to all intents and purposes in the place of the assignor.[3]

Important consequences follow from these definitions.[4] If a tenant is forbidden to assign its lease but is not prevented from subleasing the premises, the tenant may use a sublease to bring about a result almost identical to an assignment.[5] All the tenant must do is keep a reversion. If the tenant does not keep a reversion, the

---

[1] Technically, one does not assign a lease; rather, one assigns one's interest in a lease. The tenant's interest is possession, the landlord's interests are rent and the reversion. Common parlance uses the expression *assignment of lease* and this book does also. However, the technical difference is very much alive. Cedar Point Apartments, Ltd. v. Cedar Point Inv. Corp., 693 F.2d 748 (8th Cir. 1982), *cert. denied*, 461 U.S. 914, 103 S. Ct. 1893 (1983), *on remand*, 580 F. Supp. 507 (E.D. Mo. 1984), *judgment affirmed as modified*, 756 F.2d 629 (8th Cir. 1985).

[2] For an excellent discussion and academic recommendation of the abolition of the distinction between subleases and assignments, see Curtis, *Assignments and Subleases: An Archaic Distinction*, 17 Pac. L.J. 1247 (1986).

[3] 2 W. Blackstone, Commentaries on the Laws of England 326-27 (1765-1769).

[4] 3 G.W. Thompson, Commentaries on the Modern Law of Real Property § 1210 (J.S. Grimes repl. vol. 1980) (hereinafter Thompson).

[5] 3 Thompson § 1211.

transaction is an assignment, and the lease is breached. The safest and most common reversion is effected by a sublease for a term that is one day less than the balance of the tenant-sublandlord's term.[6] Many other attempts to retain a reversion have caused litigation and split the jurisdictions:[7] the tenant's reservation of a right to terminate the sublease on the occurrence of a stated event (usually subrent default); the tenant's reservation of greater rent than the rent prescribed in the master lease; and the tenant's reservation of a right of reentry on the subtenant's default.[8] Once again, a sublease for at least one day less than the sublandlord's term is the surest way to avoid an inadvertent assignment.

Unless the tenant's landlord agrees to be bound by the sublease,[9] a subtenant has no relationship with the tenant's landlord; rather, a subtenant has rights against, and obligations to, the tenant. If the tenant forfeits its lease with the landlord, the subtenant cannot avoid the loss of its sublease; for that reason, in fact, an amendment of the lease between the landlord and the tenant does not bind the subtenant unless it agrees to the amendment.[10] If the prime lease is amended after the sublease in such a way as to delay tenant's possession, the tenant cannot demand that the subtenant accept the delayed possession of the premises, and the subtenant is excused from performance. The sublease depends on the continued existence of the lease.[11] The subtenant's lot is a hapless one. For that reason, the subtenant asks for an agreement in the form set forth in § **24.3**; by this nondisturbance agreement, the subtenant protects its possession by means of an agreement with the landlord.

By the same token, the landlord has no relationship with the subtenant. As a result, except for the possibility of merger discussed in § **32.12**, the landlord can safely ignore the subtenant.[12] However, the landlord may want the subtenant as its own tenant if the landlord-tenant lease is terminated. To assure itself of a lease with the subtenant, the landlord asks the subtenant to enter into an attornment agreement such as that in § **24.3**; by this agreement, the subtenant agrees to treat the landlord as its landlord under the tenant-subtenant lease if the landlord-tenant lease is terminated.

Because restrictions against assignment and subleases are restraints on alienation, courts construe the restrictions strictly and in favor of free alienability. As a

---

[6] I M.R. Friedman, Friedman on Leases § 7.403 (1983) (hereinafter Friedman).

[7] I Friedman § 7.403(a).

[8] MCF Footwear v. Thirty-Third Equities, Inc., N.Y.L.J., May 23, 1984 at 191 (D. Ca. 1984).

[9] Marchese v. Standard Realty & Dev. Co., 74 Cal. App. 3d 142, 141 Cal. Rptr. 370 (1977).

[10] S&D Group, Inc. v. Talamas, 710 S.W.2d 680 (Tex. Ct. App. 1986), *writ refused n.r.e.*

[11] 49 Am. Jur. 2d *Landlord & Tenant* § 511 (1970); 51C C.J.S. *Landlord and Tenant* § 48(1) (1968).

[12] The protection afforded a landlord by the absence of privity with a subtenant has been overcome when principles of fairness require a subtenant to have remedies against the landlord. Tidewater Investors, Ltd. v. United Dominion Realty Trust, Inc., 804 F.2d 293 (4th Cir. 1986), recharacterized a sublease as an assignment and gave the subtenant privity of contract with the landlord to allow recourse to the landlord.

result, a tenant may be able to achieve indirectly what it cannot achieve directly. A covenant not to assign a lease is often not breached by a sublease of the premises, a transfer of a corporate tenant's stock, a transfer of a partnership interest in a partnership tenant, a mortgage of the lease, bankruptcy of the tenant, execution of judgment on the lease, or death of the tenant. A covenant not to sublease the premises is not breached by an assignment of the lease, or by a variety of arrangements by which the premises are shared;[13] in fact, a covenant not to sublease the premises (as opposed to a covenant not to sublease all or any part of the premises) is not breached by a sublease of part of the premises. Clearly, the wary landlord must protect itself against the wily tenant.

The most important—and least understood—aspect of assignments and subleases is that neither of them releases the original tenant's liability under the lease. Unless the original tenant wins the landlord's agreement to release it, the original tenant remains obligated under the lease. These results are the unavoidable conclusions from the concepts of privity of estate and privity of contract, which are discussed in § 12.3.[14]

The next two sections are helpful but not essential for the discussion that follows. Although they deal with important legal technicalities, some real estate professionals may not find these technicalities interesting.

§ 12.3   Privity

To understand fully the legal significance of assignments and subleases, one must first understand the ancient legal concept of *privity*. When applied to leases, privity means a mutual interest in the promises of a lease. A person who is in privity with another is entitled to enforce the other's promises.

Privity arises in one of two ways or in both ways: privity of contract (which is a relationship derived from contract law) and privity of estate (which is a relationship derived from real property law). The promises that may be enforced by one who has privity of contract may be different from those that may be enforced by one with privity of estate. Therefore, the nature of the privity is very important.

When a landlord and tenant enter into a lease, they are bound to one another both by privity of contract and by privity of estate. They are mutually interested in the same lease and they are mutually interested in the same premises. They may each enforce the express provisions of the lease by virtue of privity of contract, just as they may each enforce the promises that arise from privity of estate.

---

13 2 Powell § 246(1), citing authorities.

14 3 Thompson § 1215.

When a tenant assigns its interest in a lease[15] its assignee has privity of estate with the landlord;[16] they have a mutual interest in the premises. They are not in privity of contract unless the assignee assumes the tenant's obligations in the lease,[17] and the landlord agrees to be bound to the assignee. Thus, the landlord and assignee can enforce only those promises that exist by virtue of privity of estate. A tenant that assigns its lease has no right to reenter the premises if its assignee defaults; that is solely the landlord's prerogative. However, the original tenant is liable for the rent.[18]

In one case, a nonassuming assignee was held not to be liable for rents after its possession ended, even though it was held to be liable to arbitrate the issue.[19] This recognizes the general rule regarding rent obligations, but holds, in effect, that a covenant to arbitrate binds nonassuming assignees. However, there seems to be an inconsistency in this case insofar as it requires arbitration of a liability that cannot be imposed upon the nonassuming assignee.

A lender who took an assignment of a tenant's lease as collateral for the tenant's loan and who (presumably inadvertently) assumed the tenant's obligations under the lease was liable to the landlord by privity of contract.[20] *Collateral assignments*, as opposed to *absolute assignments*, are intended to give a lender a security interest in a borrower's lease. If the lender "forecloses" the assignment and becomes the landlord's tenant, the lender will be bound to those covenants that arise from privity of estate; foremost among these is the obligation to pay rent. Collateral assignments must disclaim or limit those sorts of obligations.

When a tenant subleases the premises, it has privity of contract and privity of estate with its subtenant. Their positions are analogous to the positions of the original landlord and tenant. The original landlord and the subtenant have no privity of estate or privity of contract with one another. Each of them has rights only against the tenant.

Thus, one who has privity of contract can determine its rights by reference to the lease. One who has privity of estate, but not privity of contract, must look elsewhere for its rights; those rights are discussed in § **12.4**. One who has neither privity of contract nor privity of estate is without rights. These distinctions explain several lease provisions in the context of assignments and subleases; they explain why landlords, tenants, and subtenants scramble for privity of contract and the substantial benefits that arise from express contractual arrangements.

---

[15] In this section, the assignment is presumed to be one of the entire leasehold interest.

[16] The rules are conceptually the same for an assignment (or more commonly a sale) by the landlord.

[17] 3 Thompson § 1217.

[18] Italian Fisherman, Inc. v. Middlemas, 313 Md. 156, 545 A.2d 1 (1988). An assignee has no right by virtue of the lease to recover its attorneys' fees in a dispute with the tenant/assignor merely because the lease enables the landlord to do so. Satellite Gateway Communications, Inc. v. Musi Dining Car Co., 110 N.J. 280, 540 A.2d 1267 (1988).

[19] Kelly v. Tri-Cities Broadcasting, Inc., 147 Cal. App. 3d 666, 195 Cal. Rptr. 303 (1983).

[20] South Lakeview Plaza v. Citizens Nat'l Bank of Greater St. Louis, 703 S.W.2d 84 (Mo. Ct. App. 1985).

§ 12.4   Promises Running with the Land

To recapitulate, a distinction must be drawn between promises that may be enforced by those in privity of estate and promises that may be enforced by those in privity of contract. Privity of contract allows enforcement of the contract or lease provisions. Privity of contract arises by being either the landlord or tenant or one who succeeds either of them and assumes its predecessor's obligations.

Privity of estate allows enforcement of only those promises that *run with the land*. Promises that run with the land are those that "touch and concern the land."[21] Those promises are distinguished from personal promises, which are collateral to the agreement. These technical expressions are as amorphous today as they were when they arose several centuries ago. Briefly, a promise may be said to touch and concern the land if it relates directly to the nature, quality, value, use, enjoyment, and operation of the premises.[22]

The general rule that the promise to pay rent runs with the land will illustrate two more consequences of privity of estate. If a landlord and tenant enter into a lease, they have privity of contract and privity of estate. If the tenant assigns its interest to an assignee who does not assume the lease, the landlord and assignee have only privity of estate. Since the promise to pay rent runs with the premises, the assignee must pay rent under the lease or lose the premises. The promise is said to run with the land as a burden. On the other hand, in this example, if the landlord sells the premises to a buyer who does not assume the lease, the buyer — who has only privity of estate with the assignee — may enforce the promise to pay rent. The promise to pay rent is said to run as a benefit to the land. By the same token, some promises of the landlord run with the land as a burden to the successors of the landlord and as a benefit to successors of the tenant.

To be precise, one must state not only whether lease promises run with the land but also whether they run as a benefit or as a burden to the successors of the landlord and tenant. The following promises have been found to run with the land for the benefit of the landlord's successors (by whom the promises may be enforced): promises as to rent; restrictions on the tenant's right to transfer its interest; a right to terminate the lease by notice or cancel the lease in the event of sale; the tenant's agreement to pay taxes, or make repairs, or pay insurance; clauses exculpating the landlord from damages arising from the condition of the premises; and a right to confess a judgment against the tenant.[23] The following promises have been found to run with the land as a burden upon the landlord's successors (against whom the promises may be enforced): covenants of quiet enjoyment; the return of a deposit; a payment owed to the tenant upon termination of the lease; and the tenant's options to extend the lease or purchase the premises.

---

[21] The "land" in these expressions is best understood as the interest which the landlord, tenant, and their successors have in the premises. *See generally* 3 Thompson § 1116.

[22] *See* Restatement of The Law of Property (Second)(Landlord and Tenant), Reporter's Note 3 to § 16.1(1986)(hereinafter Restatement).

[23] 2 R. Powell, The Law of Real Property § 246(2)(P.J. Rohan rev. ed. 1977).

The successors of the tenant have had the benefit of the following promises: the return of a security deposit; the purchase of improvements added by the tenant; the right to extend the term; the right to purchase the premises; the right to remove improvements to the premises; and the right to prohibit the landlord from competing with the tenant's business, although there are contrary decisions.[24] The following promises have been found to burden the successors of the tenant and to be enforceable against them: payment of rent; payment of assessments or taxes; restrictions on transfers or use; the liability of the tenant to a renewal of the lease; the liability of a tenant for the loss of improvements made by it; and the landlord's right to cancel the lease.

One more observation must be made about privity of estate. After the transfer of an estate, the transferor may not enforce promises that run with the land. Furthermore, a person entitled to enforce the promises of a lease may not enforce them against the transferor. The rights and liabilities attendant to privity of estate end with the estate. To illustrate, the tenant's assignee may compel a return of the tenant's security deposit and may forfeit its leasehold for nonpayment of rent up to the moment of—but not after—its further assignment of the lease.

The practical consequence of a covenant running with the land can be easily illustrated. If a tenant assigned its lease to an assignee that did not assume the burdens of the lease, the landlord could compel payment of rent on the basis of privity of estate with the assignee, because the promise to pay rent touches and concerns the land and runs with the land. On the other hand, in a state that construed as personal the tenant's promise to pay for insurance, the landlord could only sue its original tenant under privity of contract, because it has no privity of contract with the assignee.

The *Restatement* § 16.1 states the rule of the burden of performance after transfer:

> (1) A transferor of an interest in leased property, who immediately before the transfer is obligated to perform an express promise contained in the lease that touches and concerns the transferred interest, continues to be obligated after the transfer if:
>
> (a) the obligation rests on privity of contract, and he is not relieved of the obligation by the person entitled to enforce it; or
>
> (b) the obligation rests solely on privity of estate and the transfer does not terminate his privity of estate with person entitled to enforce the obligation, and that person does not relieve him of the obligation.
>
> (2) A transferee of an interest in leased property is obligated to perform an express promise contained in the lease if:
>
> (a) the promise creates a burden that touches and concerns the transferred interest;
>
> (b) the promisor and promisee intend that the burden is to run with the transferred interest;

---

[24] Annot., 25 A.L.R.3d 897, *Covenant restricting use of land, made for purpose of guarding against competition, as running with the land* (1969).

(c) the transferee is not relieved of the obligation by the person entitled to enforce it; and

(d) the transfer brings the transferee into privity of estate with the person entitled to enforce the promise.

(3) The transferee will not be liable for any breach of the promise which occurred before the transfer to him.

(4) If the transferee promises to perform an express promise contained in the lease, the transferee's liability rests on privity of contract and his liability after a subsequent transfer is governed by subsection (1)(a).

It also states the rule of the benefit of promises:[25]

(1) A transferor of an interest in the leased property retains the benefit of an express promissory obligation under the lease, which benefit he held before the transfer, to the extent the benefit is not assigned by the transferor and does not run with the transferred interest.

(2) A transferee of an interest in the leased property is entitled to the benefit of an express promissory obligation under the lease to the extent the benefit is assigned to him by the transferor or it runs with the transferred interest.

(3) The benefit of an express promissory obligation under the lease runs with the transfer of an interest in the leased property if:

(a) the promise touches and concerns the transferred interest;

(b) the promisor and promisee intend that the benefit is to run with the transferred interest;

(c) the transferor does not withhold the benefit of the promise from the transferee; and

(d) the transfer brings the transferee into privity of estate with the person obligated to perform the promise.

§ 12.5   An Absolute Prohibition

With some exceptions, the general rule of assignments of leases and subleases of the premises is that they are permitted unless they are expressly prohibited;[26] therefore, if the lease is silent, the tenant may assign the lease or sublease the premises. The real estate professional must know that, aside from restrictions in the lease, there are common law exceptions to this general rule and that there may be statutory restrictions on assignments or subleases.

Statutory prohibitions affecting assignment are usually related to short-term leases.[27] Texas law affects all leases,[28] but may be modified by agreement.[29]

---

[25] Restatement § 16.2.

[26] 51C C.J.S. *Landlord & Tenant* §§ 30-32, 37(1)(a), (b) (Supp. 1981); 3 Thompson § 1205; Collia v. McJunken, 358 S.E.2d 242 (W. Va.), *cert. denied*, 484 U.S. 944, 108 S. Ct. 330 (1987).

[27] Restatement § 15.1; 3 Thompson § 1206.

[28] Tex. Rev. Civ. Stat. Ann. art. 5237 (Vernon 1962).

[29] Marshall v. Smith, 199 S.W.2d 555 (Tex. Civ. App. 1946).

Some statutes prescribe free alienability in the absence of a contrary agreement.[30] A prohibition of assignment is often implied when the basis for the lease is a special personal service or skill. Sharecropping is a common example, because the landlord's share is related to its tenant's skill. The *Restatement* § 15.1(2) recognizes this exception. However, percentage leases (which some retail tenants consider to be modern sharecropping) do not imply a restriction on assignments. The notion that the nature of the tenant has a bearing on the strictures surrounding assignment finds its way into shopping center leases, in which the tenant mix is important to the shopping center's success.[31]

The *Restatement* § 15.1 takes this view:

> The interests of the landlord and of the tenant in the leased property are freely transferable, unless:
> (1)   a tenancy at will is involved;
> (2)   the lease requires significant personal services from either party and a transfer of the party's interest would substantially impair the other party's chances of obtaining those services; or
> (3)   the parties to the lease validly agree otherwise.

If the landlord is not satisfied that there is a legal restriction against assignment and subletting, and perhaps even if it is, the landlord will first suggest a provision that maintains its complete control of the premises:

FORM 12-1
ASSIGNMENT—AN ABSOLUTE PROHIBITION

Tenant will not assign this lease in part or in full and tenant will not sublease all or part of the premises.[32]

This provision is condoned by *Restatement* § 15.1(3) and a California statute.[33] So restrictive are judicial constructions of this prohibition that this form does not prevent assignments by operation of law and management arrangements. Even this form needs to be enhanced in the ways described in § **12.9**.

This suggestion evokes a prompt response from the tenant, because its potential rights to assign and sublet provide flexibility in business planning. For a small tenant, these rights give the operators an opportunity to retire from business without working to the end of their lease; since death does not release a sole proprietor, an assignment right may avoid a crushing estate liability. To a chain store tenant, these rights are important if it merges with another chain store

---

[30] *See* Restatement § 15.1, n.2.

[31] *Resolving Disputes Under Percentage Leases*, 51 Minn. L. Rev. 1139 (1967).

[32] Stern v. Thayer, 56 Minn. 93, 57 N.W. 329 (1894), appears to support a provision such as Form 12-1. However, since courts often paraphrase or characterize provisions instead of stating them verbatim, one can never be sure what the leases actually said.

[33] Cal. Civ. Code §§ 1995.010-.270 (West 1989).

whose existing locations overlap the tenant's locations; assignments and subleases may be used to dispose of unneeded stores. For any enterprise the extent of these rights may determine the ability to incorporate, take in partners, sell corporate stock, and sell the lease as part of a sale of all assets. Thus the tenant objects to such a provision.

Someone else objects to this absolute prohibition: the tenant's guarantor. Taking over a failing tenant's business may be the only way for a guarantor to limit or avoid its losses. For the same reason, a guarantor insists on notice of the tenant's default and an opportunity to cure it.

Some real estate professionals argue that a strict prohibition may intimidate an unsuccessful retail tenant and, in fact, ultimately hurt the landlord. Such a tenant will lose interest in its operations and the shopping center, will not bring an attractive prospective assignee to the landlord's attention, and may simply move out, leaving unpaid rent and a vacancy.[34]

The landlord responds with a sincere expression of the importance of its control over the premises. In a shopping center development, the landlord will have chosen its tenants with a careful view toward a good tenant mix; it may even have granted some tenants the exclusive right to conduct a certain business. Uncontrolled assignment or subleasing threatens these plans. Moreover, since different businesses pay percentage rent at different rates, the landlord may lose money if a tenant paying at a low rate with high volume (for example, a supermarket) assigns its lease to a business with a low volume (for example, a gourmet food shop) that pays at the same low percentage rent rate. Lastly, some tenants draw customers to the shopping center and thus increase the sales of all tenants, while some tenants attract customers only to their own businesses and do not enhance the business of other tenants.

In an office building, the landlord will not want a sublease or an assignment to another of its existing tenants in the office building if that tenant's lease is about to expire, because the landlord would prefer to release its own space to its own tenant.

In a single-tenant lease site, the landlord has less concern, but still wants to be certain that a responsible entity occupies its building.

Finally, there are economic realities of which both landlord and tenant are aware. Despite the current trend toward shorter terms, adjustments of rent, and recapture provisions,[35] a lease may have such a low rent or other favorable terms that the lease is itself an asset. Landlords and tenants differ on the ownership of that asset. Landlords point out that tenants are not in business to make money on their leaseholds; tenants respond that they are no more particular than landlords about their sources of revenue, and that the landlord did not offer to take back the lease if it turned out to be a liability. After their discussion, which may be quite animated, a compromise is proposed.

---

[34] Orrico, *Assignment, Subletting and Subordination*, in National Association of Realtors, Guide to Commercial Property Leasing 70 (1963).

[35] *See* § **12.12.**

§ 12.6   Requirement of Landlord's Consent

The compromise is:

FORM 12-2
ASSIGNMENT—REQUIRING LANDLORD'S CONSENT

Without landlord's prior written consent, tenant will neither assign this lease in part or in full, nor sublease all or part of the premises.

The landlord does not believe it has made a great concession; it has gone no further than to state the obvious proposition that the landlord and tenant may modify their agreement by the tenant's offer, and the landlord's acceptance, of a new tenant or a subtenant. The tenant is encouraged because its real estate professional recalls a business law principle to the effect that parties to a contract cannot act unreasonably. The tenant concludes that the mere requirement of the landlord's consent implies that the landlord cannot unreasonably withhold its consent.

Unless the premises are in one of relatively few states,[36] the tenant is wrong.[37] These few states express the minority position that a landlord cannot unreasonably withhold its consent to a proposed assignment or subleasing if the lease simply forbids assignment or subleasing without its consent.[38] The rationale of

---

[36] A 1984 study found 12 states that allowed arbitrary withholding of consent: Alabama, Alaska, Arkansas, California, Colorado, Florida, Idaho, Illinois, Kansas, Louisiana, Massachusetts, and Ohio. The survey also found twelve states that did not. *Reasonable Consent Forced on Owner*, Com. Lease L. Insider, Feb. 1984, at 3. Colorado and California have since changed their positions. For the old and new Colorado positions, see Quail & Feuerstein, *May the Landlord Unreasonably Withhold Consent to Assignment?*, 12 Colo. Law. 1631 (1983), and Quail, *May the Landlord Unreasonably Withhold Consent to Assignment?—An Update*, 16 Colo. Law. 799 (1987). Arizona seems to have joined the growing minority. Tucson Medical Center v. Zoslow, 147 Ariz. 612, 712 P.2d 459 (Ct. App. 1985) (adopting Restatement § 15.2(2)). Ohio has also changed its position. F&L Center Co. v. Cunningham Drug Stores, Inc., 19 Ohio App. 3d 72, 482 N.E.2d 1296 (1984). *See generally* Kehr, *The Changing Law of Lease Assignments*, 11 Real Est. Rev. 54 (1981); Guerra, *The Approval Clause In a Lease: Toward a Standard of Reasonableness*, 17 U.S.F.L. Rev. 681 (1983).

[37] Annot., 21 A.L.R.4th 188, *When lessor may withhold consent in lease prohibiting assignment or subletting of leased premises without lessor's consent* (1983).

[38] Homa-Goff Interiors, Inc. v. Cowden, 350 So.2d 1035 (Ala. 1977) (dealing with sublease in which landlord hurt his case by leasing to proposed tenant after tenant defaulted); Hendrickson v. Freericks, 620 P.2d 205 (Alaska 1980); Cohen v. Ratinoff, 147 Cal. App. 3d 321, 195 Cal. Rptr. 84 (1983); Fernandez v. Vasquez, 397 So.2d 1171 (Fla. Dist. Ct. App. 1981); 21 A.L.R.4th 181, *When lessor may withhold consent under unqualified provision in lease prohibiting assignment or subletting of leases premises without lessor's consent* (1983) (dealing with assignment); Funk v. Funk, 102 Idaho 521, 633 P.2d 586 (1981) (dealing with sublease); Arrington v. Walter E. Heller Int'l Corp., 30 Ill. App. 3d 631, 333 N.E.2d 50 (1975) (dealing with sublease); Jack Frost Sales, Inc. v. Harris Trust & Sav. Bank, 104 Ill. App. 3d 933, 60 Ill. Dec. 703, 433 N.E.2d 941 (1982); Associates Comm'l Corp. v. Bayou Management, Inc., 426

this newer rule is that a lease is a contract, not a conveyance, and that it is governed by the contract principles of good faith and commercial reasonableness. The reasoning in some of these cases has been criticized. In several, the courts need not have gone into the issue of reasonableness, because the cases could have been decided simply on the basis of the landlord's bad faith.[39]

The anfractuous California experience with this issue is instructive. In late 1983, a California appellate court abandoned hundreds of years of common law precedents—and the decisions of the California Supreme Court—to rule that landlords have an obligation to be reasonable when considering assignments proposed by their tenants.[40] In January 1984, another California appellate court followed with a similar decision.[41]

Less than a year later, the second court declined to follow its earlier decision and returned to the traditional rule.[42] In refusing to impose a reasonableness standard, the court said that "to hold that there is a triable issue of fact concerning whether the [landlords] unreasonably withheld their consent when they had already contracted for that right, creates only mischief by building further uncertainty in the interpretation of an otherwise unambiguously written contract."[43] The court suggested that the legislature was the only proper forum in which the unbroken line of judicial precedent should be broken.[44]

So. 2d 672 (La. Ct. App. 1982) (dealing with sublease); Granite Trust Bldg. Corp. v. Great Atl. & Pac. Tea Co., 36 F. Supp. 77, 78 (D. Mass. 1940) (in which court said, "It would seem to be the better law that when a lease restricts a lessee's rights by requiring consent before these rights can be exercised, it must have been in the contemplation of the parties that the lessor be required to give some reason for withholding consent"); Shaker Bldg. Co. v. Federal Lime & Stone Co., 28 Ohio Misc. 246, 57 Ohio Op. 2d 486, 277 N.E.2d 584 (1971) (dealing with sublease); Annot., 54 A.L.R.3d 679, *Construction and effect of provision in lease that consent to subletting or assignment will not be arbitrarily or unreasonably withheld* (1973); Marmont v. Axe, 135 Kan. 368, 10 P.2d 826 (1932); Warmack v. Merchant Nat'l Bank, 272 Ark. 166, 612 S.W.2d 733 (1981); Boss Barbara, Inc. v. Newbill, 97 N.M. 239, 638 P.2d 1084 (1982); Tucson Medical Center v. Zoslow, 147 Ariz. 612, 712 P.2d 459 (Ct. App. 1985), Newman v. Hinky-Dinky Omaha-Lincoln, Inc., 229 Neb. 382, 427 N.W.2d 50 (1988). The Idaho Supreme Court extended the reasoning in its landlord-tenant cases to a case involving the vendor's unreasonable withholding of its consent to a vendee's assignment of a land purchase contract, while imposing a standard of good faith and reasonableness. Cheney v. Jemmett, 107 Idaho 829, 693 P.2d 1031 (1984). The Colorado Supreme Court declined an opportunity to adopt Restatement § 15.2(2) in Vista Village Mobile Home Park v. Basnett, 731 P.2d 700 (Colo. 1987), *rev'g* Basnett v. Vista Village Mobile Home Park, 699 P.2d 1343 (Colo. Ct. App. 1984). The Connecticut Supreme Court has changed its law to impose upon a landlord a duty of good faith and fair dealing when considering an assignment. Warner v. Konover, 210 Conn. 150, 553 A.2d 1138 (1989).

[39] The Alabama and Florida cases involved the landlords' demands for additional money; in the California case, the landlord refused to consider the proposal at all.

[40] Cohen v. Ratinoff, 147 Cal. App. 3d 321, 195 Cal. Rptr. 84 (1983).

[41] Schweiso v. Williams, 150 Cal. App. 3d 883, 198 Cal. Rptr. 238 (1984).

[42] Kendall v. Ernest Pestana, Inc., 40 Cal. 3d 488, 709 P.2d 837, 220 Cal. Rptr. 818 (1985).

[43] *Id.*

[44] *Id.*

One critic considered these cases and suggested that the judicial failure to distinguish good faith (which is a subjective standard requiring only a sincerely believed basis for objection) from reasonableness (which is an objective standard shown by reference to the shared experiences of all people) shows a lack of reasoning.[45] This criticism is unduly harsh, because most of the cases use good faith and reasonableness interchangeably.

The California Supreme Court agreed to hear the matter. When it spoke, its voices were neither clear nor harmonious.[46] The majority concluded that in a commercial lease permitting assignments only with the landlord's prior consent, a landlord may withhold its consent only if it has a commercially reasonable objection to the assignee or the proposed use. Two justices dissented, adopting for their opinion a part of the appellate court decision that the majority had reversed.

For the real estate professional, the decision made its most important observations in two footnotes. In footnote 14, the majority opinion noted that the question of an absolute restriction was not presented, but that the *Restatement* § 15.2(2) would validate such a prohibition "if freely negotiated." The *Restatement* does not give an example of a freely negotiated provision. If a prohibition is agreeable, it would seem that the lease at minimum should explain the circumstances that gave rise to the agreement for that provision and should state any consideration or "trade-off" that induced the tenant to accept it. Because most real estate professionals agree that tenants will rarely, if ever, agree to an absolute provision, another approach is needed.

An alternative is presented in footnote 17 of the opinion. There, the California Supreme Court said "nothing bars the parties to commercial lease transactions from making their own arrangements respecting the allocation of appreciated rentals if there is a transfer of the leasehold."[47] Most real estate professionals will be wary of reserving all of the appreciated rentals for the landlord unless the provision is "fully negotiated," as discussed in the preceding paragraph. In practice, a tenant with no benefit from the highest appreciated rentals will not be motivated to get the best terms in its assignment. See **§ 12.12** regarding the recapture and profit sharing provisions.[48]

---

[45] Zankel, *Commercial Lease Assignments and the Age of Reason: Cohen v. Ratinoff*, 7 Real Prop. L. Rep. 29 (1984).

[46] Kendall v. Ernest Pestana, Inc., 40 Cal. 3d 488, 709 P.2d 837, 220 Cal. Rptr. 818 (1985). The Ninth Circuit had foreseen the California Supreme Court's decision. Preston v. Mobil Oil Corp., 741 F.2d 268 (9th Cir. 1984).

[47] Despite what appears to be the California Supreme Court's imprimatur on these provisions, a California appellate court has found that one "unreasonably restrains alienation, contravenes policy, and this is void as a matter of law." Carma Developers (Cal.), Inc. v. Marathon Dev. Cal. Inc., 211 Cal. App. 3d 1360, 259 Cal. Rptr. 708, *review granted*, ____ Cal. 3d ____, 783 P.2d 183, 264 Cal. Rptr. 824 (1989). The appellate court never mentioned the footnote.

[48] For further discussions of Kendall, see DiSciullo, *The Kendall Case: Momentum for a Reasonableness Standard in Lease Transfer Clauses*, 1 Prob. & Prop. 32 (May/June 1987); Gurwitch & Fleisher, *Kendall v. Ernest Pestana, Inc.: The Doctrines of Good Faith and*

At about the same time as this case was decided by the California Supreme Court, an intermediate appellate court in California upheld the landlord's right to be arbitrary when its only motivation was to improve its financial position;[49] the viability of that decision seemed doubtful.

A California intermediate appellate court held in 1989 that a recapture provision (similar to that in § **12.12**) allowing a landlord to terminate a lease of premises when its tenant requests consent to sublease is an unreasonable restraint on alienation and void as a matter of public policy. The provision in question allowed termination if permission "were hereby requested" and thus gave the landlord complete control over subleases (and presumably all dispositions of the leasehold).[50]

All of the decisions and much of the voluminous literature written about them were silenced in 1989 when the California legislature took up the gauntlet dropped in 1984:[51]

1995.210 (a)   Subject to the limitations in this chapter, a lease may include a restriction on transfer of the tenant's interest in the lease.

(b)   Unless a lease includes a restriction on transfer, a tenant's rights under the lease include unrestricted transfer of the tenant's interest in the lease.

1995.220.   An ambiguity in a restriction on transfer of a tenant's interest in a lease shall be construed in favor of transferability.

1995.230.   A restriction on transfer of a tenant's interest in a lease may provide that the transfer is subject to any express standard or condition, including, but not limited to, a provision that the landlord is entitled to some or all of any consideration the tenant receives from a transferee in excess of the rent under the lease.

1995.250.   A restriction on transfer of a tenant's interest in a lease may require the landlord's consent for transfer subject to any express standard or condition for giving or withholding consent, including, but not limited to, either of the following:

(a)   The landlord's consent may not be unreasonably withheld.

(b)   The landlord's consent may be withheld subject to express standards or conditions.

Commercial Reasonableness in Commercial Leases, 9 Cal. Real Prop. L. Rep. 61 (Apr. 1986), Coskran, *Lease Transfer Restraints: Must Consenting Adults Be Reasonable?*, 4 Cal. Real Prop. J. 15 (Spring 1986); Block & Greg, *Kendall v. Pestana: Standard of Reasonableness Applied to Commercial Assignment Clauses*, 18 Pac. L.J. 327 (1986), Lane, *Kendall v. Ernest Pestana, Inc.: Landlords May Not Unreasonably Withhold Consent to Commercial Lease Assignments*, 14 Pepperdine L. Rev. 81 (1986); Kassoy & Mumford, *Assigning and Subletting Commercial Leases: Can Landlords Raise the Rent after Kendall?*, L.A. Law., Jan. 1988, at 37 (generally answering affirmatively); Hayner, *Assignment of Commercial Leases—The Reasonableness Standard and Withholding Consent: Kendall v. Ernest Pestana, Inc.*, 36 De Paul L. Rev. 285 (1987); *Commercial landlords must be reasonable*, 72 A.B.A. J. 90 (1986); Johnson, *Correctly Interpreting Long Term Leases Pursuant to Modern Contract Law: Toward a Theory of Relational Leases*, 74 Va. L. Rev. 751 (1988).

[49] Hamilton v. Dixon, 168 Cal. App. 3d 1004, 214 Cal. Rptr. 639 (1985).

[50] Carma Developers (Cal.), Inc. v. Marathon Dev. Cal. Inc., 211 Cal. App. 3d 1360, 259 Cal. Rptr. 908 (1989), *review granted*, _____ Cal. 3d _____, 783 P.2d 183, 264 Cal. Rptr. 824 (1989).

[51] Cal. Civ. Code §§ 1995.010–.270 (West 1989).

1995.260.   If a restriction on transfer of the tenant's interest in a lease requires the landlord's consent for transfer but provides no standard for giving or withholding consent, the restriction on transfer shall be construed to include an implied standard that the landlord's consent may not be unreasonably withheld. Whether the landlord's consent has been unreasonably withheld in a particular case is a question of fact on which the tenant has the burden of proof. The tenant may satisfy the burden of proof by showing that, in response to the tenant's written request for a statement of reasons for withholding consent, the landlord has failed, within a reasonable time, to state in writing a reasonable objection to the transfer.

The legislature enunciated the public policy "to enable and facilitate freedom of contract by parties to commercial real estate leases" and expressly disapproved contrary judicial pronouncements.

The California statute created different rules to recognize the various judicial decisions that have recently held sway with regard to the landlord's duties when a lease is silent about its standards for consent. As a result, landlords and tenants are in theory bound by the legal principles that were in effect at the time their leases were made, presumably the principles they assumed would obtain in the absence of their contrary agreement. For leases executed before September 23, 1983, the landlord may unreasonably withhold its consent. For leases executed between September 23, 1983, and December 31, 1989, the landlord may not unreasonably withhold its consent. For leases executed after December 31, 1989, the landlord may not unreasonably withhold its consent unless a contrary agreement is made. Of course, the statute condones contrary agreements.

Many of the reported cases have involved situations in which the tenant did not seek its landlord's consent before making the assignment or sublease. In the landlord's suit for breach of the lease, the tenant asked the court to determine the suitability of the assignee or sublessee and to find that no breach had occurred because the landlord could not have reasonably refused if the tenant had asked. The courts rule — and tenants should learn — that it is imperative for a tenant to present an assignee or sublessee and give the landlord an opportunity to refuse the proposal. A landlord need not consider an assignee or subtenant who occupies the premises before the matter is presented to it. An assignment without required consent, even though an apparent formality because the landlord had no reasonable basis to object, is a default permitting termination.[52]

In the improbable situation that an absolute prohibition is desired and no standard of reasonableness is to be imposed on the landlord, the provision should emphasize its intention, saying, perhaps:

FORM 12-3
ASSIGNMENT — LANDLORD'S RIGHT TO BE
ARBITRARY AND CAPRICIOUS

Tenant will not assign this lease in whole or in part and will not sublease the premises in whole or in part without landlord's prior written consent. Landlord may

---

[52] Healthco, Inc. v. E&S Realty Assoc., 400 Mass. 700, 511 N.E.2d 579 (1987).

withhold its consent arbitrarily and capriciously. Landlord and tenant have fully bargained for this provision with the intention that landlord has absolutely no obligation to consider a proposed assignment or sublease.

§ 12.7 Requirement of Consent Not to Be Unreasonably Withheld

As § **12.6** suggested, a standard of reasonableness may be inferred even if it is not expressed. In those states that do not make that inference, and in most negotiations, when pressed by the tenant for some compromise on the issue of consent, the landlord yields and proposes:

FORM 12-4
ASSIGNMENT—SUBLEASE REQUIRING LANDLORD'S CONSENT, WHICH WILL NOT BE UNREASONABLY WITHHELD OR DELAYED

Without landlord's prior written consent, which the landlord agrees will not be unreasonably withheld or delayed, tenant will neither assign this lease in whole or in part nor sublease all or part of the premises.

This provision equates delayed and withheld consent. As a practical matter, a prospective assignee or subtenant will be lost if a response is not prompt. By including delay in this provision, the tenant assures itself that the landlord will make a decision and that it will not wait until the opportunity has passed only to grant its consent. When this provision is reached, the tenant finally has meaningful rights.[53] The landlord no longer has its (rapidly vanishing) common law right to withhold its consent arbitrarily and capriciously.

This means that the landlord may not withhold its consent for reasons of "personal taste, sensibility, or convenience."[54] In a leading case, the philosophical principles of an orthodox Jewish institution compelled it to refuse to consent to a subleasing to Planned Parenthood Foundation of America; the court said that subjective criteria are not sufficient and that "[t]o the extent that rejection of a proposed subtenancy is based upon the supposed need or dislikes of the landlord, a policy of judicial disapproval of such subjective criteria is discernible."[55]

The landlord's personal taste is not the only irrelevancy when reasonableness is the standard. The landlord cannot refuse to consent unless it receives additional

---

[53] Todres & Lerner, *Assignment and Subletting of Leased Premises: The Unreasonable Withholding of Consent*, 5 Fordham Urb. L.J. 195 (1977); Pundeff, *The Anti-Assignment Clause and the Landlord's Legitimate Interests*, 11 Real Est. L.J. 146 (1982).

[54] Broad & Branford Place Corp. v. J.J. Hockinjos Co., 132 N.J.L. 229, 232, 39 A.2d 80, 82 (1944).

[55] American Book Co. v. Yeshiva Univ. Dev. Found., Inc., 59 Misc. 2d 31, 34, 297 N.Y.S.2d 156, 161 (Sup. Ct. 1969).

rent as a condition to approval;[56] nor because the landlord may lose one of its tenants in another building by consenting to that same tenant as a subtenant;[57] nor because the proposed subtenant would compete with it;[58] nor because of the assignee's race;[59] nor because it wishes to prevent the assignee's competition with the landlord's store.[60] Generally speaking, the landlord cannot reasonably go beyond the terms of the lease in determining whether to give its approval;[61] by the same token, the tenant's request for concessions beyond the scope of the lease enables the landlord to refuse its consent.[62]

Courts recently considering the issue of reasonableness have held that a landlord's refusal to consent to the assignment of a lease or to consent to a sublease was unreasonable in the following situations:

1. An assignee proposed to bind itself to each and every provision of the prime lease, its financial status was secure, and landlord's general manager refused consent based primarily upon his subjective belief that a representative of the proposed assignee should have contacted him to discuss its financial status prior to making the application to assign. In its decision, the court stated that "such subjective concerns and personal desires cannot play a role in landlord's decision to withhold its consent to an assignment of a lease, and the hearing court properly held that the defendant had unreasonably withheld its consent."[63]

2. In a situation in which the sublease fully protected the landlord's bargain under the prime lease, the court stated: "The landlord has no reasonable basis for withholding consent if the landlord remains assured of all the benefits bargained for in the prime lease."[64] The dispute centered on the tenant's right to exercise an option to lease additional space and then sublet the additional space to a third party at a rate double that payable under the prime lease.

---

56 Campbell v. Westdahl, 148 Ariz. 432, 715 P.2d 288 (Ct. App. 1986). Chanslor W. Oil & Dev. Co. v. Metropolitan Sanitary Dist., 131 Ill. App. 2d 527, 266 N.E.2d 405 (1977); Ringwood Assocs. Ltd. v. Jack's of Route 23, Inc., 153 N.J. Super. 294, 379 A.2d 508 (1977), aff'd, 166 N.J. Super. 36, 398 A.2d 1315 (1978); Polk v. Gibson Prod. Co. of Hattiesburg, 257 So. 2d 225 (Miss. 1972) (landlord's refusal to consent to sublease was deemed unreasonable when rent was based in part on gross income and gross income was reduced by sublease).

57 Krieger v. Helmsley-Spear, Inc., 62 N.J. 423, 302 A.2d 129 (1973).

58 Edelman v. F.W. Woolworth Co., 252 Ill. App. 142 (1929).

59 List v. Dahnke, 638 P.2d 824 (Colo. App. 1981).

60 L&H Invs., Ltd. v. Belvey Corp., 444 F. Supp. 1321 (W.D.N.C. 1978).

61 *But see* United States v. Toulmin, 253 F.2d 347 (D.C. Cir. 1958) (landlord appears not to have been bound by terms of lease).

62 Mitchell's, Inc. v. Nelms, 454 S.W.2d 809 (Tex. Civ. App. 1970), n.r.e.

63 Ontel Corp. v. Helasol Realty Corp., 130 A.D.2d 639, 515 N.Y.S.2d 567, 568 (1987).

64 1010 Potomac Assoc. v. Grocery Mfrs. of Am., Inc., 485 A.2d 199, 210 (D.C. 1984). For the District of Columbia rules, see Sobel, *Assignment/Subletting Under a Lease*, Wash. Area Realtor, June 1987, at 46.

3. A proposed assignee corporation was financially responsible, having incorporated with $25,000 cash and an approved, SBA-guaranteed $200,000 loan; a $5,000 security deposit had been tendered; the landlord had been given the security assignment of all fixtures and inventories; a personal financial statement and copies of the SBA loan agreements had been provided; and the type of business to be conducted by the assignee was identical in nature to that of the tenant. The court held: "The trial court had before it considerable evidence that the corporation which was proposed was financial responsible and no evidence that it was financially irresponsible."[65]

4. A landlord did not inquire into any aspect of the suitability of a proposed tenant but claimed only that it was given insufficient time to respond to the proposal under the circumstances. However, the jury found that the landlord did not reasonably withhold consent to sublease because of insufficient time to act. The landlord had claimed that it was not unreasonable for it to require additional time to respond to the sublease proposal, because the four unions that formed the corporation owning the building had a policy against any subleasing, and it was unreasonable to expect that the executive committee of the corporation could convene, deliberate, and act to change the policy within such a short time.[66]

5. A landlord refused to consent to the assignment of a lease to another tenant in the same building who required additional space and was renting on a month-to-month basis. The court held: "Where provision is made in a lease permitting assignment of rights thereunder, limited only by the requirement of prior consent of the lessor, such consent may not be withheld unless the prospective assignee is unacceptable, using the same standards applied in the acceptance of the original lessee."[67]

6. A landlord that refused to consent to an assignment because of the assignee's doubtful creditworthiness was unreasonable when the assignee's performance was guaranteed by a substantial business person.[68]

7. An Indiana appellate court found that a landlord had been unreasonable in basing a refusal to consent to an assignment on the use provision: the lease prescribed a music store and the proposed assignee was a carpet store. Since the landlord sought many different users after the tenant moved out, it was clear that the landlord had no allegiance to the music

---

[65] Vranas and Assoc., Inc. v. Family Pride Finer Foods, Inc., 147 Ill. App. 3d 995, 498 N.E.2d 333, 340, 101 Ill. Dec. 151 (1986), *appeal denied*, 113 Ill. 2d 586, 505 N.E.2d 363, 106 Ill. Dec. 57 (1987).

[66] United Unions, Inc. v. Webster & Sheffield, 521 A.2d 273 (D.C. 1987); Stern's Gallery of Gifts, Inc. v. Corporate Property Investors, Inc., 176 Ga. App. 586, 337 S.E.2d 29 (1985), *cert. denied*.

[67] Shaker Bldg. Co. v. Federal Lime & Stone Co., 28 Ohio Misc. 246, 277 N.E.2d 584, 587, 57 Ohio Op. 2d 486 (1971).

[68] Adams Harkness & Hill, Inc. v. N.E. Realty Corp., 361 Mass. 552, 281 N.E.2d 262 (1972).

store use. Thus, it had acted unreasonably.[69] Here again, the obligation to use reasonable efforts to mitigate implies an obligation to be reasonable to avoid a default, even if it means a change in the use.

A landlord's refusal to consent to the assignment of a lease has been found to be reasonable in the following cases:

1. A California landlord properly refused an assignment that would place the landlord in a less beneficial financial position than it had bargained for and could expect to continue from the present lessee under a percentage lease agreement. It was undisputed that the lessor would suffer substantial financial detriment upon the proposed assignment, while the lessee stood to gain at least $1,250 per month above the minimum rent it would be required to pass through to the lessor. The court stated: "To force Lessor to accept the minimum $2,750 figure of the original lease while Lessee pockets $1,250 per month for providing an assignee who cannot generate more than $2,750 for Lessor is out of touch with commercial reality. Refusing to consent to highway robbery cannot be deemed commercially unjustified."[70]

2. Prior to the assignment of a lease to a spinoff division of a Fortune 500 company, the landlord was not provided with any financial information concerning assignee. The landlord did not have any projections of the proposed assignee's cash flow with which to determine whether there would be money left over, after paying the existing debts, to maintain the premises, pay taxes, and pay the rent. The court stated in its opinion: "A landlord is entitled to know something about projected income as well as about existing assets, as least when the assets are so encumbered."[71]

3. In Colorado, it was reasonable for a landlord to reject a proposed assignment when there was evidence to support the trial court's finding that the landlord refused to approve the assignment because it believed that a specialty restaurant of the type the proposed assignee planned to run would not be successful at that location. However, in reaching its decision, the court noted that "landlords have no right to refuse to permit an assignment on purely racial grounds." It further stated that "arbitrary considerations of personal taste, convenience, or sensibility are not proper criteria for withholding consent under" a lease provision which requires consent to an assignment.[72]

4. A Minnesota hospital-landlord was reasonable in refusing a competitive sublease when its arrangements with its physician-tenants, including

[69] Sandor Dev. Co. v. Reitmeyer, 498 N.E.2d 1020 (Ind. Ct. App. 1986).

[70] John Hogan Enters., Inc. v. Kellogg, 187 Cal. App. 3d 589, 594, 231 Cal. Rptr. 711, 714 (1986).

[71] National Distillers & Chem. Corp. v. First Nat'l Bank of Highland Park, 804 F.2d 978, 981 (7th Cir. 1986).

[72] List v. Dahnke, 638 P.2d 824, 825 (Colo. Ct. App. 1981).

allowances to the physicians, were meant to enhance the hospital's business. The court noted that a landlord was reasonable in withholding consent to a sublease that would defeat the purpose of the lease.[73]

5. A federal district court in Florida held that a landlord could rightly refuse to consent to a sublease that was extended approximately 26 years beyond the date of the primary lease. The court stated that the landlord's refusal to consent to this assignment "was based on commercial reasonableness and was made in good faith."[74]

6. A landlord is not unreasonable to withhold its consent if it doubts the financial strength of the proposed assignee, using the standard of a reasonable person in the position of a landlord owning and leasing commercial property. An Idaho court found that a "reasonable person" was justified in having apprehensions about a proposed assignee's obligations when the proposed assignee provided incomplete financial information and there was a risk that guaranties would be cancelled.[75]

7. It is reasonable for a landlord to refuse a proposed sublease because of its wish to enhance the potential for percentage rentals contemplated by the primary lease. A North Carolina court concluded that the landlord's desire to maintain a restaurant operation in the premises, in light of the nature of the building and the desire for percentage rentals, constituted reasonable grounds for withholding consent.[76] During lease negotiations, the landlord will insist that the percentage rent an assignee pays be commensurate with the assignee's business; that is, as a condition to an assignment the percentage rent rate may be increased. The tenant's response is often that such an adjustment makes an assignment more difficult at the time when the tenant most needs or wants to make an assignment. Put differently, the lease is less attractive to an assignee who does not get the benefit of low percentage rent rate. This is no different from the recurrent question of who gets the bonus value in the lease. One way around the issue is a negotiated division of the profits on assignment or sublease; see § **12.12**.

8. A guarantee of rent payments is not enough to compel a landlord to accept an assignee if the tenant's performance of its other obligations (such as promises to repair the premises and indemnify the landlord against certain claims) is not assured.[77]

---

[73] Medinvest Co. v. Methodist Hosp., 359 N.W.2d 714 (Minn. Ct. App. 1984), *review denied*, Mar. 21, 1985.

[74] Amjems, Inc. v. F.R. Orr Construction Co., 617 F. Supp. 273, 279 (S.D. Fla. 1985).

[75] Fahrenwald v. LaBonte, 103 Idaho 751, 653 P.2d 806 (Ct. App. 1982).

[76] Jones v. Andy Griffith Products, Inc., 35 N.C. App. 170, 241 S.E.2d 140, *review denied*, 295 N.C. 90, 244 S.E.2d 258 (1978). *See* Haack v. Great Atl. & Pac. Tea Co., 603 S.W.2d 645 (Mo. Ct. App. 1980) (tenant-sublandlord had never paid percentage rent). *See also* John Hogan Enters., Inc. v. Kellogg, 187 Cal. App. 3d 589, 231 Cal. Rptr. 711 (1986).

[77] Johnson v. Jaquith, 189 So. 2d 827 (Fla. App. 1966).

9. A Hawaiian landlord justifiably refused consent to an assignment to an undercapitalized corporation when the principals would not guarantee the lease.[78]

10. A California landlord that operates a store in its center may be able to withhold its consent to a sublease to a competitor.[79]

11. Landlords can base their decisions on the use provision. Of course, if the use is not specified, the landlord may be hard-pressed to object to the proposed use.[80] At the other end of the spectrum are cases with restricted uses; in one such case, a Louisiana landlord's refusal to consent to assignment to an orthodontist was sustained when the use was specified as general dentistry only.[81] A specification of a French restaurant operated by someone with five years' experience defeated a proposed assignment to an East Indian restaurant.[82] A landlord can reasonably refuse when it is given no information about the proposed use.[83]

12. When a law firm, which occupied part of an office building and was obligated to make its law library available to other tenants in the building, proposed to assign its lease to a bank, the landlord was held to be reasonable in withholding its consent until it was assured that the proposed assignee could furnish that same law library service.[84]

In an effort to state objective standards of reasonableness, the following criteria have been suggested for the jury's consideration of the landlord's good faith and commercial reasonableness:[85]

1. Financial responsibility of the proposed assignee or subtenant

2. Identity or business character of the proposed assignee or subtenant

3. Legality of the proposed use

4. Nature of the use and occupancy.

The California Law Review Commission[86] sets forth these criteria for assessing reasonableness of consent:

---

[78] Kahili, Inc. v. Yamamoto, 54 Haw. 267, 506 P.2d 9 (1973).

[79] Pay 'n Pak Stores, Inc. v. Superior Court (Miller), 210 Cal. App. 3d 1404, 258 Cal. Rptr. 816 (1989).

[80] Roundup Tavern, Inc. v. Pardini, 68 Wash. 2d 513, 413 P.2d 820 (1966) (retailer's assignment to a bar).

[81] Van Geffen v. Herbert, 439 So. 2d 1257 (La. App. 1983).

[82] Le Vert-Gallant, Inc. v. W&M Properties, Inc., N.Y.L.J., at 6, col. 4 (Sup. Ct. Apr. 1, 1987). The requirement of experience was given considerable weight.

[83] Kroger Co. v. Rassford Indus. Corp., 25 Ohio Misc. 43, 261 N.E.2d 355 (Com. Pl. 1969).

[84] Leonard, Street & Deinard v. Marquette Assocs., 353 N.W.2d 198 (Minn. Ct. App. 1984).

[85] American Book Co. v. Yeshiva Univ. Dev. Found., Inc., 59 Misc. 2d 31, 297 N.Y.S.2d 156, 161 (Sup. Ct. 1969).

[86] 9 Calif. L. Rev. Comm'n Rep. 418 (1969).

1. Credit rating of assignee or sublessee
2. Similarity of proposed new use to old use
3. Nature, quality, and character of assignee or sublessee
4. Requirements of assignee or subtenant for utilities or services from landlord
5. Anticipated volume of business of assignee or tenant (in leases requiring percentage rent)
6. Overall impact of assignee or sublessee on common facilities, other tenants in the building, or adjacent property of landlord.

To these criteria, a Canadian commentator[87] would add:

1. The time elapsed since the last change in the business operated at the premises
2. The name of the proposed transferee's business
3. The "drawing power" of the proposed transferee
4. The consideration being paid to the transferor (because a high price payable over time may affect the proposed transferee's ability to carry on its business)
5. The resulting tenant mix.

That commentator would also insist upon a transfer of all the premises for the full balance of the term.

In the case of leases requiring percentage rent, the landlord should be certain that the percentage rent is as appropriate for the assignee's use as it was for the assignor's use. If a jewelry store replaces a chain drug store, the percentage rent should be increased to correspond more closely to the percentage commonly required in jewelry stores, that is, from 1 to 5 percent to 5 to 10 percent according to the schedule in § **6.19**. This is a recurrent problem when a tenant with high volume but low percentage rent rate assigns or subleases to a low volume user with no change in the rate.[88] A related problem arises when a tenant's assignee is in the same business as the tenant, but the landlord believes the assignee is not likely to be as successful as the tenant. In the absence of a restriction against assignment or proof that the landlord entered into the lease in reliance on the tenant's special skill, the landlord cannot prevent the assignment.[89]

---

[87] Posen, *Assigning and Subletting*, in Shopping Centre Leases (H.M. Haber ed. 1976).

[88] Carter v. Safeway Stores, Inc., 154 Ariz. 546, 744 P.2d 458 (Ct. App. 1987) (involving a supermarket's sublease to a clothing store). Waterbury v. T.G.&Y. Stores Co., 820 F.2d 1479 (9th Cir. 1987), involved a similar experience of a California landlord. Although the lease provided that the percentage rent of an assignee would be the assignor's average percentage rent, the assignor was so successful that the landlord regretted its change to the percentage rent provision. It should have said the percentage rent payable by the assignor was the greater of that due under the lease or the average percentage rent paid by the assignor.

[89] Rowe v. Great Atl. and Pac. Tea Co., 61 A.D.2d 473, 402 N.Y.S.2d 593, *rev'd on other grounds*, 46 N.Y.2d 62, 385 N.E.2d 566, 412 N.Y.S.2d 827 (1978).

There are several steps that landlords can take (in addition to adjusting the percentage rate) when a percentage rent base is assigned. The landlord can add the last percentage rent paid (on a monthly basis) to the minimum rent, adjust the minimum rent to market rate at the time of the assignment, and adjust the minimum rent by a cost of living factor from the date of the term commencement until the date of the assignment.

Assignments of office leases require somewhat less care by the landlord than do assignments of shopping center leases. Although many office uses make substantially the same demands on an office building, there are some uses that are more burdensome than others. They include business or secretarial schools, personal finance companies, employment agencies, and messenger services. Office building landlords should be certain to consider a proposed assignee's use before consenting to an assignment; merely requiring office use is not sufficient.

The landlord is disturbed to learn how burdensome it can be to be reasonable. Thus, the landlord endeavors to limit its liability if it fails to be reasonable.

§ 12.8   Limiting the Tenant's Remedies

Some landlords have paid dearly for the unreasonable exercise of their rights to prevent an assignment or sublease. In one case, the tenant approached the landlords for consent to an assignment in connection with a sale of the tenant's business. The landlords, which were not bound by a "reasonableness" standard in the lease, required a renegotiation of rent and other lease provisions. When the tenant could not get consent for an assignment, it changed its sales contract into one which involved a sale of its corporate stock. The landlords claimed that their consent to a sale of stock was also necessary, although the lease did not say so. When the sale of the business was lost, the tenant sued the landlords on a theory of tortious interference with the sales contract. In upholding the tenant's lower court victory, a California appellate court noted that the landlords' concern about the assignment was "only incidental to their predominant motive of terminating the existing lease to obtain a new lease with more favorable terms to them-selves."[90] The landlords had made the mistakes of (1) not inquiring into the proposed assignee's creditworthiness, (2) expressing an interest only in improving their position, and (3) failing to show that any of their legitimate interests were threatened.[91] Incidentally, the court reiterated California's rule that a sale of

---

[90] Richardson v. La Rancherita La Jolla, Inc., 98 Cal. App. 3d 73, 159 Cal. Rptr. 285, 290 (1979). A similar case recurred in California with a lease that required the landlord's consent to any assignment. Sade Shoe Co. v. Oschin & Snyder, 162 Cal. App. 3d 1174, 209 Cal. Rptr. 124 (1984). In considering whether the complaint was legally sufficient to establish claims of interference with prospective advantage and contractual relationship, the court said that the fact that the lease may have allowed the landlord to withhold its consent arbitrarily did not furnish justification or privilege to interfere with the transaction of which the assignment was a part.

[91] Richardson v. La Rancherita La Jolla, Inc., 98 Cal. App. 3d 73, 159 Cal. Rptr. 285 (1979).

corporate stock does not breach the tenant's mere promise not to assign its lease.[92]

Some courts have ruled for tenants when malicious interference alone is shown,[93] while other courts have demanded that the tenant prove that the assignment or sublease failed only because of the landlord's conduct. A New York court[94] considering a claim of "illegal interference with precontractual negotiations" denied it because there was no allegation of illegality and no showing that the negotiations would have succeeded but for the alleged interference.[95]

A frustrated prospective assignee may also have a claim against a landlord whose consent has been unreasonably withheld.[96] A broker may likewise have a claim.[97]

In view of these cases, a landlord will insist upon a provision that exonerates it from monetary liability if it is found to have been unreasonable; of course, it will only bind the tenant and not a litigious assignee or broker.

FORM 12-5
ASSIGNMENT—EXONERATION FROM DAMAGES FOR UNREASONABLE REFUSAL TO CONSENT

If tenant believes that landlord has unreasonably withheld its consent, tenant's sole remedy will be to seek a declaratory judgment that landlord has unreasonably withheld its consent or an order of specific performance or mandatory injunction of landlord's agreement to give its consent. Tenant will not have any right to recover damages or to terminate this lease.

Although there are procedural devices by which an adjudication may be accelerated,[98] few assignees or subtenants will agree to await the outcome of litigation; without the assurance of an assignee or subtenant in the event of victory, no tenant will want to undertake litigation. From a tenant's view, this sort of provision may be less appropriate in an office or single tenant lease than in a shopping center lease where the criteria (of which tenant mix is one) are somewhat subjective and the landlord may have an honest but unreasonable objection. On behalf of a tenant, a prudent real estate professional will limit this provision's exculpatory effect to those situations in which the landlord is found

---

[92] *Id.*, *citing* Ser-Bye Corp. v. C.P.&G. Mkts., Inc., 78 Cal. App. 2d 915, 179 P.2d 342 (1947).

[93] Landry v. Hornstein, 462 So. 2d 844 (Fla. Dist. Ct. App. 1985).

[94] Susskind v. IPCO Hosp. Supply Corp., 45 A.D.2d 915, 373 N.Y.S.2d 627 (1975).

[95] Optivision, Inc. v. Syracuse Shopping Center Assocs., 472 F. Supp. 665 (N.D.N.Y. 1979) (follows Susskind).

[96] Pinellas County v. Brown, 450 So. 2d 240 (Fla. Dist. Ct. App. 1984).

[97] Donald G. Culp Co. v. Reliable Stores Corp., 14 Ohio App. 3d 161, 470 N.E.2d 193 (1983) (although the broker under a theory of tortious interference with contract did not recover, because the court felt that the landlord had been reasonable in requiring a restoration bond as a condition to the assignment).

[98] Goldstein, *Provisions for Subletting or Assigning a Commercial Lease (with Form)*, 28 Prac. Law. 31 (1982).

unreasonable in the application of objective criteria. To the earlier provision, a tenant would add:

Tenant may recover damages if landlord is found either to have acted in bad faith, or to have acted unreasonably in determining the proposed assignee's or subtenant's creditworthiness, identity, business character, use, and the lawfulness of the use.

The tenant will also want assurances that the landlord will respond promptly to its proposals of an assignee or subtenant. Like justice, consent delayed is consent denied. So the tenant adds:

Landlord's consent to a proposed assignment or sublease will be conclusively presumed from its failure to respond within fifteen (15) days after its receipt of tenant's proposal.

Although the time period will be a source of friction, the landlord and tenant can come to some agreement along these lines.

To avoid claims from tenants, in any event, a landlord should:

1. State in its lease as clearly and extensively as possible the standards that will be employed in considering an assignment or sublease
2. Insist that all of the information necessary for it to make a decision about a proposed assignment or sublease is delivered to it before a decision is made
3. Respond as promptly as possible to proposed assignments or subleases
4. Not insist upon changes to the lease or economic incentives as a condition to approvals
5. Not meet with the proposed assignee or subtenant except in the tenant's presence, and then only to gather the information necessary to make an informed decision
6. Respond in writing, stating specific reasons for refusing a proposed assignment or sublease or, preferably, stating the ways in which the assignment or sublease may be made acceptable.

§ 12.9   Redefining the Assignment and Sublease

Because public policy not only favors the free alienability of property but also abhors the forfeiture of valuable rights, prohibitions of assignments and sub-leases are strictly construed against the restriction. A prohibition of assignments does not forbid subleases, and vice versa; a prohibition of assignments does not forbid assignments by operation of law, nor encumbrances of the leasehold (even though the effect may be an assignment if the security interest is foreclosed). A prohibition of a sublease of the premises usually does not prevent a sublease of a part of the premises;[99] easements, concessions, vending machine arrangements, and licenses are not subleases. In order to avoid the many traps that the law has laid, the cautious landlord will define assignment and subletting very broadly. This provision addresses changes in control of the tenant or the lease.[100]

FORM 12-6
**ASSIGNMENT—OTHER TRANSACTIONS REQUIRING
LANDLORD'S CONSENT**

These transactions will also require landlord's prior written consent:

(a)   an assignment by operation of law;

(b)   an imposition (whether or not consensual) of a lien, mortgage, or encumbrance upon tenant's interest in this lease;

(c)   an arrangement (including without limitation management agreements, concessions, and licensees) that allows the use and occupancy of all or part of the premises by any one other than tenant;

(d)   a transfer of voting control of tenant (if tenant is a corporation);

(e)   a transfer of more than 50% of the interest in the capital of tenant (if tenant is a partnership).

The provisions of clause (a) are necessary to avoid the transfer of the tenant's interest in the lease to its receiver, trustee in bankruptcy, executor, or legatee, or to a purchaser of the lease or the tenant's voting stock at a judicial sale. In contrast to the usual methods of effecting an assignment or sublease, transfers by operation of law[101] are not voluntary. As a rule, assignments by operation of law do not breach a prohibition of assignments.[102] For example, a transfer of a lease to the tenant's legatee did not breach the tenant's covenant not to assign the lease.[103] **Form 12-6** may be too broad because it may prevent a corporate merger in which the assignment may be said to be by operation of law; an exception for corporate mergers is discussed with regard to clause (d). However, in a Maryland case,[104] a transfer of a lease by operation of law to the successor corporation violated the prohibition of assignments.

Clause (b) prevents a transfer that might occur when the lender forecloses on the leasehold. This provision is also too broad. A tenant may sell the leasehold as part of a sale of its business; assuming that the sale of the business was not a default (perhaps because it was a permissible sale of stock), in such a transaction the tenant may accept purchase money financing secured by the leasehold. As written, clause (b) would prevent a sale. Therefore, a prudent tenant might insist

---

[99] Annot., 56 A.L.R.2d 1002, *Subleasing or renting part of premises as violation of lease provision as to subletting* (1957).

[100] Bauer & Mantini, *Change of Control*, in 2 Shopping Centre Leases (H.M. Haber ed. 1982).

[101] Dodier Realty & Inv. Co. v. St. Louis Nat'l Baseball Club, 361 Mo. 981, 238 S.W.2d 321 (1951).

[102] 3 Thompson § 1212.

[103] Burns v. McGraw, 75 Cal. App. 2d 481, 171 P.2d 148 (1946).

[104] Citizens Bank & Trust Co. of Md. v. Barlow Corp., 295 Md. 472, 456 A.2d 1283 (1983).

upon an exclusion from clause (b) of "liens, mortgages, or encumbrances incidental to a transaction for which landlord's consent is not required by the provisions of this paragraph." Although only the most perspicacious tenant would divine the need to ask for the landlord's consent in advance, when a tenant assigns its lease in connection with a sale of its business and takes a security interest in the lease to assure payment of the price for the business, the tenant must determine whether the "reassignment" necessitates the landlord's consent.[105]

Although the landlord's intentions are honorable when clause (c) is proposed, once again the draftmanship is too sweeping. The landlord wants to be certain that the tenant does not effectively sublease the premises by giving a stranger the right to use and occupy them. Often an office building tenant anticipates growth and leases more space than it needs; it may wish to share some portion of the premises until its growth occurs. This clause causes considerable consternation to a shopping center tenant that may wish to have a department run by a concessionaire, or to provide leased vending machines for customer convenience. The simple solution is to set a limit to the fraction of the area of the premises that may be occupied by others.

Because a lease is an asset of the corporate tenant, transfer of corporate stock effects a transfer of the lease.[106] This device has been used with great success in avoiding the prohibitions against assignment.[107] This clause (d), then, has several objectionable aspects. First, it cannot apply either to a tenant whose stock is publicly traded or to a tenant that makes a public offering of its stock. Second, in closely held companies, it will prevent, for example, three of five equal owners from selling their interests in unrelated transactions over a 10-year period. Third, corporate flexibility is impaired because subsidiaries and affiliated companies cannot be created to act as separate entities. Fourth, the corporation cannot sell additional shares in order to raise capital. Fifth, one shareholder cannot transfer its shares to another shareholder. Sixth, a transfer by bequest is prohibited. Any restriction on transfer of stock ownership should be considered by a tenant in light of its employee stock ownership plans. In professional corporations, which are required by statute to redeem the shares of a retired, deceased, or inactive professional, such a prohibition is intolerable. By its terms, such a provision is

---

[105] *See* Italian Fisherman, Inc. v. Middlemas, 313 Md. 156, 545 A.2d 1 (1988) (this nicety was not observed).

[106] Annot., 12 A.L.R.2d 179, *Conditions accompanying or following dissolution of lesser corporations, as breach of covenant against assignment or sublease* (1950); Rubinstein Bros. v. Ole of 34th St., Inc., 101 Misc. 2d 563, 421 N.Y.S.2d 534 (Civ. Ct. 1979). *See also* Annot., 39 A.L.R.4th 879, *Merger of consolidation of corporate lessee as breach of clause in lease prohibiting, conditioning, or restricting assignment or sublease* (1985) (suggesting that sales of corporate assets, as opposed to transfer of corporate stock, are more likely to breach such a clause).

[107] *But see* Korvette's, Inc. v. Hills-Trumbull Corp., N.Y.L.J., May 28, 1976, at 5, col. 3 (Sup. Ct. 1976) (court found lease breached when, after landlord refused to consent to proposed assignment, tenant formed a new subsidiary corporation in order to make permitted sublease and then sold corporate stock).

violated by the enlargement of the tenant's board of directors and the adoption of cumulative voting; in these common occurrences, no shares have changed hands. The strictures of such a clause may be relieved by a provision such as

FORM 12-7
ASSIGNMENT—MODIFICATION OF CORPORATE
NON-ASSIGNMENT PROVISION

Tenant may assign all or part of this lease, or sublease all or a part of the premises, to:

(a)   any corporation that has the power to direct tenant's management and operation, or any corporation whose management and operation is controlled by tenant; or,

(b)   any corporation a majority of whose voting stock is owned by tenant; or

(c)   any corporation in which or with which tenant, its corporate successors or assigns, is merged or consolidated, in accordance with applicable statutory provisions for merger or consolidation of corporations, so long as the liabilities of the corporations participating in such merger or consolidation are assumed by the corporation surviving such merger or created by such consolidation; or

(d)   any corporation acquiring this lease and a substantial portion of tenant's assets; or

(e)   any corporate successor to a successor corporation becoming such by either of the methods described in (c) or (d), so long as on the completion of such merger, consolidation, acquisition, or assumption, the successor has a net worth no less than tenant's net worth immediately prior to such merger, consolidation, acquisition, or assumption.

Some provisions (such as the one in **Form 12-7**) allow mergers if the surviving corporation's net worth—or creditworthiness—is at least equal to that of the tenant. This is a useless restriction. Unless the acquiring corporation has a negative net worth, the surviving corporation's net worth will always be equal to or greater than the tenant's. Some leases appear to go further by requiring the acquiring corporation to have a greater net worth than the tenant. This is not helpful. If the tenant's net worth is low (perhaps as the result of unsuccessful operations), an equally weak corporation could acquire it. Net worth tests are usually expressed in such a way that the net worth need not be maintained after the assignment; it need only exist at the time of the assignment. As a result, assets may be transferred out of the surviving corporation after the assignment and it may be left a worthless shell. An apparent solution is to require the surviving corporation to maintain its net worth as a continuing condition to the effectiveness of the assignment. This is not a fair solution since it requires more from the surviving corporation than it required from the tenant itself. Needless to say, if the real estate professional must succumb to a net worth test, the term must be defined. Tenants can manipulate these sorts of modifications to the strict prohibitions on assignments or subleases. For example, a corporate tenant could assign its lease to a subsidiary and sell its stock in the subsidiary, thus transferring the lease. Real estate professionals may wish to enlarge **Form 12-7** by prohibitions of any transactions used in order to transfer the lease, and by provisions that transfers to subsidiaries are allowed for so long as the subsidiaries remain subsidiaries of the tenant.

A partnership tenant has understandable reservations about clause (e). Incorporation is impossible. The retirement of senior partners over a long period is precluded, as is the admission of new partners by expansion of the capital and interests in profits and losses. Although, on the theory that a partnership is an entity and not an aggregate, admission of a new partner is not a default,[108] clause (e) speaks specifically to the magnitude of the change and not to the admission of the partner. A two-person partnership must be particularly careful of "dissolution" in broad prohibitions against assignment, because when one partner dies, the surviving partner no longer has a partnership. Unlike a partnership with more than two partners, two-person partnerships cannot be reformed after a partner dies. Most courts are sympathetic to the survivor; however, a Texas court held that a withdrawing partner's assignment of its partnership interest to its partner was a prohibited assignment.[109] In a case involving a due-on-sale clause in a mortgage, a Connecticut court held that a change in the general partners of a limited partnership was not a sale.[110] In preparing a lease with this case in mind, the real estate professional may state that any change in the membership of the tenant-partnership is an assignment.

§ 12.10   Imposing Further Conditions to Consent

Once it has agreed to give its consent, the landlord will usually add further conditions to its consent:

FORM 12-8
ASSIGNMENT—PROHIBITION OF FURTHER ASSIGNMENT

Landlord's consent to one assignment or sublease will not waive the requirement of its consent to any subsequent assignment or sublease.

This provision is meant to avoid the result in *Dumpor's Case*:[111] the giving of one consent required by a lease ends the requirement for future consents. To be precise, the rule in *Dumpor's Case* is not applied to consents to subleases, only to consents to assignments.[112] The rule has been mercilessly criticized but rarely disavowed. As recently as 1971, a New York court wrote, "The written consent to

---

[108] Rubinstein Bros. v. Ole of 34th St., Inc., 101 Misc. 2d 563, 421 N.Y.S.2d 534 (Civ. Ct. 1979); I Friedman § 7.303b.

[109] Heflin v. Stiles, 663 S.W.2d 131 (Tex. Civ. App. 1983).

[110] Fidelity Trust Co. v. BVD Assocs., 196 Conn. 270, 492 A.2d 180 (1985).

[111] 4 Coke 119B, 76 Eng. Rep. 1110 (1578).

[112] 3 Thompson § 1213.

the first assignment obviated the necessity for consent to further assignments,"[113] and at least one other New York court has followed the rule. The simple provision in **Form 12-8** avoids such results.

In order to give an informed consent to a proposed assignment or sublease, the landlord needs some information.

FORM 12-9
ASSIGNMENT — SUBMISSION OF INFORMATION

If tenant requests landlord's consent to a specific assignment or sublease, tenant will give landlord (i) the name and address of the proposed assignee or subtenant, (ii) a copy of the proposed assignment or sublease, (iii) reasonably satisfactory information about the nature, business, and business history of the proposed assignee or subtenant, and its proposed use of the premises, and (iv) banking, financial or other credit information, and references about the proposed assignee or subtenant sufficient to enable landlord to determine the financial responsibility and character of the proposed assignee or subtenant.

A tenant does not owe its landlord a duty of care in selecting an assignee and is not liable to its landlord for negligence if the premises are damaged after the insolvent assignee vacates the premises.[114] Unlike most leases, the one in this case released the original tenant (which was acting as a nominee) upon an assignment.

The landlord will also insist that:

FORM 12-10
ASSIGNMENT — FURTHER DOCUMENTS TO BE
PROVIDED BY TENANT

Landlord's consent to an assignment or sublease will not be effective until: a fully executed copy of the instrument of assignment or sublease has been delivered to landlord; in the case of an assignment, landlord has received a written instrument in which the assignee has assumed and agreed to perform all of tenant's obligations in the lease; and landlord has been reimbursed for its attorneys' fees and costs incurred in connection with both determining whether to give its consent and giving its consent.

This provision requires the assignee's assumption of all the tenant's responsibilities in the lease, not just those that accrue after the date of assignment. This avoids any question of whether the tenant's obligations run with the land, because it creates privity of contract as well as privity of estate between the landlord and

---

[113] Nipet Realty, Inc. v. Melven's Restaurant & Bar, Inc., 67 Misc. 2d 790, 327 N.Y.S.2d 2 (Cir. Ct. 1971); Kaskel Electric, Inc. v. Leonard Nones Studios, Inc., N.Y.L.J. July 7, 1988, at 25, col. 5 (Civ. Ct. N.Y. Cty.).

[114] Shadeland Dev. Corp. v. Meek, 489 N.E.2d 1192 (Ind. Ct. App. 1986).

assignee. The tenant and assignee must arrange between themselves for the payment and performance of obligations that have accrued but are not yet due.
   The landlord will usually add:

FORM 12-11
ASSIGNMENT—NO RELEASE OF TENANT

Landlord's consent to an assignment or sublease will not release tenant from the payment and performance of its obligations in the lease, but rather tenant and its assignee will be jointly and severally primarily liable for such payment and performance. An assignment or sublease without landlord's prior written consent will be void at landlord's option.

A tenant-assignor should realize that, after an assignment, it remains liable by privity of contract for payment of rent and performance of its other promises in the lease. This rule continues the tenant-assignor's liability through extensions and renewals of the lease;[115] however, an assignor is not obligated for its assignee's unpaid rent accrued during a holdover period to which the landlord consents.[116] Courts are divided on the question of whether the original tenant remains liable primarily or merely as a surety, in much the same way as courts divide on the question of whether a mortgagor remains primarily liable or liable only as a surety when it sells its encumbered property.[117] The form of the tenant's assignment and the landlord's consent to it should address this issue. In order to preserve its rights against the tenant-assignor, the landlord must be certain to give it any notices and cure rights that the lease provides.[118] In a shopping center lease, the landlord may also insist that the minimum rent be increased to the greater of (1) market minimum rent or (2) the average minimum rent and percentage rent paid by the assignee during its occupancy of the premises. The landlord could also insist upon a recapture or profit sharing provision such as those discussed in § **12.12**.
   Leases should provide that assignments made in contravention of the prohibition are void at landlord's option. Otherwise, the assignment may be effective and the landlord may have only a claim for damages from the breach (if any could be shown). A purchase contract that fell prey to judicial scrutiny provided:

> Purchaser shall have the right to assign this agreement to any partnership which [sic] is a general partner; provided however, that purchaser shall have such right of assignment only if such assignee or transferee shall in writing expressly assume and agree to perform and discharge each and every obligation and liability of purchaser set forth in this agreement.

---

[115] Annot., 10 A.L.R.3d 818, *Liability of lessee who assigns lease for rent accruing subsequently to extension or renewal term* (1966).

[116] Meredith v. Dardarian, 83 Cal. App. 3d 248, 147 Cal. Rptr. 761 (1978).

[117] 3 Thompson § 1220.

[118] Caneva v. Miners & Merchants Bank, 335 N.W.2d 339 (S.D. Sup. Ct. 1983).

The court held that this paragraph amounted to a restriction on delegation of duties and not a restriction on the assignment of rights.[119] The court was influenced by the fact that the purchaser's name was followed by "and/or assigns," and that the binding effect provision[120] included "assigns."[121]

Finally, when a lease is guaranteed, the landlord often conditions its consent on the guarantor's ratification of the assignment. This may avoid the guarantor's defense that its risk was changed or enlarged without its consent.

§ 12.11   Relationship of Prohibitions of Assignment and Sublease to Default Provisions

When a landlord balks at the suggestion that its consent to an assignment or subletting should not be unreasonably withheld, the tenant ought to point out the interrelationship of the default provisions and the provisions regarding assignment and sublease.[122]

Some of the cases in which courts have held that the landlord's consent to a proposed assignment or sublease cannot be unreasonably withheld, even in the absence of an express requirement, have considered the landlord's claim for rent from a defaulting tenant. The courts held that the landlords could not recover rent because they failed to mitigate their damages by their refusal to allow a proposed sublease or assignment.[123] This is a familiar doctrine in contract law. Its application to leases recognizes the convergence of contract law and real property law. On the strength of this argument, the tenant may demand a reasonableness standard as a condition to the landlord's recovery of rent accruing after default.

By the same token, states that have adopted the contract law rule that a landlord must mitigate its damages[124] have opened the door for the tenant's argument that a landlord cannot unreasonably withhold its consent to a proposed assignment or sublease if the effect will be a default by its tenant. Put differently, it is illogical to require mitigation on default but not to require conduct that would avoid a default. Needless to say, this argument is of no benefit to a tenant who wants to profit from its sublease or assignment.

---

[119] Cedar Point Apartments, Ltd. v. Cedar Point Inv. Corp., 693 F.2d 748 (8th Cir. 1982), *cert. denied*, 461 U.S. 914, 103 S. Ct. 1893 (1983), *on remand*, 580 F. Supp. 507 (E.D. Mo. 1984), *judgment aff'd as modified*, 756 F.2d 629 (8th Cir. 1985).

[120] *See* § **32.28**.

[121] Cedar Point Apartments, Ltd. v. Cedar Point Inv. Corp., 693 F.2d 748 (8th Cir. 1982), *cert. denied*, 461 U.S. 914, 103 S. Ct. 1893 (1983), *on remand*, 580 F. Supp. 507 (E.D. Mo. 1984), *judgment aff'd as modified*, 756 F.2d 629 (8th Cir. 1985).

[122] I Friedman § 7.304a.

[123] Danpar Assoc. v. Somersville Mills Sales Room, Inc., 182 Conn. 444, 438 A.2d 708 (1980). However, the Connecticut Supreme Court held that a landlord may arbitrarily withhold its consent to an assignment, but it must mitigate its damages after its tenant defaults.

[124] See § **30.9**.

§ 12.12   Recapture and Profit Sharing

The recapture provision[125] is a recent addition to the landlord's arsenal of anti-assignment weaponry. In some cases a recapture provision gives the landlord a right to accept an assignment or sublease that the tenant intends to make with a third party; in others it also allows the landlord to terminate the lease. A variation allows the tenant to assign or sublease as long as the landlord shares in the tenant's profits. In any case, the result is that the landlord can recapture part or all of the value of the lease. This provision also impedes an assignment or sublease, because prospective assignees or subtenants are loath to negotiate their best deals only to find that the landlord has taken it. Coupled with short-term leases and periodic adjustments of rent, this provision virtually eliminates any bonus value in the lease. Recapture and profit-sharing provisions are more common in office building leases than in shopping center leases where shorter terms, percentage rents, and much more stringent restrictions on assignments or subleases inhibit such transfers by the tenant.

FORM 12-12
ASSIGNMENT—LANDLORD'S RIGHT TO RECAPTURE

If tenant intends to assign all or part of this lease or to sublease all or any portion of the premises, it will first submit to landlord the documents described in [**Form 12-9**], and will offer in writing:

(a)   with respect to a prospective assignment, to assign this lease to landlord without cost; or,

(b)   with respect to a prospective sublease, to sublease to landlord the portion of the premises involved (the "leaseback area")

(i)   for the term specified by tenant in its offer,

(ii)   at the lower of (A) tenant's proposed subrent or (B) the rate of base monthly rent and additional rent then in effect according to this lease, and

(iii)   on the same terms, covenants and conditions contained in this lease and applicable to the leaseback area. The offer will specify the date on which the leaseback area will be made available to landlord; however, that date will not be earlier than thirty (30) days nor later than one hundred eighty (180) days after landlord's acceptance of the offer. Tenant may withdraw the offer at any time before it is accepted. If the prospective sublease results in all or substantially all of the premises being subleased, then, if landlord accepts the offer, landlord will have the option to extend the term of its sublease for the balance of the term of this lease less one day.

---

[125] *See generally* Seneker, *Enforceability of Recapture Clause in Commercial Lease Transactions*, 5 Real. Prop. L. Rep. 1 (1982). Hambro Org. v. Benco Int'l Import Corp., N.Y.L.J., Mar. 10, 1982, at 7, col. 1 (App. Div. 1982), *cited in* Goldstein, *Provisions for Subletting or Assigning a Commercial Lease (with form)*, 28 Prac. Law. 31 (1982), held that a recapture provision does not violate New York's statutory prohibition of unconscionable lease provisions.

Landlord will accept or reject the offer within thirty (30) days after it receives the offer. If landlord accepts the offer, tenant will then execute and deliver to landlord, or to anyone designated by landlord, an assignment or sublease, as the case may be, in either case in a form reasonably satisfactory to landlord's counsel. If landlord accepts the offer, this lease will terminate on the date set forth in the offer for the delivery of the leaseback area and landlord and tenant will be relieved of their obligations to each other as of that date. If landlord rejects the offer, or fails to accept the offer within such period, tenant may assign the lease or sublease the sublease area according to the instruments described in [**Form 12-9**]; however, any sublease will be subject to the provisions of this paragraph as though the subtenant were the tenant under this lease.

Any sublease made to landlord or its designee will:

(a)   permit landlord to make further subleases of all or any part of the leaseback area and (at no cost to tenant) to make, at landlord's expense, all changes, alterations, installations, and improvements in the leaseback area as landlord may deem necessary for such subletting;

(b)   provide that tenant will at all times permit reasonably appropriate access to the common facilities in the leaseback area and to and from the leaseback area and common areas of the building;

(c)   negate any intention that the estate created under such sublease be merged with any other estate held by landlord or tenant;

(d)   provide that landlord will accept the leaseback area "as is" except that landlord, at tenant's expense, will perform all work and make all alterations required to separate the leaseback area from the remainder of the premises and to permit lawful occupancy, so that tenant will have no other cost or expense in connection with the subletting of the leaseback area; and

(e)   provide that at the expiration of the term of the sublease tenant will accept the leaseback area in its then-existing condition, subject to the obligations of landlord to make such repairs to the leaseback area as may be necessary to preserve the leaseback area in good order and condition, ordinary wear and tear excepted.

Performance by landlord, or its designee, under a sublease of the leaseback area will be deemed performance by tenant of any similar obligation under this lease, and any default by landlord, or its designee, under any sublease will not be a default under a similar obligation contained in this lease. Tenant will not be liable for any default under this lease or deemed to be in default under this lease if the default is occasioned by or arises from any act or omission of subtenant under the sublease or if it is occasioned by an act or omission of any occupant holding under the sublease.

The objections raised to rights of first refusal to lease in § **4.21** and rights of first refusal to purchase in § **4.24** are applicable to recapture provisions and should be considered when reviewing them. Tenants should be certain that recapture rights are triggered by an actual offer that the tenants intend to accept and not merely by a proposal subject to negotiation.

A tenant ought to require its landlord to repay the unamortized cost of the tenant's own improvements if the landlord exercises a recapture right; presumably the tenant would have been made whole in these costs if it had assigned the lease or sublet the premises without hindrance by the recapture provision. A profit sharing provision may be:

FORM 12-13
ASSIGNMENT—PROFIT SHARING ON ASSIGNMENT OR SUBLEASE

Without affecting any of its other obligations under this lease, tenant will pay landlord as additional rent one-half of any sums or other economic consideration that (a) are received by tenant as a result of an assignment or subletting (other than the rental or other payments that are attributable to the amortization over the term of this lease of the cost of nonbuilding standard leasehold improvements that are part of the assigned or sublet portion of the premises and have been paid for by tenant), whether or not denominated rentals under the assignment or sublease, and (b) exceed in total the sums which tenant is obligated to pay landlord under this lease (prorated to reflect obligations allocable to that portion of the premises subject to such assignment or sublease). The failure or inability of the assignee or subtenant to pay tenant pursuant to the assignment or sublease will not relieve tenant from its obligations to landlord under this paragraph. Tenant will not amend the assignment or sublease in such a way as to reduce or delay payment of amounts that are provided in the assignment or sublease approved by landlord.

The tenant must be certain to recover certain costs before the "profit" is calculated. These include: the amortization of original leasehold improvements in the subleased premises made at the tenant's expense; the brokerage fees incurred in making the sublease; the amortization of improvements made for the subtenant; and the tenant's incidental costs of the sublease, such as attorneys' fees. Some tenants also insist upon including any rent paid between the date on which they vacated the premises (if they did) and the date on which the subtenant took occupancy. For itself, the landlord will want all revenue or other value received by the tenant in connection with the assignment or sublease to be considered in determining the landlord's share of the profits; this includes without limitation base rent, bonus payments, and additional rent (such as a share of operating expenses). If the lease had a rent abatement, the landlord and tenant must determine whether profit is measured against the face rate or the effective rate.

The tenant should insist that it is released from liability if any part of the premises is recaptured or made subject to the profit sharing provision; the landlord will not want to release the tenant if the recapture or profit sharing occurs in connection with a sublease.

If a profit sharing provision is used in a retail lease, the landlord and tenant should consider how it affects a sale of all of the tenant's assets including the lease.[126] If the tenant cannot convince the landlord to exclude such transactions from the ambit of the profit sharing provision, the tenant may try to avoid its effect by its allocation of the purchase price to fixtures, inventory or goodwill. The landlord may want to provide that the lease must be appraised in connection with any of those transactions and that the profit sharing be based upon the appraised value.

---

[126] E. Halper, Shopping Center and Store Leases § 10.01(n) (Supp. 1984).

§ 12.13 Lenders' Concerns about Assignments and Subleases

The lenders' concerns about assignments and subleases are that:

1. To maintain the original creditworthiness of the lease, the original tenant should not be released when an assignment occurs
2. The new tenant's creditworthiness should be proven
3. The new tenant should assume the tenant's obligation under the lease
4. The assignment should not result in a default under existing exclusive use provisions
5. No major tenant should have a right to assign during any period in which the shopping center is initially leasing up with satellite tenants.

§ 12.14 Preparing a Form of Assignment

The form of assignment found in *Commercial Real Estate Leases: Forms* requires the assignee's assumption of the tenant/assignor's liability under the lease. An assumption will avoid any possibility that the assignee is bound only by those covenants that run with the land; the assignee will have privity of contract with the landlord. This form does not provide for the release of the tenant/assignor from its liability under the lease. To the contrary, this form makes it clear that the tenant/assignor will be bound by the lease even if it is amended. Many tenants request such a release and landlords usually refuse to give it. As a general rule, the tenant/assignor remains liable during any renewal or extension of the lease.[127] However, a landlord may inadvertently release its tenant/assignor if (without the tenant/assignor's consent) the landlord makes an agreement with the assignee that changes the terms of the lease in such a way as to increase the tenant/assignor's liability under the lease.[128] Tenants should also consider the other surety defenses that are discussed with regard to guarantees in § **3.16**.

The assignor's primary concern should be its liability if the assignee defaults. Unlike its posture in a sublease, the assignor has nothing but the assignee's indemnity (if that). The assignor may not even get a notice of default and may first hear about the default when it is sued. At that point, of course, the assignor cannot cure the default or do anything other than defend itself in an indefensible position. Assignors should try to get notice and cure rights that extend beyond the assignee's notice and cure periods (if any), and should take back a collateral assignment of the lease to assure assignee's performance of the lease. Since the collateral assignment itself will usually be subject to the prohibitions of assignments in the lease, the assignor/tenant must get the landlord's consent to it.

---

[127] Annot., 10 A.L.R.3d 818, *Liability of lessee who assigns lease for rent occurring subsequently to extension of renewal term* (1966).

[128] Walker v. Rednallok Co., 299 Mass. 591, 13 N.E.2d 394 (1938).

When an assignment of two leases made no mention of security deposits, the Virginia Supreme Court ruled that the tenant was entitled to them because it remained liable under the leases.[129]

§ 12.15   Preparing a Form of Sublease

The form of sublease found in *Commercial Real Estate Leases: Forms* pertains to a sublease of a part of office premises in which the subleased premises are in existence. There is no standard form of sublease. In fact, there is no need to call a sublease a sublease — it may be called a lease. The name is not important. Rather, what is important is that if the tenant/sublandlord's rights are terminated, the subtenant's rights are terminated. As in a lease with the fee owner (in which termination occurs upon the foreclosure of a mortgage encumbering the fee), the sublease can be terminated by termination of the prime lease (or *head lease*, as it is also called).[130]

Subtenants usually ask for a representation that there are no defaults under the master lease, that the master lease is in effect, and that the sublandlord has exercised any renewal option on which the subtenant's term depends. A cautious tenant/sublandlord may warrant only that it has paid the rent and other charges and has received no notice of default; if it can get an estoppel certificate from the landlord, it should. If the sublease concerns all or almost all of the premises for almost the entire term (and is virtually an assignment), the subtenant may ask for: (1) the right to exercise — and to prevent the sublandlord's exercise of — rights to terminate the master lease (such as those rights that may arise in connection with casualty damage or condemnation); (2) the right to compel the sublandlord to renew the lease (if renewals are available) so long as the subtenant has renewed the sublease;[131] and (3) the right to cure the sublandlord's defaults (such as rent defaults) under the master lease and to charge the cost of cure against the subrent. The subtenant will insist upon the tenant/sublandlord's agreement not to exercise any termination rights in the master lease.

The real estate professional will recognize a structural similarity between the relationship of first lender, landlord, and tenant (which is more fully discussed in **Chapter 24**) and the relationship of prime landlord, tenant, and subtenant. Any action by the first lender or the prime landlord affects the tenant or subtenant, as

---

[129] Jones v. Dokos Enterprises, Inc., 233 Va. 555, 357 S.E.2d 203 (1987).

[130] *See* Berkman, Jerome, *Negotiable Issues in Commercial Sublease,* 13 Real Est. L.J. 28 (1984) (discussion of much greater breadth than title implies).

[131] In Ministers, Elders & Deacons of Reformed Protestant Dutch Church v. 198 Broadway Inc., 59 N.Y.2d 170, 451 N.E.2d 164, 464 N.Y.S.2d 406 (1983), the New York Court of Appeals held that a subtenant who occupies a part of the premises subject to a master lease has no right to compel its sublandlord-tenant to renew the master lease when the sublease is expressly made subject to the master lease. *See* Annot., 39 A.L.R.4th 824, *Sublessee's rights with respect to primary lessee's option to renew lease* (1985). *See also* Regional Pacesetters, Inc. v. Eckerd Drugs of Georgia, Inc., 183 Ga. App. 196, 358 S.E.2d 481 (Ga. App. 1987).

the case may be. In both of these situations, a three-party agreement is appropriate,[132] because it creates a direct relationship between the first lender or prime landlord and the tenant or subtenant. With some modifications, the form of nondisturbance agreement in § **24.3** is an appropriate three-party agreement for the sublease.

Although no particular form is necessary for the sublease, the tenant using the sublease cannot create greater rights for its subtenant than it has under the prime lease for itself; for example, the tenant cannot grant a renewal option that would extend the term of the sublease beyond the term of the prime lease. In order to avoid any inconsistencies, many tenants use the prime lease as the form of the sublease. Others incorporate the terms of the prime lease by reference. The incorporation of the master lease will result in several awkward or inappropriate provisions in the sublease.[133] The landlord's rights to terminate the lease after prescribed casualty damage or condemnation should not be available to the tenant/sublandlord. The limitation of tenant's recourse to the landlord's interest in the building must be reconsidered; perhaps the subtenant's claims are limited to the tenant's leasehold. The tenant/sublandlord cannot give a broad covenant of quiet enjoyment and cannot be liable for a failure of landlord's title. The waiver of subrogation should be examined to be certain that the subtenant has its benefit.

In a New York case, the sublease made reference to the master lease, incorporated it, and subjected the sublease to it. The subtenant objected to the payment of its share of "pass-through" costs that the tenant/sublandlord paid pursuant to the master lease. The tenant prevailed with the assistance of some judicial prestidigitation.[134] The landlord's problem could have been avoided by a specific statement of the tenant's responsibility for those costs in a manner similar to paragraph 6 of **Form 12-14**.

Many subleases state that the termination of the prime lease will terminate the sublease. Certainly, this is true; however, such a provision may excuse the sublandlord who caused the termination of the prime lease (for example, by defaulting in its rent payment to the landlord). The subtenant should not accept any such exculpation for liability caused by the sublandlord's own default. A tenant is liable to its subtenant if the tenant's duties under the sublease are breached by the landlord's exercise of its rights under the master lease, because the subtenant has no reason to know what the master lease provides.[135] A

---

[132] I Friedman § 7.704b contains a lengthy discussion of the need for these agreements.

[133] Goldberg, *Preparing the Sublease*, N.Y. St. B.J., Dec. 1986, at 25. This article is required reading for real estate professionals involved in subleases.

[134] NPS Eng'rs & Constructors, Inc. v. Underweiser & Underweiser, 73 N.Y.2d 996, 539 N.E.2d 100, 541 N.Y.S.2d 344 (1989).

[135] Occidental Sav. & Loan Ass'n v. Bell Fed. Credit Union, 218 Neb. 519, 357 N.W.2d 198 (1984); Nybor Corp. v. Ray's Restaurant, Inc., 29 N.C. App. 642, 225 S.E.2d 609, *review denied*, 290 N.C. 662, 228 S.E.2d 453 (1976). *But see* Frankfurt v. Decker, 180 S.W.2d 985 (Tex. Civ. App. 1944); Gulden v. Newberry Wrecker Service, Inc., 154 Ga. App. 130, 267 S.E.2d 763 (1980) (subtenant had notice "by implication" that the sublandlord's term was shorter than purported sublease).

defaulting subtenant whose sublandlord surrenders the prime lease in order to mitigate its damages from the subtenant's breach is liable for rent accruing after the surrender in excess of amounts saved on prime lease.[136]

Once the sublandlord has created a sublease that gives the subtenant no greater rights than the prime lease gives the tenant/sublandlord, the sublandlord is legally protected. Practically, however, one obstacle must be overcome. What happens if the landlord breaches one of its obligations to the tenant/sublandlord, thus preventing the tenant/sublandlord's performance? This is a dilemma about which sublandlords and subtenants can argue endlessly. The sublandlord explains that it is giving the subtenant what it has, but that it cannot be responsible for its landlord's breaches. The subtenant contends that it has no relationship with the landlord, that it is paying the tenant/sublandlord, and that it expects performance from the tenant/sublandlord. In fact, however, the tenant has no ability to cure many of its landlord's defaults, such as failure to provide utilities or elevator service. In those circumstances, the tenant and subtenant may agree that the subtenant will have the tenant's rights against the landlord and that, if the tenant's rent is abated, the subtenant's rent will be proportionately abated.

The tenant/sublandlord and subtenant must still resolve all the questions attendant upon their sharing the premises, the common areas serving the premises, the means of access, and the services to the premises.

Finally, when notice provisions are repeated verbatim or incorporated by reference, there is a risk that the tenant who receives a notice on the last day of a notice period will be unable to pass on the notice in a timely fashion. For example, consider a casualty damage provision that enables the landlord to keep the lease in effect by giving notice within 60 days after the occurrence of its election to repair the damage. If no notice is given, the provision continues, the tenant may cancel the lease. If the landlord gives its tenant a notice on the 60th day, the tenant may be unable to give its subtenant the same notice on the same day; as a result, the subtenant may cancel the sublease while the tenant remains bound by the lease. Consequently, notice periods under the sublease should be extended to enable the tenant to receive notice from the landlord give notice to the subtenant. Subtenants will, however, insist upon sufficient advance notice to cure their sublandlord's defaults.

---

[136] Schneiker v. Gordon, 732 P.2d 603 (Colo. 1987), *rev'g*, 609 P.2d 3 (Colo. Ct. App. 1984).

CHAPTER 13

SIGNS

§ 13.1   Introduction

In the absence of a prohibition, and so long as it does not injure the reversion, a tenant of a single tenant building may install signs on the premises, including the walls and the roof,[1] and a tenant of less than all of a building may install signs on the exterior building boundary of its premises, but not the roof.[2] The right to install signs includes painted signs. The reason for this broad entitlement is the law's refusal to distinguish between the inside and the outside of the premises.

The latitude given to the tenant should not lead the real estate professional toward laxity in considering the question of signs. For one thing, most multitenant leases define the premises in such a way as to exclude the roof and walls; given such a definition, a tenant who installed signs on the outside of its premises would be a trespasser. With or without such a careful definition of the premises, most leases make specific provisions for signs. Those provisions may be found in a base provision entitled "Signs," in the rules and regulations, or in both.

§ 13.2   Signs in Single Tenant Leases

A typical landlord's form of single tenant lease will provide for signs in this way:

---

[1] 1C C.J.S. *Landlord & Tenant* § 329 (1968).

[2] III M.R. Friedman, Friedman on Leases § 33.1 (1983).

FORM 13-1
SIGNS—SINGLE TENANT BUILDING (LANDLORD'S FORM)

Except for signs that are located inside the building and are not visible outside the building, no signs will be placed at any place on the premises without the prior written consent of landlord to their size, design, color, location, content, illumination, composition or material and mobility. All signs will be maintained by tenant in good condition during the term of this lease. Tenant will remove all signs at the end of this lease and repair and restore any damage caused by their installation or removal.

The tenant of a single tenant building is in the best position to argue for minimal restrictions on its signs. This is particularly true if the building is not part of a loosely integrated development such as an industrial park; in those cases, restrictive covenants or a sign code may make it necessary for the tenant to conform to prescribed sizes and styles. Aside from such exceptions, many tenants in single tenant buildings negotiate a provision such as:

FORM 13-2
SIGNS—SINGLE TENANT BUILDING (TENANT'S FORM)

Tenant may install signs on the premises in accordance with federal, state, and local statutes, laws, ordinances, and codes.

Although the landlord may be willing to grant such a provision, it should insist that the tenant dismantle and remove the signs at the end of the term and repair any damage to the improvements and land. The landlord should not return the security deposit until the tenant has removed its signs and repaired the damage done to the premises.

§ 13.3   Signs in Office Building Leases

A typical provision for signs in an office building is:

FORM 13-3
SIGNS—OFFICE BUILDING

Without landlord's prior written permission, tenant will not attach any sign on any part of the outside of the premises or the building, or on any part of the inside of the premises that is visible outside the premises, or in the halls, lobbies, windows or elevator banks of the building. Permitted signs will comply with the requirements of the governmental authorities having jurisdiction over the building. At its expense, tenant will maintain all permitted signs and will, at the end of this lease, and at its expense, remove all permitted signs and repair any damage caused by their removal. If tenant fails to do so, landlord may remove all unpermitted signs without notice to tenant and at tenant's expense. Landlord may name the building and change the name, number or designation of the building. Tenant will not use the name of the building for any purpose other than the address of the building. Landlord will provide a directory in a conspicuous place in the building with names of tenants of the building. Tenant will be given one line on the building directory. Landlord will also provide one suite identification sign adjacent to the main entry door of the premises in landlord's standard form. Tenant will pay landlord's reasonable charges for changing the directory listing and identification sign at tenant's request.

Although it is true that a very important office building tenant can prevail upon its landlord to put the tenant's name on the building or the curtilage, most office building tenants must be content with severely limited signs. These include the building directory, the floor directories, and the office sign, and, rarely, signs in the elevator cars. The number of directory strips are related to the size of the tenant's premises. The tenant ought to insist upon as many strips on the building directory as it can reasonably use. For example, it is not unusual for a visitor to know an individual's name but not the name of the individual's firm. Similarly, office tenants often list their important officers under the company's name, in addition to listing the officers under their own names. Parent companies list their affiliated companies that also do business at the premises. The right to add more names and to change existing names should also be given to the tenant.

Floor directories seem to be inflexible. There, only the tenant's name will appear.

Suite signs are usually building standard and uniform; a commercial tenant ought to ask for the right to display its logo on its suite sign. If the tenant is a full-floor user, it will have the right to install its own sign in its elevator lobby. Tenants should have the right to install signs inside their own premises.

Some tenants are adamant about the name of the building and particularly insistent that it not bear the name of a competitor.

Signs are an appropriate topic for the most favored tenant provision discussed in § 2.4. A tenant can demand that no other tenant of comparable size have a better ratio of directory strips to rentable area or a right to other signs that the first tenant does not have.

§ 13.4 Signs in Shopping Center Leases

Shopping center leases must consider signs.[3] Tenants are concerned about them because signs are a means of advertising. Landlords are concerned about signs because they can be gaudy affronts to the shopping center. Consequently, shopping center leases strictly control signs. Among shopping centers, the need to control signs varies. The close proximity of many clashing signs in a small

---

[3] E. Halper, Shopping Center and Store Leases § 6.04 (Supp. 1984), and *Slugging It Out Over Shopping Center Signs*, Leasing Prof., Apr. 1986, at 1.

shopping center presents a more formidable assault on the eyes than do a few different signs throughout a large shopping center. One provision is:

FORM 13-4
SIGNS—SHOPPING CENTER

(a)   Tenant will purchase and erect one sign on the front of the premises not later than the date on which tenant opens for business or within thirty (30) days after the date of commencement of this lease, whichever is sooner, in accordance with landlord's sign criteria attached to this lease as Exhibit _____. Tenant will maintain, repair, and replace the sign as required by landlord during this lease. At the end of this lease, the sign will immediately become the property of landlord.

(b)   Tenant will keep the display windows and signs of the premises well lighted during business hours and until 12:00 midnight each night or such earlier time as may be prescribed by any applicable policies or regulations adopted by any utility or governmental agency, and will maintain adequate night lights after that hour or period.

(c)   Without the prior written consent of landlord, tenant will not place or permit to be placed (1) any sign, advertising material, or lettering upon the exterior of the premises or (2) any sign, advertising material, or lettering upon the exterior or interior surface of any door or show window or at any point inside the premises from which the same may be visible from outside the premises. Upon request of landlord, tenant will immediately remove any sign, advertising material, or lettering that tenant has placed or permitted to be placed in violation of the provisions of the preceding sentence, and if tenant fails so to do, landlord may enter the premises and remove such sign, advertising material, or lettering at tenant's expense. Tenant will comply with such regulations as may from time to time be promulgated by landlord governing signs, advertising material, or lettering of all tenants in the retail area; however, tenant will not be required to change any sign or lettering that was in compliance with applicable regulations at the time it was installed or placed in, on, or about the premises.

The exhibit to which reference is made in this form sets forth sign criteria. These criteria establish uniformity in the shopping center by prescribing the size, shape, color, materials, construction, installation and location of the tenant's facade sign.

Shopping center signs are of three predominant varieties: pole, or pylon, signs, of which monument signs are a variation; facade signs; and window signs. Roof signs are generally prohibited.

Pole signs themselves come in several varieties. Many large shopping centers have one or more pole signs that advertise only the center itself. Some developers of small shopping centers resist putting the name of the largest tenant on the shopping center sign. They believe that the shopping center will come to be known by that tenant's name anyway, so there is no sense in wasting space on the sign. No mention is made of any tenants. This is also true of monument signs, which are simply pretty pole signs without the pole. When tenants are allowed to display their names on the pole sign, the first tenants—who are usually also the largest tenants—take the first choice and the largest share. The smaller tenants are then allocated the rest of the pole as they sign their leases. The result can be visual discord. The tenant ought to assure itself of the number of pole signs that will grace its center, the positions it will be allowed to occupy on them, the size of the signs it will be permitted to post, the cost and responsibility for buying and maintaining the sign, and the possibility of using its logo (if it has one) instead of the standard shopping center sign.

The landlord should give some thought to the way in which it or its tenants will pay for the sign. Some landlords include the cost of removing the tenant's sign as one of the costs that the tenant must pay at the end of its lease, presumably from its security deposit.

Facade signs are found on the fascia of shopping centers, that is, just above the plate glass window on the building itself. In enclosed malls, facade signs may be found on the outside of the stores occupied by anchor tenants; if all mall tenants are allowed to post signs on the backs of their premises, the center can quickly lose its appeal. When facade signs are used, the landlord will prescribe the size and format for the signs and the criteria by which they must be governed. Landlords should be particularly sure to prohibit moving and flashing signs, and to reserve the right to remove the signs when necessary to repair or maintain the shopping center.

A final kind of sign found in a shopping center is the window sign. Although landlords try to prohibit window signs, because they tend to be flimsily and tastelessly constructed, tenants like them because they afford an inexpensive way to advertise sales and special promotions. Supermarkets are the foremost proponents of the window sign. In an effort to avoid lease restrictions, tenants often use signs that are not attached to the windows but to standards set back a short distance from the window. By the same token, a landlord who wants to prohibit window signs should also prevent interior signs that are attached to large displays or structural elements of the premises, or are visible from outside the premises.

For better or for worse, shopping center signs are limited only by the human imagination. The kinds of signs mentioned in this chapter are but a few of the many possibilities in use. There are also banners, both in and out of the parking lot; sandwich boards, both ambulatory and stationary; and television, both closed circuit and open.

For a landlord, control over signage is essential to maintaining the appearance of the shopping center. For a tenant, signage is a useful way to make itself known to the shopping center patrons. A tenant must be mindful of unique aspects of its premises (for example, a tenant on the second floor needs extra signs so shoppers will know that it is there) and the signs that have been permitted for its co-tenants. In the final analysis, the landlord and tenant are both interested in the tenant's success, the shopping center's success, and the best ways to assure a steady stream of customers to both of them.

CHAPTER 14

RULES AND REGULATIONS

§ 14.1   Introduction

Most leases for multitenant developments contain rules and regulations either as part of the lease or as an exhibit to it. Compliance with the rules and regulations is a covenant of the tenant. The difference between the covenants contained in the body of the lease and the rules and regulations is only that the rules and regulations are not as obviously important to the landlord. Nevertheless, the tenant's breach of the rules and regulations is a default under the lease. Although a tenant may assert that a violation of the rules and regulations is such a minor breach that forfeiture is too harsh, there is no assurance that a court will find any rule or regulation to be immaterial. Consequently, the tenant should review the rules and regulations very carefully in order to be certain that it can comply with them. The rules and regulations typically deal with "housekeeping" matters that the tenant must be certain are consonant with its operations.

The customary provision inserted by a landlord with regard to its rules and regulations is that:

FORM 14-1
RULES AND REGULATIONS—LEASE PROVISION

Tenant will faithfully observe and comply with the rules and regulations attached to this lease, and all modifications and additions from time to time promulgated by landlord. Landlord will not be responsible to tenant for the nonperformance of any such rules and regulations by any other tenant or occupant of the building.

This means that the landlord may unilaterally change the lease. A prudent tenant will require that any modification or addition must be:

1.   Reasonable and consistent with rules and regulations imposed in similar properties

2.   No more burdensome or costly than the rules and regulations initially proposed

3.   Subject to the other lease provisions

4.   Related only to the common areas and not to the premises

5.   Uniformly enforced

6.   Effective only after the tenant has had reasonable notice of their enactment.

A landlord should not promise that all tenants will comply, but rather that "substantially all" tenants will do so; this will avoid the possibility that the rules and regulations will be annulled if a large tenant refuses to be bound by them.

§ 14.2   Rules and Regulations for Shopping Centers

Rules and regulations for shopping centers will be similar to:

FORM 14-2
RULES AND REGULATIONS FOR A SHOPPING CENTER

1.   The sidewalks, halls, passages, exits, entrances, stairways, and elevators (if any) of the shopping center will not be obstructed by tenant or used by tenant for any purpose other than ingress to and egress from the premises. The halls, passages, exits, entrances, elevators, and stairways are not for the general public, and landlord will in all cases retain the right to control and prevent access to them by all persons whose presence, in the judgment of landlord, would be prejudicial to the safety, character, reputation, and interests of the shopping center and its tenants; however, such access will be permitted to persons with whom any tenant normally deals in the ordinary course of its business, unless such persons are engaged in illegal activities. No tenant and no employee or invitee of any tenant will go upon the roof of the shopping center.

2.   No sign, placard, picture, name, advertisement, or notice visible from the exterior of the premises will be inscribed, painted, affixed, or otherwise displayed by tenant on any part of the shopping center without the prior written consent of landlord. Landlord will adopt and furnish to tenant general guidelines relating to signs inside the shopping center and the sales floor. Tenant agrees to comply with those guidelines. All approved signs or lettering on doors will be printed, painted, affixed, or inscribed at the expense of the tenant by a person approved in writing by landlord. Material visible outside the shopping center will not be permitted.

3.   The premises will not be used for lodging or the storage of merchandise held for sale to the public, and unless ancillary to a restaurant or other food service use specifically authorized in the lease of a particular tenant, no cooking will be done or permitted by tenant on the premises. The preparation of coffee, tea, hot chocolate, and similar items for tenants and their employees and invitees will be permitted.

4.   Landlord will furnish tenant with two keys free of charge. Landlord may make reasonable charge for any additional keys. Tenant will not have any keys made. Tenant will not alter any lock or install a new or additional lock or any bolt on any door of the premises without the prior written consent of landlord; tenant will furnish landlord with a key for each of those locks. Tenant, upon the termination of its tenancy, will deliver to landlord all keys to doors in the shopping center that have been furnished to tenant.

5.   Tenant will not use or keep in the premises or the shopping center any kerosene, gasoline, or inflammable or combustible fluid or material, or use any method of heating or air conditioning other than that supplied by landlord. Tenant will not use, keep, or permit to be used or kept any foul or noxious gas or substance in the premises, or permit or suffer the premises to be occupied or used in a manner offensive or objectionable to landlord or other occupants of the shopping center by reason of noise, odors, or vibrations, or interfere in any way with other tenants or those having business in the shopping center.

6.   In the case of invasion, mob, riot, public excitement, or other circumstances rendering such action advisable in landlord's opinion, landlord may prevent access to the shopping center by such action as landlord may deem appropriate, including closing entrances to the shopping center.

7.   The toilet rooms, toilets, urinals, wash bowls, and other apparatus will not be used for any purpose other than that for which they were constructed, and no foreign substance of any kind whatsoever will be thrown in them. The expense of any breakage, stoppage, or damage resulting from the violation of this rule will be borne by the tenant who, or whose employees or invitees, caused the breakage, stoppage, or damage.

8.   Except with prior written consent of landlord, tenant will not sell, or permit the sale in the premises, or use or permit the use of any common area for the sale of newspapers, magazines, periodicals, or theatre tickets. Tenant will not carry on, or permit or allow any employee or other person to carry on, the business of stenography, typewriting, or any similar business in or from the premises for the service or accommodation of occupants of any other portion of the shopping center. The premises will not be used for manufacturing of any kind, or any business or activity other than that specifically provided in the lease.

9.   Tenant will not use any advertising media that may be heard outside of the premises, and tenant will not place or permit the placement of any radio or television antenna, loudspeaker, sound amplifier, phonograph, searchlight, flashing light, or other device of any nature on the roof or outside of the boundaries of the premises (except for tenant's approved identification sign or signs) or at any place where they may be seen or heard outside of the premises.

10.   All loading and unloading of merchandise, supplies, materials, garbage, and refuse will be made only through such entryways and elevators (if any) and at such times as landlord will designate. In its use of the loading areas, tenant will not obstruct or permit the obstruction of the loading area and at no time will park or allow its officers, agents, or employees to park vehicles in the loading areas except for loading and unloading.

11.   Landlord will have the right, exercisable without notice and without liability to any tenant, to change the name and street address of the shopping center.

12.   The freight elevator, if any, will be available for use by all tenants in the shopping center, subject to reasonable scheduling that landlord in its discretion may

deem appropriate. The persons employed to move such equipment in or out of the shopping center must be acceptable to landlord. Landlord will have the right to prescribe the weight, size, and position of all equipment, materials, furniture, or other property brought into the shopping center. Heavy objects will, if considered necessary by landlord, stand on wood strips of such thickness as is necessary to distribute the weight properly. Landlord will not be responsible for loss of or damage to that property from any cause, and all damage done to the shopping center by moving or maintaining that property will be repaired at the expense of tenant.

13.   The directory of the shopping center (if any) will be provided for the display of the name and location of tenants, and landlord reserves the right to exclude any other names from the directory. Any additional name that tenant desires to place upon the directory must first be approved by landlord, and, if so approved, a charge will be made for the additional name.

14.   No curtains, draperies, blinds, shutters, shades, screens, or other coverings, hangings, or decorations will be attached to, hung, or placed in, or used in connection with any window of the shopping center without the prior written consent of landlord.

15.   Tenant will assure that the doors of the premises are closed and locked and that all water faucets, water apparatus, and utilities are shut off before tenant or tenant's employees leave the premises, so as to prevent waste or damage. For any default or carelessness in this regard, tenant will pay for all injuries sustained by other tenants or occupants of the shopping center or by landlord.

16.   Landlord may waive any one or more of these rules and regulations for the benefit of any particular tenant or tenants, but no waiver by landlord will be construed as a waiver of those rules and regulations in favor of any other tenant or tenants, nor prevent landlord from enforcing any those rules and regulations against any or all of the tenants of the shopping center.

17.   These rules and regulations are in addition to and will not be construed to modify, alter, or amend, in whole or in part, the lease.

18.   Landlord reserves the right to make such other and reasonable rules and regulations as its judgment may from time to time be needed for the safety, care, and cleanliness of the shopping center, and for the preservation of good order in it.

§ 14.3   Rules and Regulations for Office Buildings

Rules and regulations for office buildings may be:

FORM 14-3
RULES AND REGULATIONS FOR AN OFFICE BUILDING

1.   Landlord may from time to time adopt appropriate systems and procedures for the security or safety of the building, any persons occupying, using, or entering the building, or any equipment, finishings, or contents of the building. Tenant will comply with landlord's reasonable requirements relative to such systems and procedures.

2.   The sidewalks, halls, passages, exits, entrances, elevators, and stairways of the building will not be obstructed by any tenants or used by any of them for any

purpose other than for ingress to and egress from their respective premises. The halls, passages, exits, entrances, elevators, escalators, and stairways are not for the general public, and landlord will in all cases retain the right to control and prevent access to such halls, passages, exits, entrances, elevators and stairways of all persons whose presence in the judgment of landlord would be prejudicial to the safety, character, reputation and interests of the building and its tenants, provided that nothing contained in these rules and regulations will be construed to prevent such access to persons with whom any tenant normally deals in the ordinary course of its business, unless such persons are engaged in illegal activities. No tenant and no employee or invitee of any tenant will go upon the roof of the building, except such roof or portion of such roof as may be contiguous to the premises of a particular tenant and may be designated in writing by landlord as a roof deck or roof garden area. No tenant will be permitted to place or install any object (including, without limitation, radio and television antenna, loud speakers, sound amplifiers, micro-wave dishes, solar devices, or similar devices) on the exterior of the building or on the roof of the building.

3.   No sign, placard, picture, name, advertisement or notice visible from the exterior of tenant's premises will be inscribed, painted, affixed or otherwise displayed by tenant on any part of the building or the premises without the prior written consent of landlord. Landlord will adopt and furnish to tenant general guidelines relating to signs inside the building on the office floors. Tenant agrees to conform to such guidelines. All approved signs or lettering on doors will be printed, painted, affixed or inscribed at the expense of the tenant by a person approved by landlord. Other than draperies expressly permitted by landlord and building standard mini-blinds, material visible from outside the building will not be permitted. In the event of the violation of this rule by tenant, landlord may remove the violating items without any liability, and may charge the expense incurred by such removal to the tenant violating this rule.

4.   Other than draperies expressly permitted by landlord and building standard mini-blinds, no curtains, draperies, blinds, shutters, shades, screens or other coverings, hangings or decorations will be attached to, hung or placed in, or used in connection with any window of the building or the premises.

5.   The sashes, sash doors, skylights, windows, heating, ventilating, and air conditioning vents and doors that reflect or admit light and air into the halls, passageways or other public places in the building will not be covered or obstructed by any tenant, nor will any bottles, parcels, or other articles be placed on any window sills.

6.   No show cases or other articles will be put in front of or affixed to any part of the exterior of the building, nor placed in the public halls, corridors, or vestibules without the prior written consent of landlord.

7.   No tenant will occupy or permit any portion of the premises to be occupied as an office for a public stenographer or typist, or for the possession, storage, manufacture, or sale of liquor or narcotics, in any form, or as a barber or manicure shop, or as a public employment bureau or agency, or for a public finance (personal loan) business. No tenant will permit the premises to be used for lodging or sleeping or for any immoral or illegal purpose. No tenant will use or permit the use of the premises in any manner which involves the unusual risk of injury to any person. No tenant will engage or pay any non-salaried employees on the premises, except those actually working for tenant on the premises. No tenant will advertise for laborers giving an address at the building. No cooking will be done or permitted by any

tenant on the premises, except in areas of the premises that are specially constructed for cooking and except that use by the tenant of Underwriters' Laboratory approved equipment for brewing coffee, tea, hot chocolate, and similar beverages will be permitted, provided that such use is in accordance with all applicable federal, state, and city laws, codes, ordinances, rules and regulations.

8.   No tenant will employ any person or persons other than the cleaning service of landlord for the purpose of cleaning the premises, unless otherwise agreed to by landlord in writing. Except with the written consent of landlord, no person or persons other than those approved by landlord will be permitted to enter the building for the purpose of cleaning it. No tenant will cause any unnecessary labor by reason of such tenant's carelessness or indifference in the preservation of good order and cleanliness. If tenant's actions result in any increased expense for any required cleaning, landlord reserves the right to assess tenant for such expenses. Janitorial service will not be furnished on nights to offices that are occupied after business hours on those nights unless, by prior written agreement of landlord and tenant, service is extended to a later hour for specifically designated offices.

9.   The toilet rooms, toilets, urinals, wash bowls, and other plumbing fixtures will not be used for any purposes other than those for which they were constructed, and no sweepings, rubbish, rags, or other foreign substances will be thrown in such plumbing fixtures. All damages resulting from any misuse of the fixtures will be borne by the tenant who, or whose servants, employees, agents, visitors, or licensees, caused the same.

10.   No tenant will in any way deface any part of the premises or the building of which they form a part. Without the prior written consent of landlord, no tenant will lay linoleum, or other similar floor covering, so that the same will come in direct contact with the floor of the premises. If linoleum or other similar floor covering is desired to be used, an interlining of builder's deadening felt will be first affixed to the floor, by a paste or other material, soluble in water, the use of cement or other similar adhesive material being expressly prohibited. In those portions of the premises in which carpet has been provided directly or indirectly by landlord, tenant will at its own expense install and maintain pads to protect the carpet under all furniture having casters other than carpet casters.

11.   No tenant will alter, change, replace, or rekey any lock, or install a new lock or a knocker, on any door of the premises. Landlord, its agents, or employees will retain a pass (master) key to all door locks on the premises. Any new door locks required by tenant or any change in keying of existing locks will be installed or changed by landlord following tenant's written request to landlord and will be at tenant's expense. All new locks and rekeyed locks will remain operable by landlord's pass (master) key. Landlord will furnish each tenant, free of charge, with two (2) keys to each door lock on the premises, and two (2) building/area access cards. Landlord will have the right to collect a reasonable charge for additional keys and cards requested by any tenant. Each tenant, upon termination of its tenancy, will deliver to landlord all keys and access cards for the premises and building which have been furnished to such tenant.

12.   The elevator designated for freight by landlord will be available for use by all tenants in the building during the hours and pursuant to such procedures as landlord may determine from time to time. The persons employed to move tenant's equipment, material, furniture or other property in or out of the building must be acceptable to landlord. The moving company must be a locally recognized professional mover, whose primary business is the performing of relocation services, and

must be bonded and fully insured. A certificate or other verification of such insurance must be received and approved by landlord prior to the start of any moving operations. Insurance must be sufficient, in landlord's sole opinion, to cover all personal liability, theft, or damage to the project, including but not limited to floor coverings, doors, walls, elevators, stairs, foliage, and landscaping. Special care must be taken to prevent damage to foliage and landscaping during adverse weather. All moving operations will be conducted at such times and in such a manner as landlord will direct, and all moving will take place during non-business hours unless landlord agrees in writing otherwise. Tenant will be responsible for the provision of building security during all moving operations, and will be liable for all losses and damages sustained by any party as a result of the failure to supply adequate security. Landlord will have the right to prescribe the weight, size, and position of all equipment, materials, furniture, or other property brought into the building. Heavy objects will, if considered necessary by landlord, stand on wood strips of such thickness as is necessary to properly distribute their weight. Landlord will not be responsible for loss of or damage to any such property from any cause, and all damage done to the building by moving or maintaining such property will be repaired at the expense of tenant. Landlord reserves the right to inspect all such property to be brought into the building and to exclude from the building all such property which violates any of these rules and regulations or the lease of which these rules and regulations are a part. Supplies, goods, materials, packages, furniture and all other items of every kind delivered to or taken from the premises will be delivered or removed through the entrance and route designated by landlord, and landlord will not be responsible for the loss or damage of any such property unless such loss or damage results from the negligence of landlord, its agents, or employees.

13.   No tenant will use or keep in the premises or the building any kerosene, gasoline, or inflammable or combustible or explosive fluid or material or chemical substance, other than limited quantities of such materials or substances reasonably necessary for the operation or maintenance of office equipment or limited quantities of cleaning fluids and solvents required in tenant's normal operations in the premises. Without landlord's prior written approval, no tenant will use any method of heating or air conditioning other than that supplied by landlord. No tenant will use or keep or permit to be used or kept any foul or noxious gas or substance in the premises, or permit or suffer the premises to be occupied or used in a manner offensive or objectionable to landlord or other occupants of the building by reason of noise, odors or vibrations, or interfere in any way with other tenants or those having business in the building.

14.   Landlord will have the right, exercisable upon notice and without liability to any tenant, to change the name and street address of the building.

15.   Landlord will have the right to prohibit any advertising by tenant mentioning the building, which, in landlord's reasonable opinion, tends to impair the reputation of the building or its desirability as a building for offices, and upon written notice from landlord, tenant will refrain from or discontinue such advertising.

16.   Tenant will not bring any animals (except "seeing eye" dogs) or birds into the building, and will not permit bicycles or other vehicles inside or on the sidewalks outside the building except in areas designated from time to time by landlord for such purposes.

17.   All persons entering or leaving the building between the hours of 6 p.m. and 7 a.m. Monday through Friday, and at all hours on Saturdays, Sundays, and holidays will comply with such off-hour regulations as landlord may establish and modify

from time to time. Landlord reserves the right to limit reasonably or restrict access to the building during such time periods.

18.   Each tenant will store all its trash and garbage within its premises. No material will be placed in the trash boxes or receptacles if such material may not be disposed of in the ordinary and customary manner of removing and disposing of trash and garbage without being in violation of any law or ordinance governing such disposal. All garbage and refuse disposal will be made only through entryways and elevators provided for such purposes and at such times as landlord designates. Removal of any furniture or furnishings, large equipment, packing crates, packing materials, and boxes will be the responsibility of each tenant. Such items may not be disposed of in the building trash receptacles, nor will they be removed by the building's janitorial service, except at landlord's sole option and at the tenant's expense. No furniture, appliances, equipment, or flammable products of any type may be disposed of in the building trash receptacles.

19.   Canvassing, peddling, soliciting, and distribution of handbills or any other written materials in the building are prohibited, and each tenant will cooperate to prevent the same.

20.   The requirements of the tenants will be attended to only upon application by written, personal, or telephone notice at the office of the building. Employees of landlord will not perform any work or do anything outside of their regular duties unless under special instructions from landlord.

21.   A directory of the building will be provided for the display of the name and location of tenants and such reasonable number of the principal officers and employees of tenants as landlord in its sole discretion approves, but landlord will not in any event be obligated to furnish more than one (1) directory strip for each 2,500 square feet of rentable area in the premises. Any additional name(s) which tenant desires to place in such directory must first be approved by landlord, and if so approved, tenant will pay to landlord a charge, set by landlord, for each such additional name. All entries on the building directory display will conform to standards and style set by landlord in its sole discretion. Space on any exterior signage will be provided in landlord's sole discretion. No tenant will have any right to use any exterior sign.

22.   Tenant will see that the doors of the premises are closed and locked and that all water faucets, water apparatus, and utilities are shut off before tenant or tenant's employees leave the premises, so as to prevent waste or damage, and for any default or carelessness in this regard tenant will make good all injuries sustained by other tenants or occupants of the building or by landlord. On multiple-tenant floors, all tenants will keep the doors to the building corridors closed at all times except for ingress and egress.

23.   Tenant will not conduct itself in any manner which is inconsistent with the character of the building as a first quality building or which will impair the comfort and convenience of other tenants in the building.

24.   Neither landlord nor any operator of the parking areas within the project, as the same are designated and modified by landlord, in its sole discretion, from time to time (the "parking areas"), will be liable for loss of or damage to any vehicle or any contents of such vehicle or accessories to any such vehicle, or any property left in any of the parking areas, resulting from fire, theft, vandalism, accident, conduct of other users of the parking areas and other persons, or any other casualty or cause. Further, tenant understands and agrees that: (a) Landlord will not be obligated to

provide any traffic control, security protection, or operator for the parking areas; (b) Tenant uses the parking areas at its own risk; and (c) Landlord will not be liable for personal injury or death, or theft, loss of, or damage to property. Tenant indemnifies and agrees to hold landlord, any operator of the parking areas, and their respective employees and agents harmless from and against any and all claims, demands, and actions arising out of the use of the parking areas by tenant, its employees, agents, invitees, and visitors, whether brought by any of such persons or any other person.

25.   Tenant (including tenant's employees, agents, invitees, and visitors) will use the parking areas solely for the purpose of parking passenger cars, small vans, and small trucks and will comply in all respects with any rules and regulations that may be promulgated by landlord from time to time with respect to the parking areas. The parking areas may be used by tenant, it agents, or employees for occasional overnight parking of vehicles. Tenant will ensure that any vehicle parked in any of the parking areas will be kept in proper repair and will not leak excessive amounts of oil or grease or any amount of gasoline. If any of the parking areas are at any time used (a) for any purpose other than parking as provided above; (b) in any way or manner reasonably objectionable to landlord; or (c) by tenant after default by tenant under the lease, landlord, in addition to any other rights otherwise available to landlord, may consider such default an event of default under the lease.

26.   Tenant's right to use the parking areas will be in common with other tenants of the project and with other parties permitted by landlord to use the parking areas. Landlord reserves the right to assign and reassign, from time to time, particular parking spaces for use by persons selected by landlord, provided that tenant's rights under the lease are preserved. Landlord will not be liable to tenant for any unavailability of tenant's designated spaces (if any), nor will any unavailability entitle tenant to any refund, deduction, or allowance. Tenant will not park in any numbered space or any space designated as: RESERVED, HANDICAPPED, VISITORS ONLY, LIMITED TIME PARKING, or similar designation.

27.   If the parking areas are damaged or destroyed, if the use of the parking areas is limited or prohibited by any governmental authority, or if the use or operation of the parking areas is limited or prevented by strikes or other labor difficulties or other causes beyond landlord's control, tenant's inability to use the parking spaces will not subject landlord or any operator of the parking areas to any liability to tenant, and will not relieve tenant of any of its obligations under the lease, and the lease will remain in full force and effect. Tenant will reimburse landlord upon demand for, and tenant indemnifies landlord against, any and all loss or damage to the parking areas, or any equipment, fixtures, or signs used in connection with the parking areas, and any adjoining buildings or structures caused by tenant or any of its employees, agents, invitees, or visitors.

28.   Tenant has no right to assign or sublicense any of its rights in the parking areas, except as part of a permitted assignment or sublease of the lease; however, tenant may allocate the parking spaces among its employees.

29.   No act or thing done or omitted to be done by landlord or landlord's agent during the term of the lease in connection with the enforcement of these rules and regulations will constitute an eviction by landlord of any tenant, nor will it be deemed an acceptance of surrender of the premises by any tenant, and no agreement to accept such termination or surrender will be valid unless in a writing signed by landlord. The delivery of keys to any employee or agent of landlord will not operate as a termination of the lease or a surrender of the premises unless such

delivery of keys is done in connection with a written instrument executed by landlord approving the termination or surrender.

30. In these rules and regulations, tenant includes the employees, agents, invitees, and licensees of tenant and others permitted by tenant to use or occupy the premises.

31. Landlord may waive any one or more of these rules and regulations for the benefit of any particular tenant or tenants, but no such waiver by landlord will be construed as a waiver of such rules and regulations in favor of any other tenant or tenants, nor prevent landlord from enforcing any such rules and regulations against any or all of the tenants of the building after such waiver.

32. These rules and regulations are in addition to, and will not be construed to modify or amend, in whole or in part, the terms, covenants, agreements, and conditions of the lease.

Rules 24 through 28, inclusive, are used when there are parking areas. Such rules may also be set forth in a separate parking license or other document by which parking spaces are assigned.

§ 14.4   Rules and Regulations for
Single Tenant Buildings

A lease of a single tenant building does not usually have rules and regulations, because the tenant's control of—and responsibility for—the premises is greater than that of a shopping center or office building tenant. If the single tenant building is subject to protective or restrictive covenants, the tenant is expressly required to comply with them.

CHAPTER 15

MERCHANTS' ASSOCIATIONS, PROMOTION FUNDS, AND ADVERTISING FUNDS

§ 15.1 Introduction to Merchants' Associations

The success of a shopping center is enhanced by having diverse tenants whose enterprises complement one another. The careful developer initiates this diversity in its selection of tenants, and the careful tenant encourages this diversity by its insistence on an exclusive use. Once this diversity is assured, tenants must cooperate in order to achieve their common goals. Toward this end, there is the *merchants' association*, which is an unincorporated association or a not-for-profit corporation formed to advance the interests of the tenants.[1]

The merchants' association has greatest utility in larger shopping centers, where a clear image or theme of the tenants may be discerned. In neighborhood shopping centers, the tenant mix is likely to be more haphazard and the merchants less likely to have any interest in an association. Before agreeing to join any small center which has an association, the tenant ought to be certain that other tenants support the association.

Merchants' associations are imperfect experiments in democracy. In part, their problems arise from the fact that they are foisted upon tenants who give

---

[1] See *Promotional Funds, Merchant's Associations and Tenant Advertising for Shopping Center Tenants,* Leasing Prof., Sept. 1986, at 2.

insufficient thought to the reasons for having them. The preparation of an altogether satisfactory provision for a merchants' association is impossible. As this chapter illustrates, the real estate professional can usually say what is wrong with the provision but cannot improve upon it.

§ 15.2   Purposes of Merchants' Associations

Merchants' associations do very well at coordinating such things as grand openings, holiday promotions, and center-wide sales. They also provide an effective way for the tenants to express their common concerns to the landlord without the need for separate meetings. When merchants' associations endeavor to regulate employee parking, they are usually successful. However, when they try to fix business hours or to do any of the other things that the alert tenant will have negotiated with its landlord, their usefulness quickly disappears. When their purposes make any reference to pricing, large tenants are likely to avoid them for fear of price-fixing claims. Needless to say, the tenant ought to be certain that it is not committing itself to an organization that is inimical to its own interests.

§ 15.3   Requirements of Merchants' Associations

If the tenant is comfortable with the goals of the association, it must carefully examine the extent of its obligations. Most shopping center leases require the tenant to join the association, pay dues to the association, participate in the association, and obey the rules adopted by the association.

With regard to the obligation to join the association, the tenant must be certain that all or substantially all the other tenants join the association. Broadbased membership will give the association some meaningful power with the tenants, and will also fund the association with enough money to accomplish its goals. Tenants can protect themselves by insisting that their obligation to join the association be conditioned upon all or substantially all the other tenants joining the association upon the same terms as they have. Most tenants will want to be able to drop out of the association if the membership falls below a substantial percentage.

Landlords are ill-advised to promise that all tenants will join the association; rather, they should assure only substantial membership. A promise of unanimous membership may disadvantage the landlord if an important tenant agrees to move into the center so long as it need not join the association. Landlords will attempt to tie the definition of substantial to the number of tenants, while tenants will try to tie it to the percentage of leased area. This disparity of interest arises from the landlord's goal of having an association as soon as possible and the tenant's goal of having co-contributors to the association's treasury.

§ 15.4 Payments to Merchants' Associations

As anyone familiar with democracy would suspect, merchants' associations are beset with problems when questions of dues and votes arise. Those who pay the most dues believe they should have the most votes, while those who pay little dues believe votes should not be bought with dues. In any event, landlords must require dues to operate the merchants' association. They ought to provide not only for dues but also for special assessments. Special assessments are necessary for emergencies and for the more-than-likely possibility that the association will run out of money from time to time. Most leases of shopping centers yet to be built also have a one-time charge for grand opening expenses.

Tenants will want to know exactly when their obligation to pay dues begins. Of course, this is most important when a long build-out of the tenant's premises occurs before its business is open to the public. In addition to relating the payment obligation to the opening of business, the alert tenant will want to defer its obligations until a certain level of occupancy of the shopping center is achieved. Large tenants will want either to reduce their percentage rent by their merchants' association dues and assessments or, less preferably, to include their dues and assessments in their minimum rent for purposes of calculating percentage rent.

Initial dues are usually set on a per square foot basis, for example, 20 cents per square foot, based on the landlord's estimate of a reasonable budget for the association. The tenant is not impudent to want to see the budget; after all, it is the tenant's money. After the association is operating, it sets dues on a per square foot basis. Most anchor tenants will not want to pay on this basis because they are then supporting the association as well as making their own expenditures for advertising. As a compromise, landlords frequently agree to a sliding scale by which the contribution per square foot decreases as the area of the premises increases. This issue will also arise in the context of voting, discussed in § **15.5**.

Inflation will erode the value of fixed dues. Accordingly, most leases have a provision for adjusting the dues by reference to a cost of living index. The consumer price index is not a talisman; indeed, the cost of newspaper advertising in the shopping center's community may be a more appropriate index. Of course, special adjustments should not be automatic but should be the result of a vote of the association.

In the vast majority of shopping center leases, the landlord is required to contribute one-quarter to one-third of the amount which the tenants contribute. Because the landlord prospers from its tenants' sales, this custom is understandable. Many tenants, however, are not fully satisfied by the landlord's agreement to pay a share of the association's budget. They want the landlord to pay dues for unleased space, or the difference between the actual collected dues and the dues which would have been collected if the center had been 95 percent leased to other dues-paying tenants. The tenant's justification for this demand is that it is unfair for a small share of tenants to bear the entire cost of the advertising and grand opening campaigns, and also that an underfunded campaign will be puny and insulting to the shopping center. Often a compromise is reached when the tenant agrees to pay its dues and the landlord agrees to pay its stated share (but nothing for the unleased space), but with the grand opening and advertising campaigns delayed until the center is more fully occupied.

On the subject of payments, two small issues are worthy of mention. First, very few leases provide for the proration of dues for partial months of occupancy, whether they occur at the beginning or the end of a lease. Second, landlords rarely give any thought to the disposition of their own contributions when the association is dissolved. Often, those provisions state that the association's cash on hand will be distributed to the tenants in the proportion of their voting rights; as a result, the landlord's contributions will be distributed among the tenants.

§ 15.5   Voting in Merchants' Associations

Like dues, voting is a very sensitive topic. Every tenant starts with the heartfelt precept of "one person, one vote." This conviction vanishes when a tenant realizes that it pays more rent than its neighbor; then the tenant recommends that the voting be proportional to the area each tenant occupies. That idea especially pleases the anchor tenant, which occupies the largest single premises. Just when the issue seems to be resolved, the smallest tenant reminds everyone that the anchor tenant has just convinced the association that its dues should not be based on its area. Therefore, the small tenant continues, it is not fair to allocate voting rights out of proportion to the dues contribution. In the end, a consensus may be reached that voting will be in proportion to each tenant's contribution to the monthly dues collected by the association. As a result, non-contributors will not vote and large tenants having a sliding scale for contributions will not automatically control the merchants' association.

Any tenant who considers a shopping center with a merchants' association ought to demand that the association can be abolished by a vote of the association. Otherwise, although the tenants could agree to let the association fall into disuse, the landlord would have the right to assert a default under their leases.

§ 15.6   Concluding Thoughts about Merchants' Associations

The real estate professional may feel some exasperation when it considers provisions for merchants' associations. This feeling is entirely justified, because such provisions are protocol for a series of complicated relationships among the tenants of a shopping center. The task would be difficult even if the real estate professional knew all the tenants and their unique needs. Since the provisions are prepared without benefit of that knowledge, the task is impossible. At best, the real estate professional can hope only to express generally agreeable goals whose cost will be borne in a generally fair way after a generally fair vote.

The following form has the virtues and unavoidable vices of any provision for a merchants' association:

FORM 15-1
MERCHANTS' ASSOCIATION

The tenant will become a member of, participate fully in, and remain in good standing in the Merchants' Association (as soon as the same has been formed) limited to tenants occupying premises in the shopping center, and abide by the regulations of such association. Each member tenant will have one vote and the owner will also have one vote in the operation of the association. The objects of the association will be to encourage its members to deal fairly and courteously with their customers, to sell their merchandise or services at fair prices, to follow ethical business practices, to assist the business of the tenants by sales promotions and center-wide advertising, and in particular to help the interests of members of the association. Tenant agrees to pay minimum dues to the Merchants' Association in the amount of $_____ per month (calculated on the basis of 15 cents per square foot per year of area of the premises), subject, however, to annual adjustments, approved by a majority vote of the members of the association, increasing said dues to the extent required by increases in the costs of promotional, public relations, and advertising services. In any event, the continuing monthly contributions to the association will be adjusted annually by a percentage equal to the percentage increase or decrease from the base period of the United States Department of Labor, Bureau of Labor Statistics Cost of Living Index, provided that index has increased or decreased by at least ten percent or more from the base period. The term "base period" will refer to the date on which that index is published which is closest to the date of the formation of the Merchants' Association. Tenant also agrees to pay to the Merchants' Association an initial assessment, in addition to the foregoing dues, in the amount of $_____ (calculated on the basis of _____ cents per square foot of the area of the leased premises) for the purposes of defraying the promotional and public relations expenses to be incurred by the Merchants' Association in connection with the joint opening of the shopping center. Owner will pay to the Merchants' Association for the purpose of promotion of such joint opening an amount equal to one-third of the aggregate assessments payable by all members of the association for such promotion, and will pay to the Merchants' Association for the continuing promotion of the shopping center an amount equal to one-fourth of the aggregate monthly dues payable by the members of the association. Nothing in the by-laws or regulations of the said association will be in conflict with the provisions of this lease, including without limiting the generality of the foregoing any reasonable rules and regulations adopted pursuant to the provisions of Section _____ of this lease, or in any wise shall affect the rights of the owner.

§ 15.7 Promotion Funds and Advertising Funds

Unlike merchants' associations, which are usually controlled by tenants, promotion funds are created, controlled, and managed by landlords (who may have an advisory board of tenants) to advertise their shopping centers.[2] Some landlords use them only for grand openings; others use them throughout the lease for special events such as holidays. The funds may be raised by monthly charges, periodic flat fees, periodic fees based on leasable area, or additional rent payable on demand. In theory, these funds are used only to advance the interests of both landlord and tenants by enhancing the image and business of the shopping center. Tenants often disagree with the paternalistic assumption that underlies promotion funds: that the landlord can do a better job of advertising than its tenants. Tenants should be concerned about the availability of their contributions to satisfy their landlord's creditors; they also resent the accrual of interest on their contributions to the landlord. The promotion fund therefore should be held in trust and should bear interest for all the tenants. Finally, tenants should not agree to contribute to a promotion fund unless at least 90 percent of the leasable area of the shopping center also contributes.

To appreciate advertising funds, one must look to their origins. In the early history of shopping centers, landlords realized that small tenants took space next to anchor tenants and awaited the spillover of their customers. Doing no more, many tenants failed. As a remedy, landlords began to require that their tenants buy advertising; usually this was expressed as a number of cents per square foot per month. This approach proved difficult to enforce.

As a result, landlords began to require that tenants deposit the advertising dollars they would have been required to spend under the old approach. When the tenant showed the landlord it had spent the required amount on advertising, the landlord reimbursed the tenant's expenditure from the amount the tenant had contributed to the advertising fund. In effect, the advertising fund is a security deposit to assure performance of the tenant's promise to advertise. As such, many of the same questions a tenant asks about the safety and return of security deposits should be asked about advertising funds.

---

[2] *Id.*

PART V
GIVING THE TENANT RIGHTS

CHAPTER 16

LANDLORD'S SERVICES

§ 16.1   Introduction

An office lease, among all leases, usually makes the most extensive provision for the landlord's services. The shopping center lease does not require the landlord to provide any services except those that are incidental to its maintenance of control over the common areas; see **§ 17.9**. The lease of a single tenant building, by its nature, does not contemplate any efforts from the landlord.

In preparing provisions for the landlord's services, the real estate professional must remember that every service has an associated cost and that the indiscriminate promise to provide services can result in a costly lease for the landlord. Providing services is as much one of the landlord's costs as is its mortgage. Consequently, the real estate professional must carefully consider the costs of landlord's services.

The tenant has several significant concerns about the landlord's services. One of those concerns is immediately raised when a lease provides that the landlord will furnish its services "so long as the tenant is not in default under the lease." Tenants must eliminate this provision. Its effect is to enable the landlord to evict the tenant (or at least make the premises untenantable by discontinuing services) without the benefit of the impartial judicial determination that traditionally precedes an eviction.

Tenants are also concerned about the availability of additional services, if needed, at a reasonable additional charge. Finally, tenants are interested in a fair and uniform allocation of the cost of the landlord's services. If the landlord promises to give free services to just one tenant, then the cost of those services will be paid ratably by the other tenants. As a result, the real estate professional is careful of operating expenses, and particularly the exclusion from them of services that are provided to any tenant without charge in excess of the proportionate amount in which they are furnished to other tenants.

§ 16.2   Short Provision for Landlord's Services

Small office buildings often use a simple expression of the landlord's services:

FORM 16-1
LANDLORD'S SERVICES (SHORT FORM)

So long as tenant is not in breach of this lease, landlord agrees to furnish to the premises during reasonable hours of generally recognized business days, to be determined by landlord at its sole discretion, and subject to the rules and regulations of the building of which the premises are part, electricity for normal lighting and fractional-horsepower office machines, heat and air conditioning required in landlord's judgment for the comfortable use and occupation of the premises, and janitorial service, all in a manner comparable to that of similar buildings.

The tenant may take some comfort from this provision because it is familiar with services provided by similar buildings; however, one can see that this provision invites disagreement. What happens if some similar buildings begin to offer security services or, worse, new utilities that this particular building is not constructed to provide? Because of the large array of landlord's services, landlords and tenants are always well advised to come to a complete understanding about them.

Office building services include, for example, (1) water; (2) heating; (3) cooling; (4) electricity; (5) elevators; (6) janitorial; (7) security; (8) freight elevators; and (9) common area maintenance of restrooms and hallways. Each of these can be extensively described. The real estate professional must also specify the hours and the days on which the services will be furnished. The tenant can use the longer description of landlord's services in § **16.3** as a basis for clarifying what services are to be provided.

§ 16.3   Long Provision for Landlord's Services

A fuller statement of the landlord's services[1] is:

FORM 16-2
LANDLORD'S SERVICES (LONG FORM)

(a) *Landlord's Maintenance.* Landlord will maintain the common areas of the project, including lobbies, stairs, elevators, corridors, and restrooms, the windows in the building, the mechanical, plumbing and electrical equipment serving the building, and the structure of the building in reasonably good order and condition,

---

[1] For a landlord's form of building services agreement, see *Pro-Landlord Services Clause for Office Buildings*, Leasing Prof., Oct. 1986, at 6.

except for damage occasioned by the act of tenant, which will be repaired by landlord at tenant's expense.

(b) *Landlord's Services.* Landlord will furnish the premises with (1) electricity for lighting and the operation of low-wattage office machines (such as desktop calculators and typewriters) during business hours (as that term is defined in this section), but landlord will not be obligated to furnish more than 1.3 watts per rentable square foot for nonlighting power and 1.5 watts per rentable square foot for building standard fluorescent lighting; (2) heat and air conditioning reasonably required for the comfortable occupation of the premises during business hours; (3) access and elevator service during business hours; (4) lighting replacement (for building standard lights) during business hours; (5) restroom supplies; (6) window washing with reasonable frequency, as determined by landlord in its sole discretion; and (7) cleaning service during the times and in the manner that those services are customarily furnished in comparable office buildings in the area. Tenant will have the right to purchase for use during business hours the services described in clauses (1) and (2) in excess of the amounts that landlord has agreed to furnish so long as (i) tenant gives landlord reasonable prior notice of its desire to do so, and (ii) the excess services are reasonably available to landlord and to the premises, and (iii) tenant pays as additional rent (at the time the next payment of base monthly rent is due) the cost of such excess services from time to time charged by landlord. Tenant will have the right to purchase for use during nonbusiness hours the services described in clauses (1) through (7), inclusive, in excess of the amounts that landlord has agreed to furnish, so long as (i) tenant gives landlord reasonable prior notice of its desire to do so, and (ii) the excess services are reasonably available to landlord and the premises, and (iii) landlord agrees in its sole discretion to furnish the excess services, and (iv) tenant pays as additional rent (at the time the next payment of base monthly rent is due) the cost of the excess services from time to time charged by landlord. Landlord will not be in default under this section or be liable for any damages directly or indirectly resulting from, nor will the rental reserved in this section be abated by reason of, (i) the installation, use, or interruption of use of any equipment in connection with the furnishing of any of those services, (ii) failure to furnish or delay in furnishing any such services when the failure or delay is caused by accident or any condition beyond the reasonable control of landlord or by the making of necessary repairs or improvements to the premises or to the building, or (iii) the limitation, curtailment, rationing, or restrictions on use of water, electricity, gas, or any other form of utility serving the premises or the building. Landlord will use reasonable efforts diligently to remedy any interruption in the services. The term "business hours" means 7:00 a.m. to 6:00 p.m. on Monday through Friday, except holidays (as that term is defined in this paragraph), and 8:00 a.m. to 12:00 noon on Saturdays, except holidays. The term "holidays" means New Year's Day, Presidents' Day, Memorial Day, Independence Day, Labor Day, Thanksgiving Day, Christmas Day, and such other national holidays as may be established by the United States government.

(c) *Tenant's Costs.* Whenever equipment or lighting (other than building standard lighting) is used in the premises by tenant and it affects the temperature otherwise maintained by the air conditioning system, landlord will have the right, after notice to tenant, to install supplementary air conditioning facilities in the premises or otherwise modify the ventilating and air conditioning system serving the premises, and the cost of those facilities and modifications will be borne by tenant.

Tenant will also pay as rent the cost of providing all cooling energy to the premises in excess of that required for normal office use or during hours requested by tenant when air conditioning is not otherwise furnished by landlord. If tenant installs lighting or equipment requiring power in excess of that furnished by landlord pursuant to paragraph (b)(1), tenant will pay for the cost of the excess power as rent, together with the cost of installing any additional risers, meters, or other facilities that may be necessary to furnish or measure such excess power to the premises.

Because the landlord has agreed to furnish its services, its failure to do so is a breach of its obligations under the lease. Since most of the services are available from public utilities, an interruption is not likely to arise from any fault of the landlord (except, perhaps, nonpayment). In recent memory, and except for accidents and "blackouts" over large areas or interruptions occasioned by work affecting the systems, public utility services have been interrupted only by federal regulations designed to conserve energy. As a result of the likelihood that landlords will not be at fault for interruption of services, they make a reasonable request in what is known as a breakdown provision:

FORM 16-3
LANDLORD'S SERVICES—BREAKDOWN PROVISION

Landlord will not be liable to tenant or any other person or entity, for direct or consequential damage, or otherwise, for any failure to supply any heat, air conditioning, elevator, cleaning, lighting, security, or other service that landlord has agreed to supply during any period when landlord uses reasonable diligence to supply such services. Landlord reserves the right to discontinue such services, or any of them, temporarily at such times as may be necessary by reason of accident, unavailability of employees, repairs, alterations or improvements, strikes, lockouts, riots, acts of God, governmental preemption in connection with a national or local emergency, any rule, order, or regulation of any governmental agency, conditions of supply and demand that make any product unavailable, landlord's compliance with any mandatory governmental energy conservation or environmental protection program or any voluntary governmental energy conservation program, the request, consent or acquiescence of tenant, or any other happening beyond the control of landlord. Landlord will not be liable to tenant or any other person or entity for direct or consequential damages resulting from the admission to or exclusion from the building or project of any person. In the event of invasion, riot, public excitement, or other circumstances rendering such action advisable in landlord's sole opinion, landlord will have the right to prevent access to or from the building by such means as landlord, in its sole discretion, may deem appropriate, including without limitation locking doors and closing parking areas and other common areas. Landlord will not be liable for damages to person or property or for injury to, or interruption of, business for any discontinuance permitted under this paragraph _____, nor will that discontinuance in any way be construed as an eviction of tenant or cause an abatement of rent or operate to release tenant from any of tenant's obligations under this lease.

Tenants react with hostility to the landlord's suggestion that rent will abate only after a few days of interruption have passed. Tenants point out, with some merit, that the rent abates from the date of destruction of the premises and not from a few days after the destruction. Tenants believe that the premises are as untenantable when they do not have the landlord's services as when they are destroyed. Tenants often ask for the right to terminate the lease if the landlord's failure to furnish services continues for an extended period of time. This suggestion will be resisted by most landlords. Landlords' lenders are also concerned about such opportunities for tenants to escape from their leases. As a compromise, some landlords will agree to allow the tenant to terminate the lease if the services are not provided for an extended period of time, so long as the landlord's failure to provide its services is not the result of generally prevailing circumstances, such as a government regulation or unavailability. Another area of compromise involves distinguishing the most essential services (for example, elevator service in a high-rise building) from less essential services (such as hot water in the restrooms, or air conditioning when windows can be opened). The tenant then has the right to terminate only upon the cessation of the most important services.

Landlords often ask their tenants to give them notice of any defects in the building systems. Occasionally, the landlord asks to be excused from any obligation to repair building systems until some time has passed after the tenant has given notice of the breakdown. This is true whether or not the landlord knows about the breakdown or should have known about it with only modest building management. Tenants should resist these usually vague requirements because it is they that suffer the interruption of services during the notice period. Furthermore, these provisions obligate the tenant to advise its employees of their duties as the tenant's agents. If the tenant cannot escape the provision entirely, it should make clear that its failure to give landlord notice will not be a default under the lease or otherwise allow the landlord to make any claim against it.

CHAPTER 17

COMMON AREAS

§ 17.1   Introduction

In contrast to the premises, which are under the tenant's control, *common areas* are those parts of a multitenant development that the landlord controls, and that are intended for use by more than one tenant. Common areas include hallways, stairways, corridors, elevators, walks, restrooms, yards, porches, cellars, roofs, common rooms, plumbing, heating and sprinkler systems, and utility lines. In shopping centers, an important common area is the parking area.[1] Regardless of its importance, many leases subsume parking areas in common areas and give parking areas short shrift.

Although common areas are not direct sources of revenue, the landlord still has great interest in them. Their appearance contributes to the image and success of the development and they may be converted to revenue-producing purposes in the future. Therefore, the landlord does not want to give up control of the common areas.

On the other hand, the landlord has legal obligations with respect to the common areas in its development. It must keep the common areas reasonably safe for those who are permitted to use them, including the landlord's tenants and persons who visit those tenants. If one of those persons is injured in a common

---

[1] Keay, *Parking Provisions*, in Shopping Centre Leases 533 (H.M. Haber ed. 1976).

area by a defect of which the landlord had actual knowledge, or which it could have discovered with an ordinary inspection, the landlord will be liable.[2]

Tenants, of course, look for the unrestricted right to use common areas, but they want their landlords to maintain, repair, clean, supervise, light, secure, and insure them. This is the landlord's dilemma: it can neither give up control of the common areas, nor can it truly keep control of them. Fortunately, the landlord has tenants that want to use the common areas — and, to some degree, control them — in exchange for taking some of the landlord's risk. The landlord will lose some control and will avoid some risk, while the tenant will get some control and incur some risk. In part, provisions regarding common areas may be understood as a negotiation of these risks and benefits.

In shopping center leases, common area provisions are much more than methods of allocating risk. They are also significant methods of allocating costs. If tenants share common area costs, then the definition of common areas governs the costs that the tenants will share. As the definition expands, the tenants' costs increase.

The discussions in §§ **4.6** and **4.7** are relevant to this chapter and should be considered with regard to it.

§ 17.2   Common Areas in Office Buildings

The description of the premises in an office building lease will often mention the tenant's rights in the common areas. Some office buildings, such as those with retail facilities, have more extensive common areas than others. When this is so, the landlord will want to expand on the usual provision and state:

FORM 17-1
COMMON AREAS — OFFICE BUILDING

The term "common areas" means all areas and facilities in the project that are provided and designated from time to time by landlord for the general nonexclusive use and convenience of tenant with other tenants of the project and their respective employees, invitees, licensees, or other visitors, and may include, without limitation, the hallways, entryways, stairs, elevators, driveways, walkways, terraces, docks, loading areas, restrooms, and trash facilities. Landlord grants tenant, its employees, invitees, licensees, and other visitors a nonexclusive license for the term to use the common areas in common with others entitled to use the common areas, including without limitation, landlord, and other tenants of the building, and their respective employees and invitees, and other persons authorized by landlord, subject to the terms and conditions of this lease. Without advance notice to tenant (except with respect to matters covered by subsection (a) of this paragraph) and without any liability to tenant in any respect, landlord may:

---

[2] See § **18.1**.

(a)   establish and enforce reasonable rules and regulations concerning the maintenance, management, use, and operation of the common areas;

(b)   close off any of the common areas to any extent required in the opinion of landlord and its counsel to prevent a dedication of any of the common areas or the accrual of any rights by any person or the public to the common areas, so long as such closure does not deprive tenant of the substantial benefit and enjoyment of the premises;

(c)   temporarily close any of the common areas for maintenance, alteration, or improvement purposes;

(d)   select, appoint, or contract with any person for the purpose of operating and maintaining the common areas, subject to such terms and at such rates as landlord deems reasonable and proper;

(e)   change the size, use, shape, or nature of any such common areas, so long as such change does not deprive tenant of the substantial benefit and enjoyment of the premises. So long as tenant is not thus deprived of the substantial use and benefit of the premises, landlord may change the arrangement or location of, or both, or regulate or eliminate the use of any concourse, garage, or any elevators, stairs, toilets, or other public conveniences in the project, without incurring any liability to tenant or entitling tenant to abatement of rent and such action will not constitute an actual or constructive eviction of tenant;

(f)   erect one or more additional buildings on the common areas, expand the building to cover a portion of the common areas, convert common areas to a portion of the building, or convert any portion of the building to common areas, so long as any such change does not deprive tenant of the substantial benefit and enjoyment of the premises. Upon erection or change of location of the buildings, the portion of the project on which buildings or structures have been erected will no longer be deemed to be a part of the common areas, except to the extent the building contains common areas. If any changes in the size or use of the building or common areas are made, landlord will make an appropriate adjustment in the rentable area of the building and in tenant's share of the operating expenses payable pursuant to paragraph [operating expense paragraph] of this lease.

The tenant must assure itself that the landlord will not close or change the common areas in such a way as to limit the tenant's ease of access to its premises.

§ 17.3   Common Areas in Shopping Centers—Grant

The common area provision in a shopping center lease usually begins with the landlord's grant of rights in the common areas:

FORM 17-2
COMMON AREAS—SHOPPING CENTER
(GRANT OF RIGHTS IN COMMON AREAS)

Landlord grants tenant and tenant's customers and invitees the nonexclusive right to use the common areas, in common with others to whom the landlord has granted or will grant a similar right.

This form assumes that common areas is defined elsewhere in the lease; **Form 17-3** defines common areas.

Landlords should give a right or license in preference to an easement. An easement creates an interest in real property. If the common areas are condemned, the tenant may have a compensable claim. If the tenant is deprived of the use of the common areas for any other reason, it may have a claim against its landlord.

In those rare leases in which no express provision is made for the tenant's right to use the common areas, the tenant should insist upon insertion of such a provision.

A Pennsylvania landlord was unsuccessful in its efforts to terminate the lease of a tenant that had used part of the common area for sale, display, and storage of its goods. The lease did not specifically prohibit the tenant's use of the common areas.[3]

§ 17.4 — Definition

Shopping center leases will usually define the common areas as the next step after granting a right to use them. Since shopping centers are designed in different ways, there is no uniform definition of common areas. As an example, one lease may define common areas like this:

FORM 17-3
COMMON AREAS—SHOPPING CENTER (DEFINITION)

The term "common areas" means the parking areas, roadways, pedestrian sidewalks, driveways, sidewalks, mall, whether open or closed, delivery areas, trash removal areas, landscaped areas, security areas, public washrooms, and all other areas or improvements that may be provided by landlord for the common use of the tenants in the shopping center.

On the one hand, the landlord's definition should be sparing because it will lose some control of the common areas. On the other hand, the definition will be a limiting factor in the costs that the landlord can recover from the tenants according to the provision in § **17.6**.

In theory, the landlord should avoid illustrating the common areas on a site plan because the site plan may be construed as a representation by the landlord that the shopping center will always look as it does on the plan;[4] however, in practice, the site plan is a powerful incentive for tenants to choose the landlord's shopping center over another. In one famous case arising in Illinois,[5] a tenant

---

[3] 202 Marketplace v. Evans Prods. Co., 824 F.2d 1363 (3d Cir. 1987).

[4] Annot., 56 A.L.R.3d 596, *Construction and operation of parking space provision in shopping center lease* (1974).

[5] Walgreen Co. v. American Nat'l Bank & Trust Co. of Chicago, 4 Ill. App. 3d 549, 281 N.E.2d 462 (1972).

objected to the construction of a kiosk in the parking areas. The tenant based its objection on the site plan attached to its lease, which stated that there would be 463 parking spaces; the lease contradicted this provision by saying that there would be 460 parking spaces. Even though the kiosk would have eliminated only three parking spaces, the court ordered the owner of the kiosk to remove it and it ordered the landlord not to construct any improvements in the parking area. The holding was based upon the court's belief that the site plan created an easement for ingress and egress, as well as for parking, and that the construction of the kiosk violated these easements.

In another Illinois case, the landlord proposed to add a new restaurant to an existing shopping center; to do so, the site plan had to be changed. A tenant successfully opposed the addition because the landlord had not adequately reserved the right to change the common areas. Even though the lease stated the landlord's obligations when an addition was made (and thus implied that additions would be made), the court ruled that the landlord had promised a development in strict conformity with its site plan.[6]

When a New York landlord leased a large part of the parking area in its shopping center to a restaurant, a tenant in the shopping center sued for a full abatement of its rent. Although the court ruled that the tenant had waived its claim for a full abatement when it continued to pay rent, the court decided that the tenant was entitled to damages (including lost profits) arising out of the landlord's breach.[7]

A Texas landlord constructively evicted a tenant when the landlord's construction of a theater substantially reduced the tenant's parking, access, and storage. The tenant vacated after three months of the disruption. Although the disruption was bound to end when construction was completed, the court concluded that the three-month interference was permanent deprivation sufficient to sustain the constructive eviction claim.[8]

As these examples[9] show, the real estate professional must conclude that the landlord should clearly reserve rights in the common areas; **Form 17-4** illustrates that reservation.

§ 17.5 —Landlord's Reserved Rights

The landlord wants to do more than imply that the site plan is not immutable. The landlord wants to make it perfectly clear that the site plan is subject to change by providing:

---

[6] Madigan Bros., Inc. v. Melrose Shopping Center Co., 123 Ill. App. 3d 851, 463 N.E.2d 824 (1984). *But see* La Pointe's, Inc. v. Beri, Inc., 73 Or. App. 773, 699 P.2d 1173 (1985).

[7] 487 Elmwood, Inc. v. Hassett, 107 A.D.2d 285, 486 N.Y.S.2d 113 (1985).

[8] Briargrove Shopping Center Joint Venture v. Vilar, Inc., 647 S.W.2d 329 (Tex. Civ. App. 1982).

[9] For the civil law experience in Louisiana, see Jaynes, *Obligations—Specific Performance of Obligations To Do or Not To Do in Louisiana*, 57 Tul. R. Rev. 1577 (1983), discussing J. Weingarten, Inc. v. Northgate Mall, Inc., 404 So. 2d 896 (La. 1981).

FORM 17-4
COMMON AREAS—SHOPPING CENTER
(LANDLORD'S RESERVED RIGHTS IN THE COMMON AREA)

Landlord reserves the following rights with respect to the common areas:

(a)   To establish reasonable rules and regulations for the use of the common areas (including without limitation the delivery of goods and the disposal of trash);

(b)   To use or permit the use of such common areas by others to whom landlord may grant or may have granted such rights in such manner as landlord may from time to time designate, including but not limited to truck and trailer sales and special promotional events;

(c)   To close all or any portion of the common areas to make repairs or changes, to prevent a dedication of the common areas or the accrual of any rights to any person or the public, or to discourage noncustomer use or parking;

(d)   To construct additional buildings in the common areas and to change the layout of such common areas, including the right to add to or subtract from their shape and size, whether by the addition of building improvements or otherwise;

(e)   To enter into operating agreements with respect to the common areas; and

(f)   To do such other acts in and to the common areas as in landlord's judgment may be desirable.

The wary tenant will consider this provision a harbinger of sinister changes to come. This provision gives the landlord unfettered power to deal with the common areas as though there were no tenants; as such, it violates the compromise which the landlord and tenant reached with respect to the common areas. These common area provisions will be vigorously argued. In addition to the landlord's other promises regarding the common areas (see § **17.9**), the tenant wants to be assured that:

1.   The landlord will not build any barriers (from fences to planters to bumper guards) in the common areas. Barriers may guide traffic away from the tenant or may impede access to the tenant.

2.   There will be a constant ratio of parking spaces to leasable area in the shopping center (for example, 4.5 spaces per 1,000 feet); assurance of a ratio is preferable to a fixed number of parking spaces. Some tenants go so far as to prescribe dimensions of parking spaces (with consideration of compact and full-sized cars) and the angle for parking spaces (60 degrees being easier for patrons but 90 degrees allowing more parking spaces in the same area).

3.   There will be a designated parking area for its employees. Usually employee parking is behind the shopping center or on the perimeter of the parking area. Landlords may prohibit employee parking outside of the designated areas and often ask for a list of the license plate numbers of the tenant's employees.

4. The landlord will not let anyone other than tenants and their customers use the parking lots. The landlord may want the right to let other people use the parking areas after business hours.

5. The landlord will not impose parking fees.

The landlord will resist the suggested prohibition of parking fees in the shopping center. After all, the landlord owns the land and should be allowed to use it freely; furthermore, the landlord argues, it has no reason to impose charges that will diminish its tenants' revenues or the desirability of its shopping center. The landlord may offer the tenant the right to validate parking at some bargain rate. Validation is a mixed blessing; small tenants may be unable to afford validation costs as easily as large tenants and may become less competitive. The tenants will want the landlord to reduce common area maintenance charges by the amount of parking fees and to apply parking charges in a nondiscriminatory manner; the landlord may respond that the tenant does not prescribe the use of the landlord's other revenue from the shopping center and that it should not start with parking fees. Often a landlord will accede to the wishes of a majority of the tenants when a decision to impose parking fees is made, and will usually agree that parking charges should not be excessive. Tenants try, but landlords often resist, to prohibit parking fees unless other shopping centers in the vicinity are charging them. At any rate, the tenant's employees should not be charged for parking.

§ 17.6   —Expenses

The common area maintenance expenses, which are often called *CAM charges*, are passed on to the tenants in the proportions discussed in § 17.7. Before their allocation is determined, the landlord will offer a definition of costs it may spread among the tenants:

FORM 17-5
COMMON AREA—SHOPPING CENTER CHARGES

Tenant will pay landlord as a common area charge tenant's proportionate share of all costs paid or incurred by landlord in operating and maintaining the common areas, including without limitation: cleaning, window washing, landscaping, lighting, heating, air conditioning, maintaining, painting, repairing, and replacing (except to the extent proceeds of insurance or condemnation awards are available) the enclosed malls and other enclosed common areas; maintaining, repairing, replacing, cleaning, lighting, removing snow and ice from, painting, and landscaping all vehicle parking areas and other outdoor common areas, including any shopping center pylon and sign; providing security; seasonal holiday decorations; removing trash from the common areas; providing public liability, property damage, fire, and extended coverage and such other insurance as landlord deems appropriate; total compensation and benefits (including premiums for workmen's compensation and other insurance) paid to or on behalf of employees; personal property taxes; supplies; fire protection and fire hydrant charges; steam, water, and sewer charges; gas, electricity, and telephone utility charges; licenses and permit fees; supplying music to the common areas; reasonable depreciation of equipment used in operating and maintaining the common areas and rent paid for leasing such equipment; administrative costs equal to ___% of all common area costs and expenses.

Some commentators have suggested that the term *common area expense* is too narrow and that landlords should use a term such as *occupancy costs* or *operating costs*. The reason is that landlords may want to pass on expenses that do not relate to common areas, for example, casualty insurance that covers the entire shopping center, or structural repairs that are not provided for common use.[10]

In shopping centers, as in office buildings, landlords and tenants are unable to agree on what costs should be considered operating expenses (and thus shared by the tenants) and what costs should be considered capital costs (and thus borne by the landlord, or at least amortized over some period of time and borne by the tenants). The foundation of the tenant's position is the fact that the rent represents compensation for the capital asset (the premises); as a result, the argument goes, the landlord is being paid twice if it is allowed to recover the cost of capital improvements as part of operating expenses.

The tenant's contention at first appears unassailable. On examination, faults appear. In the first place, a low-quality capital asset is likely to require more maintenance; thus, a landlord could charge less rent for poorer premises but charge the tenant more for maintaining it. Conversely, a very fine shopping center may have low operating expenses; for premises in that shopping center, however, the tenants pay high rent. Thus, it is not entirely true that the rent is the tenant's payment for the landlord's capital asset. Operating expense are also payments for capital assets.

Furthermore, the distinction between capital expenses and operating expenses is blurred. Some costs relate to the present (such as utility costs), and some costs relate to both the present and the near term (such as cleaning equipment) but not the long term. Most landlords and tenants can agree that these near-term capital costs should be amortized over their appropriate useful lives and treated as an expense over that period; usually, landlords recover interest costs on those amortized expenses.

Needless to say, the landlord will want the right to pass on every imaginable expense. The tenant will want to minimize these expenses and will want to exclude as many costs as it possibly can. To this end, many of the exclusions from office building expenses in **Form 6-8** should be considered. Tenants should assure themselves of the right to inspect and copy their landlord's accounts and

---

[10] Foster, *Common Area, Occupancy or Operating Costs*, in Shopping Centre Leases 271 (H.M. Haber ed. 1976). See Alexander, *Common Area Costs—Reduce the Tensions*, J. Real Est. Dev., Winter 1988, at 63, for a property management specialist's view of common area costs in shopping centers.

allocations of common area maintenance expenses.[11] A Maryland appellate court has ruled that a tenant has a right to an itemized statement of common area maintenance charges even though the lease does not require it.[12]

§ 17.7   —Allocation of Expenses

The traditional basis for allocating common area charges in a shopping center has been the proportion of the tenant's leasable area to the leasable area of the shopping center.[13] Nevertheless, allocations can be made in the proportions of lineal feet of frontage on the mall or parking area, sales areas (as distinguished from storage area), or minimum rents.[14]

The practice of imposing a fixed charge per square foot (or even an escalating charge based on an index) is becoming less common as landlords and their lenders see the inadequacy of these provisions. There is a trend toward allocations that are not based on the proportion of each tenant's leasable area to the entire leasable area of the shopping center. One study[15] has observed the practice of allocating expenses based on the portion that the leasable area of the premises bears to the leased area of the shopping center. Following this practice, if one-half of a 100,000 square foot shopping center is occupied and the tenant occupies 5,000 square feet, it will pay 10 percent of the operating expenses (5,000 divided by 50,000 = 10 percent); if expenses were allocated on the traditional basis of leasable area, it would only pay 5 percent. In this newer method, all of the expenses are allocated to the tenants that lease space in the shopping center. Put differently, the leased space bears the expense allocable to the unleased space. Traditionally, the burden of the unleased space was borne by the landlord.

That same study suggests that several responses to this sort of proposal:

1. Allocate on the basis of leased area, but use a floor of, say, 80 or 90 percent of the shopping center being leased.

2. As a variation of the first response, have a sliding floor that increases over time.

3. Use a minimum amount that the tenant will pay. Most tenants will respond with the suggestion of a maximum amount; however, landlord's lender may be concerned about a "cap" on the tenant's contribution to common area maintenance charges.

---

[11] Foster, *Common Area, Occupancy or Operating Costs*, in Shopping Centre Leases 271 (H.M. Haber ed. 1976).

[12] P.V. Properties, Inc. v. Rock Creek Village Assocs. Ltd., 77 Md. App. 77, 549 A.2d 403 (1988).

[13] Skolnick, *Shopping Center Lease Negotiations: Some Problems of Representing Small Tenants*, 49 N.Y. St. B.J. 28 (1977).

[14] Morris, *Shopping Centers—The Role of the Lawyer*, 1955 U. Ill. L.F. 681, 698.

[15] Fox, *Common Area Charges: How to Make Sure Tenants Pay Their Fair Share*, Comm. Lease L. Insider, Dec. 1989, at 1.

4.   Use the term leased and occupied as opposed to simply leased, or use a variation based upon space that is leased and occupied and for which the tenant is paying rent. As the number of qualifiers increases, the likelihood that each of them is met decreases and the denominator will stay low. This is to the landlord's advantage.

These variations may be used in concert with each other and are the shopping center analog of the grossing up provision discussed in § **6.12** with regard to office buildings.

A provision that relates the tenant's premises to the entire shopping center is:

FORM 17-6
COMMON AREAS—SHOPPING CENTER
(TENANT'S SHARE OF COMMON AREA CHARGES)

Tenant's common area charge will be determined by multiplying the total cost incurred by landlord by a fraction, the numerator of which is the number of square feet of floor area within the premises and the denominator of which is the total number of square feet of floor area leased and occupied within all the buildings in the shopping center.

The tenant ought to assure itself that the leasable space in the shopping center includes all of the shopping center, any kiosks in the shopping center, and any other single tenant buildings that benefit from the common areas (by reciprocal easement agreements, for example) even if they are not within the boundaries of the shopping center. Any space that is omitted in calculating the total leasable space will increase the tenant's cost because the denominator (the total space) is lower in comparison to the numerator (the tenant's space). The tenant may insist that all the leasable space in the shopping center be subject to the same provision as the tenant.

Some tenants derive greater benefits from the common areas than other tenants. This may be the result of a tenant's use of part of the common areas for sales; department stores often conduct sidewalk sales in the common areas, while other tenants may be prohibited from doing so by the rules and regulations. Other tenants use the common areas more than other tenants. On a per square foot basis, restaurants attract more customers than clothing stores and thus put greater burdens on the common areas. Finally, in enclosed malls, some tenants may be inaccessible from the mall because their only entrances are from the parking area. In most cases, all tenants share expenses in the proportions of their leasable areas. Although the negotiation of a perfectly fair agreement is impossible, the small tenant should point out these inequities when discussing its rental rate, and when suggesting that it be allowed to offset its common area charges against its percentage rent.

The tenant might also want to prevent the landlord from recovering more than all of the actual common area maintenance costs. This can happen quite innocently if the sum of the tenants' sharing ratios turns out to be greater than 100 percent; this mistake can be the result of an accidental mismeasurement. To take an absurdly simple example, if a shopping center with 100,000 leasable feet were divided into six stores of 10,000 leasable feet and eight stores of 5,000 leasable feet, the tenants of those stores would pay 10 percent and 5 percent, respectively, of the common area maintenance charges. If the developer's leasing agent were to calculate 11,000 leasable feet for one of the larger spaces, the landlord would recover 101 percent of its actual costs: eight contributors for a total of 40 percent, five contributors for a total of 50 percent, and one 11 percent contributor, for a grand total of 101 percent. These sorts of mistakes are not necessarily inadvertent; they may, in fact, be deliberate.

Another way in which landlords can profit from their expenses occurs when certain high-traffic or otherwise desirable areas of a shopping center (such as food courts) pay more common area charges than other areas. For example, tenants in a premium zone may agree to pay 110 percent of their proportion of common area expense because they are told—and they believe—that those areas have greater need for janitorial services as a result of the high traffic count. Tenants display a remarkable desire to believe that they are in the eye of a merchandising storm and that they should pay for the benefit they are convinced they have. They never think to ask whether other tenants are also paying a bonus share. When the tenant of less desirable space makes its lease, it has no way of knowing that a bigger share of the expenses is being picked up by its co-tenant in the high-traffic areas. The result is that the landlord has more than all its costs reimbursed by its tenants.

A similar example of this double recovery occurs with respect to real estate taxes. Taxes must be separately assessed for both common areas and other improvements in order for the tenant to be certain that it is not paying the same real estate taxes as a common area charge and as an escalation of other real estate taxes. A tenant may be able to rescind its lease if common area maintenance charges and taxes are misrepresented.[16]

If there are single tenant buildings in the common areas, the tenant ought to learn whether the tenants of those buildings are paying the real estate taxes assessed on the improvements they occupy. If those taxes are included in common area expenses and spread among all tenants, an unjust distortion occurs.

§ 17.8   —Payment of Expenses

Common area provisions in shopping centers usually conclude with a statement of how the common area maintenance (CAM) charges are paid:

---

[16] Magnaleasing v. Staten Island Mall, 563 F.2d 567 (2d Cir. 1976).

FORM 17-7
COMMON AREAS—SHOPPING CENTER
(PAYMENT OF COMMON AREA CHARGES)

Tenant's common area maintenance charge will be paid in monthly installments on the first day of each month in an amount estimated by landlord. Within ninety (90) days after the end of the period used by landlord in estimating landlord's cost, landlord will furnish to tenant a statement of the actual amount of tenant's proportionate share of such common area maintenance charge for such period. Within fifteen (15) days after its receipt of such statement, tenant will pay to landlord any excess of the actual amount of tenant's common area maintenance charge over the estimated amounts paid by tenant. If the estimated amounts paid by tenant exceed the actual amount of tenant's common area maintenance charge for the period as shown by the statement, the excess will be credited against the next monthly installment due from tenant.

Some landlords charge CAM monthly, others quarterly. Strong tenants may be able to negotiate a right to deduct CAM charges from their percentage rent. Needless to say, the tenant should be certain that any overpayment at the end of the term is refunded, because there is no future amount due from tenant against which to charge it.

§ 17.9 —Landlord's Obligations

The vast majority of shopping center leases never state any of the landlord's obligations with respect to the common areas. When the landlord's obligations are mentioned, the provision is usually perfunctory; "the landlord will maintain the common areas in its sole discretion." For the most part, however, tenants seem to believe that their landlords will render the services for which they are entitled to charge the tenant. Of course, the right to charge for services and the obligation to render services are entirely different matters.

Tenants should insist that their landlords agree to:

1. Maintain, repair, restore, repaint, and replace the common areas, including without limitation landscaping, asphalt, and utilities serving the common areas

2. Provide security services

3. Keep the common areas illuminated until some period after the shopping center closes

4. Clean the common areas and keep them free of accumulations of snow, ice, and debris

5. Maintain public liability and property damage insurance for injuries or damage occurring in the common areas.

In an enclosed mall, the landlord's obligations may also include maintaining the heating, ventilating, and air conditioning system. When specifying its obligations with respect to the common areas, the landlord must be certain to define common area expenses in a way that includes the cost of performing its obligations. Otherwise, the landlord will incur a cost for which it is not entitled to reimbursement.[17]

---

[17] *See generally Tenant Checklist for Common Area Control*, Leasing Prof., Jan. 1988, at 7.

PART VI

PRESERVING THE PREMISES

CHAPTER 18

REPAIRS AND MAINTENANCE

§ 18.1   Common Law Rules

The common law considered the tenant the owner of its premises for the term of its lease. In the absence of the landlord's breach of its (very rare) express warranty regarding the premises, the tenant had no claim against its landlord for any defective condition of the premises. Moreover, the landlord had no responsibility to maintain or repair the premises during the term.[1] These rules led to the conclusion that the landlord had no liability for injury to the tenant (or anyone else) for the condition of the premises.[2]

These rules are subject to several significant exceptions. A landlord has an obligation to repair the premises, and has liability to its tenant and others on the premises from unreasonable risks of physical harm:

---

[1] 3 G.W. Thompson, Commentaries on the Modern Law of Real Property § 1230 (J.S. Grimes repl. vol. 1980) (hereinafter Thompson).

[2] *See generally* W. Prosser, Prosser on Torts § 63 (5th ed. 1984); 2 R. Powell, The Law of Real Property § 233 (P.J. Rohan rev. ed. 1977) (hereinafter Powell); Restatement of the Law of Torts (Second) §§ 355, 356 (1965); Restatement of the Law of Real Property (Second) (Landlord and Tenant) ch. 17, Introductory Note (1977) (hereinafter Restatement). 3 Thompson §§ 1239, 1241, and ch. 24 is very helpful in this area.

1. If the landlord negligently repairs the premises,[3] or negligently fails to make repairs,[4] whether or not the landlord is obligated to make repairs.

2. If the landlord knows or should have known of a defective condition on the premises at the time of leasing (the concealed trap doctrine).[5]

3. On (a) common areas that the landlord entirely controls but that tenants are allowed to use, or (b) any part of the landlord's property that is necessary to the safe use of the premises. The landlord's liability under (a) is limited to injuries occurring in areas where users may reasonably be expected to go when the areas are used for their intended purposes. The landlord's liability under (b) refers to areas such as walls, roofs, and foundations.[6] However, a tenant who is found to have taken control of a part of the common areas may be liable for injuries that occur on them.[7]

4. If the landlord fails to perform its statutory obligation to repair the premises.[8]

5. If the landlord agrees to make repairs and breaches its agreement.[9] A tenant-sublandlord was held not liable for personal injuries sustained on the premises it has subleased to its subtenant because the tenant-sublandlord had not agreed to maintain the premises; as a result, the general rule that a landlord is not liable in such circumstances prevailed.[10]

---

[3] 2 Powell § 234(2); R. Schoshinski, American Law of Landlord and Tenant §§ 4:5 and 4:6 (1980) (hereinafter Schoshinski); W. Prosser, Prosser on Torts § 63 (5th ed. 1984); Restatement of the Law of Torts (Second) § 362 (1965); Restatement § 17.7; P. Rohan, 7 Current Leasing Law & Techniques § 8.02(2)(C) (1989).

[4] Scholey v. Steele, 59 Cal. App. 2d 402, 138 P.2d 733 (1943); Flagler Co. v. Savage, 368 S.E.2d 504 (Ga. 1988).

[5] 12 Powell § 234(2)(a); Schoshinski § 4:3; Young v. Garwacki, 380 Mass. 162, 402 N.E.2d 1045 (1980); P. Rohan, 7 Current Leasing Law & Techniques § 8.02(2)(1) (1989); Stephens v. Lafayette Ins. Co., 534 So. 2d 1099 (La. App. 1989).

[6] Restatement of the Law of Torts (Second) § 361 (1965); Restatement § 17.4; 2 Powell § 234(2)(b); Schoshinski § 4:4; Burks v. Blackman, 52 Cal. 2d 715, 344 P.2d 301 (1959); P. Rohan, 7 Current Leasing Law & Techniques § 8.02(2)(B) (1989); Hall v. Quivira Square Dev. Co., 9 Kan. App. 243, 675 P.2d 931 (1984).

[7] Wilson v. Allday, 487 So. 2d 793 (Miss. 1986).

[8] 2 Powell § 234(2)(e); Schoshinski § 4:8; P. Rohan, 7 Current Leasing Law & Techniques § 8.02(2)(e) (1989); 3 Thompson § 1240.

[9] Restatement § 17.5; Restatement of the Law of Torts (Second) § 357 (1965); P. Rohan, 7 Current Leasing Law & Techniques § 8.02(2)(d) (1989).

[10] Wright v. Mr. Quick, Inc., 109 Ill. 2d 236, 486 N.E.2d 908. (1985). *See* Richmond Medical Supply v. Clifton, 235 Va. 584, 369 S.E.2d 407 (1988) (allowing claim arising out of damage that vandals were able to do because landlord had not fulfilled its promise to repair premises); A. Brown, Inc. v. Vermont Justin Corp., 148 Vt. 192, 531 A.2d 899 (1987); McDevitt v. Terminal Warehouse Co., 304 Pa. Super. 438, 450 A.2d 991 (1982); Ridley v. Newsome, 754 S.W.2d 912 (Mo. Ct. App. 1988) (landlord's unsuccessful effort to repair leaking roof showed that it was responsible to do so).

6.   (Theoretically) if the tenant seeks indemnity for third-party claims against it and the landlord is liable under one of these other theories.[11]

7.   If the landlord knows that the premises will be used for admission of the general public and that the tenant will not put the premises in good condition before admitting the public.[12]

The landlord cannot escape liability under these rules merely by delegating its responsibilities to an independent contractor.[13]

The common law rule that generally excused the landlord from liability to those injured on its leased property has been so attenuated by these exceptions that some courts have adopted as the landlord's duty the basic negligence standard of reasonable care for foreseeable risks.[14] Even the well-recognized rule that a landlord is not liable for injuries sustained from known and obvious conditions has eroded. The Idaho Supreme Court recognized an exception when a tenant's employee is injured, because the employee might take risks in order to keep a job and an employer may be insured by workers' compensation laws.[15]

In a revolutionary application of the theory of strict liability, the California Supreme Court held that an apartment owner is liable to its residential tenant for injuries sustained from a hidden defect, in this case a nontempered-glass shower door.[16] Strict liability is based in part on the proposition that manufacturers and distributors of defective products should be responsible for the injuries caused by those products. Furthermore, the theory goes, the buyers of those products are unable to inspect the products adequately in order to arrive at an informed judgment about their safety. The court reasoned that residential landlords are in the business of making and marketing housing and that tenants are unable to inspect their premises properly. The ruling is particularly surprising in view of the facts of the case: the defendant-owner had not built the premises, was unaware of the defect, and had purchased the premises when they were 10 years old.

Although that case concerned residential premises (and, in fact, the cited precedents are primarily residential cases), the conceptual basis is not insupportable

---

[11] 2 Powell 2 § 234(2)(f); P. Rohan, 7 Current Leasing Law & Techniques, § 8.02(2)(f) (1989).

[12] W. Prosser, Prosser on Torts § 63 (5th ed. 1984); Restatement of the Law of Torts (Second) § 359 (1965); Restatement § 17.2; P. Rohan, 7 Current Leasing Law & Techniques § 8.02(3)(b) (1989); Cisu of Florida, Inc. *ex rel.* Aetna Cas. & Sur. Co. v. Porter, 457 So. 2d 1118 (Fla. Dist. Ct . App. 1984).

[13] Restatement of the Law of Torts (Second) § 420 (1965); Restatement §§ 19.1-19.3. *See also* Wright v. Mr. Quick, Inc., 109 Ill. 2d 236, 486 N.E.2d 908 (1985) (tenant not excused merely by subtenant's assumption of obligation to repair and maintain premises).

[14] W. Prosser, Prosser on Torts § 63 (5th ed. 1984); P. Rohan, 7 Current Leasing Law & Techniques §§ 8.02(1), 8.02(3)(a) (1989).

[15] Keller v. Holiday Inns, Inc., 107 Idaho 593, 691 P.2d 1208 (1984).

[16] Becker v. IRM Corp., 38 Cal. 3d 454, 698 P.2d 116, 213 Cal. Rptr. 1213 (1985).

in the commercial lease context. However, an intermediate California appellate court refused to extend the rule of that case to commercial tenants.[17]

Although a tenant cannot damage the premises by its negligence or waste, when a tenant promises not to "commit any undue waste on the premises," it will be liable for damages caused by its failure to clean drains and downspouts.[18] The tenant has no obligation to repair the premises—and any ordinary wear and tear to the premises—unless the repairs are minor matters that prevent decay or waste of the premises.[19] When a tenant unconditionally agrees to repair the premises, its obligations extend so far as total destruction by fire or other casualty.[20] When tenant agrees to make all necessary repairs to the premises, it does not agree to make structural repairs such as the replacement of a wall.[21] The tenant's agreement to surrender the premises in the same condition as they were delivered amounts to a covenant to repair; for this reason, the provision for repairs and the provision for surrender must be examined together.

The outcome of these common law rules is that neither the landlord nor the tenant has any obligation to maintain or repair the premises during the term of the lease. Considering that these rules originated in leases of agricultural land (in which the improvements were of little or no consequence), there should be nothing surprising about them. The landlord bears the risk of this rule because it suffers the damage to its reversion. Add to this the judicial trend toward finding implied covenants of landlords and one can see that the prudent landlord is certain to avoid the common law rule by express provisions in the lease. The prudent tenant is equally likely to resist any of these changes.

§ 18.2   Practical Overview

Landlords and tenants should agree on the theory behind repair provisions, that is, that the tenant should return the premises to the landlord in the condition in which they were received (except wear and tear incidental to the tenant's reasonable use of the premises), and that the tenant should take care of the premises to the extent appropriate for the nature and term of the tenancy. There, however, agreement may end. The tenant may say that it will be responsible for

---

[17] Mora v. Baker Commodities, Inc., 210 Cal. App. 3d 771, 258 Cal. Rptr. 669 (1989) (based in part on fact that cause of injury, part of "enormous refrigeration system," was not "placed on the market and into the stream of commerce").

[18] Western Assets Corp. v. Goodyear Tire & Rubber Co., 759 F.2d 595 (7th Cir. 1985).

[19] "The express covenant to repair binds the covenantor to make good any injury which human power can remedy, even if caused by storm, flood, fire, inevitable accident or the act of a stranger." Zuccarello v. Clifton, 12 Tenn. App. 286 (1933), *cited in* Berry, *Avoiding Lease Drafting Pitfalls*, Tenn. B.J. 11 (May 1983). Leavitt v. Fletcher, 92 Mass. 119 (1865), *cited in* 2 Powell § 233(3) n.117.

[20] Fiorntino v. Mason, 233 Mass. 451, 124 N.E. 283 (1919), *cited in* ABA Comm. on Leases, *Fire Insurance and Repair Clauses in Leases*, 5 Real Prop., Prob. & Tr. J. 532, 533-34 (1970).

[21] Expert Corp. v. LaSalle Nat'l Bank, 145 Ill. App. 3d 665, 496 N.E.2d 3 (1986).

repairing defects that it has caused, while the landlord will want the tenant to be responsible for repairs that become necessary during the term of the lease for any reason. The difference—a moral issue of fault, as opposed to an economic issue of risk allocation without fault—seems to be the real issue when repair provisions are negotiated.

When considering the maintenance and repair provisions of any lease, the real estate professional must have some familiarity with the premises and the use that will be made of them. Obviously, a tenant will be more willing to agree to maintain new, first-class premises that have been custom-finished for it than for dilapidated, underutilized premises that the tenant accepts as is. A tenant should expect greater responsibility for premises that it is leasing for a long term than for premises it is leasing for a short term; the tenant in a long-term lease expects obligations commensurate with its rights.[22]

In general, the tenant's burdens of maintenance and repair increase as one goes from leases of office building premises and shopping center premises to leases of single tenant premises. Leases of single tenant premises make the tenant virtually the owner of the premises; the scope of the tenant's responsibility is obvious. Shopping center premises seem to take more abuse than office building premises. Shopping center landlords expect periodic remodeling and impose greater maintenance obligations as part of the tenant's increased freedom. Finally, office building premises tend to undergo minimal changes after the initial improvements are made. The office building tenant often has the lowest level of responsibility for repairs.

The next two sections contain repairs provisions for office building and shopping center leases. In § **18.5**, the tenant's comments are explained. They apply with equal force to any multitenant premises. In § **18.6**, a single tenant lease provision that makes the tenant solely responsible for the premises is set out.

§ 18.3   Repairs Provisions in Shopping Center Leases

A shopping center lease will typically contain a repairs provision such as:

FORM 18-1
REPAIRS—SHOPPING CENTER

(a)   Tenant will at all times during the term of this lease keep and maintain, at its own cost and expense, in good order, condition, and repair the premises (including without limitation all improvements, fixtures, and equipment on the premises), and will make all repairs and replacements, interior and exterior, above or below ground, and ordinary or extraordinary. Landlord will keep in good order, condition,

---

[22] Glazerman, *Asbestos in Commercial Buildings: Obligations and Responsibilities of Landlords and Tenants*, 22 Real Prop., Prob. & Tr. J. 661 (1987), contains a comprehensive discussion of the repair provision and asbestos. This article has become the preeminent policy analysis.

and repair the foundations, and exterior walls (excluding the interior of all walls and the exterior and interior of all doors, plate glass, display, and other windows excluding interior ceiling) of the premises, except for (i) any damage caused by any act, negligence, or omission of tenant or tenant's employees, agents, contractors, or customers, (ii) reasonable wear and tear, and (iii) any structural alterations or improvements required by any governmental agency by reason of tenant's use and occupancy of the premises. Tenant will reimburse landlord for tenant's pro rata share of the costs that landlord incurs in performing its repair and maintenance obligations with respect to the shopping center. Tenant's pro rata share will be in the same proportion as the area of the premises bears to the total area of the shopping center. Reimbursement by tenant to landlord for its share of such costs will be made in the manner set forth in paragraph ____. As a condition precedent to all obligations of landlord to repair the shopping center, tenant will notify landlord in writing of the need for such repair. If landlord fails to commence the making of repairs within thirty (30) days after such notice, and the failure to repair has materially interfered with tenant's use of the premises, tenant's sole right and remedy for such failure on the part of the landlord will be to cause such repairs to be made and to charge landlord the reasonable cost of such repairs. If the repair is necessary to end or avert an emergency and if landlord after receiving notice from tenant of such necessity fails to commence repair as soon as reasonably possible, tenant may do so at landlord's cost, without waiting thirty (30) days.

(b) Tenant's obligation to keep and maintain the premises in good order, condition, and repair include without limitation all plumbing and sewage facilities in the premises, floors (including floor coverings), doors, locks, and closing devices, window casements and frames, glass and plate glass, grilles, all electrical facilities and equipment, HVAC systems and equipment, and all other appliances and equipment of every kind and nature, and all landscaping upon, within, or attached to the premises. In addition, tenant will at its sole cost and expense install or construct any improvements, equipment, or fixtures required by any governmental authority or agency as a consequence of tenant's use and occupancy of the premises. Tenant will replace any damaged plate glass within forty-eight (48) hours after the occurrence of such damage.

(c) Landlord will assign to tenant, and tenant will have the benefit of, any guarantee or warranty to which landlord is entitled under any purchase, construction, or installation contract relating to a component of the premises that tenant is obligated to repair and maintain. Tenant will have the right to call upon the contractor to make such adjustments, replacements, or repairs that are required to be made by the contractor under such contract.

(d) Landlord may at landlord's option employ and pay a firm satisfactory to landlord, engaged in the business of maintaining systems, to perform periodic inspections of the HVAC systems serving the premises and to perform any necessary work, maintenance, or repair of it. In that event, tenant will reimburse landlord for all reasonable amounts paid by landlord in connection with such employment. Reimbursement will be made in the manner set forth in paragraph ____.

(e) Upon the expiration or termination of this lease, tenant will surrender the premises to landlord in good order, condition, and repair, ordinary wear and tear excepted. To the extent allowed by law, tenant waives the right to make repairs at landlord's expense under the provisions of any laws permitting repairs by a tenant at the expense of a landlord.

The real estate professional should note that the landlord's obligations in paragraph (a) of **Form 18-1** are related to identifiable parts of the shopping center. The landlord's obligations are not expressed in terms of repairs "that are reasonable and necessary" or "that involve capital costs" or "that maintain or improve the shopping center." Those vague expressions invite disagreements. For example, a lease that obligated the landlord to make "necessary" repairs meant that the landlord had to replace fluorescent bulbs in the tenant's premises.[23]

§ 18.4   Repairs Provisions in Office Building Leases

A typical office building repairs provision is:

FORM 18-2
REPAIRS—OFFICE BUILDING

Tenant will, at its sole cost and expense, maintain the premises and the fixtures and appurtenances in the premises as and when needed to preserve them in good working order and condition. Tenant will immediately advise landlord of any material damage to the premises or any damage to the building. All damage or injury to the premises and to its fixtures, appurtenances, and equipment or to the building or to its fixtures, appurtenances, and equipment that is caused by tenant, its agents, employees, or invitees, will be repaired, restored, or replaced promptly by tenant at its sole cost and expense. Such repairs, restorations, and replacements will be in quality and class equal to the original work or installations. Landlord will have the right to supervise the making of repairs, restorations, and replacements by tenant and to charge tenant for its reasonable cost of doing so, and all those repairs, restorations, and replacements will be performed by a contractor approved in advance by landlord. If tenant fails to maintain the premises or to make those repairs, restorations, or replacements, they may be made by landlord at the expense of tenant and the expense (including 15% for landlord's overhead) will be collectible as additional rent and will be paid by tenant within fifteen (15) days after delivery of a statement for the expense.

§ 18.5   Comments on the Typical Multitenant Provision

The typical office building and shopping center provision will require the tenant to keep the premises in good repair and condition and to surrender them to the landlord in the same condition as they were delivered to the tenant. The tenant will try to minimize the burdens of this broad agreement. The tenant will first say that it should be allowed to return the premises together with improvements that

---

[23] Laurel Lea Shopping Center v. Parker, 457 So. 2d 822 (La. Ct. App. 1984).

the lease allows it to make. This will avoid the necessity of the tenant undoing any previous work it has been permitted to do.

Tenants will also insist that reasonable wear and tear be excepted from the condition in which the premises are returned. Some landlords are concerned that their tenants will never maintain the premises and will return them at the end of the term saying that cumulative wear and tear is permitted. These landlords often insist that the tenant agree that the premises be returned with the exception of "reasonable wear and tear since tenant's last performance of its maintenance obligations under the lease." At this point, the repair provision merges into the surrender provisions discussed in § **21.2**.

The most intense discussion will usually occur when the tenant asks that it be further excused from damage caused by fire or other casualty. Landlords usually respond to the question of fire by agreeing to that exception only if the tenant is not responsible for the fire. Although this response seems entirely reasonable, it cuts against the release and waiver of subrogation that the tenant has previously negotiated. If the premises are destroyed by fire, and the tenant is the cause of the fire, the insurance that the landlord has obtained (presumably at the tenant's expense) should be the sole source of recovery for the landlord. Any modification to the repairs provisions that requires the tenant to repair the fire damage it causes will create confusion when the landlord's insurer exercises its rights of subrogation.

When the landlord considers the question of excusing the tenant from "other casualty," it usually agrees to release the tenant from any obligation to repair damage caused by an insured casualty. This raises the question of which casualties are insured and which are not. In order to make this determination, the tenant must describe the coverages that the landlord will maintain. Some landlords are willing to do this because their coverages are prescribed by their lenders, are not subject to negotiation, and are not likely to change. Many tenants are satisfied with the description of the landlord's insurance and the landlord's promise to maintain that insurance through the term of the lease. However, those tenants fail to resolve the significant question of damage that is caused by an uninsured loss.

Some tenants feel that they are not obligated to pay for uninsured losses if they use the term insurable casualty instead of insured casualty. Since almost every peril is insurable, the landlord gives up the right of recovery for many causes of damage if it agrees to exclude insurable casualties from the scope of the tenant's repair obligations. Even so, the term insurable is not clear; for example, is flood an insurable risk? For some premises it is, because there are policies available for certain federally designated flood hazard areas. For premises located in a flood plain, it may not be insurable. So, is flood an insurable risk?

Some landlords prefer to use the term unavoidable casualty instead of insured or insurable casualty. The few cases that have considered the meaning of unavoidable suggest that it is a very narrow term including "events or accidents which human prudence, foresight, and sagacity cannot prevent."[24]

---

[24] Tays v. Ecker, 6 Tex. Civ. App. 188, 24 S.W. 954, 955 (1894).

Landlords and tenants usually arrive at a compromise that excuses the tenant from any obligation to repair the premises if the damage is not caused by the tenant and if the loss is not one that is insured. From the tenant's standpoint, a somewhat better way to express this is that the damage must be under the reasonable control of the tenant and not covered by insurance that the landlord has or has agreed to have.

When drafting a repair provision, real estate professionals must be careful to close all the gaps in responsibility. For example, a lease may emphatically provide that "the landlord will have absolutely no obligation to repair, maintain, replace, or restore the roof." Although the landlord is exonerated, by that provision alone the tenant does not become responsible for the roof. In fact, no one is responsible for the roof. As a result, the responsibility will fall on the one who first has a compelling need to repair the roof—the landlord to protect its building or the tenant to protect its goods and use of the building. These gaps may be avoided by allocating specific responsibility to either the landlord or the tenant and then providing that all other responsibility is to be borne by the other.

Many tenants insist that they will not make structural repairs. A *structural change* has been generally defined as:

> such a change as to affect a vital and substantial portion of the premises, as would change its characteristic appearance, the fundamental purpose of its erection, or the uses contemplated, or a change of such a nature as would affect the very realty itself—extraordinary in scope and effect, or unusual in expenditure.[25]

Since the term has been interpreted otherwise in many cases in which the equities were different (such as an insurance company's obligation to repair structural damage or a short-term tenant's responsibility to make structural repairs), the term should be avoided.

The landlord should repeat the often-forgotten rule that the landlord will not be obligated to make any repairs until it has been given notice that they must be made. It should limit its repair obligations to the cost of the improvements and should clearly disclaim any intent that it be liable to tenant for the tenant's consequential damages.

Landlords and tenants often disagree about the responsibility for repairs toward the end of the lease term. The tenant believes that it should not pay the entire cost of repairs because it will have the benefit of the premises only for the short duration of the term.[26] The landlord, on the other hand, points out that the tenant's use and occupancy has led to the need for the repairs. The tenant's view is prospective and the landlord's view retrospective. As a compromise, tenants will often agree to pay so much of the amortized cost of the repairs as falls within the balance of the term. Thus, a $10,000 repair that had a useful life of 10 years and no salvage value would be amortized on a straight line basis of $1,000 per year; a

---

[25] United States v. Cox, 87 F. Supp. 288, 289 (W.D. Mo. 1949).

[26] "Why so large cost, having so short a lease, Dost thou upon thy fading mansion spend?" W. Shakespeare, *Sonnet 146, in* 2 The Annotated Shakespeare 788 (A.L. Rowse ed. 1978).

tenant with three years remaining on the lease would thus pay $1,000 per year for each of its last three years. This issue also arises in connection with the tenant's obligation to comply with legal requirements, and is discussed in that context in **Chapter 11**. Many of the principles courts employ in deciding whether the tenant is obligated to make expensive alterations in order to fulfill its obligation to comply with laws are considered when courts decide whether a tenant is obligated to make expensive repairs; the cost-benefit test is probably foremost among a court's considerations.

In leases of new premises, tenants rightly ask that they be excused from any obligation to repair defects in materials or workmanship if the defects appear within one year after the completion of construction. Landlords agree with tenants on this point because they have construction warranties for at least that period of time. Also, tenants of new premises ask for assignment of contractors' warranties with respect to their premises. Often, construction warranties are not assignable. In that event, tenants merely require their landlords to pursue enforcement of the warranties. These sorts of agreements are common in net leases and are rare in shopping center or office building leases.

§ 18.6   Repairs Provisions in Single Tenant Leases

This provision endeavors to shift all of the risks of repair and maintenance to the tenant:

FORM 18-3
REPAIRS—SINGLE TENANT BUILDING

Tenant will, at its sole cost and expense, maintain the premises and make repairs, restorations, and replacements to the premises, including without limitation the heating, ventilating, air conditioning, mechanical, electrical, elevator, and plumbing systems, structural roof, walls, and foundations, and the fixtures and appurtenances to the premises as and when needed to preserve them in good working order and condition, and regardless of whether the repairs, restorations, and replacements are ordinary or extraordinary, foreseeable or unforeseeable, capital or noncapital, or the fault or not the fault of tenant, its agents, employees, invitees, visitors, and contractors. All such repairs, restorations, and replacements will be in quality and class equal to the original work or installations. If tenant fails to make those repairs, restorations, or replacements, landlord may make them at the expense of tenant and the expense will be collectible as additional rent due and payable by tenant within fifteen (15) days after delivery of a statement for the expense.

This provision underscores the importance of including both the land and the improvements in the single tenant's premises. When the premises include the land, the tenant will be obligated to maintain landscaping, underground utility lines (since the utilities themselves are responsible for their lines only on the property line), and sidewalks. The tenant has sole and exclusive control of its premises. The tenant and not the landlord is responsible for injuries to third parties as a result of improper maintenance or repairs. This is true despite the fact that the landlord has rights to approve the repairs a tenant makes.

Single tenant leases usually discuss the need for the tenant to make repairs during the last two or three years of the lease term. When substantial repairs are required toward the end of the lease terms, tenants usually win the right to cancel the lease or to pay only a portion of the expense.

When the intention is to allocate all the risks to the tenant, a clear and broad provision is well-advised. Such a provision may help to overcome the rules stated by one Illinois court:

> Where a lease contains a clause making the lessee generally responsible for repairs, the expense of repairing subsequently discovered defects falls upon the lessee. . . . If, however, the required alterations or additions are of a substantial or structural nature and are made necessary by extraordinary or unforeseen future events not within the contemplation of the parties at the time the lease was executed, the obligations of making such alterations and additions falls on the lessor.[27]

When a landlord agrees to "repair and maintain" the roof and "to keep it in good order and condition," the landlord must replace the roof if it cannot be repaired adequately.[28]

---

[27] Mandelke v. International House of Pancakes, Inc., 131 Ill. App. 3d 1076, 477 N.E.2d 9, 12 (1985) (citation omitted). In that case, the court found the landlord liable for certain unexpected repairs; the repair provision was much narrower than the one in **Form 18-3**.

[28] Dayton-Hudson Corp. v. Macerich Real Estate Co., 751 F.2d 219 (8th Cir. 1984).

CHAPTER 19

ALTERATIONS

§ 19.1   The Law

Traditionally, the rule has been that a tenant may not make alterations to its premises unless its lease allows it to do so,[1] and that a landlord may terminate a lease if its tenant makes alterations without the landlord's consent.[2] A tenant who makes alterations without approval is guilty of waste, for which the tenant is liable to the landlord and for which the landlord may seek monetary damages or injunctive relief. This has been true whether or not the alterations and improvements are valuable additions, so-called *ameliorative waste*.

An emerging rule is more flexible.[3] It considers the effect of the alterations and improvements on the reversion, the term of the lease, the nature of the improvements, and the necessity for them. Modern courts are less likely to hold a tenant liable for alterations and improvements that have a beneficial, or ameliorative, effect on the reversion. As the term increases, the permissibility of alterations and improvements also increases.[4] Alterations and improvements, such as painting, that do not affect the structure of the building find greater judicial indulgence than do alterations that affect the architectural soundness of the

---

[1] Halsell v. Scurr, 297 S.W. 524 (Tex. Civ. App. 1927), *writ dismissed;* 3 G.W. Thompson, Commentaries on the Modern Law of Real Property § 1140 (J.S. Grimes repl. vol. 1980).

[2] Cohen v. Power Inv. Co., 188 Colo. 34, 532 P.2d 731 (1975).

[3] R. Schoshinski, American Law of Landlord and Tenant § 5:22 (1980), and Rowe v. Wells Fargo Realty, Inc., 166 Cal. App. 3d 310, 212 Cal. Rptr. 374 (1985).

[4] Annot., 57 A.L.R.2d 954, *What constitutes alterations or changes in premises within lease provision permitting making thereof by lessee* (1958).

premises. Finally, improvements that are necessary for the initial or continued use of the premises are often permitted;[5] these improvements include remodeling of premises that have become obsolete.

The *Restatement* § 12.2 suggests that a tenant should have the right to make changes to the physical condition of its premises if (1) the changes relate to the tenant's reasonable use of the premises, and (2) the changes are reasonably necessary in order to effectuate such use. In deciding what changes are permissible, these factors, among others, will be considered: the effect on the reversion; the nature of the use (whether commercial or residential); the term of the lease; the location, past use, and physical attributes of the premises; and the magnitude of the changes. The *Restatement* § 12.2 requires the tenant to restore the premises to their original condition in most cases.

Several statutes deal with the tenant's right to alter its premises. At least one adopts the strict common law rule,[6] while another gives some helpful guidelines regarding a tenant's right to make alterations:

> When a person having an estate for life or for years in land proposes to make an alteration in, or a replacement of a structure or structures located thereon, then the owner of a future interest in such land can neither recover damages for, nor enjoin the alteration or replacement, if the person proposing to make such alteration or replacement complies with the requirements hereinafter stated as to the giving of security and establishes the following facts:
>
> a. That the proposed alteration or replacement is one which a prudent owner of an estate in fee simple absolute in the affected land would be likely to make in view of the conditions existing on or in the neighborhood of the affected land; and
>
> b. That the proposed alteration or replacement, when completed, will not reduce the market value of the interests in such land subsequent to the estate for life or for years; and
>
> c. That the proposed alteration or replacement is not in violation of the terms of any agreement or other instrument regulating the conduct of the owner of the estate for life or for years or restricting the land in question; and
>
> d. That the life expectancy of the owner of the estate for life or the unexpired term of the estate for years is not less than five years; and
>
> e. That the person proposing to make such alteration or replacement, not less than thirty days prior to commencement thereof, served upon each owner of a future interest, who is in being and ascertained, a written notice of his intention to make such alteration or replacement, specifying the nature thereof, which notice was served personally or by registered mail sent to the last known address of each such owner of a future interest.[7]

---

[5] Fred v. Moseley, 146 S.W. 343 (Tex. Civ. App. 1912), *no writ.*

[6] Wis. Stat. Ann. § 704.05(3) (West 1969).

[7] N.Y. Real Prop. Acts. Law § 803(1) (McKinney 1937). *See* National Bank of N. Am. v. Brook Shopping Center, Inc., 115 A.D.2d 461, 495 N.Y.S.2d 696 (1985), *appeal denied,* 68 N.Y.2d 603, 497 N.E.2d 706, 506 N.Y.S.2d 1026 (1986) (upheld bank tenant's construction of automated teller machine without landlord's consent).

Once the improvements are made, the tenant may not remove them,[8] nor is the tenant entitled to compensation for them[9] unless it is wrongfully evicted from the premises. When the lease is silent, the tenant is responsible for increased real property taxes arising out of improvements that the tenant may remove at the end of the lease.[10] If a lease allows the tenant to sublet the premises, the courts will infer a right for the tenant to make improvements in connection with the subletting. This rule obtains even if the lease forbids alterations and improvements.[11]

§ 19.2   Further Considerations

These principles make it clear that, at the time it enters into a lease, a tenant must consider the alterations it contemplates making to the premises. In office building and shopping center leases, the initial improvement of the premises will be made by the landlord and tenant according to the workletter or a finish allowance. Thus, the tenant's real concern has to do with the additional improvements it will want to make during the term of the lease. The tenant should also consider at the outset any rights it may have to remove the alterations and improvements it makes.

When a tenant asks that it be allowed to make alterations and improvements to the premises, the landlord's first concern, but not necessarily its greatest concern, will be the possibility of changes to the structural integrity of the premises. Therefore, many landlords prohibit alterations and improvements to those parts of the premises that are considered to be structural. Although the structural components of office building, shopping center, and single tenant premises may vary widely, a structural change is usually thought of as:

> such a change as to affect a vital and substantial portion of premises, changing its characteristic appearance, fundamental purpose of its erection, or uses contemplated, or a change of such nature as to affect the very realty itself, extraordinary in scope and effect, or unusual in expenditure.[12]

Generally, tenants will agree not to make such structural changes.

Landlords often prohibit improvements in excess of a fixed cost. This limitation is used in addition to, and occasionally in lieu of, the limitation to nonstructural improvements. The tenant's objections to a fixed-cost limitation

---

[8] Williams v. Gardner, 215 S.W. 981 (Tex. Civ. App. 1919), *no writ.*

[9] Mayberry v. Campbell, 356 S.W.2d 827 (Tex. Civ. App. 1962), *writ refused n.r.e.*

[10] Nesley v. Rockwood Spring Water Co., 285 Pa. Super. 507, 428 A.2d 161 (1981).

[11] Fair West Bldg. Corp. v. Trice Floor Coverings, Inc., 394 S.W.2d 707 (Tex. Civ. App. 1965), *no writ.*

[12] United States v. Certain Lands Situate in Kansas City, 66 F. Supp. 572, 575 (D. Mo. 1946).

are twofold. As costs increase, a fixed-cost limitation will permit even less alteration than the landlord and the tenant had originally agreed. Furthermore, the tenant will be precluded from making substantial improvements in order to keep up with retail competition or to refurbish an office. For these reasons, although tenants accept the right to make alterations up to a fixed amount without the landlord's consent, tenants usually ask their landlords to back down from the fixed-cost limitation because of the protection afforded by the limitation on structural improvements. Tenants may then ask that the landlord's consent to nonstructural alterations not be unreasonably withheld or delayed.

Occasionally, landlords prohibit only improvements that reduce the value of the premises or the reversion. The difficulty with this limitation is that the harm is one that will occur, if at all, at the end of the term, and that it is more speculative and less susceptible to proof than a change to a defined part of the structure.

Once landlord and tenant have agreed upon a standard for permissible improvements, the landlord should consider the further conditions that it will impose. By far the most important is the approval of the landlord's lenders. A landlord who has given its tenant extensive rights to improve the premises, but who has signed a mortgage that prohibits extensive improvements (as most mortgages do), will be in default of one of its obligations. As a further condition to making improvements, the tenant must agree to pay any increased real property taxes or insurance premiums allocable to its improvements; if those costs are spread among other tenants, they would be unfairly subsidizing the tenant's improvements. If substantial alterations will interrupt retail business operations, the landlord ought to require the tenant to pay an amount equal to the likely percentage rent during the period of the business interruption. If the tenant's alterations involve slab penetrations, the tenant should be required to restore the premises to its original condition.

Some landlords insist upon the right to make the improvements with their contractors. Tenants ought to resist this request unless it is assured that the landlord's contractors will be as competitive as those the tenant can find. All leases give the landlord the right to post appropriate notices under the mechanics', materialmen's, or laborers' lien statutes in order to insulate themselves against their liens.

Tenants should be careful of provisions that state that the tenants' improvements will become the landlord's property at the end of the term. Most tenants are able—and intend to—remove restaurant equipment, certain fixtures (such as stained glass partitions), security systems, computer wiring, and private telephone systems.

The tenant in a long-term lease stands in a different position from the short-term tenant. Courts give the long-term tenant greater latitude in making improvements to the premises. The long-term tenant has undertaken many more of the risks of ownership than has the short-term tenant; accordingly, it justly demands greater rights than the short-term tenant. The long-term tenant will want as close to carte blanche as the landlord and its lenders can tolerate. This will include the right to make ameliorative structural improvements and will often include the right to demolish and rebuild the premises. When those sorts of improvements are contemplated, the landlord and tenant must both be particularly careful of the landlord's lender's requirements.

§ 19.3   Alterations Provisions in Office Building Leases

In an office building lease,[13] the alterations provision will resemble:

FORM 19-1
ALTERATIONS—OFFICE BUILDING

(a) *Permission Required*. During the term, tenant will not make or allow to be made any alterations, additions, or improvements to any part of the premises, or attach any fixtures or equipment to the premises, without first obtaining landlord's written consent. All alterations, additions, and improvements consented to by landlord, as well as any capital improvements that are required to be made to the building as a result of the nature of tenant's use of the premises:

(1)   Will be performed by contractors approved by landlord and subject to conditions specified by landlord (which may include requiring the posting of a mechanics' or materialmen's lien bond); and

(2)   At landlord's option, will be made by landlord for tenant's account, in which event tenant will reimburse landlord for their cost (including 15% of their cost for landlord's overhead) within ten (10) days after receipt of a statement of their cost.

(b) *Landlord's Property*. Subject to tenant's rights in paragraph d, all alterations, additions, fixtures, and improvements, whether temporary or permanent in character, made in the premises by tenant or landlord, will immediately become landlord's property and, at the end of the term, will remain on the premises without compensation to tenant, unless when consenting to alterations, additions, fixtures, or improvements, landlord has advised tenant in writing that such alterations, additions, fixtures, or improvements must be removed at the end of this lease.

(c) *Free-Standing Partitions*. Tenant will have the right to install free-standing work station partitions, without landlord's prior written consent, so long as no building or other governmental permit is required for their installation or relocation; however, if a permit is required, landlord will not unreasonably withhold its consent to the relocation or installation. The free-standing work station partitions for which tenant pays will be part of tenant's trade fixtures for all purposes of this lease. All other partitions that are installed in the premises will be landlord's property for all purposes of this lease.

(d) *Removal*. If landlord has required tenant to remove any or all alterations, additions, fixtures, and improvements that are made in the premises pursuant to this paragraph, prior to the expiration of this lease or within ten (10) days after its termination, tenant will remove the alterations, additions, fixtures, and improvements at tenant's sole cost and will restore the premises to the condition in which

---

[13] See *Tenant Alterations—a Clash of Many Interests*, Leasing Prof., Nov. 1986, at 1, for tenant's checklist of an alterations provision and landlord's form of alterations provision for an office building lease.

they were before the alterations, additions, fixtures, and improvements were made, reasonable wear and tear excepted.

Office building tenants usually demand the right to make alterations that do not affect the building's structure or its heating, ventilating, air conditioning, plumbing, electrical, or mechanical systems. So long as there are adequate safeguards against mechanics' liens and adequate supervision, most landlords accede to this request. Most landlords also give tenants the right to remove the improvements and fixtures that they install at their own expense, so long as they repair damage done by the removal.

§ 19.4   Alterations Provisions in Shopping Center Leases

Shopping center leases will contain an alterations provision like:

FORM 19-2
ALTERATIONS—SHOPPING CENTER

Tenant will not make or cause to be made any alterations, additions, or improvements to or of the premises or any part of the premises, or attach any fixture or equipment to the premises, without first obtaining landlord's written consent. Any alterations, additions, or improvements to the premises consented to by landlord will be made by tenant at tenant's sole cost and expense according to plans and specifications approved by landlord, and any contractor or person selected by tenant to make them must first be approved by landlord. Landlord may require, at its option, that tenant provide landlord at tenant's sole cost a lien and completion bond, or payment and performance bond, in an amount equal to twice the estimated cost of any contemplated alterations, fixtures, and improvements, to insure landlord against any liability for mechanics' or materialmen's liens and to insure the completion of such work. All alterations, additions, fixtures, and improvements, whether temporary or permanent in character, made in or upon the premises either by tenant or landlord (other than furnishings, trade fixtures, and equipment installed by tenant), will be landlord's property and, at the end of the term of this lease, will remain on the premises without compensation to tenant. If landlord requests, tenant will remove all such alterations, fixtures, and improvements from the premises and return the premises to the condition in which they were delivered to tenant. Tenant will immediately and fully repair any damage to the premises occasioned by the removal.

§ 19.5   Alterations Provisions in Single Tenant Leases

Alterations provisions in single tenant leases may be:

FORM 19-3
ALTERATIONS — SINGLE TENANT PREMISES

Tenant will not make any alterations, additions, or improvements to the premises without landlord's prior written consent; however, landlord's prior written consent will not be necessary for any alteration, addition, or improvement that (a) costs less than $_____, including labor and materials; (b) does not change the general character of the premises or reduce the fair market value of the premises below its fair market value prior to the alteration, addition, or improvement; (c) is made with due diligence, in a good and workmanlike manner, and in compliance with all laws as that term is defined in paragraph [compliance with laws paragraph]; (d) is promptly and fully paid for by tenant; and (e) is made under the supervision of an architect or engineer reasonably satisfactory to landlord and in accordance with plans and specifications and cost estimates approved by landlord. Landlord may designate a supervising architect to assure compliance with the provisions of this paragraph, and if it does, tenant will pay the supervising architect's charges. Promptly after the completion of any alteration, addition, or improvement, tenant will give landlord a copy of "as built" drawings of the alteration, addition, or improvement. Subject to tenant's rights in paragraph [surrender paragraph], all alterations, additions, fixtures, and improvements, whether temporary or permanent in character, made in or upon the premises by tenant, will immediately become landlord's property and, at the end of the term of this lease, will remain on the premises without compensation to tenant. By notice given to tenant no less than ninety (90) days prior to the end of this lease, landlord may require that any alterations, additions, fixtures, and improvements made in or upon the premises be removed by tenant. In that event, tenant will remove the alterations, additions, fixtures, and improvements at tenant's sole cost and will restore the premises to the condition in which they were before the alterations, additions, fixtures, and improvements were made, reasonable wear and tear excepted.

Because the cost of removal and restoration can be great, prudent tenants ask for their landlord's agreement that proposed alterations need not be removed at the end of the term.

§ 19.6 Lenders' Concerns about Alterations

First of all, landlords should make all of a tenant's rights to alter the premises subject to the lenders' prior approval. If the tenant has the right to remove its improvements, it should also be obligated to repair the damage caused by doing so. Generally, landlords will want to avoid any obligation to purchase the tenant's improvements. If they must obligate themselves to do so, they should limit their obligation to the period of their ownership and should provide that their covenant to do so is personal and not binding upon any lender that succeeds to its title.

Lenders usually reject leases in which the landlord agrees to make additions to the premises on behalf of the tenant. Lenders are reluctant to run the risk of succeeding to this sort of an obligation because it will require the lender to make a larger investment in the development than it contemplated in its original loan.

When a tenant demands that the landlord agree to make substantial additions for the tenant, there are several approaches that lenders find more palatable than an absolute obligation. One approach is for the landlord to give the tenant the right to make additions and to recover its investment from percentage rent. Many lenders are comfortable with this sort of provision because they will not have to invest any more money; however, they will restrict the tenant's recovery of its investment to the percentage rent attributable to sales derived from the addition.

If the tenant insists on a stronger commitment from the landlord to make additions to the tenant's premises, the landlord's lenders will find the agreement more acceptable if: (1) the tenant is not allowed to cancel its lease if the landlord fails to do so; (2) the tenant agrees to give the lender notice of the landlord's default and an opportunity to cure the landlord's default; and (3) the landlord's failure to do the work allows the tenant only to do the work and to offset the cost of the work against percentage rent and rent in excess of a specified dollar amount (presumably the lowest minimum rent that the lender can use to support its loan).

When the landlord is obligated to make an addition for a tenant, its obligation should be conditioned upon the tenant's increased sales that justify the addition, or increased rent that pays the amortized cost of the addition, and the nonexistence of violations of other covenants that have been made with regard to the shopping center (for example, parking ratios). In no event should a landlord agree to do specified work for a specified price unless the tenant agrees to pay any amount by which the construction bids exceed the specified price. There is simply no way for a landlord to know the price of the work it agrees to do in the future, and no lender wants to succeed to a potential liability.

CHAPTER 20

MECHANICS' LIENS

§ 20.1   Introduction
§ 20.2   Mechanics' Lien Provision

§ 20.1   Introduction

Mechanics' liens did not exist at common law. They are statutory creations intended to assure payment of mechanics, materialmen, suppliers, laborers and others (such as architects) for the contributions they make to improvements. Since the statutes vary from state to state, generalizations about their scope and application are necessarily broad. The real estate professional must consider the applicable statute when preparing a provision regarding mechanics' liens.

In the absence of its landlord's consent to the work,[1] courts generally hold that a tenant cannot subject its landlord's reversion to a mechanics' lien for work that the tenant has done to the premises.[2] The tenant can only subject its leasehold to such a lien. Moreover, the reversion usually cannot be subjected to a lien for work performed in compliance with the tenant's obligation to maintain and repair the premises.[3] A percentage rent lease does not make the tenant the agent of the landlord so as to subject the reversion to a mechanics' lien.[4] Some Ohio courts have allowed a contractor to recover from a landlord on an unjust enrichment theory; these decisions have been criticized.[5]

---

[1] *See* Beaudet v. Saleh, 149 A.D. 772, 539 N.Y.S.2d 567 (1989), *appeal denied,* 74 N.Y.2d 610, 545 N.E.2d 868, 546 N.Y.S.2d 554 (1989) (New York court required affirmative act of consent as condition to subject fee to mechanics' lien.

[2] 3 G.W.Thompson, Commentaries on the Modern Law of Real Property § 1143 (J.S. Grimes repl. vol. 1980).

[3] Annot., 74 A.L.R.3d 330, *Enforceability of mechanics' lien attached to leasehold estate against landlord's fee* (1976).

[4] Hall v. Peacock Fixture & Elec. Co., 193 Conn. 290, 475 A.2d 1100 (1984).

[5] Calkins, *Contractor's Recovery From Landlord on Contracts with Tenant: the Equitable Limitations,* 16 Real Est. L.J. 195 (1988), discusses equitable theories on which tenant's contractors have recovered from landlords and the limitations imposed by *Restatement of Restitution* § 110.

Still, there are two common situations in which the tenant's work can result in liens on the reversion: when the lease requires the tenant to do the work, or when the landlord requests that the work be done. There is an elusive distinction between work that the lease requires the tenant to do (which may create a lien) and work that the tenant does to discharge its repair and maintenance obligations (which will not create a lien). An Idaho case tried to explain the difference. In it, the landlord asked its tenant to cure several electrical violations pursuant to the general repair and maintenance provision. When the tenant failed to pay for the repairs, the electrical contractor asserted a mechanics' lien against the property. The court sustained the claim, saying that the landlord's request (1) made the "general" obligation into a "specific" one, and (2) amounted to "a ratification or a consent for the work to be done."[6]

A Tennessee case suggests that work done for a tenant may subject the reversion to a lien if the tenant is acting as the landlord's agent in having the work performed.[7] In that case, however, the landlord was not held responsible because it had no control over the tenant's dealings with the lien claimant, the lease did not require the improvements which the tenant made, the landlord was not obligated to pay for the tenant's improvements, and the tenant was permitted to remove its improvements at the end of the lease.[8]

§ 20.2 Mechanics' Lien Provision

Leases usually have a provision to this effect:

FORM 20-1
MECHANICS' LIENS

Tenant will pay or cause to be paid all costs and charges for work done by it or caused to be done by it, in or to the premises, and for all materials furnished for or in connection with the work. Tenant will indemnify landlord against and hold landlord harmless from all liabilities, liens, claims, costs, and demands on account of the work. If any lien is filed against the premises, tenant will cause the lien to be discharged of record within ten (10) days after it is filed. If tenant desires to contest the lien, it will furnish landlord, within the ten-day period, security reasonably satisfactory to landlord of at least 150% of the amount of the lien, plus estimated costs and interest. If a final nonappealable judgment establishing the validity or

---

[6] Christensen v. Idaho Land Developers, Inc., 104 Idaho 458, 459, 660 P.2d 70, 71 (Ct. App. 1983).

[7] Hussman Refrigeration, Inc. v. South Pittsburgh Assocs., 697 S.W.2d 588 (Tenn. Ct. App. 1985).

[8] *See also* Lentz Plumbing Co. v. Fee, 235 Kan. 266, 679 P.2d 736 (1984) (refused to attach lien to fee after end of lease on theories of agency, estoppel, and merger of estates). *See generally* Frei & Garner, *The Landlord's Liability for Mechanics' Liens for Improvements to Leased Premises,* in Int'l Council of Shopping Centers, Shopping Center Legal Update, Summer 1986, at 6.

existence of the lien for any amount is entered, tenant will satisfy it at once. If tenant fails to pay any charge for which a lien has been filed, and does not give landlord such security, landlord may, at its option, pay the charge and related costs and interest, and the amount so paid, together with reasonable attorneys' fees incurred in connection with it, will be immediately due from tenant to landlord as additional rent. Nothing contained in this lease is the consent or agreement of landlord to subject landlord's interest in the premises to liability under any lien law. If either landlord or tenant receives notice that a lien has been or is about to be filed against the premises, or that any action affecting title to the premises has been commenced on account of work done by or for tenant or labor or materials furnished to or for tenant, it will immediately give the other written notice of the notice. At least fifteen (15) days prior to the commencement of any work (including without limitation any maintenance, repairs, alterations, additions, improvements, or installations) in or to the premises, by or for tenant, tenant will give landlord written notice of the proposed work and the names and addresses of the persons supplying labor and materials for the proposed work. Landlord will have the right to post notices of nonresponsibility or similar notices on the premises in order to protect the premises against liens.

Tenants should not have any strong objection to the thought behind this provision; it merely asks them to pay for what they order. However, they may insist on the right to discharge the lien within some period after they have notice of it, and not within some period after it is filed. A tenant is well-advised to ask for the right to contest any mechanics' lien so long as it posts a bond or cash collateral sufficient to assure that the reversion is not jeopardized. Some landlords will insist that the collateral be posted with a title insurance company and that the title insurance company insure the landlord's title against loss from the mechanics' lien.

Tenants should also scrutinize the provision carefully in order to be certain that it relates only to work done for the tenant at the tenant's request. The tenant should not agree to defend the landlord against every claim that is asserted against the premises, especially claims for work done by the landlord for the tenant's initial occupancy.

Since most leases prohibit work to the premises without the landlord's prior written consent, the landlord will have another opportunity to protect itself against mechanics' lien claims when the tenant asks for its approval to proposed improvements. Under the New York statute, a landlord that consents to its tenant's work will expose its own title to a mechanics' lien claim.[9] At that time, the landlord can require surety bonds as a condition to its approval. If the local laws allow them, waivers of liens might be sought as a further condition; New York does not allow such lien waivers, but its neighbor Pennsylvania does.[10] Finally, in connection with a tenant's work on the premises, the landlord may record the

---

[9] Harner v. Schechter, 105 A.D.2d 932, 482 N.Y.S.2d 124 (1984).

[10] Annot., 74 A.L.R.3d 505, *Release of waiver of mechanic's lien by general contractor as affecting right of subcontractor or materialman* (1976); Annot., 76 A.L.R.2d 1087, *Validity and effect of provision in agreement not to file mechanic's liens* (1961).

lease, post notices of nonresponsibility, or do whatever else local law provides for its protection.

A landlord may be well-advised to terminate a lease rather than accept a surrender of its tenant's leasehold that is subject to a mechanics' lien claim; by accepting a surrender, the landlord may be deemed to have accepted the leasehold subject to the lien claim. The landlord's dilemma when a tenant proposes to alter the premises is clear; it wants to exert control in order to protect its property, but not so much control that it is deemed responsible for payment of its tenant's work.

CHAPTER 21

SURRENDER

§ 21.1   Early Termination of Lease

The term *surrender* is used in two different senses in leases. One refers to early termination of the lease, and the other refers to the redelivery of the premises at the end of the term. In the first sense, a surrender occurs either by the landlord's and tenant's express agreement or by operation of law. When the landlord and tenant agree that the term should end before its expiration date, they agree to the surrender of the lease. Their agreement must be expressed in writing.[1]

A surrender by operation of law is a more troublesome doctrine. In contrast to a surrender by an express agreement, which states the understanding and intention of the landlord and the tenant, a surrender by operation of law is a judicial inference, based on conduct of the landlord and tenant from which the court infers that they intended and agreed to a surrender of the lease. In other words, the court says, the landlord and tenant have acted so inconsistently with their lease that, if they had thought about it, they would have made an express agreement to surrender the lease. Often, surrender by operation of law results from unwitting conduct or ambiguous circumstances, such as a new lease between landlord and tenant, a substitution of a new tenant for the old tenant, the tenant's abandonment of the premises with acceptance of the premises by the landlord, abandonment with resumption of possession by the landlord, abandonment with the landlord's acceptance of the keys, or abandonment with attempted or actual reletting of the premises by the landlord. A New York landlord that assisted a tenant in moving out (and billed the tenant a small amount for damages) in order to make room for a new tenant could not go back to the old tenant when

---

[1] 2 R. Powell, The Law of Real Property § 247(5) (P.J. Rohan ed., rev. 1977) [hereinafter Powell]; 202 Marketplace v. Evans Prods. Co., 593 F. Supp. 1133 (E.D. Pa. 1984) (applying Pennsylvania law), *aff'd*, 824 F.2d 1363 (3d Cir. 1987). Hargis v. Mel-Mad Corp., 46 Wash. App. 146, 730 P.2d 76 (1986), shows importance of a properly worded termination agreement.

the lease with the new tenant failed to materialize; the landlord's actions effected a surrender by operation of law.[2]

An Illinois landlord that enters into new leases with other tenants after the first tenant has vacated its premises does not necessarily accept its old tenant's surrender of its premises.[3] In this case, the old tenant's lease expired on March 31, 1986. By the end of 1985, the tenant had moved out and the landlord entered into two new leases for the entirety of the space. One of the leases was to begin on May 1, 1986, and the other on February 15, 1986. The original tenant asserted that the landlord had accepted its proffered surrender of the premises by entering into the new leases, irrespective of their commencement dates. The court concluded that entry into the leases was not sufficient to effect a surrender, but that the delivery of possession to one of the tenants during the term of the old lease was. Thus the landlord could not recover the rent from both its old tenant and its new tenant for the overlapping period of those two leases.

Surrender poses another very interesting problem to the landlord: its relationship to the tenant's subtenants. Basically, the subtenants are protected.[4] The real question is the degree to which the landlord is protected. In some jurisdictions, the subtenant's obligation to pay rent is discharged, either because the landlord and subtenant are not bound by privity of contract or because the subtenant's obligation to pay rent was extinguished when its landlord (the tenant) surrendered the estate (the leasehold) to which the subrent related. In those cases, the landlord has no recourse for its rent. Occasionally, judicial fictions have been created to save the landlord from this injustice; for example, some courts have said that an assignment of the subleases was implied by the surrender, thus giving the landlord privity of contract with the subtenant and rights against the subtenant. These niceties are discussed more fully in the context of a landlord's remedies after a tenant's default (§§ **30.7** through **30.12**) and merger (§ **32.12**), because the rules of surrender by operation of law are very important in the preparation of default provisions related to the tenant's abandonment of the premises.

Although the case law is sparse,[5] both voluntary and involuntary lease terminations may be attacked as fraudulent transfers under § 548 of the Bankruptcy Code.[6] Section 548 enables a trustee or debtor-in-possession to avoid a transfer of the debtor's property that was made or incurred within one year before the date of the filing of the petition, if the debtor voluntarily or involuntarily

---

[2] Riverside Research Institute v. KMGA, Inc., 68 N.Y.2d 689, 497 N.E.2d 669, 506 N.Y.S.2d 302 (1986).

[3] Checkers, Simon & Rosner v. Lurie Corp., 864 F.2d 1338 (7th Cir. 1988).

[4] 2 Powell § 247(5).

[5] Goodman, *Avoidance of Lease Terminations as Fraudulent Transfers*, 43 Bus. Law. 807 (1988), is the best discussion of the statutes and case law.

[6] 11 U.S.C. § 548 (1986). Fraudulent transfer is a misnomer. Fraud in the sense that it is commonly used, that is, deceit or deliberate misrepresentation, is not a necessary part of a fraudulent transfer; compare § 548(a)(1) to § 548(a)(2). Fraudulent transfers are also distinct from fraudulent conveyances under many state statutes.

(1)   made such transfer or incurred such obligation with actual intent to hinder, delay, or defraud any entity to which the debtor was or became, on or after the date that such transfer was made or such obligation was incurred, indebted; or

(2)(A)   received less than a reasonably equivalent value in exchange for such transfer or obligation; and

(B)(i)   was insolvent on the date that such transfer was made or such obligation was incurred or became insolvent as a result of such transfer or obligation;

(ii)   was engaged in business or a transaction, or was about to engage in business or a transaction, for which any property remaining with the debtor was an unreasonably small capital; or

(iii)   intended to incur, or believed that the debtor would incur, debts that would be beyond the debtor's ability to pay as such debts matured.

"Value" under § 548(d)(2)(A) means "property, or satisfaction or securing of a present or antecedent debt of the debtor. . . ."

If the trustee or debtor-in-possession proves that a fraudulent transfer has occurred, then, under § 550 of the Bankruptcy Code, it may recover the property from the person who has it (which may not be the initial transferee) or it may recover the value of the property from the initial transferee or subsequent transferee, unless the subsequent transferee gave value in good faith (that is, unmindful of the voidability of the transfer). Obviously, if the landlord accepts the surrender of the tenant's premises and relets them, and then is found to have participated in a fraudulent transfer when the surrender occurred, it will have liability to the tenant that is dispossessed if the trustee or debtor-in-possession elects to recover the premises.

The foremost commentator on this subject[7] has suggested the following ways in which a landlord might reduce its risks of a fraudulent transfer:

1.   Terminate the lease involuntarily, such as by judicial proceeding, rather than voluntarily by agreement. The imprimatur of a court may support the termination.

2.   Give the tenant something more than relief from liability in consideration of the termination. This is, of course, an effort to give reasonably equivalent value under § 548(d)(2) of the Bankruptcy Code. The landlord might support this exchange by an appraisal of the leasehold in comparison to the tenant's liability.

3.   Provide for automatic permanent increases in rents on default. The thought behind this suggestion is to limit the value of the lease; however, it may run afoul of state laws regarding penalties and it will always be very difficult to negotiate with a tenant.

4.   Impose conditions to any purchase option or right of first refusal on the tenant's performance of the lease and compliance with strict deadlines. See § 5.14 regarding the enforceability of strict deadlines.

---

[7] See Goodman, *Avoidance of Lease Terminations as Fraudulent Transfers,* 43 Bus. Law. 807 (1988).

5. Strictly enforce the termination provision upon insolvency of the tenant. Note that this enforcement is upon insolvency and not bankruptcy, in which the ipso facto provision would not be enforced. However, a landlord runs the risk of terminating a lease of an insolvent tenant when the tenant is still paying rent and is able to continue to do so.

6. Prohibit lease assignments if the lease is in default. This prohibition may run into problems if tenant responds to the landlord's suit for rent by saying that the landlord failed to mitigate its damages by accepting a proposed assignee.

7. Force the tenant's bankruptcy. This will avoid a fraudulent transfer, but will create the problems attendant upon leases in bankruptcy.

In any lease termination, the landlord should get whatever comfort it can from the tenant and responsible third parties that the tenant is not in financial distress under § 550 of the Bankruptcy Code.

In conclusion, although there is not a great deal of law addressing lease terminations as fraudulent transfers, one may be certain that ever vigilant creditors, trustees, and debtors-in-possession will look to bargain terminations as a source of recovery for the debtor.

§ 21.2 Redelivery at End of Term

The other sense in which the term *surrender* is used in leases involves the redelivery of the premises at the end of the term. Most leases provide:

FORM 21-1
END OF TERM

At the end of this lease, tenant will surrender the premises in good order and condition, ordinary wear and tear excepted. If tenant is not then in default, tenant may remove from the premises any trade fixtures, equipment, and movable furniture placed in the premises by tenant, whether or not the trade fixtures or equipment are fastened to the building. Tenant will not remove any trade fixtures or equipment without landlord's prior written consent if the trade fixtures or equipment are used in the operation of the building or if the removal of the fixtures or equipment will impair the structure of the building. Whether or not tenant is then in default, tenant will remove the alterations, additions, improvements, trade fixtures, equipment, and furniture as landlord has requested in accordance with paragraph [alterations and improvements paragraph]. Tenant will fully repair any damage occasioned by the removal of any trade fixtures, equipment, furniture, alterations, additions, and improvements. All trade fixtures, equipment, furniture, alterations, additions, and improvements not removed will conclusively be deemed to have been abandoned by tenant and may be appropriated, sold, stored, destroyed, or otherwise disposed of by landlord without notice to tenant or to any other person and without obligation to account for them. Tenant will pay landlord all expenses incurred in connection with landlord's disposition of such property, including without limitation the cost of repairing any damage to the building or the premises caused by removal of such property. Tenant's obligation to observe and perform this covenant will survive the end of this lease.

This form may be used in leases of multitenant developments; with minor modifications, it is appropriate for single tenant buildings. In single tenant leases, the premises are usually required to be returned broom-clean, although some landlords accept "ordinary wear and tear since the date of the last required maintenance or repair."

When the tenant's use is hard on a building (such as the storage and sale of heavy equipment), the landlord may not want to exclude normal wear and tear from the surrender obligation. The landlord may want the premises returned in the condition in which they were let or, as a compromise, may accept normal wear and tear that can be repaired at a small stated cost.[8]

A Colorado appellate court held that a landlord was not entitled to damages when it leased premises for a candle manufacturing plant and the premises were returned with wax on the walls and floors.[9] The court found this to be ordinary wear within the term of the lease that required the premises to be returned "in good order and condition as when same were entered upon . . . ordinary wear excepted." The court emphasized that this sort of wear was to be expected, given the nature of the use. Rulings such as this disturb landlords, which seem to equate "ordinary wear" with "minimal wear" and not to the intended use of the premises. Once again, the Colorado landlord's solution was to expand upon the boilerplate surrender language by stating that the "premises must be free of accumulation of wax." Landlords must consider the use being made of their premises in order to fashion an appropriate surrender provision.

The tenant's obligation to remove its alterations, additions, and improvements and to restore the premises to its original condition seems fair and reasonable; however, it can be very expensive and can be used by a landlord to euchre a termination payment out of a tenant.

The surrender provision in **Form 21-1** is no more than the statement of several well-established rules of law that would be operative without any provision at all:

1. A tenant must vacate the premises at the end of the term.

2. The premises must be returned to the landlord in the same condition in which they were delivered to the tenant, normal wear and tear excepted.

3. The tenant is liable for any damage arising from its negligence, waste, or nuisance.[10]

---

[8] *See* Wolff v. Manville Forest Prods. Corp., 486 So. 2d 1085 (La. Ct. App. 1986), involving a floor damaged by the tenant's use of the premises for storing heavy equipment.

[9] Chew v. International Soc'y for Krishna Consciousness, Inc., 738 P.2d 57 (Colo. Ct. App. 1987).

[10] *See* Urban Management Corp. v. Ford Motor Credit Co., 263 So. 2d 404 (La. Ct. App. 1972) (tenant held liable for its shoddy repairs).

4. The tenant must remove its personal property and clean out its debris.

5. The tenant must remove alterations that it made without the landlord's consent, but it may leave alterations that were made with the landlord's consent, unless, of course, the landlord's consent was conditioned upon the removal of those alterations.

6. Unless the tenant is at fault, the tenant is not liable for damage caused by fire or accidental damage.

Even though these legal principles are implicit parts of any lease, most real estate professionals express them because it is easier to point to express provisions than legal theory if the need arises.

A landlord has three remedies against a tenant that has failed to make the repairs necessary in order to surrender the premises in the condition that the lease requires: (1) it may seek specific performance of the tenant's repair obligation; (2) it may sue the tenant for the cost of the repairs; or (3) it may sue the tenant for the loss in the market value of the premises. If a subsequent tenant makes the repairs, the landlord may still sue for their cost as its damages for the tenant's breach of promise regarding redelivery.[11]

Several courts have held a tenant responsible for the cost to repair premises left in disrepair even though the landlord was not actually harmed.[12]

The surrender provision assumes greater importance when it is seen in the context of the repair provision and the casualty damage provision. These three provisions are related. Unless the real estate professional is careful to harmonize these provisions, the lease may have inconsistent obligations in the event of casualty damage to the premises. The repair provision may require the tenant to repair the damage, the casualty damage provision may excuse the tenant if the damage is of sufficient magnitude, and the surrender provision may obligate the tenant to give up the premises in their original condition diminished only by normal wear and tear. For example, most tenants would insist that **Form 21-1** be amended to allow them to surrender the premises "ordinary wear and tear and fire or other casualty excepted." Conceptually, the surrender provision is the culmination of the tenant's repair obligation, diminished by casualty damage and normal wear and tear.

---

[11] Polster, Inc. v. Swing, 164 Cal. App. 3d 427, 210 Cal. Rptr. 567 (1985) (incoming tenant made repairs and landlord re-leased premises at reduced rate). *See* Martinez v. Ball, 721 S.W.2d 580 (Tex. Ct. App. 1986) landlord granted damages for tenant's failure to repair damage to premises). *See generally* Iverson v. Spang Indus., 45 Cal. App. 3d 303, 119 Cal. Rptr. 399 (1975).

[12] Polster, Inc. v. Swing, 164 Cal. App. 3d 427, 210 Cal. Rptr. 567 (1985) (new tenant had agreed to make repairs); Sharlin v. Neighborhood Theatre, Inc., 209 Va. 718, 167 S.E.2d 334 (1969) (same); Farrell Lines, Inc. v. City of New York, 30 N.Y.2d 76, 281 N.E.2d 162, 330 N.Y.S.2d 358 (1958) (landlord intended to demolish premises); Nielson v. Okies, 503 S.W.2d 614 (Tex. Ct. App. 1973) (landlord recovered more than it had spent because court believed it would have further expense in future). *But see* Dalamagas v. Fazzina, 36 Conn. Supp. 523, 414 A.2d 494 (1979) (landlord could not collect damages for condition of premises because it had recovered losses in new lease).

The surrender provision may also have very important income tax consequences. As one court has said:

> In the context of a lease, where the terms of the lease require the lessee to return the leased property to the lessor upon expiration of the agreement in the same condition as at the beginning of the lease, or its equivalent in value, or otherwise fully protect the lessor from economic loss, no deduction for depreciation of the leased property is allowable.[13]

The case involved personal property and equipment, imposed substantial replacement and repair obligations on the tenant, and required the tenant to surrender the premises in "first class" condition. The court also said:

> On the other hand, a lessor may be entitled to depreciation under the terms of a lease requiring the lessee only to make all necessary repairs and replacements and to maintain the property in good condition during the term of the lease, *where it can be demonstrated that the lessor will suffer economic loss during the term of the lease.*[14]

Although the court limited its ruling "to the particular and somewhat unique facts of this case,"[15] its reasoning is generally applicable.

§ 21.3   Fixtures

No discussion of surrender (as the term is used in § 21.2) is complete without a discussion of fixtures. The term *fixtures* invites confusion: it refers both to articles of personal property that become part of real property and to articles of personal property that do not become part of real property. The law of fixtures grew out of the feudal landlord-tenant rule law that personal property that was attached to leased premises became part of the leased premises and thus could not be removed by the tenant at the end of its term. This rule was sensible enough when fixtures were likely to be part of improvements necessary in order to make the premises useful for agricultural purposes.[16] However, it was unacceptable for commerce after the Industrial Revolution. Commercial tenants often affixed personal property to their premises in order to carry on their trades. As a result, English law carved out an exception to the rule of fixtures and allowed the tenant to remove its *trade fixtures* so long as it repaired any damage to the premises.

---

[13] Hibernia Nat'l Bank in New Orleans v. United States, 740 F.2d 382, 387 (5th Cir. 1984).

[14] *Id.* at 387 (emphasis added).

[15] *Id.* at 390.

[16] R. Schoshinski, American Law of Landlord and Tenant § 5:29 (1980) [hereinafter Schoshinski].

On the other hand, the common law rule continued to hold that fixtures other than trade fixtures could not be removed from the premises. As a result, the distinction between fixtures and trade fixtures was very important. American law developed in a more liberal way than English law. A now-famous case decided in the middle of the nineteenth century[17] differed from the English rule that a tenant could not remove fixtures (other than trade fixtures) that were affixed to the premises, and said:

> [T]he united application of the following requisites will be found the safest criterion of a fixture.
> 1st.　Actual annexation to the realty, or something appurtenant thereto.
> 2d.　Appropriation to the use or purpose of that part of the realty with which it is connected.
> 3d.　The intention of the party making the annexation to make the article a permanent accession to the freehold—this intention being inferred from the *nature* of the article affixed, the *relation* and *situation* of the *party* making the annexation, the structure and mode of annexation, and the purpose or use for which the annexation has been made.[18]

Modern American jurisprudence requires a trade fixture:

1. To be affixed to the building or other realty by the tenant
2. To be intended for use in connection with the pursuit of a business, trade or profession
3. Not to become part of the building or other realty under the terms of the lease
4. To be intended to be removed upon vacation of the premises
5. Not to be in substitution for an essential part of the building or other real property
6. To be removable without having its essential characteristics changed or rendered valueless for further use
7. To be removable without substantial injury to the building or other realty.[19]

---

[17] Teaff v. Hewitt, 1 Ohio St. 511 (1853) (cited in Schoshinski § 5:29).

[18] *Id*. at 529-30 (emphasis by the court). The continuing vitality of this rule is illustrated by Brown v. Dubois, 40 Ohio Misc. 2d 18, 532 N.E.2d 223 (1988), finding the carpet was not a removable fixture.

[19] Even, *A Critique of Lease Terms and Their Effect on Insurance Administration*, 7 Forum 130 (1972); Annot., 39 A.L.R. 1044, *What amount to permanent improvements within provision of lease against their removal* (1925); Annot., 53 A.L.R. 697, *Conclusiveness of appraisal of buildings or other improvements under provision of lease for compensation to tenant on termination of lease* (1928); Annot., 110 A.L.R. 480, *Right to remove fixtures or improvements placed upon property by one holding under lease as affected by renewal or new lease made to him or his successor without reservation of the right to remove* (1937); Annot., 92 A.L.R. 1381, *Rights as between surviving spouse and holder of leasehold interest under a lease from deceased spouse in respect of improvements made pursuant to provisions of lease* (1934).

This extensive list has been reduced to three fundamental differences between fixtures and trade fixtures: annexation, adaptability, and intention.[20] The degree of annexation of the fixture to the property—or, conversely, the ease of its removal from the premises—is an important element in determining whether an item of property is a fixture. As to adaptability, an item is more likely to be considered a fixture if it is uniquely adapted to the premises in which it is installed. Both annexation and adaptability may be considered to be merely evidence of the most important determinant of a fixture: intention.[21] The governing intention is usually that of the tenant, because it is presumed that the tenant does not want to enrich its landlord by installing its fixtures only to have them become part of the landlord's property. A gas station tenant's intention to remove its underground storage tanks convinced a New York federal court that they were removable trade fixtures.[22]

The law of fixtures has several quirks. For one thing, if a lease ends and the landlord and tenant enter into a new lease for the same premises, the trade fixtures installed under the old lease are considered to have been abandoned and to have become the landlord's property. This is one point at which the distinction between a renewal (which is a new lease) and an extension (which is the continuation of an existing lease) is crucial. In some jurisdictions, another peculiarity of the law of fixtures allows a tenant to remove its trade fixtures for a reasonable time after the end of the term. However, a tenant that waited two and a half years after the end of its term to remove its trade fixtures lost its right to do so; although the court recognized the possibility that this 390-foot steel-frame tower might have been a trade fixture that could have been removed after the term, the tenant had waited too long to do so.[23]

In order to avoid these traps, a properly written agreement is necessary. Such an agreement will supersede the common law of fixtures. In preparing this agreement, the real estate professional should consider fixtures at the same time as he or she considers alterations, improvements, and additions. The provisions should be uniform with regard to all of them. The landlord will want the tenant's agreement to remove its fixtures, alterations, improvements, and additions at or before the end of the term; this will avoid the tenant's right to remove its fixtures after the end of the term. The tenant will insist upon the right to remove its trade fixtures. Although tenant's right to remove "fixtures" has been construed to mean only "trade fixtures" (to prevent a tenant from removing toilets, sinks, fuse boxes, and lights, which are also commonly called "fixtures"),[24] a well-drawn provision will refer specifically to "trade fixtures." See **Form 21-1**.

---

[20] Garfinkle, *How Objects Become Fixtures*, 1 Prac. Real Est. Law. 19 (1985). *See* R&D Amusement Corp. v. Christianson, 392 N.W.2d 385 (N.D. 1986) (North Dakota's expression of the law of trade fixtures and leases; the decision emphasizes items 2 and 7 of this list).

[21] II M.R. Friedman, Friedman on Leases § 24.5 (1983) [hereinafter Friedman].

[22] Shell Oil Co. v. Capparelli, 648 F. Supp. 1052 (S.D.N.Y. 1986).

[23] Southern Mass. Broadcasters, Inc. v. Duchaine, 26 Mass. App. Ct. 497, 529 N.E.2d 887 (1988), *review denied*, 403 Mass. 1106, 532 N.E.2d 690 (1988).

[24] Green v. Harper, 700 S.W.2d 565 (Tenn. Ct. App. 1985).

When fixtures are an important part of the lease, the landlord and tenant should consider recording a short-form lease or memorandum of the lease in order to give third parties notice of rights that may be inconsistent with appearances. For example, if the tenant has a right to remove its fixtures, the short-form lease or memorandum of lease should say so.[25] Finally, a tenant that intends to install substantial fixtures should express its rights in any estoppel certificate given to a lender or purchaser of the premises.[26]

A fixture between landlord and tenant may not be a fixture between seller and buyer, or between borrower and lender. The same piece of property may be characterized differently in each of these relationships. The Uniform Commercial Code offers some uniformity in the law of fixtures,[27] but only to the extent that it pertains to lenders against the personal property. It does not affect the law of landlord and tenant with regard to fixtures, although it does give the lender some rights that may affect the landlord.[28] As a result, provisions of a lease will govern the interests of landlord and tenant in fixtures installed pursuant to the lease.

The tenant's loss of fixtures that it has the right to remove may be a significant compensable claim if the premises are condemned. A tenant may have this claim even if it has no claim for the unexpired portion of its lease.[29]

---

[25] Schoshinski § 5:32.

[26] Garfinkle, *How Objects Become Fixtures,* 1 Prac. Real Est. Law. 19 (1985).

[27] U.C.C. § 9-313 (1990).

[28] U.C.C. §§ 9-313(4), 9-313(5) (1990). Section 9-313(5) states:

A security interest in fixtures, whether or not perfected, has priority over the conflicting interest of an encumbrancer or owner of the real estate where (a) the encumbrancer or owner has consented in writing to the security interest or has disclaimed an interest in the goods as fixtures; or (b) the debtor has a right to remove the goods as against the encumbrancer or owner. If the debtor's right terminates, the priority of the security interest continues for a reasonable time.

[29] II Friedman § 13.4.

CHAPTER 22

DAMAGE AND DESTRUCTION

§ 22.1   The Law

According to the common law rule, when leased premises were damaged or destroyed, the lease was not affected, and the tenant's obligation to pay rent was not abated. These conclusions followed from the common law view of a lease as a conveyance in which the landlord's obligations ended and the tenant's obligations began at the time of delivery of possession. This same view led to the conclusion that the landlord had no obligation to repair the premises during the term of the lease. The common law rule regarding the consequences of damage to the premises is less relevant today, because it is often overruled by statute and because it is almost always avoided by private agreement in leases.[1]

The statutes mitigating the harsh common law rule usually provide that the damage or destruction of the premises terminates the lease, unless the tenant is at fault. These statutes also allow the landlord and tenant to agree that the common law rule will control their leases and that the statutes will have no effect.

On the rare occasion courts have had to apply a modern common law rule, they have either held to the old rule or fashioned a new rule that fixes the tenant's

---

[1] *See generally* ABA Comm. on Leases, *Fire Insurance and Repair Clauses in Leases*, 5 Real Prop. Prob. & Tr. J. 532 (1970).

liability by the degree to which the premises have been destroyed. Under this new rule, courts have been reluctant to continue the tenant's rent liability for premises that are no longer useful to the tenant.[2] Some courts have ignored the old common law rule and found that the destruction of leased premises frustrated the purpose of the lease and therefore terminated it.[3]

The law of damage and destruction has one important quirk. Prepaid rent is not apportioned. As a result, if the premises are destroyed in the middle of a month for which the tenant has paid its rent, the landlord is entitled to all—not just half—the rent. A contrary lease provision requiring apportionment will be enforced by a court.

Real estate professionals pay far too little attention to damage and destruction provisions. Although the likelihood of damage or destruction may be remote, the consequences are certain and catastrophic. Blasé reliance on insurance is misplaced; although insurance is a palliative, it is not a cure and certainly not a preventative. These provisions must be read, considered, and negotiated.

§ 22.2   Landlord's and Tenant's Concerns

When considering a casualty damage provision, the real estate professional should fully answer four questions:

1. What sort of casualty damage affects the lease?
2. If the lease is affected, what happens to the rent?
3. If the lease is affected, what happens to the premises?
4. If the lease is affected, what happens to the lease?

The real estate professional can easily get lost in a casualty provision that fully answers some of those questions but does not adequately answer them all. For the landlord, the most important issues are satisfaction of the concerns of its present or prospective lenders, discussed in § **22.10**, and, to a lesser extent, the concerns of its insurance consultants. For the tenant, the most important issues are whether it can use the premises and, if so, what they will cost.

The ensuing discussion is organized around questions that a real estate professional should ask and possible answers that the lease, or a recommended addition to the lease, should give. A question asked with regard to one part of the casualty provision may be answered in another part. These are not immutable

---

[2] Annot., 99 A.L.R.3d 738, *Modern status of rules as to tenant's rent liability after injury to or destruction of demised premises* (1980); Annot., 61 A.L.R.2d 1445, *Condition of premises within contemplation of provision of lease or statute for cessation of rent or termination of lease in event of destruction of or damage to property as rebuilt of fire, calamity, the elements, act of God or the like* (1958).

[3] Albert M. Greenfield & Co. v. Kolea, 475 Pa. 351, 380 A.2d 758 (1977).

divisions between the parts; however, a complete casualty provision should completely answer all the questions in one part or another.

§ 22.3   —Is the Lease Affected?

This section discusses the threshold issue presented by casualty damage: is the lease affected?[4] Subsequent sections discuss the possible effects.

For the reasons described in § 22.1, casualty damage need not affect the lease; in practice, however, all commercial leases make provision for the possibility of casualty damage.

The question whether casualty damage affects the lease is answered in one or more of four ways:

(a)   The first way in which casualty provisions are written begins with the extent of the damage. In this answer, casualty damage in a multi-tenant project affects the lease if it affects a stated percentage of the project of which the premises are a part or, usually (but not always), a stated percentage of the premises. If casualty damage to the premises does not affect the lease, the tenant must insist that it does; otherwise, the tenant will have damaged premises and nothing it can do about it. In a single tenant building, the casualty damage is measured by reference to the building.

When considering damage to the project, the tenant must consider first what is meant by the project. For example, in a shopping center, is the project defined as the buildings and the parking area or just one of them? In an office lease, does the project include the parking area and retail space, or just the office areas? The tenant must decide whether there are areas (other than those prescribed in the casualty provision) so important to the tenant's use of its premises that damage to them must affect the lease.

Assume, for example, that a shopping center lease provides that damage to 15 percent of the parking area affects the lease. In fact, the tenant may not care about the parking area on the other side of the shopping center, but it may be vitally concerned about the 10 parking spaces in front of its entrance. The tenant must add those spaces as areas of the shopping center that, if damaged, will affect the lease. As a further example involving a shopping center lease, a tenant may want its lease affected by casualty damage to an anchor tenant's premises, even though no other part of the shopping center is affected.

As an example in the office building, the tenant must be assured of uninterrupted elevator access to the premises, regardless of the extent of the damage to the project. If the tenant and its visitors cannot reach the premises, what use are they? Thus, a casualty provision with no reference to impaired access to the premises is insufficient for the tenant.

---

[4] *See* Breslow, *Negotiating the Casualty Loss Clause of a Commercial Lease,* J. Real Est. Dev., Summer 1988, at 84.

(b)   Another style in which casualty provisions are written states that a casualty affects the lease if the cost to repair it exceeds a stated amount or a stated percentage of the value of the project. The tenant must ask many of the same questions it does with respect to casualty damage that affects a portion of the project or premises. To a tenant, the cost to repair casualty damage—and the value of the damaged part of the project—are relevant only as indications of the disruptions of its business; typically, as the magnitude of the damage increases, so does the magnitude of the disruption.

However, it is quite possible that substantial damage to a distant part of a project—on the other side of a mall—has no effect on a tenant. On the other hand, the destruction of neighboring premises in a shopping center—although a small part of the center's value—may shut down an otherwise unaffected tenant during the repair period.

Again, the tenant returns to its fundamental concern: how are its premises affected? Knowing that it cannot change the landlord's form lease with respect to the effect on other tenants, the tenant demands that casualty damage affect its lease if it affects the usefulness of its premises, regardless of the value or extent of the casualty.

(c)   A third casualty provision is tied to the time needed to repair the casualty; if it can be repaired within a stated period, then there is no effect on the lease. This sort of provision is practically and analytically similar to a provision based on the extent of the casualty. The tenant must relate the casualty and the time to repair it to the effect on the tenant's use of its premises.

In this approach to casualty damage, the tenant must be wary of the way in which the time needed to repair the damage is measured. If the provision says something like "the lease will terminate if the damage cannot be repaired within 90 days," two questions beg for answers. First, does the 90-day period begin from the date of the damage or the date on which repair is begun? If it is the latter, there is no limit to the duration of the disrepair. Second, is the 90-day period subject to extensions for force majeure? If it is, repair can last indefinitely.

A New Hampshire case illustrates the problems with a reconstruction provision based on the time needed to build. After a fire in a restaurant, the landlord terminated the lease based on a provision that allowed termination if the repairs could not be accomplished within 90 days after they were begun; however, the lease required the landlord to rebuild if the work could be "substantially completed" within the 90-day period. After the landlord built an office building on the site, the tenant sued. The tenant's construction experts testified they could "substantially" rebuild the restaurant within 90 days after they started; significantly, the 90-day period did not include time to clean up the rubble of the old restaurant. The tenant won.[5]

When a lease gives the landlord a cancellation right when casualty damage is so extensive that it cannot be repaired within 120 days, the landlord cannot cancel the lease if it has decided to rebuild before the cancellation right is exercised. In

---

[5] Restaurant Operators, Inc. v. Jenney, 128 N.H. 708, 519 A.2d 256 (1986).

other words, the landlord must act in good faith and not use its cancellation right as a ruse to end an unfavorable lease.[6]

(d)   A final approach to casualty damage is to tie its effect on the lease to the insurance available for repair. A lease may provide that rent is abated if the premises are damaged by an *insured risk*, or if the premises are damaged by an *insurable risk*. First of all, insurable risks is an ambiguous term. Does it include standard fire policy risks, or extended fire policy risks, or "all-risk" policy risks, or risks (such as flood in some cases) that are insured under special programs? One expert has observed: "Primarily all losses or risks may be insured against unless contrary to public policy, such as a loss caused by the insured's willful misconduct, or unless prohibited as illegal by decisional or statute law or by administrative regulation."[7] In contrast to insurable risks, which contemplate what may have been available, insured risks are limited to those risks for which insurance is actually in effect; if there is no insurance in effect, there are no insured risks. Provisions using the terms insurable risks or insured risks raise the possibility that a loss may occur from a risk that is neither insured nor insurable. The casualty damage provision rarely states what happens if one of these losses occurs. If the landlord's repair obligation is tied to the collection of sufficient insurance proceeds, the tenant must await the results of an insurance claim process that could take years, if contested. Since casualty insurance policies always have a deductible, it is necessary for the tenant to insist that insurance proceeds are sufficient if, when added to the deductible, they cover the cost of repair.

Tenants wonder why their premises should not be rebuilt just because the landlord failed to obtain insurance (perhaps in breach of the lease), or failed to have adequate coverages or amounts (over which the landlord has complete control). Often, insurance proceeds are insufficient because the landlord's mortgage lender asserts its right to take the proceeds and discharge the mortgage loan to the extent of the proceeds. In order for the tenant to assure itself that the mortgage lender will use the proceeds to restore the premises and the development, the tenant must either have an agreement with the lender that insurance proceeds will be used to repair the premises or the lease must be prior to the mortgage. An agreement between landlord and tenant will not suffice, because it will not bind existing and future mortgage lenders with priority over the lease.

The sufficiency of insurance proceeds depends on what degree of repair is necessary. Most frequently, the landlord is required to restore a multitenant development to its condition prior to the casualty. Put differently, the landlord must redo its original work. However, the original work included only building standard for the office tenant, and a shopping center tenant's shell. Who is to rebuild the over-standard work and who will supply the allowance?

---

[6] Adams Drug Co. v. Knobel, 64 N.Y.2d 768, 475 N.E.2d 450, 485 N.Y.S.2d 983, *reargument dismissed,* 64 N.Y.2d 1041, 478 N.E.2d 211, 489 N.Y.S.2d 1028 (1985), *appeal after remand,* 129 A.D.2d 401, 513 N.Y.S.2d 674 (1987).

[7] G. Couch, Cyclopedia of Insurance Law § 39:2 (R.A. Anderson 2d ed., M.S. Rhodes rev. vol. 1983).

When negotiating these provisions the real estate professional must remember that it cannot successfully change the casualty provision in the form lease used by the landlord with existing tenants and to be used with other tenants. For a simple example, suppose the form lease says, "This lease will terminate if 20 percent of the parking area is damaged." The tenant cannot reasonably expect its landlord to reduce that percentage to 10 for one tenant if it has not done so for other tenants. If it did, the landlord would be bound to repair the premises for one tenant when the other tenants' leases were terminated. Thus, the tenant's task is to identify casualty damage that does not affect the lease proposed by the landlord and to negotiate an amendment by which that casualty damage does affect the tenant's own lease.

§ 22.4   — Is the Rent Affected?

Once it is determined that the lease is affected by the casualty, the real estate professional must determine what parts of the lease are affected. Invariably, rent is one of them. With regard to the rent, the landlord and tenant must first decide what they mean by rent. Is it only the base monthly rent? Or, in the shopping center lease, is it the base monthly rent, percentage rent, common area maintenance charges, real estate taxes, insurance, and merchants' association dues? In the office building lease, does the rent include operating expenses and real estate taxes (if separately charged)? Generally, operating expenses are not abated, because lenders reject leases that allow it, and also because there is no reason for the tenant not to pay for the costs (perhaps reduced by the casualty) of operating the project.

Although casualty damage usually leads to a rent abatement, there is no compelling reason that it should. The tenant's obligations for rent (and whatever other charges would be subject to abatement) are risks that the landlord or tenant can insure. If the tenant must pay the rent without abatement, the tenant has an insurable interest for which business interruption insurance may be appropriate; the landlord would be the loss payee. If, on the other hand, the rent is abated, the landlord has an insurable interest in the rent stream. Once again, rent insurance is best carried by the insured under the fire policy; the cost is likely to be less and the settlement to be faster. Whether by abatement or rent insurance, however, tenants should avoid a rent expense when they have no revenue from which to pay it.

If the rent is abated, when does the abatement begin and when does it end? Often a lease will provide that the abatement begins on a day other than that on which the casualty occurred, for example, the date on which landlord learns of the casualty, or the date on which it decides whether to rebuild the premises. The tenant is favored by a provision that abates rent from the date of the casualty. Most rent abatements continue until the premises are substantially repaired or until the landlord redelivers possession; in any event the abatement cannot end before a certificate of occupancy is issued for the premises and possession is delivered to the tenant. Once again, the tenant prefers a rent abatement that ends when its premises are useful, which means that the tenant improvements must be completed. If the tenant is responsible for their completion, the abatement must continue for a period after the landlord finishes its basic work.

A retail tenant ought to insist upon an abatement that recognizes the reality of its business. For example, an abatement that begins in August and ends two weeks before Christmas is not useful to a tenant that has lost its Christmas season and must resume its business in the slack months of the new year. That tenant should have insisted upon an abatement through June of the new year.

Finally, once the landlord has decided the standard that will govern whether an abatement occurs, the landlord must decide the basis on which the rent will be abated. Rent is usually abated on the basis of either the share of the premises that are rendered untenantable (for example, a 25 percent abatement if 25 percent of the premises are destroyed), or the degree to which the value of the premises to the tenant is reduced. To a tenant, this latter method is favorable. Consider an office tenant who cannot reach its premises because the elevator lobby or elevators are impassable; although its premises are intact, the value of the premises to the tenant is nil. Or consider an ice-cream parlor whose walk-in freezer is destroyed; although the serving area and most of the storage area remains, the tenant cannot run its business.[8]

§ 22.5 —How Are the Premises Affected?

To answer the next question—what will happen to the premises?—the landlord and tenant must determine whether the premises will be rebuilt. It is quite unusual for the landlord to be required to rebuild the tenant's premises to their condition before the casualty. Rather, landlords usually agree to rebuild shopping center premises to the condition in which they were delivered to the tenant, that is, a shell, or to rebuild office premises to building standard. In other words, tenants are responsible for redoing their tenant improvements without a tenant finish allowance.

In one case, when the lease obligated the landlord to rebuild the premises after a fire, the landlord did so but did not rebuild the improvements made by the tenant. The tenant refused to accept the rebuilt premises. The Ohio Supreme Court ruled that a trial was necessary to determine who was responsible for reconstruction of a tenant's improvements.[9] The lesson of this case is that the lease must state clearly whether it is the improvements made by the landlord or the tenant, or both, that the landlord or tenant, as the case may be, is obligated to rebuild.

One can see that a tenant whose premises have been destroyed is in the same position as it was before a lease began. Accordingly, all the questions that it asked at the outset of the lease must be asked and answered again. In practice, however,

---

[8] Pollack, *Clauses in a Shopping Center Lease*, 20 Prac. Law. 63, 76 (1974).

[9] Toledo's Great Eastern Shoppers City, Inc. v. Abde's Black Angus Steak House No. III, Inc., 24 Ohio St. 3d 198, 494 N.E.2d 1101 (1986).

landlords agree to no more than allowing their tenants to rebuild their tenant improvements in a rent-free period after the landlord has done its required work.

Tenants ought to insist that their landlords promptly commence reconstruction and diligently pursue it to completion. Tenants should also ask for a right to cancel if the work is not completed within a stated period after the casualty. Landlords resist this suggestion because they may be delayed for reasons beyond their control and miss a critical deadline. Usually a compromise can be reached by which the completion date is extended for force majeure and the time to settle the insurance proceeds.

§ 22.6 — How Is the Lease Affected?

Finally, with respect to their concern about the effect casualty damage will have on their lease, the landlord and tenant should realize that, as § **22.1** has shown, there is usually no rule that casualty damage must have any effect on the lease. Their agreement will control the effect, and it may be a simple affirmation that the lease will continue as though no casualty had occurred. In that case, the landlord and tenant would agree upon the responsibility for repair and each would insure its liabilities and its losses. That sort of agreement is made in single tenant leases as illustrated in § **22.9**. In multitenant developments, the repair by each tenant of its premises is not feasible. As a result, in leases of those developments, landlords and tenants negotiate for termination rights based upon the same criteria involved in the decision of whether rent will abate and whether the landlord will repair the development: the degree of the damage. Tenants are almost always able to win an agreement that their leases will terminate if their premises are, or the development is, substantially destroyed. If the lease is to be terminated on account of substantial destruction, the tenant must be certain that the lease apportions prepaid rent to the date of termination.

The consequences of less catastrophic casualty are negotiable. Tenants often ask for the right to terminate their leases if almost any casualty occurs. In large part, those tenants act in good faith, because they want to be able to resume their businesses as soon as possible. However, some of them do not act in such good faith; they consider their right to terminate an opportunity to reevaluate their leases and, perhaps, under the threat of termination, to compel a renegotiation. One way to manage the effect of casualty on a lease is to give the landlord greater cancellation rights as the commitment of the tenant (in financial strength and lease term) diminishes.

Landlords, on the other hand, want to be able to evaluate the feasibility of repair, and should resist the tenant's suggestion that it have the right to terminate if minor casualty damage occurs. Realistically, most tenants cannot find new premises and improve them before most repairs are done; tenants that move also lose the goodwill associated with their premises. As a last resort for a strong tenant that wants the right to terminate if a minor casualty occurs, the landlord can respond that it should have the same right. This puts the tenant at the same risk of a disingenuous decision by its landlord, but the provision may be of little practical value if the landlord's lender objects.

Tenants—especially retail tenants—are often required to operate in the balance of the premises during the repair period. Reduced operations may not be feasible or economical. Tenants should ask for the right to be the good faith arbiter of their operations.

Many leases provide that the lease may be terminated by either the landlord or the tenant if there are only a few years remaining in the term. Some tenants ask for the right to exercise their renewal options if a casualty occurs in order to prevent termination of the lease. Although the suggestion sounds reasonable, landlords should be careful not to obligate themselves to rebuild an entire development because one tenant has extended its lease; if it must concede the point, a landlord should condition its obligations on tenants occupying a specified number of square feet remaining obligated for a specified minimum period of time.

The real estate professional cannot consider casualty damage provisions without considering insurance provisions. For the most part, casualty damage provisions deal with risks for which insurance is available. As a result, the landlord and tenant should not fail to reach an agreement because of casualty damage provisions for which adequate insurance is available. However, mere availability is not enough. For example, a tenant may be able to insure some of the profits it will lose as a result of a fire, but it usually cannot insure all its profits for the balance of the term, nor can it insure the intangible losses that it will sustain from losing its visibility and its advertising. Consequently, the casualty damage provisions must be used in concert with insurance provisions.

Regardless of the form of the casualty damage provision, the landlord must be certain that the tenant waives any statutory rights that it may have to cancel the lease if the premises are damaged or destroyed.

§ 22.7   Damage and Destruction in Office Building Premises

A typical provision for damage or destruction to the office building premises states:

FORM 22-1
DAMAGE AND DESTRUCTION—OFFICE BUILDING

(a)   If the premises or the building are damaged by fire or other insured casualty, landlord will give tenant written notice of the time that landlord has determined in its reasonable discretion will be needed to repair the damage, and the election (if any) that landlord has made according to this section. The notice will be given before the thirtieth (30th) day (the "notice date") after the fire or other insured casualty.

(b)   If the premises or the building are damaged by fire or other insured casualty to an extent landlord has determined in its reasonable discretion can be repaired within one hundred twenty (120) days after the notice date, landlord will promptly begin to repair the damage after the notice date and will diligently pursue the completion of such repair. In that event this lease will continue in full force and effect except that monthly rent will be abated on a pro rata basis from the date of the damage until the date of the completion of such repairs (the "repair period") based on the proportion of the rentable area of the premises that tenant is unable to use during the repair period.

(c)   If the premises or the building are damaged by fire or other insured casualty to an extent landlord has determined in its reasonable discretion can not be repaired within one hundred twenty (120) days after the notice date, then (1) landlord may cancel this lease as of the date of the damage by written notice given to tenant on or before the notice date or (2) tenant may cancel this lease as of the date of the damage by written notice given to landlord within 10 days after landlord's delivery of a written notice that the repairs cannot be made within one hundred twenty (120) days. If neither landlord nor tenant so elects to cancel this lease, landlord will diligently proceed to repair the building and premises and monthly rent will be abated on a pro rata basis during the repair period based on the proportion of the rentable area of the premises that tenant is unable to use during the repair period.

(d)   If the premises or the building are damaged by uninsured casualty, or if the proceeds of insurance are insufficient to pay for the repair of any damage to the premises or the building, landlord will have the option either to elect to repair the damage or to cancel this lease as of the date of the casualty by written notice to tenant on or before the notice date.

(e)   If any damage by fire or other casualty is the result of the willful conduct or negligence or failure to act of tenant, its agents, contractors, employees or invitees, monthly rent will not be abated. Tenant will have no right to terminate this lease on account of any damage to the premises, the building, or the project, except as set forth in this lease.

For both the landlord and the tenant, this provision provides certainty. If certain conditions are met—such as the landlord's statement that the rebuilding may be completed within one hundred twenty (120) days—then the lease continues. However, a price is exacted for this certainty. There is no impartial arbiter of the time required for rebuilding. Often, tenants ask for an architect's certificate about the time required for rebuilding. Still, the tenant runs the risk of collusion between the landlord and its architect. Some tenants protect themselves by demanding that their leases may not be terminated unless the leases of similarly affected tenants are also terminated. This will prevent the landlord from picking and choosing between desirable and undesirable leases.

The landlord protects itself in this provision because it requires the tenant to rebuild the nonstandard tenant improvements that the tenant installed at the outset of the lease. Thus, in the lease, the landlord will require the tenant to maintain insurance on the tenant's improvements so that the tenant will have funds available with which to do its reconstruction work. The tenant will ask that prepaid rent be abated after the date of damage or destruction, in addition to the abatement of rent due after the date. Once again, because the lease was considered a conveyance, the landlord was entitled to the full amount of the rent at the outset of the lease, and there was no common law rule of rent abatement on account of the damage or destruction of the premises.

This provision is unfair to the tenant insofar as rent abates from the notice date and not from the date of the casualty damage. Often these provisions state that rent will abate to the extent that the premises are rendered untenantable or unusable by the tenant. Those provisions are unfair to a tenant because they do not consider the common areas on the tenant's floor or elsewhere in the building (such as lobbies) whose use is part of the value of the premises.

The real estate professional must be realistic when it looks at damage and destruction provisions in office leases. Fire damage in these buildings is either minimal or catastrophic. As a result, office leases will not usually condition repair on a percentage of the building damaged (for example, "less than fifty percent of the area of the building being destroyed"), because it is unlikely that only 40 percent will be damaged. The damage would be so great that the entire building would have to be renovated or demolished, even if some tenants were not disturbed at all. The tenant's principal concern is its ability to terminate the lease as soon as possible after damage or destruction so that it may find replacement premises.

If the tenant has been given an abatement of rent as an inducement to enter into the lease, it should be sure that the casualty provision extends its rent abatement for the period of any repair. Otherwise, it will have lost its inducement by virtue of the casualty provision.

§ 22.8   Damage and Destruction in Shopping Center Premises

A provision for damage and destruction in a shopping center lease might say:

FORM 22-2
DAMAGE AND DESTRUCTION—SHOPPING CENTER

(a)   If the premises or the portion of the shopping center necessary for tenant's occupancy is damaged or destroyed during the term of this lease by any casualty insurable under standard fire and extended coverage insurance policies, landlord will repair or rebuild the premises to substantially the condition in which the premises were immediately prior to such destruction.

(b)   Landlord's obligation under this paragraph will not exceed the lesser of (1) with respect to the premises, the scope of building standard improvements installed by landlord in the original construction of the premises or (2) the extent of proceeds received by landlord of any insurance policy maintained by landlord.

(c)   The minimum rent will be abated proportionately during any period in which, by reason of any damage or destruction not occasioned by the negligence or willful misconduct of tenant or tenant's employees or invitees, there is a substantial interference with the operation of the business of tenant. The abatement will be proportional to the area of the premises that tenant may be required to discontinue for the conduct of its business. The abatement will continue for the period commencing with the destruction or damage and ending with the completion by the landlord of the work, repair, or reconstruction that landlord is obligated to do.

(d)   If the premises, or the portion of the shopping center necessary for tenant's occupancy, is damaged or destroyed (1) to the extent of 10% or more of the then-replacement value of either, (2) in the last three (3) years of the term of this lease, (3) by a cause or casualty other than those covered by fire and extended coverage insurance, or (4) to the extent that it would take, in landlord's opinion, in excess of ninety (90) days to complete the requisite repairs, then landlord may either terminate this lease or elect to repair or restore the damage or destruction. If this lease is not terminated pursuant to the preceding sentence, this lease will remain in full force and effect. Landlord and tenant waive the provisions of any law that would dictate automatic termination or grant either of them an option to terminate in the event of damage or destruction. Landlord's election to terminate under this paragraph will be exercised by written notice to tenant given within sixty (60) days after the damage or destruction. The notice will set forth the effective date of the termination of this lease.

(e)   Upon the completion of any of the work, repair or restoration by landlord, tenant will repair and restore all other parts of the premises, including without limitation nonbuilding standard leasehold improvements and all trade fixtures, equipment, furnishings, signs, and other improvements originally installed by tenant. Tenant's work will be subject to the requirements of paragraph [alterations paragraph].

(f)   During any period of reconstruction or repair of the premises, tenant will continue the operation of its business in the premises to the extent reasonably practicable.

Insofar as the shopping center tenant is concerned about damage to its own premises, its concerns are akin to the concerns of the office building tenant. However, those concerns are only a small part of the shopping center tenant's concerns.[10]

Because the shopping center is an integrated development, in which the tenants are mutually dependent upon one another, the effect of damage or destruction on other tenants in the shopping center is almost as important to the shopping center tenant as damage or destruction of its own premises. If an anchor tenant will be out of business for a year during reconstruction, the small tenant's sales volumes will fall. Moreover, if an anchor tenant terminates its lease as a result of casualty damage, the small tenant may never recover.

Another concern of the shopping center tenant is the reconstruction of other parts of the shopping center that attracted customers. These would certainly include parking areas.

The shopping center tenant is also concerned about the time when it must reopen. Almost no retail tenants would initially reopen their doors in June or July,

---

[10] E. Halper, Shopping Center and Store Leases ch. 15 (1984), contains a helpful discussion of how restoration is accomplished after casualty damage or condemnation. Halper, *Insurance, Destruction Clauses Revisited*, N.Y.L.J., Mar. 28, 1984, at 1, col. 1, has a detailed discussion of the entire casualty provision.

or in December. Sales drop off during those summer months, and the tenant who opens in December is unable to carry on effective Christmas business. The shopping center tenant who must reopen in off-season months may want to consider an agreement that it will only pay a percentage of sales until it has had an opportunity to restock and advertise in accordance with its usual practices. A retail tenant that negotiates a rent abatement should have a proportional reduction of its breakpoint, and its common area maintenance charges. What the shopping center tenant really wants is an agreement by the landlord that its rebuilt premises will not be considered ready for the tenant's occupancy unless the conditions of the tenant's initial occupancy are met.[11]

§ 22.9   Damage and Destruction in Single Tenant Premises

In keeping with the spirit of shifting to the single tenant almost all the rights and incidents of ownership, the risk of damage or destruction to the premises falls squarely on the single tenant:

FORM 22-3
DAMAGE AND DESTRUCTION—SINGLE TENANT BUILDING

(a)   *General*. If the premises are damaged or destroyed by reason of fire or any other cause, tenant will immediately notify landlord. If the building is damaged or destroyed by fire or any other cause, tenant will promptly repair or rebuild the building at tenant's expense, so as to make the building at least equal in value to the building existing immediately prior to the occurrence and as similar to it in character as is practicable and reasonable. Landlord will apply and make available to pay to tenant the net proceeds of any fire or other casualty insurance paid to landlord, after deduction of any costs of collection, including attorneys' fees, for repairing or rebuilding as the same progresses. Payments will be made against properly certified vouchers of a competent architect in charge of the work and approved by landlord. Landlord will contribute out of the insurance proceeds towards each payment to be made by or on behalf of tenant, for the repairing or rebuilding of the building, under a schedule of payments to be made by tenant and not unreasonably objected to by landlord, an amount in such proportion to the payment by tenant as the total net amount received by landlord from insurers bears to the total estimated cost of the rebuilding or repairing. Landlord, however, may withhold from each amount so to be paid by landlord 15% of the amount until the work of repairing or rebuilding is completed and proof has been furnished to landlord that no lien or liability has attached or will attach to the premises or to landlord in connection with the repairing or rebuilding. Upon the completion of rebuilding and the furnishing of the proof, the balance of the net proceeds of the insurance will be paid to tenant. If the proceeds of insurance are paid to the holder

---

[11] See § **5.9**.

of any mortgage on landlord's interest in the premises, landlord will make available net proceeds of the insurance in accordance with the provisions of this paragraph. Before beginning the repairs or rebuilding, or letting any contracts in connection with the repairs or rebuilding, tenant will submit for landlord's approval, which landlord will not unreasonably withhold or delay, complete and detailed plans and specifications for the repairs or rebuilding. Promptly after receiving landlord's approval of those plans and specifications, tenant will begin the repairs or rebuilding and will prosecute the repairs and rebuilding to completion with diligence, subject, however, to strikes, lockouts, acts of God, embargoes, governmental restrictions, and other causes beyond tenant's reasonable control. Tenant will obtain and deliver to landlord a temporary or final certificate of occupancy before the premises are reoccupied for any purpose. The repairs or rebuilding will be completed free and clear of mechanics' or other liens, and in accordance with the building codes and all applicable laws, ordinances, regulations, or orders of any state, municipal, or other public authority affecting the repairs or rebuilding, and also in accordance with all requirements of the insurance rating organization, or similar body, and of any liability insurance company, insuring landlord against liability for accidents related to the premises. Any remaining proceeds of insurance after the restoration will be tenant's property.

(b)   *Landlord's Inspection.* During the progress of the repairs or rebuilding, landlord and its architects and engineers may, from time to time, inspect the building and will be furnished, if required by them, with copies of all plans, shop drawings, and specifications relating to the repairs or rebuilding. Tenant will keep all plans, shop drawings, and specifications at the building, and landlord and its architects and engineers may examine them at all reasonable times. If, during the repairs or rebuilding, landlord and its architects and engineers determine that the repairs or rebuilding are not being done in accordance with the approved plans and specifications, landlord will give prompt notice in writing to tenant, specifying in detail the particular deficiency, omission, or other respect in which landlord claims the repairs or rebuilding do not accord with the approved plans and specifications. Upon the receipt of that notice, tenant will cause corrections to be made to any deficiencies, omissions, or other respect. Tenant's obligations to supply insurance, according to paragraph [insurance paragraph] will be applicable to any repairs or building under this paragraph.

(c)   *Landlord's Costs.* The charges of any architect or engineer employed by landlord to pass upon any plans and specifications and to supervise and approve any construction, or for any services rendered by the architect or engineer to landlord as contemplated by any of the provisions of this lease, will be paid by tenant as a cost of the repair or rebuilding. The fees of the architect or engineer will be those that are customarily paid for comparable services.

(d)   *No Rent Abatement.* Monthly rent and additional rent will not abate pending the repairs or rebuilding except to the extent to which landlord receives a net sum as proceeds of any rent insurance.

(e)   *Damage During Last Three Years.* If at any time during the last three years of the term, as extended according to paragraph [term paragraph], the building is so damaged by fire or otherwise that the cost of restoration exceeds fifty percent (50%) of the replacement value of the building (exclusive of foundations) immediately prior to the damage, either landlord or tenant may, within thirty (30) days after the damage, give notice of its election to terminate this lease and, subject to the further provisions of this paragraph, this lease will cease on the tenth (10th) day after the delivery of the notice. Monthly rent will be apportioned and paid to the time of termination. If this lease is so terminated, tenant will have no obligation to repair or rebuild, and the entire insurance proceeds will belong to landlord.

The single tenant will usually want to be excused from its obligations to rebuild toward the end of its term. Landlords should not object to such a provision as long as they receive adequate fire insurance proceeds. Some landlords ask for the rent or a portion of the rent that would be lost in the last few years.

§ 22.10 Lenders' Concerns about Damage and Destruction

Although many commentators have observed that lenders' concerns about casualty damage and condemnation are very similar, one fundamental difference between casualty damage and condemnation makes the lease provision with regard to casualty damage more complicated. The difference is that the premises can usually be restored after destruction, but they cannot be restored after condemnation. Therefore, the real estate professional must consider the circumstances in which the premises will be restored after casualty damage.

Generally, mortgages provide that the lender may have the insurance proceeds after damage to the premises. This provision is sensible enough in view of the fact that the lender's collateral has been converted into cash. Thus, the landlord must negotiate more liberal mortgage provisions regarding casualty damage if it wishes to have any latitude at all with its tenants' leases. Stated differently, the landlord must be careful not to make promises to its tenants if its mortgage makes it impossible to fulfill those promises.

Before specifically discussing the two broad categories of casualty damage provisions, several more of the lender's concerns should be acknowledged. Lenders do not object to an abatement of rent during the period from the casualty to the completion of repair, because they can require landlords to carry rent insurance that will continue their income stream without interruption. Generally, lenders seem to feel that tenants should not have any right to terminate their leases unless the premises will be untenantable for at least six months. The lender's best case is one that gives the landlord the sole right to cancel, but that, if it does not elect to cancel, requires it to restore the premises with reasonable diligence, subject to delays occasioned by adjustment of the insurance claims and force majeure. The real estate professional can easily imagine why tenants have such difficulties with this position: they have no idea how long they will be out of business in the premises.

The first large category of destruction provisions is that in which the landlord is obligated to repair the premises. Lenders prefer the provisions in which the landlord can repair the premises only if the mortgage is not in default and the leases of the affected premises are not in default. They also prefer provisions in which the landlord is obligated to rebuild only to the extent of the insurance proceeds, and only if the repair can be effected in a stated period or, alternatively, only if the cost to repair the casualty damage is less than a stated percentage of the value of the project. Lenders will not allow the proceeds to be used for reconstruction if the tenants have cancellation rights that may result in a new — but empty — building. Tenants object to this provision unless the provisions for the landlord's insurance are clearly stated. Finally, lenders like their borrowers to have the right to cancel their leases if the remaining balance of the term is short.

When the tenant is obligated to restore the premises, lenders like to be certain that the tenant will do so only if the insurance proceeds and any necessary shortfall in those proceeds are available to the tenant. The tenant's option to cancel the lease is acceptable if more than half of the premises is destroyed and there is a short remaining term of the lease. Furthermore, lenders occasionally will want insurance trustees (banks, savings and loans, title insurance companies, or themselves) to hold the funds that will be used for the tenant's restoration and to disburse them according to the usual standards of construction loans (for example, upon assurance that there are no mechanics' liens and that there is always a sufficient balance in the construction fund to complete the restoration). Finally, lenders like the tenant to be obligated to restore the premises to substantially the same condition in which they were prior to the casualty.

It is of utmost importance that the landlord's repair obligations be identical in all the leases in a multitenant development. Inconsistent provisions may lead to absurd results. For example, if one lease provides that the landlord must restore the premises if they may be repaired within 90 days, and another lease requires that they must be restored if they may be repaired within 180 days, then the landlord may be compelled to restore one tenant's premises but not another's. Since different premises can be destroyed to different degrees, most leases provide a second standard for a landlord's repair obligation: namely, that if a stated part of the development is rendered untenantable, the landlord need not restore any tenant's premises.

The real estate professional can hardly overstate the case for adequate insurance: it is the lender's last — and perhaps only — resort. If insurance proceeds are insufficient, a borrower with a nonrecourse loan may walk away from the project. Even a well-intentioned borrower that cannot make up the shortfall may be compelled to default. In those events, the only ones left to rebuild are the tenant and the lender. Since they usually have no agreement about the matter, their agreement will be reached by a negotiation in which their respective commitments to the premises (the lender's usually being greater) and their respective prospects from the premises (the tenant's usually being greater) will drive them.

CHAPTER 23

CONDEMNATION

§ 23.1   Condemnation and Eminent Domain

In the sense in which it is used in leases, the term *condemnation* refers to a taking of private property for public use, and is derived from the old legal term for a sentence of forfeiture. In leases, the term does not include its common usage, that is, a public authority's expression of disapproval of the condition of a building.

The term *eminent domain* is often used instead of condemnation. Eminent domain denotes the sovereign's inherent preeminent dominion over private property for public purposes. Strictly speaking, it is proper to say that condemnation occurs as the result of the exercise of the right of eminent domain.

When analyzed, condemnation appears to be composed of four elements, (1) a taking (2) of property (3) for a public purpose (4) upon payment of just compensation (as required by the Fifth Amendment of the United States Constitution). In discussing leases, all those matters are taken for granted, and only two issues remain: the effect of the condemnation on the lease and the allocation of the compensation between landlord and tenant.[1] In the usual case, since the landlord has lost its reversion and the tenant has lost its leasehold, each of them has a compensable property right. If the lease terminates by its terms upon condemnation, then the tenant has no compensable interest. On the other hand, a tenant with an option to purchase may be entitled to the award in excess of the purchase price.[2]

This chapter first explains the law of the several sorts of condemnation, and then applies these legal principles to office building, shopping center, and single tenant premises. The real estate professional should bear in mind that condemnation is governed by applicable federal and state law.[3]

§ 23.2   Total Taking

The *Restatement* § 8.1(1) succinctly states: "If there is a taking by eminent domain of all of the leased property for all of the lease term, the lease is terminated." The rule is entirely sensible, because the subject matter of the lease has vanished and there is no landlord or tenant. This rule is in keeping with the common law rule.[4]

However, the termination of the lease is not the end of the story; the compensation, or award, must be divided between landlord and tenant.[5]

The landlord's loss is composed of:

1.   The loss of the reversion

2.   The loss of the income stream during the term of the lease

3.   The loss of any improvements that would have been the landlord's at the end of the lease.

---

[1] *See Condemnation of Leasehold Interests,* 3 Real Prop. Prob. & Tr. J. 226 (1968). P. Rohan & M. Reskin, Condemnation, Procedures & Techniques—Forms ch. 11 (1968), has many helpful forms. Goldberg, Merrill, and Unumb, *Bargaining in the Shadow of Eminent Domain: Valuing and Apportioning Condemnation Awards between Landlord and Tenant,* 34 U.C.L.A. L. Rev. 1083 (1987), contains a normative analysis of the questions of valuation, allocation, and litigation versus negotiation in the condemnation process.

[2] San Diego v. Miller, 13 Cal. 3d 684, 532 P.2d 139, 119 Cal. Rptr. 491 (1975).

[3] P. Rohan, 7 Current Leasing Law & Techniques § 10.01(2) (1984), sets forth the various federal and state laws.

[4] Elliott v. Joseph, 163 Tex. 71, 351 S.W.2d 879 (1961); Annot., 43 A.L.R. 1176, *Condemnation of premises or part thereof as affecting rights of landlord and tenant inter se* (1926); Annot., 3 A.L.R.2d 286, 328, *Elements and measure of lessee's compensation for taking or damaging leasehold in eminent domain* (1949).

[5] 2 R. Powell, The Law of Real Property § 247(2)(a) (P.J. Rohan ed., rev. 1977).

The tenant's loss is composed of:

1. The amount (that is, the present economic value of the future payments) by which the fair market rental value of the premises exceeds the rent that the lease obligates the tenant to pay
2. The loss of its improvements and fixtures.[6]

As a general rule, neither the landlord nor the tenant is entitled to compensation for loss of profits, goodwill,[7] income from a business conducted on the premises, or costs of removal. The reason that these losses are not recoverable is variously stated: that the real property and not the business is being taken, that the business is severable from the property, that goodwill is not property, or that the damages are too speculative.

If condemnation awards were always sufficient to pay the entire losses of both the landlord and the tenant, there would be almost no reason for condemnation provisions. There are, however, very few states that give condemnation awards on the aggregate of the interests in the condemned property, because the aggregate can far exceed the value of the unencumbered fee. The prevailing rule is the *unit rule* as opposed to the *aggregate of the interests rule*. Under the unit rule, the condemned property is evaluated as a unit with due consideration of all factors affecting its value.[8]

Applying the unit rule in condemnation proceedings of property subject to a lease, the market value of the entire property is determined without regard to the component interests. The standard is the usual one: what would a willing buyer be willing to pay for the property if he or she were under no compulsion to buy, and what would a willing seller be willing to accept for the property if he or she were under no compulsion to sell? Then the leasehold is evaluated. Its value is the amount by which the worth of the use and occupancy of the premises according to the lease (including renewal rights) exceeds its fair market rental value. The fair market rental value is the willing landlord-willing tenant standard. The owner's reversion is equal to the market value of the entire property less the value of the leasehold.[9] One can readily see that problems arise when a valuable leasehold leaves little or nothing for the owner.

Stealthy landlords' leases often provide that they terminate automatically upon condemnation of part or all of the premises. The effect of this agreement is to

---

[6] Annot., 17 A.L.R.4th 337, *Eminent domain; measure and elements of lessee's compensation for condemnor's taking or damaging of leasehold* (1982).

[7] Annot., 58 A.L.R.3d 566, *Goodwill or "going concern" value as element of lessee's compensation for taking leasehold in eminent domain* (1974).

[8] Cal. Civ. Proc. Code § 1248(1) (West 1972) is an example of the unit rule.

[9] Colley v. Carleton, 571 S.W.2d 572 (Tex. Civ. App. 1978), *no writ*.

deny the tenant any claim for its unexpired term. No more need be said by the lease.[10] Tenants should be careful of this simple provision.

Condemnation, like damage and destruction, brings to the fore one of the peculiarities of real estate law: rent is not apportionable. As a result, if the tenant has prepaid rent for a period during which its premises are condemned, the landlord may keep the rent for the entire period and need not refund the unused portion.

§ 23.3   Partial Taking

Although it has been soundly criticized and is contrary to common sense, the majority rule holds that the effects of a partial taking are:

1. The tenant's obligation to pay the rent continues without abatement
2. The landlord is not entitled to any award for the diminution of its income stream (because there is none)
3. The tenant is entitled to an award for the diminished value of its leasehold.

The effect is to give the tenant the present value of the excess of its payments during the balance of the lease term over the fair market rental value of the leasehold as condemned. The landlord gets nothing except the right to receive what has been given to the tenant. If the tenant becomes insolvent, the landlord will have nothing at all.

A minority rule abates the rent when a partial taking occurs, and gives the landlord the value of the property taken. This rule is adopted by the *Restatement* § 8.1(2):

> Except to the extent the parties to a lease validly agree otherwise, if there is a taking by eminent domain of less than all of the leased property or for less than all of the lease term, the lease:
>
> (a)   is terminated if the taking significantly interferes with the use contemplated by the parties; and
>
> (b)   is not terminated if the taking does not significantly interfere with the use contemplated by the parties, but the tenant is entitled to an abatement of the rent to the extent prescribed in § 11.1.

Section 11.1 (Rent Abatement) says in part, "If the tenant is entitled to an abatement of its rent, the rent is abated to the amount of that proportion of the rent which the fair rental value after the event giving the right to abate bears to the fair

---

[10] City of Rochester v. Northwestern Bell Tel., 431 N.W.2d 874 (Minn. Ct. App. 1988), *review denied*, Jan. 13, 1989.

rental value before the event." These peculiar rules compel a landlord to use its lease to supersede the common law.[11]

§ 23.4   Temporary Taking

A temporary taking does not affect the fee but rather the leasehold, because it is, in effect, the taking of a tenancy.[12] For that reason, the tenant is entitled to the entire award and remains liable for the rent. In this unique instance among possible takings, the tenant is entitled to recover the cost of removing its goods. The rule is different, however, if the term of the temporary taking exhausts the balance of the leasehold term (for example, a taking of seven years when there are only two years left on the lease). In that case, the tenant is entitled to the amount by which the value of the remaining term exceeds what the tenant must pay for that term.

On closer analysis, however, the rules pertaining to temporary takings that do not exhaust the term have the same effect on the landlord as do the rules pertaining to partial takings; the landlord is at risk that the tenant may not pay the rent as it becomes due even though it has been paid to the tenant in the condemnation proceedings. The *Restatement* § 8.1 (set forth in § **23.3**) does not distinguish temporary takings from partial takings; rather, it considers the degree to which the taking interferes with the use contemplated by the landlord and tenant.

The vast majority of temporary takings of improvements arise in wartime; however, unimproved parts of shopping centers are often taken temporarily for street improvements. Since the common law rule seems so just and so sensible, and since temporary takings are rare, very few leases expressly provide for them.

§ 23.5   Condemnation of Office Buildings

Traditionally, office buildings have been built in the most valuable and densely developed parts of urban centers. Recently, office parks have been built nearer to centers of suburban growth. In either case, office buildings are expensive — and thus unlikely — targets for condemnation; temporary takings are more likely but still very rare.

The belief that condemnation of an office building is improbable leads many real estate professionals to slight the condemnation provisions in their leases.

---

[11] Annot., 96 A.L.R.2d 1140, *Validity, construction and effect of specific provision of a lease or statute relating to rights and compensation of lessee in event of condemnation* (1964).

[12] *See generally* Goldstein, *Some Considerations in Drafting a Condemnation Clause to Cover Temporary Takings (with Form),* Prac. Real Est. Law, May 1985, at 67.

Regardless of the degree to which they believe that condemnation should be discussed, almost all real estate professionals would agree that, in office building leases, a victory in negotiating the condemnation provision is not worth a loss in negotiating the rent, operating expense, or, for that matter, almost any other provision of the lease.

A succinct and fair provision is:

FORM 23-1
EMINENT DOMAIN—OFFICE BUILDING

If all of the premises are taken by exercise of the power of eminent domain (or conveyed by landlord in lieu of that exercise), this lease will terminate on a date (the "termination date") that is the earlier of the date on which the condemning authority takes possession of the premises or the date on which title to the premises is vested in the condemning authority. If more than 25% of the rentable area of the premises is taken, tenant will have the right to cancel this lease by written notice to landlord given within twenty (20) days after the termination date. If less than 25% of the rentable area of the premises is taken, or if the tenant does not cancel this lease according to the preceding sentence, the monthly rent will be abated in the proportion of the rentable area of the premises taken to the rentable area of the premises immediately before the taking, and tenant's share will be appropriately recalculated. If all or substantially all of the building or the project is taken, landlord may cancel this lease by written notice to tenant given within thirty (30) days after the termination date. In the event of any taking, the entire award will be paid to landlord and tenant will have no right or claim to any part of it; however, tenant will have the right to assert a claim against the condemning authority in a separate action and so long as landlord's award is not reduced by the claim, for (i) tenant's moving expenses; (ii) leasehold improvements owned by tenant; and (iii) tenant's leasehold estate.

§ 23.6   Condemnation of Shopping Centers

The substantial area needed for shopping centers necessitates their development in suburban areas where sufficient land is available. Since shopping centers are intended to be in urban and suburban growth patterns, parts of shopping centers are frequently condemned for roadways that serve the newer growth. The parts of shopping centers that are most likely to be taken are those that abut public roadways. Because the buildings are set back from the roadways, the taking usually involves entrances, pole signs, and parking. The buildings themselves will be taken only after the parking areas have already been taken, so this kind of taking is rare.

Since the premises are much less likely to be taken than are the common areas that serve them, tenants should carefully consider those portions of the shopping center (other than their own premises) that are essential or helpful to their business's success. These include not only parking and loading areas, but also curb cuts, entrances, interior access, and anchor tenants. Although few tenants could cogently argue that every entrance to the shopping center is essential for their businesses, many tenants could argue that the presence of major tenants does have a direct bearing on their own prosperity. Thus, tenants should carefully note portions of the shopping center whose loss would affect them. Some of these areas can be shown on a site plan, and of course the location of major tenants can be identified.

A typical condemnation provision in a shopping center lease is:

FORM 23-2
EMINENT DOMAIN—SHOPPING CENTER

(a)   The term "total taking" means the taking of the fee title or landlord's master leasehold estate to so much of the premises or a portion of the shopping center as is necessary for tenant's occupancy, by right of eminent domain or other authority of law, or a voluntary transfer under the threat of the exercise of the right of eminent domain or other authority, that the premises are not suitable for tenant's intended use. The term "partial taking" means the taking of only a portion of the premises or the shopping center that does not constitute a total taking.

(b)   If a total taking occurs, this lease will terminate as of the date of the taking. The phrase "date of the taking" means the date of taking actual physical possession by the condemning authority or an earlier date on which the condemning authority gives notice that it is deemed to have taken possession.

(c)   If a partial taking of more than ____% of the leasable area of the premises occurs during the term of this lease, either landlord or tenant may cancel this lease by written notice given within thirty (30) days after the date of the taking, and this lease will terminate as to the portion of the premises taken on the date of the taking. If the lease is not terminated, this lease will continue in full force and effect as to the remainder of the premises. The minimum rent payable by tenant for the balance of the term will be abated in the proportion that the leasable area of the premises taken bears to the leasable area of the premises immediately prior to the taking, and landlord will make all necessary repairs or alterations to make the remaining premises a complete architectural unit. Tenant will have no right to cancel this lease if ____% or less of the leasable area of the premises is taken.

(d)   All compensation and damages awarded for the taking of the premises, any portion of the premises, or the whole or any portion of the common areas or shopping center will belong to landlord. Tenant will not have any claim or be entitled to any award for diminution in value of its rights under this lease or for the value of any unexpired term of this lease; however, tenant may make its own claim for any separate award that may be made by the condemnor for tenant's loss of business or for the taking of or injury to tenant's improvements, or on account of any cost or loss tenant may sustain in the removal of tenant's trade fixtures, equipment, and furnishings, or as a result of any alterations, modifications, or repairs that may be reasonably required by tenant in order to place the remaining portion of the premises not taken in a suitable condition for the continuance of tenant's occupancy.

(e)   If this lease is terminated pursuant to the provisions of this paragraph, then all rentals and other charges payable by tenant to landlord under this lease will be paid to the date of the taking, and any rentals and other charges paid in advance and allocable to the period after the date of the taking will be repaid to tenant by landlord. Landlord and tenant will then be released from all further liability under this lease.

§ 23.7   Condemnation of Areas of a Shopping Center Other than Premises

The premises are the most obvious, but not the only, property whose loss by condemnation will affect the shopping center tenant.[13] In this regard, the discussion in § 4.6 may be helpful.

Parking is, of course, vital to any shopping center tenant. Many tenants do no more than negotiate their right to terminate the lease if the ratio of parking spaces to leasable area or the number of parking spaces is diminished. What these tenants fail to notice is that some parking areas are much more important than other parking areas; thus, parking in a distant part of the shopping center can be completely taken with less effect on a tenant than the taking of 25 percent of the parking spaces within 100 feet from its front doors. Thus, key parking areas should be designated as areas whose loss gives the tenant some rights. The tenant should also consider whether the taking of distant areas may lead to an encroachment upon its parking area when cars that parked in the taken area are pushed into other parts of the parking areas.

When confronted with the tenant's suggestion that it should have the right to terminate its lease if certain parking areas are taken, many landlords ask that they have the right to continue the tenant's lease if they are able to provide alternative parking. Tenants routinely ask that the alternative parking be adjacent to the existing shopping center (for example, not across a street) and that it not be located at too great a distance from their premises. Most tenants insist that alternate parking behind the shopping center is an inadequate substitute, because the backs of most shopping centers are unappealing entrances for customers and unfit areas for customer parking.

Traditionally, landlords and tenants have been content with the right to substitute alternative parking areas. In reality, however, as the areas around the shopping centers are developed, land for substitute parking areas may not be available. If it is, it may be exorbitantly expensive. For this reason, many landlords insist upon a right to install parking structures on the common areas. With a parking structure, the landlord has an opportunity to replace the parking spaces that were lost in condemnation. Unfortunately, the construction of a parking garage is likely to interfere with the visibility of most tenants' premises; this is less true in enclosed malls. As a result, tenants should be cautious about accepting substitute parking in the form of a parking structure.

---

[13] E. Halper, Shopping Center and Store Leases ch. 13 (1984), contains a useful discussion of condemnation in shopping center leases.

In some circumstances, a landlord may be able to prevent its tenants' exodus when a condemnation of part of the parking areas occurs. Consider a shopping center in which all leases provided (with remarkable imprudence on the landlord's part) that the tenants could terminate their leases if the ratio of parking spaces to leasable area fell below 5:1. If condemnation left a 4.5:1 ratio, the landlord could close so much of the leasable area as was necessary in order to restore the 5:1 ratio. The rent that the landlord would forgo in order to mitigate its loss may be compensable in the condemnation proceedings. In any event, the landlord has saved its shopping center.

Since the presence of anchor tenants is vital to a shopping center, some tenants demand the right to cancel their leases if an anchor tenant cancels its lease because of a condemnation. Just as landlords should demand an opportunity to replace parking, so also should they demand a right to replace anchor tenants. The anchor tenants may leave because their premises are taken or, in the more likely event, because they have a right to leave on account of some taking of the common areas. A landlord may be able to attract a different anchor tenant to the abandoned premises or, if the premises have been taken, to replace the premises in a different part of the shopping center.

There are other parts of shopping centers that may be so important to a tenant that it needs the right to cancel its lease if any of those parts are taken. These include the tenant's loading areas—not only the dock itself but also access and sufficient unobstructed areas for trucks to back into the loading dock.

§ 23.8 Consequences of Condemnation

Once the landlord and tenant have agreed upon those takings that affect the tenant's interests, they must then agree upon the consequences of those takings. The simplest provision is one that allows the tenant to cancel its lease if any of those vital parts of the shopping center are taken. Landlords must resist this heavy-handed suggestion. Instead, the landlord and tenant must come to some conclusion about an abatement of the rent. When considering rent abatements after condemnation, landlords and tenants must bear in mind the fundamental distinction between rent abatements after damage and destruction and rent abatements after condemnation. In the former, the abatement is temporary, continuing only for so long as is required for the restoration of the premises. In the latter, there may be two abatements: (1) while the premises are being restored to an architecturally sound unit; and (2) for the duration of the lease. These permanent abatements of rent distinguish abatements in condemnation from abatements in damage and destruction, and they must be very carefully considered by landlords.

The landlord and tenant can readily agree that the operative question is the effect of the taking on the tenant's business. After that initial agreement, however, landlord and tenant diverge. The landlord feels that the tenant's continued operation at the premises is indication of the insignificance of the taking to its business; on the other hand, landlords are unwilling to let tenants be the judge of that impact by giving them unrestricted rights of cancellation. Tenants cannot immediately assess the effect of a condemnation. If the taking occurs during slack business months (which usually coincide with the best times for construction), then the tenant will not know if its business has been affected until it can compare its peak months before and after the taking. This means that the tenant may need several months in order to evaluate the effect of a taking.

The agreement that the landlord and tenant can make in theory—that the viability of the tenant's business should not be affected by a taking—can be brought about by an abatement of rent that gives the tenant the same profitability. That, however, requires time to gather data, and leaves the landlord and tenant in limbo during the interim. As a result of these complications, most condemnation provisions in shopping centers finally provide:

1. For cancellation if the entire premises are taken
2. For temporary abatement during restoration of the premises in the event of a partial taking of the premises
3. For a permanent abatement of the minimum rent in the proportion that the floor area taken bears to the initial floor area of the premises
4. For rights of cancellation upon the taking of vital areas to the tenant and
5. For cancellation if a specified portion of the common areas or a specified number of parking spaces are taken or if the prescribed parking ratio cannot be maintained as a result of the taking.

In lieu of a formula, some leases provide that the rent will be "equitably abated" if a part of the premises or shopping center is taken. Although this compromise ends their discussion, the landlord and tenant have accomplished little with this provision except to assure themselves of a disagreement if a partial taking occurs. A better objective standard provides that the rent will be adjusted to the portion of the rent payable before the taking that the rental value of the premises after the partial taking bears to the rental value of the premises before the partial taking.

§ 23.9 Landlord's Restoration of Premises

Landlords must be absolutely certain not to commit themselves to restoration in excess of the net award in condemnation after deducting attorneys' fees and amounts paid to the landlord's mortgagees. This is particularly true when anchor tenants insist that their minimum rent be abated in the proportion of the costs of the construction of the premises that is recovered by the landlord in condemnation. In addition to the lender's concerns discussed in § **23.12**, landlords must consider the consequences of the condemnation with regard to their lenders. If the lender takes the entire award, and tenants are allowed to abate their rents, the landlord may have insufficient rental income with which to pay its monthly debt service. This is particularly true if no adjustment is made to the amortization of the balance of the debt, but rather the original payments are continued.

§ 23.10 Allocation of Condemnation Award

Deciding the allocation of a condemnation award between landlord and tenant can be a hard-fought battle, but it really need not be. In the first place, the tenant must be made to realize that it will have no premises if landlord's lender believes it is not adequately secured with its mortgage and the landlord's leases. One element of the lender's security is the certainty that its mortgage will be paid when its security is converted into cash. As a result, the landlord and tenant should be able to agree that the lender should be entitled to be repaid its debt before there is any discussion between the landlord and the tenant.

The next area of inquiry arises when some portion of the condemnation award remains after the lender has been repaid. When the landlord has invested cash in the premises, it has a cogent argument that it should be repaid its investment before the tenant has any opportunity to share in the excess award.

What happens, however, when the landlord has no investment in the premises and a portion of the award remains after the landlord's lender is repaid? This is solely a matter of negotiation. The tenant will argue that its lease created the value on which the award was based; this is an invitation to circularity, because the shopping center created the leases, which created the value, and so on. The tenant's other argument is that it is entitled to a share of the award by common law. The landlord has no simple response to these arguments. Its answer is another invitation to circularity, that is, that the landlord created the shopping center.

The most difficult negotiation occurs if the tenant has a substantial investment in the premises, which usually occurs when the landlord delivers only a shell, and part of the award is left after payment of the lender. When the landlord has no investment in the premises, the tenant can fairly claim that it should be compensated for its investment. In that case, the landlord and tenant merely negotiate the distribution. When both the landlord and the tenant have an investment in the shopping center, there is usually an insufficient amount of money to pay both of them. The simplest way to allocate the award is to add up the landlord's investment in the shopping center and the tenant's book value of its improvements, to allocate to the landlord that part of the total of which its investment is the numerator, and to give the tenant the rest. When the landlord and tenant discuss the book value of the tenant's improvements, the landlord will want the fastest possible writeoff of those costs and the tenant, of course, will want the slowest possible writeoff. Since the tenant will probably use the fastest possible writeoff for federal income tax purposes, the landlord should insist that the book value for the tenant's tax purposes be used.

In this regard, it should be noted that if the tenant has no right to assign its lease, there is no assurance that it will never receive any value for its leasehold. Thus, its argument for a share of the award in that circumstance is weakened.

§ 23.11   Condemnation of Single Tenant Premises

The condemnation of single tenant premises involves the same legal principles as condemnation of shopping center or office premises.

FORM 23-3
CONDEMNATION—SINGLE TENANT BUILDING

(a)   *Termination.* If (i) all of the premises are taken in a condemnation, or (ii) a portion of the premises are taken in condemnation and tenant determines in good faith that it will be economically unfeasible to operate its business in any facility that could be reconstructed on the remaining portion of the premises, this lease will terminate and all obligations under it will cease as of the date upon which possession is taken by the condemnor. Upon such termination, the rent will be apportioned and paid in full by tenant to landlord to that date, all rent prepaid beyond that date will be repaid by landlord to tenant, and tenant will comply with paragraph (e). If, after a partial condemnation of the premises, tenant remains in possession of the remaining portion of the premises after the date on which the condemnor takes possession of the portion of the premises taken in condemnation, then the remaining portion will be deemed sufficient for the reasonable operation of tenant's business and this lease will terminate only with respect to the portion of the premises possessed by the condemnor.

(b)   *Partial Condemnation.* If there is a partial condemnation and this lease has not been terminated pursuant to paragraph (a), landlord will promptly restore the building and other improvements on the land to a condition and size as nearly comparable as reasonably possible to their condition and size immediately prior to the taking; the time of restoration will be extended for time lost due to causes beyond landlord's reasonable control. Tenant will pay the costs of restoration as the work progresses within fifteen (15) days after delivery of an invoice to it. Landlord agrees to pay to tenant, when received, the proceeds of any condemnation award recovered in excess of counsel and appraiser's fees and other costs incurred in collecting the proceeds (the "net condemnation proceeds"), up to the total amount paid by tenant for the cost of restoration. In that event, there will be an equitable abatement of the minimum annual rent according to the value of the premises before and after the taking, commencing from and after the date on which the condemnor takes possession; however, the minimum annual rent will be at least equal to the percentage of the minimum annual rent payable prior to the condemnation produced by multiplying any first mortgage encumbering the premises by a fraction whose numerator is the sum equal to its original principal amount, less the net condemnation proceeds retained by landlord or the holder after the payment of all costs of restoration, and whose denominator is the original principal amount of the mortgage.

(c)   *Award.* If a condemnation affecting tenant occurs, tenant will have the right to make a claim against the condemnor for removal expenses, business dislocation damages and moving expenses to the extent that such claims or payments do not reduce the sums payable by the condemnor to landlord. Tenant waives all claims against landlord and all other claims against the condemnor, and tenant assigns to landlord all claims against the condemnor including, without limitation, all claims for leasehold damages and diminution in value of tenant's leasehold.

(d)   *Temporary Taking.* If the condemnor takes possession for a fixed period of time or for the duration of an emergency or other temporary condition, then this lease will continue in full force and effect without any abatement of rent, but the amounts payable by the condemnor with respect to any period of time prior to the expiration or sooner termination of this lease will be paid by the condemnor to landlord and the condemnor will be considered a subtenant of tenant. Landlord will apply the amount received from the condemnor applicable to the rent due (net of the costs to landlord for its collection, or as much of it as may be necessary for that purpose) toward the amount due from tenant as rent for that period. Tenant will pay landlord any deficiency between the amount paid by the condemnor and the amount of the rent, or landlord will pay tenant any excess of the amount of the award over the amount of the rent.

(e)   *Effect of Termination of Lease.* For the purposes of this paragraph, these phrases have the following meanings: (i) "Subject property" means the premises, if any portion remains after a condemnation, all outstanding rights and claims against the condemnor at the time of settlement, and that portion of the proceeds of condemnation, if any, received by landlord equal to or less than the purchase price; (ii) "Purchase price" means the unpaid principal balance secured by the first mortgage encumbering the premises at the time when landlord is no longer entitled to possession, together with accrued interest to the date of settlement and other sums secured by the mortgage. If this lease terminates in accordance with the provision of paragraph (a), then tenant will be deemed irrevocably to have offered to purchase the subject property from landlord upon the terms and conditions of this paragraph (e), and landlord will be deemed to have accepted the offer unless it rejects the offer in writing within ninety (90) days after the termination of this lease. Tenant will pay the purchase price to landlord; settlement will occur at a location determined by landlord that is reasonably convenient for tenant within forty-five (45) days after expiration of the ninety (90) day period; and the subject property shall be conveyed free and clear of the first mortgage, but subject to all other encumbrances and restrictions existing at the execution of this lease, utility and public road rights-of-way hereafter created, all encumbrances and restrictions that are created or suffered by tenant, and all encumbrances and restrictions to which tenant has consented; and tenant will pay all realty transfer taxes, if any.

When the tenant has made substantial improvements to the premises, a different provision may be necessary.

In considering **Form 23-4**, assume that the tenant leased a shell and made $500,000 of improvements to the premises. Thus, it will not accept any condemnation provision that does not make allowance for its contribution to the value of the premises. Of course, it may agree to a share that decreases as its improvement costs are amortized.[14]

There are alternatives. The landlord and tenant may have decided to allow common law rules to govern. They may have decided to give the landlord the capitalized value of the rent payable and the tenant the balance; if the lease were made of vacant land for a very long term, so that the reversion was worth very

---

[14] Olschwang, *Negotiating a Commercial Lease,* 12 Real Est. Rev. 74 (1983).

little, this approach might be sensible, because the landlord would be receiving relatively little rent for its unimproved property.

If the tenant leased vacant land and built all the improvements, one approach might be to apportion the award by giving the landlord the portion that the value of the ground bears to the award and giving the tenant the portion that the value of the improvements bears to the award. This appears to ignore the landlord's right to improvements as part of its reversion. Still, if the tenant's depreciated value of the improvements is used, the tenant's eventual loss of them is taken into account; for example, on a 10-year straight-line depreciation without salvage value, the tenant is entitled to $50,000 less of the award for each elapsed year of the lease.

The landlord and tenant may eventually agree on a provision such as:

FORM 23-4
CONDEMNATION—SINGLE TENANT BUILDING

(a) *Total Taking.* If, by exercise of the right of eminent domain or by conveyance made in response to the threat of the exercise of that right (in either case a "taking"), all of the premises are taken or if so much of the premises are taken that the premises (even if the restorations described in subparagraph (b) were to be made) cannot be used by tenant for the purposes for which they were used immediately before the taking, this lease will end on the earlier of the vesting of title to the premises in the condemning authority, or the taking of possession of the premises by the condemning authority (in either case the "ending date"). If this lease ends according to this subparagraph (a), prepaid rent will be appropriately prorated to the ending date. The award in a taking subject to this subparagraph (a) will be allocated according to subparagraph (d).

(b) *Partial Taking.* If, after a taking, so much of the premises remains that the premises can be used for substantially the same purposes for which they were used immediately before the taking, (i) this lease will end on the ending date as to the part of the premises that is taken, (ii) prepaid rent will be appropriately allocated to the part of the premises that is taken and prorated to the ending date, (iii) beginning on the day after the ending date, rent for so much of the premises as remains will be reduced in the proportion of the floor area of the building remaining after the taking to the floor area of the building before the taking, (iv) at its cost, tenant will restore so much of the premises as remains to a sound architectural unit substantially suitable for the purposes for which they were used immediately before the taking, using good workmanship and new first-class materials, all according to alterations paragraph, (v) upon the completion of restoration according to clause (iv), landlord will pay tenant the lesser of the net award made to landlord on account of the taking (after deducting from the total award attorneys', appraisers' and other costs incurred in connection with obtaining the award, and amounts paid to the holders of mortgages affecting the premises) or tenant's actual out-of-pocket cost of restoring the premises, and (vi) landlord will keep the balance of the net award.

(c) *Tenant's Award.* In connection with any taking subject to subparagraph (a) or (b), tenant may prosecute its own claim by separate proceedings against the condemning authority for damages legally due to it (such as the loss of fixtures that tenant was entitled to remove, and moving expenses) only so long as tenant's award does not diminish or otherwise adversely affect landlord's award.

(d) *Allocation of an Award for a Total Taking.* If this lease ends according to subparagraph (a), the condemnation award will be paid in the order in this subparagraph to the extent it is sufficient:

(1) First, landlord will be reimbursed for its attorneys' fees, appraisal fees, and other costs incurred in prosecuting the claim for the award;

(2) Second, landlord will be paid for lost rent and the value of the reversion as of the ending date;

(3) Third, tenant will be paid its adjusted book value as of the date of the taking of its improvements (excluding trade fixtures) made to the premises. In computing its adjusted book value, improvements will be conclusively presumed to have been depreciated or amortized for federal income tax purposes over their useful lives with a reasonable salvage value;

(4) Fourth, the balance will be divided equally between landlord and tenant.

The allocation in subparagraph (d) is based upon the assumption that no mortgage encumbers the reversion. If there is a mortgage, provision must be made for the lender.

§ 23.12 Lenders' Concerns about Condemnation

Every real estate professional has heard a landlord say that it is willing to accede to one request or another of the tenant, but its lender will not allow it to do so. Often, this is just a convenient ruse. In the case of condemnation provisions, that response is honest.

Because the development of which the premises are a part is the security for the lender's investment, that is, its loan, the lender wants the award in any condemnation; the proceeds of that award have replaced its security. The mortgage will almost invariably require all condemnation awards to be paid to the lender.

When the entire development is taken, the lender will be fully paid by the award, because the award typically will exceed its loan. When less than the entire development is taken, the lender will still have the right to the entire award, no matter how slight the diminution of the value of its security. The lender may relinquish its rights if the landlord/borrower uses the award to rebuild the development; any amount remaining after rebuilding would usually be paid to the lender, because that excess represents the amount by which its security has been damaged but not rebuilt.

With these thoughts in mind, the real estate professional can deduce several conclusions. In the first place, without its lender's consent, the landlord should not employ a form lease that unconditionally obligates the landlord to rebuild after a partial taking. Otherwise, if the lender takes the entire award, the landlord must use its own money to perform its lease covenants.

Second, a tenant ought to consider carefully the consequences of the subordination of its leasehold to the landlord's mortgage. As a result of that subordination, the tenant's share of any award will be subject to the terms of the mortgage and the mortgagee may take the entire award. If that happens, the award available to a tenant for the bonus value of its lease, and its purchase and renewal options, will be lost. In addition, if the tenant's fixtures and leasehold improvements are made subject to the mortgage, the lender will receive that portion of the award that is made for those fixtures and improvements. Clearly, in these circumstances and others, the subordination provisions are very important to the tenant.

Needless to say, if the tenant itself has a mortgage of its leasehold, the tenant's lender will be entitled to the award up to its loan and the tenant will be entitled to the balance.

As this discussion has shown, the landlord's concerns and its lender's concerns with regard to condemnation are virtually identical. However, one fine distinction should be observed. As a shorthand way of protecting their lenders, many landlords provide that the tenant cannot share any condemnation award unless the lender has first been paid in full. Obviously, this is intended to assure the lender that all of the condemnation award will be available to discharge its debt. Still, after foreclosure, there is no mortgage debt to be discharged, and that shorthand provision will leave the lender/landlord and the tenant in the position of sharing just as though there had been no mortgage. In order to close this gap, cautious real estate professionals provide that if the lender owns the property at the time of the condemnation, then the award will be paid first to the lender to the extent of its equity in the development (principal, interest, costs of foreclosure, and costs of carrying the development after foreclosure) before any part of the award is paid to the tenant.

§ 23.13 Deceptive Role of Some Mortgages

The landlord's solicitous concern for its lender may prompt it to insist that all mortgagees be paid before the tenant sees any part of an award. Tenants should reflect carefully on this provision. If the landlord takes some of the value out of the premises in the form of a second mortgage or other refinancing (such a wraparound), it will have effectively assured itself of being paid before the tenant is paid. This is because the discharge of all mortgages will discharge the landlord's indebtedness to its secondary lenders. This is also true when the landlord becomes a purchase money mortgagee after the sale of the premises. In this event, again, payment of all mortgages assures that the landlord escapes unscathed.

When tenants intend to make substantial investments in their premises, they should insist that only the first mortgage be paid before they share in any excess award. The landlord must refine this suggestion by providing that secondary financing proceeds that are invested in the property be considered first mortgages for purposes of the tenant's suggestion, and that only mortgages whose proceeds have gone or will go to the landlord are considered secondary financing. This negotiation is very delicate, because of the lender's concerns discussed in § 23.12.

PART VII

PROTECTING THE LANDLORD

CHAPTER 24

SUBORDINATION

§ 24.1   Introduction and General Rules

Almost without exception, leases contain subordination provisions stating that the rights of the tenant under the lease will be subject to the rights of any lender whose mortgage affects the premises. As a result, the foreclosure of the mortgage will terminate the lease; in other respects, the tenant's rights will not be enforceable until the lender's rights are satisfied. Subordination provisions are made not so much for the landlord's direct benefit as they are in anticipation of the requirements of its lenders. In turn, the lender's requirements depend upon the relative priority of mortgages of the reversion and leaseholds.[1]

As a general rule, a lease will not be subordinate to a mortgage, but rather will be prior to the mortgage, if the lease is recorded, or the tenant is in possession, before the mortgage is recorded. In some cases discussed in § **32.4**, a lease will not be subordinate to a mortgage if the lender has notice of the lease before the mortgage is recorded. On the other hand, a lease will be subordinate to a mortgage if it is made after the mortgage is recorded, or if it contains a provision that makes it subordinate to the mortgage, or if a separate subordination agreement is given by the tenant. If the lender wants to be subordinate to the lease, it may assure itself of subordination by recording its mortgage after the lease is made; but all will be for naught if the lease contains an automatic subordination provision, because the lease will be subordinate to the mortgage even though the mortgage is recorded after the lease.

The decision that the lender makes about the primacy or subordination of its mortgage will not be made without knowing what effect the foreclosure of its mortgage will have on leases that affect the premises. Since it is universally the

---

[1] *See generally Subordination—A Review of the Basics,* Leasing Prof., Nov. 1987, at 1.

rule that the foreclosure of a mortgage will not affect a lease to which the mortgage is subordinate, the important questions are presented when the mortgage is superior to the lease. The states are almost evenly divided on the question whether the foreclosure of the mortgage or deed of trust automatically extinguishes a subordinate lease, or whether foreclosure extinguishes a subordinate lease only if the tenant has given notice.[2]

In states that allow foreclosures by a power of sale contained in a deed of trust, for the most part a subsequent lease will be automatically terminated by the foreclosure of the deed of trust. In other words, the lender cannot avoid the result that its foreclosure will end the lease.

In states that allow foreclosure by sale through a judicial proceeding, two rules have emerged. One holds that the sale automatically terminates subordinate leases. The other holds that the sale does not terminate subordinate leases unless the tenants are made parties to the judicial proceedings;[3] these instances give lenders complete control over the subordinate leases.[4]

§ 24.2 Significance to Lender

The desirability to a lender of being subordinate to a lease depends upon the worth of the lease to the lender and the consequences of the foreclosure of the lender's mortgage. If the lender has determined as a matter of its underwriting that it need not rely upon a particular lease, the consequences of its foreclosure on that lease are of less interest to the lender than they are if it has concluded that it

---

[2] Feinstein & Kiels, *Foreclosure: Subordination, Nondisturbance and Attornment Agreements,* Prop. & Prob., July/Aug. 1989, at 38. That study identifies the "automatic" jurisdictions as: California, Colorado, District of Columbia, Georgia, Hawaii, Idaho (automatic cut-off if lease is unrecorded; if lease recorded, lessee must be made a party), Indiana, Iowa, Kentucky, Louisiana, Maine (lease is terminated by entry and possession), Massachusetts (lease is terminated by entry and possession), Michigan, Minnesota, Mississippi, Missouri, New Hampshire, North Carolina, Oklahoma, Oregon, Pennsylvania, Rhode Island, South Dakota, Tennessee, Virginia, West Virginia, Wisconsin, and Wyoming. The same article identifies the following states as ones that terminate leases only if the tenant is made a party to the proceeding: Alabama (lease terminated only if notice given of foreclosure sale), Alaska, Arizona, Arkansas, Connecticut, Delaware, Florida, Illinois (if mortgage foreclosure, lessee must be made party; if by power of sale in deed of trust, lease automatically terminates), Kansas, Maryland (if mortgage or deed of trust authorizes and advertisement of sale discloses, sale can be made subject to subsequent, that is, subordinate leases), Montana, Nebraska, Nevada, New Jersey, New Mexico, New York, North Dakota, Pennsylvania (lessee does not become a party, but must be served notice of action), Puerto Rico, South Carolina, Texas, Utah, Vermont (debtor retains possession during redemption period), and Washington.

[3] M.R. Friedman, I Friedman on Leases § 8.1 (1983).

[4] *See* Gearen, Vranicar, & Becker, *Into Harms' Way: Now that Harms v. Sprague Has Established the Lien Theory of Mortgages in Illinois, Does Foreclosure Cut Off a Junior Lease or Can a Mortgagee Elect to Reserve Them?,* 34 De Paul L. Rev. 409 (1985) (discussing Illinois precedents but providing an overview of common law principles).

definitely does want the lease to continue after foreclosure. In making that determination, the lender will consider not only the revenue from the lease but also the duties that the landlord (or the lender as landlord's successor) must discharge in order to keep the tenant; for example, a lease that a tenant may terminate if the landlord does not make prescribed improvements may be one that the lender decides should be subordinate to its mortgage.

If a lender has determined that a particular tenant or the cash flow from a particular lease is important to it, and it has found that the unavoidable effect of its foreclosure will be to terminate the lease, the lender will want to make an agreement with the tenant that the tenant will remain after any foreclosure. This would usually be true of major tenants whose rent is essential to repay the loan. The lender may be willing to take its chances with smaller tenants whose loss would not be significant to the lender.

The agreement by which the tenant agrees to remain after foreclosure and to treat the lender as its landlord is called an *attornment agreement*. The tenant is said to "attorn" to the lender as its new landlord; by way of historical interest, the concept of attornment goes back many centuries in the common law to a time when the transfer of the reversion was not effective until the tenant attorned to its new landlord, usually by paying its rent.[5]

The dual goals of effecting a subordination of the lease and avoiding its automatic termination on foreclosure are achieved by the subordination and attornment provisions:

FORM 24-1
SUBORDINATION AND ATTORNMENT

(a) *Subordination.* This lease and tenant's rights under this lease are subject and subordinate to any ground lease or underlying lease, first mortgage, first deed of trust or other first lien encumbrance or indenture, together with any renewals, extensions, modifications, consolidations, and replacements of them (each a "superior lien") that now or at any subsequent time affects the premises or any interest of landlord in the premises or landlord's interest in this lease and the estate created by this lease (except to the extent that the recorded instrument evidencing the superior lien expressly provides that this lease is superior to the superior lien). This provision will be self-operative and no further instrument of subordination will be required in order to effect it. Nevertheless, tenant will execute, acknowledge and deliver to landlord, at any time and from time to time, upon demand by landlord, documents requested by landlord, any ground landlord or underlying lessor or any mortgagee, or any holder of a deed of trust or other instrument described in this paragraph, to confirm or effect the subordination. If tenant does not execute, acknowledge, and deliver any of those documents within twenty (20) days after written demand, landlord, its successors and assigns will be entitled to execute, acknowledge, and deliver those documents on behalf of tenant as tenant's attorney-in-fact. Tenant

---

[5] 3 G.W. Thompson, Commentaries on the Modern Law of Real Property § 1200 (1980) repl. vol. by J.S. Grimes), tells the story of attornment.

constitutes and irrevocably appoints landlord, its successors and assigns, as tenant's attorney-in-fact to execute, acknowledge, and deliver those documents on behalf of tenant.

(b) *Attornment.*   If the holder of any mortgage, indenture, deed of trust, or other similar instrument described in paragraph (a) succeeds to landlord's interest in the premises, tenant will pay to it all rents subsequently payable under this lease. Tenant will, upon request of any one succeeding to the interest of landlord, automatically become tenant of, and attorn to, the successor without change in this lease. The successor will not be bound by (i) any payment of rent for more than one month in advance, or (ii) any amendment or modification of this lease made without its written consent, or (iii) any claim against landlord arising prior to the date that the successor succeeded to landlord's interest, or (iv) any claim or offset of rent against landlord. Upon request by the successor and without cost to landlord or the successor, tenant will execute, acknowledge, and deliver documents confirming the attornment. The document of attornment will also provide that the successor will not disturb tenant in its use of the premises in accordance with this lease. If tenant fails or refuses to execute, acknowledge, and deliver those documents within twenty (20) days after written demand, the successor will be entitled to execute, acknowledge, and deliver those documents on behalf of tenant as tenant's attorney-in-fact. Tenant constitutes and irrevocably appoints the successor as tenant's attorney-in-fact to execute, acknowledge, and deliver those documents on behalf of tenant.

In deference to their first mortgage lenders, landlords should avoid provisions by which the leases are subordinate "to all present and future mortgages affecting the premises." The first mortgage lender's concern is that the foreclosure of a subsequent mortgage will terminate a valuable lease that has been made subordinate to the subsequent mortgage by virtue of the expansive subordination provision. This gives the subsequent mortgage lender an opportunity to threaten the first mortgage lender with termination of a valuable lease unless the first mortgage lender cures or pays off the subsequent mortgage.

Tenants ought to be aware of one common, and meaningless, part of the usual subordination provision, including the one in **Form 24-1**. That is the statement made by the landlord that the landlord's lender will recognize the tenant in the event of foreclosure. Since the lender is not a party to the lease, one may justifiably wonder how the landlord's promise can bind it. A tenant's assurance can only come from the holder of the mortgage to which its lease is subordinate.

Some real estate professionals wonder why the mortgage is not simply subordinated to the lease in those states in which the automatic termination rule is in effect; if a foreclosure occurs, they reason, the lease will not be affected. The reason that mortgages are not subordinated in those circumstances is the possible conflict between the lease and the mortgage as to the division of condemnation awards and the proceeds of insurance.[6] These possibilities are avoided by the

---

[6] *See* § **23.10.**

nondisturbance agreement among the lender, the landlord, and the tenant discussed in § **24.3**.

§ 24.3   Significance to Tenant

The meaning of subordination to a tenant is the risk of the loss of its leasehold without its fault. This may mean not only the expenses of moving and the loss of leasehold improvements, but also the loss of an advantageous rent rate and the goodwill associated with a location. A tenant may try to protect itself against these risks by agreeing that it will subordinate its lease only to a lien for indebtedness that is:

1. A first lien.
2. Held by an institutional lender, which is usually defined as a bank, savings and loan association, thrift institution, trust company, insurance company or pension fund.
3. Fully amortized in installments that the tenant can, in the worst case, afford to discharge on the landlord's behalf. The tenant will insist upon the right to pay the indebtedness if the landlord does not and to deduct its payments from the rent. This right is meaningful only in a single tenant lease.

The likelihood that a landlord will consent to such an intrusion is small. The tenant can rightly object to complete subordination if it has made expensive leasehold improvements; in that case, the tenant has legitimate interests in fire insurance proceeds and condemnation awards.

Ultimately, the tenant's comfort must come from the holder of the mortgage to which its lease is subordinate. This comfort is effected with an instrument entitled a *nondisturbance agreement*, which assures the tenant that the holder of the mortgage will not disturb the tenant's possession so long as the tenant is not in default under its lease. The lender uses this agreement to assure itself that the tenant will not take the opportunity of foreclosure to assert termination of its lease, and also that the tenant will attorn to the lender as the tenant's landlord if a foreclosure occurs.

When the landlord, tenant, and lender are unable to agree on a nondisturbance agreement, the tenant can suggest that the landlord be personally liable for the tenant's cost of relocation. The personal liability is an exception to the landlord's usual exculpation, illustrated in **Form 29-1**, and may be worthless if the landlord is insolvent. A further suggestion is that the landlord post a bond for tenant's relocation costs if the tenant is dispossessed.

When the landlord, tenant, and lender reach agreement, the instrument becomes a nondisturbance and attornment agreement by which the lender and the tenant agree to recognize one another in the event of foreclosure. Such an agreement is also called a *recognition agreement*. Under any name, it looks like:

FORM 24-2
SUBORDINATION—NONDISTURBANCE, ATTORNMENT, ESTOPPEL, AND SUBORDINATION AGREEMENT

THIS NONDISTURBANCE, ATTORNMENT, ESTOPPEL, AND SUBORDINATION AGREEMENT is made on _____, 19_____, by landlord, tenant, and lender.

Landlord and tenant have entered into the lease with respect to the premises. The premises are part of the property. Lender has agreed to make the loan to landlord and to accept the mortgage as security for repayment of the loan and performance of landlord's obligations related to the loan. However, as a condition to making the loan, lender has required a subordination of the lease to the mortgage. Tenant is willing to subordinate the lease to the mortgage so long as tenant is assured that its possession of the premises will not be disturbed. Accordingly, landlord, tenant, and lender agree that:

1. *Definitions.*

(a)   Date: _____, 19_____.

(b)   Landlord: _____.

(c)   Lease: the Lease Agreement dated _____, 19_____, between landlord and tenant.

(d)   Lender: _____, its successors and assigns, and anyone else who succeeds to landlord's interest in the lease through foreclosure (both judicial and power-of-sale), or deed in lieu of foreclosure.

(e)   Loan: a loan of $_____ by lender to landlord.

(f)   Premises: the subject matter of the lease.

(g)   Property: the real property described in Exhibit A to this agreement.

(h)   Tenant: _____.

(i)   Mortgage: the Loan Agreement, Mortgage, Security Agreement, and Assignment of Rents, all dated _____, 19_____, between landlord and lender, and any extensions, modifications, renewals, substitutions, replacements, or consolidations of any of them.

2. *Nondisturbance.*   So long as no event of default under the lease has occurred, lender will not disturb tenant's possession of the premises.

3. *Attornment.*   If lender succeeds to landlord's interest in the lease, tenant will be bound to lender according to the lease for the balance of the term of the lease and any extension of the lease as if lender were the landlord under the lease, and tenant will attorn to lender as its landlord, immediately upon lender's succeeding to the interest of landlord under the lease; however, tenant will not be obligated to pay rent to lender until tenant receives written notice from lender that it has succeeded to the interest of landlord in the lease. Subject to paragraph 4, upon such attornment the rights and obligations of tenant and lender will be the same as they would have been if lender had been landlord under the lease.

4. *Limitation on Lender's Obligations.*   If lender succeeds to the interest of landlord in the lease, lender will not be:

(a)   liable for any act or omission of landlord or any predecessor of landlord (including landlord); or

(b) subject to any offsets or defenses that tenant may have against landlord or any predecessor of landlord; or

(c) bound by any rent or additional rent or advance rent that tenant may have paid for more than the current month to any prior landlord (including landlord) and all such rent will remain due and owing without regard to such advance payment;

(d) bound by any amendment or modification of the lease made without its consent and written approval; or

(e) required to complete the building of which the premises are a part; or

(f) bound by any promise by landlord or any predecessor of landlord not to compete with tenant; or

(g) responsible to return tenant's security deposit pursuant to the lease.

5. *Subordination.* Subject to the terms of this agreement, the lease now is, and will be, subject and subordinate to the mortgage. This agreement will not limit lender's rights under the mortgage.

6. *Estoppel.* Landlord and tenant certify to lender that:

(a) the lease is in effect and unmodified;

(b) the term of the lease will commence or did commence on _____, 19____, or within sixty (60) days after tenant's receipt of a written notice from landlord advising that the premises have been substantially completed, whichever occurs later, and full rental will then accrue or is now accruing under the lease;

(c) all conditions required under the lease that could have been satisfied as of the date have been met;

(d) no rent under the lease has been paid more than thirty (30) days in advance of its due date;

(e) no default exists under the lease;

(f) tenant, as of the date, has no charge, lien, or claim of offset under the lease or otherwise, against rents or other charges due to become due under the lease;

(g) the lease constitutes the entire agreement between them;

(h) lender will have no liability or responsibility with respect to tenant's security deposit;

(i) the only persons, firms, or corporations in possession of the premises or having any right to the possession or use of the premises (other than the record owner) are those holding under the lease; and

(j) tenant has no right or interest in or under any contract, option, or agreement involving the sale or transfer of the premises.

7. *Limitation on Tenant's Rights.* In the absence of lender's prior written consent, tenant will not:

(a) prepay the rent under the lease for more than one (1) month,

(b) enter into any agreement with landlord to amend or modify the lease, or

(c) voluntarily surrender the premises or terminate the lease without cause.

8. *Curing Defaults; Landlord's Termination.* If landlord fails to perform any of its obligations under the lease, tenant will give written notice of the failure to lender and lender will have the right (but not the obligation) to cure such failure. Tenant will not take any action with respect to such failure under the lease, including without limitation any action to terminate, rescind, or avoid the lease or to withhold any rent under the lease, for a period of thirty (30) days after receipt of such written notice by lender; however, in the case of any default which cannot with diligence be cured within said thirty-day period, if lender proceeds promptly to cure such failure and prosecutes the curing of such failure with diligence and continuity, the time within

which such failure may be cured will be extended for such period as may be necessary to complete the curing of such failure with diligence and continuity. If landlord exercises its right to terminate the lease pursuant to paragraph [damage and destruction] or paragraph [condemnation] of the lease, lender will have the right (but not the obligation) to elect to repair or restore the premises. Lender will give tenant notice of its election (if at all) within _____ (_____) days after landlord terminates the lease. If lender so elects to repair or restore the premises, landlord's termination of the lease will be ineffective and lender will have the right to repair or restore the premises within the periods set forth in relevant paragraphs of the lease.

9. *Amendments and Binding Effect.* This agreement may be modified only by an agreement in writing signed by landlord, tenant, and lender. Subject to paragraph [transfer of the premises] of the lease, this agreement will inure to the benefit of and will be binding upon landlord, tenant and lender, their successors and assigns.

10. *Counterparts.* This agreement may be executed in several counterparts and, when executed by landlord, tenant, and lender, will constitute one agreement, binding upon them, even though they are not signatories to the original or the same counterpart.

11. *Notices.* All notices under this agreement will be in writing and will be considered properly given if mailed by first-class United States mail, postage prepaid, registered or certified with return receipt requested, or if personally delivered to the intended addressee, or by prepaid telegram. Notice by mail will be effective two (2) days after deposit in the United States mail. Notice given in any other manner will be effective when received by the addressee. For purposes of notices, the addresses of landlord, tenant, and lender are:

Landlord:

_____

_____

_____

Tenant:

_____

_____

_____

Lender:

_____

_____

_____

Any of them may change its address for notice to any other location within the continental United States by the giving of thirty (30) days' notice in the manner set forth in this paragraph.

Landlord, tenant, and lender have executed this agreement as of _____, 19_____.

LANDLORD: TENANT: LENDER:

_____   _____   _____

By _____   By _____   By _____

Many landlords prefer to attach a copy of the nondisturbance, attornment, and subordination agreement to their leases. This avoids any arguments when the form must be signed. Most nondisturbance agreements such as **Form 24-2** make it clear that the tenant has no monetary claims (or claims of offset) against the lender for past defaults of the landlord. However, they do not make it clear whether a tenant can terminate its lease on account of the landlord's past defaults; if a tenant cannot, it has lost a valuable right.

The real estate professional will immediately observe the similarity of the nondisturbance and attornment agreement to the agreement that a prime landlord gives to its tenant's subtenant on the occasion of a sublease. A moment's reflection will reveal that the structures of the two transactions are identical. The prime landlord is in the position of the lender, the tenant/sublandlord is in the position of the landlord, and the subtenant is in the position of the tenant, in the sublease and loan transactions, respectively.

By the same token, a landlord should not unequivocally promise to deliver nondisturbance agreements to its tenant. Even if the present lender has indicated its willingness to provide one, the landlord cannot be certain what its future lenders may say. The landlord cannot be sure what will happen if a buyer of the development seeks purchase money financing; if its lender refuses to give a nondisturbance agreement, an advantageous sale may be lost. Thus, landlords should agree only to use reasonable efforts to get nondisturbance agreements in the future. Some tenants reserve the right to cancel their leases if the landlord does not deliver nondisturbance agreements from existing lenders within a reasonable period after the lease begins.

Tenants must be insistent that the nondisturbance agreement is broader than a mere agreement not to dispossess it. The tenant wants all of its rights—such as the landlord's construction obligation, and the tenant's expansion rights and exclusive rights—recognized and protected.

The real estate professional should not leave nondisturbance agreements without an awareness of the argument against their usefulness. This argument is applicable to a tenant in a multitenant development that has an institutional first mortgage lender. The argument begins by stating the obvious: a nondisturbance agreement is irrelevant in a successful development because the lender will be paid and the tenant will not be threatened with dispossession after foreclosure. Thus, nondisturbance agreements are necessary only if a development is not successful and the possibility of foreclosure is real. There, however, the lender is faced with a difficult choice: will it foreclose, extinguish subordinate leases of paying tenants, and try to revive the development with new untried tenants, or will it keep existing paying tenants and try to lease the vacant space? Lenders, the argument continues, will take the first choice, because there is no reason for them to believe that they can lease vacant space any more successfully than their borrowers. Put differently, the landlord and its lender have the same problem.

This argument against nondisturbance agreements is less persuasive when burdensome leases are the only reason for the foreclosure. If the leases were made when market conditions strongly favored tenants, the rents may be low and the terms may be long. In that situation, the lender's only hope may be termination of the unfavorable leases, and a nondisturbance agreement is the only hope of a tenant whose favorable lease is subordinate to the first mortgage.

CHAPTER 25

LANDLORD'S ACCESS

§ 25.1   General Access Provisions

The landlord should expressly reserve the right to enter the premises after they are leased. Otherwise, the landlord usually has no right to enter the premises.[1] If it does, the landlord will breach its covenant of quiet enjoyment and may be liable to its tenant as a trespasser.[2] Some cases hold that the landlord has a limited implied right to enter the premises in order to comply with governmental regulations, to prevent waste, to demand and collect rent, and to prevent injuries for which it may be liable.[3]

A common provision states:

FORM 25-1
LANDLORD'S ACCESS

Landlord, its agents, employees, and contractors may enter the premises at any time in response to an emergency, and at reasonable hours to (a) inspect the premises, (b) exhibit the premises to prospective purchasers, lenders, or tenants, (c) determine whether tenant is complying with its obligations in this lease, (d) supply cleaning service and any other service that this lease requires landlord to provide, (e) post notices of nonresponsibility or similar notices, or (f) make repairs that this lease requires landlord to make, or make repairs to any adjoining space or utility services, or make repairs, alterations, or improvements to any other portion of the

---

[1] 51C C.J.S. *Landlord and Tenant*, § 318 (1968); Higby v. Kirksey, 163 S.W. 315 (Tex. Civ. App. 1914), *writ refused*; Restatement of the Law of Property (Second) (Landlord and Tenant) § 6.1 (1977).

[2] *See* Magliocco v. Olson, 762 P.2d 681 (Colo. Ct. App. 1987), *cert. denied*, Oct. 11, 1988 (Colorado landlord successfully defended trespass claim because of express right to enter premises).

[3] 51C C.J.S. *Landlord and Tenant*, § 318 (1968).

building; however, all work will be done as promptly as reasonably possible and so as to cause as little interference to tenant as reasonably possible.

Tenant waives any claim of injury or inconvenience to tenant's business, interference with tenant's business, loss of occupancy or quiet enjoyment of the premises, or any other loss occasioned by such entry. Landlord will at all times have a key to unlock all of the doors in the premises (excluding tenant's vaults, safes, and similar areas designated in writing by tenant in advance). Landlord will have the right to use any means that landlord may deem proper to open doors in the premises and to enter the premises in an emergency. No entry to the premises by landlord by any means will be a forcible or unlawful entry into the premises, or a detainer of the premises, or an eviction, actual or constructive, of tenant from the premises, or any part of the premises, nor will the entry entitle tenant to damages or an abatement of rent or other charges that this lease requires tenant to pay.

The breadth of this provision disturbs many tenants. The landlord's right to enter in order to verify the tenant's compliance with the lease is an unrestricted license to enter. The landlord's entry to make repairs—especially to prepare adjacent premises for another tenant—should not be an inconvenience to the tenant. With the possible exception of repairs that are made to the tenant's own premises and that do not interfere with the conduct of its business, the landlord's entry should be during off hours. Some tenants demand that their landlords pay for any damage that they cause to the tenants' premises, tenants' improvements, and property in the premises.

Tenants should ask for a few days' advance notice of the landlord's visits, and it should ask that the landlord's visits occur only during business hours. Obviously, entry in response to an emergency should not require prior notice. If proprietary processes are used by an industrial tenant, notice and execution of a confidentiality agreement by all visitors should be required. Tenants whose work is subject to national security regulations must closely regulate and supervise their landlords' entries.

§ 25.2   Considerations for Shopping Center Tenants

In shopping center leases, landlords reserve the right to enter the premises near the end of the term (60 to 90 days before the expiration date) in order to post "for rent" signs. Tenants should resist this reserved right, because those signs detract from the tenant's business. Landlords can post their signs elsewhere on the perimeter of the shopping center and show prospective tenants through the premises. If the tenant capitulates on this issue, it should be certain that the size of the signs is appropriately limited and that no "for rent" signs can be posted before the date on which the tenant must exercise any renewal or extension rights. Tenants should not allow the landlord to post "for sale" signs on the premises. Such a sign invariably hurts a retail tenant.

CHAPTER 26

INDEMNIFICATION, WAIVER, AND RELEASE

§ 26.1   Introduction

Although *indemnification, waiver*, and *release* are distinct legal concepts, many leases use one broad provision to encompass them all. However, the distinctions among them should be observed. When a tenant waives or releases its claims against the landlord, the landlord's liability to the tenant is eliminated to the extent of the waiver or release. When a tenant indemnifies its landlord, it waives its own claims and becomes responsible for the claims of others. Because the tenant assumes the landlord's liability, indemnification is tantamount to insurance.

To confuse the matter further, a waiver or release is often referred to as an *exculpatory provision*, even though, in some leases, the term is used to describe the express limitation on a landlord's liability, such as that discussed in **Chapter 29**. These two kinds of exculpatory provisions are very similar but not identical. The release relieves the landlord of liability for certain mishaps; the landlord will never have liability if those mishaps occur, but it may have liability for other occurrences. The other exculpatory provision limits the recourse of a claimant against the landlord; the landlord always has liability, but the tenant may not be able to find any asset with which to satisfy its claims. If the release provision is broad enough and enforceable, there would be no need for the limitation of the tenant's recourse, because the claimant would have no claim. On the other hand, if there is no release, but there is an enforceable limitation on the tenant's recourse, the landlord would have limited its exposure to whatever it was willing to risk, presumably its interest in the premises or the development of which the premises are a part.

§ 26.2   Indemnification

Indemnifications are insurance contracts; in fact, they are the products that insurance companies usually sell. The tenant who gives its landlord an indemnification agrees to act as its landlord's insurer, that is, to substitute its liability for its landlord's liability. Among other things, this may mean that the tenant is liable even though it is not at fault.

Indemnifications are found in three general circumstances:

1. If only the tenant is at fault
2. If both the landlord and the tenant are at fault
3. If only the landlord is at fault.[1]

When a tenant considers a landlord's proposed indemnification, it should resist the third choice without compromise. The first choice is fair. The second choice should be resisted strenuously but not without some flexibility; like the first choice, it is a risk against which the tenant can be insured.

The real estate professional should not be surprised to learn that courts look askance at indemnifications and construe them strictly.[2] In order to convince a court that a valid indemnification has been given, there must be clear and unequivocal evidence of the tenant's intention to indemnify its landlord. In order to determine the tenant's intention, some courts require specific language in the indemnification provision, while other courts infer the tenant's intentions from that provision and the rest of the agreement.[3] An indemnification negotiated at arm's length by a sophisticated landlord and tenant can be upheld in New York, despite a statutory prohibition against an owner's indemnification for its own negligence.[4]

Indemnification provisions usually express a long list of matters against which the landlord is indemnified. Well-established legal principles make it clear that the landlord is most interested in being indemnified against "loss, liability and expense." An indemnification against liability arises when the liability arises (even though a loss has not been sustained), while an indemnification against loss arises only later, when the indemnitee sustains a loss.[5] A landlord's indemnification

---

[1] Lindblad, *Risk Implications in Lease Agreements*, 1979 Ins. L.J. 307.

[2] *See* discussion and cases collected in DiSciullo, *Negotiating a Commercial Lease From the Tenant's Perspective*, Real Est. L.J., Summer 1989, at 27.

[3] Annot., 4 A.L.R.4th 798, *Tenant's agreement to indemnify landlord against all claims as including losses resulting from landlord's negligence* (1981).

[4] La Vack v. National Shoe, Inc., 124 A.D.2d 352, 507 N.Y.S.2d 293 (1986). For judicial enforcement of a landlord's indemnification of its tenant, *see* Reeves v. Welch, 127 A.D.2d 1000, 512 N.Y.S.2d 749 (1987).

[5] *See* 755 Seventh Ave. Corp. v. Carroll, 266 N.Y. 157, 194 N.E. 69 (1935). In this case, Earl Carroll personally guaranteed a landlord that Earl Carroll Realty Corporation, the tenant, would

provision should clearly express a tenant's agreement to indemnify the landlord against the consequences of its own negligence.[6] A strong public policy prohibits insurance—and by extension indemnifications—against a loss arising from a landlord's intentional, deliberate or willful acts; indemnifications of that breadth must be unalterably opposed.

In order to arrive at the appropriate breadth of indemnification provisions in leases of office buildings, shopping centers, and single tenant buildings, the real estate professional ought to understand the legal basis for the landlord's liability. The landlord's liability for personal injury or property damage is related to the degree of its possession and control of the property on which the claimant is injured or the property is damaged.[7] If the landlord has no possession or control of the property, then the landlord will not have any liability for injury or damage on it. For example, a landlord would generally not have any liability for injury or damage in the shopping center tenant's premises or the office building tenant's premises. Therefore, it is entirely appropriate for the office building or shopping center tenant to indemnify its landlord for injury or damage occurring in or on its premises, so long as the injury or damage does not result from the landlord's act or negligence. As to those areas over which the landlord retains possession and control, such as the common areas of a shopping center, the tenant should not indemnify the landlord. In fact, one of the typical costs in common area charges is the landlord's insurance for loss or damage in those areas.

This allocation of responsibility on the basis of control leads to the conclusion that the tenant of a single tenant building should properly indemnify its landlord against damage or injury occurring anywhere on the premises. Because the landlord has given up possession and control of the premises and property to the tenant, it is entitled to a broader indemnification.

With these principles in mind, one can see that the landlord will propose a form of indemnification provision such as:

FORM 26-1
INDEMNIFICATION

Tenant will indemnify landlord, its agents, and employees against, and hold landlord, its agents, and employees harmless from, any and all demands, claims, causes of action, fines, penalties, damages (including consequential damages),

---

pay the costs of building a new theater on its leased premises. When the tenant failed to pay for some work, mechanics' liens were placed against the premises and eventually foreclosed. Not only that, the mortgage lender foreclosed soon after the mechanics' lienors. Carroll claimed that the landlord had not sustained any damage because it had lost the property anyway. The court upheld the landlord's claim because its liability for payment of the liens arose before the loan foreclosure, and thus the guarantee was operative.

[6] Goodyear Tire & Rubber Co. v. Jefferson Const. Co., 565 S.W.2d 916 (Tex. 1978); Foster v. Kenimer, 167 Ga. App. 567, 307 S.E.2d 30 (1983).

[7] See § **18.1** for some important exceptions to this rule.

losses, liabilities, judgments, and expenses (including, without limitation, attorneys' fees and court costs) incurred in connection with or arising from: (a) the use or occupancy of the premises by tenant or any person claiming under tenant; (b) any activity, work, or thing done or permitted by tenant in or about the premises; (c) any acts, omissions, or negligence of tenant, or any person claiming under tenant, or the employees, agents, contractors, invitees, or visitors of tenant or any such person; (d) any breach, violation, or nonperformance by tenant, or any person claiming under tenant, or the employees, agents, contractors, invitees, or visitors of tenant or any such person, of any term, covenant, or provision of this lease or any law, ordinance, or governmental requirement of any kind; or (e) except for loss of use of all or any portion of the premises or tenant's property located within the premises that is proximately caused by or results proximately from the negligence of landlord, any injury or damage to the person, property, or business of tenant, its employees, agents, contractors, invitees, visitors, or any other person entering upon the premises under the express or implied invitation of tenant. If any action or proceeding is brought against landlord, its employees, or agents by reason of any such claim, tenant, upon notice from landlord, will defend the claim at tenant's expense with counsel reasonably satisfactory to landlord.

This provision is fairly even-handed. It does not expressly seek indemnification against the landlord's own negligence; nevertheless, the tenant will want to make it clear that the landlord is not indemnified against the consequences of its own negligence or willful misconduct. This provision allows the landlord to defend itself; the landlord will want to do so if the tenant is financially unsound and there is no insurance. The prudent tenant will want to limit this provision to claims that occur during the term of the lease, and to limit its exposure to the extent that insurance against such risks is sufficient to discharge them in full.

Since the landlord's insurer is entitled to the benefit of the tenant's indemnification for losses that the insurer pays,[8] tenants should further limit their indemnification to matters against which the landlord is not—or, better yet, cannot be—effectively insured.[9]

Although some tenants vehemently oppose indemnification provisions, most sophisticated tenants realize that their risks under such provisions are insurable by the contractual liability coverage in their commercial general liability insurance. Of course, the limits of liability under such a policy may be less than the extent of the tenant's exposure under its indemnification. This, however, is no different from the tenant's risk that any of its liability coverage is insufficient, and should be addressed by the tenant with its risk management consultant.

Indemnities are often given "to the extent of insurance." This requires the indemnitee to advise the indemnitor of the extent of indemnification that it desires. The indemnitee must then require the indemnitor to obtain appropriate insurance. Although real estate professionals often object to this provision, it is

---

[8] Hartford Fire Ins. Co. v. Chicago Tunnel Terminal Co., 12 Ill. App. 2d 539, 139 N.E.2d 770 (1956); 46 C.J.S. *Insurance* § 1209 (1946).

[9] *See* Friedman, *Selected Problems in Store Leasing*, 15 Prac. Law. 41, 48 (1969).

merely a decision between the landlord and tenant about who will pay for certain insurance coverages and whose insurance company will pay the loss for which the indemnification is given.

The tenants in office buildings and shopping centers[10] are not out of line to request indemnification by the landlord against the tenant's loss, liability, and expense arising out of either injury or damage in the common areas, or landlord's default in its obligations under the lease. After all, in one way or another, the tenant is paying for the landlord's insurance against those risks in the common areas. Many landlords, for inexplicable reasons, consider such a request to be blasphemous. This response is unnecessary, since a moment's reflection will reveal that landlord can grant the tenant's request by getting contractual liability coverage as part of its commercial general liability policy. The landlord may also be able to add the tenant as an additional insured on its liability policy. In drafting the landlord's indemnification of its tenant, the landlord's real estate professional should bear in mind that its indemnification of the tenant is different from tenant's indemnification of the landlord, because the landlord's indemnification will be for injury or damage occurring in the common areas, while the tenant's indemnification will be for injury or damage occurring in the premises.

§ 26.3 Waiver and Release

The provisions for waiver and release of claims by the tenant against the landlord—the so-called exculpatory provisions—excuse the landlord from liability to its tenant for any sort of damage arising out of any sort of conduct.[11] As one might guess, exculpatory provisions are disfavored by courts and are carefully scrutinized when they are interpreted,[12] because they effectively allow the landlord to injure the tenant with impunity.

Several well-recognized exceptions to exculpatory provisions have been established by the courts. A landlord cannot exculpate itself from its fraudulent conduct or from its concealment of a defect of which it has knowledge.

---

[10] Annot., 48 A.L.R.3d 1163, *Liability of lessee of particular premises in shopping center for injury to patron from condition on portion of premises not included in his leasehold* (1973).

[11] Annot., 49 A.L.R.3d 321, *Validity of exculpatory clause in lease exempting lessor from liability* (1973). For a helpful discussion of the matter and a form which worked for a Pennsylvania landlord, see Princeton Sportswear Corp. v. H&M Assocs., 335 Pa. Super. 381, 484 A.2d 185 (1984), *rev'd*, 510 Pa. 189, 507 A.2d 339, *appeal after remand*, 358 Pa. Super. 325, 517 A.2d 963 (1986), *appeals denied*, 516 Pa. 642, 533 A.2d 713, and 517 Pa. 608, 536 A.2d 1332 (1987).

[12] 2 R. Powell, The Law of Real Property § 234(4) (P.J. Rohan ed. rev. 1977) [hereinafter Powell]; R. Schoshinski, American Law of Landlord and Tenant § 4:10 (1980) [hereinafter Schoshinski]. *See* First Nat'l Bank of Elgin v. G.M.P., 148 Ill. App. 3d 826, 499 N.E.2d 1039 (1986) (scrutiny of entire lease superseded release provision by itself and made tenant liable for damage by fire it had caused).

Exculpatory provisions are further limited by other principles in some jurisdictions. For example, some courts distinguish between a landlord's passive negligence and its active negligence.[13] Passive negligence is the landlord's failure to do something it is required to do, while active negligence is its incorrect doing of something it is required to do. For obvious reasons, the active/passive distinction has been criticized. Other courts have limited exculpatory provisions when they are believed to be against public policy.[14] This, of course, requires a case-by-case analysis of each provision. Many courts have refused to enforce exculpatory provisions when they arise in the context of residential leases (as opposed to commercial leases). This is especially true of exculpatory provisions found in leases of public housing authorities. Many courts have refused to allow an exculpatory provision to excuse a landlord's performance of duties imposed by statute.[15] Finally, several states have enacted legislation that limits or annuls exculpatory provisions.[16]

When a tenant is confronted with the landlord's form of exculpatory provision, it may wish to respond by limiting the provision's scope to exclude those recognized limitations. Nevertheless, a landlord's exculpatory provision might look like:

FORM 26-2
WAIVER AND RELEASE

Tenant waives and releases all claims against landlord, its employees, and agents with respect to all matters for which landlord has disclaimed liability pursuant to the provisions of this lease. In addition, tenant agrees that landlord, its agents, and employees will not be liable for any loss, injury, death, or damage (including consequential damages) to persons, property, or tenant's business occasioned by theft, act of God, public enemy, injunction, riot, strike, insurrection, war, court order, requisition, order of governmental body or authority, fire, explosion, falling objects, steam, water, rain or snow, leak or flow of water (including water from the elevator system), or rain or snow from the premises or into the premises or from the roof, street, subsurface or from any other place, or by dampness or from the breakage, leakage, obstruction, or other defects of the pipes, sprinklers, wires, appliances, plumbing, air conditioning, or lighting fixtures of the building, or from construction, repair, or alteration of the premises, or from any acts or omissions of any other tenant, occupant, or visitor of the premises, or from any cause beyond landlord's control.

---

[13] Queen Ins. Co. of Am. v. Kaiser, 27 Wis. 2d 571, 135 N.W.2d 247 (1965).

[14] Schoshinski § 4:12.

[15] Tenants Council of Tiber Island-Carrollsburg Square v. DeFranceaux, 305 F. Supp. 560 (D.D.C. 1969).

[16] N.Y. Gen. Oblig. Law § 5-321 (McKinney 1963) is one such state statute. California has another. *See* Cal. Civ. Code § 1668 (West 1872) (exculpation from one's own negligence is against public policy). However, in a lease of a mini-warehouse space, an exculpatory provision was upheld because there was no persuasive public policy. Cregg v. Ministor Ventures, 148 Cal. App. 3d 1107, 196 Cal. Rptr. 724 (1983).

This form has been used in multi-tenant projects. With minor modifications, it will serve for single tenant buildings. A similar provision effectively protected a Minnesota landlord from liability on account of bursting pipes.[17]

Like indemnification provisions, exculpatory provisions should not result in irreconcilable conflict, because the claims that the landlord hopes to be waived and released are risks against which the prudent tenant will be likely to purchase insurance. Landlords should not, however, eliminate their exculpatory provisions just because the tenant can insure the risk. There is a considerable body of law holding that the tenant's customers, invitees, and employees cannot recover against the landlord if the tenant has released the landlord.[18] These cases are based on the rationale that the claim arises through the tenant and cannot be any broader than the tenant's rights. Therefore, since the tenant has waived its rights, the claimant through the tenant has no rights.

On the other hand, there is also a body of law which holds that strangers to the lease cannot be bound by its terms.[19] In any event, the landlord may have some benefit from the provision and the tenant will not be hurt if it purchases insurance against the risks from which the landlord is exculpated.

---

[17] Fena v. Wickstrom, 348 N.W.2d 389 (Minn. Ct. App. 1984). For a form that worked for a Pennsylvania landlord, see Princeton Sportswear Corp. v. H&M Assocs., 335 Pa. Super. 381, 484 A.2d 185 (1984), *rev'd*, 510 Pa. 189, 507 A.2d 339, *appeal after remand*, 358 Pa. Super. 325, 517 A.2d 963 (1986), *appeals denied*, 516 Pa. 642 and 533 A.2d 713, 517 Pa. 608, 536 A.2d 1332 (1987).

[18] Annot., 12 A.L.R.3d 958, *Effect, on nonsigner, of provision of lease exempting landlord from liability on account of condition of property* (1967).

[19] Schoshinski § 4:11.

CHAPTER 27

SECURITY DEPOSITS

§ 27.1   Preparing and Reviewing a Security Deposit Provision

Every well-written lease requires the tenant to post a security deposit, although creditworthy tenants are usually excused from this obligation. Some landlords waive a creditworthy tenant's security deposit for so long as it maintains its creditworthiness. If the tenant's net worth subsequently falls below a stated amount, those landlords can require a security deposit.

For other tenants, the question is not whether they will post security deposits, but how much their security deposits will be.[1] The amount of a security deposit is negotiated with reference to the marketplace and the tenant's credit. However, a landlord that makes substantial initial improvements to the premises and amortizes its cost as part of the rent is certainly entitled to a larger security deposit than a landlord who delivers premises "as is" for improvement at the tenant's cost. Landlords in the latter category may take security interests in the tenant's own improvements.[2]

The real estate professional can learn about security deposits by considering a typical provision and the questions it addresses:

FORM 27-1
SECURITY DEPOSIT

Tenant has deposited $_____ with landlord as security for tenant's payment of rent and performance of its other obligations under this lease, and any renewals or

---

[1] *See The Pro-Landlord Security Deposit Clause,* Leasing Prof., Mar. 1987, at 6.

[2] *See* Ungar, *Get Extra Security on Tenant Installations With Chattel Mortgage,* Com. Lease L. Insider, May 1989, at 1.

extensions of this lease. If tenant defaults in its payment of rent or performance of its other obligations under this lease, landlord may use all or part of the security deposit for the payment of rent or any other amount in default, or for the payment of any other amount that landlord may spend or become obligated to spend by reason of tenant's default, or for the payment to landlord of any other loss or damage that landlord may suffer by reason of tenant's default. If landlord so uses any portion of the security deposit, tenant will restore the security deposit to its original amount within five (5) days after written demand from landlord. Landlord will not be required to keep the security deposit separate from its own funds and tenant will not be entitled to interest on the security deposit. The security deposit will not be a limitation on landlord's damages or other rights under this lease, or a payment of liquidated damages, or an advance payment of the rent. If tenant pays the rent and performs all of its other obligations under this lease, landlord will return the unused portion of the security deposit to tenant within sixty (60) days after the end of the term; however, if landlord has evidence that the security deposit has been assigned to an assignee of the lease, landlord will return the security deposit to the assignee. Landlord may deliver the security deposit to a purchaser of the premises and be discharged from further liability with respect to it.

The following questions—and possible answers—arise with regard to this provision and security deposits generally:

1. What is the purpose of the security deposit? It assures payment of rent and the tenant's performance of its other obligations under the lease. It is not liquidated damages, it is not advance rent, and it is not consideration for the landlord's execution of the lease. Among many reasons to avoid these provisions are the possible inadequacy of the liquidated damages in comparison to actual damages, and the immediate taxability to the landlord of bonus consideration or advance payment.[3] The tenant cannot deduct bonus consideration or advance payment as rent for tax purposes; the amount must be amortized over the term of the lease.

2. Must the security deposit be segregated from the landlord's own funds? A security deposit may be kept in an escrow account, or in an account separate from the landlord's other funds and not commingled with it, or in trust. State statutes, which almost invariably are limited to residential rental agreements, often impose one of these limitations.[4] If the landlord becomes a debtor under the Bankruptcy Code, the tenant has no priority claim to its commingled deposit. Depending upon its bargaining position, the tenant may prevail upon the landlord to accede to one of these limitations.

3. Must the landlord use the security deposit before exercising its other rights under the lease, or are its rights cumulative?

---

[3] *See Don't Get Taxed on Security Deposits*, Com. Lease L. Insider, July 1986.

[4] 2 R. Powell, The Law of Real Property § 231(2)(b) (P.J. Rohan ed., rev. 1977) contains a lengthy analysis of these state statutes.

4. To what defaults does the security deposit apply: nonpayment of rent only, or all defaults?

5. Is the security deposit to be replenished if it is used, or is it a one-time deposit?

6. Is the security deposit a limitation on damages?

7. Does an assignment of the lease include an assignment of the security deposit?

8. Does the security deposit bear interest? A tenant will try to convince the landlord that it should. Occasionally, a tenant proposes a discounted deposit that is to be considered a full deposit. The approach gives the tenant the benefit of the time value of money without requiring the landlord to pay interest. The landlord, however, will have less than it wanted if it needs the full security deposit before the discount period has passed.

9. Should the security deposit be reduced as the lease term progresses or if the tenant makes leasehold improvements that enhance the landlord's reversion? Tenants often demand that it should. A landlord should resist the suggestion with particular strength if it has doubts about the tenant's willingness to perform its obligations under the lease or if the landlord has expended a substantial amount of money in the initial improvement of the premises.

10. Does the security deposit pertain if the lease is extended or renewed?

11. If the security deposit must be returned at the end of the lease, how does the landlord protect itself from breaches that occur afterward, such as the tenant's failure to remove its trade fixtures or to repair damage caused in the course of doing so?

12. May other collateral be substituted for a cash security deposit? An agreement allowing substitution says (this form assumes that the term security deposit has been defined elsewhere in the lease):

FORM 27-2
SECURITY DEPOSIT—ALTERNATE SECURITY

After no less than fifteen (15) days' prior notice to landlord, tenant may substitute alternate security for its security deposit according to this paragraph:

(1) The term "alternate security" means obligations of the United States of America having a market value at all times of at least ____% of the security deposit.

(2) As a continuing condition to its right to substitute alternate security, tenant will always maintain on deposit with landlord alternate security whose market value is equal to ____% of such security deposit. If the market value of the alternate security falls below ____% of the security

deposit (whether by reason of a decrease in market value, or by landlord's application of the alternate security according to this paragraph) and tenant fails to deposit sufficient additional alternate security within five (5) days after notice from landlord, then in addition to any other rights that landlord may have under paragraph _____ [the basic security deposit provision] on account of tenant's failure to restore its security deposit landlord may sell the alternate security and hold the proceeds (less landlord's cost of sale) as a security deposit subject to the provisions of paragraph _____ [the basic security deposit provision].

(3)   So long as tenant is not in default under this lease, the earnings of the alternate security will be paid to tenant by landlord promptly after landlord receives them or, if the earnings are paid directly to tenant, tenant may keep them. At any time after tenant defaults under this lease, the earnings of the alternate security will be kept by landlord or, if the earnings are paid directly to tenant, tenant will remit them to landlord promptly after they are received.

(4)   The alternate security may be used by landlord for any purpose for which the security deposit may be used. Tenant authorizes landlord to sell all or part of the alternate security at any time after landlord would be entitled to apply the security deposit. The sale may be conducted at public or private sale, and landlord may be the purchaser, and the proceeds of sale (less landlord's cost of sale) will be applied according to the provisions of paragraph _____ [the basic security deposit provision].

(5)   Tenant may exercise its rights under this paragraph more than once. The alternate security will be returned to tenant whenever a cash security deposit replaces alternate security. The cash security deposit will be returned to tenant whenever tenant deposits alternate security.

13.   Is repayment of the security deposit secured? Landlords must vehemently resist any lien on title to secure repayment of the security deposit.

14.   Tenants sometimes suggest that they should post only part of the security deposit at the outset of their leases and should increase their deposits in installments during the initial period of the lease. This leaves the landlord with the bleak prospect that it may be unable to get a security deposit when it is most needed, that is, when the tenant's financial condition has deteriorated. Other tenants point proudly to their credit and ask that they be required to post a small security deposit, with an increase to follow if the lease is assigned. Since the original tenant remains liable under the lease in the event of an assignment, this is not particularly persuasive.

15.   To whom should the security deposit be returned? The provision in **Form 27-1** allows the landlord to return the deposit to the original tenant unless it has evidence that the deposit has been assigned to the tenant's assignee. These provisions are made to protect the landlord. In their absence, a landlord may improperly refund the deposit, because an assignment of lease, without more, does not necessitate an assignment of the security deposit.

16. What happens to the security deposit if the premises are sold? The provision should state that the landlord is excused from liability. Otherwise, it remains liable for the security deposit's return. If the provision excuses the landlord from its obligation to return the security deposit, the tenant should insist that any transferee must assume the landlord's obligation to return the tenant's security deposit as a condition of the release of the landlord.[5]

Any concession made to a tenant with respect to its security deposit — and, for that matter, in most other respects — should be personal to the tenant and should not inure to the benefit of any successor or assign.

§ 27.2 Lender's Obligation to Return Security Deposits

The rule in the few jurisdictions that have considered the question is that the lender, as transferee, does not become liable for the return of the security deposit by taking the reversion.[6]

The logic underlying this rule is that the landlord's covenant to return the security deposit exists by virtue of privity of contract, and it is not a covenant that runs with the land; therefore, the original landlord remains contractually bound to return the security deposit.[7] When a tenant deposits a sum of money with its landlord as security for the performance of the covenants of the lease, the deposit is considered a pledge and the landlord/pledgee is liable as such, not solely as landlord, for its return.[8] In other words, the promise to return a security deposit is a personal obligation stemming from the relationship of the tenant as pledgor and the original landlord as pledgee.[9] The liability to return a security deposit does not run with the reversion, and one who purchases the property subject to the lease is not liable for return of the security deposit if there is no evidence that the purchaser assumed the obligation of returning the deposit.[10]

There are several ways that responsibility for the return of security deposits passes from an original landlord to a successor landlord or lender. The successor landlord can agree to be responsible for return of the security deposits, thus

---

[5] Rosenman, *Tenant Security and Advance Rent,* in 2 Shopping Centre Leases (H.M. Haber ed. 1982).

[6] R. Schoshinski, American Law of Landlord and Tenant § 6:35 (1980).

[7] Mullendore Theatres v. Growth Realty Investors Co., 39 Wash. App. 64, 691 P.2d 970 (1984); 1 P.M.K., Inc. v. Folsom Heights Dev. Co., 692 S.W.2d 395 (Mo. Ct. App. 1985).

[8] Tuteur v. P.&F. Enters., Inc., 21 Ohio App. 2d 122, 255 N.E.2d 284 (1970).

[9] Partington v. Miller, 122 N.J.L. 388, 5 A.2d 468 (1939).

[10] 5 A.2d at 471; Tuteur v. P.&F. Enters., Inc., 21 Ohio App. 2d 122, 255 N.E.2d 284, 292 (1970).

affirmatively assuming the obligation.[11] The liability to return the security deposits passes to the successor landlord when the deposits are actually transferred to the successor landlord or lender.[12] Finally, if a security deposit is to be applied to a later installment of rent, the successor landlord or lender, upon receipt of the reversion, is bound by the covenant to apply the deposit to rent for the designated period because the rental obligation runs with the land.[13]

§ 27.3 Lenders' Other Concerns about Security Deposits

Lenders object to provisions that characterize the security deposit as prepaid rent, because tenants may have claims for refunds or credits. Lenders prefer provisions that have the security deposits held in trust by landlords; however, they recognize landlords' resistance to the trust fund idea. Lenders do not want any liability as a successor to the landlord for the return of the security deposit. When the mortgage is subordinate to a lease, the real estate professional must be particularly careful to provide that the tenant's only recourse for its deposit is to the landlord and that the tenant cannot assert any lien, claim, or offset against the lender, the rent, or the premises.

---

[11] Federated Mortgage Investors v. American Sav. & Loan Ass'n of Cal., 47 Cal. App. 3d 917, 121 Cal. Rptr. 137 (1975). The principle of *Federated* has been followed by a California appellate court in a slightly different question regarding security deposits: between a foreclosing lender and an assignee of the security deposits for collateral purposes. Enoch Packing Co. v. Equitable Fed. Sav. & Loan, 198 Cal. App. 3d 621, 243 Cal. Rptr. 789 (1988), *review denied and ordered not to be officially published,* Apr. 27, 1988. The collateral assignee prevailed.

[12] McDonald's Corp. v. Blotnik, 28 Ill. App. 2d 732, 328 N.E.2d 897 (1975).

[13] Bay View State Bank v. Liber, 33 Wis. 2d 539, 148 N.W.2d 122 (1967).

COVENANT OF QUIET ENJOYMENT

§ 28.1   General Rules

The common law covenant of quiet enjoyment promises the tenant that its possession of the premises will not be disturbed by the landlord; by anyone having an interest in the premises by, through, or under the landlord; by anyone having title paramount to the landlord's title; or by anyone having any lawful claim to the premises.[1] The covenant of quiet enjoyment is an implied covenant; in other words, it is implicit in a lease even though the lease says nothing about it.[2] Furthermore, even states that have abolished implied covenants in grants by deed have not abolished the implied covenant of quiet enjoyment in leases.[3] The covenant of quiet enjoyment is an independent covenant, that is, the landlord must assure the tenant's quiet enjoyment even if the tenant does not pay its rent or perform its other covenants in the lease.[4] The covenant of quiet enjoyment survives and must be confronted.

The reason a landlord will make an express covenant is to avail itself of the rule that an express covenant will supersede an implied covenant.[5] If a landlord

---

[1] 51C C.J.S. *Landlord and Tenant* § 323(2) (1968).

[2] Boyle v. Bay, 81 Colo. 125, 254 P. 156 (1927); 3 G.W. Thompson, Commentaries on the Modern Law of Real Property § 1129 (1980); City of New York v. Mabie, 13 N.Y. 151 (1855); Doyle v. Lord, 64 N.Y. 432 (1876).

[3] I American Law of Property § 3.47 (A. Casner ed. 1952) (although some states have reached different conclusions); 51C C.J.S. *Landlord and Tenant* § 323(1) (1968); 2 R. Powell, The Law of Real Property § 225(3) (P.J. Rohan ed., rev. 1977); R. Schoshinski, American Law of Landlord and Tenant §§ 3:3-3:9 (1980).

[4] 51C C.J.S. *Landlord and Tenant* § 323(2) (1968); Leveites v. Gottleib, 115 Misc. 218, 187 N.Y.S. 452 (Sup. Ct. 1921).

[5] 51C C.J.S. *Landlord and Tenant* § 323 (1968).

wishes to protect itself, it is only sensible to replace a broad implied covenant by a lesser express covenant; otherwise, the landlord is no further than the point at which it began. Many leases, however, have poor provisions that do no more than state the common law rule:

FORM 28-1
COVENANT OF QUIET ENJOYMENT—
NO PROTECTION FOR THE LANDLORD

Landlord covenants that tenant's use and enjoyment of the premises will not be disturbed during the term of this lease.

The breadth of this provision affords the landlord no protection from its common law duties.

One aspect of the covenant against which the landlord needs protection is the breadth of the warranty. It protects the tenant against any paramount title—even one of which the landlord may be unaware—and is riskier for the landlord in much the same way as a general warranty deed is riskier for a grantor than a special warranty deed or a deed with covenants against grantor's acts.

With these thoughts in mind, a landlord may suggest:

FORM 28-2
COVENANT OF QUIET ENJOYMENT—AN ILLUSION

So long as tenant pays the rent, and performs all of its obligations in this lease, tenant's possession of the premises will not be disturbed by landlord, its successors, and assigns.

As far as the tenant is concerned, this provision gives too little: nothing more than a landlord's promise not to undo what it has done.[6] With this covenant, it is unlikely that the landlord would be liable to the tenant if the tenant were evicted as a result of the foreclosure of a prior mortgage.[7]

Some real estate professionals suggest on behalf of tenants that the tenant will not be disturbed by anyone claiming "by, through, or under landlord." In effect, this covenant promises that the tenant will not be dispossessed by the landlord or holders of mortgages that the landlord makes. Most tenants are still not satisfied. They ask about holders of mortgages that existed before the landlord came into title. This leads back to the question of the breadth of the landlord's covenant.

The cautious landlord's response is to name the paramount title holders against which it will defend the tenant and to state:

---

[6] III M.R. Friedman, Friedman on Leases § 29.201 (1983).

[7] Burr v. Stenton, 43 N.Y. 462 (1871), *cited in* III Friedman § 29.302.

FORM 28-3
COVENANT OF QUIET ENJOYMENT—
CAUTIOUS LANDLORD'S PROVISION

So long as tenant pays the rent, and performs all of its obligations in this lease, tenant's possession of the premises will not be disturbed by landlord, or anyone claiming by, through or under landlord, or by the holders of the mortgages described in paragraph _____.

In appropriate circumstances, this provision would refer to ground leases.

One can see the difference between a covenant that names the superior mortgages (such as **Form 28-3**) and a covenant that assures quiet possession against all claims "except deeds of trust, mortgages, and ground leases." A tenant should not accept the latter provision. It excuses the landlord from liability in the common situation in which a tenant is dispossessed by a lender or ground landlord.[8] To the contrary, a tenant may discharge a lien that is superior to its lease if it is necessary to do so in order to protect its possession; then the tenant is subrogated to the lender's rights against the landlord.[9]

The landlord's liability in this covenant is not extinguished by its sale of the premises; the covenant runs with the land as a promise for the benefit of the tenant and its successors made by the landlord and its successors. For this reason, a landlord who has sold the premises may be sued by its tenant's assignee. The landlord protects itself against this risk by a provision such as that set forth in **Chapter 29**.

Many tenants do not understand that the covenant of quiet enjoyment does not prevent the landlord's lender from foreclosing. This covenant is the landlord's promise, not the lender's promise. Certainly, in most cases, the dispossessed tenant has a claim against its landlord, although provisions such as the one set forth in **Chapter 29** may limit the tenant's recourse. However, the tenant cannot rely on the landlord's covenant to avoid dispossession. The tenant's protection is found in the nondisturbance agreement described in § **24.3**.

By far the greatest modern significance of this covenant is its place in the tenant's arsenal of claims against landlords who have delivered premises in a condition that does not meet with the tenant's approval. See § **5.11** for a fuller discussion of its use in that context.

§ 28.2 Limitations of Covenant

The covenant of quiet enjoyment is not breached by a taking of premises pursuant to the exercise of the power of eminent domain, because the taking is not the

---

[8] *See* 220 West 42 Assoc. v. Ronbet Newmark Co., 53 A.D.2d 829, 385 N.Y.S.2d 304 (1976), *aff'd*, 40 N.Y.2d 1000, 359 N.E.2d 701, 391 N.Y.S.2d 107 (1976).

[9] Annot., 1 A.L.R.4th 286, *Lessee's right of subrogation in respect of lien superior to his lease* (1948).

result of the landlord's conduct or a defect in landlord's title.[10] Nor is the covenant of quiet enjoyment breached if the tenant's use of the premises is disturbed by strangers to title. Typically, these are trespassers against whom the tenant has its own rights. A more difficult question is presented when the tenant's use is disturbed by other tenants of the property of which the premises are a part.[11] Some courts do not give the tenant relief against its landlord because the tenant has rights against the other tenants. One notable exception has survived for more than a century; if the tenant is disturbed by the lewd and immoral conduct of another tenant, the covenant of quiet enjoyment is breached if the landlord does not stop the offensive behavior.[12]

On the other hand, some courts come to the tenant's rescue, especially if the tenant is disturbed by conduct that is a breach of the offending tenant's lease. These decisions are based upon the fact that the landlord's remedy of forfeiture of the offending tenant's lease is better than the tenant's remedy of a claim of nuisance or trespass. A Florida landlord, for example, breached the covenant when a dance studio tenant disturbed the use and possession of a neighboring tenant. The landlord was obligated to take steps to preserve the quiet possession of the complaining tenant.[13] If a tenant believes that the disturbance of its possession amounts to a constructive eviction, it must act promptly — and in any event before the disruption ends.[14]

There are several recent cases, involving the landlord's disturbance of the tenant's possession, which suggest that a claim for compensatory damages for breach of the covenant of quiet enjoyment may be appropriate even though a claim of eviction is not.[15]

As § **14.1** illustrates, the prudent landlord tries to avoid any claim that it must enforce its rules and regulations.

The covenant of quiet enjoyment is not breached unless there is an actual disturbance of the tenant's use and enjoyment of the premises.[16] A sale, a sale by foreclosure, a sale by taxing authority, an appointment of a receiver, or an

---

[10] 3 Thompson § 1133.

[11] Annot., 1 A.L.R.4th 849, *Landlord and tenant: constructive eviction by another tenant's conduct* (1980); 3 Thompson § 1133.

[12] Gilhooley v. Washington, 4 N.Y. 217 (1850).

[13] Barton v. Mitchell Co., 507 So. 2d 148 (Fla. Dist. Ct. App. 1987) (disturbance amounted to a constructive eviction).

[14] Segalas v. Moriarty, 211 Cal. App. 3d 1583, 260 Cal. Rptr. 246 (1989) (tenant vacated six months after the disturbance involving a neighboring restaurant's tenant finish ended).

[15] Broadway Copy Serv. Inc. v. Broad-Wall Co., 77 A.D. 285, 431 N.Y.S.2d 13 (1980); Bijan Designers v. St. Regis-Sheraton, 142 Misc. 2d 175, 536 N.Y.S.2d 951 (Sup. Ct.), *aff'd,* 150 A.D. 244, 543 N.Y.S.2d 296 (1989).

[16] *But c.f.* Conference Center, Ltd. v. TRC-The Research Corp. of New England, 189 Conn. 212, 455 A.2d 857 (1983), which held that the institution of foreclosure proceedings may (a) give rise to the tenant's "commercial insecurity" under Uniform Commercial Code § 2-609 and *Restatement (Second) of Contracts* § 251, thereby obliging the landlord to provide reasonable assurances of the tenant's continued possession, and (b) be a constructive eviction. This case is unique.

expiration of the term of the landlord's lease (if the tenant is actually a subtenant) will not give rise to a claim unless the tenant's use is disturbed. Furthermore, the disturbance must be substantial; entry by a landlord to make repairs required by law, for example, is not substantial.

There is some question whether the covenant is breached by the landlord's failure to put the tenant into possession of the premises. The remedies for the landlord's failure are discussed in § 5.2.

§ 28.3   Inappropriate Uses

In at least two situations, the covenant must be limited. One is a sale-leaseback in which the seller becomes the tenant and the buyer becomes the landlord.[17] Obviously, the landlord-buyer should not give assurances against anything but its own acts. Another example is the landlord acting in a fiduciary or representative capacity; its covenant should also be carefully circumscribed, if not expressly disclaimed.

---

[17] *In re* Lumbermans Mortgage Co., 712 F.2d 1334 (9th Cir. 1983).

CHAPTER 29

LIMITATION ON TENANT'S RECOURSE: SALE OF PREMISES

§ 29.1   Introduction

Many commercial leases have some form of two closely related exculpatory provisions. They are used in addition to, not in lieu of, the exculpatory provisions in § **26.3**, because they differ from those provisions. In one of these related provisions, the landlord limits the tenant's recourse against landlord on account of the landlord's breach. In the other, the landlord limits the duration of its liability under the lease to the duration of its ownership of the premises. These provisions will be considered separately.

§ 29.2   Limitation on Tenant's Recourse

A landlord will typically present a provision such as:

FORM 29-1
LIMITATION ON TENANT'S RECOURSE

Tenant's sole recourse against landlord, and any successor to the interest of landlord in the premises, is to the interest of landlord, and any successor, in the premises and the building of which the premises are a part. Tenant will not have any right to satisfy any judgment that it may have against landlord, or any successor, from any other assets of landlord, or any successor. In this paragraph the terms "landlord" and "successor" include the shareholders, venturers, and partners of landlord and

475

successor as well as the officers, directors, and employees of landlord and successor. The provisions of this paragraph are not intended to limit tenant's right to seek injunctive relief or specific performance, or tenant's right to claim the proceeds of insurance (if any) specifically maintained by landlord for tenant's benefit.

The problem that the tenant will have with this provision is simple: What can it do if its landlord fails to perform its duties under the lease? Considering the tenant's obligation to pay rent "without deduction or offset" in most leases, the tenant may have to pay rent even though its landlord is in default.

The tenant's inability to collect a money judgment against the landlord's other assets means it must be satisfied that the landlord's interest in the premises and the building of which the premises are a part is sufficient to cover any likely judgment. Moreover, many leases limit the tenant's recourse to the landlord's interest in the premises, which is, in many cases, a small fraction of its interest in the building of which the premises are a part. There is no realistic way for the tenant to assure itself of the adequacy of the landlord's interest in the premises and building. To do so, it would have to know the value of the building and the encumbrances against it. Furthermore, the tenant would have to be able to control the future value and encumbrances of the building. Finally, it would have to know the number of claims similar to its claim that might be asserted against the landlord's interest.

The tenant's task is impossible, but its concerns are real. For example, in exchange for its waiver of any claims against the landlord for personal injury and property damage, the tenant has been given the landlord's assurance that the landlord's insurer will waive its rights of subrogation against the tenant. If the insurer does not waive its right of subrogation, the tenant may be sued for a loss for which it thought it was not liable. Without recourse to the landlord, the tenant has no claim. By the same token, the tenant wants to get its security deposit back at the end of the lease; how does it know that the interest of the landlord in the building and premises is sufficient to assure its return? Although this provision allows the tenant to seek insurance proceeds maintained for the tenant's benefit, it says nothing about condemnation proceeds to which the tenant may be entitled, or escrow funds for taxes, insurance, or common area maintenance charges that the tenant has paid in advance or overpaid. If the landlord has promised the tenant improvements or renovations of the premises, the landlord should be personally obligated to provide them. For those occasions when the landlord has the tenant's money or has promised to spend its money for the tenant's benefit, the tenant should have personal recourse against the landlord. Finally, if the tenant is evicted when its landlord's lender forecloses, the tenant's claim for breach of the covenant of quiet enjoyment cannot be pursued against the landlord's lost equity.[1]

When a landlord argues for these exculpation provisions, it often asks rhetorically whether the tenant would hesitate to enter into the lease if the landlord were

---

[1] Skolnick, *Shopping Center Lease Negotiations: Some Problems of Representing Small Tenants,* 49 N.Y. St. B.J. 28 (1977).

a corporation with the premises as its sole asset. This is a variation of the proposition that the tenant is not relying on its landlord's credit. The tenant may rightly respond, "No, if my landlord-to-be were a thinly capitalized corporation with substantial obligations to me, I would insist on a guaranty or other assurance of performance." The facetious tenant may add, "O.K. Let me incorporate a shell corporation to be the tenant and we will be even."

In the final analysis, these exculpation provisions are desirable for a landlord, but not essential. When a landlord claims that its lenders will not allow it to remove the exculpation language because the lenders do not want liability on the leases if they foreclose, it gives the tenant the opportunity to respond that, if the lenders are the real concern, the lenders (but not the landlord) can be exculpated. A similar response is appropriate when the landlord claims that it would be unable to sell the premises to certain institutional investors, because they will not abide by the prospect of recourse; the tenant can offer to abate its recourse against these institutional investors.

Since these provisions are fought bitterly, landlords and tenants should consider possible compromises. When dealing with a partnership landlord, one compromise provides that the other assets of the partnership will be available to the tenant. This requires disclosure of the landlord's other activities and, perhaps, some limitations on sales of partnership assets and partnership distributions (in order to preserve the assets for which the tenant has negotiated), but it evidences good faith. Another compromise allows the tenant to discharge a personal judgment against the landlord only by offset against its rent. In effect, this is really no more than the tenant's right to garnish its own rent, and the tenant probably has that right without saying so. However, it is attractive to the tenant because it allows the tenant to abate its rent to the extent of its judgment, and it is attractive to the landlord because the landlord need not satisfy the judgment from separate assets. Of course, if the judgment exceeds the rent reserved, the tenant may suffer, but that is part of the compromise. If this arrangement is agreeable, the tenant must get the landlord's lender's consent in a proper adaptation to the nondisturbance agreement set forth in § **24.3**.

In some circumstances, there are sound reasons for variations on the landlord's exculpation; for example, trustees should not have personal liability for actions taken in their representative capacities, and beneficiaries should not be personally responsible for assets beyond their control.[2]

§ 29.3   Sale of Premises

When the landlord wishes to limit its liability after its sale of the premises, it will add to the form in § **29.2** a provision such as:

---

[2] Halper, *People and Property: Exculpation Clauses in Occupancy Leases,* 8 Real Est. Rev. 85 (1977).

FORM 29-2
SALE OF PREMISES

If landlord, or any subsequent owner of the premises, sells the premises, its liability for the performance of its agreements in this lease will end on the date of the sale of the premises, and tenant will look solely to the purchaser for the performance of those agreements. For the purposes of this paragraph, any holder of a mortgage or deed of trust that affects the premises at any time, and any landlord in any lease to which this lease is subordinate at any time, will be a subsequent owner of the premises when it succeeds the interest of the landlord or any subsequent owner of the premises. Tenant will attorn to any subsequent owners of the premises. The provisions of this paragraph are made in addition to, and not in lieu of, the provisions of paragraph [limitation on tenant's recourse paragraph].

This provision endeavors to end the landlord's liability if it sells the premises or loses them to foreclosure. As a general rule, the landlord would not be relieved of its liability under the lease on those occasions, just as the tenant would retain its liability under the lease if it were to assign the lease. The justification for this provision, to the extent there is one, arises out of the demands of the landlord's lender (who does not wish continuing obligations under leases it inherits) and out of the problems associated with the running of covenants with the land as burdens upon the landlord and as benefits to the tenant. For example, the landlord may be liable for a breach of the covenant of quiet enjoyment even after it has parted with the premises. Although prospective purchasers are said to justify this provision, they can be given comfort about the tenant's possible claims by the estoppel certificates described in § **32.15**. In practice, a tenant with claims against its landlord will rate them in any estoppel certificate it is asked to give to a prospective purchaser and use the vulnerability of the sale to settle its claims.

Form 29-2 seems to forgive the landlord's past defaults if it sells the premises. (This is quite different from waiving the landlord's liability for matters that occur after its sale. Landlords routinely agree to make the provision clearly reflective of the latter notion.) The release of the landlord from liability according to this provision has its own risks. In addition to the concerns that the tenant has with regard to the limitation on its recourse, the tenant wants to be assured that the so-called personal covenants of the landlord will be fulfilled. The construction of the premises is the most important of these covenants in the usual lease. In a shopping center, the landlord's covenant not to compete with the tenant, or not to lease to a competitor of the tenant within a specified radius, may be as important as the initial preparation of the premises. If the landlord is freed of its obligations under the lease, it may compete with the tenant or build another shopping center that has tenants who are competitive with the tenant.[3] Its release may allow it to breach other promises made in the lease, such as the confidentiality of the tenant's financial reports. The real estate professional must read the lease

---

[3] On the other hand, the original landlord can be liable for a breach of an exclusive by a subsequent owner. Renee Cleaners, Inc. v. Good Deal Super Mkts. of N.J., Inc., 89 N.J. Super. 186, 214 A.2d 437 (1965).

carefully and exclude those sorts of promises from the scope of a provision such as **Form 29-2**. In any event, the tenant ought to be certain that the landlord is released on sale only if a solvent purchaser assumes and agrees to perform the landlord's promises, such as the return of the security deposit.

PART VIII

DEFAULT AND ARBITRATION

CHAPTER 30

DEFAULT

§ 30.1   Landlord's Default

Although landlords try mightily to exonerate themselves from any real responsibility under their leases, some obligations to their tenants are inescapable. The rights and remedies available to a tenant if its landlord defaults flow from the dependence or independence of the landlord's and tenant's promises. If the landlord's promises are legally independent of the tenant's promises, the tenant must still perform its promises and pursue a separate claim for damages occasioned by the landlord's breach. If, on the other hand, the landlord's and tenant's promises are legally dependent, then the tenant may suspend performance of its covenants until the landlord resumes performance. Typically, the tenant would either apply its rent to the cost of performing the landlord's covenants, or withhold its rent until the landlord fulfills its covenants. Although the dependence of covenants rule has considerable judicial support in residential leases, it is only slowly gaining that support in commercial leases.[1]

One of the landlord's most important obligations in any lease is to pay encumbrances that affect the premises in order to prevent the dispossession of tenants by foreclosure and the resultant breach of the landlord's covenant of quiet enjoyment. In multitenant developments, the landlord's other obligations usually have to do with the provision of services and the maintenance and repair of the structure and common areas. In single tenant buildings, the tenant usually has all the obligations of ownership, other than the landlord's obligation to pay encumbrances that affect the premises.

The feasibility of an office building or shopping center tenant curing its landlord's defaults seems remote, because the cost will be prohibitive. In fact, at a manageable cost, a tenant can cure many of its landlord's defaults with regard to the premises; the tenant can hire cleaning crews, install space heaters, and replace or repair many parts of the premises. However, landlords of multitenant developments are wise to resist the tenant's substitution of its judgment for the landlord's with respect to matters about which reasonable people can differ, for example, good condition and repair. Moreover, a typical landlord will not allow any of its tenants to make repairs to the structure of the development or the systems that serve it. The right to cure the landlord's defaults, if given at all, must be carefully delineated.

In a single tenant building, the rent obligation is likely to be greater than the mortgage obligation, so the tenant's payment of its landlord's mortgage is feasible. Furthermore, in a single tenant building, the cost to cure the landlord's other defaults (if it has any other obligations) will be nearer to the tenant's rent than it will be to the rent of a tenant in a multitenant development.

Landlords usually give their tenants the right to cure the landlord's defaults as long as the landlord acknowledges its responsibility after it is given notice of its defaults and an opportunity to cure them. After all, landlords reason, they cannot justly prohibit their tenants from doing what they as landlords promised and failed to do.

A form of tenant's right to cure landlord's default may say:

FORM 30-1
DEFAULT — TENANT'S PERFORMANCE OF
LANDLORD'S COVENANTS

If (a) landlord fails to discharge fully any of its obligations imposed by a mortgage that is superior to this lease, or (b) landlord fails to pay any real estate taxes and assessments affecting the premises, or (c) landlord fails to make any repairs that this lease or any law requires it to make, then tenant may (but will not be required to)

---

[1] Restatement of the Law of Property (Second) (Landlord and Tenant) § 7.1 (1977) supports the dependence of covenants rule in commercial leases, although it does not adopt any position with regard to the dependence of rent on tenantability.

discharge those obligations, or pay those taxes and assessments, or make those repairs, as the case may be. If it does, all amounts paid by tenant in doing so and all costs and expenses incurred by tenant in connection with doing so (together with interest at _____% per annum from the date of tenant's payment of the amount or incurring of each cost or expense until the date of full repayment by landlord) will be payable by landlord to tenant on demand. If landlord fails to make the repayment, in addition to any other rights it may have, tenant will have the right to offset the amount of the repayment against its rent and other charges under this lease; however, tenant will have no lien or claim against the premises or the building.

§ 30.2 Lenders' Concerns about Tenant's Cure Rights

Generally, lenders strenuously object to any provision that gives a tenant a broad right to cure its landlord's defaults and to deduct the cost to cure from its rent. Nevertheless, many lenders do allow these rights if the leasehold is threatened by the landlord's default and if the expense is one that would be a normal use of the landlord's cash flow. In other words, if the landlord's default is directly related to the security for the loan and not merely to the convenience of the tenant, the lender will look more favorably on the tenant's rights to cure.

The landlord's failure to pay its mortgage is one default that lenders will usually allow tenants to cure. However, the right to cure will only be available with respect to mortgages that are prior to the lease and thus threaten the continuation of the lease after foreclosure. Because a tenant has the right to protect itself against a superior lien (even if the lease does not say so),[2] this right to cure does no more than express the rights that the tenant has if its landlord breaches its lease. If the tenant is given the right to cure defaults in mortgages that are subordinate to its lease, then prior mortgages may become, in effect, subordinated to later mortgages; there will be no rent available to the prior lender if the tenant has paid it to a subsequent lender in order to cure its landlord's default on the subsequent loan. This is one of the reasons that first lien lenders dislike subordination provisions that automatically subordinate the lease to all mortgage liens. If the lease is subject to a second mortgage lien on which the landlord defaults, the tenant's use of the default will leave no money for payment of the first lien. The first lien lender will be compelled to foreclose eventually or to "make a deal" with the holder of the second mortgage lien.

Lenders will often allow tenants to pay real estate taxes and assessments that by law are superior to the lease. However, lenders will not allow this to continue after their foreclosures, nor will they usually allow tenants to spend more than a fixed amount or a stated percentage of their rent to cure those defaults.

Lenders will sometimes allow a tenant to cure its landlord's failure to make required repairs or to comply with building codes. These cure rights are often

---

[2] Annot., 1 A.L.R.2d 286, *Lessee's right of subrogation in respect of a lien superior to his lease* (1948).

limited in the same way as rights to cure tax defaults. Tenants should insist that they not be obligated to give notice and an opportunity to cure a default in making repairs if the landlord's default has resulted in an emergency.

The tenant's rights to cure defaults invariably require prior notice to the landlord and the lender and an opportunity for both of them to cure the default. Lenders need more time to cure a default than landlords. First of all, the lender must wait until the landlord's cure period has passed in order to see whether any cure is necessary. Next, the lender must then decide whether it wishes to cure. Last, the lender may want to foreclose before it cures; it may not have adequate access to cure before foreclosure and may not want to incur substantial costs before it owns the premises.

§ 30.3   Introduction to Tenant's Default

Too many real estate professionals give too little attention to lease provisions regarding tenant's default.[3] They base their casual attitude on the irrebuttable fact that the landlord's array of remedies is inconsequential to a tenant that has no money, where there is no money, there is no money, they say, no matter how many remedies the landlord may have. This common belief is subject to several just criticisms. The most important objection is that this view fails to distinguish remedies from defaults. Not until a default has occurred do the landlord's remedies come into play. The real estate professional's task is to limit those occurrences that are deemed defaults, and thus to delay or avoid the landlord's right to exercise its remedies.

The opinion that default provisions are not a proper subject for vigorous negotiation arises from the dubious proposition that defaults are harbingers of the tenant's imminent doom. Not all are. Some arise inadvertently and others are susceptible to cure without any real risk or inconvenience to the landlord. The real estate professional must protect the tenant against costly or irreversible consequences of those defaults.

Finally, the default provisions are of paramount importance to any guarantors of the lease. If the real estate professional is careless about the meaning of default and the landlord's remedies, the guarantors of the lease will ultimately suffer. Thus, although the undercapitalized tenant may escape the consequences of inattention because it is unable to respond to a judgment, the substantial guarantors bear the brunt of the landlord's remedies. When the real estate professional is involved with the guaranteed lease, the default provisions should be as vigorously negotiated as they would be if the guarantors were the tenant; in effect, they are.

---

[3] *See* Leasing Professional, Sept. 1988, at 1 (discussion of default provisions, with forms).

§ 30.4   Tenant's Default and Other Parts of the Lease

The default provisions do not stand alone—other parts of the lease affect them. For example, the lease provisions regarding notices have a direct impact on the default provisions. If the default provisions require the landlord to give notice to the tenant before it exercises any of its remedies, the method of giving notice and the time in which notices become effective are important parts of the default provisions.

The default provisions also affect other parts of the lease. As an illustration, many leases condition the tenant's renewals or options upon it not being in default at the time of its exercise of those renewals or options. These renewals and options are often so beneficial to the tenant that landlords are eager to fall upon any excuse to avoid them. Tenants must therefore be certain they do not lose these valuable rights because of a poorly written provision that cuts off the tenant's rights because of a minor and long-forgotten default.

On the other hand, the default provisions should make clear that the termination of the lease on account of the tenant's default also terminates the tenant's purchase options. In the absence of any such provision, termination would be the result in the vast majority of leases; however, courts have sustained purchase options after a lease termination, holding that the options are divisible from the lease and independent of the lease.[4]

§ 30.5   Landlord's Right to Cure

Some of the tenant's possible defaults, such as failure to provide insurance or to make repairs, are not so serious that the landlord will want to terminate the lease. In those cases, the landlord may wish to perform the tenant's covenant on its behalf and charge it for the cost of doing so.

Because one alternative to the landlord's cure is the tenant's default under the lease, most tenants readily give the landlord this right to cure. Those tenants feel that they are no worse off if the landlord cures its default and recovers its costs to do so. In fact, even without such a provision, the landlord may have a common law right to cure the tenant's defaults if the landlord mitigates its damages by doing so. Still, both landlords and tenants should approach this provision with care.

The landlord will want to be certain that it has the right, but not the obligation, to cure the tenant's default; this will avoid a reversal of their roles by which the landlord becomes liable to the tenant for the landlord's default. The landlord will also want to characterize the amounts that it advances as additional rent, for this will assure the landlord of the summary possessory remedies available for

---

[4] Annot., 10 A.L.R.2d 884, *Termination of lease as termination of option to purchase therein contained* (1950).

nonpayment of rent. If the failure to reimburse the landlord for its advances to cure the tenant's default is not itself a default, the landlord may be unable to terminate the lease and will be relegated to a suit for damages.[5]

For itself, the tenant will insist that it be given notice of the default before the landlord cures it. The landlord should grant this request as long as it does not apply to emergencies in which the delay incurred by giving notice would prevent a worth while cure. The tenant will insist that the landlord incur only reasonable cost. Landlords balk at this suggestion for two reasons. First, they do not want to argue about the reasonableness of their costs. Second, when all is said and done, the tenant could have avoided the argument by performing its own promises.

FORM 30-2
DEFAULT—LANDLORD'S PERFORMANCE OF
TENANT'S COVENANTS

If tenant fails to pay when due amounts payable under this lease or to perform any of its other obligations under this lease within the time permitted for their performance, then landlord, after ten (10) days' prior written notice to tenant (or, in case of any emergency, upon such notice, or without notice, as may be reasonable under the circumstances) and without waiving any of its rights under this lease, may (but will not be required to) pay the amount or perform the obligation.

All amounts paid by landlord and all costs and expenses incurred by landlord in connection with the performance of any of those obligations (together with interest at the prime rate from the date of landlord's paying the amount or incurring each cost or expense until the date of full repayment by tenant) will be payable by tenant to landlord on demand. In the proof of any damages that landlord may claim against tenant arising out of tenant's failure to maintain insurance, landlord will not be limited to the amount of the unpaid insurance premium but rather landlord will also be entitled to recover as damages for the breach, the amount of any uninsured loss (to the extent of any deficiency in the insurance required by the provisions of this lease), damages, costs, and expenses of suit, including attorneys' fees, arising out of damage to, or destruction of, the premises occurring during any period for which tenant has failed to provide such insurance.

§ 30.6   Events of Default

As the first three sections of this chapter suggested, lease provisions regarding default actually encompass two subtopics: defaults and remedies. Defaults are occurrences that allow the landlord to exercise its remedies. The default provisions themselves are often divided into two categories: those that define *defaults* and those that define *events of default*. Events of default occur after defaults and after the passage of time, or the giving of notice, or the failure to cure. In order to

---

[5] Haddad v. Francis, 40 Conn. Supp. 567, 537 A.2d 174 (1986), *aff'd*, 13 Conn. App. 324, 536 A.2d 597 (1988) (landlord's advance of insurance premiums).

illustrate the difference, consider the obligation to pay rent on the first day of each month. Certainly it is a default not to pay the rent on that first day, but it may not be an event of default unless the failure to do so continues for a stated period after notice.

The distinction is important for two reasons. The landlord's remedies depend on there being defaults, and some of the tenant's rights (renewals and expansion options, as examples) depend on there being no defaults. If the landlord has the right to pursue its remedies immediately after a default, then the tenant has no grace period, no notice, and no opportunity to cure. By the same token, if the tenant's right to renew is dependent upon there being no default, then the tenant may lose valuable rights because of a default of which it is unaware.[6]

Although the terminology is helpful and common, the importance of defaults and events of default does not lie merely in semantics. Regardless of the terms that a lease employs, the tenant ought to ask for a grace period (in which interest and late charges do not accrue on the unpaid amount), a notice, and an opportunity to cure its defaults. The consequences of a forfeited lease and liability for damages are too drastic to allow a default without notice and an opportunity to cure. The grace period is helpful, but it is not as essential as notice and cure.

Some landlords refuse to give tenants a grace period for payment of rent, because their lenders do not give them a grace period for mortgage payments. While notice and cure are appropriate for most other tenant defaults, some landlords refuse to give notice or cure for nonpayment of rent, because they believe that tenants should know whether or not they have paid their rent. Tenants respond that rent payments can be misplaced and that they deserve a chance to save their leases after notice that the landlord has not received payment. For example, a South Carolina court enforced forfeiture of a lease when a misaddressed rent check was late even though a replacement check (and late charge) were promptly tendered. The onerous lease provision for late payment allowed a 10 percent late charge, or rent acceleration, or forfeiture.[7] Even if termination is not allowed, the court may award a landlord its attorneys' fees and court costs.

As a compromise that is preferable to losing its lease, the tenant may prefer to pay late charges and interest. If the landlord and tenant are unable to agree upon notice of nonpayment of rent, and cannot reach a compromise, they should consider the applicable eviction statutes; often these statutes require that the landlord give its tenant three days or five days after notice within which to pay the rent or surrender the premises. When such a statute is in effect, the issue of notice of nonpayment of rent is not so momentous. In addition to statutory protections, judicial interventions often assist tenants; for example, when a New York lease allowed a landlord to terminate a lease at any time after rent remained unpaid for

---

[6] *See* Eskridge v. Macklevy, Inc., 468 So. 2d 337 (Fla. Dist. Ct. App.), *review denied*, 478 So. 2d 54 (Fla. 1985) (an example of the tenant's loss of a valuable purchase option on account of a long-standing default).

[7] Hairston v. Carolina Wholesale Furniture Co., 291 S.C. 371, 353 S.E.2d 701 (Ct. App. 1987).

five days, the New York Court of Appeals refused to allow a termination when the tenant paid before the landlord gave notice of termination.[8]

Because the statutes of many states favor tenants, some tenants take advantage of them by persistently defaulting and waiting for the last possible moment to cure. In an effort to avoid the recurrent irritation of frustrated eviction attempts, some landlords provide that a default is not curable if it has occurred before. For example, a second failure to pay rent in timely fashion is not a curable default. One can go on to divide uncurable defaults into monetary and nonmonetary defaults and to allow a different number of defaults for each kind before the uncurable one occurs. Such a provision is, of course, entirely different from the provision in paragraph (a) of **Form 30-3** that says only that notice will not be given after the first one in any 12 months. Despite the attraction those provisions may have, the real estate professional should be aware that state statutes may nevertheless override contract provisions.

In several cases, tenants have successfully challenged default notices that were sent by the landlord's attorney when the lease specified that the landlord had to give notices.[9] Other courts have not been so literal.[10] To be safe, a lease provision might omit the source of notice and base a default on a failure to pay "after notice," or a lease may use a notice provision such as **Form 32-24**.

Although real estate professionals think first of terminating the lease when a tenant defaults, there are other (and sometimes better) remedies available to the landlord; they are introduced in § **30.7**. Furthermore, termination—or forfeiture—is a serious remedy which courts assiduously try to avoid.[11] Finally, at common law and in many states, a landlord cannot terminate a lease unless it has first given notice and made demand for performance; tenants should not waive these notices or demands. A termination following an improper notice (such as a notice to vacate within 15 days as opposed to a notice to cure within 10 days that the lease required) will be ineffective.[12]

In the following provision, the term *rent* has been defined elsewhere in the lease to mean all the tenant's monetary obligations, not just the monthly payments that are usually considered rent. In a lease that uses the event of default terminology, the first part of the default provision may provide:

---

[8] TSS-Seedman's, Inc. v. Elota Realty Co., 72 N.Y.2d 1024, 531 N.E.2d 646, 534 N.Y.S.2d 925, *reargument denied,* 73 N.Y.2d 852, 534 N.E.2d 335, 537 N.Y.S.2d 496 (1988).

[9] Siegel v. Kentucky Fried Chicken of Long Island, Inc., 108 A.D.2d 218, 488 N.Y.S.2d 744 (1985), *aff'd,* 67 N.Y.2d 792, 492 N.E.2d 390, 501 N.Y.S.2d 317 (1986); 117-07 Hillside Ave. Realty Corp. v. RKO Century Warner Theaters, Inc., 151 A.D.2d 732, 543 N.Y.S.2d 151 (1989).

[10] Arnold v. Krigbaum, 169 Cal. 143, 146 P. 423 (1915).

[11] 2 R. Powell, The Law of Real Property § 231(3) (P.J. Rohan ed., rev. 1977) [hereinafter Powell]. See Annot., 54 A.L.R.4th 595 *Commercial leases: application of rule that lease may be canceled only for "material" breach* (1987) for surprising examples of defaults that have and have not been the bases for termination.

[12] Korte v. National Super Markets, Inc., 173 Ill. App. 3d 1066, 528 N.E.2d 10 (1988).

FORM 30-3
DEFAULT—EVENTS OF DEFAULT

The following occurrences are "events of default":

(a)   Tenant defaults in the due and punctual payment of rent, and the default continues for five (5) days after notice from landlord; however, tenant will not be entitled to more than one (1) notice for default in payment of rent during any twelve-month period, and if, during the twelve (12) months after any such notice, any rent is not paid when due, an event of default will have occurred without further notice;

(b)   Tenant vacates or abandons the premises;

(c)   This lease or the premises or any part of the premises are taken upon execution or by other process of law directed against tenant, or are taken upon or subjected to any attachment by any creditor of tenant or claimant against tenant, and the attachment is not discharged within fifteen (15) days after its levy;

(d)   Tenant files a petition in bankruptcy or insolvency or for reorganization or arrangement under the bankruptcy laws of the United States or under any insolvency act of any state, or is dissolved, or makes an assignment for the benefit of creditors;

(e)   Involuntary proceedings under any bankruptcy laws or insolvency act or for the dissolution of tenant are instituted against tenant, or a receiver or trustee is appointed for all or substantially all of tenant's property, and the proceeding is not dismissed or the receivership or trusteeship is not vacated within sixty (60) days after the institution or appointment;

(f)   Tenant fails to take possession of the premises on the commencement date of the term; or

(g)   Tenant breaches any of the other agreements, terms, covenants, or conditions that this lease requires tenant to perform, and the breach continues for a period of thirty (30) days after notice by landlord to tenant.

Unlike many default provisions, paragraph (a) of this one gives the tenant notice (albeit only once each 12 months) and an opportunity to cure before an event of default has occurred. With regard to paragraph (b), the terms *vacate* and *abandon* are not synonyms. Vacating is a temporary interruption of possession. To abandon is to vacate without intending to return.[13] The law of abandonment, having as it does a subjective element, has been criticized as unpredictable, and it has been suggested that abandonment be proven by a failure to pay rent coupled with vacation of the premises, both continuing after notice from the landlord.[14] Tenants should resist a default based upon mere vacating.

Many lawyers feel that the events of default in paragraphs (d) and (e) are superseded by § 365(e)(1) of the Bankruptcy Code, which prohibits automatic termination of executory contracts such as leases on account of a bankruptcy. Some real estate professionals argue for these paragraphs by saying that the

---

[13] *See* Trustees of Net Realty Holding Trust v. Avco Fin. Servs. of Barre, Inc., 144 Vt. 243, 476 A.2d 530 (1984); Foureal Co. v. Nat'l Molding Corp., 74 Misc. 2d 316, 344 N.Y.S.2d 598 (1973) (discussions of differences between "vacated" and "vacant" premises).

[14] Note, *New Approach to Adjudicating Tenant's Abandonment of Premises*, 9 Cardozo L. Rev. 1811 (1988).

Bankruptcy Code may be amended in order to allow a termination on account of bankruptcy. Other real estate professionals argue that if a tenant's bankruptcy is dismissed or the tenant is not discharged, the landlord may have the right to terminate the lease because a bankruptcy has occurred and the tenant is not protected by the Bankruptcy Code.[15]

The tenant should ask that the provision in paragraph (g) be expanded to provide that, if the default by its nature cannot be cured within 30 days or if the tenant is prevented from curing the default by reasons beyond its control, then the cure period will be extended in order to allow the cure. Most landlords grant this request, but condition it upon the tenant's prompt commencement and due diligence in effecting the cure.

These are the basic events of default. Special circumstances demand special provisions. Often, leases provide that a prohibited assignment is an event of default. In a guaranteed lease, a landlord may want the guarantor's death, insolvency, or attempted rescission or termination of the guaranty to be a default. In a guaranteed retail lease, the guarantor's breach of a radius restriction may also be a breach.

If the credit of the tenant depends upon a subsidiary or parent (whether or not the lease is guaranteed), the insolvency of the parent or subsidiary may be an appropriate event of default. If the parent's or subsidiary's principal operations are abroad, the expropriation or commencement of proceedings comparable to bankruptcy proceedings should also be considered as events of default.

§ 30.7 Remedies

When a tenant has abandoned the premises,[16] the landlord may (a) accept the surrender, consider the lease terminated, and resume possession of the premises; (b) do nothing and sue the tenant for each installment of rent as it becomes due or sue the tenant for all the rent at the end of the term; or (c) take possession of the premises for the tenant's account, relet the premises for the tenant's account, and hold the tenant liable for the difference between what the tenant owed and what the landlord received on reletting.[17] These are the basic remedies that leases provide. To them are added rent acceleration and all other legal remedies by a

---

[15] That view has been upheld in Miller v. Parlor Furniture of Hickory, Inc., 79 N.C. App. 639, 339 S.E.2d 804, *review denied, appeal dismissed,* 316 N.C. 732, 345 S.E.2d 389 (1986), *cert. denied,* 484 U.S. 1043, 108 S. Ct. 777 (1988).

[16] Gunther, *Lessor's Remedies for Lessee's Unjustified Abandonment of Premises,* 30 Loy. L. Rev. 901 (1984), discusses Louisiana's unique laws in this area.

[17] Gould v. Vitiello, 526 So. 2d 1018 (Fla. Dist. Ct. App. 1988); Truitt v. Evangel Temple, Inc. 486 A.2d 1169 (D.C. 1984).

provision such as paragraph (c) of **Form 30-4**.[18] Of course, state statutes may also govern many of the landlord's remedies.[19]

§ 30.8   — Termination

Termination of the lease is permitted only if the lease or applicable statute gives the landlord the right to do so.[20] Without the right to terminate the lease, the landlord can only sue for late rent.[21] Termination can also come about by the landlord's acceptance of the tenant's surrender; see **§ 21.1**. In case of surrender and acceptance, the landlord and tenant are relieved of any mutual obligations accruing after the date on which the surrender is accepted, and the tenant owes the landlord only the rent through that date. Termination is a drastic remedy that courts award sparingly.[22]

Since termination ends the tenant's rent obligation, landlords employ a "survival clause" such as that in this section and in paragraph (a) of **Form 30-4** to convert the rent obligation to an obligation to pay damages on account of the tenant's breach. With a survival provision, the landlord can continue to collect "rent" in the guise of "damages."

In 1985 the Supreme Court of New Jersey answered a very difficult question: When a landlord terminates a lease with a survival provision and then leases the premises at a greater rent than the defaulting tenant was obligated to pay, who should get the excess rent that accrues during the balance of the defaulting

---

[18] When an event of default has occurred, a landlord has some or all of the following remedies: ejectment; summary proceedings, forcible entry and detainer proceedings, or unlawful detainer proceedings (the claim has various names in different jurisdictions); rent acceleration; appointment of a receiver (an appropriate remedy when the landlord wanted to preserve subtenant's rental payments); repossession or self-help; declaratory action; a suit for breach of contract; and a right to cure. 2 Powell § 250(1). Although liquidated damages are enforceable under Kentucky law, a provision requiring the tenant to pay 12 months' rent on account of one month's default is an unenforceable penalty. *In re* Robinson, 49 Bankr. 575 (W.D. Ky. 1985). For the unique procedural issues in New York, see Ross, *Converting Nonpayment to Holdover Summary Proceedings: The New York Experience with Conditional Limitations Based upon Nonpayment of Rent,* 15 Fordham Urban L.J. 289 (1987). For D.C. procedures, see Bunn, *Commercial Landlord-Tenant Eviction: A.D.C. Guide,* Wash. Law, Sept./Oct. 1986, at 34.

[19] See P. Rohan, 7 Current Leasing Law & Techniques § 7.02 (1989) for the statutory schemes.

[20] *See* Barnett v. Dooley, 186 Tenn. 611, 212 S.W.2d 598 (1948) (landlord has no right to terminate lease upon tenant's default unless lease allows it to do so), *cited in* Berry, *Avoiding Lease Drafting Pitfalls,* Tenn. B.J., May 1983, at 11, 14. *See generally* Kane & Nussbaum, *How to Protect Against a Tenant's Default Under a Commercial Lease (with Form),* 1 Prac. Real Est. Law 9 (1985) (excellent discussion of appropriate bankruptcy provisions); Chervin & Binder, *What Rights Does the Commercial Landlord Have When the Tenant Goes Bankrupt?,* 2 Prac. Real Est. Law. 51 (1986).

[21] Dillingham v. Williams, 165 S.W.2d 524 (Tex. Civ. App. 1942), *writ refused.*

[22] *See* E. Halper, Shopping Center and Store Leases § 16.01(b) (Supp. 1984) (a valuable discussion of the many ways in which courts avoid terminating leases).

tenant's term? By a 4-3 margin, the court held that the landlord should; however, a lengthy dissent argued that the tenant should get the excess.[23]

Because the decision was close and the case has been widely discussed, one can profitably consider the case with care. When the tenant defaulted, the landlord elected to terminate the lease and to hold the tenant liable for rent due after termination pursuant to a survival provision in the lease. That provision said:

> In the event that the relation of the Landlord and Tenant may cease or terminate by reason of the reentry of the Landlord under the terms and covenants contained in this lease or by the ejectment of the Tenant by summary proceedings or otherwise, or after the abandonment of the premises by the Tenant, the Tenant shall remain liable and shall pay in monthly payments the rent which accrues subsequent to the reentry by the Landlord, and the Tenant shall pay as damages for the breach of the covenants contained in this lease the difference between the rent reserved and the rent collected and received, if any, by the Landlord, during the remainder of the unexpired term, such difference of [sic] deficiency between the rent reserved and the rent collected, if any, shall become due and payable in monthly payments during the remainder of the unexpired term, as the amounts of such difference or deficiency shall from time to time be ascertained.

At the time of termination, eight months remained on the lease. The landlord leased the premises for a term that overlapped the last four months of the unexpired term of the defaulting tenant's lease. For those four months, the landlord received approximately $10,000 more that it would have received if the defaulting tenant had performed its obligations under the old lease. When the landlord sued the old tenant (among other claims) for four months' rent due when the premises were vacant, the tenant argued that it should be given credit for the excess rent that the landlord collected during the unexpired balance of its term.

A majority of the court disagreed, stating that "when the reletting yields a higher rent than does the original lease, . . . the credit due the breaching tenant is to be limited to the period during which the second tenant leased the premises." Put differently, a defaulting tenant's credit for excess rent in any month after termination is compared to the rent received from the new tenant in that month and cannot exceed that rent.

After a lengthy discussion of the origins of survival provisions, the dissenting opinion characterized a claim under a survival provision as a claim for damages and not for rent. As such, under contract principles, the landlord cannot be in a better position as a result of a breach than it would have been if the tenant had fully performed its obligations under the lease. Consequently, the dissenters continued, when a tenant's breach enables a landlord to relet its premises for a profit, the damages must be reduced by the profit. Unlike the majority's holding, the minority concluded that the defaulting tenant's credit is calculated not by a

---

[23] New Jersey Indus. Properties, Inc. v. Y.C. & V.L., Inc., 100 N.J. 432, 495 A.2d 1320, 1325, 1326 (1985).

month-to-month comparison but by reference to the old rent due and the new rent received during the remaining balance of the original term.

The majority and minority conceded that the case raises a moral issue: Can a tenant benefit from its own default? The prestige of the court that rendered the opinion, the quality of both the majority opinion and the dissent, and the fundamental moral issue all make it certain that this case will be the basis for a great deal of litigation.

The dissenting opinion in the New Jersey case relied on a District of Columbia Court of Appeals case.[24] There, the landlord sought to recover rent for the period from tenant's abandonment until the beginning of the new tenant's term. The tenant responded that the landlord had suffered no damages because the new lease produced more rent from the premises through the end of the old tenant's lease than the old tenant's lease would have produced. The court held for the tenant, saying, "When a landlord benefits financially from abandonment of the premises by the original tenant, he suffers no damages, and is not entitled to recover any money from that tenant." In effect, the tenant's liability for rent before releasing was extinguished by the advantageous new lease.

At issue in these cases, of course, is the dual nature of the lease as a conveyance (in which only rent is recoverable) and as a contract (in which damages are recoverable). The Colorado Supreme Court confronted the distinctions between contract remedies and real property remedies.[25] The decision is noteworthy for its extensive discussion of the dual nature of a lease. In that case, the subtenant abandoned the premises before the end of its term. The tenant-sublandlord negotiated a surrender of the master lease. Under real property principles the tenant-sublandlord would not be entitled to subrents after its surrender, but under contract principles the tenant-sublandlord would have been entitled to amounts due from the subtenant through the balance of the sublease (less rents due under the master lease). The court awarded the contract damages.

The lease should not provide that it terminates automatically when a default occurs. The occurrence of a default should give the landlord the option to terminate the lease. The landlord may not want to terminate the lease for every default. On the other hand, when a default occurs and the landlord is concerned that the tenant may file for bankruptcy, the landlord must move quickly to terminate the lease.[26] A lease that is properly terminated according to the lease

---

[24] Truitt v. Evangel Temple, Inc., 486 A.2d 1169 (D.C. 1984).

[25] Schneiker v. Gordon, 732 P.2d 603 (Colo. 1987), *rev'g* Gordon v. Schneiker, 609 P.2d 3 (Colo. Ct. App. 1984).

[26] One bankruptcy court has held that six hours is too quick. *In re* Law Clinic of Mott & Gray, P.C., 39 Bankr. 73 (E.D. Pa. 1984). The landlord's demand for payment against a threat to terminate the lease implied a reasonable time for payment, and six hours was not reasonable. *See also In re* Bricker, 43 Bankr. 344 (D. Ariz. 1984). A bad-faith termination before a bankruptcy will not be considered valid under state law. *In re* 29 Newbury St., Inc., 75 Bankr. 650 (D. Mass. 1987), *appeal denied,* 856 F.2d 424 (1st Cir. 1988) (involving the landlord's unjustified charges for cost of living adjustments).

and state landlord/tenant law before bankruptcy proceedings are begun will not be an asset of the bankrupt estate, and the landlord will avoid the vagaries of the bankruptcy court.[27] On the other hand, a lease that is not terminated before the bankruptcy will be a part of the bankruptcy estate.[28] For this reason, landlords prefer to give only the minimum notice required by state law in order to terminate a lease.

§ 30.9 — Maintaining the Lease

Maintaining the lease, and suing for damages or rent as it comes due, is another one of the landlord's choices when the tenant abandons the premises; see paragraph (b)(1) of **Form 30-4**. This is a traditional remedy that arose when leases were considered conveyances and not contracts; its best recommendation is that it assures the landlord of the benefit of its bargain (usually with interest).[29] One justification for this rememdy is that it does not require the landlord to do anything (such as reenter) that might support the tenant's claim of surrender and acceptance. Another justification is that a defaulting tenant should be enabled to impose a duty on its innocent landlord to relet the premises.[30] However, it may require multiple suits unless the balance of the term is shorter than the applicable statute of limitations, in which event all the claims on the lease can be joined in one litigation. Another drawback to this "wait-and-see" approach is that the landlord quickly develops a substantial claim against a tenant that may be insolvent when the landlord sues to collect. Last, and of greatest importance, this remedy raises significant questions about the landlord's duty to mitigate its damages, as discussed in § **30.15**.

§ 30.10 — Reentry

Reentering and releasing require care. If the landlord is deemed to have accepted the tenant's surrender of the premises, the tenant will have no liability for rent due after its surrender.[31] A provision similar to **Form 30-4** rescued a landlord from a tenant's claim of surrender.[32] When a landlord strictly complies with the lease provisions for reentry without termination, a court may award the remaining rent and the landlord's fees.[33] Most real estate professionals try to avoid an inadvertent

---

[27] However, see § **21.1** regarding fraudulent conveyances.

[28] Charthouse, Inc. v. Maxwell, 40 Bankr. 231 (N.D. Ill. 1984).

[29] E. Halper, Shopping Center and Store Leases § 16.05 (1989).

[30] Reid v. Mutual of Omaha Ins. Co., 776 P.2d 896 (Utah 1989).

[31] Wheeler v. Thomas, 328 S.W.2d 891 (Tex. Civ. App. 1959), *no writ.*

[32] Collet v. Am. Nat'l Stores, Inc., 708 S.W.2d 273 (Mo. Ct. App. 1986).

[33] LIC, Inc. v. Baltrusch, 215 Mont. 44, 692 P.2d 1264 (1985).

acceptance of surrender by using a lease that gives the landlord the right to reenter and release. Landlords should advise their tenants of the intended effect of the reentry. The landlord's damages are the difference between the rent reserved in the lease and the rent realized from the re-leasing;[34] the landlord's claim against its abandoning tenant ripens when the landlord re-leases for a new term that is as long as the balance of the old term.[35]

§ 30.11 — Rent Acceleration

Acceleration of the rent is a contract remedy for anticipatory breach. In order to have an anticipatory breach, the tenant must abandon the premises or refuse to take possession of them and refuse to pay future rent.[36] The damages are the difference between the present value of the rent reserved in the lease and the cash (that is, present) market value of the lease for its unexpired term.[37] Put slightly differently, if all the rent were accelerated and paid, the tenant would have fully paid its rent obligations under the lease; it would own its leasehold, subject only to its other obligations under the lease. If all the rent were accelerated, but reduced by the accelerated rent that landlord had received (or could receive) to release the premises for the balance of the term, then the landlord would be made whole from the tenant's breach. It would have the new tenant's rent (assuming it was paid for the balance of the term) and it would have any difference between what the old tenant was to pay and the new tenant is to pay.

When computing the accelerated rent, the real estate professional confronts the difficulty of accelerating unknown future amounts that are payable as rent and are part of the landlord's damages: for example, operating expenses in office building leases, taxes and maintenance and insurance in single tenant leases, and common area maintenance charges in shopping center leases. Although the landlord knows the base rent that will be due for the balance of the term, it does not know the tenant's share of escalations.

A well-known variation of this problem — accelerated percentage rent — may provide some assistance. When a shopping center lease is breached, the landlord loses the percentage rent that would have been payable during the balance of the term. The amount is more speculative than the landlord's costs: the costs are inescapable even though they are not quantifiable, while the tenant's gross sales are neither inescapable nor quantifiable, because the business may fail. The ironic fact is that computation of future percentage rent may be necessary at a time when the business has failed, and if anything is certain it is that the tenant will have no more gross sales.

---

[34] Evons v. Winkler, 388 S.W.2d 265 (Tex. Civ. App. 1965), *no writ.*

[35] Marathon Oil Co. v. Rone, 83 S.W.2d 1028 (Tex. Civ. App. 1935), *no writ.*

[36] Thieneman v. Kahn, 433 So. 2d 761 (La. Ct. App.), *writ denied,* 440 So. 2d 731 (La. 1983).

[37] Maida v. Main Bldg. of Houston, 473 S.W.2d 648 (Tex. Civ. App. 1971), *no writ;* Cantile v. Vanity Fair Properties, 505 S.W.2d 654 (Tex. Civ. App. 1974), *writ refused n.r.e.*

Aside from this unfortunate reality of the situation, a good deal of thought has been given to the computation of lost percentage rent.[38] The simplest method takes the average historical percentage rent and presumes that an equal amount would have accrued during the balance of the term. Choosing the proper historical period (if it is less than the full term) means that the landlord must take the past three years of the term, for example, or such lesser period of the term as has elapsed since the commencement date, and then find the average percentage rent for that period. Having reduced the percentage rent to a monthly amount, the landlord is in a position to calculate the base rent and the percentage rent that could have been expected over the remaining term of the lease. A landlord could also determine the lost percentage rent by reference to the highest annual percentage rent paid by the tenant; obviously, this favors the landlord. Finally, the landlord could use the percentage rent paid for the year before the default; this may favor the tenant.[39]

By similar reasoning, the other unknown amounts—including operating expenses, real estate taxes and assessments, utilities, maintenance, and common area maintenance charges—can be approximated. These expenses, as well as percentage rent, often increase over time and may not, in fact, be level amounts over the remaining term. This makes the arithmetic more difficult but not impossible.

The landlord that chooses to make provision for these amounts should do so in its lease and should not await litigation in which the amounts will be attacked as speculative. Nevertheless, few landlords recover the full reserved base rent, let alone the expected percentage rent and other costs.

To review, the real estate professional should note that rent acceleration and a demand for possession are inconsistent; if the entire rent is paid, the tenant should have an unquestionable right to possession, so long as it performs its other obligations under the lease.[40] *Restatement* § 12.1 comment K, makes several important observations about rent acceleration:

1. If the landlord terminates the lease after the accelerated rent has been paid (which the landlord could do only on account of another default by the tenant), the landlord must return the excess prepaid rent (less the landlord's related expenses) to the tenant.

2. Rent acceleration without prior demand by the landlord may be unconscionable.

3. Rent acceleration without a discount for the present payment of future obligations may be unconscionable.

---

[38] Landis, *Problems in Drafting Percentage Leases,* 36 B.U.L. Rev. 190, 236-38 (1956).

[39] Grossman v. Barney, 359 S.W.2d 475 (Tex. Civ. App. 1962), *writ refused n.r.e.*

[40] 2 Powell § 231(3).

The *Restatement* analogizes this situation to the prepayment of a promissory note. When payment of a promissory note is accelerated, the borrower immediately gives back what it has received. Put differently, the installments due on a promissory note have an interest component. The sum of the installment payments is principal and interest. When the principal balance is paid, the interest that would have been due on future installments is not payable. Similarly, there is an implicit interest component on rent payments, which are, in effect, installment payments for the leasehold. When rent is accelerated and declared due and payable in full, the interest component of the rent payments must be deducted from the accelerated amount, just as interest ended when the promissory note was paid in full.

That deduction arrives at the present value of the future rent payments. Of course, if the rent payments are fully paid, the tenant owns its leasehold "free and clear" with no rent obligation. If the landlord takes back the premises, it must further reduce the present value of the future rent payments by the present value of the leasehold, that is, the future rent payments that it can expect to receive from a new tenant. Without deduction of those expected future rent payments, the landlord has both the new tenant's payment of future rent and the leasehold for which the old tenant has paid.

§ 30.12   —Retained Jurisdiction

The real estate professional can see that the traditional methods of measuring the landlord's damages after the tenant's default are not precise, prompt or efficient. The landlord that waits until the end of the term to sue for accrued rent may be able to calculate it precisely, but will not be able to receive it promptly after the breach; in fact, by the time the lease ends, the landlord may be unable to find the erstwhile tenant or to collect from it even if it is found.

Termination with rent acceleration may give a landlord judgment promptly after the tenant's default, but the award will be imprecise. If the landlord does not collect the equivalent of the present value of the rent that was deducted from the present value of the unpaid rent, it will not be made whole, but if the landlord collects more than that rent, the tenant will have been penalized.

A landlord that sues for accrued and unpaid rent in separate actions from time to time will admittedly have prompt, precise awards, but at an exorbitant cost.

In order to make the landlord's damages more precisely calculable and more immediately and efficiently recoverable, one innovative commentator[41] has suggested that trial courts retain jurisdiction of the litigation between a landlord and defaulting tenant. At the first hearing, the tenant's breach and the landlord's

---

[41] Kwall, *Retained Jurisdiction in Damage Actions Based on Anticipatory Breach: A Missing Link in Landlord-Tenant Law,* 37 Case W. Res. L. Rev. 273 (1986).

damages to the date of hearing would be adjudicated. However, unlike traditional litigation, the court would not lose jurisdiction after it rendered its decision. Rather, it would retain jurisdiction over the matter and the landlord and tenant. Subsequently, from time to time, the landlord would simply prove its damages since the last hearing in a very brief proceeding in which default was not an issue, although presumably the landlord's mitigation efforts might be.

Recognizing the inadequacies of the traditional procedures, the Utah Supreme Court has endorsed the retained jurisdiction concept.[42] The opinion is valuable reading, not only with regard to the retained jurisdiction concept, but also with regard to the court's reasoning for adopting the rule that the landlord must mitigate its damages upon tenant's abandonment of the premises. The opinion described how retained jurisdiction should work: When a landlord's action for breach of a lease is tried before the expiration of the lease term, and the finder of fact determines that the tenant has breached the lease, the amount awarded should represent only those rents that have come due as of the time of trial. This judgment will be immediately enforceable. Rents accruing after the trial, on the other hand, may be recovered through what would amount to rather brief supplemental proceedings. To provide this remedy, the trial court should retain jurisdiction of the underlying action. After additional unpaid rents have accrued, the landlord may return to the court, without the risks and burdens that attend the filing of a new action, for a simple determination of additional losses suffered through the date of the supplemental proceedings and whether the landlord has fulfilled its ongoing duty to mitigate. Under the law-of-the-case doctrine, the initial determination of the tenant's liability would govern in any supplemental proceedings.

§ 30.13 — Form

A form of landlord's remedies is:

FORM 30-4
DEFAULT—LANDLORD'S REMEDIES

If any one or more events of default set forth in paragraph [tenant's default paragraph] occurs, then landlord may, at its election, either:

(a) Give tenant written notice of its intention to terminate this lease on the date of the notice or on any later date specified in the notice, and, on the date specified in the notice, tenant's right to possession of the premises will cease and the lease will be terminated (except as to tenant's liability set forth in this paragraph (a)), as if the expiration of the term fixed in the notice were the end of the term of this lease. If this lease is terminated pursuant to the provisions of this paragraph (a), tenant will

---

[42] Reid v. Mutual of Omaha Ins. Co., 776 P.2d 896 (Utah 1989).

remain liable to landlord for damages in an amount equal to the rent and other sums that would have been owing by tenant under this lease for the balance of the term if this lease had not been terminated, less the net proceeds, if any, of any re-letting of the premises by landlord subsequent to the termination, after deducting all of landlord's expenses in connection with the reletting, including without limitation, the expenses set forth in paragraph (b)(2). Landlord will be entitled to collect those damages from tenant monthly on the days on which the rent and other amounts would have been payable under this lease if this lease had not been terminated and landlord will be entitled to receive those damages from tenant on those days. Alternatively, at the option of landlord, if this lease is terminated, landlord will be entitled to recover from tenant (A) the worth at the time of award of the unpaid rent that had been earned at the time of termination; (B) the worth at the time of award of the amount by which the unpaid rent that would have been earned after termination until the time of award exceeds the amount of the rent loss that tenant proves could reasonably have been avoided; (C) the worth at the time of award of the amount by which the unpaid rent for the balance of the term of this lease after the time of award exceeds the amount of the rent loss that tenant proves could reasonably be avoided; and (D) any other amount necessary to compensate landlord for all the detriment proximately caused by tenant's failure to perform its obligations under this lease or that in the ordinary course of things would be likely to result from that failure. The "worth at the time of award" of the amount referred to in clauses (A) and (B) is computed by allowing interest at the highest rate permitted by law. The worth at the time of award of the amount referred to in clause (C) is computed by discounting the amount at the discount rate of the Federal Reserve Bank of _____ at the time of award. For the purpose of determining unpaid rental under clause (C), the monthly rent reserved in this lease will be deemed to be the sum of the rent due under paragraph [the minimum rent paragraph] and the amounts last payable by tenant pursuant to paragraph [the operating expense paragraph] for the calendar year in which the award is made; or

(b) (1) Without demand or notice, reenter and take possession of the premises, or any part of the premises; repossess the premises as of landlord's former estate; expel tenant and those claiming through or under tenant from the premises; and remove the effects of both or either, without being deemed guilty of any manner of trespass and without prejudice to any remedies for arrears of rent or preceding breach of covenants or conditions. If landlord elects to reenter, as provided in this paragraph (b), or if landlord takes possession of the premises pursuant to legal proceedings or pursuant to any notice provided by law, landlord may, from time to time, without terminating this lease, relet the premises or any part of the premises, either alone or in conjunction with other portions of the building of which the premises are a part, in landlord's or tenant's name but for the account of tenant, for such term or terms (which may be greater or less than the period that would otherwise have constituted the balance of the term of this lease) and on such terms and conditions (which may include concessions of free rent, and the alteration and repair of the premises) as landlord, in its uncontrolled discretion, may determine. Landlord may collect and receive the rents for the premises. Landlord will not be responsible or liable for any failure to relet the premises, or any part of the premises, or for any failure to collect any rent due upon reletting. No reentry or taking possession of the premises by landlord will be construed as an election on landlord's part to terminate this lease unless a written notice of such intention is given to tenant.

No notice from landlord under this lease or under a forcible entry and detainer statute or similar law will constitute an election by landlord to terminate this lease unless the notice specifically says so. Landlord reserves the right following any reentry or reletting, or both, to exercise its right to terminate this lease by giving tenant written notice, and, in that event, the lease will terminate as specified in the notice.

(2)   If landlord elects to take possession of the premises according to this paragraph (b) without terminating the lease, tenant will pay landlord (i) the rent and other sums that would be payable under this lease if such repossession had not occurred, less (ii) the net proceeds, if any, of any reletting of the premises, after deducting all of landlord's expenses incurred in connection with such reletting, including without limitation all repossession costs, brokerage commissions, legal expenses, attorneys' fees, expenses of employees, alteration, remodeling, repair costs, and expenses of preparation for reletting. If, in connection with any reletting, the new lease term extends beyond the existing term or the premises covered by reletting include areas that are not part of the premises, a fair apportionment of the rent received from such reletting and the expenses incurred in connection with such reletting will be made in determining the net proceeds received from reletting. In addition, in determining the net proceeds from reletting, any rent concessions will be apportioned over the term of the new lease. Tenant will pay such amounts to landlord monthly on the days on which the rent and all other amounts owing under this lease would have been payable if possession had not been retaken, and landlord will be entitled to receive the rent and other amounts from tenant on those days.

(c)   Suit or suits for the recovery of the rents and other amounts and damages set forth in this paragraph may be brought by landlord, from time to time, at landlord's election, and nothing in this lease will be deemed to require landlord to await the date on which the term of this lease expires. Each right and remedy in this lease will be cumulative and will be in addition to every other right or remedy in this lease or existing at law or in equity or by statute or otherwise, including without limitation suits for injunctive relief and specific performance. The exercise or beginning of the exercise by landlord of any right or remedy will not preclude the simultaneous or later exercise by landlord of any other rights or remedies. All rights and remedies are cumulative and nonexclusive.

In states such as New York and Minnesota, which allow a tenant to redeem a canceled leasehold, landlords usually conclude the default provision with the tenant's waiver of redemption rights.

§ 30.14   Special Bankruptcy Provisions

The Bankruptcy Code affects the landlord's rights upon the tenant's bankruptcy in several ways. One of those has to do with the enforceability of use provisions discussed in §§ 10.14 and 10.15. Another limitation is the clear unenforceability of so-called ipso facto provisions, which state that the commencement of bankruptcy proceedings automatically terminates the lease. Moreover, a landlord cannot reserve the right to terminate the lease at its option because of the commencement of bankruptcy proceedings. Finally, there is an express limitation on the landlord's damages:

> [I]f such claim is the claim of a lessor for damages resulting from the termination of a lease of real property, such claim exceeds—
>
> (A) the rent reserved by such lease, without acceleration, for the greater of one year, or 15 percent, not to exceed three years, of the remaining term of such lease, following the earlier of—
>
> (i) the date of the filing of the petition; and
>
> (ii) the date on which such lessor repossessed, or the lessee surrendered, the leased property; plus
>
> (B) any unpaid rent due under such lease, without acceleration, on the earlier of such dates. . . .[43]

An assignee of a lease ought to be certain that the bankruptcy default (to the extent it is enforceable at all) is enforceable only against the current owner of the leasehold. In other words, the assignor's bankruptcy is not a default. A typical provision may be:

> Any such proceeding or action involving bankruptcy, insolvency, reorganization, arrangement, assignment for the benefit of creditors, or appointment of a receiver or trustee will be considered to be an event of default only if the proceeding, action, or remedy is taken or brought by or against the then holder of the leasehold under this lease.

§ 30.15 Duty to Mitigate

As § **12.11** suggested with respect to assignments and subleases, the modern lease is now more likely to be considered as a contract than a conveyance. Among other things, this means that the landlord has an obligation to be reasonable in granting or withholding its consent to a proposed assignment or sublease. This contract principle of the implied duty to act reasonably has equal applicability to lease defaults. Many courts refuse to hold a tenant liable for damages on account of its breach of its lease if the breach has been occasioned by the landlord's unreasonable refusal of a proper assignee or subtenant. See § **12.11**. Put somewhat differently, courts will not give relief to a landlord who refused an opportunity to avoid or reduce its losses. Of course, this is just another way to express the implied contractual duty to mitigate one's damages. This principle is the law's recognition of the unconscionability of allowing a person to recover damages that might have been avoided.

The real estate professional should not lose sight of the fact that these are contract law rules, not originally a part of real property law. States that do not

---

[43] 11 U.S.C. § 507(b)(7)(A) & (B).

import these contract rules to leases have completely different rules regarding the tenant's default. However, states that recognize a duty to mitigate damages on lease defaults should also recognize a landlord's duty to be reasonable in lease assignments and subleases, and vice versa.

Two subsidiary contract law principles are relevant, and each arises in response to one question: What happens when a landlord relets the premises during the unexpired term of the defaulting tenant's lease for greater rent than the defaulting tenant was obligated to pay? According to the contract principle that one cannot benefit from one's own default, the defaulting tenant is not entitled to have any part of the excess rent applied to reduce its obligations.[44] On the other hand, according to the contract rule that the landlord should be put in the same position—but not a better position—than it would have been if the tenant had performed, those excess rents should be applied to reduce the tenant's liability.[45] See the discussion in § **30.8**.

When leases are viewed as conveyances, and not as contracts, a landlord has no duty to mitigate its damages when its tenant abandons the premises. This rule arose from the belief that the landlord's duties were fully executed when it granted the estate. The landlord had every right to expect performance by the tenant in the form of payment of rent. Under the traditional rule, the landlord could pursue any of three remedies after a tenant abandoned its premises:

1. The landlord could treat the tenant's abandonment of the premises as a surrender of the premises and terminate the tenancy.

2. The landlord could stand by and sue for rent as it became due.

3. The landlord could relet the property and pursue the tenant for the difference between what it was obligated to pay and what the landlord was able to recover by releasing.

The traditional view is certainly on the descent. Modern courts are increasingly likely to consider leases as contracts when confronting the landlord's obligation to mitigate its damages. In fact, a 1984 study concluded that 20 states imposed on landlords a duty to mitigate their damages when their tenants abandon the premises; the other states did not require mitigation, or did not have any rule, or had a modified rule.[46] At least two states require mitigation by statute.[47]

---

[44] New Jersey Indus. Properties, Inc. v. Y.C. & V.L., Inc., 100 N.J. 432, 495 A.2d 1320 (1985).

[45] Truitt v. Evangel Temple, Inc., 486 A.2d 1169 (D.C. 1984).

[46] *States Enforce Duty to Mitigate,* Com. Lease L. Insider, Sept. 1984, at 8. The states requiring mitigation are: Arizona, California, Colorado, Connecticut, Hawaii, Indiana, Iowa, Kansas, Michigan, Nebraska, Nevada, New Jersey, North Carolina, North Dakota, Ohio, Oregon, South Carolina, Tennessee, Washington, and Wisconsin. For a Connecticut case, see Rokalor, Inc. v. Conn. Eating Enters., Inc., 18 Conn. App. 384, 558 A.2d 265 (1989).

[47] Cal. Civ. Code § 51.2 (West 1970); Ill. Ann. Stat. ch. 110, § 9-213.1 (Smith-Hurd 1984), discussed in Sclar, *Landlord's Remedies When Tenant Abandons the Premises—Illinois Requires Landlords to Mitigate Damages,* 13 Real Est. L.J. 270 (1984).

When the landlord is under a duty to mitigate its damages, it must use due diligence or reasonable diligence (or similar efforts) to do so.[48] In a commercial lease transaction, the landlord's obligation to mitigate damages has been formulated in this way:

> Following abandonment of the leased premises, the landlord cannot stand idly and look to the tenant for damages in the amount of the rent which would accrue during the remainder of the leasehold term. The lessor has the duty to make a reasonable effort to mitigate damages by finding a suitable tenant.[49]

Once again, this general statement gives little guidance to a practitioner asked in specific circumstances what a landlord must do in order to mitigate its damages or to avoid the consequences of not having done so.

The reasonableness of a landlord's conduct in mitigating its damages is gleaned from the many cases that address this issue. For illustration, a landlord has been found not to have mitigated its damages in the following situations:

1. An Iowa landlord took no affirmative action to sublet except to place a "For Rent" sign in the window. The landlord did not place any ads in the newspaper or contact a realtor, and when approached by two prospective tenants it did not fully explore the opportunities to rent the premises.[50]

2. When a North Dakota landlord placed the premises for lease at a substantial increase over what he had been receiving previously, he had not made a good faith effort to mitigate damages. In reaching its decision, the court stated: "If seeking a higher rent inhibits the re-rental of the premises, it cannot be found to be in good faith. There was testimony which showed that the higher rent figure was firm and did deter the re-rental."[51]

3. On appeal from a judgment in favor of a landlord on its claim for breach of a commercial lease, an Oregon appellate court remanded the case, finding that the jury instructions inconsistently placed the burden of proof as to mitigation on both parties. The court held that, in attempting to prove mitigation of damages, the landlord has the burden of proof to show that it made a reasonable effort to find a suitable tenant. Furthermore, if there are tenants available to lease the space, the landlord has the burden to show why they are not suitable tenants.[52]

---

[48] Annot., 21 A.L.R.3d 534, *Landlord's duty, on tenant's failure to occupy, or abandonment of, premises, to mitigate damages by accepting or procuring another tenant* (1968); Weissenberger, *The Landlord's Duty to Mitigate Damages: A Survey of Old Law and New Trends,* 53 Temp. L.Q. 1 (1980).

[49] United States Nat'l Bank of Or. v. Homeland, Inc., 291 Or. 374, 631 P.2d 761, 765 (1981).

[50] Vawter v. McKissick, 159 N.W.2d 538 (Iowa 1968).

[51] Mar-son, Inc. v. Terwaho Enters., Inc., 259 N.W.2d 289, 292 (N.D. 1977).

[52] Portland Gen. Elec. v. Hershiser, Mitchell, Mowery & Davis, 86 Or. App. 40, 738 P.2d 593, *review denied,* 304 Or. 149, 743 P.2d 167 (1987).

4. When a Colorado landlord receives a substantial "entry premium" from a new tenant that leases the premises of a defaulting tenant before the end of the defaulting tenant's term, the entry premium must be applied to mitigate the landlord's damages, that is, set off against the defaulting tenant's arrearages.[53]

However, landlords have been found to have mitigated their damages in other cases:

1. An Arizona landlord advertised the property in a newspaper, placed a large sign on the property, and contacted several brokers about the property. The facts that there was a delay in the attempt to relet the premises, due to the substantial cleanup required, and that the landlord set the monthly rental at $3,000 when the defaulting tenant was paying $2,771 did not persuade the court that the landlord failed to mitigate its damages.[54]

2. Even though a North Dakota landlord did not hire a real estate agent, he prevailed on the defense that he failed to mitigate damages by presenting evidence that he made more than 140 contacts with 50 prospective tenants. The landlord also presented the testimony of an experienced commercial realtor that the higher monthly rent sought by him was a reasonable rental for the property at the time.[55]

3. In Oregon, when the tenant has not abandoned, and thus made it impossible for the landlord to relet, the tenant will not carry the burden of its defense that the landlord failed to mitigate its damages.[56]

4. An Arizona landlord who made reasonable efforts to relet the space at a fair rental value was entitled to summary judgment on the issue of its duty to mitigate. Fair rental value was determined by affidavit of the landlord's leasing agent/realtor. The agent made contact with numerous tenants, the vacancy was advertised in a local newspaper, the premises were shown to various prospective tenants, and advertising literature was mailed to businesses of a similar nature. In its decision, the court stated: "While a landlord has a duty to make efforts to rent the abandoned premises at a fair rental, the law only requires that these efforts be 'reasonable' not heroic."[57]

5. An Iowa landlord exercised reasonable diligence to mitigate damages even though he did not take action for four months after he was informed the tenant was abandoning the lease. The landlord promptly placed ads in

---

[53] La Casa Nino, Inc. v. Plaza Esteban, 762 P.2d 669 (Colo. 1988).

[54] Butler Products Co. v. Roush, 153 Ariz. 500, 738 P.2d 775 (Ct. App. 1987).

[55] Ruud v. Larson, 392 N.W.2d 62 (N.D. 1986).

[56] Amvesco, Inc. v. Key Title Co. of Bend, 77 Or. App. 333, 713 P.2d 614 (1986).

[57] Wingate v. Gin, 148 Ariz. 289, 714 P.2d 459 (Ct. App. 1985).

well-read circulations, put up several signs on the property, and eventually obtained a rental once the tenant conclusively stated he was abandoning the lease.[58]

6. In light of a Colorado lease provision providing that the landlord may "reenter the premises . . . and relet the premises at such rental and upon such other terms and conditions as landlord in its sole discretion may deem advisable," the landlord did not fail to mitigate its damages by attempting to relet for $11 or $12 per square foot, rather than the $8 charged the tenant in the lease. The court interpreted the lease provision to permit reletting at the current commercial rate, and the landlord asserted that $11 or $12 per square foot was the current commercial rate.[59]

7. A Nebraska landlord did not fail to mitigate its damages by finding a tenant who refused to pay the amount of rent the former tenant paid. There was evidence that the subsequent tenant was the only one interested in the premises and that the landlord, in advertising or listing the premises, had requested an amount greater than what the subsequent tenant ultimately agreed to pay. In its decision, the court stated: "The evidence indicates the [landlord] found another lessee who, while refusing to pay the amount of rent which defendants paid, paid a sum that we cannot say was unreasonable as a matter of law."[60]

8. A Louisiana landlord fulfilled its duty to mitigate its damages by attempting to release the offices vacated by the tenant at fair market rate, even though the efforts to release had been unsuccessful. The evidence established that the landlord attempted to re-lease the offices at approximately $15.75 per square foot rather than the $10.50 paid by the defaulting tenant. The court found that a market study introduced by the landlord, comparing its asking price with the price of comparable office space in the area, was conclusive of the fair market rate. In reaching its decision, the court stated that "it would not be reasonable to expect [landlord] to offer the space at less than a fair market rate."[61]

The issue of mitigation of damages raises the interesting question whether the landlord is obligated to accept a dramatically lower rental rate. For example, assume that the tenant is renting at $10 per square foot, and the tenant abandons the premises. To mitigate its damages, does the landlord have to relet the premises at $10? Certainly it does. Does the landlord have to relet at $1? That is a more difficult question. It appears that the landlord is only obligated to accept fair rental value for the premises to meet its burden of mitigating damages.

---

[58] Harmsen v. Dr. MacDonald's, Inc., 403 N.W.2d 48 (Iowa Ct. App. 1987).

[59] Del E. Webb Realty & Management Co. of Colo. v. Wessbecker, 628 P.2d 114, 116 (Colo. Ct. App. 1980), *cert. denied* (Apr. 27, 1981).

[60] Middagh v. Stanal Sound, Ltd., 222 Neb. 54, 382 N.W.2d 303, 309 (1986).

[61] Easterling v. Halter Marine, Inc., 470 So. 2d 221, 224 (La. Ct. App.), *writ denied,* 472 So. 2d 920 (La. 1985).

In an Oregon case, the tenant claimed that the landlord had an obligation to mitigate damages by reletting at less than the fair rental value and for use other than a dental clinic. In finding that the landlord had fulfilled his obligation to mitigate damages, the court stated:

> In order to mitigate the damages occasioned by a lessee's breach of a lease, the landlord should not be required to substantially alter his obligations as established in the pre-existing lease. Thus, in the present case plaintiff was not required to rent the premises to persons not working in dentistry or related fields, since the offices were part of a dental clinic occupied by two other dentists and were designed for that special use. Nor should plaintiff be required to rent the premises below their fair rental value. Defendant did not produce any evidence that $375 per month was not the fair rental value of the dental offices.[62]

In another Oregon case, the court determined that reasonable efforts at mitigation of damages had been made because the landlord attempted to relet the premises at fair rental value.[63] Although the court was considering whether the landlord had mitigated damages by attempting to relet at a higher rental rate, its decision centered on its conclusion that a landlord satisfied the duty to mitigate its damages by attempting to relet at fair rental value. In determining fair rental value, the court stated that the rent paid for similar premises was relevant.

Prudent landlords take the following steps when their tenants abandon the premises in order to show that reasonable efforts have been made to mitigate:

1. Advertising the premises for lease
2. Listing the premises with real estate brokers
3. Putting up signs of the availability of the premises for lease
4. Determining the fair market rental value from brokers or appraisers
5. Documenting delays caused by the tenant, such as holding over or poor condition of the premises
6. Keeping records of calls made by the landlord and responses to calls on the property
7. Staying out of the premises, except to show the premises to prospective tenants or to maintain and preserve them.

On the other hand, tenants take the following steps to show the surrender of the premises and termination of the lease:

1. Staying off the premises
2. Removing their signs from the premises
3. Vacating the premises entirely
4. Giving the keys to the premises back to the landlord or its agent

---

[62] Foggia v. Dix, 265 Or. 315, 509 P.2d 412-14 (Ct. App. 1973).

[63] United States Nat'l Bank of Or. v. Homeland, Inc., 291 Or. 374, 631 P.2d 761 (1981).

5.   Taking whatever posture they must in order to prepare an argument that the landlord has accepted their surrender of the premises and thus terminated the lease obligations.

§ 30.16   Landlord's Lien

Landlord's liens arise in any of three ways, and occasionally in more than one way. First of all, there is the contractual landlord's lien.[64] Next, there is the statutory landlord's lien.[65] Finally, there is the landlord's remedy of distress (or right of distraint), which is not truly a lien but has a similar effect.[66]

Distress or *distraint* is an old common law remedy that enabled the landlord to seize any property found on the premises and hold it as security for past due rent. Distress has two features that have generally distinguished it from the landlord's other lien remedies: (1) the landlord was allowed to take any property which it found on the premises, not just the property of the tenant; and (2) the landlord did not really have a lien until it had taken possession of the property. As one might guess, the distress remedy did not promote the orderly resolution of rent disputes and did not give comfort to innocent depositors of merchandise who found their property the subject of distress. The rough justice of distress has thus given way to statutory liens, although distress persists in some states and has been modified by statute in many instances. In fact, the distress remedy has been the target of intense constitutional challenge as a violation of the tenant's right to due process of law.[67] Although some may try to distinguish its use in commercial settings from its use in residential ones (from which the leading cases have sprung), a landlord should approach distraint with the greatest circumspection.[68]

Statutory landlord's liens exist in several states. The fundamental difference between this lien and distress is that this nonconsensual lien attaches at the beginning of the tenancy and not at the time that the property is taken by the landlord. As a result, this lien is prior to liens that attach to the property after the

---

[64] R. Schoshinski, American Law of Landlord and Tenant § 6.23 (1980) [hereinafter Schoshinski]; 52 C.J.S. *Landlord & Tenant* §§ 606-618 (1968).

[65] Schoshinski § 6:22; 52 C.J.S. *Landlord & Tenant* §§ 619-673 (1968). See 1988 Okla. Sess. Law. Serv. (No. 3) 484 (West), for that state's statute governing the disposition of personal property of an evicted or abandoning tenant.

[66] Schoshinski § 6:21; 52 C.J.S. *Landlord & Tenant* §§ 674-715 (1968). Sachs v. Curry-Thomas Hardware, Inc., 464 So. 2d 597 (Fla. Dist. Ct. App. 1985), is an unusual case under Florida law involving the priority of a statutory landlord's lien over a subsequent security interest that arose after several new tenants and new leases.

[67] Schoshinski § 6:24; *see also* Korngold, *Can Distraint Stand Up as a Landlord's Remedy?*, 5 Real Est. L.J. 242 (1977) (discussing constitutional issues with special emphasis on Pennsylvania law). In McCrory v. Johnson, 296 Ark. 231, 755 S.W.2d 566 (1988), the Arkansas Supreme Court invalidated a prejudgment attachment of a defaulting tenant's personal property.

[68] Riccardi, *Liens for the Commercial Landlord,* 39 Baylor L. Rev. 523 (1987), discusses statutory liens and security interests under Article 9 of the Uniform Commercial Code, with emphasis on Texas law.

term begins. Although some statutory liens attach to all property in the premises, the more common statute provides a lien only on the tenant's property and (if applicable) crops. Insofar as commercial leases are concerned, the most impor- tant aspect of statutory liens is that they are often not applicable to commercial tenancies, but rather are limited to residential and agricultural tenants.[69] How- ever, when they exist, a landlord's statutory lien may be at odds with a contractual or consensual lien.

A contractual or consensual landlord's lien arises from an agreement between the landlord and its tenant, by which the tenant grants a security interest in its property for the benefit of the landlord. It has been attacked in the context of residential tenancies, in which the rental agreement and the lien may be considered an adhesion contract. In commercial leases, the contractual or consensual lien is generally deemed to be a nonpossessory security interest governed by Article 9 (Secured Transactions) of the Uniform Commercial Code (UCC). As such, a proper security agreement and filing of a financing statement are necessary in order to perfect the security interest.[70] In most states that have considered the question, the contractual lien is independent of the statutory lien and the distress remedy, so a landlord may have the benefit of all these remedies.

The real estate professional should be aware of problems with the UCC's resolution of priorities between consensual landlord's liens and non-consensual statutory liens.[71] UCC § 9-102 states that Article 9 deals only with security interests created by contract, and § 9-104(b) adds that Article 9 does not apply to "landlord's liens." However, it does not specify whether the landlord's liens are the consensual ones or the non-consensual ones, or both. The early case law[72] — which has become the rule—holds that the exclusion in § 9-104(b) is only of consensual landlord's liens. In other words, statutory liens that arise without agreement are not subject to Article 9. If a dispute arises between a security interest created pursuant to Article 9 and a non-consensual landlord's lien, a court will look to the law existing before the UCC was enacted. On the other hand, landlord's liens created by contract are subject to Article 9; for the real estate practitioner, this requires perfection of the landlord's security interest according to local law.

---

[69] P. Rohan, 7 Current Leasing Law & Techniques § 7.02(5)(c) (1984) (examining statutes of jurisdictions having provisions for either distress or landlord liens or having expressly abolished distress for certain kinds of leases); 2 Powell § 230(2); Bank of N. Am. v. Kruger, 551 S.W.2d 63 (Tex. Civ. App. 1967), *writ refused, n.r.e.*; Goldie v. Bauchet Properties, 15 Cal. 3d 307, 540 P.2d 1, 124 Cal. Rptr. 161 (1975).

[70] Bank of N. Am. v. Kruger, 551 S.W.2d 63 (Tex. Civ. App. 1967), *writ refused, n.r.e.;* Goldie v. Bauchet Properties, 15 Cal. 3d 307, 540 P.2d 1, 124 Cal. Rptr. 161 (1975).

[71] The topic can be fully understood by reading Harvey, *Article 9's Exclusion of Consensual Landlord's Lien: King Furniture City Revisited,* 16 U.C.C. L.J. 360 (1984); Riccardi, *Liens for the Commercial Landlord,* 39 Baylor L. Rev. 523 (1987), (valuable general discussion emphasiz- ing Texas law); Wilcox & Harty, *The Relative Priority of a Landlord's Lien and Article 9 Security Interest,* 35 Drake L. Rev. 27 (1985-86), McLaughlin & Cohen, *Article 9 and Non-Consensual Liens,* N.Y.L.J., Oct. 12, 1988, at 3, col. 1.

[72] *In re* King Furniture City, Inc., 240 F. Supp. 453 (E.D. Ark. 1965).

A landlord may have both a consensual lien subject to Article 9 and a non-consensual lien not subject to Article 9. Since there may be limitations to the scope of the non-consensual lien,[73] landlords are well advised to take advantage of both opportunities. The UCC provision begs for legislative clarification.

The tenant who finds the errant express provision for a landlord's contractual lien ought to resist it, not as a matter of mere reflex but as one of reflection. If the tenant intends to borrow against any of its inventory or to buy any of its equipment on an installment plan, its lender or seller might want assurances that the inventory or equipment is free of any other claims. Furthermore, if the tenant's business were to fail, it would not want conflicting claims on its limited resources. If the tenant cannot avoid the contractual lien, by all means it must be certain that only its tangible personal property is subject to the lien; its accounts receivable, contract rights, and other intangibles must be excluded.

In addition, in those states which still have distress and statutory lien remedies, the tenant will want to amend the lease to eliminate those rights. A tenant might insist upon a provision such as:

FORM 30-5
DEFAULT—WAIVER OF LANDLORD'S LIEN

Landlord waives any statutory liens, and any rights of distress, with respect to tenant's property. This lease does not grant a contractual lien or any other express or implied security interest to landlord with respect to tenant's property.

Landlord, on the other hand, must be certain to comply with the requirements of the Uniform Commercial Code both with respect to the security agreement, which may be included in the lease, and with respect to the filing of financing statements and (if necessary by reason of the term of the lease) continuation statements. Cautious landlords will insist that the failure to provide a continuation statement will be a default under the lease.

A contractual landlord's lien, that is, security agreement, looks like this:

FORM 30-6
DEFAULT—LANDLORD'S LIEN

To secure the payment of all rent and its performance of this lease, tenant grants to landlord an express first and prior contractual lien and security interest on all property (including fixtures, equipment, chattels, and merchandise) that may be placed in the premises, and also upon all proceeds of any insurance that may accrue to tenant by reason of the destruction or damage of that property. Tenant will not remove that property from the premises (except in the ordinary course of business) without the written consent of landlord until all arrearages in rent have been paid. Tenant waives the benefit of all exemption laws in favor of this lien and security

---

[73] Tex. Prop. Code Ann. § 54.021 (Vernon Supp. 1987), for example, limits the lien to the current year's rent and is subject to several exemptions.

interest. This lien and security interest is given in addition to landlord's statutory lien and is cumulative with it. Upon the occurrence of an event of default, these liens may be foreclosed with or without court proceedings by public or private sale, so long as landlord gives tenant at least fifteen (15) days' notice of the time and place of the sale. Landlord will have the right to become the purchaser if it is the highest bidder at the sale. Contemporaneously with its execution of this lease, and if requested by landlord after such execution, tenant will execute and deliver to landlord Uniform Commercial Code financing statements in form and substance sufficient (upon proper filing) to perfect the security interest granted in this paragraph. If requested by landlord, tenant will also execute and deliver to landlord Uniform Commercial Code continuation statements in form and substance sufficient to reflect any proper amendment of, modification in, or extension of the security interest granted in this paragraph.

CHAPTER 31

ARBITRATION

§ 31.1 Introduction
§ 31.2 Possible Arbitration Provisions

§ 31.1 Introduction

On occasion, a commercial lease will provide for arbitration as a means of resolving some or all disputes that the landlord and tenant may have. Long-term leases and ground leases more frequently have arbitration provisions; these leases implicitly acknowledge the impossibility of planning for all contingencies and plan only for a means of meeting them. There is clearly a public policy favoring arbitration as an alternative method of dispute resolution.[1] In fact, so strong is the public policy that a Hawaiian appellate court on its own motion characterized a dispute over an option price as an arbitration even though the litigants denied it was.[2]

When an arbitration provision is contemplated, the landlord and tenant must first consult the law of the state that will govern the lease. Some states have enacted the Uniform Arbitration Act and leave no question about the enforceability of arbitration provisions.[3] Other states adhere to the older view that an

---

[1] United States Arbitration Act, 9 U.S.C. § 1–208( ); Shearson/American Express, Inc. v. McMahon, 482 U.S. 220 (1987).

[2] Beclar Corp. v. Young, 750 P.2d 934 (Haw. Ct. App. 1988).

[3] Alaska, Alaska Stat. §§ 09.43.010-.180 (1972); Arizona, Ariz. Rev. Stat. Ann. §§ 12-1501 to -1518 (1984); Arkansas, Ark. Stat. Ann. §§ 34-511 to -532 (1981); Colorado, Colo. Rev. Stat. §§ 13-22-201 to -223 (1975); Delaware, Del. Code Ann. tit. 10, §§ 5701–5725 (1953); District of Columbia, D.C. Code Ann. §§ 16-4301 to -4319 (1981); Idaho, Idaho Code §§ 7-901 to -922 (1975); Illinois, Ill. Ann. Stat. ch. 10, §§ 101–123 (Smith-Hurd 1961); Indiana, Ind. Code Ann. §§ 34-4-2-1 to -22 (West 1969); Kansas, Kan. Stat. Ann. §§ 5-401 to -422 (1973); Maine, Me. Rev. Stat. Ann. tit. 14, §§ 5927–5949 (1967); Maryland, Md. Cts. & Jud. Proc. Code Ann. §§ 3-201 to -234 (1957); Massachusetts, Mass. Gen. Laws Ann. ch. 251, §§ 1–19 (West 1960); Michigan, Mich. Comp. Laws Ann. §§ 600.5001–.5035 (West 1963); Minnesota, Minn. Stat. Ann. §§ 572.08-.30 (West 1957); Missouri, Mo. Stat. Ann. §§ 435.350–.470 (Vernon 1980); Nevada, Nev. Rev. Stat. §§ 38.015–.205 (1969); New Mexico, N.M. Stat. Ann. §§ 44-7-1 to -22 (1978); North Carolina, N.C. Gen. Stat. §§ 1-567.1–.20 (1973); Oklahoma, Okla. Stat.

agreement to submit future disputes to arbitration may be revoked before the arbitration begins. Under a narrow arbitration provision, an arbitrator is without power to determine whether an arbitratable issue has been submitted to it within the time limits set forth in the lease. A court must make that determination.[4]

Arbitration has several virtues and several vices. Among its virtues is speed. An arbitration can often be conducted more quickly than a trial; however, if either the landlord or tenant goes to court to stay arbitration (by asserting, for example, that the dispute is not subject to the lease's arbitration provisions or that the claimant has waived its right to arbitration), the ensuing judicial proceedings will be lengthier than any arbitration and the result may be only to compel arbitration. The accelerated pace may lessen involvement of the parties' management, who might spend considerable time answering discovery requests and appearing at depositions if the matter were litigated. Another recommendation of arbitration is its cost. Arbitration often costs less than a judicial proceeding; however, this cost saving is more apparent than real in many cases, because the evidence must be as carefully and completely presented at an arbitration as it must be at a trial. Arbitration also allows the landlord and tenant to designate arbitrators who are experts on the issue being arbitrated. It may reduce the likelihood of punitive damages and may facilitate settlement. Finally, arbitration is conducted in privacy, so the landlord and tenant are able to present evidence that they may be reluctant to present in open court.[5]

Arbitration nevertheless has three significant vices. One is that the arbitrator does not have the power of a court to do such things as appoint receivers or issue temporary restraining orders or injunctions. An injunction may be the only meaningful remedy when a tenant begins a business in violation of a radius provision, for example.

Another drawback to arbitration is that basic litigation procedures are unavailable. There is no requirement for discovery before the hearing. The arbitrator need not take testimony or consider documentary evidence, and, even if the arbitrator does, the rules of evidence do not control admissibility. As a matter of fact, the arbitrator does not have to hold a hearing on the dispute. A proper arbitration provision avoids these shortcomings.

Finally, the arbitrator's decision, which is not required to be written, is subject to review on very narrow grounds:

Ann. tit. 15, §§ 801–818 (West 1978); Pennsylvania, 42 Pa. Cons. Stat. Ann. §§ 7301–7320 (Purdon 1980); South Carolina, S.C. Code Ann. §§ 15-48-10 to -240 (Law. Co-op. 1976); South Dakota, S.D. Codified Laws Ann. §§ 21-25A-1 to -38 (1971); Tennessee, Tenn. Code Ann. §§ 29-5-301 to -320 (1983); Texas, Tex. Rev. Civ. Stat. Ann. arts. 224 to 238-6 (Vernon 1966); Wyoming, Wyo. Stat. §§ 1-36-101 to -119 (1977).

[4] Silverstein Properties, Inc. v. Paine, Webber, Jackson & Curtis, Inc., 65 N.Y.2d 785, 482 N.E.2d 906, 493 N.Y.S.2d 110 (1985).

[5] Sigman, Harry C. *Understanding Arbitration,* ALI-ABA Court Materials J., Dec. 1989, at 47, is a helpful discussion with emphasis on the federal and California statutes.

1. Where the award was procured by corruption, fraud, or undue means

2. Where there was evident partiality or corruption in the arbitrators, or either of them

3. Where the arbitrators were guilty of misconduct in refusing to postpone the hearing, upon sufficient cause shown, or in refusing to hear evidence pertinent and material to the controversy, or of any other misbehavior by which the rights of any party have been prejudiced

4. Where the arbitrators exceeded their powers, or so imperfectly executed them that a mutual, final, and definite award upon the subject matter submitted was not made.[6]

A party to a valuation arbitration cannot have relief from a valuation based on a method that does not meet with its approval.[7] Nor can a party to an arbitration successfully get a judicial award of attorneys' fees if the arbitrator rules that each party must pay its own counsel.[8] Such an award is outside the scope of permissible review. An award apparently based on a misreading of a lease will be sustained; in such a case, the Louisiana Supreme Court said "Because of the strong public policy favoring arbitration, arbitration awards are presumed to be valid. Errors of fact or law do not invalidate a fair and honest arbitration award. . . . Therefore, misinterpretation of a contract by an arbitration panel is not subject to judicial correction."[9] The Florida Supreme Court ruled that an error of law is not sufficient to invalidate an arbitration award on the statutory basis that the arbitrator exceeded its authority.[10]

Some commentators believe that arbitration is not the proper way to answer questions about the interpretation of a lease, about the enforceability of a lease, or about the truthfulness of the people involved in the lease.[11] Their view is that interpretation and enforceability are traditionally legal questions that the judge resolves in any litigation, while truthfulness is an issue about which one may wish to have the several opinions of a jury.

Other commentators have suggested that arbitration is the proper forum to decide "sound accounting practices," time of "completion of construction," appraisal of electricity usage in rent inclusion provisions, compliance with workletters,[12] use, occupancy, and gross sales issues, cost of living increases, and appraisal and revaluation provisions.[13]

---

[6] 9 U.S.C. § 10(a)–(d). The federal arbitration act served as a model for many state statutes.

[7] Board of Educ. of Chicago v. Gorenstein, 179 Ill. App. 3d 388, 534 N.E.2d 579 (1989).

[8] New Shy Clown Casino, Inc. v. Baldwin, 737 P.2d 524 (Nev. 1987).

[9] National Tea Co. v. Richmond, 548 So. 2d 930 (La. 1989) (citations omitted).

[10] Schnurmacher Holding, Inc. v. Noriega, 542 So. 2d 1327 (Fla. 1988) (arbitrator's award was contrary to a Florida statute).

[11] E. Halper, *Shopping Center and Store Leases* § 19.03 (Supp. 1984).

[12] Goldstein, *The Value of Arbitration Provisions in Leases*, 22 Prac. Law. 53 (1976).

[13] N. Hecht, Long Term Lease Planning and Drafting ch. 9 (1974).

Without exception, all commentators agree that the issue of rent default should not be resolved in arbitration.

§ 31.2 Possible Arbitration Provisions

Real estate professionals realize that arbitrators should be presented with a specific question and not vested with broad authority to decide any question that arises under the lease. Put differently, the landlord and tenant should give careful consideration to the issues that will be resolved by arbitration and should state that only those issues will be so resolved. For example, the provision dealing with the cost of living adjustments may conclude:

FORM 31-1
ARBITRATION—COST OF LIVING ADJUSTMENTS

If the cost of living index is no longer published, and if the landlord and tenant are unable to agree upon a substitute index, then they will submit the question of the substitute index to arbitration according to paragraph [arbitration]. In deciding what the substitute index should be, the arbitrators will be bound by the relevant provisions of this paragraph regarding the cost of living index.

This provision assumes that the lease defines cost of living index and substitute index.

In practice, leases employ any one of several provisions. One simply provides:

FORM 31-2
ARBITRATION (SHORT FORM)

Any question that this lease requires to be resolved by arbitration will be submitted to the American Arbitration Association and will be decided according to its rules.

This is sufficient to initiate arbitration.

The American Arbitration Association has promulgated this provision:

FORM 31-3
ARBITRATION—AMERICAN ARBITRATION ASSOCIATION'S
STANDARD ARBITRATION CLAUSE

Any controversy or claim arising out of or relating to this contract, or the breach thereof, shall be settled by arbitration in accordance with the Commercial Arbitration Rules of the American Arbitration Association, and judgment upon the award rendered by the Arbitrator(s) may be entered in any Court having jurisdiction thereof.

Since the American Arbitration Association's rules permit the initiating party to recover from the other party if the other party fails to attend or obtain an adjournment, arbitration provisions should say that the arbitration is subject to those rules.[14]

Another form of the provision includes rules for the arbitration process. Subjects that should be covered are:

1. How arbitration is initiated
2. How the arbitrator or arbitrators are identified. Some real estate professionals recommend the use of more than one arbitrator in order to avoid an unreasonable ruling by one person
3. What qualifications (if any) the arbitrators must have
4. Whether the landlord and tenant are allowed to choose partial arbitrators
5. What happens if the landlord or tenant fails to choose an arbitrator
6. How the arbitrators chosen by the landlord and tenant choose a third arbitrator
7. The time periods within which the landlord and tenant must act and the time periods within which the arbitrators must convene and then issue their decision, failing any of which the landlord or tenant may resort to judicial proceedings
8. The allocation of the costs of arbitration and the costs that the landlord and tenant incur in presenting their own cases
9. The finality and appealability of the arbitrators' decision.

An extended arbitration provision may look like:

FORM 31-4
ARBITRATION (LONG FORM)

These procedures will govern any arbitration according to this lease:

(a)   Arbitration will be commenced by a written demand made by landlord or tenant upon the other. The written demand will contain a statement of the question to be arbitrated and the name and address of the arbitrator appointed by the demandant. Within ten (10) days after its receipt of the written demand, the other will give the demandant written notice of the name and address of its arbitrator. Within ten (10) days after the date of the appointment of the second arbitrator, the two arbitrators will meet. If the two arbitrators are unable to resolve the question in dispute within ten (10) days after their first meeting, they will select a third arbitrator. The third arbitrator will be designated as chairman and will immediately give landlord and tenant written notice of its appointment. The three arbitrators will meet within ten (10) days after the appointment of the third arbitrator. If they are unable to

---

[14] IFG Leasing Co. v. Snyder, 77 Or. App. 394, 713 P.2d 630 (1986) (opinion does not say whether real estate lease was involved).

resolve the question in dispute within ten (10) days after their first meeting, the third arbitrator will select a time, date, and place for a hearing and will give landlord and tenant thirty (30) days' prior written notice of it. The date for the hearing will not be more than sixty (60) days after the date of appointment of the third arbitrator. The first two arbitrators may be partial. The third arbitrator must be neutral. All of the arbitrators must have these qualifications: [qualifications of arbitrators].

(b)   At the hearing, landlord and tenant will each be allowed to present testimony and tangible evidence and to cross-examine each other's witnesses. The arbitrators may make additional rules for the conduct of the hearing or the preparation for it. The arbitrators will render their written decision to landlord and tenant not more than thirty (30) days after the last day of the hearing.

(c)   If the one of whom arbitration is demanded fails to appoint its arbitrator within the time specified or if the two arbitrators appointed are unable to agree on an appointment of the third arbitrator within the time specified, either landlord or tenant may petition a justice of the _____ Court of the State of _____ to appoint a third arbitrator. The petitioner will give the other five (5) days' prior written notice before filing its petition.

(d)   The arbitration will be governed by the Arbitration Law of the State of _____ and, when not in conflict with that law, by the general procedures in the Commercial Arbitration Rules of the American Arbitration Association.

(e)   The arbitrators will not have power to add to, modify, detract from, or alter in any way the provisions of this lease or any amendments or supplements to this lease. The written decision of at least two arbitrators will be conclusive and binding upon landlord and tenant. No arbitrator is authorized to make an award of punitive or exemplary damages.

(f)   Landlord and tenant will each pay for the services of its appointees, attorneys, and witnesses, plus one-half (1/2) of all other proper costs relating to the arbitration.

(g)   The decision of the arbitrators will be final and non-appealable, and may be enforced according to the laws of the State of _____.

PART IX
MISCELLANEOUS PROVISIONS

CHAPTER 32

MISCELLANEOUS

§ 32.1   Submission of the Lease

At the end of negotiations, the landlord will submit its form lease to the tenant. The lease will be complete and ready for the tenant's signature. Of course, the landlord will not have signed the lease, and, as an invariable rule, the landlord will not sign it until the tenant has. Some tenants may be tempted to use the prepared lease for negotiating better offers from other prospective landlords. Other tenants may consider the lease an open offer. To avoid these misuses of the lease[1] a provision is properly made that:

FORM 32-1
MISCELLANEOUS—NO OFFER

The submission of this lease to tenant is not an offer to lease the premises, or an agreement by landlord to reserve the premises for tenant. Landlord will not be bound to tenant until tenant has duly executed and delivered duplicate original leases to landlord and landlord has duly executed and delivered one of those duplicate original leases to tenant.

There are, however, good reasons for a tenant to get an actual offer. It may want to get estimates for the cost of its improvements, or to get necessary licenses and permits. In those cases, the tenant deserves the comfort of knowing that its premises will be available when its preliminary work is finished. Of course, the allotted time is a matter of negotiation.

The tenant's concern that its preliminary work not be wasted is often addressed by mutual execution of a lease that gives the tenant a right to cancel the lease if stated conditions are not satisfied. This approach is unavoidable in some circumstances; for example, like many states, California requires an applicant for a liquor license to have a lease for the premises to be licensed.[2] The problem with giving the tenant a cancellation right is that the tenant may inadvertently become obligated under the lease. In considering a lease that provided that it was "contingent upon" transfer of a license to the tenant, a Pennsylvania court ruled that the tenant was liable under the lease until the transfer was denied.[3] If that tenant had been given an offer, it would simply have declined the offer when the transfer was denied.

---

[1] A provision similar to **Form 32-1** was enforced in 20/20 Vision Center, Inc. v. Hudgens, 256 Ga. 129, 345 S.E.2d 330 (1986).

[2] Cal. Bus. & Prof. Code § 24040 (West 1964).

[3] Village Beer & Beverage, Inc. v. Vincent D. Cox & Co., 327 Pa. Super. 99, 475 A.2d 117 (1984).

A provision such as **Form 32-1** is not a panacea for a landlord.[4] A landlord may be liable to a tenant if the landlord's agent misleads a tenant into thinking that the landlord has signed the lease that the tenant signed and submitted.[5]

Inadvertent lease obligations recall the essential lease provisions—premises, rent, and term—as discussed in **Part II**. The essential lease provisions are not only necessary to have a lease, but they are also sufficient. As a result, many landlords have signed informal agreements or letters of intent without realizing that they had actually entered into a lease. When deciding whether a lease has resulted from preliminary discussions, courts consider the materiality of the issues that were left undecided. Material issues include rent and manner of payment, plans and specifications, and the location of the premises; failing agreement on those issues, no lease results. However, leases have occurred despite the absence of an express agreement about maintenance, insurance, assignment and subleasing, and store hours.[6]

A disturbing case[7] was decided in connection with Tyson's Corner Shopping Center in Fairfax County, Virginia.[8] There, the developer asked a prospective tenant, Lansburgh's, for a letter supporting the developer's application for rezoning. In appreciation for this letter, the developer told Lansburgh's that if the development proceeded, "[W]e will give you the opportunity to become one of our contemplated center's major tenants with rental and terms at least equal to that of any other major department store in the center." When the development proceeded without Lansburgh's and Lansburgh's sued, the trial court ordered the developer to give Lansburgh's a lease, and the court of appeals affirmed the trial court. The court believed that the leases with other major tenants provided sufficient details to enable the developer to prepare a lease "at least equal to that of any other major department store in the center."

In another case,[9] the landlord and a prospective tenant executed a detailed letter of intent in which, among other things, the landlord agreed to withdraw the premises from the market and to negotiate a lease with the prospective tenant.

---

[4] When a landlord rejects a lease and offers another one that the tenant refuses, the landlord cannot then sign the one it refused. Elbert v. Dr. Scholl's Foot Comfort Shops, Inc., 137 Ill. App. 3d 550, 484 N.E.2d 1178 (1985).

[5] Greenstein v. Flatley, 19 Mass. App. 351, 474 N.E.2d 1130 (1985).

[6] *See* Annot., 85 A.L.R.3d 414, *Requirements as to certainty and completeness of terms of a lease in agreement to lease (1978); cases collected in Casual Writing Leads to Binding Lease*, Com. Lease L. Insider, Mar. 1985, at 1-2. *See also* Feeley v. Michigan Ave. Nat'l Bank, 141 Ill. App. 3d 187, 490 N.E.2d 15 (1986), *appeal denied*, (was decided on somewhat formal grounds in favor of the existence of a lease). Kaufman, *Writing the Effective Lease Proposal Letter*, Com. Real Est. Inv. J., Winter 1986, at 27, contains a thorough and useful sample proposal for an office lease and an explanation of its terms.

[7] Ammerman v. City Stores Co., 394 F.2d 950 (D.C. Cir. 1968).

[8] The Tyson's Corner Shopping Center case also helped to make much of the law concerning the antitrust implications of certain "exclusive use" provisions. See § **10.8**.

[9] Channel Home Centers Div. of Grace Retail Corp. v. Grossman, 795 F.2d 291 (3d Cir. 1985).

The landlord used the letter for its financing, the tenant submitted a draft lease, and they each pursued their respective duties under the letter of intent. When a competitor of the prospective tenant approached the landlord, the landlord broke off discussions with the first prospective tenant. The court found that the letter of intent was sufficient to be a lease and that the trial court should take evidence of the intentions of landlord and tenant. Here again, the landlord and tenant crossed the line between a mutual expression of interest and an agreement. This case illustrates how one signatory to a letter of intent may believe — or at least argue — that it had a lease when only the letter of intent was signed.

§ 32.2   Brokers

In most leasing transactions, the landlord is more likely than the tenant to have retained the services of a broker,[10] and the landlord is usually liable for the broker's commission. As a result, leases contain provisions by which the landlord seeks to protect itself from claims of brokers whom it has not employed. A typical provision states:

FORM 32-2
MISCELLANEOUS — BROKERS (LANDLORD'S PROVISION)

Tenant has not dealt with any broker or finder other than _____ with regard to the premises or this lease. Tenant will indemnify landlord against any loss, liability, and expense (including attorneys' fees and court costs) arising out of claims for fees or commissions from anyone other than _____ with whom tenant has dealt with regard to the premises or this lease. Landlord agrees to pay any commission or fee owing to _____.

Cautious tenants will often take issue with the breadth of this provision and will suggest that it be drafted in a more evenhanded way:

FORM 32-3
MISCELLANEOUS — BROKERS (TENANT'S PROVISION)

Landlord and tenant warrant to each other that neither of them has consulted or negotiated with any broker or finder with regard to the premises or this lease other than _____. Tenant agrees to indemnify landlord against any loss, liability, and expense (including attorneys' fees and court costs) arising out of claims for fees or commissions from anyone other than _____ with whom tenant has dealt with regard to the premises or this lease. Landlord agrees to indemnify tenant against any loss, liability, and expense (including

---

[10] *See generally* Cohen, *Leasing Brokerage and Commissions,* 10 Real Est. Rev. 49 (1981).

attorneys' fees and court costs) arising out of claims for fees or commissions from anyone other than _____ with whom landlord has dealt with regard to the premises or this lease. Landlord agrees to pay any commission or fee owing to _____.

§ 32.3   No Recordation

Leases often state:

FORM 32-4
MISCELLANEOUS—NO RECORDATION

Tenant's recordation of this lease or any memorandum or short form of it will be void and a default under this lease.

The landlord hopes by this provision to avoid the difficulty of expunging the recorded lease of a tenant who has vacated the premises. Since many states prohibit the recordation of instruments that are not acknowledged, and since most leases are not acknowledged, tenants have been known to add acknowledgments of their signatures to a copy of a signed lease and then to record it. When local law has required it, some have attached an affidavit that the lease is accurate and then recorded it.

Occasionally, a lease will state that its recordation is "ineffective" or "void" or "of no force and effect"; **Form 32-4** is typical. Since, as **§ 32.4** shows, recordation gives notice, and notice is equivalent to knowledge, one may wonder whether such a provision can be expected to compel someone to forget what he or she has seen.

On the other hand, some states require leases to be recorded if they are longer than a specified period (often three years); failing recordation, those leases may be wholly ineffective, or effective only between the landlord and tenant and not third persons.[11]

Moreover, in several circumstances, the tenant would be remiss in not recording its lease. For a full appreciation of these circumstances, an understanding of the law of notice is necessary.

§ 32.4   Notice, Possession, and Recordation

Before considering the notion of notice, it is necessary to understand the problem that notice is intended to solve and the people whom notice is intended to protect.

---

[11] 2 R. Powell, The Law of Real Property § 222(2) (P.J. Rohan ed., rev. 1977) [hereinafter 2 Powell].

Notice is no more than a device to assist in resolving conflicting claims to the premises and protecting innocent people.[12]

Suppose a landlord leases the premises to a tenant one moment and the next moment, without disclosing the lease, sells the premises to a purchaser who itself intends to occupy the premises. The tenant will not be likely to record its lease, but the purchaser will be most likely to record its deed. The purchaser's rights will prevail over the tenant's rights and the tenant will be left to its claims against its erstwhile landlord.

The result is different if the tenant records its lease before the deed. The result is also different if the tenant takes possession of the premises before the deed is recorded. In those cases, the purchaser's rights will not prevail and the purchaser will be left with a claim against its seller.

The salient differences between these results are recordation and possession.[13] They both give rise to the essential determinant: notice. A person with actual knowledge of another person's rights conferred in an unrecorded document is also on notice of those rights without need for possession or notice by recordation.[14]

The tenant's possession of the premises, which need not be actual occupancy but merely a conspicuous sign, puts a purchaser on notice of the tenant's rights. Although the authorities differ on the sort of notice (actual, constructive, or inquiry) that possession gives, it is clear that a subsequent purchaser, mortgagee, or tenant will not be accorded the sacrosanct status of an innocent party if it does not make adequate inquiry as to the rights of a tenant in possession.

The depth of the inquiry varies from case to case because it must be a reasonable inquiry in the circumstances. Merely asking the owner is insufficient; if fraud is afoot, the owner is involved. At the very least, inquiry must be made of the person in possession; the possessor will be precluded from later asserting a position that is contrary to the one it stated to the inquirer. Research into recorded instruments is also necessary; this, however, may not reveal unrecorded modifications of which the inquirer nevertheless has notice by virtue of the possession.[15]

Recordation is another way in which a tenant can protect itself against the rights of innocent parties. As between the landlord and tenant, in the absence of any statutory requirements, a lease is valid whether or not it is recorded. Not all states permit recording of leases; in those states, priority and innocence are determined by common law principles.

---

[12] *See generally,* ABA Committee on Leases, *Some Considerations to Be Observed in the Recording of Leases,* 12 Real Prop., Prob. & Tr. J. 256 (1977); 3 G.W. Thompson, Commentaries on the Modern Law of Real Property §§ 1104-1106 (1980) [hereinafter 3 Thompson].

[13] Sieger v. Standard Oil Co., 155 Cal. App. 2d 649, 318 P.2d 479 (1957) (holding that notice is imparted by recordation or possession).

[14] Hudson Oil Co. v. Shartstop, 111 Cal. App. 3d 488, 168 Cal. Rptr. 801 (1980).

[15] *See generally* III M. R. Friedman, Friedman on Leases ch. 31 (1983) [hereinafter III Friedman] (on recordation).

§ 32.5   Importance of Recordation

The legal principles of notice make it clear that recordation is very important to a tenant in several situations. When the tenant has a lease for premises that are not yet in existence, recordation is critical because the tenant cannot give notice of its rights by its possession. When the tenant has rights to property beyond the premises, recordation is also advisable because, again, there is no possibility of notice from possession. This situation arises when the landlord gives its covenant not to lease to competing businesses or the landlord grants the tenant an option to expand its premises.[16]

When a tenant has the benefit of an exclusive use, it also has the burden of giving proper notice. For example, if the exclusive use affects two parcels held in separate ownerships, the tenant must be sure that it records its lease (or memorandum of lease or short-form lease) in such a way as to appear in a title search of either ownership.[17]

Tenants should also record their leases when they have options to purchase the premises or rights to remove their improvements (as opposed to trade fixtures), because case law divides over the extent of notice given by mere possession.[18] Generally, however, possession gives notice of the tenant's purchase rights.

Once the landlord and tenant have decided to record the lease, they must choose between recording the full lease, a short-form lease, or notice or memorandum of lease. The choice is discussed in § 32.6. Once the lease is recorded, of course, any amendments must also be recorded.

§ 32.6   Memorandum of Lease and Short-Form Lease

The protection afforded by recordation brings with it the burdens of recording: cost and disclosure. The cost can be substantial in light of the length of many leases; there may also be a recording tax for long-term leases with purchase options if the agreements are construed as sales.[19] Public disclosure of the business terms of the lease is the greatest barrier to recording; ironically, this reluctance usually arises from the landlord's belief that it has not been paid enough and from the tenant's belief that it has paid too much. A lesser concern is the burden on the public records resulting from the recordation of enormous leases of which the vast majority is irrelevant to the general public.

Most of these objections can be overcome by recording a short-form lease or a notice or memorandum of lease; however, the real estate professional must be assured not only of the lawfulness of recording such documents but also of the quantum of notice afforded by recording them. Recordation of a document that is

---

[16] See § 10.5 regarding exclusive uses.

[17] Genovese Drug Stores, Inc. v. Conn. Packing Co., 732 F.2d 286 (2d Cir. 1984).

[18] Annot., 37 A.L.R.2d 1112, *Possession of real property by tenant as charging another purchaser with notice of tenant's agreement with owner-landlord to purchase property* (1954).

[19] Rifkin, *Transfer Taxes: A National Survey,* 19 Real Prop., Prob. & Tr. J. 1035 (1984).

not legally allowed to be recorded does not give any notice at all. Recordation of a document that gives notice of some details of the lease may or may not give notice of other details of the lease.[20]

Short-form leases and memoranda or notices of leases set forth information of which the landlord and tenant wish to give public notice by recordation. The information includes the essential lease information (except rent, which is either omitted or stated nominally) and information about purchase options, renewal or extension rights, expansion rights, and exclusive uses. These documents are governed by applicable recording statutes and judge-made law regarding the effect of recordation. When recording statutes allow only grants or conveyances to be recorded, a short-form lease is used; a short-form lease contains an actual present grant. When these statutes give memoranda of leases the effect of notice, then memoranda are used in accordance with law.

A typical memorandum of lease is that offered by North Carolina statute:

FORM 32-5
MISCELLANEOUS—MEMORANDUM OF LEASE

(Name and address or description of lessor or lessors) hereby lease(s) to (name and address or description of lessee or lessee) for a term beginning the _____ day of _____, 19____, and continuing for a maximum period of _____, including extensions and renewals, if any, the following property:

(here describe the property)

(If applicable: There exists an option to purchase with respect to this leased property, in favor of the lessee which expires the _____ day of _____, 19 _____, which is set forth at large in the complete agreement between the parties.)

The provisions set forth in a written lease agreement between the parties dated the _____ day of _____, 19____, are hereby incorporated in this memorandum.
[Seal]
[Seal]
(Acknowledgment as required by law.)[21]

This form resembles a short-form lease because it contains a present grant, but (as will be shown in **Form 32-6**) it differs from a short-form lease because it does not fully describe other rights and obligations. Another North Carolina statute[22] makes it clear that other forms "sufficient in law" may be used. Other states have made similar allowances for memoranda of leases.[23] A short-form lease may look like:

---

[20] Annot., 89 A.L.R.3d 901, *Recorded real property instrument as charging third party with constructive notice of provisions of extrinsic instrument referred to therein* (1979).

[21] N.C. Gen. Stat. § 47-118 (1984).

[22] *Id.* at § 47-117.

[23] Me. Rev. Stat. Ann. tit _____, § 33-201 ( ); Conn. Gen. Stat. Ann. § 47-19 (West 1964).

FORM 32-6
MISCELLANEOUS—SHORT-FORM LEASE

THIS SHORT-FORM LEASE is made as of _____, 19 ____ by _____ ("landlord"), and _____ ("tenant").

RECITALS:

Landlord and tenant have entered into a lease dated _____, 19____ (the "lease") with respect to certain premises commonly known as 100 First Street, City of _____, County of _____, State of _____ (the "premises"). Landlord and tenant wish to give notice of the lease. Accordingly they agree:

1. *Agreement.* Landlord leases to tenant, and tenant leases from landlord, the real property commonly known as:

_____ Street
City of _____
County of _____
State of _____
(the "premises"), and more particularly described as
Lot _____,
Block _____,
_____ SUBDIVISION,
City of _____,
County of _____,
State of _____.

2. *Term.* The term of the lease begins _____, 19____ and ends _____, 19____, inclusive. The lease gives tenant the following rights:

[RENEWAL OR EXTENSION PROVISION]

3. *Option to Purchase.* The lease gives tenant the following rights:

[OPTION TO PURCHASE]

4. *Exclusive Use.* The lease provides:

[EXCLUSIVE USE]

5. *The Lease.* The terms of this short-form lease are subject to the lease, and any amendments, renewals, or extensions of the lease. The lease (except for the provisions relating to the rent) may be examined at the premises.

LANDLORD:

_____

By: _____

Title: _____

TENANT:

_____

By: _____

Title: _____

ACKNOWLEDGMENTS

In order to avoid misstating any provision of the lease a short-form lease or notice of lease or memorandum of lease should recite the entire provision to which it makes reference. This is particularly true of special provisions such as options to purchase or expand, or exclusives. In **Form 32-6** those provisions would be the renewal or extension provision, option to purchase, and the exclusive use.

§ 32.7   Leasehold Title Insurance

Several circumstances prompt a tenant to search its landlord's title. The tenant may be concerned about the number of mortgages and the terms of those mortgages to which the tenant has agreed to subordinate its leasehold. Another tenant may want to assure itself that no other tenants have exclusive uses of record. A third tenant may want to verify the terms of restrictive covenants with which it has agreed to comply. Yet another tenant may have substantial bonus value in its lease. A last tenant may have a purchase option whose value is dependent on encumbrances of record. In these circumstances, and others, the tenant may want leasehold title insurance.

Leasehold title insurance first became available around 1970, when demand led the American Land Title Association to promulgate forms of title insurance policies for leasehold owners. The leasehold owner's form—and all the other American Land Title Association forms—were most recently revised in 1987. The leasehold owner's form is identical to the owner's policy form to the extent of the insurance afforded, Schedule B, and the exclusions; Schedule A in each is substantially identical. However, they differ with regard to three important aspects of the conditions and stipulations: definition of the estate or interest that is insured,[24] valuation of the estate or interest insured,[25] and miscellaneous items of loss.[26]

---

[24] A.L.T.A. Leasehold Owner's Policy § 1(h) (1987).

[25] *Id.* at § 14.

[26] *Id.* at § 15.

The rights insured by a leasehold policy are the rights of the leasehold estate, that is, "the right of possession for the term or terms described in Schedule A hereof subject to any provisions contained in the Lease which limit such right of possession." The leasehold policy insures only possession, and does not go so far as to assure the tenant that any other obligations of the landlord are enforceable. Therefore, leasehold title insurance does not give the tenant assurance (for instance) that it can compel its landlord to furnish utilities according to the lease.

The basic loss that the policy will pay is the present value of the fair market rental value of the leasehold over the rent reserved in the lease:

> If, in computing loss or damage incurred, it becomes necessary to determine the value of the estate or interest insured by this policy, the value shall consist of the then present worth of the excess, if any, of the fair market rental value of the estate or interest, undiminished by any matters for which claim is made, for that part of the term stated in Schedule A then remaining plus any renewal or extended term for which a value option to renew or extend is contained in the lease, over the value of the rent and other consideration required to be paid under the lease for the same period.

For example, if a tenant loses its leasehold to an insured risk, and if the fair market rental value of its leasehold is $50,000 per year, and if its rent reserved is $45,000 per year, and if the lease has a remaining term of 10 years (including renewals, if any), then the policy will pay the present value of $50,000, payable $5,000 each year for 10 years. Of course, the amount recoverable under the policy is limited to the lesser of the tenant's actual loss or the face amount of the policy.

The policy pays miscellaneous items of loss:

> (a) The reasonable cost of removing and relocating any personal property which the insured has the right to remove and relocate situated on the land at the time of eviction, the cost of transportation of that personal property for the initial twenty-five miles incurred in connection with the relocation, and the reasonable cost of repairing the personal property damaged by reason of the removal and relocation. The costs referred to above shall not exceed in the aggregate the value of the personal property prior to its removal and relocation.
>
> "Personal property," above referred to, shall mean chattels and property which because of its character and manner of affixation to the land, can be severed therefrom without causing appreciable damage to the property severed or to the land to which the property is affixed.
>
> (b) Rent or damages for use and occupancy of the land prior to the eviction which the insured as owner of the leasehold estate may be obligated to pay to any person having paramount title to that of the lessor in the lease.
>
> (c) The amount of rent which, by the terms of the lease, the insured must continue to pay to the lessor after eviction for the land, or part thereof, from which the insured has been evicted.
>
> (d) The fair market value, at the time of the eviction, of the estate or interest of the insured in any sublease of all or part of the land existing at the date of the eviction.

(e) Damages which the insured may be obligated to pay to any sublessee on account of the breach of any sublease of all or part of the land caused by the eviction.

A tenant who obtains title insurance should be certain to have it endorsed or reissued in the event of an assignment of its leasehold.

Significantly, a leasehold title policy is not the proper policy by which to insure a tenant's right to purchase the premises, even if that right is granted in the lease; for that purpose, the tenant should obtain an owner's policy of title insurance.

Most importantly, leasehold title insurance does not cover the tenant's improvements to the premises. If there is a failure of title, the title insurer will not be obligated to pay the tenant for any losses of its improvements. As a general rule, the proper way to insure tenant improvements is by an owner's policy of title insurance; some states may allow protection by an endorsement to the leasehold policy.

§ 32.8   Holding Over

Holding over is the expression used to describe the conduct of a tenant that remains in possession of the premises after its term has ended. Although many tenants view it lightly, holding over may have catastrophic results for them. The tenant's attention to this seemingly minute detail is well-deserved.

For reasons that are lost in the history of the common law, a landlord had two choices when its tenant held over after its term. The landlord could evict the tenant, or it could bind the tenant to another term. The landlord—not the tenant—had the election.[27]

If the landlord decided to bind its tenant to another term, the new term was on all the terms of the old term,[28] except the duration of the new term varied. Some decisions held it was a fixed term, while some held it was a periodic term, that is, one that continued automatically for one period after another unless terminated by the landlord or tenant.[29] Usually, a new one-year term came about if the original term was longer than a year or was from year to year. On the other hand, if the original term was less than a year, or for periods of less than a year, a new tenancy of less than a year resulted. The renewal term did not, however, exceed one year. Other decisions came to substantially the same conclusion by reference to the payment periods for rent instead of the original term. In any event, the tenant was bound for a term that it may not have wanted. The rule of holding over is harsh for a tenant who is caught by this ancient precept. As a result, the common law rule has been modified in many states.

---

[27] Shepherd & Mitchell v. Cummings, 41 Tenn. 354 (1860); *see generally* R. Schoshinski, American Law of Landlord and Tenant § 2:23 (1980) [hereinafter Schoshinski].

[28] Cottonwood Mall Co. v. Sine, 767 P.2d 499 (Utah 1988) (carrying over tenant's obligation to pay landlord's attorneys' fees incurred in enforcement of lease).

[29] Schoshinski § 2:10.

On the other hand, a tenant may find that holding over works to its advantage. The general rule now is that if a tenant holds over after the end of its lease, and if its landlord accepts rent, a year-to-year renewal or extension of the term results.[30] This unexpected result is a surprise to many landlords. However, the landlord's acceptance of a full month's rent for a month in which the term expired (part of the rent thus pertaining to a period after the end of the term) does not create a holdover term against the landlord's wishes.[31]

If the consequences of holding over are prescribed in the lease itself, courts will abide by the agreement of the landlord and tenant. The real estate professional may avoid any possibility of an unintended result by providing:

FORM 32-7
MISCELLANEOUS—HOLDING OVER

If tenant remains in possession of the premises after the end of this lease, tenant will occupy the premises as a tenant from month to month, subject to all conditions, provisions, and obligations of this lease in effect on the last day of the term.

Like most, this form provides that the terms of the lease govern any holdover. Litigation has arisen when a holdover tenant has exercised a purchase option which was available during the term. Does the right continue? A New Hampshire court has decided that it does not.[32] In an unusual case, the South Dakota Supreme Court extended a tenant's right of first refusal into the holdover period, thus upsetting a sale made without regard to the tenant's perceived rights.[33] As a result of the uncertainty, in the appropriate situation the real estate professional may want to make it clear that a purchase option, right of first refusal, renewal, or extension right does not continue into the holdover period.

Some leases provide a greater rent (for example, twice the minimum rent) for the holdover period. This is a negotiable matter. When providing for greater rent, the real estate professional should characterize the payment as rent or liquidated damages for the holding over. Any suggestion that the payment is a penalty should be scrupulously avoided.[34]

Many states have statutes that entitle the landlord to premium rental (two or three times the prevailing monthly rent, for examples) if the tenant holds over.

---

[30] Annot., 45 A.L.R.2d 827, *Landlord's consent to extension or renewal of lease as shown by acceptance of rent from tenant holding over* (1956); *see* Penmanta Corp. v. Hoelis, 520 N.E.2d 120 (Ind. App. 1988) (rule rescued landlord from loss of exculpatory provision in holdover situation).

[31] City v. Hart, 175 Cal. App. 3d 92, 220 Cal. Rptr. 349 (1985) (landlord had said it would not renew lease).

[32] Carroll v. Daigle, 123 N.H. 495, 463 A.2d 885 (1983).

[33] Williams v. Williams, 347 N.W.2d 893 (S.D. 1984).

[34] Annot., 23 A.L.R.2d 1318, *Validity and construction of lease provision requiring lessee to pay liquidated sum for failure to vacate premises or surrender possession at expiration of lease* (1952).

Often the application of these statutes is conditioned upon the tenant's willfulness, or failure to quit after promising to do so, or loss in an eviction action.[35]

More importantly, some leases state that the tenant becomes a tenant at sufferance after the end of the term. A tenant at sufferance is the lowest claim of occupancy that one can have, and as such it has the fewest rights. Presumably, the goal of such a provision is to enable the landlord to give the least possible notice required by law. The unintended result may be to invalidate the tenant's property damage insurance pursuant to a rule that a tenant at sufferance does not have an insurable interest in its improvements to the premises.[36]

Finally, in addition to the election that the landlord has of binding the tenant to a new term, the landlord has the right to claim use and occupation of the premises. This is the rental value of the premises for the period of the holdover. It may be the previous rental rate or a new, independently established rental rate.[37] The landlord may also claim special damages caused by the tenant's failure to surrender the premises. These are losses that the holdover tenant could have foreseen and that the landlord could not avoid. They may include attorneys' fees, court costs, and the loss of a new tenant.[38] However, in one case, when a tenant held over and caused the landlord to lose not only a lease for the tenant's premises but also a lease for other premises, the tenant was not held liable for the landlord's loss because the loss was not foreseeable at the time the lease was executed.[39]

Lest the landlord's panoply of remedies overshadow the benefit that having some holdovers confers on a landlord, the real estate professional should remember that the landlord has its space rented on a sufficiently short term to allow it to accommodate the expansion of existing tenants and the requirements of new tenants.

§ 32.9   Time of the Essence

A lease will often provide:

---

[35] Ala. Code § 6-6-314 (1940); Ark. Stat. Ann. § 18-16-106 (1987); Cal. Civ. Proc. Code §§ 735, 1174(b) (West 1982), *construed in* Sasson v. Katash, 146 Cal. App. 3d 119, 194 Cal. Rptr. 46 (1983); Del. Code Ann. tit. 25, § 5509(c) (1974); D.C. Code Ann. § 45-1407 (1981); Fla. Stat. Ann. § 83.06 (West 1967), *construed in* Eli Einbinder, Inc. v. Miami Crystal Ice Co., 317 So. 2d 126 (Fla. Dist. Ct. App. 1975); Idaho Code § 6-317 (1985), *construed in* Pearson v. Harper, 87 Idaho 245, 392 P.2d 687 (1964); Ill. Ann. Stat. ch. 110, para. 9-202 (Smith-Hurd 1970); Iowa Code Ann. § 562.2 (West 1989); Minn. Stat. Ann. § 557.08 (West 1988); Miss. Code Ann. § 89-7-25 (1972).

[36] J. Appelman, 4 Insurance Law and Practice § 2193 (1969, Supp. 1982).

[37] Restatement of the Law of Property (Second)(Landlord and Tenant) § 14.5 (1977) [hereinafter Restatement].

[38] Restatement § 14.6.

[39] Prudential Ins. Co. of Am. v. United States, 801 F.2d 1295 (11th Cir. 1986), *cert. denied*, 479 U.S. 1086, 107 S. Ct. 1289 (1987).

FORM 32-8
MISCELLANEOUS—TIME OF THE ESSENCE

Time is of the essence of each and every provision of this lease.

In considering this provision, courts have taken two divergent paths. Some courts have held that this provision means that performance by one party at a specified time or within a specified time is so important that it is a condition to performance by the other party.[40] Other courts are less stringent; they rule that this provision is not conclusive, and that it may be nullified by contradictory statements in the same contract.[41]

Contrary to the impression of some real estate professionals, this provision is not necessary in order to enable a nondefaulting party to assert a breach of the contract. A breach can be asserted whether or not this provision is in the agreement.[42] Many real estate professionals believe that this provision will serve to deprive a tenant of valuable renewal rights; however, despite this provision, courts have recently begun to find ways around the loss of valuable rights.[43]

This provision is contradicted by the usual force majeure provision that excuses timely performance when supervening causes prevent it. This provision may also have the unintended effect of penalizing the landlord for late delivery of possession (when force majeure is not applicable) and giving the tenant a right to cancel the lease or sue for damages.

All in all, the real estate professional may conclude that this provision should be used sparingly and only with reference to the particular obligation to which it is relevant. The general applicability of this provision may have unforeseen and undesirable results.

§ 32.10   No Light, Air, and View Easements

American law does not usually imply in leases an easement for light, air, or view.[44] There are, however, cases in which the easement has been implied as an appurtenance to the premises.[45] Leases occasionally say:

---

[40] *E.g.,* Providence Ins. Co. v. LaSalle Nat'l Bank, 118 Ill. App. 3d 720, 455 N.E.2d 238 (1983).

[41] Hayes Mfg. Corp. v. McCauley, 140 F.2d 187, 190 (6th Cir. 1944); Stratton v. Tejani, 139 Cal. App. 3d 204, 187 Cal. Rptr. 231 (1982).

[42] Rocky Mountain Gold Mines v. Gold, Silver & Tungsten, 104 Colo. 478, 93 P.2d 973, 982 (1939).

[43] Mazzotta v. Bornstein, 104 Conn. 430, 133 A. 677, 680 (1926).

[44] Mannino v. Conoco Realty Corp., 86 N.Y.S.2d 855 (Sup. Ct. 1949); I Friedman § 3.3 (1983).

[45] Tomburo v. Liberty Freehold Theater Corp., 131 N.J. Eq. 513, 25 A.2d 909 (1942).

FORM 32-9
MISCELLANEOUS—NO LIGHT AND AIR EASEMENT

The reduction or elimination of tenant's light, air, or view will not affect tenant's liability under this lease, nor will it create any liability of landlord to tenant.

This provision is particularly worthwhile if the premises are in the first of several buildings to be built in a project; an early tenant will be precluded from making claims that it has lost these easements as the project is developed.

§ 32.11   No Partnership

Shopping center leases in which percentage rent is payable commonly provide:

FORM 32-10
MISCELLANEOUS—NO PARTNERSHIP

This lease is not intended to create a partnership or joint venture between landlord and tenant, or to create a principal-and-agent relationship between them. The percentage rent is intended only as a method of computing rent.

The purpose, of course, is to avoid any inference that the landlord and tenant have become partners as to each other or as to strangers. One consequence of a partnership as to strangers is that the landlord becomes liable with the tenant for the expenses of the business conducted on the premises. A consequence of being partners as to each other is that the landlord is entitled to share the profits of the tenant's business.

The law is well-settled that the mere sharing of profits as part of rent does not create a partnership.[46] The Uniform Partnership Act says:

> The receipt by a person of a share of the profits of a business is prima facie evidence that he is a partner in the business, but no such inference shall be drawn if such profits were received in payment . . . as . . . rent to a landlord.[47]

Two states have enacted statutes to the same effect.[48]

A partnership is more likely to be found as the landlord's and tenant's community of interests grows: sharing of expenses and losses and joint rights of management and control are important indications of a partnership. When an

---

[46] Notes and Legislation, *Percentage Leases—Aspects of the Relationship of Lessor and Lessee,* 16 N.Y.U. L.Q. Rev. 284 (1939); I Friedman § 6.101 (1983); Annot., 131 A.L.R. 508, *Lease or tenancy agreement as creating partnership between lessor and lessee* (1941); 68 C.J.S. *Partnerships* § 20(4) (1950); 52A C.J.S. *Landlord & Tenant* § 798 (1968); 59 Am. Jur. 2d *Partnerships* § 57 (1971).

[47] Uniform Partnership Act § 7(4)(b), 6 U.L.A. 39 (1969).

[48] N.Y. Partnership Law § 11(4) (McKinney 1948); N.C. Gen. Stat. § 42.1 (1950).

office building lease has a profit sharing provision (such as that shown in § **12.12**), the real estate professional may wish to add a no partnership provision.

§ 32.12   No Merger

The term *merger* may occur in at least three different senses in a lease. In one sense, mergers affecting corporate tenants are considered in connection with the prohibition of assignments of the lease. In another sense, merger is used like the entireties provision discussed in § **32.20**, by which all promises or agreements made in lease negotiations are said to be merged into the lease that survives as the sole and entire agreement of the landlord and tenant. Finally, merger is used to describe the consequences of one person owning both the landlord's reversion and the tenant's leasehold. This section deals with this last use of the term.

Merger usually comes about when the tenant surrenders its lease to the landlord,[49] or when the tenant's assignee buys the landlord's reversion. In those circumstances, the reversion and the leasehold merge to form the fee. The importance of merger is greatest when there is a subtenant or leasehold mortgagee. If the lease is surrendered, and thus extinguished, what happens to the subtenant or mortgagee whose interest depends on the lease?[50]

The traditional (but waning) view has been that the subtenant could remain in possession without paying rent. The formal concepts of common law compelled this anomalous outcome. Since the landlord had neither privity of contract nor privity of estate with the subtenant, the landlord had neither a claim for rent nor a right to possession. In modern times, these harsh rules have been relaxed but not entirely abandoned. A similar result occurred if a tenant with an option to purchase exercised its option; the landlord's lender could not compel the payment of rent nor could it dispossess the tenant/owner through foreclosure. Newer cases seem to protect the rights of leasehold mortgagees. These lenders do not lose their security when the leasehold and reversion merge.[51]

Leases try to avoid merger by providing:

FORM 32-11
MISCELLANEOUS—NO MERGER

The surrender of this lease by tenant or the cancellation of this lease by agreement of tenant and landlord or the termination of this lease on account of tenant's default will not work a merger, and will, at landlord's option, terminate any subleases of part or all of the premises or operate as an assignment to landlord of any of those subleases. Landlord's option under this paragraph will be exercised by notice to tenant and all known subtenants in the premises.

---

[49] *See generally* III Friedman ch. 39; Schoshinski § 8:13.

[50] *See* Friedman § 7.703.

[51] 3 Thompson § 1204; 6424 Corp. v. Commercial Exch. Prop. Ltd., 171 Cal. App. 3d 1221, 217 Cal. Rptr. 803 (1985).

In leases that give the tenant an option to purchase, the real estate professional should be certain to state that the deed delivered pursuant to the option will negate any merger of the leasehold and fee.

§ 32.13   Modification and Financing Conditions

Very often, leases are signed before development begins and before the landlord has permanent financing for its project. In those circumstances, the landlord is uncertain whether its future lender will accept its form lease. In an effort to avoid the loss of financing on account of an unacceptable lease form, many leases provide:

FORM 32-12
MISCELLANEOUS—MODIFICATION AND
FINANCING CONDITIONS

Landlord has obtained financing and intends to obtain further financing that is secured by mortgages or deeds of trust encumbering the premises. Landlord may also elect to enter into a ground lease of the premises. If any mortgage lender requires any modification of this lease as a condition to such financing or pursuant to rights of approval set forth in the mortgage or deed of trust encumbering the premises, or if any ground lessee requires any modification of this lease as a condition to such ground lease or pursuant to rights of approval set forth in the ground lease, tenant agrees to execute such modification, so long as such modification (a) does not increase the rent or tenant's share of any costs in addition to rent, (b) does not materially interfere with tenant's use or occupancy, and (c) if requested by a mortgage lender with a lien on the premises as of the date of this lease, or a ground lessee in effect as of the date of this lease, has been requested prior to thirty (30) days after the date of this lease. If tenant refuses to execute any such modification within ten (10) days after it is delivered to tenant, landlord will have the right by notice to tenant to cancel this lease. Upon such cancellation landlord will refund any unearned rent or security deposit, and neither landlord nor tenant will have any liability under this lease after the date of cancellation.

One may doubt the value of this provision as anything more than an agreement to agree. If the landlord has a serious problem in its lease form, the tenant is the beneficiary and, as such, is likely to be reluctant to give up its advantage. On the other hand, a minor problem will not prevent a lender from approving the lease form.

In any event, a tenant should certainly amend this broad provision in much the same way as it amends the provisions regarding rules and regulations. The tenant should not agree to amend its lease in any way that increases the tenant's costs, or diminishes the tenant's rights, or increases the tenant's obligations. In other words, the tenant should refuse to give its landlord an unqualified agreement to make lease modifications.

If the landlord knows its lender's form of estoppel certificate or subordination agreement, the landlord should attach them as exhibits to the lease.[52]

The provision in **Form 32-12** is somewhat similar to a provision that gives the landlord the right to cancel the lease if its lender does not approve it:

FORM 32-13
MISCELLANEOUS—LENDER'S APPROVAL

Landlord's obligations under this lease are subject to the approval of the lender furnishing the permanent loan for the building. If that lender disapproves of this lease within _____ (_____) days after tenant executes this lease, landlord will have the right to cancel this lease, without any liability, by written notice of cancellation given to tenant within ten (10) days after landlord learns of the disapproval. If no written notice of cancellation is given to tenant within thirty (30) days after the date of this lease, this lease will continue in full force and effect.

§ 32.14   Consents and Approvals

In order to assure themselves that their landlords will not be capricious or dilatory, tenants often suggest a provision such as:

FORM 32-14
MISCELLANEOUS—CONSENTS AND APPROVALS

Whenever this lease requires landlord's consent or approval, landlord will not withhold its approval or consent unreasonably or in bad faith, and landlord will not unreasonably delay its response to tenant's request for its approval or consent. Landlord will be deemed to have given its consent or approval to any request made by tenant if landlord does not respond to tenant in writing within _____ (_____) days after landlord's receipt of the request. If landlord withholds its consent or approval, its response will explain its reasons for doing so.

Landlords usually resist the breadth of this proposal. Instead, they agree to consider the request on a case-by-case basis.

§ 32.15   Estoppel Certificates

The estoppel certificate is a status report on the lease.[53] It is usually presented by the landlord to its prospective lenders and purchasers with the intention that they

---

[52] See § **32.15**.

[53] One commentator has recommended landlord estoppel letters in the nature of a concise statement of the representations that the tenant would like the landlord to make. The idea is admittedly novel. Ruschman, *Protecting the Commercial Tenant with a Landlord Estoppel Letter (with Form)*, Prac. Real Est. Law., Sept. 1989, at 15.

rely on its contents. Generally, estoppel certificates can be requested only by the landlord; however, tenants should demand the right to require them for the benefit of their prospective assignees or subtenants. A tenant will be precluded from asserting a claim that is contrary to statements made in its estoppel certificate.[54]

The failure to provide an estoppel certificate from an important tenant (or to an assignee) can frustrate a financing or sale or assignment. An estoppel certificate delayed will have the effect of an estoppel certificate denied: an opportunity will be lost. In order to avoid the consequences of a delayed certificate, the estoppel certificate provision should state that a proffered certificate will be presumed to be correct if a response is not received within a short period.

Such a self-proving certificate requires that the offeror complete the information it desires; otherwise, there will be no presumptively correct certificate. Attaching a copy of the lease and any amendments to it assures an accurate certificate. Some landlords resist the notion of attaching a copy of the lease for fear that they might inadvertently omit part of it. In addition to the truism that the landlord ought to have accurate records, a further reason for attaching a copy is prompted by this rhetorical question: Would a landlord prefer to learn of its inaccurate records before a sale or financing—or after a sale or financing in which the buyer or lender relied on the landlord's inaccurate records?

Another way in which a landlord tries to protect itself against unresponsive tenants is to provide that it is empowered to act as the tenant's attorney-in-fact in executing the certificate if the tenant fails to do so. A provision in a lease for estoppel certificates often states:

FORM 32-15
MISCELLANEOUS—ESTOPPEL CERTIFICATES

Within no more than _____ (_____) days after written request by landlord, tenant will execute, acknowledge, and deliver to landlord a certificate stating (a) that this lease is unmodified and in full force and effect, or, if the lease is modified, the way in which it is modified accompanied by a copy of the modification agreement, (b) the date to which rent and other sums payable under this lease have been paid, (c) that no notice has been received by tenant of any default that has not been cured, or, if such a default has not been cured, what tenant intends to do in order to effect the cure, and when it will do so, (d) that tenant has accepted and occupied the premises, (e) that tenant has no claim or offset against landlord, or, if it does, stating the circumstances that gave rise to the claim or offset, (f) that tenant is not aware of any prior assignment of this lease by landlord, or, if it is, stating the date of the assignment and assignee (if known to tenant), and (g) such other matters as may be reasonably requested by landlord. Any certificate may be relied upon by any prospective purchaser of the premises and any prospective mortgagee or benefici-ary under any deed of trust or mortgage encumbering the premises. If landlord submits a completed certificate to tenant, and if tenant fails to object to its contents within _____ (_____) days after its receipt of the completed certificate, the matters

---

[54] Spiegel v. Stanley Nelson, Inc., 458 So. 2d 1175 (Fla. Dist. Ct. App. 1984), *review denied,* 471 So. 2d 44 (Fla. 1985).

stated in the certificate will conclusively be deemed to be correct. Furthermore, tenant irrevocably appoints landlord as tenant's attorney-in-fact to execute and deliver on tenant's behalf any completed certificate to which tenant does not object within _____ (_____) days after its receipt.

In order to avoid any disagreement about the form of the estoppel certificate, many landlords attach the form to their leases and negotiate at the outset any objections that the tenant raises. When this is done, however, the landlord should still use **Form 32-15**, just in case a future lender has a different form or different requirements.

The following form of estoppel certificate contemplates the attachment of the form of the lease about which the certificate is requested. This mandates the attachment of the full lease, any "side agreements," and any amendments. Care is required in order to be certain that the certificate is complete and correct. This form is intended for use in connection with a sale of the premises and the use of borrowed money by the buyer. With minor changes, it may be used for assignments by tenants or refinancings without a sale. This form complements the nondisturbance agreement in § **24.3**.

FORM 32-16
MISCELLANEOUS—ESTOPPEL CERTIFICATE

LANDLORD: _____

TENANT: _____

LEASE DATED: _____,19____

PREMISES: _____

SECURITY DEPOSIT: $_____

PURCHASER: _____

PURCHASER'S ADDRESS: _____

LENDER: _____

LENDER'S ADDRESS: _____

EFFECTIVE DATE: _____,19____

Tenant certifies to purchaser and to lender, their successors and assigns, that as of the date of tenant's execution of this instrument:

(a) the lease is unmodified and in full force and effect, and there are no other agreements between landlord and tenant with respect to the lease, the premises, or the building of which the premises are a part;

(b) tenant has accepted possession of the premises, and any improvements required by the terms of the lease to be made by landlord have been completed to the satisfaction of tenant;

(c)   rental and other amounts payable under the lease have been paid to the date of tenant's execution of this instrument and will be paid through the effective date;

(d)   landlord is not in default under any of the terms of the lease;

(e)   no notice has been received by tenant or given by tenant of any default under the lease that has not been cured, and there are no circumstances that with the passage of time or giving of notice would be a default by landlord or tenant under the lease;

(f)   the address for notices to be sent to tenant is set forth in the lease;

(g)   tenant has no charge, lien, or claim of offset under the lease or against rent or other charges due or to become due under the lease and tenant has no outstanding claim for credit or reimbursement on account of tenant's improvements to the premises;

(h)   the amount of any security or other deposit returnable to the tenant pursuant to the lease is set forth above and the amount of any rental and other amounts paid more than thirty (30) days prior to the date on which they are due under the lease are set forth in the lease;

(i)   a correct copy of the lease and all amendments and side agreements to it are attached to this instrument as Exhibit _____; and

(j)   tenant has no right or option to purchase the premises or any part or all of the building of which they are a part, or to renew or extend the lease, or to expand the premises, except as set forth in Exhibit _____.

Tenant further warrants to purchaser, its successors and assigns, and lender that tenant (except as set forth in the lease): has not paid and will not pay any rent under the lease more than thirty (30) days in advance of its due date; prior to the effective date, will not surrender or consent to the modification of any of the terms of the lease or to the termination of the lease by landlord, and will not seek to terminate the lease by reason of any act or omission of landlord until tenant will have given written notice of such act or omission to purchaser and lender at their addresses above and until a reasonable period of time has elapsed following the giving of such notice, during which period purchaser and lender will have the right, but will not be obligated, to remedy such act or omission; will notify purchaser in writing at purchaser's address above prior to the effective date if any of the statements made by tenant in this instrument are materially false or misleading, or omit to state a material fact, as a result of any circumstances occurring or becoming known to tenant after the date of tenant's execution of this instrument; understands it may be prevented from taking a position after the effective date that is inconsistent with the statements made by it in this instrument.

Date of execution: _____
Tenant's signature _____

When used for a shopping center lease, the landlord should also have the tenant state that no other tenant in the shopping center is breaching the tenant's exclusive use. If the lease involves a base year or base amount for operating expenses, some estoppel certificates include that information. A tenant that has the right to remove its fixtures (other than trade fixtures) or its improvements should say so in any estoppel certificate it gives.

§ 32.16   No Waiver

Landlords usually provide in their leases that they will not lose any of their rights no matter how remiss they may be in enforcing them. A typical provision says:

FORM 32-17
MISCELLANEOUS—NO WAIVER

No waiver of any condition or agreement in this lease by either landlord or tenant will imply or constitute its further waiver of that or any other condition or agreement. No act or thing done by landlord or landlord's agents during the term of this lease will be deemed an acceptance of a surrender of the premises, and no agreement to accept a surrender will be valid unless in writing signed by landlord. The delivery of tenant's keys to any employee or agent of landlord will not constitute a termination of this lease unless landlord has entered into a written agreement to that effect. No payment by tenant, nor receipt from landlord, of a lesser amount than the rent or other charges stipulated in this lease will be deemed to be anything other than a payment on account of the earliest stipulated rent. No endorsement or statement on any check, or any letter accompanying any check or payment as rent, will be deemed an accord and satisfaction. Landlord will accept the check for payment without prejudice to landlord's right to recover the balance of such rent or to pursue any other remedy available to landlord. If this lease is assigned, or if the premises or any part of the premises are sublet or occupied by anyone other than tenant, landlord may collect rent from the assignee, subtenant, or occupant and apply the net amount collected to the rent reserved in this lease. That collection will not be deemed a waiver of the covenant in this lease against assignment and subletting, or the acceptance of the assignee, subtenant, or occupant as tenant, or a release of tenant from the complete performance by tenant of its covenants in this lease.

Each sentence of this provision was prompted by a case holding that the landlord waived some of its rights by the conduct described in the sentence.[55] Although

---

[55] 52A C.J.S. *Landlord & Tenant* § 737 (1968); 49 Am. Jur. *Landlord and Tenant* §§ 1066, 1073, 1095, 1096, 1100 (1970). In Betancourt v. Garcia, 49 Bankr. 620 (D.P.R. 1985), the court held that a landlord's acceptance of rent was evidence that it had approved a sublease from the tenant to its wholly owned corporation. Step Ahead, Inc. v. Lehndorff Greenbriar, Ltd., 171 Ga. App. 805, 321 S.E.2d 115 (1984), illustrates the ways in which a landlord can inadvertently accept an otherwise prohibited sublessee. A landlord that accepts renewal rent for 15 months cannot say the tenant had no renewal rights because of a default in the primary term. Bernstein v. 1000 Second Ave. Corp., N.Y.L.J. at p. 6, col. 4 (App. Div. Nov. 25, 1986). Another case on the effect of the acceptance of rent is S.E. Nichols, Inc. v. Am. Shopping Centers, 115 A.D.2d 856, 495 N.Y.S.2d 810 (App. Div. 1985). Fay Corp. v. Bat Holdings I, Inc., 682 F. Supp. 1116 (W.D. Wash. 1988), reaches a similar result regarding enforcement of a "gold clause" (entitling the landlord to collect payment in gold) and a waiver that cost the landlord a 20-fold rent increase. In Holman v. Halford, 518 So. 2d 442 (Fla. Dist. Ct. App. 1988), a landlord that failed to object to three improper subleases could not terminate the lease on account of another. Presumably, however, the landlord had revived its right to terminate the lease if another improper sublease occurred.

this provision is comprehensive, real estate professionals will want to research the law of their states in order to determine whether other circumstances have also resulted in a waiver. Although real estate professionals often show little concern about no-waiver provisions, they do deserve careful attention; no-waiver provisions are often enforced.[56]

Tenants often have rights that are dependent upon there being no default in their covenants in the lease; renewals, assignments, and purchase options are examples. If the landlord can assert a long-past default, the tenant's rights may be defeated.[57] A Florida landlord was able to avoid a purchase option because of the tenant's 10-year-old default.[58] As § **30.6** illustrated, a tenant will want to protect itself from the forfeiture of valuable rights because of an (almost) long-forgotten default.

The no-waiver provision may be raised in response to a defense that the statute of limitations has run. If that response were successful, the tenant would have had its rights substantially reduced. The tenant may want to avoid this result by limiting the impact of the provision to claims for which the statute of limitations has not passed.

The law of waiver has evolved in connection with two kinds of covenants to which waiver may apply: continuous and noncontinuous covenants. A continuous covenant requires repeated performance by the tenant. Although the payment of rent is the foremost example, other important continuous covenants are promises to maintain the premises, and to maintain insurance on the premises. A noncontinuous covenant requires a single act by the tenant; construction or demolition of improvements is a typical noncontinuous covenant.

In the case of continuous covenants, the tenant's persistent late payment of rent without objection from the landlord is a waiver by the landlord of its right of prompt payment. In order to resurrect its right to insist upon prompt payment, the landlord must give notice that its rights are going to be enforced strictly; the landlord cannot go along with a course of conduct and then abruptly rely on it as a basis for a forfeiture of the lease. Of course, if the landlord had always insisted upon performance and had objected to late payments, the tenant would have been forewarned and the landlord would have been better able to declare a default without further notice. In Illinois, the purchaser of a shopping center was able to

---

[56] S.H.V.C., Inc. v. Roy, 188 Conn. 503, 450 A.2d 351 (1982); Giller Inds. v. Hartley, 644 S.W.2d 183 (Tex. Civ. App. 1982); Cottonwood Plaza Assocs. v. Nordale, 132 Ariz. 228, 644 P.2d 1314 (Ct. App. 1982).

[57] Summa Corp. v. Richardson, 93 Nev. 228, 564 P.2d 181 (1977), *appeal after remand*, 95 Nev. 399, 596 P.2d 208 (1979).

[58] Eskridge v. Macklevy, Inc., 468 So. 2d 337 (Fla. Dist. Ct. App.), *review denied*, 478 So. 2d 54 (Fla. 1985). Entrepreneur, Ltd. v. Yasuna, 498 A.2d 1151 (D.C. 1985), is a case in which the landlord's acceptance of rent and failure to give a tenant notice and an opportunity to cure an ongoing default (in this case, an alleged failure to comply with laws) prevented it from avoiding the tenant's purchase option.

insist upon a tenant's submission of certified gross sales reports, even though the predecessor owner had not demanded them.[59]

In a California case, the tenant expanded its premises and encroached on areas outside of the premises. Even though the landlord accepted rent for five years after these breaches, the court held that the landlord had not waived its right to terminate the lease because it had shown its willingness to make a new agreement for the new construction and the encroachment area. The court felt it could not penalize the landlord for trying to reach an amicable settlement of the breach.[60]

A Virginia tenant unsuccessfully claimed that the landlord's breach of its promise to enforce uniform hours of operation in a shopping center for seven years was a continuous breach that entitled the tenant to raise its claim after the statute of limitations had run.[61]

A noncontinuous covenant raises entirely different questions. Once the breach has occurred and a waiver of the breach has occurred, the landlord can neither insist upon performance nor forfeit the lease for nonperformance. The most striking case of a noncontinuous covenant arose in a 200-year lease that required the tenant to construct a building within 25 years after the term began. Although the building was not built within 25 years after the term began, the landlord accepted rent after that date and was found to have waived performance of the construction obligation. As a result, the landlord, who had probably believed it would have improved property at the end of the lease, faced the prospect that unimproved land would be returned to it.[62]

The effect of nonperformance of a noncontinuous covenant may be avoided by converting the covenant into a continuous covenant. A provision such as "tenant will demolish the shed before the second anniversary of the commencement of the term of this lease" may be expressed as "tenant will demolish the shed either before the second anniversary of the commencement of the term of this lease, or at any time after the second anniversary, within ninety (90) days after landlord requests tenant to do so." The landlord may also refer to other provisions of the lease (such as that shown in § 30.5) that allow it to perform tenant's covenants and to charge tenant for its cost to do so.

One commentator has mentioned the peculiarity of waiver: "when the tenant is in default, the landlord is penalized for accepting what is due to it."[63] Put differently, when a tenant defaults, the landlord can only preserve the default by declining the rent. However, the Arizona Supreme Court ruled that the landlord's acceptance of rent from a tenant who remains in possession after an alleged default (in this case a breach of the use provision) does not prohibit it from a judgment of eviction.[64]

---

[59] LaSalle Nat'l Bank v. Helry Corp., 136 Ill. App. 3d 897, 483 N.E.2d 958 (1985).

[60] Thriftimart, Inc. v. Me & Tex, 123 Cal. App. 3d 751, 177 Cal. Rptr. 24 (1981).

[61] Westminster Inv. Corp. v. Lamps Unltd., Inc., 237 Va. 543, 379 S.E.2d 316 (1989).

[62] United States Trust Co. v. Broadwest Realty Corp., 201 Misc. 769, 106 N.Y.S.2d 432 (Sup. Ct. 1951).

[63] II Friedman § 16.503.

[64] DVM Co. v. Bricker, 137 Ariz. 589, 672 P.2d 933 (1983).

In most cases, the landlord pays to keep the tenant in default.[65] Believing that waiver arose in order to avoid the landlord's harsh remedy of forfeiting the lease, that same commentator suggests that the rigorous doctrine of waiver be supplemented by the equitable doctrine of estoppel. In this way the landlord would not be allowed to forfeit the lease if the tenant could cure its default and give the landlord the benefit of its bargain.

The landlord should not be entirely downcast by the law of waiver.[66] A waiver of one default does not prevent forfeiture on account of another one. Moreover, the waiver of a right to forfeit the lease for a breach does not prevent a suit for damages for that same breach. If a landlord accepts rent after an impermissible assignment and thus waives its right to forfeit the lease for that breach, it may be entitled to the difference between market rental rates and lease rental rates as damages.[67]

§ 32.17   Joint and Several Liability

Although the effect is merely to repeat the universal rule,[68] many leases state that all signatories to the lease are jointly and severally liable under the lease:

FORM 32-18
MISCELLANEOUS—JOINT AND SEVERAL LIABILITY

If tenant is composed of more than one signatory to this lease, each signatory will be jointly and severally liable with each other signatory for payment and performance according to this lease.

§ 32.18   Authority

When dealing with corporate tenants, landlords often insist on a corporate resolution authorizing the lease; see § **3.7** for a form of corporate resolution. In

---

[65] *See, e.g.,* Waters v. Taylor, 527 So. 2d 139 (Ala. Civ. App. 1988) in which a landlord unsuccessfully sought four years of past cost of living adjustments; although it seems unfair to collect money long after it was due, it seems equally unfair to lose a loan made to a tenant that had interest free use of the money for several years. J.E.M. Enters., Inc. v. Taco Pronto, Inc., 145 Ga. App. 573, 244 S.E.2d 253 (1978), involved a landlord's assurance that it could not collect real estate taxes otherwise due under the lease and a refusal to allow it to do so.

[66] II Friedman § 16.5 has a fine discussion of waiver in leases; *see also* 2 Powell § 250(3).

[67] Food Pantry, Ltd. v. Waikiki Business Plaza, Inc., 58 Haw. 606, 575 P.2d 869 (1978). *But see* Gonsalves v. Gilbert, 44 Haw. 543, 356 P.2d 379 (1960) (landlord may commit waiver despite nonwaiver provision).

[68] 52 C.J.S. *Landlord and Tenant* § 526 (1968); A. Corbin, Corbin on Contracts § 937 (1-vol. ed. 1952).

addition, those landlords ask for an express warranty of the signatories' authority:

FORM 32-19
MISCELLANEOUS—AUTHORITY

If tenant signs this lease as a corporation, each of the persons executing this lease on behalf of tenant warrants to landlord that tenant is a duly authorized and existing corporation, that tenant is qualified to do business in the state in which the premises are located, that tenant has full right and authority to enter into this lease, and that each and every person signing on behalf of tenant is authorized to do so. Upon landlord's request, tenant will provide evidence satisfactory to landlord confirming these representations.

A similar representation is sought from partnership tenants.

§ 32.19   Captions, Exhibits, Gender, and Number

These minor housekeeping matters cannot possibly be objectionable. One can hardly imagine that their presence or absence could affect the outcome of any litigation.

FORM 32-20
MISCELLANEOUS—CAPTIONS, EXHIBITS, GENDER, AND NUMBER

The captions and table of contents are inserted in this lease only for convenience of reference and do not define, limit, or describe the scope or intent of any provisions of this lease. The exhibits to this lease are incorporated into the lease. Unless the context clearly requires otherwise, the singular includes the plural, and vice versa, and the masculine, feminine, and neuter adjectives include one another.

§ 32.20   Entire Agreement

In order to avoid an assertion by the tenant that there are oral agreements ancillary to the lease, which are usually barred by the statute of frauds and the parol evidence rule,[69] a lease usually states that it is the entire agreement of the landlord and tenant and that all their agreements, discussions, and promises are integrated into it. This is often called the *entireties* or *integration provision*:

---

[69] Wilkerson v. PIC Realty Corp., 590 S.W.2d 780 (Tex. Civ. App. 1979), *no writ*.

FORM 32-21
MISCELLANEOUS—ENTIRE AGREEMENT

This lease contains the entire agreement between landlord and tenant with respect to its subject matter and may be amended only by subsequent written agreement between them. Except for those that are set forth in this lease, no representations, warranties, or agreements have been made by landlord or tenant to one another with respect to this lease.

This provision should prompt the tenant's real estate professional to ask the tenant what other promises have been made. Often these promises are made in promotional materials or renderings or models of the development of which the premises are a part. These promises should be expressed in the lease. Although the law is sparse, the tenant may have difficulty in avoiding a lease because the development differs from the promotional literature.[70]

An equally interesting—and an equally undeveloped—area of the law concerns the point at which "sales talk" (which no one expects to be honest) becomes a representation forming the basis for a claim of deceit. Traditionally, courts have allowed owners to give their opinions of the value of their property: a statement such as "these premises are worth $25 per square foot" is not actionable if the premises prove to be worth $20 per square foot. On the other hand, to say to a prospective tenant that "Jones is willing to pay $25 per square foot" is to deceive the prospective tenant if Jones is not willing to pay that much.[71]

Although the entireties provision is usually believed to be useful to protect the landlord, tenants should consider its value to them. For example, the provision may help a retail tenant whose landlord is disappointed in the tenant's sales, and asserts that the tenant induced the landlord to make the lease by a real or imagined misrepresentation about its prospective sales volume.

Insofar as the entireties provision inhibits judicial construction of a lease, it is against public policy. A court will not allow a fraud to be concealed by an entireties provision,[72] nor will it exclude testimony that bears upon the intentions of the landlord and tenant.[73] For this reason, real estate professionals should save early drafts of a lease, because the drafts may illuminate the intention of the landlord and tenant. In a North Carolina case, the deletion of a provision from the first draft of a lease was used to help a court to construe the final lease; the

---

[70] *See* Annot., 43 A.L.R.3d 1386, *Statements in promotional or explanatory literature issued by lessor to lessee as grounds for relief from lease contract* (1972) (considers residential landlord-tenant case law).

[71] Kabatchnick v. Hanover-Elm Bldg. Corp., 328 Mass. 341, 103 N.E.2d 692 (1952), *discussed in* Annot., 30 A.L.R.2d 918, *Misrepresentation by lessor, in negotiations for lease, as to offers of rental received from third persons, as actionable fraud* (1953).

[72] Barash v. Pa. Terminal Real Estate Corp., 26 N.Y.2d 77, 256 N.E.2d 707, 308 N.Y.S.2d 649 (1970); Betz Laboratories, Inc. v. Hines, 647 F.2d 402 (3d Cir. 1981).

[73] Garden State Plaza Corp. v. S.S. Kresge Co., 78 N.J. Super. 485, 189 A.2d 448 (1962), *cert. denied*, 40 N.J. 226, 191 A.2d 63 (1963), *cited in* II Friedman § 26.6 n.2.

provision in the first draft had allowed the tenant to make certain renovations that the landlord later said that the tenant should not be allowed to make.[74] Although the decision does not set forth the factual basis of the claim, a federal district court in Maine held that a shopping center tenant may have a claim under that state's Unfair Trade Practices Act.[75] Such a theory may allow a tenant to go beyond the "four corners" of the document.

§ 32.21 Amendments

A provision regarding lease amendments appears by itself or in the company of the entire agreement provision in § **32.20**. Usually, it says:

FORM 32-22
MISCELLANEOUS—AMENDMENT

This lease can be amended only by a written document signed by landlord and tenant.

The purpose of this provision is obvious: to prevent any assertion of oral modifications. In this sense, it does no more than repeat the statute of frauds and parol evidence rule as most states use them. This provision cannot be used to effect an injustice; as New York's highest court has said, "the prohibition of oral waiver may itself be waived."[76]

§ 32.22 Severability

In order to avoid the possibility that one illegal provision may taint the entire lease and prompt a court to refuse to enforce any part of it, many leases include a provision such as:

FORM 32-23
MISCELLANEOUS—SEVERABILITY

If any provision of this lease is found by a court of competent jurisdiction to be illegal, invalid, or unenforceable, the remainder of this lease will not be affected, and in lieu of each provision that is found to be illegal, invalid, or unenforceable, provision will be added as a part of this lease that is as similar to the illegal, invalid, or unenforceable provision as may be possible and be legal, valid, and enforceable.

---

[74] Asheville Mall, Inc. v. F.W. Woolworth Co., 76 N.C. App. 130, 331 S.E.2d 772 (1985), *appeal after new trial*, 83 N.C. App. 532, 350 S.E.2d 875 (1986), *review denied*, 319 N.C. 402, 354 S.E.2d 709 (1987).

[75] Fishermen's Net, Inc. v. Weiner, 608 F. Supp. 1283 (D. Me. 1985).

[76] Beatty v. Guggenheim Exploration Co., 225 N.Y. 380, 381, 122 N.E. 378 (1919).

These provisions originated in legislative draftsmanship when a new statute was hoped to be substantially, if not entirely, immune to constitutional attack. The provision was the legislature's statement that it would have enacted the statute even if the objectionable part had been omitted. Courts have said repeatedly that a severability provision will not save a statute that is wholly dependent on an invalid provision; on the other hand, courts have invalidated only a part of a statute without the legislative declaration.[77]

With regard to private agreements (including lease agreements) that contain unenforceable noncompetition agreements, the modern judicial trend is to enforce the provision insofar as it is reasonable in duration and territorial scope.[78] When the tenant is relying upon a particular provision whose legality may be questioned, or whose scope may be reformed by a court, such as an exclusive use, the tenant may not wish this rule to apply. In fact, the tenant may say that the exclusive use provision is a material inducement to its making the lease and that the invalidation or judicial modification of the provision will enable the tenant to terminate the lease.

§ 32.23   No Construction Against
Preparer of Lease

If a court is unable to interpret a lease after all of the interpretive rules have been exhausted, the court may decide that there is no agreement at all. On the other hand, the court may conclude that the landlord and tenant reached an agreement in their lease and that the only obstacle to an adjudication is the interpretation of conflicting or ambiguous provisions.[79] In this event, the court may rule in favor of the interpretation that goes against the preparer of the lease.

Courts are most likely to do this when a form document has been offered by the landlord and accepted by the tenant without modification or negotiation.[80] The mere use of a form does not by itself call into play this rule of interpretation; some forms, such as the American Institute of Architects form construction contract, may have been propounded by both the landlord and the tenant.[81]

In order to avoid the adverse interpretation, landlords' leases often provide:

---

[77] 82 C.J.S. *Statutes* § 94 (1953).

[78] Annot., 61 A.L.R.3d 397, *Enforceability insofar as restrictions would be reasonable, of contract containing unreasonable restrictions on competition* (1975).

[79] 2 Powell § 222(5)(c).

[80] Sirtex Oil Indus., Inc. v. Erigan, 403 S.W.2d 784 (Tex. 1966).

[81] A. Corbin, Corbin on Contracts § 559 (1952).

FORM 32-24
MISCELLANEOUS—NO CONSTRUCTION AGAINST PREPARER OF LEASE

This lease has been prepared by landlord and its professional advisors and reviewed by tenant and its professional advisors. Landlord, tenant, and their separate advisors believe that this lease is the product of all of their efforts, that it expresses their agreement, and that it should not be interpreted in favor of either landlord or tenant or against either landlord or tenant merely because of their efforts in preparing it.

If this provision is a part of a printed form, and if it is false, it would prove the point it sought to avoid: the inequality of the bargaining strengths of the landlord and tenant.

§ 32.24 Notices

The provision for notices usually states:

FORM 32-25
MISCELLANEOUS—NOTICES

Any notice, request, demand, consent, approval, or other communication required or permitted under this lease will be written and will be deemed to have been given only (a) when personally delivered, or (b) when served pursuant to the Federal Rules of Civil Procedure, or (c) on the _____ day after it is deposited in any depository regularly maintained by the United States Postal Service, postage prepaid, certified or registered mail, return receipt requested, addressed to:

Landlord: _____

With a copy at the same time to: _____

Tenant: _____

With a copy at the same time to: _____

Notices may be given by an agent on behalf of landlord or tenant. Either landlord or tenant may change its addresses or addressees for purposes of this paragraph by giving ten (10) days' prior notice according to this paragraph. Any notice from landlord to tenant will also be deemed to have been given if delivered to the premises, addressed to tenant, whether or not tenant has vacated or abandoned the premises.

Despite its apparent harmlessness, this provision ought to be carefully reviewed. A New York landlord's notice given by its attorney was found ineffective because only the landlord was allowed to give it.[82] A tenant ought to be certain that it has the right to receive notices at more than one address (such as its corporate headquarters and also its attorneys' offices). Often tenants object to notices by personal delivery to any occupant of the premises; some occupants may not be employed by the tenant, and, among those who are, some may not handle notices properly. Of course, a tenant ought to assure itself that it gives notices in the same manner as it receives them, because some landlords' leases prescribe a more difficult way for tenants to give notices.

Some leases refer to business days in the notice provision and elsewhere. Unless business days (or holidays) are defined, such a provision is unclear.

Leases usually specify the way in which notices must be given. In the absence of specification, a dispute about the giving of notice will be the testimony of the landlord against that of the tenant. Hand delivery is commonly allowed but is useless unless a receipt acknowledges delivery. Notice by the statutory method prescribed for the commencement of lawsuits is reliable but costly. Ordinary mail gives a landlord a presumption of delivery, but that presumption can be overcome. Registered mail or certified mail — with return receipt requested — are the preferred methods of giving notices.

Registered mail is appropriate when sending things of value (for example, jewelry) because the sender is paid the declared value (which determines the cost of mailing) of the lost item. Certified mail is used for items of no intrinsic value, such as notices under leases. It costs much less than registered mail.

A certificate of mailing is first-class mail but not registered or certified mail. The certificate is completed by the sender with its name and address and the addressee's name and address. A postal clerk verifies the information, stamps the date on the certificate, and mails the letter. Although the sender has proof that the mail was sent, it has no proof that the mail was received. In this important regard, a certificate of mailing differs from registered or certified mail.

A prescription of a method that is "sufficient" does not mean that other methods may not be.[83] Thus the prescribed methods should be the "only" or "sole" ways for notice to be given.

§ 32.25 Attorneys' Fees

Since an agreement by landlord and tenant with respect to attorneys' fees will usually be enforced by a court,[84] most leases contain a provision such as:

---

[82] 117-07 Hillside Ave. Realty Corp. v. RKO Century Warner Theaters, Inc., 151 A.D.2d 732, 543 N.Y.S.2d 151 (1989).

[83] Bijan Designer for Men, Inc. v. St. Regis Sheraton Corp., 150 A.D.2d 244, 543 N.Y.S.2d 296 (1989) (Sup. Ct. 1989).

[84] 2 Powell § 250(3)(b); Annot., 77 A.L.R.2d 735, *Construction and effect of lease provision relating to attorneys' fees* (1961); *see* Fitzgerald v. Lake Shore Animal Hospital, Inc., 183 Ill. App. 3d 655, 539 N.E.2d 311 (1989) (Illinois appellate court remanded an unreasonably high award).

FORM 32-26
MISCELLANEOUS—ATTORNEYS' FEES

If landlord and tenant litigate any provision of this lease or the subject matter of this lease, the unsuccessful litigant will pay to the successful litigant all costs and expenses, including reasonable attorneys' fees and court costs, incurred by the successful litigant at trial and on any appeal. If, without fault, either landlord or tenant is made a party to any litigation instituted by or against the other, the other will indemnify the faultless one against all loss, liability, and expense, including reasonable attorneys' fees and court costs, incurred by it in connection with such litigation.

For the landlord, it is important to have the tenant's agreement to pay the landlord's attorneys' fees incurred in any third-party action; this would include mechanics' liens and personal injury claims. It is also important for a landlord to be able to recover its attorneys' fees in any litigation involving the tenant, and not just litigation for the recovery of rent—as opposed to possession.[85]

The tenant's greatest concern is that the agreement be mutual with respect to claims between landlord and tenant. If the tenant prevails in a case between them, the landlord pays the tenant's attorneys' fees and vice versa. This is only fair.[86]

Although this provision specifies costs of appeal, an Illinois court has held that costs of appeal are recoverable by a successful litigant even though they are not included in the attorneys' fees provision.[87]

The real estate professional may consider adding a definition of successful litigant to this provision.[88] What happens, for example, if the landlord sues for $10,000, and the tenant counterclaims for $5,000, and each wins, leaving the landlord ahead $5,000? Some courts have said that the successful litigant is the one with the net judgment. However, what happens if the landlord sues to forfeit the lease, and the tenant asserts a counterclaim for monetary damages, and each wins? There is no net judgment. In this instance, some courts have said that the successful litigant is the one that wins the main issue. At least one court has awarded attorneys' fees to both litigants when each prevailed on its issue. The real estate professional may want to consider a definition of successful litigant as one who recovers the net judgment in claims for monetary damages, and the one who recovers substantially the relief it sought in claims that do not involve monetary damages. There may still be two successful litigants. Of course, if a claim is frivolous, a litigant may be entitled to attorneys' fees and costs, pursuant to statutes in many states.[89]

---

[85] *See* Gergora v. Flynn, 486 So. 2d 5 (Fla. Dist. Ct. App.), *review denied*, 500 So. 2d 544 (1986) (restricting landlord's recovery because of narrow provision).

[86] N.Y. Real Prop. Law § 234 (McKinney Supp. 1975) obligates the landlord to pay the tenant's attorneys' fees if the tenant prevails and the lease allows the landlord to recover its attorneys' fees if it prevails. This statute pertains only to residential leases.

[87] Losurdo Bros. v. Arkin Distrib. Co., 125 Ill. App. 3d 267, 465 N.E.2d 139 (1984).

[88] *See Who Wins Legal Fees: Owner or Tenant?*, Com. Lease Law Insider, Nov. 1984, at 7.

[89] *See* Briarwood v. Faber's Fabrics, Inc., 163 Mich. App. 782, 415 N.W.2d 310 (1987), *appeal denied*, June 7, 1988.

§ 32.26   Waiver of Jury Trial

In order to avoid the legal expense of preparing for a jury trial and, particularly, the delay in getting a jury trial, many landlords provide in their leases that:

FORM 32-27
MISCELLANEOUS—WAIVER OF JURY TRIAL

Landlord and tenant waive trial by jury in any action, proceeding or counterclaim brought by either of them against the other on all matters arising out of this lease or the use and occupancy of the premises (except claims for personal injury or property damage). If landlord commences any summary proceeding for nonpayment of rent, tenant will not interpose (and waives the right to interpose) any counterclaim in any such proceeding.

As a general rule, such contractual waivers of the right to a jury trial have been upheld.[90] However, since the right to a jury trial is highly esteemed, the waiver provision will be carefully scrutinized and strictly construed. One commentator, acknowledging the dearth of cases directly on point, has suggested that the provision:

1. be conspicuous (perhaps with capital letters or bold face type)
2. emphasize its knowing and voluntary character
3. be located near the signatures or separately initialled.[91]

If a court concludes that a "buried" waiver was not understood by the tenant, the waiver may be lost.[92] Therefore, when the lease itself is invalid, the waiver will not be effective.[93] When the provision allows a jury trial, but does not require it, a jury trial will be granted. A waiver of jury trial in actions between landlord and tenant will not preclude a jury in claims involving third-party litigants.[94] Of course, when no objection is raised to a pending jury trial, a "waiver of the waiver" may be found. A Maryland statute that required a tenant to deposit into escrow allegedly past due rent as a condition to the tenant's right to a jury trial was found unconstitutional because it deprived the tenant of property without the process of law.[95]

---

[90] 47 Am. Jur. 2d *Jury* §§ 86-89 (1969), Annot., 73 A.L.R.2d 1332, *Validity and effect of contractual waiver of trial by jury* (1960).

[91] Loewy & Swank, *Waiving Jury Trials in Commercial Leasing Cases*, Prob. & Prop., Nov./Dec. 1989, at 50.

[92] Gaylord Dep't Stores of Ala., Inc. v. Stephens, 404 So. 2d 586 (Ala. 1981).

[93] Wesley v. Brinkley, 198 Misc. 783, 100 N.Y.S.2d 966 (N.Y. Mun. Ct. 1950).

[94] Tilden Fin. Corp. v. Malerba, Abruzzo, Downes & Frankel, 89 Misc. 2d 1074, 393 N.Y.S.2d 499 (N.Y. App. Term 1977).

[95] Lucky Ned Pepper's, Ltd. v. Columbia Park & Recreation Ass'n, 64 Md. App. 222, 494 A.2d 947 (1985).

The tenant's usual objection is that a jury trial may be desirable in some circumstances, such as claims involving personal injury or property damage; in fact, those claims have usually prompted courts to construe the waiver strictly and to allow a jury trial if at all possible. The landlord's basic goal can be achieved by the tenant's waiver of a jury trial only in landlord's summary proceedings to recover possession. If the tenant cannot limit the waiver to that narrow scope, it should retreat to a demand that it be allowed to prosecute its counterclaims in a separate action with a jury trial. Usually, the landlord will be pleased to recover possession in summary proceedings and to defer its defense of other claims to a later date. Applying that state's statutes, a New York court has ruled that a provision barring consolidation of actions is unconscionable, unenforceable, and against public policy since it interferes with the administration of justice.[96] Finally, the tenant ought to insist that it be allowed to bring its counterclaims in the summary proceedings — and to have a jury trial of them — if the applicable rules of civil procedure require it to do so.

Without prompting from any lease provisions, some California courts have required issues unrelated to possession — both a tenant's defenses[97] and a landlord's claims on nonrent lease covenants[98] — to be raised in a claim separate from the summary proceedings. However, one California court has allowed a commercial tenant's claim of retaliatory eviction (a traditional residential tenant's defense)[99] to be tried in a summary proceeding. In that unusual case, the tenant claimed that its landlord was evicting it solely because the tenant refused to perjure itself in litigation involving the landlord.[100]

§ 32.27   Governing Law and Venue

Almost every lease has a provision such as:

---

[96] Ultrashmere House, Ltd. v. 38 Town Assocs., 123 Misc. 2d 102, 473 N.Y.S.2d 120 (1984). *But see* Middletown Plaza Assocs. v. Dora Dale of Middletown, Inc., 621 F. Supp. 1163 (D. Conn. 1985) (Connecticut court applying New York law dismissed defendant-tenant's counterclaims, raised in an action for nonpayment of rent, because tenant waived its right to assert counterclaims in proceedings for nonpayment of rent under lease).

[97] Nork v. Pacific Coast Medical Enters., Inc., 73 Cal. App. 3d 410, 140 Cal. Rptr. 734 (1977); Mobil Oil Corp. v. Handley, 76 Cal. App. 3d 956, 143 Cal. Rptr. 321 (1978); Mobil Oil Corp. v. Superior Court of Los Angeles County, 79 Cal. App. 3d 486, 145 Cal. Rptr. 17 (1978).

[98] Vasey v. Cal. Dance Co., 70 Cal. App. 3d 742, 139 Cal. Rptr. 72 (1977).

[99] Schoshinski §§ 12:1-12:13.

[100] Custom Parking, Inc. v. Superior Court of Marin County, 138 Cal. App. 3d 90, 187 Cal. Rptr. 674 (1982). *See also* E.S. Bills, Inc. v. Tzucanow, 38 Cal. 3d 824, 700 P.2d 1280, 215 Cal. Rptr. 278 (1985) (trial of issues extraneous to the issue of possession allowed in limited circumstances under California's eviction statute).

FORM 32-28
MISCELLANEOUS—GOVERNING LAW AND VENUE

This lease will be governed by the law of _____ and will be
construed and interpreted according to that law. Venue on any action arising out of
this lease will be proper only in the District Court of _____
County, State of _____ .

On examination, this provision has three parts: governing law, construction and
interpretation, and venue.

Courts and commentators tend to make unqualified statements that the law
which governs a lease is the law of the state in which the premises are located.[101]
A more correct statement would be that some parts of the lease (those that create
an interest in real property, or are in rem) are governed by the law of the state in
which the premises are located, and that other parts of the lease (those that create
personal rights and obligations or are in personam) are governed by the law of the
state in which the lease was made.[102] The Restatement of the Conflict of Laws is
in accord.[103] By way of example, the issue of surrender is governed by the law of
the state in which the premises are located.[104] The law of the state in which the
lease was made governs the question of the landlord's lien.[105]

In the interest of conformity, real estate professionals are always well-advised
to state the governing law of the lease. Although there appears to be no problem
when the landlord, tenant, and premises are located in the same state, sales of the
premises and assignments of the lease may lead to unforeseen diversity of
citizenship among landlord and tenant. Of course, if form documents are being
used, the real estate professional may as well eliminate the need to consider
citizenship in each lease it drafts. So long as the transaction is not repugnant to
the public policy of the chosen state, and so long as there is an appropriate
relationship between the chosen state and the transaction, the choice of governing
law should be upheld by courts which consider it.[106]

The next issue presented is the distinction between *interpretation* and *construction*. Although they are often used interchangeably by courts and real estate
professionals, these words have different meanings. When a lease is before a
court, the judge will try to determine the intention of the landlord and tenant. To
do so, the court will first give meaning to the words and expressions of the lease;
this is interpretation. When the interpretation is completed, the court will give
legal effect to the lease; this is construction. One popular example is a provision
that a purchaser must pay for goods only if the purchaser is completely satisfied

---

[101] 51C C.J.S. *Landlord and Tenant* § 4 (1968); 3 Thompson § 1052.

[102] Annot., 15 A.L.R.2d 1199, *Law governing validity and construction of, and rights and
obligations arising under, a lease of real property* (1951).

[103] Restatement of the Conflict of Laws (Second) § 341 (1969).

[104] Ten-Six Olive, Inc. v. Curby, 208 F.2d 117 (8th Cir. 1953).

[105] Lee Wilson & Co. v. Fleming, 203 Ark. 417, 156 S.W.2d 893 (1941).

[106] 16 Am. Jur. 2d *Conflict of Laws* § 46 (1979).

with them. This may be interpreted to mean that the purchaser may refuse to pay for any reason. However, this provision may have the legal effect—that is, may be construed to mean—that the purchaser may not unreasonably refuse to pay. There are numerous rules and a great deal of case law that discuss interpretation and construction; they are beyond the scope of this book.[107]

Finally, this provision dictates the place of trial in any dispute between the landlord and tenant. In order to be effective, the selection should be exclusive and not permissive: the provision should state that the chosen place of trial is the only proper one. The selection will be enforced unless it is unreasonable, unfair, or unjust.[108]

§ 32.28 Binding Effect

Almost every legal document provides:

FORM 32-29
MISCELLANEOUS—BINDING EFFECT (SHORT FORM)

The benefits of this lease and the burdens of this lease will inure to the benefit of and will be binding upon the heirs, successors, personal representatives, and assigns of landlord and tenant.

This self-explanatory statement may be no more than it seems. If so, it contradicts the usual assignment provision that any assignment will be void (thus, not conferring any benefit on successors and assigns) unless the landlord consents to it. With that possibility in mind, many real estate professionals modify the standard provision to read:

FORM 32-30
MISCELLANEOUS—BINDING EFFECT
(WITH LIMITATION OF ASSIGNS)

This lease will inure to the benefit of, and will be binding upon, the successors and permitted assigns of landlord and tenant.

As modified, the provision avoids confusion. Still, one wonders what else is meant by this provision. Bearing in mind that leases are not terminated by the death of the landlord or tenant, or the dissolution of a corporation or partnership, the real estate professional may conclude that the provision is no more than a redundant statement of the law, because the successors are bound even without this provision.

---

[107] II Friedman ch. 26 is a fine discussion, while A. Corbin, Corbin on Contracts §§ 532-559 (1960), is the basic text.

[108] M/S Bremen v. Zapata Off-Shore Co., 407 U.S. 1 (1972).

Perhaps this provision is meant to answer any lingering questions about which covenants run with the land, so as to bind successors and assigns of the landlord and tenant. If this is the case, the provision contradicts the provisions discussed in **Chapter 29** that endeavor to limit the liability of the landlord's successors and assigns. In conclusion, this small provision may be changed to:

FORM 32-31
MISCELLANEOUS—BINDING EFFECT (LONG FORM)

This lease will inure to the benefit of, and will be binding upon, landlord's successors and assigns except as provided in paragraph [sale of the premises paragraph]. This lease will inure to the benefit of, and will be binding upon, tenant's successors and assigns so long as the succession or assignment is permitted by paragraph [assignments and subleases paragraph].

Although this binding effect provision is found in almost every legal document, its origin is unclear. In leases, it seems to relate to at least two ancient legal doctrines. One is that the tenant was not bound to its landlord's transferee unless it accepted the transferee as its landlord and attorned to it.[109] Thus, the provision seeks to bind the tenant to the landlord's transferee without the tenant's consent. Another ancient legal doctrine is *Spencer's Case,* from 1583.[110] That famous case laid down the rule of real covenants, that is, those that run with the land, as discussed in § **12.4**. This case also held that covenants with regard to matters that were not in existence at the time of the lease (for example, improvements to be constructed) bound successors to the landlord and tenant only if the word "assigns" was used; otherwise, the promise was said to be personal.

The following peculiar binding effect provision led to litigation about the personal liability of the signatories: "26. BINDING EFFECT. This agreement shall be binding upon the parties personally in addition to their corporations, hereto their heris[sic], successors and assigns." No one—including the landlord, the tenant, an arbitrator, and two courts—could agree on its effect.[111]

The historical digression offers a succinct conclusion to this book. Two time-worn precedents are now changed by the lowliest lease provision to reflect modern business precepts: the prohibition of assignments and the limitation of recourse against landlords. But even as the business and law of leases develop, they hark back to their origins in feudal England.

---

[109] 3 Thompson § 1200; III Friedman § 36.1.

[110] 5 Coke 16a, 77 Eng. Rep. 72 (1583).

[111] Diversified Realty, Inc. v. McElroy, 41 Wash. App. 171, 703 P.2d 323 (1985).

TABLE OF AUTHORITIES

Case	*Book §*
McDevitt v. Terminal Warehouse Co., 304 Pa. Super. 438, 450 A.2d 991 (1982)	§ 18.1
McDonald's Corp. v. Blotnik, 28 Ill. App. 2d 732, 328 N.E.2d 897 (1975)	§ 27.2
MCF Footwear v. Thirty-Third Equities, Inc., 191 (100) N.Y.L.J. at 15, col. 15M (May 23, 1984)	§ 12.2
McKnight-Seibert Shopping Center, Inc. v. National Tea Co., 263 Pa. Super. 292, 397 A.2d 1214 (1979)	§ 10.10
McLane & McLane v. Prudential Ins. Co., 735 F.2d 1194 (9th Cir. 1984)	§ 5.15
McQuinn v. City of Guntersville, 277 Ala. 328, 169 So. 2d 771 (1964)	§ 2.3
Medico-Dental Bldg. Co. v. Horton & Converse, 21 Cal. 2d 411, 132 P.2d 457 (1942)	§ 10.6
Medinvest Co. v. Methodist Hosp., 359 N.W.2d 714 (Minn. Ct. App. 1984), *review denied* (Mar. 21, 1985)	§ 12.7
Mendel v. Golden-Farley of Hopkinsville, Inc., 573 S.W.2d 346 (Ky. Ct. App. 1978)	§ 10.7
Mercury Inv. Co. v. F.W. Woolworth Co., 706 P.2d 523 (Okla. 1985)	§ 10.12
Meredith v. Dardarian, 83 Cal. App. 3d 248, 147 Cal. Rptr. 761 (1978)	§ 12.10
Michigan Ave. Nat'l Bank v. Evans, Inc., 176 Ill. App. 3d 1047, 531 N.E.2d 872 (1988), *appeal denied*, 125 Ill. 2d 567, 537 N.E.2d 811 (1989)	§ 6.17
Middagh v. Stanal Sound Ltd., 222 Neb. 54, 382 N.W.2d 303 (1986)	§ 30.15
Middletown Plaza Assocs. v. Dora Dale of Middletown Inc., 621 F. Supp. 1163 (D. Conn. 1985)	§ 32.24
Miles Shoes, Inc. v. Brainerd Village, Inc., (Tenn. Ct. App., E.D., Dec. 11, 1967)	§ 5.9
Miller v. Parlor Furniture of Hickory, Inc., 79 N.C. App. 639, 339 S.E.2d 804, *review denied, appeal dismissed,* 316 N.C. 732, 345 S.E.2d 389 (1986), *cert. denied,* 108 S. Ct. 777 (1988)	§ 30.6
Ministers, Elders & Deacons of Reformed Protestant Dutch Church v. 198 Broadway Inc., 59 N.Y.2d 170, 451 N.E.2d 164, 464 N.Y.S.2d 406 (1983)	§ 12.15
Mitchell v. Exhibition Foods, Inc., 184 Cal. App. 3d 1033, 229 Cal. Rptr. 535 (1986)	§ 4.22
Mitchell's, Inc. v. Nelms, 454 S.W.2d 809 (Tex. Civ. App. 1970), *n.r.e.*	§ 12.7
Mobil Oil Corp. v. Handley, 76 Cal. App. 3d 956, 143 Cal. Rptr. 321 (1978)	§ 32.24
Mobil Oil Corp. v. Superior Court of Los Angeles County, 79 Cal. App. 3d 486, 145 Cal. Rptr. 17 (1978)	§ 32.24
Monmouth Real Estate Inv. Trust v. Manville Foodland, Inc., 195 N.J. Super. 262, 482 A.2d 186 (App. Div. 1984), *cert. denied,* 99 N.J. 234, 491 A.2d 722 (1985)	§ 10.5
Monte Corp. v. Stephens, 324 P.2d 538 (Okla. 1958)	§ 10.11
Moon v. Haeussler, 153 A.D.2d 1002, 545 N.Y.S.2d 623 (1989)	§ 4.25
Moore v. Greenville Restaurants, 287 S.C. 295, 337 S.E.2d 892 (Ct. App. 1985)	§ 6.18

LIST OF FORMS

INDEX